The Prince of Providence

The True Story

of Buddy Cianci,

America's Most

Notorious Mayor,

Some Wiseguys,

and the Feds

 RANDOM HOUSE NEW YORK

THE **Prince** OF **Providence**

MIKE STANTON

All rights reserved under International and Pan-American
Copyright Conventions. Published in the United States by Random House,
an imprint of The Random House Publishing Group, a division
of Random House, Inc., New York, and simultaneously in
Canada by Random House of Canada Limited, Toronto.

Random House and colophon are registered trademarks
of Random House, Inc.

Library of Congress Cataloging-in-Publication data is available.
ISBN 0-375-50780-9

Random House website address: www.atrandom.com

Printed in the United States of America on acid-free paper

9 8 7 6 5 4 3

Book design by Barbara M. Bachman

Title-page photograph by Michael Delaney, The Providence Journal

To Susan

Willy: Well, I got on the road, and I went north to Providence. Met the Mayor.

Biff: The Mayor of Providence!

Willy: He was sitting in the hotel lobby.

Biff: What'd he say?

Willy: He said, "Morning!" And I said, "You got a fine city here, Mayor." And then he had coffee with me.

ARTHUR MILLER, *Death of a Salesman*

CONTENTS

A Knock on the Door

Providence is an old city, built on seven hills like ancient Rome, and situated at the head of Narragansett Bay in Rhode Island.

When Dennis Aiken, a young FBI agent, learned that he was being transferred there in 1978, he cringed. Aiken was from Clarksdale, Mississippi, birthplace of Muddy Waters and home of the blues. He thought he was being sent to Long Island, and this southern boy wanted no part of New York. His boss pulled out a map of the United States and pointed to Providence, a spot on the map beneath the curved arm and fist of Cape Cod—the armpit of New England.

It was a long way from Houston, Texas, Aiken's last assignment. Providence was an alien world of old buildings and narrow streets, a crabbed seaport and faded factory town, carved up into balkanized neighborhoods— the old-moneyed Yankees on College Hill, the Italians on Federal Hill, the Irish on Smith Hill.

But for Aiken, Providence was also paradise. In law enforcement parlance, Providence was "a target-rich environment."

Providence was the capital of the New England Mafia. Providence, Jimmy Breslin once wrote, is "where the best thieves in the world come from."

Providence was also the capital of Rhode Island, an incestuous city-state where politics had been dominated since colonial times by a rich cast of visionaries and freethinkers, rascals and rogues, patriots and privateers. Founded by Roger Williams in 1636 as a haven for religious freedom after the Puritans banished him from Massachusetts, Providence was, in a sense, America's first safe house. The colony, whose motto was "Hope," became a refuge for Jews, Catholics, Baptists, and Quakers, who fled Massachusetts to escape whipping, branding, ear-cropping, tongue-boring, and hanging. But even the tolerant Williams found that individualism could be carried too far, as colonists resisted paying taxes and bowing to any government authority. The colony's wide-open mores opened the door to land speculators and sharp merchants. The Puritans called it "Rogue's Isle." Cotton Mather described the colony as "the fag end of creation" and "the sewer of New England." By the early eighteenth century, its venturesome sea captains were leaders in the notorious Triangle Trade, exchanging rum for African slaves and Caribbean molasses, a key ingredient in rum. "I would plow the ocean into pea-porridge to make money," said one Rhode Island privateer. When the Revolution dawned, Rhode Island was the first colony to declare independence from Great Britain and the last to join the new union. Later, Moses Brown helped finance America's first textile mill, based on plans smuggled out of England, and the colony became the birthplace of the industrial revolution. Rhode Island grew rich, restrictive, and Republican. Robber barons built mighty companies like Fruit of the Loom, exploiting tens of thousands of immigrants from Ireland, Italy, and other countries. At the dawn of the twentieth century, Providence was a national economic power—and a hotbed of political corruption.

"The political condition of Rhode Island is notorious, acknowledged and it is shameful," muckraker Lincoln Steffens wrote in 1904. "Rhode Island is a state for sale, and cheap."

Aiken learned that lesson firsthand when he put together a case against the speaker of the Rhode Island House, for taking bribes from a furniture salesman. Armed with a search warrant, the FBI agent went into the speaker's home and cut a swatch of carpet from under his bed that matched the new carpet in the speaker's office at the State House. The case ended in two hung juries, which taught Aiken that Providence wasn't easy.

While he was in Providence, Aiken also got to know its colorful mayor, Vincent A. "Buddy" Cianci, Jr.

In his second term, Cianci was a spellbinding speaker and ubiquitous politician who, in a line borrowed from Andy Warhol, joked that he would attend the opening of an envelope. He was a Republican who had beaten the Democratic machine, the anticorruption candidate who had come out of nowhere in 1974 to be elected Providence's first Italian-American mayor in a city ruled by Irish bosses.

Cianci's résumé—grandson of immigrants, son of a doctor, former mob prosecutor—and his dynamic leadership of a dying urban center convinced many that he had a bright national future. He had been friendly with President Gerald Ford and had spoken at the 1976 Republican National Convention. The mayor had his eye on the United States Senate, and from there, perhaps, a spot on the Republican ticket as a vice-presidential candidate. As audacious as it seemed, some said that Buddy Cianci had the potential to be the nation's first Italian-American president. Short of that, there was always Hollywood; a producer once offered Cianci his own sitcom.

Then there was the other Buddy. This was the Buddy Cianci who helped inspire a recurring character played by comedian Jon Lovitz on *Saturday Night Live*—the Pathological Liar. This was the mayor of insider deals and cash in envelopes, of political hacks and mobsters on the city payroll. This was the ruthless Buddy who took a sadistic glee in crushing his opponents and settling old scores, the dark Buddy who had been accused in law school of raping a woman at gunpoint.

"He's a survivor in a wicked world," said Frederick Lippitt, who ran against him twice. "If he's out to get you, your head's going to be in your lap before you know it's been cut off."

The second Buddy soon came under Dennis Aiken's microscope. Acting on tips about payoffs for city contracts, Aiken began constructing a profile of the mayor, gathering background information that could be used later in a full-scale investigation. Trailed by aides, Cianci would approach Aiken in the marble corridors of City Hall and ask the FBI agent what he was doing. Aiken would answer that he was conducting surveillance. Cianci would sort of chuckle, make a wisecrack, and walk quickly away.

In 1981 Aiken left Providence. He was promoted to run the FBI's office in West Palm Beach, Florida. He rose through the ranks, to chief of the Bureau's Public Corruption Unit. He wrote the book on corruption, *The FBI Field Guide to Public Corruption*. Along the way, Aiken married a woman from Rhode Island. In 1994 FBI director Louis Freeh announced an initiative to put several hundred senior agents back in the field. Aiken, bored with his desk job in Washington, jumped at the chance.

This time, he asked to be sent back to Providence.

In his absence, the city that *The Wall Street Journal* in 1983 had called "a smudge beside the fast lane to Cape Cod" had undergone a remarkable transformation. The grimy railroad yards and parking lots that had bisected downtown were gone. Rivers that had been smothered in ribbons of concrete had been uncovered and moved. Authentic Venetian gondolas glided along the water, past impressive stone and brick buildings that spoke to Providence's storied past as a maritime power and a factory town. At night, thousands congregated to behold WaterFire, a series of meditative bonfires on iron pyres in the rivers, accompanied by music ranging from New Age to opera. With its nationally acclaimed restaurants and devotion to the arts, Providence had become a mecca for tourists and a trendy place to live, a poster child for the rebirth of the American city.

Presiding over this renaissance was a reincarnated Buddy Cianci.

Driven from office in 1984 after his conviction for felony assault—an ugly episode involving his ex-wife's suspected lover, a lit cigarette, and a fireplace log—Cianci had staged a stunning comeback in 1990. Although twenty-two people had been convicted for corruption in his first administration, Cianci convinced the voters to give him a second chance.

By the time Dennis Aiken returned to Providence in 1994, it appeared that Cianci had made the most of his comeback. He was the longest-serving active mayor in America among cities with more than 100,000 people. He was hailed as an urban messiah. An acclaimed PBS documentary, *Vote for Me*, called him "the King of Retail." He had his own marinara sauce. He traded barbs on national radio with Don Imus. He mingled with Hollywood stars. He landed a cameo—as himself—on the hit NBC television series *Providence*.

The real Providence was a much more interesting place, and Buddy was the undisputed star. He was squired about his city in a shiny black limousine with a surveillance camera on the back and a riot gun and a spare case of marinara sauce in the trunk. His driver, a husky policeman in high black boots, towered above the squat, forceful mayor. Cianci wore tailored suits and a marvelously coifed toupee and moved in a perpetual haze of cologne and cigarette smoke. At night, as he made the rounds, he carried a "to-go cup" of liquor; he favored vodka when he was campaigning because the voters couldn't smell it on his breath. He joked that every time he smoked, he helped schoolchildren, who benefited from the cigarette tax. This was vintage Buddy, repackaging vice as virtue.

He was equal parts visionary, cheerleader, rogue, and lounge singer. A city was like a woman you made love to, he said. Or, in Providence's case, many women. Cianci embraced them all—the Italian ward bosses in Silver Lake, the Ivy Leaguers on the East Side, the black-clad artists at RISD, the gays in the downtown leather bars, the newer Asian and Hispanic immigrants, the old ladies in the senior high-rises. And they all loved Buddy— they all tolerated and even reveled in his flaws—because he was funny and put Providence back on the map and made them feel good about them-selves. He was a larger-than-life political character unique to Rhode Island and yet reflective of America, which had evolved more along the lines of Roger Williams's freewheeling Providence than puritanical Plymouth. If the Puritans shunned Providence, it was because there was more of Provi-dence in them than they dared admit. Providence, wrote Brown University historian William McLoughlin, was the heart of a city-state that "epito-mizes all the ambiguities of the American dream." And Cianci, who boasted that he could ride around his city blindfolded and recognize each neighborhood by its sounds and smells, embodied Providence.

Cianci was at the peak of his popularity in the spring of 1999, when Dennis Aiken decided it was time to pay him a call. Having been reelected the previous November to a sixth term, Cianci would soon become the longest-sitting mayor in Providence history. The occasion was to be marked by big festivities, including a gala exhibit of artisans and art from the Uffizi Gallery in Florence, Italy—Providence's new sister city.

Aiken had returned to Providence wanting to believe that Cianci had learned his lesson, that the Renaissance was real. But Providence was a city of ghosts. Once he started digging beneath the surface, it didn't take Aiken long to find what he was looking for.

The FBI agent liked to warn reluctant witnesses, "You'd better be knocking on my door before I'm knocking on yours." On the morning of April 28, 1999, Aiken and another agent drove down Benefit Street, known as the Mile of History for its wealth of well-preserved colonial homes and mansions. Dappled sunshine filtered through the trees. They passed the soaring white spire of the First Baptist Church, the restored brick mansion that housed the University Club, the Rhode Island School of Design, the templelike Providence Athenaeum, and the colonnaded Providence County Courthouse, where socialite Claus von Bulow had been acquitted of trying to murder his wealthy wife.

At the imposing John Brown House, built in 1786 by the Revolution-ary War patriot, slave trader, and early benefactor of Brown University, Aiken turned onto Power Street. The street dove steeply down College Hill toward the old waterfront. Aiken turned into the first driveway, drove through a black iron gate and up a curving brick drive. He parked in front of a massive brick carriage house topped with a cupola and a patina-green steeple, got out of the car, and rang the doorbell. This was Buddy Cianci's house.

It was shortly before 9 A.M., early for the nocturnal mayor. It was an hour when Cianci might still be in bed or lounging in his robe, having a cup of coffee and a cigarette, reading the paper, and working the phones as his city came alive. The mayor liked to stay well informed, and he followed his press coverage closely. He was mentioned in several stories in that morning's *Providence Journal*—his attendance at a meeting of the city investment board, a speech at an education luncheon, an appearance with actor James Earl Jones to announce a $2.1 million Bell Atlantic grant for the planned Heritage Harbor Museum. Cianci had been in good spirits, presenting Jones with a jar of his marinara sauce and laughing when Rhode Island's lieutenant governor joked that the grant was the size of the mayor's cell-phone bill. Another story reported a no-confidence vote by police officers in Cianci's police chief, following a series of scandals involving missing evidence, including a kilo of cocaine.

Aiken and the other agent waited on the mayor's doorstep. Cianci's gravelly voice came through the intercom. Aiken said that the FBI would like to talk to him.

The door opened. Cianci, who was dressed this morning, stood peering out, surprised to see Dennis Aiken on his doorstep. He invited the two agents inside.

Aiken told Cianci that he was working on an investigation of City Hall and would like to ask the mayor a few questions. Cianci looked at the tape recorder that Aiken held and asked what this was about. He was curious but guarded.

The FBI agent did not tell the mayor that, at that moment, fifty agents were preparing to fan out across Providence, armed with search warrants for City Hall and other places. Aiken did not say that the chairman and vice chairman of the city tax board had just been arrested and handcuffed. He did not mention that the FBI had the mayor's top aide and campaign treasurer on videotape, taking bribes in his City Hall office with Cianci's smiling picture on the wall.

Cianci stared at the tape recorder suspiciously, as if wondering whether it was running. Aiken asked if he would like to cooperate. The mayor wanted to know who was involved, and whether he was involved. Aiken made it clear that he was there to ask the questions. He told the mayor that he wanted to tape-record anything Cianci had to say, so that there would be no dispute later.

The mayor replied that he didn't want to say anything into a tape recorder that could be contradicted later.

With that, Aiken and the other agent said good-bye. They got back into their car and drove down the hill the short distance to City Hall, which would soon be in an uproar as agents seized boxes of records.

Back on Power Street, Cianci holed up in his house late into the afternoon, consulting with his lawyers and advisers.

The mayor could count the FBI agents and state police detectives who had stood in Dennis Aiken's shoes over the years, hoping to take him down. They had all failed.

This was just one more challenge in a career full of challenges. Cianci had taken Providence too far, through the wilderness of the past quarter of a century, to be turned back now. So intertwined were the fortunes of the mayor and his city that he could have borrowed as his epitaph what was engraved on the tombstone of the horror writer H. P. Lovecraft in Swan Point Cemetery: I AM PROVIDENCE.

Let Aiken and the FBI and the United States Justice Department come after him. Buddy would not be beaten on his turf—not in his Providence.

They had too much history together.

The Prince of Providence

CHAPTER ONE

The Prosecutor, the Priest, and the Mob Boss

Buddy Cianci sat in the wooden pew of the courtroom, doubting a priest.

Courtroom No. 5 in the Providence County Courthouse was crowded on this spring morning in 1972, like Easter mass at St. Bartholomew's in Silver Lake, where Cianci had gone as a boy. Cianci, a thirty-one-year-old Rhode Island prosecutor, sat shoulder to shoulder with Bobby Stevenson, a beefy Irish detective who had played CYO ball for St. Michael's in South Providence.

The two men watched as a ruddy, white-haired priest made his way to the front of the room, past a larger-than-normal contingent of armed sheriffs and curious spectators. He walked past a tableful of exhibits—an army carbine, two sawed-off shotguns, pistols, revolvers, and Halloween masks of John F. Kennedy and Richard M. Nixon. The priest paused to embrace the man at the defense table, Mafia boss Raymond L. S. Patriarca.

Then Father Raymond Moriarty took the witness stand, raised his right hand, and swore to tell the truth.

Patriarca, the feared ruler of the New England rackets, the man known in the underworld as "the Mayor of Providence," was on trial for murder. Moriarty, his childhood friend, who had entered the priesthood around the time that Patriarca was arrested for rolling dice on a Sunday, had come from his parish in Maryland to testify as the Mafia chief's alibi.

Four years earlier, on the Saturday after Easter, two masked gunmen had burst into a meat market in Silver Lake and gunned down a bookmaker and his bodyguard as they did their weekly grocery shopping. Rudolph Marfeo, the bookie, fell near the front door, a drawn .38 in his hand, his left side blown apart. Anthony Melei, the bodyguard, died next to the ice cream freezer, his face shot away by Double OO buckshot. The shopkeeper and his wife dived behind the deli counter as the killers retreated.

Their getaway car roared up a steep hill beside the market, through the streets of Buddy Cianci's childhood, and sped across Laurel Hill Avenue, a few blocks north of his house. Soon, curious neighborhood boys pressed their face to the plate-glass window to see the bloody corpses as the wail of sirens signaled yet another mob hit in Providence.

The government's star witness, Boston armored-car robber Red Kelley, had testified that he planned the murders for Patriarca. He described a meeting outside a Providence restaurant two weeks before the murders, on Palm Sunday, when Patriarca snarled, "I want him dead," meaning Marfeo. The hit had been planned for the day before Easter. But it was postponed after the son of one of the gunmen found a pistol stashed in a toy chest and accidentally shot and killed his playmate on Good Friday afternoon.

Father Moriarty contradicted Red Kelley's story.

Speaking in a soft, confessional voice, the priest told the jury that he had been with Patriarca that Palm Sunday. He had gone with the mob boss to the Gate of Heaven Cemetery in East Providence, where the two men had prayed over the grave of Patriarca's wife. Afterward, they had returned to Patriarca's house on the East Side of Providence, and Father Moriarty had spent the night.

Patriarca wept during Father Moriarty's testimony and hugged him again when he stepped off the witness stand.

In the back of the courtroom, Cianci turned to Stevenson and shook his head. The priests Cianci had known as a boy at St. Bart's had listened to his confessions and taught him the Ten Commandments: *Thou shalt not steal. Thou shalt not kill. Thou shalt not bear false witness. . . .* This priest's story sounded too good to be true, Cianci said. Stevenson wondered aloud what kind of a priest would be away from his parish on Palm Sunday.

Cianci and Stevenson feared that Father Moriarty had destroyed the state's case in heavily Catholic Rhode Island, and that Patriarca would soon be free to resume running the rackets. During a recess, Cianci went downstairs to the Rhode Island attorney general's office and spoke to his bosses about his doubts.

"This doesn't sound right," Cianci told them.

Cianci, who had been assisting the lead prosecutor in the trial, offered to check out the priest's alibi. His superiors agreed. But there wasn't much time. Closing arguments were scheduled for the next day. Then the case would go to the jury.

■

LONG BEFORE PROVIDENCE was Buddy Cianci's town, it belonged to Raymond Loreda Salvatore Patriarca.

Patriarca was the last of the old-time gangsters. He came of age during Prohibition, hijacking shipments of bootleg liquor, and over the next five decades became one of the richest and most powerful mob bosses in America.

From the back room of his Coin-O-Matic vending office on Federal Hill, in the heart of Providence's Little Italy, Patriarca ran a multimillion-dollar criminal empire built on illegal gambling, loan sharking, truck hijackings, and labor racketeering. An illegal FBI bug ordered by J. Edgar Hoover in the early 1960s picked up the constant squeak of Patriarca's desk drawer as he dropped in envelopes that the wiseguys brought in tribute. They also gave him cigars, whiskey, a fur coat, a diamond ring, a gallon of spaghetti sauce—anything they could think of to keep those baleful eyes from looking on them with disfavor. One day a shoplifter stopped in to show Patriarca a London Fog raincoat that he had stolen from a downtown department store; Patriarca tried it on, found that it fit perfectly, and told the man, "Now go boost another one for yourself."

"No matter what went on in New England, Raymond got a piece of the action," recalled Patriarca underboss Vinny Teresa.

Patriarca bragged that he owned Connecticut, vowed to declare martial law to end an Irish-Italian gang war in Massachusetts, and arbitrated disputes among the Five Families in New York. He owned part of the Dunes Hotel and Casino in Las Vegas, had dealings with Jimmy Hoffa and Meyer Lansky, and was a silent partner in a Massachusetts horse track with Frank Sinatra and Dean Martin. Law enforcement lore had it that Sinatra got the engagement ring he gave Mia Farrow from Patriarca, who procured it from a wiseguy who had stolen it from Damon Runyon's widow on Cape Cod. Patriarca had once entertained an offer from some wealthy Cuban businessmen to assassinate Fidel Castro, using the same hitman who had gunned down Rudy Marfeo and Anthony Melei. Facing the prospect of prison, Patriarca received an offer of asylum from his casino partner in Haiti, the notorious dictator "Papa Doc" Duvalier. Patriarca turned him down, confident that he could beat the rap.

If someone got out of line, Patriarca would bite down hard on his cigar, his craggy face would turn white, and he'd spit out the command to "put him in the hospital," or worse. When a Bible manufacturer reported that someone was stealing Bibles from a business that Patriarca had a piece of, the mob boss warned that if he was lying, "he would wind up in the hospital with his legs broken."

But Patriarca understood that running a successful business required more than muscle and the threat of violence. Corrupting government officials was also necessary. He owned judges, politicians, and cops, whom he paid to protect his illegal gambling operations. "If you have not got the law today," he told an associate, "you can't stay in the gaming business." He advised his men to stay away from politicians, unless absolutely necessary—then "go see them with the money."

The FBI bug captured Patriarca discussing political endorsements like a ward boss. In 1964 he and an unidentified politician discussed who they were supporting in the mayor's race. Another time, a man running for lieutenant governor stopped by Coin-O-Matic, seeking Patriarca's backing, and received a lecture for being so careless as to visit in person. When Patriarca's son had trouble changing a course at the University of Rhode Island, Patriarca called the governor to straighten things out.

Patriarca's rise coincided with Providence's decline.

Born on St. Patrick's Day 1908 in Worcester, Massachusetts, Patriarca moved to Providence when he was about four years old. His father ran a liquor business on Federal Hill, a neighborhood west of downtown that teemed with Italian immigrants, among them a carpenter from Roccamonfina, Pietro Cianci, Buddy's grandfather.

The crowded tenements of Patriarca's childhood were a place of ferment as the rural Italians struggled to adapt to an urban environment dominated by Yankee factory owners and Irish cops. Even the Catholic Church was run by Irish bishops and upper-caste Northern Italian priests, who tried to ban the southerners' peasant superstitions and boisterous religious feast days. In 1920 a phalanx of Providence police officers held back one hundred Italian women trying to forcibly evict a priest from the Church of the Holy Ghost on Federal Hill. Said one early Italian leader, "We came here with high ideas, and were kicked around like dogs." Their mistreatment fueled a suspicion of authority carried over from the old country, where the people had a saying: "If you want to be rich, become a thief, a policeman, or a priest."

In choosing his career path, Patriarca could have followed many of the immigrants into one of Providence's booming factories. Thanks to immigrant labor, Providence was one of the richest cities in America in the early 1900s. It was the hub of the nation's most industrialized state, an early-day Silicon Valley of cutting-edge technology. The city boasted its "Five Industrial Wonders of the World"—the largest precision-tool factory (Brown & Sharpe), the largest file factory (Nicholson File), the largest steam-engine factory (Corliss), the largest silverware factory (Gorham), and the largest screw factory (American Screw)—plus the country's biggest textile manufacturer, Fruit of the Loom. Local factories turned out windlasses for U.S. Navy ships and the U.S. Army cannons that massacred the Sioux at Wounded Knee. Local innovators developed the first fire-sprinkler system for office buildings, a machine that made horseshoes, and a "burglarproof" safe.

Most of that wealth remained locked in the vaults of the wealthy East Siders. Although the immigrants outnumbered them, the Yankee ruling class controlled the government through a corrupt political machine that bought rural Republican votes while denying the vote to landless urban dwellers. The system was run by Boss Brayton, the half-blind Republican party chief and Providence's federal postmaster, who once secured a thirty-seven-thousand-dollar personal loan with postage stamps. Brayton's machine produced the most powerful politician in America at the turn of the century, U.S. Senator Nelson Aldrich, a descendant of Roger Williams who began his career as a grocery clerk and started his political career on the Providence City Council. Dubbed "the General Manager of the United States," Aldrich fought Teddy Roosevelt's trust-busting efforts, permitted trust lobbyists to set up shop in his Senate office, and married off his daughter to John D. Rockefeller's son in his opulent waterfront mansion on Narragansett Bay in Warwick—the house that sugar built. Curious about the political system that had produced Aldrich, the muckraker Lincoln Steffens visited Rhode Island for *McClure's* magazine in 1904 and found it to be one of the most corrupt in the nation. Vote-buying was rampant; the going rate for a man's vote was two to five dollars for an ordinary election and fifteen to thirty-five for a hotly contested race. "An honest voter," said one Brayton lieutenant, "is one who stays bought." The growing immigrant populace watched and waited.

"What has the immigrant really learned in America?" asked one Italian activist. "Justice here encourages lawlessness and corrupts the sons of honest peasants."

A. J. Liebling, the *New Yorker* magazine writer who worked as a reporter for *The Providence Journal-Bulletin* during Prohibition, recalled a waterfront lined with flophouses, tattoo parlors, and Portuguese ship chandlers' stores, where smugglers ran scotch right up Narragansett Bay. "The best liquor was to be had of a bootlegger who had a flat in a frame building behind the State House," wrote Liebling. "He felt a responsibility for the quality of the legislation that got passed under its influence."

Patriarca dropped out of school after eighth grade. He shined shoes and worked as a bellhop at the new Biltmore Hotel, an opulent Jazz Age hotel that had a rooftop chicken coop to provide guests with fresh eggs for breakfast. Patriarca worked there for two years, opening doors for the powerful businessmen and politicians who would walk across the street from City Hall. Then, in 1925, when he was seventeen, his father died. Later Patriarca would say, "I lost my father, and I guess I drifted a little."

Prohibition, another curse visited upon the immigrant population by the Yankee temperance movement, provided savvy and ruthless young men like Patriarca a quick path to the riches that America had promised. Patriarca drifted first into rum-running, then double-crossed his associates and hijacked the liquor shipments he had been paid to guard. After Prohibition, Patriarca gambled, robbed payrolls, and trafficked in white slavery, as prostitution was known.

In 1930, while a third of Providence's workers were losing their jobs to the Great Depression, Patriarca organized an Easter Sunday prison break for two criminal cohorts from the Rhode Island state prison; it failed, after a shoot-out in which two guards died. In 1933, when seventy-seven thousand workers marched through downtown Providence in support of President Roosevelt's National Recovery Act, the Providence police designated Patriarca a "public enemy," meaning that he could be picked up on sight after dark. In 1938, Patriarca's scandalous early parole by the governor of Massachusetts after a burglary conviction led to the impeachment of a state official who had been a contemporary of James Michael Curley.

Patriarca ran with Butsey Morelli's gang. Back in 1920, Morelli's gunmen had pulled off the Braintree, Massachusetts, shoe-factory payroll heist that was later pinned on Sacco and Vanzetti, the famous martyrs to anti-Italian prejudice. A guard was killed in the holdup, and Sacco and Vanzetti, two Socialists, were railroaded and executed. As Butsey later confided to another Patriarca associate: "These two suckers took it on the chin for us. That shows you how much justice there really is."

After World War II, Morelli retired. Patriarca moved swiftly to seize control of the rackets, not only in Rhode Island but throughout New England. One of his first moves was to take over the underworld's lucrative race wire. When Irish gangster Carleton O'Brien stood in his way, Patriarca's goons wrecked O'Brien's betting parlors and then shot O'Brien dead in his driveway. Next, Patriarca strong-armed his way to control of Rhode Island's vending-machine business. As the proprietor of Coin-O-Matic on Federal Hill, Patriarca claimed that he had gone straight, even as various crime commissions concluded otherwise.

In 1950, when Buddy Cianci was in grammar school, the Kefauver Committee in Washington crowned Patriarca king of the New England rackets. In 1955, when Cianci was a high school freshman, a Boston bank robber arrested by the police said that he owed Patriarca money: "I was told by a member of the Patriarca mob that I had until Thursday to get the money, or else. Patriarca is the mayor of Providence." And in 1959, when Cianci was a college freshman, Patriarca jousted with Bobby Kennedy at a U.S. Senate rackets committee hearing about his wayward youth.

"Why do a lot of young fellows do a lot of things," Patriarca asked Kennedy, "when they haven't a father?"

Patriarca cultivated an image as the Robin Hood of Federal Hill, handing out boxes of candy bars to respectful children at Halloween and quietly financing "Patriarca scholarships" so that poor youths could attend college. His neighbors said that he made the streets safe at night, and that he could quickly recover stolen cars and goods taken in house burglaries. When the hated *Providence Journal* kept writing about his mob exploits, Patriarca bought an ad in the newspaper quoting Shakespeare's *Julius Caesar*: "The evil that men do lives after them. The good is oft interred with their bones." Yellowed clippings of his early criminal career disappeared from the newspaper's morgue.

Patriarca's postwar Providence was a wide-open town that lived up to its colonial reputation as "Rogue's Isle," a city of hustlers, gamblers, and ward heelers with a film-noir skyline that curled like a fist around the head of Narragansett Bay. The great ships that had once circled the globe no longer visited the rotting piers that jutted out into the bay like a prizefighter's broken teeth. As the factories moved south and the families of returning soldiers moved to the suburbs, Patriarca reigned over a world of floating crap games, bookie parlors, and brassy nightclubs. Housewives in Silver Lake put down a dime or a nickel to play the "nigger pool," a numbers game that originated in Harlem. Judges and lawyers bought their suits from Alfredo "the Blind Pig" Rossi, a major Patriarca fence. Rossi trafficked in stolen merchandise that teams of Patriarca's boosters stole from fancy department stores around the country, shipping their catch back home like fishermen of old.

People crowded into the Celebrity Club in Randall Square to see Duke Ellington and the Rhode Island Auditorium on North Main Street to watch boxer Rocky Marciano chase the world heavyweight title. Afterward, fight fans adjourned to Manny Almeida's Ringside Lounge, a downtown bar run by Marciano's manager, an intimate of Patriarca's. Marciano knew who held the power in Providence. When someone stole a fur coat from his car, he went to Patriarca, not the police, to try and get it back.

Another boxing fan, Colonel Walter Stone, was an honest cop who tried to fight Patriarca, first as Providence's police chief and then as superintendent of the Rhode Island State Police. One night he leaped into the ring at the Arcadia Ballroom downtown to break up a melee that had begun when the brother of the losing boxer attacked the winner; flinging bodies aside, Stone quickly restored order. A governor who was in Patriarca's pocket, John Notte, fired Stone in the early 1960s, but outraged voters threw Notte out the next election and the new governor, John Chafee, reappointed Stone. In the fall of 1963, when the U.S. Senate's McClellan Committee held the explosive Valachi hearings, in which mob turncoat Joseph Valachi revealed the inner workings of the Mafia, Stone also testified regarding Patriarca, whom Valachi had identified as a member of the Mafia's national ruling commission.

Patriarca was "a shrewd, scheming individual," said Stone, "as well versed in the ways of crime today as he was in yesteryear." He was hard to nail, because he insulated himself and intimidated potential witnesses. Eddie Hannan, an ex-boxer who thought about testifying against a Patriarca hit man he had seen shoot Tiger Balletto in the Bella Napoli Café, was strangled to death with baling wire, his body left in the Federal Hill dump. There was a saying on the Hill: "Better to be judged by twelve than carried by six."

"Certainly if we had the cooperation of the citizen, we could cope with the situation, but when you don't have it, certainly you can't," Stone testified. "Law enforcement on a state and local level I would say is not in any position to compete with them."

But by the late 1960s, a growing number of citizens felt that things had gotten out of control. They were tired of reading about gangland slayings and shootings in broad daylight. One afternoon, bullets smashed through the window of Angelo's restaurant on the Hill, narrowly missing a waitress and sending diners diving to the floor. The streets of Providence, said Stone, had turned into "a jungle."

The police became jaded by the violence. They found Baby Curcio one winter's night, slumped behind the wheel of his car in his pajamas in the city's North End, six bullet holes in his head and neck. A junkie, Baby had made the mistake of burglarizing the house of Patriarca's brother. It was so cold that his blood wouldn't run, so the coroner allowed the police to tow the car to headquarters, with Baby's corpse still behind the wheel. On the way, the two detectives stopped off at the Everready Diner on Admiral Street for a cup of coffee. Thawing out inside, the detectives sent the counter boy to see if the guy in the car wanted anything. The boy came rushing back inside, chalk white, lips shivering, as if he'd just seen a ghost.

In 1966 Rhode Islanders elected Herbert DeSimone, a Republican long shot, as attorney general. He upset a four-term Democrat who had denied the existence of the Mafia in Rhode Island. The Ivy League–educated DeSimone, who had been a football star at Brown University, wanted to be governor. He saw political advantages in going after Patriarca. A gang-buster image would help him overcome anti-Italian prejudice among suburban voters.

One of DeSimone's campaign volunteers was a recent law-school graduate with his own political ambitions, Buddy Cianci.

RIDING DOWNTOWN WITH his mother for singing lessons behind City Hall, or going with his father to dinner at Federal Hill's Old Canteen, where Raymond Patriarca had a private room upstairs, Buddy Cianci didn't imagine himself as mayor of Providence.

He had bigger dreams.

In second grade, little Buddy stood up at the Laurel Hill Avenue Elementary School and announced that he was going to be president of the United States. Whether he said so because of an early interest in politics or a love of the spotlight was anyone's guess. But one thing was clear—Buddy wanted to be loved, and when he wasn't, it hurt.

He was the Golden Son, the only boy in an immigrant family that had found success in the New World, and much was expected of him. His father, Dr. Vincent Albert Cianci, was one of thirteen children, the son of an immigrant carpenter and the first in his family to attend college. A proctologist, he had an office in a Victorian house on Pocasset Avenue, in the heart of Silver Lake. The Ciancis lived up the hill, just over the line in Cranston, in a rambling brick house, with a swimming pool, that Buddy's grandfather had built. His mother, Esther Capobianco, came from a prominent North End family—her father was a businessman active in Democratic ward politics, and her grandfather had been mayor of Benevento, an Italian hill town.

Vincent Albert Cianci, Jr., was born on April 30, 1941. Raised in a household of doting women—mother, sister, grandmother, aunts, and cousins—he was both spoiled and pushed to excel. His father wanted him to be a doctor. His mother signed him up for music lessons. He loved to eat, and battled his weight. Other kids in the neighborhood resented his superior attitude and made fun of the chubby boy whose mother dressed him in Buster Brown suits, bow ties, and white bucks. They tugged at his clothes, stepped on his shoes, shoved him around.

A neighbor, Pasquale DeSocio, whose son played with Buddy, remembered the other boys teasing him. "Once, we were painting our garage and Buddy came over in his Buster Brown suit and got paint all over it," he said. "Everyone was laughing at him."

Michael Traficante, who grew up a block away, on Heather Street, made fun of Cianci because he had more than the other kids. They envied his in-ground pool and would jump in, aggravating Cianci. "He could be a snotty little twerp," said Traficante, who went on to become the mayor of Cranston and remained friendly with him.

Once when he was mayor Cianci showed an aide a family photo album and began reminiscing. He said that his mother wouldn't let him out of the house much, and recalled a lonely childhood. In the photographs little Buddy was dressed like Little Lord Fauntleroy.

Cianci found refuge as a child performer. His music teacher, Celia Moreau, called him "a good little entertainer." By the age of seven, he was singing the theme song to Moreau's *Kiddie Revue*, a weekly radio show broadcast live on Saturday mornings from the Outlet Department Store downtown. He dressed up as a little old Italian man, with a funny hat and work clothes, tap-dancing and singing silly songs like "Where D'Ya Worka, John?"

"He was my comedy guy," recalled Moreau. "Whatever I'd tell him to do, he'd do it."

His mother also put him in church pageants around Silver Lake. One Christmas, he blanked out in the middle of "O Holy Night" but kept singing, making up the words. Buddy's Aunt Josephine recalled him as precocious, "always up to something." He could talk his way out of mischief so well, she said, that his grandmother would smile indulgently and say, "That boy's going to be president someday."

An old-time Silver Lake resident remembered the Cianci family—Buddy, his parents, and his older sister, Carol—walking into St. Bartholomew's for Sunday mass. The family always sat in the same pew, up front, but sometimes Buddy would try to detour to a different pew, only to be collared by his father. "His father would walk behind him, bada-boom, bada-bing," the man recalled, smiling. "Because Buddy was no angel."

Buddy looked up to his father and struggled to please him. Dr. Cianci, who had worked his way through medical school sorting freight for the railroad and driving a cement truck, could be hard on his son. He thought the boy was spoiled and lacked discipline.

Dr. Cianci fooled around with other women, which pained his wife. That Buddy was aware of his father's affairs was evident years later, when he told one friend about his father's reputation as a ladies' man, and joked in front of another, at a family dinner, about "Daddy's girlfriends."

The adult Buddy didn't talk much about his father, even to close friends. One day, after he had berated an aide at City Hall, another aide turned to Cianci's sister, who had stopped by, and expressed surprise at such a childish tantrum by a grown man. According to the aide, his sister explained that Buddy had had a difficult time with their father, who could be busy and distant.

Cianci's former girlfriend Wendy Materna can recall a conversation with him in the 1990s, when they were breaking up, in which she asked what had gone on between him and his father. Cianci, she said, burst into tears and never went into it. Instead, he spoke sadly about the last time that he had seen his father alive, when he boarded the train in Providence to join the army in 1967.

When Cianci was nine years old, his father enrolled him in fifth grade at the Moses Brown School, an East Side prep school across the street from Brown University. Years later Buddy would still vividly remember driving through the iron gates for the first time and up the curving drive shaded by elm trees. Ahead loomed Middle House, a massive brick building draped in ivy.

"Wow!" he said to his father. "What is *this* place?"

This was the cradle of Providence's WASPs, who bred their sons for Harvard and Williams, Yankee banks and white-shoe law firms—a world of bridge and tea dances. Founded as a Quaker school around the time of the American Revolution, the school preached the tolerance of its benefactor, Moses Brown, who had freed his slaves and clashed with his slave-trading brother, John Brown, an early benefactor of Brown University across the street. The school motto at Moses Brown was "For the honor of truth."

Cianci felt conspicuous at Moses Brown, although he was not the only Italian-American student and there was no overt prejudice. He made friends and developed fond memories of his times there. He also developed the social skills that would enable him to move in different social circles. But there was also a sense of being different, a cultural displacement after growing up across town in Silver Lake. Cianci's teachers and classmates had trouble pronouncing his name; they called him "Kee-yankee," or "Chauncey" (it's "See-ANN-see"). A classmate might make a crack about the Mafia. Cianci invited classmates to his house, but some "never invited me to their houses," he sadly told an aide years later.

"I didn't understand a lot of their lifestyle," he said. "I didn't understand a lot of their values. . . . We drove in and I saw these monstrous buildings—old and, you know, it was really another world. I mean, across the city was another world."

Cianci was an average student, "part of the pile," according to one of his teachers, King O'Dell. Classmate Robert Ellis Smith recalls him as an outsider who tried hard to be one of the gang. He was a joiner—glee club, chess club, school newspaper, wrestling, football, baseball. He got by with grit, determination, and a wisecracking sense of humor.

"Everyone on campus had noticed the Buddha," his yearbook said.

He owned a convertible and took classmates to the old Narragansett Race Track in Pawtucket to play the ponies. Seabiscuit had raced at the Narragansett, where Raymond Patriarca's men were known to "past-post" races—get down bets *after* the race. Cianci loved horses, and rode himself. For his yearbook saying, his classmates chose "The gray mare is the better horse."

Cianci was too much of an outsider to get very involved in student politics. He did serve on the snack bar committee—"without a whiff of scandal," a classmate joked. At the snack bar, in the basement of Middle House, glimpses of the future politician could be seen. Buddy would lean across the bar as he dispensed snacks during recess, telling funny stories about teachers, classmates, and characters from Silver Lake. The other students would gather around their pudgy classmate, who resembled the comedian Jackie Gleason doing his popular bartender TV skit.

At Moses Brown, Cianci defined himself through sports. A football lineman, he badgered his coach all year for a chance to carry the ball. Finally, in his last senior practice, he got his chance—and was gang-tackled so hard that he lost two teeth.

But it was as a wrestler that Cianci had his most success. On the wrestling mat—a twenty-four-foot square smelling of old leather and stale sweat—he learned some of the moves that would serve him well in City Hall. Success required a combination of aggressiveness, brute strength, leverage, and cunning.

Cianci was not a natural athlete, but he worked hard, sweating and grunting to avoid being pinned. Hopelessly behind in one match, he won by default when his opponent tripped and sprained an ankle. He was five foot nine and weighed about 185 pounds. His yearbook photos reveal a boy with a stocky torso, long, brawny arms, closely cropped hair, thick black eyebrows, and full lips curled in a smirk.

In the 1958 state semifinals, at Brown University's Marvel Gym, Cianci wrestled the defending champion, John Volpe. The match quickly became a test of survival for Cianci. Unable to pin his bigger opponent, Cianci kept scrabbling away from him like a crab to avoid being pinned. Frustrated, Volpe smashed Cianci with a forearm while trying to drag him back to the center of the mat. He was penalized a point for unnecessary roughness. At the final whistle, Cianci had escaped being pinned. Each wrestler had scored one point, but the referee, in a controversial decision, raised Cianci's hand in victory. The vocal partisans of Mount Pleasant, accustomed to winning, fell into a stunned silence.

The Buddha just smiled.

BUDDY CIANCI WAS not destined to become a doctor. He lasted just one semester at his father's alma mater, St. Louis University, then transferred to Fairfield University, where he switched from pre-med to political science. He went on to earn a master's in political science at Villanova and a law degree at Marquette University.

As he matured, Cianci grew surer of himself. He became cockier, more charismatic, quicker on his feet. Initially, he envisioned a career in international relations. Drafted by the army after law school, he received a commission as a second lieutenant in the military police. He was assigned to a military government group in Georgia that was headed to Vietnam to work with villagers in creating democratic institutions. But shortly before he was to leave for Vietnam, in 1967, his father died unexpectedly of a heart attack, on the Fourth of July.

Following his father's death, Cianci was transferred closer to home, to Fort Devens in Massachusetts. There a superior's loss was Cianci's gain. One day, a prisoner escaped by putting silver soap wrappers on his shoulders and saluting his way out of the stockade. The commanding officer was reassigned, and Cianci replaced him. He spent a year and a half at Fort Devens, watching over draft dodgers and AWOL soldiers. In 1968, after the assassination of Martin Luther King, Jr., Cianci was provost marshal of a riot squad—the only white man in the brigade, he said—that was going to be sent to Memphis. But the unit was never deployed.

Cianci had met Herb DeSimone in 1966, when between law school and the army he volunteered on his campaign for attorney general. In 1969, after Cianci's army discharge, DeSimone hired him as an assistant attorney general. The job was part-time and paid seventy-five hundred dollars a year. Cianci also launched a private law practice in his father's old doctor's office in Silver Lake.

The young lawyer's new classroom was the Sixth District Court in Providence, in the Old State House on Benefit Street. It was there, in 1776, that Rhode Island had become the first American colony to renounce its allegiance to King George III. The brick building's decline in the two hundred years since spoke to the decay that had settled into the cracks and crevices of Providence itself. In seedy halls that had known the step of George Washington, Thomas Jefferson, and John Adams, halls now pocked with broken plaster and cracked linoleum, Cianci waded into a shifting sea of thugs, prostitutes, junkies, bill collectors, winos, ward heelers, and courthouse politicians.

Security in the antiquated courtrooms was poor. One day, a two-bit mobster nicknamed "the Moron" bolted out of court while being arraigned on a gun charge and led the police on a merry chase through the East Side, over to Smith Hill, and through the new State House.

Cianci reveled in the hurly-burly of the courthouse—the camaraderie, the rivalries, the backroom politics. He prowled the courtroom as if it were a wrestling mat, flailing his arms, spinning on the balls of his feet, and perspiring freely, even in the winter. Once, a judge warned him about his habit of grunting at a witness. He had the physical presence and stamina of a bulldog, with heavy jowls, penetrating brown eyes with bags underneath, and prematurely thinning hair that he combed across a broad forehead.

Out of court, Cianci had a rakish, man-about-town swagger. He was a nocturnal creature, eating and drinking, working and playing late into the night. His iron constitution seemed impervious to illness or lack of sleep. But getting him out of bed in the morning could be a challenge. Minutes before court, Cianci would sweep up to the courthouse in a chauffeured black Cadillac with an opera light on the ceiling. His driver, who also fetched his dry cleaning and brought him sandwiches, was a young man whom Cianci had represented in a worker's compensation case.

Some in the office smiled at Cianci's flamboyance. "That's Buddy," they'd say. But others grumbled that Cianci was overly ambitious, and only for himself. A political junkie, he went to lunch with DeSimone and other Republican leaders to plot strategy. He worked on DeSimone's unsuccessful campaigns for governor in 1970 and 1972, and would have been appointed to a high-ranking position, possibly chief of staff, had DeSimone won.

DeSimone's successor as attorney general, Republican Richard Israel, praised Cianci's abilities and aggressiveness but felt that he had his eye on bigger things and wasn't a team player. He rarely attended staff meetings and was habitually late for court.

"I'd get calls from judges looking for him, and I'd threaten to fire him," recalled William Dimitri, the chief of the Criminal Division. "But he was a damn good prosecutor. He'd rush in late, the judge would chew him out, and then he'd dive into the case."

Stephen Fortunato, a schoolmate from Moses Brown and Silver Lake, saw Cianci's swashbuckling style up close. Returning home from college in the early 1970s to launch his own law practice, Fortunato paid a visit to Cianci's office on Pocasset Avenue. Cianci sat in his heavily furnished chamber, all dark wood and leather, wheeling and dealing. At times he seemed to carry on three conversations at once, barking at his secretary, dispensing advice to Fortunato, and talking to clients on the speakerphone about settling this case or closing that real estate deal. He told Fortunato about his driver and boasted about how well his practice was doing.

Later Fortunato faced Cianci in court. Fortunato defended a man being prosecuted by Cianci in the death of his estranged wife. The man had caught her having an affair and strangled her. Then he tried to make it look like an accident that had occurred during a sexual-arousal technique known as "burking," which involves partial strangulation during oral sex. The killer contended that the death was accidental. But Cianci argued that the marks on the woman's neck proved that she had been deliberately strangled.

"This woman didn't die with a penis in her mouth," Cianci shouted during his closing argument—she had been strangled. The man was convicted.

Cianci had graduated to prosecuting felonies in superior court by then. He was also promoted to the attorney general's Organized Crime Unit, and began working closely with an up-and-coming state police detective, Vincent J. Vespia. The two had known each other as boys, through dinners with their fathers at the Old Canteen. They became best friends.

Vespia was a kick-ass cop who had grown up on the Hill, playing in the street with some of the wiseguys he now pursued. As a young trooper, Vespia had busted a former playmate with a truckload of stolen furs.

"How can you arrest me?" the man asked. "We played kick the can together."

Replied Vespia: "You went one way, I went another."

One night Vespia came crashing through the second-floor window of Willie Marfeo's crap game on Federal Hill from the bucket of a cherry picker, waving a machine gun at two dozen stunned dice players. An obese man raised his hands, and his pants fell down. Another player, a wiseguy, laughed and said it reminded him of Batman. "This is beautiful," he said. "I wouldn't have missed this pinch for the world."

Willie Marfeo's crap game was at the root of Raymond Patriarca's troubles with the law in the late 1960s. When Marfeo refused to pay tribute to Patriarca and brought heat to the Hill with the cherry-picker raid, Patriarca had him killed. When Marfeo's brother, Rudolph, took over the game and swore revenge, Patriarca had him killed, too.

Vespia and Cianci resented the bad name that the Mafia gave honest Italian-Americans and the folk-hero status that many afforded Raymond Patriarca. Vespia's father had grown up on the Hill with Patriarca but had chosen an honest path, driving a truck and later working in the city clerk's office. Vespia could remember walking down Atwells Avenue with his father as a child and stopping to chat with Patriarca, who would pat the boy's head. Later, when Vespia grew up, he visited his father in the hospital and noticed two plants on opposite sides of the room. One was from Patriarca, his father said, and the other was from Colonel Stone of the state police; Vinny's dad joked that he had separated the plants before they started fighting.

"Be a good policeman," Patriarca once told Vinny. "But don't ever frame anybody."

It was a source of pride to Vespia and Cianci to lock up mobsters and show the public that not all Italians were gangsters. As an Italian-American, Cianci said, "I wasn't proud of what these Italian-Americans were accused of doing, what they were doing. I was a very zealous prosecutor."

One of the more memorable trials that Cianci and Vespia worked on together was the Case of Bobo Marrapese and the Italian Wedding Soup.

Bobo was a squat fireplug of a man with a violent temper and a bright future in the mob. He ran the Acorn Athletic Association, a popular organized-crime haunt on the Hill, and dabbled in burglary, gambling, loan-sharking, and assault. Even a parking ticket could set him off; he once threw two chunks of concrete through an offending policeman's windshield.

The week before Christmas in 1971, Bobo went on trial for conspiracy to steal a Ford camper. Cianci invited a friend down to the courthouse to watch the show.

His star witness was Bobo's ex-girlfriend Vivian. In a raucous direct examination, she told Cianci about their tempestuous relationship. After one spat, Vivian hid the keys to all the cars that Bobo had stolen and stashed around Providence. So Bobo beat her up. But the fiery Vivian concocted a spicier revenge. She invited Bobo over for dinner and served him some of her Italian wedding soup. With Vivian's encouragement, Bobo ate one bowl of soup, then a second.

"Did you like the soup?" she asked Bobo.

He grunted that he did.

"Well, I pissed in it!" Vivian screamed.

Bobo's lawyer leaped to his feet and objected.

"Did I hear what I thought I heard?" he asked in disbelief. Cianci, who would regale people with the story years later, pantomiming Vivian ladling out the soup and making his voice raspy and nasty like hers, struggled to keep a straight face.

Bobo had his own objection to the polluted soup, Vivian told Cianci, and he beat her up again, this time breaking her arm. Later, to make it up to her, Bobo suggested a change of scenery. With winter approaching, he offered to take Vivian to Florida on a camper safari. Then he sent two of his men to steal a camper from a local car dealership.

The theft went off smoothly, but then Bobo dumped Vivian. Enraged, she called Vespia. The detective found the stolen camper sticking out of a small garage on Smith Hill, next door to the father of a Providence police officer.

Bobo took the stand in his defense, claiming that a local bartender had offered to sell him the camper, but Bobo refused, suspecting it was stolen. Cianci hammered away at his story and got him to admit that the mysterious bartender had died five weeks before the trial.

Two days before Christmas the jury convicted Bobo and his two confederates. Anticipating the immediate revocation of their bail, the three men stood in the courtroom, stripping off their gold chains, pinky rings, and watches and handing the jewelry to their wives and girlfriends as the lawyers argued about bail. Bobo's lawyer urged the judge to let the men remain free until sentencing, in the spirit of Christmas. Cianci fired back, "Why don't you just go back into your chambers, Your Honor, and put on your Santa Claus suit?"

"That's enough, Mr. Cianci," the judge intoned.

Bobo made bail that day but wound up getting three years in prison. He would be back, to commit more mob mayhem and haunt Cianci's first go-round as mayor.

After Bobo's trial, Cianci urged Vespia to join him on a holiday trip to Venezuela. At the Caracas airport, the Customs police started searching Vespia. As the detective stood spread-eagled against the wall, worrying that this was some mob setup and drugs had been planted in his suitcase, Buddy clowned around, taking Vespia's picture and egging on the searchers. "Check his shoes," said Cianci. "Check inside his belt—he has a secret compartment."

They spent a week at a swanky hotel in Caracas. Vespia would get up at seven to jog on the beach, about the time that Cianci would roll into bed. Cianci would rise at two in the afternoon and come down to the pool for breakfast. One night Vespia came back to their room to find himself locked out. Cianci, who had a girl inside, told him to go sleep by the pool, since he'd be up in a few hours anyway.

Another night after dinner Cianci asked their taxi driver if he knew of a good club where they could go and have some fun. The cabbie drove them miles up into the lush hills surrounding Caracas, to an ornate Spanish villa with verandas and wrought-iron windows, lights ablaze and music floating in the tropical air. Couples in dinner jackets and evening gowns drifted about arm in arm, like something out of a movie. Cianci and Vespia went inside, found the lounge, and sat down at the bar. As their eyes adjusted to the dimness, they noticed a bevy of voluptuous women. The ladies started cozying up to the prosecutor and the detective from Rhode Island, rubbing their shoulders, stroking their legs, slipping tongues in their ears.

Vespia turned to Cianci and said, "Buddy, I think this is a whorehouse."

Cianci slammed his fist on the bar and exclaimed, "Now I know why they made you detective."

They finished their drinks and left, without partaking. A few days later, they were on a plane to Rhode Island. Back home, the murder trial of Raymond Patriarca awaited.

THE DAY AFTER Father Moriarty testified for Raymond Patriarca, Buddy Cianci called St. Ignatius Church in Oxon Hill, Maryland, where the priest had been in 1968. Recently, he had been transferred to a church in nearby College Park. Cianci spoke to the church secretary, Margaret McNeil, and asked if she knew whether Father Moriarty had been away on April 7, 1968.

McNeil, a genteel churchwoman who had worked at St. Ignatius for fourteen years, was bewildered that a prosecutor in Rhode Island would be asking about Father Moriarty. He had not been her favorite priest; he drank too much and got into loud, violent arguments with people. He was bitter toward the diocese over a dispute involving construction of a new Catholic school. But McNeil wasn't about to go into that with Cianci. She told him she would have to consult with the new pastor, Monsignor William O'Donnell, who was still dividing his time between St. Ignatius and his former post as editor of the *Catholic Standard*, in Washington.

Cianci's request went quickly up the ladder, from O'Donnell to the archbishop of Washington, Cardinal Patrick O'Boyle. The cardinal huddled with his advisers, alarmed at the prospect of one of his priests having testified for a mob boss, and concerned about the diocese's legal exposure.

Back in Providence, Cianci waited impatiently. It was past lunchtime. Closing arguments were scheduled to begin in less than half an hour, at

2 P.M. At 1:55, the lead prosecutor, Irving Brodsky, went to the judge's chambers and asked him to delay the closings for fifteen minutes, because the state was expecting certain information from Maryland.

Finally, Cianci was back on the phone, this time in a conference call with O'Donnell in Washington and McNeil at St. Ignatius. With the archbishop's permission, McNeil had searched through church records but had found nothing to show where Father Moriarty had been on April 7, 1968.

Then she had a thought. Perhaps, if there had been a baptism that day . . . but, no, that was Palm Sunday. Baptisms were normally done on Saturday. Just to be certain, McNeil pulled out the St. Ignatius baptismal register, in which she meticulously recorded the entry of each new life in the church. It was a large, red-and-black book, bound in leather, which she kept in the safe in her office on the first floor of the rectory.

Flipping to 1968, McNeil ran her finger down the list of babies born that year. Beside each name was written the date of the baptism and the priest who had performed it. Her finger came to rest on the name of Stacy Lynn Densford.

"He had to have been here that day," she told Cianci. "He baptized a baby girl that day."

Suddenly, there was pandemonium on the phone. Everybody started talking and shouting at once. It was almost two-fifteen. In the attorney general's office Cianci relayed the news to Brodsky, who rushed downstairs to tell the judge. Patriarca's lawyers, curious about the delay, were also waiting. Brodsky told them what Cianci had discovered and asked the judge for a continuance so that Cianci could go down to Maryland and investigate further. The judge gave them until ten the next morning.

Meanwhile, Cianci was telling McNeil not to let the baptismal register out of her sight. Then he and others in the office began making a frantic series of phone calls. The U.S. marshals in Washington agreed to dispatch deputies to St. Ignatius to guard the baptismal register. There were calls to get Cianci and Bobby Stevenson, the Providence police detective, on a plane to Maryland. There was only one more flight from Providence to Washington that afternoon, and it was full. Someone found a U.S. Navy jet, which was placed on standby. Finally, the director of the airport intervened and bumped two passengers off the commercial flight to National Airport.

Cianci and Stevenson landed in Washington around 6 P.M. They were met by two sheriff's deputies from Prince Georges County. Their car sped along the Potomac River, then crossed over into the gently rolling farmland of Maryland.

St. Ignatius Church was a squat brick building on top of a hill in the farming community of Oxon Hill, about twenty miles east of Washington. Two U.S. marshals were already there when Cianci arrived. And it was a good thing. A group of Patriarca associates, including his son, Junior, and his lawyer, had beaten Cianci and Stevenson to Maryland by chartering a Lear jet, only to be turned away at St. Ignatius by the marshals.

As dusk fell over the church, a congregation gathered in the lace-curtained dining room of the rectory next door. Besides Cianci and Stevenson and the two marshals, there were the two Prince Georges County deputies and two lawyers representing Cardinal O'Boyle and Monsignor O'Donnell. Margaret McNeil sat uneasily at the table, clutching the baptismal record to her chest. She said little as the lawmen sipped the monsignor's Chivas Regal and puffed on cigars.

Cianci, wreathed in a cloud of cologne and cigar smoke, carried the unmistakable whiff of danger. His speech was fast and gravelly as he talked about how this was an important trial, how Patriarca was the big Mafia guy, the godfather for all of New England, and how he had ordered numerous people murdered. Cianci told her that, as the custodian of the baptismal register, she would have to fly back to Rhode Island with him the next morning and possibly testify. The blood drained from the woman's face. She nearly fainted.

O'Donnell eased Cianci aside and stepped in to try and lighten the mood. He made a joke about the hit movie in theaters that spring, *The Godfather*. McNeil blanched. She had just seen the movie, and now she kept flashing on the scene where the Hollywood producer wakes up to find a severed horse's head in his bed.

A policeman was sent to fetch Father Moriarty. Meanwhile, Cianci negotiated with the archbishop's lawyers. Cardinal O'Boyle was angry with the priest and wanted him to go back to Rhode Island and straighten things out. But he also wanted to cut a deal with the attorney general so that Father Moriarty would not be prosecuted.

Cianci said that he lacked the authority and called Irving Brodsky, who started screaming into the phone so loudly that Cianci had to hold the receiver away from his ear. "No fucking way I'm making any deals with any fucking cardinals!" shouted Brodsky. "Get that lying bastard back here! I want that priest on the stand tomorrow!"

Cianci told the cardinal's men that there would be no deal, and went about assembling his case against Father Moriarty. A Prince Georges deputy brought the father of the baptized girl, Allan Densford, to the rectory. Densford showed Cianci his daughter's birth certificate and dated Polaroid photographs of Father Moriarty baptizing her. The girl had been born with a bilateral hip dislocation that required surgery. So her parents had pushed for an early baptism, which was done on Palm Sunday, three weeks after she was born. Densford remembered the time vividly; Martin Luther King had just been assassinated, and riots were threatening his family's furniture store in Washington.

Cianci told Densford about the Patriarca trial and said he would be needed in court in Rhode Island the next day. The prosecutor told him that Patriarca's men were around Oxon Hill, and impressed upon him the gravity of the situation, that the information about his daughter's baptism could lead to a mob boss's conviction in a double homicide. The Prince Georges sheriffs agreed to watch the Densfords' house that night.

Later, Father Moriarty arrived at the rectory and was taken into custody by Cianci and Stevenson. The federal marshals drove Cianci, Stevenson, and Father Moriarty, wedged together in the backseat, to a motel in Alexandria.

They got two adjoining rooms and left the door open. The Providence lawmen shared one room; the priest and one marshal took the other. Cianci and Stevenson questioned Father Moriarty late into the night. He was calm and serene, insisting that he must have confused the dates.

It was nearly 4 A.M. when everyone finally went to bed. A few hours later, Stevenson was struggling to wake up Cianci and pushing him into the shower. Then they drove to National Airport, where they met Monsignor O'Donnell, Margaret McNeil, and Allan Densford and his wife, Jean. Cianci was at the ticket counter, arranging for the flight, when the terminal doors slid open. In walked Junior Patriarca and Joseph Badway, the old man's driver and proprietor of a Providence auto-body shop that was a wiseguy haunt.

"We want to talk to the priest," demanded Patriarca.

"You're not talking to anybody," replied Stevenson.

The two mobsters retreated when the federal marshal threatened to arrest them.

On the hour-long flight to Providence, the St. Ignatius contingent sat near the front of the airplane, guarded by the lawmen. The younger Patriarca and Badway sat near the back of the plane, poking their heads out to peer up the aisle.

When they got off the plane in Rhode Island, Cianci's Cadillac and driver were waiting on the tarmac. Escorted by police cars, the Cadillac sped north on Interstate 95 from the growing suburbs encircling the aging capital, through an industrial corridor of old brick factories and warehouses.

Sitting in his car with the Densfords and Margaret McNeil, who was still clinging to the baptismal register, Cianci boasted how he was going to blow the case wide open. Nobody else said much. The convoy arrived at the courthouse, which bristled with shotgun-toting policemen.

Irving Brodsky met Cianci and the group from St. Ignatius. He took one look at Moriarty, who was dressed in civilian clothes, and snapped: "Where are your priest clothes? You were wearing your priest clothes the other day."

A little while later, having changed into his priest clothes, an embarrassed Father Moriarty returned to the courtroom. Patriarca's lawyer tried to block the state's attempt to put him back on the stand. The priest had made an honest mistake, the lawyer argued, and his testimony should simply be stricken from the record; no purpose would be served in recalling him, except to expose him to ridicule and harassment in front of a crowded courtroom. But the judge refused, calling Father Moriarty's testimony the strongest evidence on Patriarca's behalf.

With Cianci once again watching from the back of the courtroom, Father Moriarty took the stand for the second time in three days. This time, there was no hug from Patriarca. Father Moriarty was sheepish, more subdued. The courtroom was hushed as everyone listened intently. The Densfords and McNeil were upstairs, in reserve, should the priest fail to recant his previous testimony.

"Father," shouted Brodsky, "were you at the home of Raymond L. S. Patriarca on April 7, 1968?"

"I was not."

During each question, Brodsky pounded the jury rail with his fist.

"Were you at any time on April 7, 1968, in the company of the defendant?"

"I was not."

"Were you at the cemetery saying prayers for the late Mrs. Patriarca on April 7, 1968?"

"I was not."

Moriarty said that he had been away from his parish for several months and so he hadn't had access to the records at St. Ignatius when Patriarca's son had called and asked him to testify. He had simply gotten confused about the dates.

Few people in the courtroom believed him. Brodsky emphasized the priest's testimony in his closing argument. Following Father Moriarty's testimony two days ago, the prosecutor told the jury, it looked as if the state's case had been destroyed. But that morning's developments cast things in a new light.

As the jury began its deliberations, Cianci basked in the glow of the media spotlight. Explaining to reporters how he'd uncovered the real story, he said that Father Moriarty's testimony was "so believable that it was unbelievable." The next day, Saturday, June 3, 1972, Cianci made his first appearance on the front page of *The Providence Journal*. A large photograph of him ran above the fold, with a story headlined PRIEST EPISODE "UNBELIEVABLE."

Meanwhile, the jurors slogged through a weekend of deliberations. On the first ballot, they voted 7–5 to convict Patriarca. Many jurors were troubled by the priest's testimony. Before "the priest thing," as the jury foreman later referred to it, not one of the jurors thought Patriarca was guilty.

Ultimately, one lie trumped another.

The jurors were also bothered by contradictions in the testimony of the government's star witness, Red Kelley. The most glaring example was Kelley's recollection of the fateful Palm Sunday meeting with Patriarca as having taken place in front of the Gaslight Lounge on Orange Street. The defense had presented testimony that the restaurant was closed at the time because of a fire. Years later, Kelley would admit that he had lied about the location of the meeting on orders from a Boston FBI agent, Paul Rico, who wanted to implicate the owner of the Gaslight. Rico would later become notorious in his own right in the 1990s, as part of a burgeoning scandal involving the Boston FBI office and its cozy relationship with gangster-informants Whitey Bulger and Stephen Flemmi.

On Sunday afternoon, after eight ballots, the jury voted to acquit Raymond Patriarca of accessory to murder. The mob boss wept at the news.

Cianci was unfazed by the verdict. "It's okay," he told Monsignor O'Donnell, now back in Maryland. "We've got other charges coming."

Margaret McNeil, relieved to get out of Providence, had to contend for a while with anonymous threatening phone calls in the middle of the night about her role in the Patriarca case. Someone sent her a Boston newspaper article reporting the verdict. Then, one day, Father Moriarty stopped by the rectory. He seemed happy, and drunk, and was eager to gloat.

"I want you to know that my friend was acquitted," he told her.

That summer Patriarca testified before a congressional committee investigating the mob's influence on horse racing. He denied knowing Frank Sinatra, who also appeared to deny his hidden interest with the mob boss in a Massachusetts racetrack. One congressman couldn't resist asking Patriarca's opinion of Mario Puzo's best-selling novel, *The Godfather*.

"It was a good book and interesting reading," replied Patriarca. "There was a lot of fiction in it. People like to read that stuff. You could come out with *The Patriarca Papers* tomorrow and make a million dollars on it."

Cianci went on to try a case involving a violent criminal, John Gary Robichaud, who had disguised himself as a priest to steal a sixty-six-thousand-dollar payroll from an armored car at the state Department of Employment Security. Robichaud was convicted, then escaped from the state prison a few months later. Cianci slept with a gun by his bed—until Robichaud's bullet-riddled body turned up a few weeks later in Massachusetts.

Then Cianci's work as a prosecutor took a turn: he was assigned to a new public-corruption unit formed by the attorney general. Not long afterward, Cianci received a tip that would lead to an investigation of the administration of the mayor of Providence, Joseph A. Doorley, Jr.

That case would be part of the genesis of Cianci's first run for public office—as the anticorruption candidate.

CHAPTER TWO

The Anticorruption Candidate

They called it Doorley's Dream.

Rising from the marshy soil near the Great Salt Cove of colonial times, on the site of an old jewelry factory, the Providence Civic Center was hailed as the salvation of a dying city. Joseph A. Doorley, Jr., the mayor of Providence, had built the Civic Center after the state's voters refused to pay for it. It was the early 1970s, desperate times for Providence. Since the suburban boom that followed World War II, the capital city's population had plummeted from 248,000 to 179,000. The federal urban-renewal funds from Lyndon B. Johnson's Great Society had dried up.

The big department stores were closing, one by one. One day teenagers pulled some mannequins out of a Dumpster, smeared the arms and legs with ketchup, and then drove around downtown with the would-be corpses sticking out of the trunk of their Karmann Ghia; the police ignored them. A Chamber of Commerce leader said that you could fire a rifle down Westminster Street at dusk and not hit anyone. Even a downtown Bible studies storefront had shut down, because there were no souls left to save.

The cynics said that Providence was beyond salvation. They predicted that Doorley's Dream would become Doorley's Icebox.

The building opened on Friday night, November 3, 1972, with a Providence Reds hockey game. The proud city fathers invited President Richard M. Nixon, who was scheduled to make a campaign stop at the state airport in Warwick, to drop the ceremonial first puck.

Not surprisingly, the Republican president declined to venture into a Democratic stronghold that hadn't elected a Republican mayor since the Great Depression. Standing on the steps of *Air Force One*, bathed in spotlights, Nixon urged Rhode Islanders to elect Herbert DeSimone as governor and John Chafee as U.S. senator the following Tuesday. The marching bands drowned out a small group of hecklers who chanted about Watergate—which was still just a third-rate burglary.

Among the crowd of ten thousand cheering Nixon supporters was Buddy Cianci, who had emerged as a key campaign adviser to DeSimone. DeSimone was considering making Cianci his chief of staff if he became governor. But when DeSimone lost, Cianci started to think more seriously about his own political future. He had toyed previously with the idea of running for mayor of Cranston, or some other office in that Republican-dominated city.

Meanwhile, in Providence, Cianci was hearing rumors of turmoil in the mighty Democratic party.

Early in 1973, a few weeks after Doorley presided over the Civic Center's grand opening, a rock-music promoter named Robert "Skip" Chernov walked into Cianci's life.

Chernov had come to the attorney general's office angry and scared. The executive director of Doorley's Civic Center had just shaken him down for a one-thousand-dollar bribe to book a Grateful Dead concert.

Doorley's Dream was about to become Cianci's Opportunity.

SKIP CHERNOV WAS an unlikely instrument for a political revolution.

With black curly hair and red velvet sport coats, he bore a striking resemblance to Tiny Tim. He did drugs, drove a Bentley, and cultivated a flamboyant hippie image that was the antithesis of the Irish Catholic, shot-and-beer Doorley, whose taste ran to Frank Sinatra.

In 1969 the mayor had banned rock concerts in Providence after Chernov promoted a Sly and the Family Stone concert at the Rhode Island Auditorium that was followed by a riot. But with the construction of the Civic Center, Doorley needed the revenues from big rock shows to pay off the bonds. And Chernov was the biggest promoter in town.

The son of an Orthodox Jewish interior decorator from Russia, Chernov had always been different. Born in South Providence, he got his start promoting rock-and-roll dance nights at Catholic Providence College, where he also ran for class president with the slogan "A Jew for you," losing by fifty-one votes.

After college he headed for the West Coast and landed in the center of the vibrant San Francisco music scene. He worked his way up from doorman at a topless bar to manager of Basin Street West, which defied the San

Francisco police by booking Lenny Bruce. Miles Davis played at Chernov's wedding. A young Janis Joplin crashed at his apartment. He went on to become a Xerox salesman in Beverly Hills, where he made a lot of money but missed the action.

In 1968, with a pregnant wife and dreams of becoming a big shot in his hometown, Chernov moved back to Providence and opened a nightclub, the Warehouse, on the grubby waterfront. He brought in up-and-coming acts like Neil Young and Deep Purple. The crowds, hungry for rock and roll, poured in—hippies, sailors, bikers, artists, businessmen, college students, secretaries. In a town where the drinking age was twenty-one, Chernov defied convention by aiming his club at youth.

He also learned two truisms of doing business in Providence: you had to cater to the mob, and you fought City Hall at your peril.

To install vending machines and game machines in the club, Chernov had to go through Raymond Patriarca's Coin-O-Matic Distributing. Other companies were cheaper, but Coin-O-Matic offered something that its rivals didn't—protection from break-ins and vandalism. When Chernov went up the Hill to close the deal, Patriarca looked over the long-haired, shabbily dressed young man who aspired to be Providence's king of rock and roll.

"Aren't you Sammy Chernov's son?" he said. "Your dad's a stand-up guy."

Chernov was indeed Sammy Chernov's boy, gregarious Sammy Chernov, whose interior-decorating fortunes had brightened one day, during World War II, when he was hired to redecorate Patriarca's brother's house and Raymond stopped by. Patriarca had taken a liking to him, and his business began to expand into areas that he had been unable to crack before. Soon Chernov was landing lucrative contracts redecorating Providence funeral homes, even the Rhode Island State House. As the business grew, the Chernovs moved into a spacious house in the upscale waterfront suburb of Barrington, one of the first Jewish families to do so.

Years later, when Skip was planning to open the Warehouse, his father advised him to see Patriarca but never to become his partner. Straight money deals were okay, but a partnership was for life—and partnerships could end badly.

The strange cultural crosscurrents of Skip Chernov's life were never more evident than the day he took Neil Young to Smith's, a popular family-style Italian restaurant on the Hill, and ran into Raymond Patriarca after a mob shooting.

Chernov liked to take his performers to Smith's, known for its succulent spareribs, to impress them so that they'd want to return to a second-rate city like Providence. The singers would get the celebrity treatment and autograph a photo to hang on the wall.

As soon as he and Young walked in, they noticed that the phone booth was splintered and saw some blood spattered on the wall. Young, who had just released his first album with Crazy Horse, *Everybody Knows This Is Nowhere*, had pulled into Providence that afternoon in a rented car, towing a U-Haul trailer with the band's equipment. Now he wanted to get the hell out.

Chernov, trying to calm him down, looked down the long, narrow restaurant and spotted Patriarca sitting in the last booth. They nodded to each other. A waiter told Chernov that there had been a mob shooting the night before; the Old Man was there to restore order.

"Who's that?" Young asked, lowering his voice. "Is that the don?"

"You don't want to know," said Chernov, but Young persisted.

Chernov conceded that it was "the don," and that it would be a sign of disrespect for them to leave. They stayed for dinner. Young left an autographed picture, inscribed, "Best ribs ever." The picture hung in Smith's until the restaurant burned a few years later. That night, Young played an inspired four-hour set at the Warehouse, prowling the stage during extended guitar solos on "Cinnamon Girl" and "Cowgirl in the Sand," for a crowd of forty-three paying customers.

If Skip Chernov could coexist with Raymond Patriarca and the mob, Joe Doorley's City Hall was another story. The Warehouse was a constant source of friction. Fights broke out at closing time, and the Providence police became a familiar presence. Chernov complained of police harassment, saying they didn't like hippies. At closing time, he played a tape of the "Hallelujah Chorus," which further irritated the police.

Nor did Chernov endear himself to City Hall by booking the MC5, the Detroit band whose signature song was "Kick Out the Jams, Motherfuckers." The MC5 had played for antiwar protesters at the 1968 Democratic National Convention in Chicago, where Doorley had chaired the Credentials Committee, and given the finger to his pal Mayor Daley. Doorley's Board of Licenses refused a permit for the MC5 concert. Chernov sued on free-speech grounds and won. The MC5 played to a packed house, without incident.

In 1969 Chernov was busted for having a cover charge on a Sunday, and later for serving beer to underage drinkers and asking them to lie about it to the police. Chernov beat the charges, but the city took away his liquor license. The Warehouse wound up in the hands of the father of Ronald Glantz, Doorley's assistant city solicitor.

Chernov bounced back. He cut a deal with Narragansett Brewery to promote the Narragansett Tribal Rock series throughout New England, booking acts like the Band and Led Zeppelin. He opened a bar, the Incredible Organ Pub, and a Mexican restaurant, Tortilla Flats, and bought and motorized a San Francisco cable car to ferry customers between the two. In 1971 he won New England closed-circuit television rights to the world heavyweight boxing match between Muhammad Ali and Joe Frazier and took in a million dollars. He bought a big house on the East Side with French gardens and a billiards room.

Chernov suffered a setback when the riot broke out after the Sly and the Family Stone concert, and Doorley banned rock concerts in Providence. Furious, Chernov wanted to take the city to court. But brewery officials counseled patience, urging Chernov to focus on concerts in other cities. A few months later the concert ban was lifted—but not by a judge. According to Chernov, it went down like this: Doorley ran a bar near City Hall. Narragansett Brewery agreed to supply him with free beer. And rock and roll returned to Providence.

ON THE MORNING of February 13, 1973, Chernov and his lawyer were ushered into Dick Israel's office and offered coffee and pastry. Someone introduced Chernov to a heavyset, balding man in a short-sleeve shirt and tie named Buddy Cianci.

Chernov proceeded to tell a story about his efforts, over the past several months, to book concerts at the Civic Center. For months, Chernov said, he had been lobbying the center's executive director, Harold Copeland, and gotten the runaround. Then, on February 2, 1973, during a telephone conversation with Copeland about a possible Grateful Dead concert, Copeland told Chernov that it would cost him $13,500 to rent the Civic Center—plus a thousand bucks, under the table, for Copeland.

Hanging up, Chernov was a nervous wreck. He told his wife, his secretary, and his business partner, Bruce Goldstein. In Chernov's opinion, Copeland was either shaking him down, setting him up, or making a sick joke. They agreed to notify their lawyer, who told the attorney general, Dick Israel.

Six days later, on a Friday, Chernov came into his office and found a message from Copeland. Angry and scared, Chernov called Doorley's office and demanded an emergency meeting with the mayor. He told Doorley's personal secretary that he didn't want to make enemies at City Hall, but that if he didn't get an appointment, the shit was going to hit the fan. But Doorley wouldn't meet with him. A few minutes after Chernov hung up with Doorley's secretary, Copeland called to say that he had a couple of open dates in April. Once again, Chernov said, Copeland brought up the thousand dollars for himself, under the table.

The following Monday, February 12, Chernov bought a tape recorder and hooked it up to the telephone in his office. There was another message to call Copeland. With Chernov's partner listening on the extension and recording the conversation, Chernov made the call. He and Copeland discussed the concert dates in April. Copeland reiterated that Chernov's expenses for renting the building would be $13,500.

"Yeah, it's the whole thing," said Copeland. "Out the door you're thirteen five."

"Right," replied Chernov.

"With me," Copeland continued.

"Well, okay," said Chernov.

"Yeah, and there's a thousand for me," Copeland said.

"Okay," said Chernov.

"Strictly under the table, and all that [blank]," said Copeland.

"Right," said Chernov.

The next morning, February 13, Chernov brought the tape to the attorney general's office and played it for the assembled prosecutors, including Cianci, who listened quietly. Israel asked Chernov if he thought Copeland was just kidding. Chernov said he didn't know but agreed to work undercover and try to deliver the bribe to Copeland. The case was assigned to state police detective Vin Vespia, Cianci's friend and a former classmate of Chernov's at Hope High School. The Providence police, who were too closely aligned with Joe Doorley, would be kept out of the loop. Israel told Chernov that Cianci would probably try the case.

Cianci didn't say much during the meeting, but Chernov did take note of one comment. The prosecutor allowed himself a Cheshire-cat grin and said, "Now I got him!"

In the following weeks, Chernov talked to Copeland again and booked a Pink Floyd concert for March 19. On the night of the show, Chernov walked into the Civic Center carrying a state police briefcase wired with a tape recorder and transmitter. He also carried ten one-hundred-dollar bills that Vespia had dusted with a fluorescent powder that would stick to the hands of anyone who handled the money. Chernov had been warned not to offer the money unless Copeland asked for it.

Outside, Vespia waited in a van. He had a warrant to search Copeland and his office.

As Chernov walked inside, he whistled a few notes to test the transmitter, not unlike the sound check that the band members of Pink Floyd were performing onstage. The psychedelic rock band from Great Britain had just released a new album, *Dark Side of the Moon*, with its hit single, "Money," featuring the *ca-ching* of cash registers. The building pulsed with sound as Chernov waited nervously, wired with his own sound system.

Chernov thought that Copeland seemed uneasy as they settled the box-office receipts. He never asked for the money. Outside, in the van, Vespia cursed, believing that Copeland had been tipped off.

Shortly thereafter, Chernov and Bruce Goldstein, his partner, attended another meeting in the attorney general's office. According to Goldstein, the attorney general was on the fence about whether to proceed, since Copeland hadn't taken the money. But Cianci spoke up forcefully in favor of pursuing the case, Goldstein recalled.

Israel said the authorities would monitor the situation. Chernov and Goldstein left the meeting relieved, figuring that that was the end of it. Since going to the authorities, they had had second thoughts about the ramifications to their concert business.

While that drama played out behind the scenes, Joe Doorley and the city were preoccupied with the fortunes of the Civic Center's primary tenant, the Providence College men's basketball team. The day before the Pink Floyd concert, the Friars upset Maryland to advance to college basketball's Final Four. The team was led by homegrown talents Ernie DiGregorio and Marvin "Bad News" Barnes, the star-crossed All-American center from South Providence who, according to local legend, had once tried to hold up a city bus wearing his Central High School letter jacket. Doorley joined a delegation of Rhode Island politicians who journeyed to St. Louis, hoping to see the Friars meet Bill Walton's mighty UCLA team for the championship. But Barnes injured his knee in the semifinals and the Friars lost to Memphis State. Doorley returned home and dreamed about what might have been.

That spring, with the Watergate scandal mushrooming, Mayor Doorley remarked that the Republicans' apparent attempt to bug the Democratic National Committee offices was no shock to him.

"Everybody assumes that the politicians are spies and cheats and liars," said Doorley, who confessed that he liked to "snoop" to find out what his political rivals were up to. "I suspect that very little of my activities are not bugged."

Doorley didn't say that he had recently been tipped off that Chernov had Copeland on tape, asking for money. The mayor had passed the rumor on to Copeland, according to Copeland's subsequent court testimony. Copeland went to Chernov, who dismissed the rumor as "absurd."

"There's always somebody trying to get somebody in this town," Chernov told him.

TWO MONTHS AFTER the Pink Floyd concert, Joe Doorley served as toastmaster at a very different kind of gathering at the Civic Center, one rife with intrigue that would have implications for the political fortunes of Buddy Cianci.

Three thousand city workers, ward heelers, and other Democratic party luminaries and soldiers—from the governor on down to sewer workers—turned out to pay tribute to a man known simply as Mr. Democrat, Lawrence P. McGarry, a lean, twinkling Irishman with a mischievous smile and a Machiavellian mind.

McGarry was the Democratic city chairman of Providence, the last of the old-time political bosses. He ran the city's Public Works Department, the hub of a patronage empire that turned out the votes on election day. A product of the "Fighting Tenth" Ward, on the city's South Side, McGarry had come up through the ranks, beginning as a teenage errand boy in the Great Depression for the party bosses who hung out at Gallagher's plumbing shop. An advancing case of multiple sclerosis made it increasingly difficult for him to get around without the aid of a cane or a wheelchair. But McGarry, an avid horse-racing fan with his own box near the finish line at Lincoln Downs, still possessed an agile political mind.

McGarry believed in unquestioned loyalty to the Democratic machine. He once warned that if the unendorsed candidate won in a certain ward, "not another leaf will be picked up in that neighborhood." But he was also a benevolent boss, a devout Catholic who attended St. Pius V Church in Elmhurst, and a sucker for a hard-luck story. He enjoyed a good cigar—the bigger, the better—and he mocked the image of the smoke-filled room by posing for a newspaper photograph with ashtrays overflowing with cigarette butts.

"The political machine is just ordinary people," he liked to say. "I never saw anything dishonest take place in a back room."

In the back room McGarry was king—and, as the crowd gathered at the Civic Center attested, Rhode Island's preeminent political kingmaker. He came to power in 1964, when he led a party revolt against the entrenched Democratic leadership and backed Joe Doorley, a spunky young councilman and lawyer educated at Notre Dame and Boston College.

Together McGarry and Doorley had restored the strength of the Democratic machine. Doorley was the out-front guy, making speeches, searching for ways to reverse Providence's postwar decline, mingling with national Democratic bigwigs. McGarry was the behind-the-scenes guy. Sitting in his wheelchair at Public Works, a brick building near the crumbling Port of Providence with its dilapidated warehouses and gasoline-storage tanks, McGarry oiled the machine—doling out patronage, receiving favor seekers, directing the troops.

But after nearly a decade, the partnership was fraying. Despite their smiles at McGarry's Civic Center tribute, Mr. Democrat and Mayor Doorley were in the process of a painful political divorce. McGarry believed that Doorley had broken faith with the machine—that the mayor had lost interest in the job and grown aloof and arrogant. Doorley's drinking also bothered McGarry. The mayor, who boasted that he could conduct all of his city business for the day between 9:30 A.M. and lunchtime, could often be found later on some bar stool, his speech slurred, his balance unsteady.

Doorley's dissolution mirrored his city's. *Providence Journal* political columnist Brian Dickinson wrote that the mayor had squandered his obvious talents for running a city. "Drained by a penchant for high living and compromised by a reliance on the dreariest sort of machine politics, he has been content to see the city drift and stagnate. Behind that rambunctious Frankie Fontaine exterior, whatever spark there used to be has flickered out."

The mayor, who bristled at any criticism, particularly from a newspaper run by Yankee Republicans, fired back that at least his high living was not at country clubs, but in working-class establishments where he could watch a ball game and live up to his reputation as "a beer-drinking, two-fisted politician."

The son of a Providence firefighter whose father had emigrated from County Roscommon, Doorley grew up in Irish working-class Elmhurst, where life revolved around family, church, and ward politics. The Democratic machine was not the corrupt monolith attacked by East Side reformers but an extended family. It had enabled the immigrants, predominantly Irish and Italian, to accumulate power and to eventually overthrow the

Yankee factory owners and Republican bosses. The machine provided order and stability. If you needed a streetlight replaced, a sidewalk fixed, a job, coal for your furnace, a Christmas turkey, even a pair of shoes or a bath—the city operated public bathhouses then—you went to your block captain, who went to his ward committeeman, who went to the ward chairman, who called downtown. In return, the machine commanded your loyalty, and your vote.

Doorley, who nurtured his idealism at Notre Dame and later as a civics teacher at La Salle Academy, a Catholic high school that educated scores of future political and business leaders, viewed Kennedy's New Frontier and Johnson's Great Society as extensions of the machine's noblest principles. Doorley had run President Kennedy's 1960 campaign in Rhode Island and been inspired to run for city council in 1962 by Kennedy's inaugural declaration that the torch had been passed to a new generation. Proud that Kennedy's political roots were in the wards of Boston, Doorley also saw a need for new ideas. He felt that Providence was falling out of the mainstream of American life. The city was losing middle-class whites faster than any city in the country except Detroit.

The Democratic machine that had run Providence since the Great Depression was suffering from atrophy. Mayor Walter Reynolds, nicknamed "Scratchy Ass" by some, had alienated party regulars by neglecting politics and patronage and catering to the big shots downtown. He had been in power for fourteen years. When Larry McGarry tried to take control of the Democratic City Committee, Reynolds fired him from his job at Public Works.

Another machine boss, City Council president Tommy Luongo, carried his patronage empire too far. A Federal Hill liquor-store owner, Luongo was said to have placed a thousand people in city, state, and federal jobs. One of them was Joe Melino, a Providence street sweeper who didn't exist but who still managed to cash his city paychecks for more than three years. In 1964, while Doorley was running for mayor, Luongo and one of his ward committeemen were convicted of cheating the city. The scandal highlighted Doorley's call for change and drove Luongo from office; he died shortly thereafter—from a broken heart, some said.

Not wanting to risk a divisive primary, Reynolds didn't run in 1964, citing his health. McGarry, who had initially favored another candidate, aligned himself with Doorley. He was a fresh, appealing face; he came from the Fifth Ward, the city's most populous; and he had a well-to-do uncle who ran a construction company and could help finance the campaign. Doorley and McGarry swept to victory over Reynolds's handpicked candidate and took control of the machine.

Joe Doorley was thirty-three years old, the youngest mayor in Providence history, and eager to get to work. The morning after his election-night celebration, he was out early with his campaign volunteers, taking down his political signs.

During the turbulent sixties, when politicians were struggling to address the ills of America's cities, Doorley stood on the ramparts of President Lyndon Johnson's Great Society. Providence was among the first to join the federal Model Cities program and to integrate its schools. Doorley pushed for fair housing laws and antipoverty programs, and obtained federal funding for the country's first urban-renewal demolition project and the second code-enforcement project. Doorley and his top policy aide, Jack Cicilline, traveled regularly to Washington and New York to learn about various urban programs. Cicilline said that federal officials were impressed that the mayor would come personally rather than just sending an aide.

"I firmly believe that the position of mayor of a large urban city is the single most important political office in America today," Doorley wrote.

Doorley's advocacy won him attention from such publications as *Time* magazine. He began traveling in national Democratic circles. He became a regular visitor to the Texas ranch of national party chairman Robert S. Strauss and ran a respectable race for national chairman himself in 1970. He headed the credentials committee in 1968, the year of the party's riotous national convention in Chicago, where Mayor Richard Daley's cops beat antiwar protesters. Daley, who sent his son, Richard, the future mayor of Chicago, to Providence College, praised Doorley's Providence machine. Doorley, in turn, joked that he was "a mini Daley."

While Doorley attacked the city's problems and cultivated his growing national image, Larry McGarry tended the machine. He was in his element chewing on a cigar, a ball game on in the background, surrounded by cronies like "Snack" McManus, who drove a yellow Cadillac, and "Taxi" Albanese, a Fourth Ward committeeman, sewer inspector, and bookmaker who didn't drive but instead took cabs from bar to bar. Taxi didn't really know how to inspect a sewer, said one councilman, but he could tell you how many miles of sewer pipe there were in Providence.

McGarry could also count. He knew how many votes there were, and how to keep them in line. His friend ex-councilman Ray Devitt recalled McGarry presiding over a Tenth Ward committee meeting in a restaurant, and making everyone join hands around the table to show that "we're all in this together." Still, politics was like sports, all about the action and winning or losing. McGarry loved to gamble, running a regular Friday-night card game in the Tenth Ward, and he loved the rough-and-tumble of ward politics.

"With Larry, you toed the mark or you were gone," said Devitt. "He played hardball."

Although he never held public office, McGarry dictated to those who did. Each week, before the City Council met, McGarry gathered the Democratic councilmen in a private room next to the council chambers at City Hall and told them how to vote. Since the Democrats controlled twenty-four of the twenty-six council seats, the caucus was where the real decisions were made. There would be some fierce battles, but McGarry saw to it that they walked out onto the floor unified.

In 1971 some councilmen complained anonymously to *The Providence Journal* about McGarry's "tyranny" in trying to dictate appointments to the new Civic Center Authority. "We've had it up to here with the 'Last Hurrah' antics and being told what we must do and how we should vote," said one.

The reference to *The Last Hurrah* showed how far behind the times Providence had fallen. The classic American political novel by Edwin O'Connor, who had been weaned on Rhode Island politics growing up in Woonsocket, depicted machine politics in Boston as going out of style in the 1950s. In Larry McGarry's Providence, the machine was still fashionable in the early 1970s. The day that the *Journal* published its story identifying the so-called dirty dozen councilmen who were unhappy with McGarry, eleven of the twelve publicly denied any rift and swore their loyalty to Mr. Democrat. End of mutiny.

Not everything was so easy to control. In the early 1970s friends noticed that McGarry would lose his balance without warning. He wasn't a drinker, so they knew something was wrong. He was diagnosed with multiple sclerosis, a degenerative nerve disease that robs the body of coordination, muscle control, and, eventually, speech and brain functions. It was a terrifying illness for anyone, but especially for a man who thrived on moving around the city and talking to people.

McGarry persevered. He required help going up stairs. He started using a cane and a wheelchair. He got a driver and continued to make the rounds. While the disease slowed him down physically, it didn't dull his mind—or diminish his growing conflict with Joe Doorley over the direction of Providence.

From Jack Cicilline's perspective as Doorley's top policy aide, the struggle between the two men reflected the desperation of the times. By the 1960s, three fourths of the nation's people lived in cities; many of these city dwellers were poor, black, and elderly, unemployed and ravaged by drugs. The changing demographics threatened the power of old political machines and cried out for new solutions. Doorley and McGarry clashed over patronage in the new federal programs and the mayor's efforts to draw minorities into the political process.

Cicilline bore the brunt of McGarry's anger. Mr. Democrat thought that Doorley should take care of his base and get rid of people like Cicilline, a young, liberal idealist with shaggy hair and glasses who had a picture of Robert Kennedy in his office. But Doorley, though a Johnson man, relied on Cicilline, a bright former student at La Salle Academy, to guide him through the maze of new federal programs and keep him in touch with the black community. Doorley created an antipoverty agency, Progress for Providence, and brought in Kennedy pal William McNamara from out of state to run it. He gave McNamara free rein to hire other outsiders and nonpolitical people from the city's poor neighborhoods.

Cicilline witnessed shouting matches in the mayor's office between Doorley and McGarry, who had three criteria for a job: if you were a friend, if you were qualified, and if you were a Democrat.

"Geez," McGarry would complain, "you're giving this guy a ten-thousand-dollar job when I have a list of people we owe jobs." Cicilline also argued with Mr. Democrat, who couldn't understand why "there's this guy in South Providence who's got a city car and a fat job, hanging around with kids."

McGarry and the Old Guard also were unhappy with Doorley's efforts to reach out to the black community. With racial tensions increasing, a loose group of neighborhood advocates, school officials, and East Side liberals convinced Doorley to push for integration and to open a magnet school in South Providence, where the mayor sent his own children.

"Larry McGarry complained that this was pissing off the whites," said Cicilline. "We'd go to a rally or a function up in Elmhurst, and people started ignoring Joe, in his own neighborhood."

Cicilline viewed McGarry as a throwback to James Michael Curley, a likeable, "you scratch my back, I'll scratch yours" politician who had fallen out of step with the times. "He didn't recognize that you needed to open the doors," says Cicilline. "I would tell him, 'Do you remember when the Irish were trying to become cops, get city jobs, and there were guys in City Hall with baseball bats, trying to keep them out?' His attitude was, 'Yeah, well, now it's our turn. We're the guys with the bats.' "

In retrospect, Cicilline said, some of the well-intentioned solutions, such as tearing down buildings and putting up high-rises, proved misguided and even made things worse. But you had to be there, to see the city burning, to feel the urgency to try something, *anything*. In blighted neighborhoods across Providence, arson was the leading pastime; on some summer weekends, weary firefighters fought several hundred fires as a haze of smoke hung over the city.

Cicilline quit in 1968, the year that Bobby Kennedy was assassinated, to pursue a private law practice, eventually becoming Rhode Island's preeminent mob lawyer. In the morning Cicilline would bring coffee to Raymond L. S. Patriarca on Federal Hill, and the two men would chat on the sidewalk. Patriarca, who had been a contemporary of Joseph Kennedy's when the Kennedy patriarch was a reputed bootlegger, had no love for the Kennedys; one day he told Cicilline that the Kennedys were "double-crossers." Eventually, the picture of Bobby Kennedy came down from Cicilline's wall. A picture of Patriarca, whom Kennedy had once pursued, took its place.

In 1968 Richard Nixon was elected president and federal funds for cities dried up. Providence continued its decline. Doorley, an austere fiscal manager, hoarded what federal money did come in to hold down taxes, neglecting new programs and capital improvements. At budget time, he sat at his desk with sharpened pencils and an adding machine, scrutinizing every expenditure. People started calling him "No Dough Joe."

Doorley, like Providence, seemed to lose his way. The tension between him and McGarry increased after the mayor passed up opportunities to run for higher office. According to Cicilline, when Doorley went away to think about a bid for Congress in 1967, after the sudden death of Congressman John Fogarty, McGarry started lining up the City Committee votes to back him for mayor. When Doorley decided not to run, he was annoyed that some people had committed to McGarry without checking with him first.

McGarry intimates said that he was never interested in succeeding Doorley himself, but that he always had a protégé, probate judge Francis Brown, in mind. Brown had been McGarry's first choice in 1964, but McGarry had switched to Doorley because he had better financial support. According to McGarry pal Ray Devitt, it was with the understanding that Doorley would eventually run for governor or Congress and make way for Brown.

In either event, when Doorley failed to step aside and run for Fogarty's seat, "that started the battle," said Devitt. Cicilline also called it a turning point, saying, "That was the beginning of the end of the relationship between Joe and Larry. That's when you heard more talk that Joe was distant. . . . They started maneuvering against him."

Quietly, McGarry complained that Doorley had stopped caring about the city. Privately, Doorley grumbled about McGarry's disloyalty. The mayor had delegated the daily affairs of the machine to McGarry, in part because he considered lines of supplicants outside the mayor's office unseemly. But, Doorley would later remind people, McGarry "made use of that power with very little credit given the mayor who gave him that power."

Another break in the relationship involved Tony Bucci, a lawyer and power broker in the Fourth Ward, the Italian North End. Bucci was a key McGarry ally who had helped Doorley get elected in 1964, part of the Irish-Italian alliance that had been critical to the machine's strength. Bucci had built a lucrative downtown law practice with the aid of his political connections. Hungry for deals and greedy for patronage, "T.B.," as he was known, was always pressing Doorley for something—either a job for someone or a deal for a private business client that Cicilline considered shady. *The Washington Post* called Bucci "Mr. Asphalt," after he represented a Providence liquid-asphalt importer in a case that went all the way to the U.S. Supreme Court. One of Bucci's clients wanted to build controversial liquefied natural gas tanks near the waterfront; the project was opposed by Doorley and nearby residents, who feared an explosion. Doorley further aggravated Bucci and McGarry in 1973 when he attended a Democratic function in the Fourth Ward hosted by a rival faction to Bucci.

One hint that Doorley's hold on the machine was weakening had come the previous year, when the mayor dressed down workers in one ward for a lackluster 1972 primary turnout, which he viewed as a tune-up for his own reelection campaign in 1974.

"We've got more city workers in that ward than voted in the primary," he groused. Doorley was so shocked at discovering that nobody was getting out the vote on election day that the shot-and-beer mayor took drastic measures, banning booze and other extracurricular activities from his political headquarters. "I don't want any bartender making book on the side in this headquarters."

Meanwhile, even Doorley's supporters worried about his drinking. The stories were multiplying around town about Doorley's drinking himself into a stupor, falling off bar stools, and being dragged home by his police driver. His lifestyle began to put a strain on his marriage. After City Council meetings, Doorley would invite councilmen across the street to the Biltmore, where he had a private room upstairs with a view of the city and an open bar. Sometimes he drank until his words slurred. When the bar on the first floor of the Biltmore closed, a cousin of Doorley's opened a taproom, the Plantations Room, with a Doorley pal, Jimmy Notorantonio, a car dealer who had the contract to sell and service police cars. Doorley, sources said, was a silent partner. (The lounge was not to be confused with Doorley's Bar, run by a relative of the mayor in a strategic spot between City Hall and *The Providence Journal*, which extended the length of a city block and was known as the world's longest bar.) The liquor was provided free, provided by various supporters and councilmen who worked in the liquor industry, according to assistant city solicitor Ronald Glantz. On Sunday mornings, Glantz said, Doorley would be in the bar, taking inventory and helping to drain the near-empty bottles.

As Doorley grew more remote, community activists tried tracking him down at the Biltmore bar. In March 1973 a St. Michael's priest protesting conditions in South Providence suffered bruises when he was forcibly ejected from a City Council meeting. Two nights later, with the priest calling his mistreatment another example of the Providence political machine, some of the activists confronted the mayor as he sat on his bar stool at the Biltmore. A few months after that, residents of a public-housing project whom Doorley had refused to see also tried the mayor there, only to chase him out as one shouted, "The S.O.B. has bolted!"

On May 19, 1973, not a word was spoken of those underlying tensions as Joe Doorley served as toastmaster at Larry McGarry's tribute. Smiling, Doorley stood in the Civic Center that he had built and praised McGarry's kingmaking abilities and his enduring political roots. The two men grinned together for the cameras.

If Doorley thought that this testimonial would fix things, he was mistaken. And the following month, when Doorley promoted two potential rivals, including McGarry protégé Francis Brown to public-safety commissioner, McGarry remarked that "the politics of owning people is gone." Around the same time, Doorley said publicly that his dispute with Tony Bucci would not dampen his relationship with McGarry; "I fully expect to be his friend for the rest of my life."

One month after the testimonial, McGarry's Democratic City Committee refused to endorse Doorley's bid for reelection in 1974. Their divorce had become public. Party insiders had seen the split coming but never thought it would be that serious.

The time was approaching when the mayor would measure loyalty by a simple test: "He's Doorley, or he's McGarry."

BY THE SUMMER of 1973, with the Doorley-McGarry feud out in the open, Buddy Cianci had two big decisions to make: Should he run for mayor? And should he get married?

He had started discussing the mayor's race early in the year with his friend Herb DeSimone, the former attorney general. After four years as a prosecutor, and after working on DeSimone's unsuccessful campaigns for governor in 1970 and 1972, Cianci felt that it was his turn. The question was what office to run for. Cianci was eager to get started, but he hadn't paid his dues in any local party organizations. He considered running for office in Cranston or Providence, as a Republican or a Democrat—whatever it would take to win.

One of his closest advisers was his good friend Mickey Farina, a Cranston real estate salesman who dabbled in local Republican politics and was looking to get back in the game. Farina had been the Cranston coordinator of DeSimone's statewide campaigns and had also managed the 1970 victory of Mayor James Taft, the heir apparent to a powerful Republican machine that was the equal of the Democratic machine in Providence. Farina had been rewarded with a job running TransVan, a federally funded agency that provided rides for Cranston senior citizens. But Taft later fired him for incompetence, saying that seniors were being stranded without rides. Others whispered that the problems were more serious, and that Taft mistrusted Farina.

Cianci and Farina met at a real estate closing around 1970 and began socializing and attending political functions together. Cianci found Farina, with his political experience, to be a good sounding board; he told Farina of his admiration for presidents like Teddy Roosevelt and John F. Kennedy, dashing, can-do politicians, and confided his ultimate dream—to one day be president.

In Cianci, Farina saw talent and promise. All they needed was an opportunity. Looking ahead to 1974, they thought about running for attorney general. But then the incumbent, Richard Israel, Cianci's boss, announced that he would seek reelection. That left mayor of Providence. Realistically, they didn't think they could win. It would be more like an audition, to show that Buddy Cianci belonged in politics. Doorley was vulnerable, and if Cianci made a strong showing, he could establish himself for some future office, said DeSimone.

Then there was the question of marriage.

After an awkward youth, when he didn't date much, one thing seemed clear about Buddy—he was not the marrying kind. Despite his chubby physique and receding hairline, he had a way with women. Many found him funny, charming, and worldly. They were drawn to his boyishness and his sad-eyed vulnerability.

When Cianci attended Fairfield University, a high school classmate attending another Connecticut college would get rides to and from school with him. Often, Cianci would stop at the Connecticut College for Women and go into one of the dormitory lounges. All the girls seemed to know him, and they crowded around to hear his stories.

During National Guard training weeks in Pennsylvania in the early 1970s, Cianci liked to frequent the strip clubs near the base, recalled another officer.

In Providence, Cianci dated a lot, which annoyed his steady girlfriend, Sheila Bentley. Buddy met Sheila in 1968 when he was out barhopping in his army uniform one night at the old Colonial Hilton in Cranston. She was with a woman Buddy knew, and caught his eye. She had the WASPy good looks that Cianci found appealing: trim, blond, elegant. Later Cianci would joke about some guy mistaking his uniform for that of a valet-parking attendant that night and tossing Cianci his car keys.

Buddy started calling Sheila, and they began dating. She had just divorced her first husband, with whom she had three young sons. The divorce, which left custody of the boys with the father, became official early in 1969, around the time that Cianci left the army and became a prosecutor.

Bentley was the daughter of a Cranston dentist who had died when she was young, leaving the family in difficult straits and forcing her mother to take a job as a telephone operator. She had gotten married before she was eighteen to Manny Gorriaran, Jr.

His father was a prominent wrestling promoter and the wealthy owner of a jewelry-manufacturing company. The year that Sheila met Buddy, her father-in-law coached the U.S. Olympic wrestling team in the 1968 Olympics in Mexico City, where he captured international headlines for punching out a Russian judge who robbed an American wrestler of the gold medal. (Upon further review, the decision was reversed and the American got the gold.)

Cianci's mother was not crazy about the relationship, but Buddy and Sheila kept seeing each other. Vincent Vespia, Cianci's state police friend, recalled nights of domestic tranquility, when he and Buddy would go over to Sheila's apartment and work on a case while she cooked them a pot roast. Sheila, who worked as a secretary, would also help Buddy out on some of his cases, doing typing and clerical work.

But she had a wild side, and could keep up with Buddy. Once, at a birthday party for Cianci at her apartment, she invited a friend into the bedroom, according to another guest, Paul Giaccobe. The people in the living room assumed she was going to show the man Cianci's present. Suddenly, shots rang out and the guests charged into the bedroom. The man was lying on the bed, looking pale and scared. Sheila stood holding a track starter's pistol and laughing. Cianci just rolled his eyes, and the party went on.

Cianci bought her a St. Bernard, which wound up at his mother's house. He joked that Bentley "helped me spend my money." He enjoyed what they had together, but he didn't seem in any hurry to settle down. He was having too much fun, carousing, taking flying lessons, running his law practice, trading political gossip.

One night Sheila worried when Buddy didn't show up at her apartment for dinner, as planned. She called a friend and asked him to meet her at Buddy's law office on Pocasset Avenue, where he had been working late. The man, who arrived with another man who also knew Cianci, walked in with Sheila and found Buddy in his private office having sex with his secretary. One man said that he left in a hurry when he saw that Cianci wasn't dressed, not wanting to stick around to see what would happen next. The other man, who stayed, said that Sheila took an unloaded gun and stormed into Cianci's office, surprising him. She pointed the gun at her naked boyfriend and made him dance around; he pleaded with her as his secretary threw her clothes on and dashed out into the night. Then Sheila started throwing and breaking things in the office, including a painting she had given Buddy, which she snatched off the wall and smashed over his head before storming out. Cianci later told Vespia that Sheila had gone for a gun that he kept in his desk for protection, but that he had prevented her from actually grabbing it.

In the spring of 1973 Bentley got pregnant.

Cianci agonized for months about what he should do. Bentley wanted to get married, but he wasn't sure. He also worried about how his decision would affect his political ambitions. He sought Vespia's advice. His friend listed the obvious choices: he could marry her, support the child, or "make other arrangements." Farina said that she gave Cianci no choice; he could ill afford a scandal as he was preparing to run for office.

While Cianci was deliberating, Vespia said, Bentley put an engagement announcement in the newspaper—without telling Cianci. Cianci's mother found out when Herb DeSimone saw the announcement and called to congratulate her—which, according to Vespia, forced Cianci to do some fast explaining to his mother.

Cianci finally decided to get married.

In August he paid $108,000 for an eighteen-room brick mansion on Blackstone Boulevard, a broad, tree-lined thoroughfare on the East Side. In September Buddy and Sheila were married. Vespia, whom Cianci had asked to make the arrangements, found a justice of the peace in Seekonk, an out-of-the-way town in nearby Massachusetts.

On the appointed day, Cianci picked up Vespia and Vespia's future wife, Judy, in his Cadillac, then swung by the house on Blackstone Boulevard. Sheila waddled out, obviously pregnant, and got in the front seat with Cianci. The mood was jolly.

"You know, Sheila, I'm never gonna forgive you for this," Cianci said drily.

"What a way to start a marriage," cracked Vespia, and all four of them burst out laughing.

Vespia made another joke about slipping the justice of the peace a hundred bucks to say the wrong words.

The ceremony was simple. Buddy and Sheila were married under a tree behind the justice's house in Seekonk. Vin was the best man, Judy the maid of honor. Cianci's mother wasn't there.

IN THE FALL of 1973 Cianci presented the case of Harold Copeland to the grand jury. On October 10, the executive director of Doorley's Dream was indicted for soliciting a bribe.

Copeland's lawyer immediately branded the indictment as "politically motivated." The mayor issued a statement that said, "I'm particularly upset because of the fact that the Civic Center is the cornerstone of the plan to rebuild downtown Providence. I earnestly hope that the present situation will not cast a shadow over the success the Civic Center has enjoyed in its first year of operation."

But the shadow continued to grow. Attorney General Dick Israel announced that an audit had discovered a forty-six-thousand-dollar discrepancy in box-office receipts. Later, questions were raised about missing tickets to a Frank Sinatra concert. Investigators went into the Civic Center with subpoenas and carted away financial records. Israel announced that the investigation was being handled by Assistant Attorney General Buddy Cianci.

Israel later said that he never would have allowed Cianci to handle the case had he known that he was thinking of running for mayor. But if Israel was unaware of Cianci's political plans, it is clear that Cianci was seriously contemplating the race.

Still, Cianci wasn't sure. Although he viewed Doorley as vulnerable, winning as a Republican would be a formidable challenge. If Cianci got swamped in his first political campaign, it might be hard, especially as a Republican, to run for office again. On the other hand, Cianci had an appealing résumé as a mob-fighting prosecutor; he had money; and he was Italian-American in a city with a large Italian-American population.

One night, after dinner with Vespia in the Old Canteen on Federal Hill, Cianci was in a whimsical mood. It was a favorite spot for both men, because their fathers had taken them to dinner there as boys. Joe Marzilli, the owner, came over and joined them for a late-night cup of coffee. Cianci debated the merits of running for mayor versus buying a boat. An inveterate doodler, he pulled out a Cross pen that Vespia had given him, engraved "Assistant Attorney General Buddy Cianci." There was no paper handy, so Cianci began writing on the linen tablecloth.

In one column he jotted down the various costs involved in buying a boat as Marzilli, who owned a boat, offered advice. In typical Cianci style, this would not be a small boat. He factored in the cost of a captain, a crew, fuel, slip fees, et cetera. Then, in another column, he wrote down the costs of running for mayor: a campaign manager, an ad agency, advertising, et cetera. Then he added up the two columns of figures. It turned out it would be cheaper to run for mayor.

But it was a later visit to the Old Canteen that would help Cianci make up his mind.

Early in 1974, he and Farina went there for lunch. Across the main dining room, Joe Doorley was also eating. The mayor sat at a large table with eight or nine of his cronies, holding court.

Cianci's ambitions were no secret. He and Farina politely nodded hello to Doorley.

"Come on over," the mayor commanded them.

They went over. Doorley, who had been drinking, introduced Cianci to his men, then announced, "This is the man who wants to be mayor and take my job away from me." The mayor's men chuckled.

"Mayor, you never know," Cianci replied politely. "There's always that possibility."

"He can beat *me?*" Doorley said to his men, who joined him in another laugh.

"Maybe I will," Cianci said affably.

They exchanged some more jabs. Doorley was clearly belittling him, but Cianci kept his cool.

"When I make my decision," Cianci said in parting, "you'll be the first to know."

Then Cianci walked away. As he moved out of earshot, he turned to Farina and said in a low, determined voice: "Let's do it, Mickey. Let's run."

In March Cianci resigned from the attorney general's office. In April he formally announced his candidacy for mayor at a rally at the Biltmore Hotel. He called himself the anticorruption candidate.

Nobody took the Republican challenger seriously. The focus was on what would happen in the Democratic party, where challengers were lining up against Doorley. From Silver Lake came Councilman Charles Pisaturo, the latest Italian-American contender hoping to become the first of his heritage to be mayor. From the South Side came a fresh-faced young lawyer, army veteran, and Catholic Youth Organization baseball coach, Francis Darigan, Jr. And from the Second Ward came Larry McGarry's protégé, Francis Brown, Doorley's public safety commissioner.

Darigan was the most impressive of the three. Tall and handsome, he had grown up in the Cathedral parish on Emmett Street, named for the Irish patriot Robert Emmett. As an altar boy, he had walked down the Canyon, a dirt trench excavated during the construction of Interstate 95, to serve mass at the Cathedral of Saints Peter and Paul. He came home from the army in 1967 to find his once-vibrant South Providence neighborhood decimated by the interstate. Darigan found it ironic that Doorley had billed the highway as "the Road to Progress," even using the interstate logo in campaign ads.

His idealism—he was an admirer of John F. Kennedy, whom he'd met in New York the week before his assassination—drove him into politics. As a new city councilman, Darigan was awed to adjourn to Doorley's private room at the Biltmore after meetings and listen to the mayor hold forth. Doorley was impressive—articulate and aggressive. He pushed through the Civic Center. But by 1974 Darigan felt that Doorley had lost interest in the job; his drinking had become a distraction and he wasn't doing anything for South Providence. Irish-Americans were fleeing to the suburbs. Darigan went to McGarry and sought his support for the Democratic nomination.

Darigan had first met Mr. Democrat in 1967, when he ran a friend's primary campaign for state senate; the friend upset the incumbent by fourteen votes. The next morning, McGarry came to their headquarters, in a tenement on Glenham Street, wearing a camel-hair coat and a soft felt hat, to offer his congratulations and his support. In 1974, Darigan tried to talk McGarry out of supporting Franny Brown. Darigan viewed Brown, a dapper, mild-mannered lawyer who favored bow ties, as a good and decent man but a weak candidate. "Franny's a nice guy, but he's vanilla," he said. But McGarry believed in loyalty. "You're only a kid," he told Darigan. "You've got a bright future. Wait in line."

That spring, McGarry swung the party endorsement to Brown. Darigan and Pisaturo remained in the race as unendorsed candidates. Furious, Doorley struck back. He fired McGarry and Brown from their city jobs and purged other disloyal city employees. He confined a boiler inspector to his desk for backing Brown. Another inspector was confined, then released after his wife, who sat on the city Democratic Committee, switched her vote to Doorley.

"If you want to sit around in a cushy job and you cut the hand that feeds you, that's your business," he said.

The mayor also warned Public Works employees loyal to McGarry about abusing their sick leave to campaign for his enemies. "They are either for me or against me," Doorley declared. "The time has come for these people to face reality."

Meanwhile, Cianci blasted away at continuing problems at the Civic Center, Doorley's Dream. The grand jury issued a report critical of the Civic Center's operations and the missing forty-six thousand dollars. Then, in July, police arrested the manager of the Civic Center's restaurant in connection with irregularities at an Elvis Presley concert. The trouble arose when concertgoers who had bought tickets arrived to find people already in their seats.

Darigan met Cianci at a candidates' forum in the basement of Grace Church that summer and was not impressed. Cianci was fat and balding, with a Nero-style haircut, and didn't seem to know the first thing about running a city. But he kept showing up at festivals, forums, and any private home that would have him. Republican councilman Malcolm Farmer III, a patrician East Side lawyer who had been a few years ahead of Cianci at Moses Brown, convinced his parents to host a cocktail party for Cianci at their impressive home on Angell Street. The Farmers invited all their snappy WASP friends, many of them East Siders in their sixties. They sat in the dining room, beneath the crystal chandelier, mesmerized by Cianci's vision and his sense of humor.

Cianci wanted to face Doorley in the fall election, because he would be an easier target. Hoping to pick off some dissident Democrats after the primary, Cianci reached out that summer to Mr. Democrat, Larry McGarry. One day, at a church festival in the Fourth Ward, Cianci and Farina encountered Ronald Glantz, a McGarry operative who was campaigning for Brown. Because of his defection from Doorley, Glantz had resigned his city job in the spring. Cianci pulled Glantz aside and asked him to consider supporting him in the fall if Brown lost. Glantz reported Cianci's offer to McGarry.

During the same period, Cianci was attacking Brown publicly, calling him a product of the same corrupt Doorley machine, a man "schooled in the covert ways of Larry McGarry." But Cianci and McGarry knew that that was just rhetoric—that Cianci needed Democratic votes. And McGarry was an astute enough politician and horseman to know that he might need a new horse to ride after the primary.

Farina, who had become Cianci's campaign manager, said that he began meeting covertly with McGarry at night. He was so conscious of security that he drove a borrowed car to McGarry's neighborhood and parked one street over, then walked to McGarry's house on Royal Avenue. Mr. Democrat would receive Farina in his basement.

McGarry wanted assurances that Cianci would take care of his people. Farina agreed. In return, according to Farina, McGarry pledged to covertly support Cianci if Brown lost.

"You'll get everything I have," he said.

■

ON SEPTEMBER 10, 1974, Joe Doorley won the Democratic primary, beating his strongest challenger, Franny Brown, by about two thousand votes. Collectively, Doorley's three challengers received twenty-eight thousand votes to Doorley's fourteen thousand.

But at the Providence Civic Center, where several thousand Doorley supporters had gathered, the mood was jubilant. Doorley had wrested the machine from Larry McGarry. Vendors sold black armbands that said, R.I.P. LARRY & TONY, referring to McGarry and his ally Tony Bucci.

Doorley called it "the sweetest victory of my life." Political observers said that he was stronger than ever, and predicted that he could run for governor or U.S. senator in 1976. His victory in November over little-known Republican Buddy Cianci was a foregone conclusion. Invoking a Frank Sinatra song that he had quoted frequently during his campaign, Doorley shouted defiantly: "We did it our way! We did it our way!"

Over at Franny Brown's headquarters, McGarry had not lost his sense of humor. He called the campaign his "last hurrah," and joked about his image as a political puppeteer, which had hurt Brown among voters ready for a change. Brown, whose political career was over, picked up on the gag and danced around like a marionette, jerking his arms and legs as McGarry manipulated invisible strings.

But McGarry had one more string to pull.

Over in Silver Lake, at the Rosario Club, several hundred Brown supporters who had gathered for a victory celebration turned their lonely eyes to Cianci. They invited the Republican challenger to come down and talk.

Some of Cianci's advisers urged him not to go. Political passions were running high in Providence; Doorley and Brown partisans had gotten into fistfights during the primary race. Nobody knew what kind of reception Cianci would receive in a neighborhood where *Republican* was a dirty word. Older residents still remembered how the last Republican mayor, "Honest John" Collins, had purged the city payroll during the Great Depression.

According to Farina, McGarry arranged for Cianci and Farina to meet first at a hotel with Tony Bucci and some other McGarry insiders. Farina said that they sought, and received, assurances that no one would get hurt if they went into the Rosario Club.

Still, some of Cianci's supporters didn't want the anticorruption candidate to cozy up to the McGarry machine. But Cianci knew that good government alone wasn't going to win him the election. Once you came down from the East Side and crossed the river into the rest of Providence, you needed political grease and muscle. You had to cut deals. You needed an organization.

"Fuck it," Cianci said. "I'm gonna go see them."

Cianci, after all, had roots in Silver Lake, and he was an Italian-American in a city that had never had an Italian-American mayor. Although Italian-Americans had become the city's largest single ethnic group, they had been subsumed in the Irish-Democratic machine, an alliance forged during the Great Depression by Dennis Roberts and Democratic party boss Frank Rao, who, incidentally, had been a distant cousin of Cianci's mother's family, the Capobiancos.

The Irish-Italian alliance spoke to the tribal nature of Providence politics. Despite the historic tensions between the two groups, political survival dictated that they work together. Sharky Almagno, a Silver Lake Democrat, described it as a matter of "You stay on your side of the fence and I'll stay on mine. . . . You can't spite yourself, lose a pair of shoes, because you don't want to vote with the Irish. You gotta go with the Irish to get your shoes." Still, Almagno said, there was a pent-up desire among Italian-Americans for a mayor of their own.

Most of Silver Lake seemed to be jammed inside the Rosario Club when Cianci walked in. The club, off Pocasset Avenue, was a low-slung hall where Italian-speaking women wearing kerchiefs served plates of pasta while the men talked politics, drank wine, and played cards. The somber mood lifted, followed by chants of "Bud-dee, Bud-dee, we're with you!" Shouting over the din, Cianci delivered a rousing speech that whipped up the crowd. He promised that they would work together and vowed to protect their jobs. He was one of them—a son of Silver Lake, a parishioner of St. Bart's.

In the coming days and weeks, the Democratic rebellion would take shape in clandestine meetings and conversations, as Doorley spurned his supporters' advice to mend fences.

Almagno, who ran Sharky's Wholesale, a Silver Lake produce stand, was in a difficult spot. Because he had backed his childhood friend Charlie Pisaturo against Doorley, he said, the mayor summoned him to City Hall and told him that none of the Seventh Ward patronage would be coming his way. "Hey," Almagno replied. "That's life in Silver Lake." After the primary, the first person to call Almagno was Larry McGarry. He had no problem with Almagno's people going with Cianci, saying, "Do what you gotta do."

One weekend, Cianci and Farina stopped by the basement of the

St. Bart's church hall, where Almagno ran the Sunday bingo, and asked for his support. Almagno's initial response was, "Is this a joke?" But the more he thought about it, the more he realized that Doorley had left him no choice. On Columbus Day Almagno gathered some of his ward people at one man's house. Cianci, all dressed up to march in the parade later, stopped by. They talked for several hours, then Cianci left to march. It took Almagno and his men another hour to decide to support Cianci.

The pundits gave Cianci little chance to win. Although he was stronger and better financed than past Republican sacrificial lambs, they said that Cianci shared one fatal weakness—he lacked an organization that could go into the wards and battle Doorley on his own turf.

What they didn't realize was that Larry McGarry was turning his organization over to Cianci.

One night, shortly after the primary, three of McGarry's men waited in the shadows at a corner in downtown Providence. One, Joseph Florio, wore a comical disguise—a trench coat and Groucho Marx–style fake eyeglasses, nose, and mustache. The other two men were Ron Glantz and Lloyd Griffin, an up-and-coming black political figure from the South Side who had worked for Doorley.

A van pulled up to the corner.

The three men climbed in. Inside were Cianci and Farina. As Farina drove the van through the streets of the darkened city, the men discussed strategy. Cianci offered his assurances that he would protect the jobs of McGarry's people. As a sign of respect, Cianci later called McGarry to offer his word directly, according to Glantz.

About three weeks later, Glantz publicly announced the formation of Democrats for Cianci. Glantz was cochairman, along with Charlie Pisaturo, Doorley's Silver Lake challenger. Glantz and Florio opened a law office in the suburb of Lincoln, created a scholarship fund, and made McGarry an officer. Every day McGarry would come to the office and hold court in the law library with his old cronies, whom he called "the Over the Hill Club."

Democrats for Cianci provided Cianci with 150 workers as well as lists of thirty-one thousand anti-Doorley Democrats that had been compiled by a Washington pollster Franny Brown had hired during the primary. Armed with those lists, Cianci created a phone bank on the third floor of his house on Blackstone Boulevard and had a host of campaign workers making calls, day and night.

Cianci showed that he meant business by taking over Brown's campaign headquarters in two crucial Democratic strongholds, the Fourth Ward, in the Italian North End, and Doorley's Fifth Ward. The transition was marked by the Changing of the Balloons—campaign volunteers popped the old Brown balloons and inflated red, white, and blue Cianci balloons. Brown volunteers and Cianci volunteers went around the city, plastering Cianci's face over Brown's campaign signs.

The insurgents met at the Imperial Club on Broadway, recalled Almagno. McGarry attended a few meetings. So did Cianci.

Cianci also met secretly with McGarry ally Tony Bucci to talk strategy, at out-of-the-way restaurants in East Greenwich and North Providence, according to Glantz, a Bucci confidant who also served as a conduit for messages between the two camps.

Doorley's allies blasted Cianci for cutting a backroom deal with Bucci and McGarry to support the controversial waterfront storage tanks that the mayor had opposed. Doorley called a press conference to report that his spies had seen Cianci, Bucci, and Glantz at the Old Canteen, "conspiring" against him.

"Buddy can have the remnants of the McGarry-Bucci machine," said Doorley. "I warn him, however, to remember what they tried to do to me during the last few years. . . . If Buddy can trust them, he can have them."

LATE IN SEPTEMBER, in the midst of the Cianci-Doorley campaign, the Civic Center's Harold Copeland went on trial for soliciting a thousand-dollar bribe from concert promoter Skip Chernov.

Chernov, the leadoff witness, was about as eager to be in court as Copeland. In the nineteen months since he had cooperated, Chernov's wife had divorced him, the police had raided his Incredible Organ Pub, a rival promoter had threatened to kill him, the mob had tried to muscle in on his business, and the Civic Center had refused his efforts to book concerts.

Shortly after Copeland's indictment, Chernov said, Raymond "Junior" Patriarca, the mob boss's son, offered to become Chernov's silent partner, guaranteeing him bookings in East Coast arenas. Patriarca also offered to make Chernov's problems with the Copeland case disappear. But Chernov, heeding the advice of his father never to become partners with the mob, declined.

Not long afterward, Chernov was forced to close the Incredible Organ after a police raid turned up a small amount of marijuana and scared away business. Meanwhile, the Civic Center Authority had denied Chernov's application to promote concerts by the Beach Boys, Cat Stevens, and James Taylor.

Chernov later said that a Civic Center official offered to let him back into Doorley's Dream if Chernov would change his testimony and say that Copeland had only been joking when he asked for the bribe. Chernov angrily refused. But as the trial approached, he was having second thoughts. "I'm dead," he moaned to his lawyer, who encouraged him to follow through.

With obvious reluctance, Chernov testified that Copeland had asked for one thousand dollars under the table. Copeland's lawyer asked Chernov if he had ever told prosecutors that it could have been a "sick joke." Chernov said he didn't know.

Copeland testified that he had only been joking. He also revealed on the stand that Doorley had warned him at the time that there were rumors around town that Chernov had him on tape, asking for money.

During the trial, Chernov felt bad as he looked at Copeland's wife, Patricia, who was convinced that her husband was the victim of a political conspiracy to get Doorley.

Copeland was convicted on October 2. The following week, Cianci blasted Doorley about the conviction. As the press conference ended, Cianci was interrupted by a telephone call. He listened for a few minutes, then smiled and dramatically waved the reporters back. Cianci announced that Doorley had attended a party for Copeland the night before at a Federal Hill restaurant, organized by Civic Center employees.

Doorley fired back that he still believed in Copeland's innocence. He called Cianci a "character assassin who makes charges based on half truths, innuendo, and the distortion of facts."

One week before the election, Doorley charged that Cianci had offered Copeland immunity to testify against the mayor.

"There are four or five people who will attest to the fact that [Cianci] was walking around offering immunity," said Doorley.

Cianci denied it. He said that Copeland was never offered immunity, but that Cianci did talk to him about the possibility of him testifying— against whom, Cianci never said. Cianci said that he couldn't say more because the investigation of Doorley—which Cianci hadn't been involved with since his resignation as a prosecutor six months earlier—"is still going on."

"It was not a political investigation in any sense of the word," said Cianci.

IN THIS YEAR of Watergate—Richard Nixon had resigned the presidency in disgrace on August 9, 1974—Cianci hammered at the anticorruption theme. He promised to release his income-tax statements and run a more open government.

"The Providence River is like the Democratic machine that has been running this city—namely, it stinks," said Cianci.

As election day approached, Buddy Cianci was everywhere, smiling and schmoozing—at factory gates, church feasts, supermarkets, senior centers, coffee hours, testimonial dinners. "Hello, may I shake your hand? I'm Buddy Cianci and I'm running for mayor," he said over and over again as he crisscrossed Providence from dawn to midnight.

Not everyone would accept the handshake. When he tried to address the longshoremen, they shouted him out of the hall and slammed the doors. With beer bottles banging off the walls, Cianci pushed the doors open and marched right back in, winning their grudging respect, if not their support.

Every day, it seemed, Cianci was introducing a new program. He sketched out his visions to revive downtown, restore the blighted neighborhoods, rebuild the waterfront, create green spaces, build housing, create jobs, improve the schools.

Doorley, who had disappeared to Florida after the primary, ran a more passive campaign. One nervous supporter urged the mayor to pay more attention to the city's elderly housing projects. He warned that Cianci, who was throwing campaign parties for senior citizens, was making "tremendous inroads."

Jean Coughlin, a Mount Pleasant housewife running for mayor as an Independent, recalled going into the senior high-rises to do ice cream socials and hearing that Cianci had been there. "The little old ladies would come up to me and say, 'Buddy came in with money and gave us a big dinner.'"

Coughlin, a member of the Republican City Committee, had been asked the previous winter to run as the party's candidate for mayor but was told that the impoverished party had no money for her campaign. Then, she said, "Mr. Cianci arrived with a fistful of money," and she was shouldered aside. Her shoestring campaign as an Independent featured an old postal truck, painted shocking pink and with a loudspeaker on top, that she drove around Providence. One day she stopped outside City Hall and shouted, "The only activity down here is the pigeons." The old men on the bench in Burnside Park clapped and cheered. She attacked the cozy relationship between the Irish pols and the Catholic Church—the only reason Doorley had pushed for the Civic Center, she said, was that the Dominican fathers at Providence College wanted it for their basketball team. Her quixotic goal was to crack the Democratic machine, as embodied in the heavy metal voting machines bristling with levers and complicated machinery. "The joke was that you couldn't break the machine," she said.

Coughlin was also critical of Cianci, calling him "a man born with a silver spoon in his mouth and raised on every advantage money can buy." Irritated, Cianci snapped that she was mentally ill and should be locked up, she said. One night Cianci's mother called Coughlin at home and screamed at her for saying negative things about her Buddy. Later, Buddy would refer to Coughlin as "the Menopausal Maniac," according to two people associated with his campaign.

But Cianci directed most of his fire at Doorley. No Dough Joe had alienated police officers by refusing to buy them winter coats. When the police union set up an informational picket line outside the Civic Center during an event attended by Doorley, the Republican challenger marched with them. Cianci vowed that when he became mayor, the officers would never have to buy another piece of clothing.

In an ominous sign of the city's shifting demographics, a group of suburban voters who had left Providence formed Commuters for Doorley, to woo Providence voters left behind. The group didn't even meet in Providence; they met at a hotel in Warwick. According to Edward Xavier, a Doorley adviser, the group disbanded after the mayor failed to show up. Instead, Xavier recalled, Doorley would invariably be found planted on some bar stool, where his cronies would make jokes about Cianci's latest proclamation.

"You give me any shit, Doorley," said one crony, "and I'll sic Buddy Cianci on you." The men would roar with laughter.

Doorley's drinking was a serious concern. According to Xavier and another member of the mayor's campaign committee, they warned him about it at a meeting following the primary. Xavier, a Fox Point councilman and truck driver, was one of the people assigned to baby-sit Doorley, with an eye toward keeping him away from Scotch. Beer was okay, said Xavier; but Doorley didn't do so well with Scotch.

One night Xavier arrived too late at the Pelham House, where Doorley had been drinking. According to Xavier, mobster Dickie Callei, who would be murdered the following year by Bobo Marrapese, had bet Doorley that he could drink him under the table. By the time Xavier got there, the mayor was so badly out of it that Xavier suspected Callei had slipped a mickey into his drink. Xavier took Doorley out of the bar and drove him around in his car until well past midnight, then left him in his driveway, alerting a trusted police captain.

About ten days before the election, according to a Doorley campaign aide, the mayor arrived drunk at a hall on Elmwood Avenue in South Providence, where several hundred black voters were waiting to hear him speak. His drinking buddy, Jimmy Notorantonio, or Jimmy Noto, as he was known, pulled up to the curb in a white Thunderbird. He and a red-faced Doorley got out. Doorley had trouble walking up the stairs to the building. Notorantonio, who had also been drinking, walked ahead of the mayor, opened the door, glanced at the crowd, and said, "Fuck this—we don't need 'em," then turned around and shut the door before Doorley could enter. The aide watched in amazement as the mayor and Jimmy Noto left.

Cianci's advisers feared a sober Doorley in a debate. But Doorley refused to debate, saying that he was sick of reporters questioning him about his personal finances and corruption at the Civic Center. Besides, he added, half jokingly, the Patriots were playing at Buffalo on Sunday.

One week before election day, Doorley struck back at the anticorruption candidate. The occasion was a gala Democratic dinner at Rhodes-on-the-Pawtuxet, a turn-of-the-century ballroom where the big bands of the forties had played. Virtually all of the state's top Democrats and more than two thousand faithful had turned out, the largest crowd in the old hall since President John F. Kennedy appeared more than a decade earlier.

Doorley sat at the head table, waiting grimly to speak. There had been rumors all day that the mayor had a surprise for Cianci. When Doorley's turn came, he stood and waved a piece of paper over his head. It was an affidavit from an insurance adjuster, delivered to the attorney general that afternoon, accusing Cianci of paying a cash kickback to falsify records in an automobile accident.

"This is the man who attacks my integrity and my character!" thundered Doorley.

Cianci watched Doorley on the eleven o'clock news with disbelief, then paced furiously about his living room. Herb DeSimone, who was there, urged him to relax; Doorley's attack was a sign of desperation.

Over the next few days, details of the accusation emerged. The accident in question had involved Cianci's wife, his car, and his driver. The insurance adjuster who said Cianci had paid him off was a former state trooper under indictment for insurance fraud. In 1970, when Cianci was dating Sheila Bentley, his driver was giving her a ride when he was sideswiped. The adjuster alleged that Cianci had given him $280 to conceal the fact that Sheila had collected unemployment benefits after going back to work.

A subsequent grand-jury investigation, after the election, would clear Cianci of any wrongdoing. But even before that, Doorley's charge backfired.

The weekend before election day, a *Providence Journal* poll predicted that Doorley would win handily, taking 54 percent of the vote to Cianci's 41.5 percent. Farina argued vehemently with the newspaper reporter before the story ran, pointing out that no self-respecting Democrat would admit favoring a Republican.

Larry McGarry's numbers told another story. Cianci was within one thousand votes of Doorley.

Late on the Saturday night before the election, Cianci walked into the East Side Diner after a long day of campaigning. He was greeted by the spontaneous applause of 150 people who rose to their feet and cheered.

Election day dawned gray and drizzly in Providence, with a promise of thunderstorms. Turnout across the city was heavy. Cianci made one last, long, mad dash to the finish line. That night, five minutes before the polls closed, not having eaten anything for hours, he stopped by a supermarket to grab a sandwich and wound up shaking hands with shoppers.

Later, Cianci plopped down on the couch in his mother's house, on Laurel Hill Avenue, and watched the returns on television with Farina. The two men drank a toast.

Cianci let out a whoop when the results came in from the Second Ward, on the East Side. He took 71 percent of the vote, more than he'd dreamed, giving him an early cushion. Over the next few hours, as the solidly Democratic wards came in, Doorley chipped away at Cianci's lead. But Doorley wasn't winning big; he barely carried his own Fifth Ward, by four hundred votes. Cianci won Silver Lake.

Cianci waited for the returns from South Providence, once solidly Irish territory that had been overtaken by poorer blacks. Cianci's campaign commercials had featured footage of blighted South Side neighborhoods that Cianci compared to "wartime Europe."

Lloyd Griffin, the black leader who had joined Cianci for the clandestine van ride, delivered big-time. He turned out a strong black vote that helped Cianci carry two more wards, including Larry McGarry's old Fighting Tenth.

Griffin also delivered on mail ballots. During the campaign he had persuaded hundreds of seniors to sign mail ballots by promising them a free day trip to Atlantic City. When the day came, the seniors were told that the buses had been canceled because of a labor dispute. In fact, no trip had ever been booked.

Cianci won only four of Providence's thirteen wards, but his commanding East Side margin and strong showing on traditional Democratic turf pulled him through. He beat Doorley by 709 votes.

Doorley's police chief, Walter McQueeney, arrived at the Laurel Hill house to drive Cianci to his campaign headquarters. The chief called Cianci "Mayor."

The celebration was already in full swing when Cianci arrived downtown at the Holiday Inn, next to Doorley's Dream—the Providence Civic Center. In the chaos of the balloon-draped ballroom, jammed with hundreds of sweating, stomping, singing, and chanting people, there was a sense of history being made. After an unbroken chain of Yankee and Irish-American mayors dating back to 1832, Cianci would be Providence's first Italian-American mayor.

As Cianci rode upstairs in the service elevator with a small group of family and supporters, one observer recalled that the mayor-elect looked at his mother with a poignant expression and asked, "Have I finally done something to make you proud of me?" She said that he had.

When Cianci made his entrance, a little before midnight, the ballroom erupted. A dozen policemen formed a flying wedge through the mob of people who wanted to shake his hand and slap his back.

"It was people fed up with the machine who got him in," said one supporter. "Buddy is the New Look in politics. He's the opposite of Watergate."

Afterward, upstairs at a smaller gathering of campaign insiders, Cianci wrapped Tony Bucci in a bear hug.

Late that night, unable to sleep, Cianci called his friend Vinny Vespia.

"Vespia," he rasped, his voice hoarse. "They're never gonna call me 'Landslide Cianci.' "

The next afternoon a car drove up to the mayor-elect's house on Blackstone Boulevard. A thin, lanky man, unable to walk, was carried by two men into the house. They set him down in a chair. Brandishing a long cigar and a twinkling smile, Larry McGarry finally came face to face with Buddy Cianci.

"Mayor," said McGarry, with a long, theatrical pause, "we'd like your support."

Later the press got wind of the meeting between the once and future powers of Providence.

"I'm a Democrat. I was born a Democrat and I will die a Democrat," McGarry explained. "But I was also born in Providence, and I have lived all my life in Providence. I will in no way be a stumbling block or try to hurt Mr. Cianci if he is trying to do something good for the city."

The mighty Providence Democratic machine would never be the same. Doorley, stung by McGarry's betrayal, said that Mr. Democrat's "sense of loyalty is like Eddy Street—one way." (Later, a Doorley aide issued a correction when it was pointed out that Eddy Street became a two-way street once it left downtown and ran into South Providence.)

"I'm laughing," responded McGarry.

Ray Devitt, McGarry's friend, said that the Democratic split of 1974 "led to good friends going to their graves not speaking to each other."

Doorley's friends on the City Council tried to give him a going-away present. They voted unanimously to rename the Providence Civic Center the Joseph A. Doorley Jr. Civic Center.

The vote came shortly after a judge fined Harold Copeland one thousand dollars for soliciting a bribe from Skip Chernov. Fired, Copeland moved back to California. Chernov, who never promoted another concert at the Civic Center, ran into him years later during a trip to the West Coast. "That didn't do either one of us any good, did it?" asked Copeland.

Cianci voiced outrage that the Civic Center would be named for a man "defeated on that very issue." The name change never went through. Instead, Doorley had to settle for the lobby.

In the aftermath of Cianci's victory, *The Providence Journal* asked, "How will he cope with this complex city, with its decaying neighborhoods, fading retail center, poverty and unemployment, street crime, shabby schools, disinterested students, racial tensions, unequal tax assessments and rising government costs?"

Responded Cianci, "It's a little frightening."

CHAPTER THREE

The Art of Politics

Snow flurries dusted the ground as the city employees' softball team warmed up at the Mount Pleasant Avenue playground in the first week of April 1975. A black limousine driven by a Providence police officer glided to a halt near the field, and a pudgy man in a sweat suit bounded out.

"Let's go!" Buddy Cianci shouted.

The new mayor grabbed a bat, stepped into the batter's box, stared down the pitcher, and popped a few fly balls to right. Then he grabbed a glove and trotted out to shortstop. The batter hit a ground ball sharply to Cianci's left. The mayor lunged and dug the ball out of the dirt. He lost his balance and rolled over, then jumped up with the ball in his glove, proud as a playful puppy.

The players cheered.

Cianci's first term as mayor had the feel of opening day, from the red, white, and blue bunting that adorned City Hall on inauguration day to the springtime air of renewal and hope. He brought a new sense of vitality and exuberance to the job, and he relished the competition with the City Council, which was controlled by his Democratic enemies.

Cianci also knew how to play hardball.

A few months into the job, he fired the city's recreation director, a Doorley holdover, for not keeping proper track of baseball equipment. When the assistant director locked Cianci's designated replacement out of the recreation office, the mayor sent the police over and fired the assistant, too. Then he ordered an investigation of recreation finances that led to the conviction of the assistant director for embezzling $765 in lunch money during a youth bus trip to the Bronx Zoo.

Not since Babe Ruth was slugging for the Providence Grays, perhaps, had the city seen someone with such star power. In national Republican circles, Cianci was a curiosity—an ethnic, urban mayor—and the party cultivated him like a rare orchid.

During his second month in office, he was invited to a private audience with President Gerald R. Ford in the Oval Office. "He wanted to know how I did it—how I, as a Republican, won in a Democratic city like Providence," said Cianci.

Cianci had visions of using City Hall as a springboard to the U.S. Senate, and from there, perhaps, landing a spot on the national party ticket as a vice-presidential candidate.

But back in Providence Cianci had a job to do: restoring hope to a dying city. His vision for his city and for his political fortunes were intertwined. He sought power, to save Providence and advance his career. That meant playing the game.

Nobody played it better than Buddy.

CIANCI WASTED NO time in getting started.

Five minutes past midnight, on January 6, 1975, Vincent Albert Cianci, Jr., was sworn in as mayor of Providence in a ceremony at his house on Blackstone Boulevard. Standing in front of his fireplace, he raised his right hand, placed his left on his mother's Bible, and took the oath of office as Providence's thirty-second mayor. His wife, Sheila, her shoulder-length blond hair glowing in the television lights, leaned over and kissed him. Their infant daughter, Nicole, crooked in her mother's left arm, looked around quizzically as more than a hundred people cheered.

"I truly hope to bring a spirit of adventure and excitement to the city of Providence during the next four years," said Cianci, choked with emotion.

The eclectic crowd ranged from East Side Brahmins to Silver Lake ward heelers, who whispered that this was different from the parties that Democrats threw. The meatballs on the buffet were Swedish. The pizza was cold and had anchovies. There wasn't a beer in sight, just lots of champagne.

The Yankees sized up the crowd with bemusement. Fred Lippitt, a Republican patrician, surveyed the Runyonesque crew, many flashing gold chains and reeking of cologne, and marveled that this was a whole new world for the Grand Old Party in Providence.

Over in a corner, Democratic power broker Tony Bucci shook hands and winked. Across the room, Republican elder statesman Herb DeSimone chatted with the two lone Republicans on the twenty-six-member City

Council. Cianci, confident and self-assured, flitted about the room, pumping hands, cracking jokes, slapping backs, issuing orders—taking charge. He thanked his supporters, Republicans and Democrats alike, and made them laugh when he welcomed them to the "Cianci Civic Center."

The next morning, Cianci and his wife stepped outside and saw the mayor's city limousine, a black Cadillac driven by a uniformed policeman. Two more policemen on motorcycles revved their engines. "Is that too much?" said Cianci, laughing with delight.

A few minutes later, the new mayor was being chauffeured along Angell Street, down ancient College Hill with its brick mansions and Ivy League buildings, past curious Brown University students. Inside the car, Cianci mused, "What if nobody shows up?"

The limousine rolled past the soaring white spire of the First Baptist Church and into downtown, through a death-defying traffic rotary known as Suicide Circle, and across a swath of concrete that carried the dubious distinction of being the world's widest bridge, covering a long stretch of the Providence River. It glided to a stop beside City Hall, a squat gray edifice that was built like its new master, low and wide. A massive wooden platform, draped in red, white, and blue bunting, had been erected in front of the one-hundred-year-old building, built in the style of the French Second Empire. President Theodore Roosevelt had addressed more than twenty thousand people here in 1902 on the evils of corporate trusts and the corruptibility of mankind. John Kennedy had spoken to an adoring crowd here on the eve of his election to the presidency in 1960.

There was a similar Camelot-like quality to Cianci's entrance into City Hall. The public was captivated by the exuberant mayor and his stylish wife. Their daughter, Nicole, wore a red-and-white snowsuit with an elephant on the left side; in the spirit of bipartisanship, Cianci had ordered a donkey sewn on the other side.

People milled around inside the mayor's grand corner office, with its carved wooden paneling, gilt wallpaper, marble fireplace, and gracefully curved chandelier. Bright winter sunlight spilled in through the huge windows facing east onto Kennedy Plaza.

"Take off your coat and stay awhile," he told Ron Glantz, one of his new aides. "We've got four years."

Outside, workers were straining to swing open the castlelike front doors of City Hall, which, under Joe Doorley, had been opened only for ceremonial occasions. Doorley, who had angered Cianci by appointing twenty-one of his supporters to city jobs on his way out the door, was vacationing in Florida.

Shortly past noon, Cianci waited as the police chief called the roll of dignitaries to take their places outside. He kidded with Larry McGarry, Mr. Democrat, who sat in his wheelchair in a black morning coat, a white carnation pinned to his lapel.

"They didn't call my name," said Cianci. "You guys are up to your old tricks."

Finally, his name was called. He and Sheila walked down the sweeping marble staircase and out into the sunshine, where they were met with a shower of applause and the salutes of white-gloved police officers.

As he took the oath for the second time that day, Cianci could see the challenges all around. Directly ahead was Burnside Park, where winos loitered near the statue of Ambrose Burnside, the incompetent Civil War general and prominent Rhode Island Republican. To his right were nineteenth-century office buildings whose upper floors had been closed off as fire hazards. To his left he noticed workmen wheeling a grand piano out of the once-elegant Biltmore Hotel, now home to a dozen or so long-term residents, some jewelry-trade offices, and the occasional overnight trucker.

Surrounding him on the platform were the twenty-six members of the City Council, overwhelmingly Democratic and largely hostile. Although they clapped politely, many had already met in secret and vowed not to give the Republican mayor anything. His election had been a fluke, they believed, and they wanted to see to it that he failed.

Back inside, the mayor joked with his secretary. "Am I on the payroll yet?" he asked. "I better be—with overtime, starting at 12:01."

Cianci grew more serious when he received word that the council had just met upstairs and elected a Doorley Democrat, Robert Haxton, to lead it. Haxton had taken sixteen of the twenty-six votes, defeating a Democratic newcomer aligned with McGarry and sympathetic to Cianci. The council immediately voted to refer all department-director nominees to committee.

Cianci glanced knowingly at one of his aides. "It looks like a short honeymoon," he said.

In the next few weeks, Cianci and Haxton clashed over the stalled appointments. The mayor pressured some of Doorley's department directors to resign. Haxton persuaded them to stay. He accused Cianci of using threats and coercion. Cianci responded by firing two directors and putting his own men in as "acting" directors.

"I started acting like a mayor today," Cianci declared.

He hung a poster of an elephant in his office, not a soft, cuddly Republican elephant but a fierce bull elephant charging angrily toward the camera, ears flared and tusks lowered. The caption said, "It's better to be the stomper than the stompee."

Cianci angrily canceled a meeting with Haxton and other council leaders to discuss the stalemate. He vowed not to negotiate patronage with "people who are trying to usurp my power."

A few weeks later Haxton was arrested by the Providence police.

Haxton, a ruddy man of forty with modish sideburns, was known as a dashing man-about-town. A *Providence Journal* feature had once rated him one of the city's most eligible bachelors. He drove a white Mercedes with a low-numbered license plate, an odd status symbol in Rhode Island, signifying stature or longevity. He lived with his parents in the city's West End and ran one of his family's chain of liquor stores.

On Sunday night, January 26, Haxton wound up at the X-rated Columbus Theater on Broadway, a once-grand boulevard west of downtown, lined with Victorian mansions that had grown seedy. He met a sixteen-year-old boy standing on the sidewalk looking at the marquee, which advertised *The Life and Times of Xaviera Hollander*.

The boy said later that Haxton had asked him to come inside with him and watch the movie, and the boy had declined. According to official accounts, Haxton went in alone; the boy went to the house of a Providence policeman he knew, Alfred Mintz.

Mintz had supported Cianci in the 1974 campaign. After Cianci took office, Mintz was transferred to a plainclothes unit. Mintz rounded up his partner, and they brought the boy back to the Columbus. As the two cops waited down the street in Mintz's gold Toyota, Mintz's partner grew uneasy because of the boy's age; he urged Mintz to call headquarters for guidance. But then Haxton emerged and gave the boy a ride. The policemen followed. After about an hour, driving around the city, the Mercedes stopped in front of a fruit stand on Hartford Avenue. The officers saw the boy get out, and Haxton drove away.

Later that night, at the police station, top police brass took a statement from the boy, who alleged that Haxton had grabbed his crotch. It was past midnight when the boy finished giving his statement.

The next day, Chief Walter McQueeney and two of his top aides went to City Hall to meet with Cianci and Ron Glantz in the mayor's office. The topic was whether to charge Haxton.

According to Glantz, police officials who had been loyal to Doorley and friendly with Haxton were reluctant to charge him. But the chief, who wanted to keep his job, wasn't about to openly defy Cianci, who wanted Haxton charged. Glantz said that Cianci also asked him, as a lawyer, about the legal procedure for removing Haxton from office. The meeting ended with a decision to charge Haxton. He was arrested later that afternoon, after attending a meeting at City Hall, and charged with committing a lewd and indecent act.

Haxton's lawyer called his arrest "one of the grossest examples of dirty politics I've ever seen." Francis Darigan, the new Democratic city chairman and Cianci's likely opponent in 1978, complained that Haxton had been set up. When Darigan went down to the police station to get Haxton, he asked a major he knew from South Providence, "What's this all about?" The major, said Darigan, couldn't look him in the eye.

Several police officers were also upset by Haxton's arrest. One, Major John J. Leyden, said that the police normally shooed away men caught cruising pickup spots at night, rather than arresting them—including Haxton, whose white Mercedes was a familiar sight to nighttime officers on patrol. Leyden also questioned the wisdom of putting the boy at risk by using him as bait. The whole case smacked of entrapment, he said.

Cianci responded that "there was no political motivation whatsoever." Asked years later about allegations that he ordered Haxton arrested, Cianci said: "That's a lie. I can't help it if he liked boys."

Haxton's arrest neutralized him as a public critic of Cianci's. Although he remained council president as his case wound through the legal system, he was never quite as vocal about the mayor as he had been that first month.

In May, after four months of sniping with the council, Cianci finally acquiesced to a private meeting with the council's majority leader to discuss their differences. Over a cordial, two-hour lunch at Camille's, on Federal Hill, the two men reached a compromise; Cianci's top-level appointees would be confirmed.

"I do have a city to run," said Cianci. As to why he was now willing to meet with the council leadership when he had refused to in January, the mayor said, "That's the art of politics."

EVERYONE FROM THE Hot Dog Lady to Antoinette Downing was welcome in Cianci's City Hall.

In his first week, the mayor dispatched his limousine to the East Side to pick up Downing, the grand dame of historic preservation in Providence. Downing had single-handedly saved many of the old mansions and colonial houses on Benefit Street, one of Providence's oldest streets, from the wrecking ball of urban renewal.

Downing and two of her society cohorts sat in the mayor's office, engaging in polite chitchat and slaughtering the pronunciation of Cianci's name with their precise Yankee diction. After listening to the women call him "Chauncey" and "Ci-AHN-cee," the mayor smirked, leaned across his desk on his elbows, and said: "It's See-ANN-see. You'll get used to it."

The Hot Dog Lady, a vendor who had been banished from downtown streets, returned to a warm welcome from Cianci. The mayor made sure that the police would give her no trouble by pulling up in his limousine and, as officers watched, buying a hot dog.

When the banks balked at cashing Social Security checks for seniors without accounts, Cianci flexed his mayoral muscles. He got the bank presidents on his speakerphone and, putting on a show for those in his office, threatened to withdraw the city deposits. The banks capitulated.

Cianci became ubiquitous. He clambered aboard a backhoe to break ground for a new community center in South Providence. He hosted the Mayor's City Celebration, a downtown festival that included folksingers, ballet dancers, karate experts, the puppet act Kukla, Fran & Ollie, and a City Hall screening of *Yankee Doodle Dandy*, about the life of Providence-born showman George M. Cohan. He dropped in at a triple-decker where a woman was sitting at her kitchen table planning a neighborhood cleanup. He showed up for the event in overalls and killed a rat.

But the mayor was not universally beloved. At the St. Patrick's Day parade on Smith Hill, in his first year, Doorley people booed and hissed and turned their backs to him. And when Cianci showed up at a banquet hall for a St. Augustine Church reunion dinner, one supporter recalled, "You'd have thought the devil had walked in there. You could hear people hissing and saying, 'What's he doing here?' " In those days, Cianci later joked, a Republican mayor intruding on Democratic turf was "about as welcome as the ayatollah at an American Legion convention." Cianci found it devastating not to be liked. But, ever mindful of his fragile margin of victory, he kept smiling and showing up, trying to win over his enemies.

"I would go to the groundbreaking of an ant," he declared.

Cianci knew that he couldn't erase decades of urban decay and solve all the city's problems overnight. Providence had one of the highest unemployment rates in the nation, at 18 percent, and also one of the highest rates of alcoholism.

During his first week in office, monkeys escaped from the decrepit zoo and ran loose through the city. During his second week, the debt-ridden Biltmore Hotel, a downtown landmark, closed because it couldn't pay its gas bill. When Cianci received the news in his office across the street, he slid out of his chair and onto the floor and cried out, "What can happen next?"

The mayor wanted people to know that there was more to life than death and taxes. He wanted to create a legacy for Providence. That's why he made a twenty-thousand-dollar budget request to buy mates for some of the animals at the zoo. "We have one yak at the zoo," he explained. "If we feed it and care for it, what do we eventually have? A dead yak."

He told attendees at a neighborhood meeting in Olneyville one night: "Let's look at the facts, one of which is that Providence is a tired old city. We can't change it overnight, but we're trying, and we're looking everywhere for the dollars to do it."

In the summer of 1975 Cianci's search brought him to Nashville, Tennessee, site of the annual convention of the national Fraternal Order of Police. Cianci wanted the convention in Providence in two years. The Rhode Island FOP delegation flew in fresh steamers to Nashville daily, and served them up with clam cakes, booze, and Cianci charm. The mayor made the rounds of each state's delegation, pressing the flesh and addressing the convention before the vote. Providence beat out New Orleans, Phoenix, and Albuquerque by eighty votes. None of those mayors came.

Cianci's winning pitch included a boast of Providence's fine Italian cuisine, which he found wanting in Tennessee. One night, in an Italian restaurant in Nashville, Cianci ordered spaghetti *al dente*, or hard-cooked. The perplexed waiter responded in his southern accent that they had spaghetti, but they were all out of *al dente*. Cianci roared with laughter.

In a gesture symbolic of his pledge to clean up City Hall, Cianci clambered up a stepladder in the old aldermans' chambers one day with a crowbar and pried loose a beam to launch a historic restoration.

He appointed his wife, Sheila, to cochair the restoration task force. Browsing in a Massachusetts antique store one day, she came across some red-leather chairs that bore a striking resemblance to the chairs long missing from the aldermans' chambers. The antique dealer said that he could get more of the chairs if she liked them.

Subsequently, an investigation found that a City Hall janitor with a drinking problem was selling the chairs to buy booze. The janitor, an ex-boxer, hired Tony Bucci as his lawyer. Bucci's defense, Cianci later said, laughing, was, "He's one of ours."

THE MANEUVERING BETWEEN the mayor and the City Council intensified as Cianci tried to pass his first budget, in the summer of 1975.

The mayor wanted to raise taxes to erase a deficit and finance his programs. The council, not wanting him to succeed, rejected his budget. The mayor threatened layoffs. The council accused him of scare tactics.

On the night of June 24, union members worried about layoffs crowded into the steamy council chambers. The debate over Cianci's budget raged for more than two hours, as whirring ceiling fans stirred the humid air and bands played on the steps outside—part of a one-hundredth-birthday celebration of City Hall organized by Cianci. At ten-thirty, exploding fireworks and aerial bombs punctuated the angry exchanges between perspiring pro- and anti-Cianci councilmen. Finally, the council rejected Cianci's budget.

The next morning Cianci called a mass union meeting at the Providence Civic Center. Only six hundred of the city's forty-five hundred union workers showed up, but they were raucously pro-Cianci. The mayor shouted that their jobs were not safe because of his foes on the council. When council leaders tried to respond, the plugs were yanked from their microphones and their voices drowned out by the boos and jeers of departing union members.

Two nights later the council rejected Cianci's budget again, creating the spectacle of Democratic union workers booing a Democratic council for opposing a Republican mayor. A *Journal* columnist said that it was like watching the College of Cardinals booing the pope.

Cianci went ahead and raised taxes anyway, through a deft maneuver of vetoing the council's stricter spending limits on him, but accepting their higher revenue projections. Council members cried foul. Larry McGarry publicly applauded Cianci's political skills—the kid learned fast, and his adversaries didn't know how to deal with a mayor from the opposing party. "They're used to saying yes and they're trying to say no and they don't know how," said McGarry.

Cianci was a political chameleon, playing off his battles with the council to impress East Side reformers that he was standing up to the machine—all the while embracing McGarry's political organization.

At a meeting of Young Republicans at Brown University, Cianci described his struggles against the remnants of an old political machine and its "do-nothing hacks" who "hang around City Hall like mannequins." At an East Side garden party, over iced tea and cake, Cianci regaled his Republican audience with tales of Doorley holdovers, including a city worker who was fired for meeting his girlfriend in the city pump house one night, only to be reinstated after a union arbitration hearing.

"The moral of the story is that everybody deserves a night in the pump house with his girlfriend," cracked Cianci. "No," muttered an East Sider, "the moral is we should all move to Warwick."

His first summer in office Cianci also dropped in, by helicopter, on Larry McGarry's annual Democratic City Committee clambake, for two thousand beer-guzzling, chowder-swilling ward heelers escaping the city heat at Francis Farm in rural Massachusetts. The mayor mingled freely. McGarry's sidekick, Snack McManus, was there, in his yellow slacks and matching yellow cigar holder, a Cianci appointee to the city tax board. So was Councilman Ray Cola, a devotee of Saint Rita who handed out medals of the saint and praised Cianci for putting a lot of Sixth Ward people to work. "As Saint Rita says, it's not what you know that counts in this country but who you know," he said. Responded Cianci: "Everybody he brings in is a cousin."

Meanwhile, Cianci was building his own patronage empire, financed by millions of dollars in federal funds. The money paid for two thousand temporary jobs and several hundred permanent jobs, as well as programs offering lucrative construction, street-paving, sidewalk-repair, and other contracts, for housing rehabilitation and neighborhood improvements. To bypass the City Council and retain control over the federal largesse, Cianci created agencies like the Mayor's Office of Community Development. The office administered the roughly nine million dollars a year that flowed to Providence as a result of the 1974 federal Community Development Act.

When the council tried to assert control, Cianci pointed to its past oversight of Progress for Providence, a high-minded antipoverty agency during the Doorley administration that had disintegrated into a scandal-ridden trough for mobsters, scam artists, and political hacks. "Progress for Providence," said Cianci, "was probably the worst disaster to hit Providence since the '38 hurricane."

The Providence Journal joined Cianci in calling his council critics hypocritical, but added that checks and balances in spending the money was not a bad idea. "Total control, however well-intentioned, still adds up to despotism," the newspaper warned.

Cianci also found himself journeying frequently to Washington, D.C., the city that he saw as his ultimate destiny, to lobby for federal assistance for his beleaguered city. Cianci was an anomaly, a young, urban, ethnic Republican, and he enjoyed a friendly relationship with the administration of President Ford, who was eager to broaden his party's base in the wake of the Watergate debacle. Cianci told the president that he owed his success to appealing to blacks, working people, and others traditionally excluded by the Republicans. "We were able to win in Providence," Cianci reported telling Ford, "because we didn't shut them out; we were able to win with them."

Back home, Cianci proved himself more of a populist, and a shrewd politician, when he bypassed the City Council and reached out directly to neighborhood groups to help decide how the federal money should be distributed. When the Doorley Democrats on the council screamed, Cianci called them obstructionists.

Cianci's Office for Community Development became a bizarre mishmash of idealism and cronyism characteristic of federal programs that attempted to address the ills of urban America in the 1970s—a blend of the old Providence and the new. Within Cianci's circle of advisers, a cadre of Republicans—East Siders and reformers—argued that good government was good politics, and so Cianci hired neighborhood activists and grassroots organizers who traditionally had been cut out of power. But then McGarry or T.B.—Tony Bucci—would call about a guy who needed a job, and Cianci would put him on the payroll. When some of the good-government types on the mayor's staff tried to argue, he would cynically remind them, "Good government will only get you good government."

Nick Easton, who was hired by the mayor's Office of Community Development, approached that question from a different perspective. A long-haired South Side radical, Easton knew what it was like to be on the outside looking in. As a director of PACE (People Acting Through Community Effort), the militant group that had futilely fought for neighborhood improvements under Joe Doorley, Easton realized that throwing stones would only take you so far.

Easton, in his mid-twenties, had grown up an exile from privilege. He was a curiosity: a Yankee Democrat. He joked that he came from fourteen generations of blue blood but only thirteen generations of green money.

His ancestor, Nicholas Easton, had been one of Rhode Island's first settlers, with Roger Williams, and one of Rhode Island's first governors. Eastons had been Quakers, opposed to the Revolutionary War and against the thriving Rhode Island slave trade. The Eastons had prospered, as farmers, merchants, and industrialists. Nick's grandfather had been an inventor, second in line in the family company. Nick's father had been raised with servants, maids, and chauffeurs. But then he lost his job in a family power struggle, and the Eastons' fortunes declined.

Young Nick lived in an extra house that belonged to his grandparents in the upper-caste waterfront suburb of Barrington, surrounded by wealth but forced to wear patches on his clothes. The experience radicalized him. Smart and opinionated, Easton earned a scholarship to Moses Brown, then waited tables to help pay his tuition at Brown University, where generations of more privileged Eastons had preceded him.

Easton had always been drawn to politics. In the blighted neighborhoods of South Providence he found an outlet after college for his radical beliefs. As a leader of PACE, he fought for safer streets, better housing, and equal opportunity. One issue of concern was the city's failure to rein in wild dogs that attacked people on the streets.

Cianci, who had stunned PACE leaders by inviting them into his office during his first week as mayor, sought to defuse their confrontational tactics by embracing them. He showed up at the group's annual congress in South Providence one night and charmed skeptical members who, the previous year, had awarded Doorley its "Tory" award in absentia. When one man complained that the city's property tax structure was unfair, Cianci invited him to serve on a study committee. "He did a job on me," the man said afterward.

PACE leaders, accustomed to battling the establishment, were wary of Cianci's motives but pragmatic enough to get what they could. The mayor appointed some PACE members to city boards and hired others to city jobs. Cianci may be acting "for the wrong reasons," said one leader, but at least people from the community were finally gaining a voice at City Hall. Another PACE leader warned: "At this point, he needs us. But if at any point we need him and he turns on us, we'll turn into snakes."

Nick Easton was hired to work in an affordable-housing program in the Office of Community Development. There he found himself surrounded by a motley crew of ward heelers and political favor seekers. Several of his coworkers never showed up at the office, which was probably a good thing, since many of them were incompetent.

Easton oversaw a group of "rehabilitation officers" who were supposed to go around the city in two-man teams, inspecting lists of abandoned buildings and writing reports on necessary repairs. But most days, one man would hand off his stack of folders to his partner and go off to his real job. Another day, his partner might reciprocate. One rehab officer was a jobber for a jewelry factory. Another worked in a shoe store. A third sold used cars.

Easton wound up, by default, as deputy director of the office's housing program. Although he was one of the only people in the office capable of running the program, he made less money than just about everyone except the secretaries. Cianci regarded Easton as a rabble-rouser and never trusted him.

"Easton!" the mayor would bark. "Why are you going around causing trouble?"

Easton can remember being called into the mayor's office and getting yelled at by Ronnie Glantz in front of Cianci. The issue was inconsequential, involving a list of job applicants that Easton had passed along to PACE leaders, but the message was clear: intimidation. Glantz, who had emerged as a key Cianci confidant, screamed at Easton that passing on the list was a federal offense, that he could go to prison. It was a routine that Cianci and Glantz also pulled with others, said Easton, to keep people in their place and remind them who was boss.

After about a year and a half, things grew so outrageous that Easton quit his job with the city. PACE officials, despite Cianci's efforts to co-opt them, blasted the mayor for hiring political hacks and detailed shoddy workmanship in the city's housing-rehabilitation program. Cianci was irked when they marched on his stately brick house on Blackstone Boulevard, which one neighbor said resembled the White House for the floodlit American flag that flew from the second-floor balcony, day and night.

In the Office of Community Development's second year of operation, the FBI began investigating allegations that federal funds had been diverted to pay contractors to repair private individuals' homes. In its third year, the federal government cut off funding for a three-mile bike trail from downtown through the East Side after the city ran afoul of competitive bidding regulations and spent more than two hundred thousand dollars without even finishing the trail. According to Kenneth Orenstein, who coordinated the office's Downtown Development and Preservation Team, one of the overseers of the bike trail sat next to him—an older, tattooed man who had been given a job because he needed health insurance. One day, the man, whose desk was next to Orenstein's, walked over to the water fountain and dropped dead of a heart attack. Orenstein also remembered the day that a group of grubby demolition contractors took over the OCD's conference room and rigged the bids for contracts to knock down dilapidated buildings. Eventually, the director of the office, a reform-minded East Sider, quit in disgust, tired of meddling from the mayor's office. Looking back on some of the people who worked for the OCD, Easton called it "one of the worst crews ever assembled."

After Easton's departure, one of Cianci's federally funded hires, the director of the office's Homestead Board, was arrested for defrauding homesteaders seeking to move into abandoned houses that had been acquired by the city. When the police did a routine criminal-background check, they discovered that the director was on parole from state prison in Massachusetts for kidnapping and rape, and had been when he was hired in 1975. Besides shaking down homesteaders, he had another sideline—running a string of prostitutes who worked the streets of downtown Providence, in sight of City Hall. On rainy days, the hookers took shelter in the Homestead Board's offices on Washington Street.

THE MOST PRIZED office in Rhode Island politics is a seat in the United States Senate.

The tiniest state has a tradition of sending senators to Washington who become giants: Nelson Aldrich, Theodore Francis Green, John O. Pastore, Claiborne Pell, and John Chafee. Each man served two decades or more, counseled presidents, shaped national and foreign policy, and steered federal dollars and patronage to his home state.

In 1975, after barely six months in office as mayor of Providence, Buddy Cianci heard the call of the most powerful club in America. Although he was young, he was hot, and some Republican leaders wanted him to run in 1976. But to get to Washington, Cianci would have to face down two dominant figures in Rhode Island politics: Pastore and Chafee.

Pastore was the epitome of the ethnic Democratic politician, a product of poor immigrant parents on Federal Hill who had gone on to become the nation's first Italian-American senator and one of its leading liberals. He was a spellbinding orator who helped pushed through Lyndon Johnson's landmark civil-rights bill and delivered the keynote address at the 1964 Democratic National Convention, a eulogy to the fallen president, John F.

Kennedy. Pastore, who had held the seat for twenty-five years, was up for reelection in 1976.

Chafee, the son of privilege and a graduate of Harvard and Yale, was a moderate Republican who had won a Purple Heart at Guadalcanal. He served three terms as Rhode Island governor in the 1960s, running as "the man you can trust," and went on to serve as navy secretary under President Nixon. Chafee had lost a fourth bid for governor in 1968, after saying that he would impose a state income tax—a race in which he stopped campaigning following the death of a daughter. Then he had lost a tough Senate race to Pell, a wealthy Newporter, in 1972. A prominent Yankee lawyer in Providence, Chafee wanted to return to public life.

The skirmishing began in the spring of 1975, when Cianci and Pastore addressed the Rhode Island Verrazzano Day banquet. Cianci talked about the contributions of Italian-Americans, then added pointedly that he and Pastore represented "the movement from one era to another in public service," suggesting that Pastore's day was done.

"That really burned him up," Cianci laughingly told people afterward.

Over the next several months, Cianci delighted in tweaking Pastore and telling derogatory stories about the senator in private. He boasted that Pastore got mad when the mayor sat in the front row at the Providence College graduation, while the senator was in the second row, with the rest of the congressional delegation.

Pastore was a short, dignified man with a bristly mustache. He was fiercely protective of his position as a role model for Italian-Americans and would storm out of restaurants on Federal Hill if he saw a mobster eating there. One Sunday morning in the late sixties, Pastore was eating alone at the counter at the East Side Diner; farther down, also eating alone, was Raymond Patriarca. They ate in silence, without acknowledging each other. As Pastore reached into his pocket to pay, a nickel fell to the floor. According to someone working there at the time, the senator and the mob boss each reached down for the nickel; Pastore got it and left without a word.

The senator liked being compared to the Rhode Island Red, a fiery bantam rooster that was the state bird. In his last campaign, in 1970, at the height of the Vietnam War, the hawkish Pastore had faced a stiff challenge from a Jesuit priest, John McLaughlin, who went on to host *The McLaughlin Report*, a national political commentary television show out of Washington.

"If I could win against Father McLaughlin, and I did, then certainly Cianci doesn't frighten me," Pastore told a Democratic audience at a summer clambake.

There was a movement afoot in the Democrat-controlled state legislature to pass a law that would have forced Cianci to step down as mayor if he wanted to run for Senate. Pastore issued a public challenge, saying that he would resign the remaining months of his term if Cianci beat him, if Cianci would promise to give up the final two years of his term as mayor if Pastore beat him. "The idea that because he's safe to turn his back on the people of Providence and then crawl back if he's beaten—the people of Rhode Island aren't going to buy that," said Pastore.

Clearly offended at what he considered Cianci's disrespectful behavior, Pastore, who had known Cianci's father, joked that he had bounced little Buddy on his knee, and that he must have bounced him one time too many, because Cianci had become a Republican. (Cianci teased that since Pastore's first name, in Italian, was Giovanni, his initials were G.O.P.)

Pastore also scolded Cianci for not working together with the state's congressional delegation in his efforts to land a federal office building for Providence. Pastore said that Cianci had been ignoring him, even though Pastore sat on the Senate committee that controlled the funds. "He should know, if he doesn't know already," that his projects "will never come to Providence without the help of John Pastore."

Cianci fired back by accusing Pastore of making "veiled threats." The dispute came to a head a few nights later, when Pastore and Cianci shared top billing at the annual banquet of the San Biagio Society. Cianci and an allied councilman criticized Pastore again over the federal building. A fuming Pastore, believing that Cianci had come to the banquet "looking for trouble," responded by lecturing the mayor. Cianci, said Pastore, was "an ill-mannered person." As Cianci listened uncomfortably, Pastore reminded him that he, John Pastore, whose political ideals had been forged in the Great Depression and the New Deal, was still the principal spokesman for Rhode Island's Italian-Americans—not some young, upstart Republican son of privilege who had yet to pay his political dues.

A few days later Cianci and Pastore studiously ignored each other as they waited with other political leaders at Green Airport to welcome President Ford, who was flying in for a political fund-raiser in Newport.

But there would be no Pastore-Cianci race. In October Pastore announced that he would not seek reelection. He was sixty-eight years old, he said, and it was time to come home. The political experts predicted that Pastore would have beaten Cianci. One of Cianci's top aides told the mayor that his mother, like leagues of older voters, would never go against Pastore. But it would have been a fiery campaign, between an old warhorse, perhaps the finest public speaker Rhode Island had ever known, and a young lion, who was winning favorable comparisons.

Pastore's announcement seemed to open the door for Cianci. The state Republican chairman said that the nomination was his, if he wanted it. It was a question of timing. On one hand, Cianci did not want to seem overeager, given his inexperience, and jeopardize a bright political future. And winning would be tough; Rhode Island had not seen a Republican senator since the Democrats had become the state's dominant party during the Great Depression. On the other hand, Senate seats didn't open up very often. Cianci should pounce while his popularity was high, especially among Italian-American voters, who would be more likely to support him with Pastore out of the race. If Cianci lost, he'd still have two years left on his term as mayor.

Cianci played it close to the vest, restricted in part by strict new federal campaign-spending laws that would have kicked in had he too openly declared his interest. One day he confessed to experiencing political vertigo. He said that he felt like he was "in an elevator on about the eighth floor of the Empire State Building, heading all the way to the roof."

But Cianci was not alone. Standing silently in the background, biding his time, was John Chafee.

THAT FALL AND winter, Chafee and Cianci circled each other warily, like the schoolboy wrestlers they had once been. The two men represented the Yankee and Italian wings of the Rhode Island Republican party, which coexisted uneasily. They were cautious but firm in their public remarks, eager to avoid a divisive primary but determined to show their resolve.

"I am positive I could get the endorsement of the Republican party if I so choose," said Cianci. The mayor added that he had conferred with Chafee, and gave the impression that Chafee would not contest him.

Countered Chafee, "In the final analysis, I don't think I will be controlled by what his [Cianci's] decision would be."

Behind the scenes, the two men jockeyed for position. At a state Republican-party dinner at the West Valley Inn in West Warwick, Cianci fumed as he waited outside for Chafee to show, wanting to upstage his rival by coming in later and being the last to speak. But Chafee, apparently sitting in a car nearby, outwaited him. Finally, after Cianci gave up and went in and started speaking, Chafee arrived and upstaged him with a huge ovation.

One of Cianci's aides, Joe Vileno, was sitting next to an elderly matron from South County, a frugal Swamp Yankee who told him in her blue-blooded voice that she didn't usually attend political functions, "but I came out for John." All the old Yankees had come out. In a low-turnout Republican primary, that kind of fealty could prove decisive. Cianci was a long way from the Fourth Ward, where Tony Bucci could turn out the Democratic vote. At that moment, recalled Vileno, "I knew there was no way we'd ever win a primary."

Other Cianci partisans weren't convinced of that. The mayor believed that he could beat Chafee. Cianci was the hottest thing in Rhode Island politics; the party endorsement was his for the taking and he could lay claim to what had become, in the minds of some ethnic-conscious voters, an Italian seat. Chafee was down and out, a two-time loser for statewide office.

The rivalry with Chafee was intertwined with Cianci's resentments and insecurities about being accepted by the WASPs. Years later, Cianci would speak bitterly, and enviously, of Chafee. He said that Chafee was a member of the privileged upper class who went to fancy barbecues while "I was out working for votes in a crowd of two thousand Puerto Ricans—hot, sweaty guys putting their arms around me so you can smell their armpits, spitting on me, asking for a job."

Early in 1976, Cianci and Mickey Farina drove down to Chafee's house in Potowomut, a peninsula jutting into Narragansett Bay in Warwick. Chafee, wanting to speak privately, came outside and sat in his car, an old station wagon, with the mayor and his political adviser. Chafee said that he wanted to run regardless of Cianci's intentions, and that he would oppose the mayor in a primary if necessary. Cianci's position was that if Chafee went against the party's endorsement he truly would be dead politically.

Not long after, according to two witnesses, Chafee came to Cianci's house on Blackstone Boulevard for Sunday brunch. Cianci had a handful of advisers there, including Farina and Herb DeSimone. Sheila Cianci, who had prepared a Jewish brunch, served the men at the large dining room table—salmon, whitefish, blintzes, strawberries and sour cream, washed down by lots of espresso. Chafee sat at the end of the table, drinking tea. Cianci, seated at the other end, was cocky and arrogant.

The conversation flowed back and forth. Farina had been pushing Cianci to run for Senate and get out of Providence; City Hall was a sewer that could drag you down if you stayed too long. Farina, who had worked in Washington, wanted to get back; he could be Cianci's chief of staff, and they could stay forever. And with Cianci's oratorical ability and charisma, who knew what opportunities might follow. The Senate was the most powerful club in America—there were only a hundred U.S. senators, and they ran the world. DeSimone, more of an elder statesman in the party, was more cautious and conciliatory. He had pointed out that there were only fifty governors, and that Cianci, who was still young and had been in office for only a year, should pay his dues and then try for the State House first. "It's not your turn to be selfish," DeSimone said. DeSimone later disputed that, saying that he never would have backed Cianci against Chafee, still one of the state's leading Republicans.

At one point during the brunch, Chafee put his head down on the table and cried. He said, "I want this more than anything. I'll be a great senator." There was an awkward silence. After Chafee left, Cianci joked about his behavior. He thought Chafee was weak. Years later, Cianci would smile and say of Chafee, "He wanted it badly. He had lost twice. He wasn't the lovable John Chafee that we knew later on."

But underneath Chafee's WASP exterior was a steely politician as tough as any ward boss. A combat veteran of World War II and the Korean War, he refused to back down. After months of attempting to build consensus in his quiet manner, Chafee decided to press ahead. When it became apparent that Cianci wasn't going to step aside, Chafee's advisers urged him to announce his candidacy, recalled his campaign chairman, Bruce Selya. Further delay, they warned, would only give Cianci more time to maneuver.

In February, shortly before publicly announcing his candidacy, Chafee went to the mayor's office to inform Cianci of his intentions. The afterhours meeting was small—Chafee and Selya, and Cianci and DeSimone. The discussion began cordially, with Chafee stating his intentions and Cianci, stalling for time, trying to persuade him to wait, and let the party decide. But when Chafee declined, Cianci blew up. He brought up a divisive primary that Chafee had faced in the early 1960s, when he ran for governor against an Italian-American Republican. Cianci threatened his own primary challenge. He raged about how unfair it was for things to be handed to people like Chafee on a silver platter. He complained that people like himself, lacking Chafee's lineage, couldn't get in the door. Chafee just sat there. Eventually, Selya and DeSimone calmed things down, and the meeting ended. Chafee had called Cianci's bluff. For all his bravado, Cianci did have doubts about whether he could have won and whether the timing was right.

It was dark when Chafee and Selya walked through Kennedy Plaza in front of City Hall. Selya offered to give Chafee a ride home, but Chafee said that he'd take the bus and Selya went back to his law office. A short time later, he heard a rapping on the door. It was Chafee, who didn't have bus fare, seeking a ride.

On Monday, February 9, Cianci publicly removed himself from the race. Campaigning on Saturday in New Hampshire, Cianci said that he had broken the news to President Ford, who had encouraged him to run, then met with Chafee on Sunday to give him the green light. After saying in December that he was "leaning very strongly" toward running, Cianci now said that he had a job to finish in Providence. He was still a young mayor; it was not yet his time. He denied that he had backed off for fear of losing. "It's a great opportunity, and if I were an opportunist, I'd be taking advantage of it."

Spared a contentious primary, Chafee went on to be elected and served twenty-two distinguished years in the Senate. He earned a national reputation as a champion of the environment and health care. When he died in 1999, his funeral at Grace Church in downtown Providence was attended by President Clinton and his wife, Hillary, several cabinet members, and dozens of senators.

In later years, political junkies would look back and speculate about what would have happened had Cianci challenged Chafee, like the split-screen films that used to run at the Ocean State Theater, presenting a fantasy boxing match between heavyweight champs Rocky Marciano and Muhammad Ali. As time passed, Cianci would regret not running.

"I thought that I had plenty of time," he said.

BUDDY CIANCI'S DECISION to pull out of the 1976 Senate race did not dampen his enthusiasm for the national political spotlight, or diminish his star. At the Republican National Convention in Kansas City that summer, he gave a nationally televised speech introducing a major speaker, former Texas governor John Connally.

Norm Roussel, Cianci's political adman, recalled the mayor's sitting in President Ford's room the afternoon before the speech, around a large conference table with Republican luminaries like Henry Kissinger, Howard Baker, and Donald Rumsfeld and members of Ford's steering committee. A White House staffer asked Cianci to introduce Connally. Cianci inquired about giving one of the speeches seconding Ford's nomination instead. That might be more prestigious, but it would be late at night. The Connally speech offered Cianci six minutes of national prime-time television exposure. He took it.

Late that night Cianci was grabbing a bite at a Denny's restaurant with Roussel, trying to figure out what to say. His eyes fell on his paper place mat, which offered an illustrated history of European immigrants—bricklayers, artisans, masons. All of a sudden, it clicked. The message dovetailed with Cianci's profile as an ethnic northeastern mayor, someone the Republicans wanted to showcase to broaden their appeal.

The next night, standing before a sea of delegates in Kemper Arena, Cianci delivered a rousing speech that fired up the crowd and won him a huge ovation. He spoke of immigrant hopes and dreams, of the need to rebuild urban neighborhoods, and of how the Democrats had taken ethnic voters for granted.

"For too long, ethnics have been treated as votes and statistics by Democratic machines that stifled their hopes, laughed at their ambitions, and scoffed at their dreams," thundered Cianci. "Our Republican ranks contain many of us who are proud that we come from Federal Hill in Providence, from the streets of the north of Boston, or from Floresville, Texas [Connally's hometown]."

Then Cianci went after Ford's Democratic opponent, Georgian Jimmy Carter, who had mispronounced *Italian* "Eye-talian" in his convention acceptance speech. "I'd like to address myself to Mr. Carter, if he's watching," said Cianci. "My name is Vincent 'Buddy' Cianci, mayor of the great city of Providence, Rhode Island. I am not an Eye-talian, but an Italo-American and proud of my ethnic background."

The speech established the dynamic young mayor as a political comer. Dick Cheney, Ford's chief of staff, sang Cianci's praises. The congratulatory telegrams rolled in, along with gifts: Scotch, provolone, salamis. Cianci freely distributed copies of his biography. It was, said Roussel, like winning the Oscar.

After the convention, President Ford appointed Cianci to his twenty-three-member campaign-strategy council and invited him to dinner at the

White House. There was talk of a place for Cianci in Washington, either as a cabinet or subcabinet official, if Ford won. On election night a plane stood by at the airport to take Cianci to Washington if Ford won. But Ford lost. Afterward, Cianci was subdued, especially after Jimmy Carter's landslide victory in Rhode Island.

Back at City Hall, Cianci's continuing battles with the Democrats were taking their toll. The ongoing budget impasse led to frequent labor unrest and a decline in city services. Residents in the West End complained about rats biting their children. In neighborhood meetings angry residents of Mount Pleasant, Federal Hill, and Fox Point protested skyrocketing taxes; some called for Cianci's impeachment.

One steamy morning, in the summer of 1977, a convoy of city trucks and private vehicles snarled Kennedy Plaza for ninety minutes to protest layoffs. Trash piled up at the rate of two hundred tons a day as sanitation workers claimed that they had "lost" the keys to their garbage trucks. Frustrated residents dumped their garbage outside the city sanitation headquarters. Sewage pumps threatened to back up into the basements of people's houses after sewage-plant workers walked off the job. Bodies lay unburied at the city's North Burial Grounds when the gravediggers refused to show. Said Cianci, "No one is panicking."

City Hall became a hostile environment, punctuated by angry shouting matches and juvenile confrontations. One night a city worker walked into the mayor's office to report that he had just overheard Councilman John Garan, a Cianci foe, talking on the telephone in the lobby of City Hall. Garan had been telling someone that "the mayor is no friend of yours." The worker had no idea what Garan was talking about, but Cianci did. The mayor had just finished drawing up a list of 182 city employees who would be losing their jobs as a result of budget cuts, and he suspected that Garan was tipping off someone on the list. When Cianci learned that Garan was holding a copy of the list, he erupted.

Cianci charged out into the second-floor hallway and, peering over the balcony, began screaming at Garan below. Then he sent an aide downstairs to order Garan off the phone. When Garan refused, the aide grabbed the receiver out of the councilman's hand and then yanked the cord out of the wall.

"Garan was being the bearer of doom," complained Cianci, defending his actions. Worse, Garan had been using the only available line to City Hall after 4 P.M., the mayor said. "If Garan had wanted to make 182 phone calls, he could have made them on another telephone."

The budget was merely one front in the wide-ranging war for control of the fractious city. In Silver Lake, a council candidate accused Cianci of threatening the jobs of city workers who backed the Democratic ticket. On the waterfront in Fox Point, Cape Verdean community leader Tia Santos charged that Cianci fired him as deputy port director for refusing to take the mayor around the neighborhood and "hit the joints with him" to expand his political base. In the Second Ward Providence's first black councilman, Democrat Philip Addison, Jr., complained that the mayor pressured the Urban League to fire him for voting against a black Cianci appointee. In South Providence the Irish felt that Cianci neglected their declining neighborhoods at the expense of the more politically important Italian wards, content to see the suburban flight of Irish Democratic voters continue.

Others accused Cianci of using his power to punish his enemies and reward his friends, something that all politicians do, but which his critics said he carried to extremes. His tax assessor resigned after a shouting match with Cianci in which he complained of political pressure over assessments. Cianci fired his building inspector, Lloyd Griffin, after Griffin alleged political interference in code enforcement. Griffin, the mercurial black South Providence leader whose mail-ballot work had helped Cianci win in 1974, also accused the mayor of telling the police to follow his building inspectors. Cianci responded that the police had been asked to check on suspected malingerers, after a tip about a Public Works truck parked outside a saloon. Larry McGarry, a close Griffin ally, warned that the firing could hurt Cianci politically but also criticized Griffin for being disloyal.

McGarry watched Cianci's maneuvering with a wary bemusement. One day in 1975 mayoral aide James Diamond appeared in McGarry's law office, in Lincoln, where Mr. Democrat had been spending his days since the 1974 campaign. The mayor had dispatched Diamond on a political mission—in essence to find out who was for Cianci and who was against him.

A native Texan, Diamond had come to Providence to study at Brown and wound up working as a grant writer for Attorney General Richard Israel when Cianci was a young prosecutor. Diamond hadn't known Cianci well or been terribly impressed—he thought he was lazy and self-centered. But after Cianci became mayor, Diamond found himself working at City Hall, writing grant proposals for federal funds. Before long, Diamond, who had computer skills, received a new assignment. Cianci summoned him to the mayor's office and told him to start building a computerized database of every citizen in Providence. The mayor wanted everyone ranked on a scale of 1 to 5 in terms of their loyalty to Buddy Cianci. According to Diamond, Cianci said that the list would be used "to reward his supporters and punish his enemies." Diamond was told to start with the prominent political people and to consult Larry McGarry, who knew all the players.

The assignment troubled Diamond, raising uncomfortable parallels with the recently fallen President Nixon and his enemies list. Diamond was especially sensitive because he had supported Nixon and felt bad about it in the wake of Watergate. (When he still supported Nixon, Diamond had angered local anti-Nixon Republicans by hiring a helicopter to photograph a "Dump Nixon" rally at the Rhode Island State House; he later said that he wanted to record the size of the crowd in case the president's enemies exaggerated it.) A devout Christian who had studied Hitler and occupied Europe at Brown, Diamond talked it over with another Cianci aide, Anthony Agostinelli, and decided not to "collaborate." (Agostinelli confirmed Diamond's recollection.)

Diamond went to see McGarry, driving up Smithfield Avenue past the St. Francis Cemetery to his basement office, and found an ally in his one-man resistance movement. Over a period of three or four months, the gangly, bearded outsider to Providence politics and the wheelchair-bound old Irish ward boss spent hours together. Diamond found McGarry to be a devout, ethical man, and saw that his alliance with Cianci was an uneasy one. McGarry shared Diamond's lack of enthusiasm for Cianci's project, not wanting to transfer all of his political secrets to a potential enemy. Instead, McGarry regaled Diamond with old political war stories about his heyday in the Tenth Ward and at Public Works. Diamond scribbled down enough names to satisfy Cianci that he was making progress but never entered anything into the computer. Finally, a job opened up in the Parks Department and Diamond left City Hall. The list was forgotten. But the mayor, as Diamond would learn in the coming years, had other ways of keeping score.

Governing a city as factionalized as Providence wasn't easy—it required hard decisions and compromise. Vincent Vespia, now a state police lieutenant, saw his old friend's ambition grow after he became mayor and his national stature increased. Cianci told him of his dream of someday being in the U.S. Senate. Vespia sat proudly in his living room and watched on television when Cianci addressed the 1976 Republican National Convention in Kansas City. Vespia got to meet visiting dignitaries like President

Ford and John Connally and joined Cianci in choice seats at the Civic Center to see Red Skelton and Frank Sinatra.

The wiseguys always came out strong for Sinatra in Providence, where the mob's presence remained strong. Providence was a city where Bobo Marrapese's bar on Federal Hill could get a liquor license but the Brown Faculty Club, which Joe Doorley had hated, could not. In fact, shortly after Cianci became mayor, the two establishments appeared back-to-back on the agenda for a licensing-board hearing. Cianci, who was sympathetic to the faculty club, laughed as he told the club's leaders the story one day over lunch. The club finally got its license.

Three days after Cianci was sworn in as mayor, Sinatra's old pal Raymond Patriarca was paroled from prison for his role in the murders of Rudy Marfeo and Anthony Melei. The speaker of the Rhode Island House had written the state parole board, attesting to Patriarca's "good moral character." Patriarca went back to Coin-O-Matic on Federal Hill, where wiseguys with no-show city jobs continued to hang out.

Vespia understood that Cianci had inherited a culture that went back years, one that no one man, not even the mayor, could change overnight. He also realized that his friend faced different choices as mayor than he had as a prosecutor. He had to play the patronage game, and if that involved cutting deals with guys who knew guys who knew guys, well, that was politics, especially in Providence. Vespia felt that Cianci made some bad choices but that it wasn't his place to say so. He was a cop, not a politician. Still, there was an old Italian saying: "Do good, and forget about it. Do bad, and worry about it."

Vespia was angry when he saw men like mobster Gerald Tillinghast on the city payroll. In the summer of 1975 a gang of thieves broke into the Bonded Vault Company in Providence, pried open 140 safe-deposit boxes, and carted away duffel bags crammed with three million dollars' worth of cash, gold, and jewelry. There was so much treasure that they left a fortune on the floor. Much of the booty had been stashed there by criminals, but the robbery had been sanctioned by Patriarca, who received a portion as tribute. Several men were later arrested, including Tillinghast, who was suspended from his job at Public Works. The following summer, following his acquittal, Tillinghast attended Larry McGarry's Democratic clambake and praised the mayor. "I have spoken to Cianci," he said, "and I am happy that he has permitted me to return to the job." Jim Diamond said that Dick Israel's former finance chairman asked Cianci how he could allow underworld figures like Tillinghast on the payroll; the chairman later told Diamond that Cianci had explained that this was the way you made deals and got things done in politics.

With a name like Tillinghast, Gerald was not your typical mobster. He was a descendant of Pardon Tillinghast, the colonial farmer, merchant, and Baptist pastor, and friend to Rhode Island's founder, Roger Williams. Tillinghasts fought in the Revolutionary War and got rich trading slaves and running textile mills. Tillinghasts married Chafees, dined at the Hope Club, served on the state supreme court, and helped run Brown University. But Gerald Tillinghast, the son of a bricklayer who came from a penniless tributary of the clan, made his money the old-fashioned way—he stole it. Hired by the city when Doorley was mayor, he developed a reputation as a notorious mobster. Two years after Tillinghast's acquittal in the bonded-vault case, Vespia was conducting surveillance on him and his brother Harold one night as they drove near the airport in a stolen yellow sedan with loan shark George Basmajian. Minutes later, after the car was obscured by a snow fence, Vespia and an FBI agent came across Basmajian's bullet-riddled body in the backseat. Vespia caught up with the Tillinghasts about a half hour later at Michael's Lounge, a mob haunt in Providence, and arrested them. There was blood all over Gerald Tillinghast's black nylon softball jacket. The Tillinghasts were convicted of murder, despite a dozen alibi witnesses, including a fellow Public Works employee, who said they were at the bar.

Cianci tried a few times to hire Vespia as his police chief, but it never worked out. The first occasion was in 1976, when Cianci forced out Doorley holdover Walter McQueeney. But Colonel Walter Stone, the head of the state police, was not a fan of Cianci's and refused to grant Vespia a leave to take the job. Vespia also wondered if he could work for Cianci, given his domineering nature. The friction between Cianci and McQueeney had been no secret. Frank Darigan, who had been elected city Democratic chairman, recalled meeting McQueeney at the Holiday Inn one day; the crusty old chief was talking about Cianci when he suddenly started crying and sobbed, "What this guy is making me do . . ." McQueeney implied that Cianci had pressured him over jobs and promotions but didn't go into detail, recalled Darigan.

When Vespia dropped out, Cianci, eager to hire an Italian-American police chief, chose Captain Robert E. Ricci, the head of detectives and, before that, head of the vice squad for ten years. Vespia considered Ricci one of the most honorable police officers he had ever known, ramrod straight and not at all political. There was no speculation about how Ricci and Cianci would get along as the mayor swore him in at a ceremony attended by several hundred people at Roger Williams Park on September 13, 1976. Standing in the white marble Temple to Music, Ricci smiled as the Providence bishop bestowed his blessing and the outgoing chief pinned the colonel's badge to his uniform. Flanked by his wife and his teenaged son and daughter, Ricci found it difficult to express his joy. "I feel my cup has runneth over," he said.

THE JOB SEEMED to bring out Buddy's best and worst sides, the cheerleader and the bully.

In the beginning there was a sense of excitement and challenge that made the job fun. At the end of the day on Friday, Cianci presided over weekly staff meetings in the conference room off the mayor's office. Takeout food would be brought in. The mayor and his aides would talk and laugh about the week's events, the crazy things that had happened. Cianci played the role of father, telling them: "We're family. I'm here for you."

Cianci's forceful personality generated a merry kind of chaos around the office when he was in. He would talk to anyone about anything, and so his appointments would back up. One day Cianci burst into hysterics after his secretary told him that the president of the Alzheimer's Foundation had forgotten about their appointment. The whimsical mayor took an owl from the zoo and set it on the mantel of his office fireplace, delighting in the fact that visitors didn't know it was alive.

People of all stations would see the mayor's black limousine outside City Hall and wander in off the street. One little old lady, known as the Flower Lady, was constantly bringing flowers for the mayor. Cianci's secretary kept after him to see her, and finally, one day, he did. When Cianci came out of his office to greet the Flower Lady, she took him by the arm and escorted him back into his own office. They were in there for so long that his secretary finally buzzed Cianci to rescue him. After the Flower Lady left, Cianci grabbed his secretary's shirt in mock anger, laughed, and said, "She hit me up for five hundred bucks."

A former police officer remembered a chaotic scene when he reported for his first day as the mayor's driver. It was St. Patrick's Day. Irish music blared through City Hall, the green beer flowed freely, and drunks staggered in the corridors. The policeman opened the door to the mayor's outer office and saw three men wrestling on the floor—two other policemen and a large man in coveralls. The secretaries were screaming for help. The man in coveralls was an unemployed carpenter, frustrated at his inability to get city work, who had gotten drunk and come down to City Hall to demand a job. Cianci burst out of his office as the officers subdued the man and said, "What the hell is going on?" The carpenter started blubbering, "Mayor, Mayor, Mayor," and then launched into his tale of woe. "Well, come on in," said Cianci, who talked to the man for a while and then ordered a city official to give him some work.

As the tensions from the constant political battles grew, Cianci became more difficult to work for. The pace became so hectic that the Friday staff meetings were phased out. The mayor was notorious for his temper tantrums. One day Cianci flew into a rage after a favor seeker slipped past his security guard and got into his office. Screaming and cursing, Cianci stormed into the reception area, where there were four or five chairs, and started throwing them into the hallway.

The mayor also became legendary for the abuse he would heap upon his police chauffeurs. One former police bodyguard, Joseph Agugiaro, remembered that Cianci would hit one particular driver about the neck and face with the car phone. Once, the day after an evening fund-raiser, Cianci had a manila envelope stuffed with contributions that had not been deposited at the bank. Hurrying to another political event in his limousine, he lost his temper as he tried, unsuccessfully, to stuff the large envelope into the small glove compartment. By the time they arrived at their destination, Cianci had dismantled the dashboard and was cursing and screaming and hitting his driver with the telephone, said Agugiaro. Politicians and other dignitaries stood around the limousine in the parking lot, waiting for the mayor's tirade to subside. Cianci ordered the policeman not to leave the car for a second, not even to go to the bathroom, and then composed himself and went inside to work the crowd.

Another former police bodyguard, Urbano Prignano, Jr., remembered a wild ride with the mayor that began on Federal Hill. A car shot through the intersection in front of them. A woman was driving and a man was hanging out the driver's window, being dragged along and trying to grab the steering wheel. The cops wanted to chase the car, but Cianci, late for an appointment, told them to keep going. They argued back and forth for a few seconds until finally the police driver swerved around the corner in pursuit, nearly sideswiping a bus. They finally forced the car to stop, and discovered that the man was one of Prignano's informants, who had been arguing with his girlfriend when she tried to drive off with his car. As Cianci and Prignano walked back to the limousine, Prignano said, the mayor turned to him and said, "If that had been a real robbery, you know I would have had to make the arrest."

Aware of his tenuous, 700-vote margin of victory, Cianci was perpetually campaigning, mindful that a swing of 351 votes would spell defeat. The mythical 351st voter always seemed to hover over his shoulder. Cianci would remind his staff, "Whoever pisses off the three hundred fifty-first voter is in trouble."

With his sharp wit, glib tongue, and agile mind, Cianci cultivated reporters and mastered the medium of television. He was cunning at slipping information to a reporter about a political foe, prefaced with the hushed caveat "You didn't hear this from me. . . ." He transformed his office into a stage set for press conferences and wore pancake makeup for the television lights. When the six o'clock news came on, Cianci sat in his swivel chair with two remote controls to flip channels on the two television sets in his office. His staff recorded the evening news so that it could be critiqued for its coverage of the mayor.

Cianci created a cult of personality that overlaid the old-fashioned political machine he had assembled. In the process, his tireless promotion of Providence blurred into self-promotion. Cianci wanted to do good for Providence, but he also needed to look good in the process.

One night Cianci decided that he wanted to go see a jazz singer at Ballard's, a nightclub in the moribund downtown. He ordered a staffer to go arrange for a front-row table, then swept into the half-empty club at the appointed hour with his retinue, as if he were Jimmy Walker.

Cianci enjoyed making a grand entrance. He used a helicopter, then professed ignorance when *The Providence Journal* reported that city workers had installed a helicopter landing pad near his East Side home. He badgered an aide, Ron Glantz, to call the major automobile companies in Detroit to see if they would provide Cianci a new official limousine, for a discount. Ford had a program to lease Lincoln Town Cars to cities, at cost, but an executive informed Glantz that Providence wasn't big enough to qualify. Finally, Glantz said, he arranged for a car with a local dealer.

The public and the media were fascinated with the Imperial Buddy. He was praised for restoring pomp and circumstance to a dying city, and for nourishing the arts and entertainment even as he became Providence's principal entertainer. When the Ringling Brothers Barnum and Bailey Circus came to town, Cianci served as honorary ringmaster. "They tell me that we have a circus going on at City Hall every single day," he quipped.

The mayor drew comparisons to Napoleon, Nero, and Caesar. About six months into his reign, Cianci showed up for work with a toupee to mask his receding hairline. He ordered photographs of himself hung in city offices and in the lobbies of Providence's fourteen federal housing projects. A *Providence Journal* editorial writer waxed poetic about "Prince Vincent" after observing him preside over a musical Midsummer Night Festival one evening outside City Hall. The writer called Cianci a throwback to the flamboyant former mayor of New York, Fiorello La Guardia, who was known as "the Little Flower."

"Bravely and confidently, he romps through the first year of his reign. Clean-cut features, strong without pudginess, endow him with a remarkable resemblance to 'the Little Flower' of happy memory. He stands in our dream on one of the higher landings of the great granite front staircase of City Hall. His smile is as broad as a crescent moon as he waves his upraised arms."

At other times, however, Cianci's self-aggrandizement was problematic. He had a tendency to shoot from the hip in search of headlines, and then not follow through on certain projects. Another *Providence Journal* editorial criticized him for jumping the gun on announcing a new federal building for Providence and for making reckless remarks that threatened to disrupt carefully laid plans for a new state courthouse in the city.

"If Mr. Cianci wants to strut on the bridge and display his gold braid, he should be aware that showmanship is not going to move the city off dead center. That takes seamanship. . . . The good ship Providence is on the rocks, and all that gold braid looks pretty silly."

IT WAS THE second Sunday in January 1978, and a sheet of ice had blanketed Providence in what was being called the worst winter storm in years. Still, Margaret Ricci, the wife of police chief Robert Ricci, thought nothing of it when her husband told her late that night that he had to go into the office to handle an emergency.

Ricci was a cop's cop, rigid and taciturn, six foot four with silver hair and a military bearing. Sixteen months after Cianci had put him in command of New England's second-largest police department, the job was still all about chasing criminals. As a beat cop in South Providence and West Elmwood, Ricci had won five commendations for outstanding police work. He was promoted to detective and rose steadily through the ranks, developing a reputation for incorruptibility as the head of the C-Squad, which fought drugs, prostitution, and gambling. Vin Vespia remembered how it had bothered Ricci when the state police sometimes conducted raids in the city without alerting the Providence Police Department, implying that some of his men were on the take and couldn't be trusted.

Now Ricci had other problems. Dressed in his uniform on an icy winter's midnight, with many of the city's residents lacking power or heat as a result of the storm, city streets impassable, and a state of emergency in effect, the chief sat in his darkened third-floor office at Providence police headquarters and pondered how it all went wrong.

Ricci was torn between his duty as a police officer and his loyalty to the mayor. For weeks he had agonized over the selection of recruits into the new police academy. Cianci had pressed him to admit five recruits whom the police selection board had rejected. As a result, three were subsequently admitted. Meanwhile, two applicants who had been rejected had filed lawsuits against the city the previous week. That weekend Ricci had met for several hours at the police station with top police brass and Cianci's acting city solicitor, Ron Glantz, to discuss the case. Ricci expected that he would have to testify. He dreaded being asked whether political pressure was a factor in choosing new police officers.

Politics has always played a role in the Providence Police Department, as it has anywhere. Politicians want certain police officers hired or promoted. Some officers, eager to advance, are influenced by political considerations about whether to aggressively pursue an investigation or drop it. A smaller number of corrupt cops are willing to gather dirt on political enemies or even set them up on bogus charges. There is an inherent tension in the relationship between a mayor and his police chief. The chief serves at the mayor's pleasure, but not for the mayor's pleasure.

In Buddy Cianci's Providence, a growing number of police officers said privately that the mayor had politicized the police department more than his predecessor Joe Doorley had. They pointed to the arrest of the City Council president, Bobby Haxton, and the aggressive investigations of political foes. In addition, with political campaigns becoming more expensive because of television, there were charges that police officers were pressured to buy and sell campaign fund-raising tickets for Cianci. When former president Ford had come to Providence the month before for a Cianci fund-raiser, officers later complained, pro-Cianci cops had pushed them to buy hundred-dollar tickets to the event. John J. Leyden, a major, said that he had received phone calls from Cianci, who said that he wanted the police veteran at his fund-raisers. Leyden, who was working extra nighttime details to support his family, put the mayor off, saying that he had five kids to feed.

Ricci had received similar calls, said Leyden, and it bothered him. Politics had no place in Ricci's life, which revolved around family and duty. He saw things in black and white, not shades of gray. He also kept things to himself. Shy and withdrawn, he was sometimes mistaken for aloof. He addressed longtime associates as "Mr." and didn't socialize with other officers, not even to attend the annual policemen's ball. Every morning he faithfully visited his elderly mother. At lunchtime the chief would grab his police radio and patrol the streets of downtown, on foot and alone. At night he went home to his family.

But Ricci, who knew every thief and bookie in Providence, didn't know how to deal with the mayor. Only a handful of Ricci's trusted lieutenants saw the strain that dealing with City Hall put on him.

Lieutenant Edward J. Collins, Ricci's personnel director, was known for the high standard of conduct he demanded from officers. One day Ricci ordered Collins to discipline a patrolman for not handling himself properly at a break-in. Collins put an administrative warning in the officer's file, then thought nothing of it, until he received a call from the mayor's office to come down to City Hall. Collins, who had never met with Cianci before, walked into the mayor's office, which he found imposing and cathedral-like. Before he could get comfortable, Cianci was all over him, screaming and cursing about the disciplinary action. Collins tried to explain, and the mayor grew angrier, yelling within inches of Collins's face. The disciplined officer's father was a key neighborhood supporter of Cianci's in South Providence. Collins, a fiery Irishman, yelled back at Cianci. Ron Glantz, who was also there, had to get between the two men to calm things down.

The next day Ricci approached Collins and apologized. Ricci felt bad, since Collins had acted on the chief's orders. It was apparent to Collins, and former Cianci aides confirm, that Ricci had been subjected to similar verbal abuse from the mayor.

Over time, Collins noticed Cianci becoming more involved in the police department. The mayor would want certain people hired and promoted. Collins pointed to the day that Cianci overruled Ricci on which officer to put in charge of the property room, which holds seized drugs and other evidence, as the day that Ricci found out he wasn't the chief. Ricci was exasperated by some of Cianci's personnel moves, said Collins, but he always went along. Collins wanted Ricci to stand up to Cianci. But Ricci said that he would remain loyal.

A few weeks before the ice storm, the mayor's office sent Ricci a list of twenty people he wanted in the next police academy class. Ricci, who didn't normally involve himself in the selection of new police recruits, passed the list on to the police selection board, which admitted fifteen. One week before the academy was to open, Ricci and other police officials were summoned to Cianci's office. Cianci was upset that some of his applicants had been rejected. One of his concerns was that the roster of those admitted did not reflect the city's affirmative-action goals for hiring more minority officers.

Captain Walter Clark, Ricci's administrative assistant, told the mayor that it would be difficult to include the rejected candidates. They had failed background checks, and one had a minor criminal record. At that point, Ricci caught Clark's eye and motioned that he wanted to leave. The meeting adjourned without any resolution.

Back at police headquarters, Ricci surprised Clark by asking him to reconsider the rejected candidates. Prior to the meeting with the mayor, Ricci had told Clark to stand firm, because the chief did not want any of the five hired. But now, as a result of Ricci's turnaround, the board agreed reluctantly to admit three of Cianci's rejects.

The week before the ice storm, two recruits who had not been selected sued the city. Ricci worried about having to testify about the selection process. He peppered Clark and Collins with questions and concerns. He obsessed about Cianci, asking what he should say about his conversations with the mayor. Ricci said that he didn't want to lie on the stand. Clark told Ricci that he didn't have to lie, that he hadn't done anything wrong. Since time immemorial, Clark reminded Ricci, politicians had attempted to influence the selection process.

On Friday night the ice storm hit. Ricci had to deal with Cianci regarding the city's emergency response to the storm. But still, he could not shake the lawsuit from his mind. He had a meeting with staff and lawyers over the weekend to discuss it, then called Clark and Collins several times on

Sunday. Clark thought he was going to quit, and screamed into the phone for him not to.

Ricci's last phone call to Clark was at 11 P.M. He was calm but downcast. He told Clark that the job was too much. "I thought the job would be chasing criminals," he said. "I can't figure out the system. Good-bye, kid."

Not long before midnight, Ricci told his wife that he had to go to the station to deal with an emergency. At 3 A.M. John Leyden was awakened by a call from Ricci's wife, who said that her husband had called and needed him at the station. Leyden called Collins, and the two men hurried downtown. Met by Leo Trambukis, the public safety commissioner, the men went upstairs to the chief's office, and found it locked. They broke through the glass with a crowbar, then pried open a second locked door to Ricci's inner office. They found Ricci lying in his anteroom, his topcoat folded neatly under his head, a single bullet wound in his head, and his police-issue .38-caliber service revolver at his side.

The three men looked at one another.

"Can you imagine this, over a job?" one of them said finally.

Who do you call when you're the police and you've just found your chief dead at headquarters? They called the coroner. Then someone called the mayor, who was home, asleep.

Shaken, Cianci called Ronnie Glantz and asked if he had heard anything. The mayor was concerned about whether Ricci had left a note, and if it mentioned Cianci. Ricci did leave a note. It said: "Leo—everything is too much. John—take care of my family."

Later that morning Cianci came to the station. He was in a state of shock. He stayed awhile, as officers reporting for morning duty stopped by and spoke in hushed tones. Hardened police officers fought back tears. The mood was equally somber at City Hall. One of Cianci's aides said that when she heard the news on the radio, her immediate reaction was that Cianci deserved a share of the blame. The aide had heard the mayor screaming at the police chief, whom she considered a good and decent man. That day she avoided Cianci.

The mayor called this day "the saddest I have experienced as mayor." He declared a thirty-day period of mourning and ordered flags lowered to half-staff.

Throughout the day, as police officials said publicly that they had no idea what had been bothering Ricci, Ted Collins agonized. After speaking to Ricci's widow and enduring a sleepless Monday night, Collins knew what he had to do. The day after Ricci killed himself, Collins went to the press.

"Bob Ricci died because he couldn't lie," said Collins. "The mayor was ramming [unqualified] men down his throat." Collins went on to detail the pressure that he said Cianci had put on the police to take unqualified recruits. "Bob Ricci did not pull that trigger," said Collins. "The system did. The mayor is also the victim of the same system, with political patronage what it is."

Publicly, the police brass lined up with Cianci, who emphatically denied ever putting any political pressure on Ricci. Privately, another ranking police official and two other knowledgeable sources, interviewed by *The Providence Journal*, backed up what Collins said about Cianci's political interference.

Walter Clark tried to put the tragedy of Ricci's death in a less emotional context when he was called to testify before a City Council committee investigating Collins's allegations. Ricci committed suicide not on January 16, said Clark, but on the day, sixteen months earlier, when he accepted the chief's job. He was overwhelmed by his administrative responsibilities and was too rigid to handle the realities of politics. Slowly, the job overwhelmed him, until he "found himself in that room without doors or windows. Clearly, there was no escape."

The Ricci tragedy, highlighting politics and patronage in the police department, was not an auspicious start to an election year in which the Democrats figured to be more unified.

Cianci didn't realize that that would soon be the least of his worries. On the day that Bob Ricci was buried, during a driving snowstorm, another storm was gathering in the Midwest, concerning a story from the mayor's past, when he was a law student at Marquette University in Milwaukee.

Five months after Ricci's death, Collins was demoted to nights. Later he was served with a three-year-old arrest warrant for code violations on tenements he owned. Cianci, dismissing Collins's charges of retribution, said that the policeman had an obligation to fix his properties.

"No person is above the law," said the mayor.

CHAPTER FOUR

Operation Snow Job

When Ron Glantz was called into the mayor's office on a January afternoon in 1978, Buddy Cianci was in a panic.

The week of Bob Ricci's suicide, Cianci learned that two reporters from *The Providence Journal* were in Milwaukee, digging into his past. They were looking into twelve-year-old allegations that Cianci had raped a woman at gunpoint during his final year at Marquette Law School.

Cianci summoned Glantz, his acting city solicitor, and Herbert DeSimone, the former Rhode Island attorney general and a trusted adviser. He ordered them to get on the first plane to Milwaukee, find the girl, and collect all the information they could. Cianci reached into his desk drawer, took out two thousand dollars in cash, and gave it to DeSimone, for expenses.

The winter of 1978 was stormy. It was snowing when Glantz and DeSimone flew into Chicago and changed planes for Milwaukee. On the cab ride from the airport, Glantz looked at Lake Michigan and noticed signs warning that the water was polluted, then saw pipes that local breweries used to draw water from the lake for making beer.

Glantz and DeSimone checked into a posh hotel, the Pfister, in downtown Milwaukee. Over the next few days they made contact with a prominent Milwaukee criminal-defense lawyer, Daniel Weiss, who had represented Cianci in the original matter; met with a lawyer who represented the woman who had accused Cianci; and went to the police station in the suburb of River Hills, where the alleged rape had taken place, to see what police files existed.

Meanwhile, *Providence Journal* reporters Randy Richard and Bert Wade were tracing some of the same steps. They interviewed the chief of police in River Hills, who had investigated the Cianci matter as a lieutenant in

1966. They also tried to talk to the woman, only to be rebuffed by her lawyer. When the reporters tried to see the original police file, it was unavailable. They were told that the records had been destroyed.

The reporters also met with Alan D. Eisenberg, a flamboyant Milwaukee lawyer and classmate of Cianci's at Marquette who had been instrumental in resurrecting the Cianci story. Eisenberg, who has been called the most obnoxious lawyer in Wisconsin, had already carved out a reputation as a hell-raiser who attacked the establishment and took on controversial cases. In 1970 he had been stripped of his law license for one year for making derogatory remarks about a county judge who later committed suicide. In 1978 Eisenberg was defending a woman accused of murdering her husband and burning their house down after enduring years of domestic violence. A poster in Eisenberg's law offices proclaimed: THE FIGHT OF THE CENTURY—MUHAMMAD ALI VS. ALAN D. EISENBERG.

Eisenberg and Cianci had become friendly early in their law-school days at Marquette. Cianci was bright and funny, Eisenberg remembered, and obviously came from money. When he arrived in Milwaukee, Cianci bought himself a new Buick Riviera, paying cash, and moved into an apartment in an upscale lakefront neighborhood known as the Gold Coast. He boasted to Eisenberg that his father was a man of great wealth, a proctologist whose patients came from all over the Northeast and included the rich and famous, even movie stars. Cianci also told Eisenberg that his ambition was to go into politics and succeed John Pastore as a U.S. senator from Rhode Island.

Cianci frequented various singles bars in Milwaukee, said Eisenberg. One bar, near Cianci's apartment, was attached to a restaurant, Chico's, run by a mob associate named Frankie LaGalbo. One night, Eisenberg and Cianci were having dinner in Chico's when a man who worked there leaped over the bar and started beating a man, punching him repeatedly in the head.

"Do you want to do something?" Eisenberg asked Cianci. "Should we try and stop it?"

"No," he says Cianci replied. "It's the Italian code of honor."

Being new in town, Cianci asked Eisenberg, who dated frequently, to introduce him to some women. Eisenberg obliged, but later three of the women complained to him about Cianci's overly aggressive advances, he said; one woman slapped him in the face for fixing her up with Cianci. When Eisenberg told Cianci, he dismissed them as liars.

On Saturday, March 5, 1966, Eisenberg noticed a short item buried inside the *Milwaukee Sentinel*, underneath a review of the Albert Camus play *The Just Assassins*, performed by the Marquette University Players. The seven-paragraph story began: "A 20-year-old telephone operator and a 25-year-old law school senior she has accused of raping her at gunpoint have agreed to take lie detector tests next week, Asst. Dist. Atty. Gerald Boyle said Friday." It went on to detail the woman's allegations that the law student had lured her to his house on the pretext of offering her a typing job, then given her a drink that she thought was drugged. When she awoke, the woman said, the law student threatened her with a gun unless she submitted. The next morning she took a taxi home and told a friend, who called the police. The story did not identify the telephone operator or the law student. It ended by saying that "no charges have been lodged."

A day or so later, when Eisenberg went to law school, the students were buzzing about the story. The senior class contained fewer than one hundred students. Someone said that the guy was Cianci. Eisenberg said that he asked him, and Cianci replied, "Yeah, it's a shakedown." He said that a local defense lawyer, Danny Weiss, was handling it.

Eisenberg heard no more of the matter until graduation, when he noticed that Cianci was not there. Nor was he present when the dean of the Marquette Law School took the graduating Class of '66 to the Wisconsin Supreme Court in Madison—a Marquette tradition—and had them sworn in to the Wisconsin bar.

THE MATTER LAY buried from the spring of 1966 until the fall of 1977, when it was revived by an only-in-Rhode-Island type of coincidence.

Alan Eisenberg was frequently quoted in the media. One day, Nancy Laffey, a young television reporter for Channel 12 in Milwaukee, interviewed him. Afterward, as they chatted, Laffey mentioned that she had grown up in Rhode Island and had worked for Channel 10 in Providence.

"I went to law school with a guy from Providence," said Eisenberg.

Laffey lit up when Eisenberg said it was Cianci. She told him some of the things that she knew about the colorful mayor of Providence. Then Eisenberg told her some things that he knew, most notably the rape allegation at Marquette.

With Eisenberg's help, Laffey pursued the story. In November 1977 they visited the police chief in River Hills, Harold Block, who had worked on the case in 1966. River Hills is one of the richest towns in Wisconsin, a quiet suburb of lavish homes hugging the Lake Michigan shore north of Milwaukee. Block had not forgotten the case. He gave Laffey police reports from the original investigation, including a handwritten statement by the victim.

The documents made for chilling reading.

In her written statement, the woman, Ruth Bandlow, said that Cianci approached her about working part-time for him, typing subscriptions for *Time* magazine. He said that he knew a friend of hers, a student at Marquette, and so she agreed to go with him, after work, to the house where he was staying in River Hills. At the house, she said, Cianci offered her a drink.

> I accepted it and after I drank it I can't really remember what happened after I blacked out. But when I came to he was on top of me. I started screaming and got hysterical and he told me if I wouldn't keep my mouth shut, he'd blow my brains out. Then he got the gun from the drawer and asked me if I thought he was kidding. He loaded it and put it to my head and said, you think I have not done this before where do you think I get all my money from. And he said no one would ever miss me because no one knew I was with him.
>
> There were certain things that interested him such as psychology, traveling and so forth. So I kept trying to keep him interested, thinking it would keep his mind of [*sic*] what he was trying to do to me. But finally I couldn't keep him off me any longer. And that is when he raped me for certain. He went downstairs after that and started mixing drinks.

Years later, in an interview with a writer for *New Times* magazine, Bandlow gave a further description of how, as Cianci tried to rape her, she threatened to tell the police.

"I told him I'd go to the police, and he said that I'd make a fool out of myself . . . that he would get away with it because he knew every nook and cranny—he was going to law school. He laughed and he said that he'd get away with it. He said he could do anything he wanted . . ." Later, she said, as Cianci wielded the gun, he told her, "Look out the window—there's a ravine there. I could throw your body down there, and no one would ever find you."

Afterward, when Cianci left the room, Bandlow said that she called a cab. "I was going to call the police, but I thought if a police car drove up, he would kill me. . . . When the doorbell rang, he got all excited, and he said, 'Who's that?' And I ran—I pushed him aside and I ran, and I opened the door. The cab driver had come to the door. He acted very cool in front of the cab driver. He says, 'We had a wonderful time, and I'll call you. . . . We'll go out to dinner sometime.' I remember that very plain."

When she got home, about seven the next morning, Bandlow told the police that all she could think about was being safe and needing to sleep. Her entire body felt numb, she said, and she could hardly walk. Bandlow had been living away from home for about a year and was renting a room in a women's residence in Milwaukee. The night after the alleged rape, she told a friend what had happened. The friend called the police. The next day, March 3, Bandlow gave her statement to the police.

On March 4, at 9 A.M., Bandlow and Cianci were ordered to appear before the Milwaukee County district attorney. Bandlow was asked to identify Cianci, who denied her accusations.

"We were in the judge's chamber at the time," Bandlow would later tell *New Times*. "When they first brought him in, he said, 'Hi there! Didn't we have a great time last night?' He acted so cool, calm and collected. . . . And they asked him if he knew me, and he said, 'Yes, I met her last night, and we had such a good time I wanted to take her out to dinner.' And I just completely . . . I don't know . . . I just flipped out. Can you imagine—my parents were there in the judge's chambers, and he walks in like that? My dad almost went after him."

Cianci and Bandlow each agreed to take lie-detector tests. But the next day a distraught Bandlow took an overdose of sleeping pills and was hospitalized for ten days.

"I didn't want to kill myself," she later explained to *New Times*. "But I was under such strain and nervous pressure. No one seemed to believe me. . . . I even felt guilty, because I did go with that man—a person that's raped always feels a little bit guilty . . . but I think anyone would have trusted him—the way he can smooth talk, and put on a front . . ."

In the meantime, the investigation continued. The police, with Cianci's consent, took evidence from the house, including a German 7.65-millimeter Ortgies pistol, a bloodstained sheet, and two glasses containing the remainder of a drink. Noting that the investigation was continuing, Lieutenant Block of the River Hills Police wrote, "No warrants have as yet been issued."

The gun was test-fired and found to be in working condition. Tests on the empty glasses for drug residue were negative; the crime-lab report said that a low-level concentration of drugs would be difficult to detect. Investigators identified semen on the bedsheet, small spots of human blood on the sheet and pillowcase, and traces of blood at the crotch area of Bandlow's panty girdle—an amount insufficient for further testing to determine whose blood.

Four weeks after the alleged crime, on March 30, 1966, Cianci and Bandlow went separately to the state crime lab in Madison to take their lie-detector tests. According to a police report written by Lieutenant Block, the state's veteran polygraph expert said that the results "showed this to be one of the most clear cut cases of rape he had ever processed in his years with the State Crime Lab. In his opinion Ruth Bandlow passed the test beyond a shadow of a doubt while Cianci failed completely on three separate testings."

Although the authorities used lie-detector tests to probe for guilt or innocence, the assistant district attorney on the case, Gerald Boyle, knew that the results themselves were not admissible in Wisconsin. The next day, March 31, Cianci and Bandlow were ordered back to the DA's office, with their lawyers, for further questioning. No progress was made at that meeting, so the parties were instructed to return on April 9 and appear before the number-two prosecutor in the Milwaukee County district attorney's office, deputy Aladin A. DeBrozzo.

On Saturday, April 9, Cianci and Bandlow, with their lawyers, returned to the DA's office. But they had barely settled into their seats when DeBrozzo received an emergency call concerning another case. The meeting was postponed for one week, until the following Saturday, April 16.

On April 16, Cianci and Bandlow returned with their lawyers to the office of the prosecutor, Gerald Boyle. According to Boyle, he told them that he didn't think there was enough evidence to support a charge of sexual assault. He based that on an examination of the physical evidence, the lapse in time between the alleged rape and Bandlow's initial report to the police, and Boyle's questioning of the taxi driver who had picked her up when she left Cianci's residence. During the meeting, Boyle said, Bandlow and her lawyer indicated that they would withdraw the criminal complaint. After the meeting, Boyle called Lieutenant Block to report that the woman had withdrawn her complaint "and is starting a civil action," according to Block's subsequent report. Two and a half months later, on June 29, Boyle wrote the River Hills police chief that "the matter concerning one Vincent Cianci, Jr. has been resolved." Boyle wrote that Bandlow had signed a letter withdrawing her criminal complaint and relayed a request from Cianci's lawyer for the police to release Cianci's possessions being held at the state crime lab.

"My attorney didn't think I was well enough to go on with the case," Bandlow later told *New Times.* "So he told me to drop the charges and settle out of court. . . . The only reason I did it was because he advised me to. Otherwise I wouldn't have."

Cianci subsequently paid Bandlow three thousand dollars, half of which went to her lawyer, to settle the matter civilly. Cianci said that the settlement had nothing to do with the woman's decision to drop the charges; he said that he paid her on the advice of his lawyer, because he was going into the army and it would have been inconvenient to return to Milwaukee to defend himself from a lawsuit.

Boyle went on to become a prominent criminal-defense lawyer in Milwaukee, where his clients included the cannibalistic serial killer Jeffrey Dahmer. Years later, Boyle said that he had heard rumors that Cianci had paid Bandlow, but that he wasn't aware of the settlement at the time and that it wouldn't have influenced his judgment.

The decision not to charge Cianci disappointed the investigating police officer, Lieutenant Block.

"We thought we had everything," Lieutenant Block told *New Times* years later, after becoming chief in River Hills. "We thought we had enough to convict him. When you think you have enough, you send it on up to the DA. Then you hope for justice."

In June 1966, in an update on the investigation, Block referred to the written conclusion of Milwaukee County district attorney Hugh O'Connell, "that in all his years of practise [sic] he had never experienced a more dastardly crime than that committed by Cianci, but due to lack of evidence prosecution was almost impossible."

AFTER GOING THROUGH the police records provided by Harold Block, television reporter Nancy Laffey spent several days searching for Ruth Bandlow. Laffey finally found her living in a Milwaukee suburb, a happily married housewife. The week before Thanksgiving, in 1977, Laffey and Eisenberg visited Bandlow at her tidy brick ranch house. Laffey had called ahead to say she wanted to discuss "a personal matter." When they arrived, they showed Bandlow a Marquette yearbook photo of Cianci.

"We're here about this man Cianci," Laffey told Bandlow, according to Laffey's later account in *New Times.*

Bandlow looked at Cianci's smiling photo and started to cry. Laffey recalled Bandlow's telling them, "I can't even look at him. . . . Look how gross he is. Look. . . . Yes, he's the one. He's the one."

Bandlow confirmed her rape accusation against Cianci and said that she had settled out of court to avoid the ordeal of a trial. She also wrote her lawyer a note authorizing him to discuss the case with Laffey and alerting him that she had disclosed to the reporter her three-thousand-dollar settlement with Cianci.

But shortly thereafter, Bandlow's lawyer called Laffey and advised her to drop the story. The lawyer wanted no further involvement in the matter, however, so when Laffey tried to talk to Bandlow again, Bandlow hired a new lawyer, Carl Krueger.

By December, Cianci's old lawyer, Danny Weiss, knew that Bandlow had talked to the television reporter. Weiss contacted Krueger to find out what was going on. Krueger called Laffey and advised her not to use any statements from Bandlow because they had been secured "by threat and intimidation." Krueger accused the reporter of threatening to publicize Bandlow's married name and put a picture of her house on television if she didn't cooperate. Any statements by Bandlow, said Krueger, had been made when she was in "a very nervous state."

The television station, Channel 12 in Milwaukee, never acknowledged making any such threat. But the message was clear. Not only had Bandlow become an unwilling source, but her lawyer warned Laffey that any story would be met with a lawsuit.

On December 16 Krueger wrote to Cianci's lawyer, Weiss, to summarize his dealings with Laffey. "In regard to an incident involving Vincent A. Cianci Jr., occurring 11 or 12 years ago, my client has no further comment," Krueger assured Weiss. "At the time of said incident, there was an investigation by the Milwaukee County District Attorney and she takes no issue with the manner in which that matter was disposed of. . . . [Bandlow] feels that this matter was disposed of 11 years ago and considers it closed."

When a similar message was conveyed to Channel 12, along with a threat of a lawsuit from Cianci's representative, the television station backed off the story.

As 1978 dawned, Cianci had managed to keep a lid on the story, without answering any questions about what had happened that night in 1966 or why he had agreed to pay the woman who accused him of raping her three thousand dollars.

But rumors of the alleged Marquette incident were making their way eastward.

Oddly, a whisper had reached Jean Coughlin, the Mount Pleasant housewife who had run for mayor of Providence as an Independent in 1974. One night during the campaign, Coughlin said that she received an anonymous phone call at home from a man who said of Cianci: "Did you know that he raped a woman at law school? He was accused of rape. He bought his way out of a mess." Coughlin didn't know what to say, and she never pursued it.

"It was hearsay," she said. "What could I do?"

Four years later, early in 1978, the story found its way from an outraged Wisconsin feminist who knew Alan Eisenberg to *The Providence Journal.* The woman, who had also contacted national newsmagazines and the networks, sent copies of the police records to Bert Wade, a woman who worked for the newspaper's "Accent/Focus" section. The police reports, with their graphic descriptions of the alleged rape, spread quickly through the newsroom in the long redbrick *Journal* building on Fountain Street, a few blocks from City Hall.

The Providence Journal, founded before the Civil War by Yankee industrialists, was a historically Republican newspaper. An afternoon edition, the *Evening Bulletin,* had been launched during the Civil War to provide the latest battlefield updates. The newspaper had built a strong national reputation for investigative reporting, having won a Pulitzer Prize in 1971 for a story by Jack White revealing that President Nixon had not paid any income tax. As Rhode Island's dominant newspaper, the *Journal,* or *ProJo,* as it was known, had the power to set the agenda for the state and to make or break politicians with its exposés detailing cronyism and corruption. Its Yankee ownership had been tightly aligned with the Republican bosses who had run the state until early in the twentieth century, and its editorial board often clashed with the ethnic Democrats who had run the state since. The *Journal* had been generally supportive of Cianci, a Republican reformer, though the newspaper would draw the mayor's ire for the occasional story pointing out Cianci confidants who had gotten city business. Cianci would yell and curse at the offending reporter, then calm down and banter with him.

The *Journal*'s editors discussed how to handle the Marquette story. They talked about the fact that Cianci had never been charged with a crime and about the story's explosiveness. But they also agreed that the police reports told a tale that warranted further investigation. Wade was teamed up with Randall Richard, a veteran investigative reporter. On Wednesday, January 18, 1978—two days after Chief Ricci's suicide—the two reporters flew to Milwaukee.

Wade seemed an unlikely choice for such a sensitive assignment. While she was the one who had obtained the police reports, she was a feature writer with no experience as an investigative reporter. A demure woman in her forties, Wade had started at the *Journal* as a copy clerk, in a journalistic era when women were often consigned to the women's pages, as they were then quaintly known. In the early 1970s, when the women's liberation movement swept across Rhode Island, with women marching into a males-only bar in downtown Providence, Wade, then assigned to the youth beat, staged her own miniprotest in the newsroom. She and another staffer complained to the new executive editor, Chuck Hauser, that some women feature writers were classified as "women's news specialists," earning less than full-fledged reporters. The paper changed its policy.

In Milwaukee, Wade and Richard made the rounds. They talked to Nancy Laffey, the television reporter, and had dinner with Alan Eisenberg. They also spoke to River Hills police chief Harold Block. But the police file that Block had copied for Laffey a few months earlier (and which the *Journal* reporters had received copies of from the Wisconsin feminist) was no longer available.

When Wade and Richard visited Bandlow at her house, she seemed nervous and upset, and refused to let them inside. She did, however, confirm that Cianci had paid her three thousand dollars to withdraw her criminal complaint.

Wade and Richard spent three days in Milwaukee, tracking down leads and trying to confirm details. They went to the district attorney and the Milwaukee County medical examiner. They also had what would prove to be a fateful interview with the dean of the Marquette Law School. During the interview, according to an affidavit submitted later by the dean, Wade told him that the problem with Cianci extended beyond the lone Marquette accusation; Wade proceeded to lay out what a court would later say were "demonstrably false accusations against Cianci in order to coax information" from the dean. Wade repeated rumors she had heard in Providence about other purported sexual incidents involving Cianci, including episodes of homosexual activity and acts involving minors.

The dean alerted someone in the Cianci camp. Soon the mayor was aware that the *Journal* was on to the story—a story that he knew could destroy his political career. Already dealing with the fallout of the Ricci suicide, Cianci flew into a panic and dispatched Herb DeSimone and Ron Glantz to Milwaukee. The mayor's men huddled with Danny Weiss and Carl Krueger. According to Glantz, a two-pronged strategy emerged: seal the records and silence Ruth Bandlow. (DeSimone confirmed making the trip, but declined to elaborate, citing attorney-client privilege.) Cianci, anxiously waiting back in Providence, called several times a day for updates. At one point Glantz asked Cianci why he had had a gun in law school.

"For protection," he recalled Cianci's replying.

Ironically, Glantz, when he had been in private practice, had defended a man who was convicted of raping a woman on a pool table in a bar in Central Falls. The prosecutor was Buddy Cianci.

Krueger told the *Journal* reporters that the records had been expunged—destroyed—at Bandlow's request, something that a criminal complainant had a right to request under Wisconsin law. But it wasn't clear that the records had, in fact, been destroyed or sealed. DeSimone later told another reporter that the village attorney in River Hills had ordered Chief Harold Block not to discuss the case publicly. Trying to warn a TV reporter off the story, DeSimone noted that as a result of that order, it would be difficult for a journalist to authenticate the documents that had been circulating.

DeSimone and Glantz also checked for any surviving medical records and tried to track down the doctor who had seen Bandlow after her rape accusation. One morning, while they were still searching for the doctor, Glantz was dressing in his hotel room, the television on, when he heard the doctor's name on the news. He raced out into the hallway to meet DeSimone, who had heard the same thing. It turned out, though, that the doctor they were looking for was dead; the one on TV was his son.

Meanwhile, the *Journal* was getting close. On Friday, January 20, the day that Cianci attended Bob Ricci's funeral in the driving snowstorm, the newspaper decided to publish the story on Sunday. On Saturday, using borrowed desks and typewriters in the newsroom of the *Milwaukee Journal,* Wade and Richard began telexing information back home. In the Providence newsroom the editors and lawyers stood by as another reporter sat down and began punching a story into the computer.

The story began:

Vincent Cianci was accused of rape while he was a law student at Marquette University in 1966 and three times failed a lie detector test in connection with the case, the Journal-Bulletin has learned.

Doane Hulick, the *Journal*'s City Hall reporter, was standing by to get a comment from Cianci. He walked over to the mayor's office at about 1 P.M. Cianci was edgy and upset. Although he and Hulick had a good professional relationship, Cianci refused to talk to him about this. Instead, he told Hulick that he wanted to meet with the *Journal*'s publisher to discuss "the conduct of one of your reporters." Eventually, two editors and the *Journal*'s lawyers met in Cianci's office with the mayor and his advisers.

During the hour-long meeting, Cianci's lawyers described Bert Wade's conversation with the Marquette Law dean. They said that she had said things about Cianci that she knew to be untrue, in an effort to pry information from the dean, slandering the mayor in the attempt. Her statements, they argued, demonstrated malicious intent, a necessary element for a public figure to prove in a libel suit. A law-school dean would testify to that. Cianci's lawyers also attacked the credibility of the newspaper's sources. Someone had dug up the Wisconsin bar's disciplinary action against Eisenberg.

When the *Journal* party returned to the newsroom at 3 P.M., the editors pulled the story from Sunday's paper, gathered up all the notes, and shipped the story to a high-security computer queue, away from prying newsroom eyes. Reporters grumbled that the paper had lost its will, been intimidated, backed down to a Republican mayor, acted too cautiously. But others realized that the paper had had no choice under the circumstances. Bert Wade had screwed up.

In the days and weeks ahead, rumors about the story that the *Journal* was sitting on spread through City Hall. Cianci's enemies on the City Council began to gloat. "We've got the bastard," councilmen said. "He's in a real jam now."

What they didn't realize was that the story hadn't merely been delayed; it was essentially dead. Although it remained on life support for a few months, the *Journal*'s editors finally pulled the plug when it became apparent that Ruth Bandlow might not cooperate in the likely event of a lawsuit by Cianci. Wade, who was briefly suspended for her conduct, went back to writing features.

The *Journal*'s decision to kill the story sent a powerful message to other local reporters with thoughts of pursuing it. When Paul Giaccobe, a former *Journal* reporter who had moved to Channel 10 television in Providence, investigated in March 1978, Herb DeSimone told him that the *Journal* had declined to run the story; the Associated Press and another Providence television station had made the same decision.

Giaccobe asked DeSimone if he had any quarrel with the existence of police documents that were a matter of public record. DeSimone launched into an Orwellian discourse on how maybe the records existed at one time, but they no longer did, officially.

DeSimone told the reporter that Cianci was at the peak of his political career. Any story would be met with a lawsuit.

"The decision is a close one—legally, ethically, morally," Giaccobe wrote to his news director. "Unless I hear differently from you, I'll consider the file inactive."

A MAYOR IS judged in many ways, from the direction he charts for his city to more elemental concerns: Is the trash picked up? Are the school buses on time? And when it snows, are the streets plowed? On such small things can votes be lost and elections turn.

In February 1978, still dealing with Chief Ricci's suicide and trying to put the Marquette rape accusation behind him, Buddy Cianci faced another challenge—snow.

The flurries began late on a Monday morning, fat flakes wafting gently out of a threatening sky. Within an hour it was snowing heavily as two massive low-pressure systems, one moving east from the northern plains, the other sweeping up the Atlantic seaboard from Cape Hatteras, converged on Providence. By midafternoon, hurricane-force winds howled across the city, driving the snow horizontally and obscuring the skyline in a veil of white.

A desperate and futile evacuation of Providence began. Cars and tractor-trailer trucks were snarled in the snow, which was piling up at a rate of an inch or two an hour. Streets were quickly rendered impassable by the advancing snow and the trapped vehicles. Thousands of people were trapped in their cars, thousands more stuck in downtown office buildings and city schools. Thousands of residents lost power and heat.

The governor, J. Joseph Garrahy, declared a state of emergency and advised Rhode Islanders to prepare for a few days of isolation. Cianci urged motorists to stay out of Providence; a panicky aide, having just surveyed the traffic nightmare outside City Hall, amplified the mayor's comments: "Just stay the hell out!"

Nearly three feet of snow—thirty-five inches—fell on Providence in the span of a little more than twenty-four hours, the worst blizzard in the city's recorded history. The death toll statewide was twenty-one. The Providence police headquarters became a temporary morgue, a makeshift hospital, and a refuge for more than fifty stranded pedestrians. Hundreds more slept on cots and on the floor at the Providence Civic Center, which one observer said looked like the hospital scene from *Gone With the Wind*. Others took refuge in downtown bars, restaurants, and hotels, where food supplies quickly dwindled to cheese and crackers and, fortuitously, plenty of liquor. Ash Wednesday services were canceled for the first time in the history of the Providence Roman Catholic diocese. Kennedy Plaza resembled Moscow's Red Square, as bundled-up pedestrians picked their way past snowdrifts taller than a grown man.

Meanwhile, where were the city's snowplows? Ominously, when a big snowstorm had struck Providence a few weeks earlier, they had all broken down. They were hardly ready this time, either, even though meteorologists had been predicting a major storm for two days. The city's plowing army was caught unawares and stranded at the Public Works garage. Privately owned plows that the city rented were stored in surrounding towns and unable to get into the paralyzed city.

And what about Buddy? After the storm ended and the sun reemerged, day after day passed and, still, the streets of Providence remained impassable, marked only by boot prints and ski tracks. In wards that hadn't seen a snowplow in nearly a week, the grumbling about the mayor intensified. Why had he kept such a low profile in the early days of the crisis? Why hadn't the city's plows been mobilized sooner? Why was Cianci's office telling the public early on that the city had more than one hundred pieces of equipment clearing the city's 420 miles of streets, when in fact the number was actually eight?

Some of Cianci's City Council foes considered meeting in emergency session to wrest control of the city from the mayor, then thought better of adding to the chaos. Others carped that Cianci was providing preferential plowing to politically important neighborhoods, like Tony Bucci's Fourth Ward.

"To say we plowed [the Fourth Ward] because it was an Italian ward that we lost by a few hundred votes is ridiculous," responded Ronnie Glantz. Echoed Cianci, "You can't plow for political or nonpolitical reasons without equipment."

The criticism was exaggerated and somewhat unfair. It would have been difficult for the most efficient plowing operation to cope with such a cataclysmic blizzard, especially with two thousand abandoned cars blocking city streets. Still, the city's sluggish response exacerbated the problem and reflected poorly on Cianci, the man in charge. Had that year's election been scheduled for February instead of November, angry voters said, Cianci would have lost in an avalanche.

The mayor's slippage—literally as well as figuratively—was evident on the second day of the storm as he struggled to make his way by snowmobile from his house on Blackstone Boulevard to City Hall. It took him two hours to navigate the two miles through a wintry wonderland. Three times he attempted to scale high drifts, like some urban Admiral Peary, and three times his snowmobile tipped over, tumbling him into the snow.

Providence became the laughingstock of the state. Long after Rhode Island's other major cities had dug out, entrepreneurial pilots on Block Island offered fifteen-dollar airplane flights over Providence, so that islanders could see the mess firsthand. A headline in the Sunday *Journal,* six days after the storm, announced, PROVIDENCE WON'T OPEN TOMORROW. As the crisis deepened and the political ramifications became apparent, Cianci fought back. The night after the storm ended, he spent four hours riding on a city payloader through the snowbound streets.

The mayor also picked a political snowball fight with the Democratic governor, Joe Garrahy, whom he blamed for not clearing Interstate 95 quickly enough to make room for cars trying to escape from Providence when the storm hit. Cianci assailed a work slowdown in the blizzard's critical early hours by the state's unionized snowplow drivers, who were in the midst of a contract squabble with the governor. Worse, in the mayor's eyes, was his belief that Garrahy had steered National Guard cleanup equipment and U.S. Army reinforcements to assist areas outside Providence first—all to discredit Cianci, a potential political rival.

Joe Garrahy, an affable former beer salesman, had come out of Joe Doorley's Elmhurst neighborhood, where he still lived, part of a coterie of influential Irish Democrats. It was no secret that Cianci, having passed on the 1976 Senate race but still looking to move up, was weighing a challenge to Garrahy that November.

Garrahy, who had struggled three hours home through the snow from a speaking engagement in Newport, had been quick to take charge of the blizzard. He petitioned President Carter to declare Rhode Island a national disaster area and went on television early to reassure citizens with his folksy manner. Throughout the crisis, Garrahy wore a red-and-blue flannel shirt that gave him a comforting presence.

It galled Cianci to be branded a villain while a rival seized the spotlight. The state had been just as poorly prepared to cope with the storm, and there had been virtually no coordination between city and state in how to respond to the blizzard. Incredibly, Providence had been left off a priority list of communities for additional army equipment because of a communications snafu between state and city officials. The operations officer for the army's snow-removal task force, who had followed priorities set by the governor, seemed troubled that more equipment wasn't sent to Providence sooner. When he finally arrived in Providence late on Friday night, he was stunned to find so little equipment there.

On Thursday, two days after the storm, Cianci skirmished with Garrahy over credit for discovering an armada of more than seventy bulldozers, front-end loaders, and other heavy equipment sitting at a naval base in southern Rhode Island, and manned by navy Seabees flown in from Gulfport, Mississippi. Cianci went on television and boasted that he had found the equipment and appropriated all of it for Providence, only to go wild later in the day when Garrahy officials said that it was the governor's decision where it would be sent.

"I'm sick and tired of taking crap. . . . The state is running the snowstorm like they're running the prisons," fumed Cianci. "The governor gave me his word and now he's backing off."

When Cianci called Garrahy's disaster-relief officials at the State House and confronted them, they relented and released the Seabees to Providence. The mayor gloated and smiled his I-told-you-so grin. When the Seabees arrived at Providence's Fields Point the next night, Cianci was at the waterfront to greet them.

The mayor established a command post at City Hall, grabbing catnaps in his office as outside his window Kennedy Plaza filled with arriving army equipment and troops. The city was placed under a military blockade, with all entrances barricaded by National Guard trucks and police cruisers to keep the streets free of curiosity seekers, who had impeded the removal effort. Cianci declared a curfew, after scattered reports of looting. Anyone who ventured into downtown, even pedestrians, required a pink pass signed by the mayor.

Through the weekend, the Seabees, working with reinforcements from the army, fanned out across Providence, attacking the snow. The army's 483rd Engineer Battalion, comprising men from Massachusetts and Connecticut, established a beachhead in Fox Point and plowed north toward College Hill and Brown University. Meanwhile, troops from the army's 36th Engineering Group, from Fort Benning, Georgia, attacked the streets of Olneyville, driving north and northwest toward the North End, Mount Pleasant, and Smith Hill.

Finally, by the middle of the second week, some ten days after the Blizzard of '78 began, the city returned to a semblance of normalcy. The storm and its aftermath had brought out the best and the worst in people, from untold acts of kindness and heroism to looting and snow rage. The Sunday after the storm, thousands of people showed their ability to triumph over adversity by walking or skiing to the Civic Center to cheer on the scrappy Providence College Friars basketball team as they upset the nationally ranked University of North Carolina. The Tarheels, advised that food supplies were low in Providence, had flown in carrying their own supply of T-bone steaks.

The blizzard also exposed the ugly side of Rhode Island politics, from the lack of preparedness to the inept coordination of the rescue effort to Cianci's shrill attempts to blame Garrahy. The outrage mounted when city Public Works employees submitted their overtime bills for the storm. Topping the list was Slim DiBello, Cianci's acting Public Works director and Tony Bucci's Fourth Ward sidekick, who put in for the equivalent of fourteen straight twenty-two-hour days.

Cianci demanded an investigation into the state's role and testified before a Senate subcommittee in Washington organized by John Chafee. But the hearing provided few answers. Nor was there ever any substantiation of Cianci's charge that Garrahy had deliberately withheld equipment from Providence. Cianci conceded that the city's response to the storm had been disappointing but hoped that voters would understand. "I would like to think that people would have some understanding that this was a disaster," he said.

In other words, Cianci might have said, Mother Nature was a Democrat.

■

THE SNOW EVENTUALLY melted, but relations between Cianci and the City Council remained icy. Their three-and-a-half-year struggle for primacy in Providence was reaching a pivotal point as the mayor geared up for his reelection campaign.

On a raw, damp morning in April 1978, Cianci strode triumphantly into the festive ballroom of the Marriott, in the shadow of the State House, to the cheers of one thousand supporters. Uniformed policemen cleared a path for the mayor as Tony Polito's Dixieland band struck up "My Buddy." Making his way to the podium and standing beneath a large photograph of himself, Cianci declared that he would run for mayor again, and not governor.

"Providence has been transformed," said Cianci, "from a machine-dominated oligarchy to a grassroots, participatory democracy."

Recent statewide polls showed Cianci's popularity slipping. Ricci's suicide and the blizzard had not helped Cianci's image, and his Democratic enemies kept harping on the city's growing deficit, rising taxes, and declining services.

The honeymoon with Larry McGarry was over, too. Cianci had cast aside his onetime Democratic mentor. Ron Glantz, who had acted as an intermediary between the two when McGarry wanted patronage jobs, said that Cianci strung McGarry along on some request until McGarry grew disgusted and said, "Just tell him it's over." When Glantz relayed the message, Cianci's reaction was "Fuck him." Cianci didn't need McGarry anymore, especially since he still had Tony Bucci.

McGarry subsequently announced that he would run in the 1978 Democratic primary for mayor, but he was sage enough to know that his glory days were behind him. He approached the race more with the nostalgic air of a historian of Providence politics than as a candidate who seriously thought he could win. He ranked Cianci as the most political mayor he had seen in more than twenty-five years, a well-meaning showman but a poor administrator. His election in 1974 had been a "fluke." Beyond the East Side and Silver Lake this year, McGarry said, "I see nothing but trouble for him."

Mingling in the crowd at the Marriott was a young freelance writer from Massachusetts, Craig Waters. He was pursuing the story of the Marquette rape accusation for New Times magazine, a small but feisty national publication based in New York that specialized in muckraking pieces.

Out in the lobby, councilman Ed Xavier, one of Cianci's most vocal critics, sat on a couch, taking attendance of "these so-called Democrats" who were with Cianci. "Good morning!" he called out over and over, his gravelly voice full of mock cheer.

At a subsequent dinner of the Republican City Committee, Cianci reminded his supporters that he controlled seven million dollars in federal money, which was about to be spent on road repairs; six million to rebuild a pedestrian mall downtown; and another four million for improvements to Roger Williams Park. The mayor also had a commanding campaign war chest that he placed at $250,000 but that Democrats believed was actually closer to $400,000—a lot of money for a mayor's race in that era.

Meanwhile, Cianci had a plan to smash his opposition on the City Council once and for all. It would go down in the annals of Providence political history as the Wednesday Night Massacre.

Council president Robert Haxton had kept a low profile since his arrest on the morals charge in connection with the boy he had picked up outside the Columbus Theater back in 1975. But he still showed up for meetings, said Democratic chairman Frank Darigan, because "we needed his vote."

The case had finally gone to trial in the fall of 1977. Haxton's lawyer felt he could show that his client had been set up as part of a political vendetta. But an entrapment defense would have opened the door for the prosecution to explore Haxton's secret life. The price of that approach was made clear when the policeman on the case, Alfred Mintz, the Cianci supporter who had since been promoted, subpoenaed a black transvestite to testify. The witness showed up in the hallway at the courthouse but never actually took the stand. Haxton's lawyer didn't pursue the entrapment defense. The only two witnesses to testify were Haxton and the boy. Haxton was convicted.

By the spring of 1978, Haxton had been sentenced and had chosen not to appeal, and Cianci decided it was time to force the council's hand. It was an opportune moment because two other Democrats on the council who had opposed the mayor, both from Federal Hill, had also been found guilty of separate crimes. Anthony Merola had been convicted of insurance fraud. Mario Turchetta was in the federal detention center in New Bedford, Massachusetts, en route to begin serving two years in prison for a racetrack tax-cheating scheme known as "10-percenting."

Cianci invoked the city charter, which stated that officeholders convicted of felonies or crimes of "moral turpitude" shall forfeit their positions, and demanded that the council remove Haxton and Merola. (Turchetta still had an appeal pending.)

"The incidence of convicted felons in the general population is about one in fifteen thousand," said Cianci. "On the Providence City Council, it's one in eight."

At a raucous meeting on April 24, the council moved reluctantly, by a vote of 13–10, to remove Haxton and Merola.

Merola, whose brother would later be convicted for the murder that month of a Federal Hill wiseguy known as "Joe Onions," marched defiantly into the council meeting with fifty backers, carrying petitions containing the signatures of three hundred more.

"This whole thing is political," said Merola, who had been convicted of defrauding an insurance company of twenty-one hundred dollars in a phony lost-wages claim following an automobile accident. "My people knew about this case even before the election. They elected me anyway. Now, what do you think that means?"

After the council voted to throw him off, Merola straightened the knot on his tie and, like General MacArthur, predicted, "I'll be back." (He ran and won in the September primary but lost in November.)

Although the council had succeeded for three and a half years in blocking Cianci's appointments, denying the mayor control of key boards and commissions and frustrating him on taxes and the budget, it had also unwittingly helped him. The more the council blocked Cianci, the more it made him look like a martyr to the voters.

"We could send them the cure for cancer," Cianci and his aides would joke, "and the vote would be fifteen to ten, against."

The council, with its collection of roguish characters and parochial interests, proved a perfect foil for the nimble Cianci. One councilman was so obsessed with having potholes in his ward repaired that Cianci and his aides called him "Councilman Pothole." Two others nearly got into a fist-fight one night at City Hall during an argument over what date to hold a public hearing. Vinny Cirelli, a leader in the Cianci opposition, held Democratic caucuses at his Old Timer's Tap on Mount Pleasant Avenue, a dark, smoky bar where you could also place bets; the bar served only Narragansett beer—"made from the sparkling waters of the Scituate Reservoir," which also happened to be Providence's drinking-water supply—until the brewery went out of business. Another councilman favored baggy, 1940s-style zoot suits.

A favorite target was Eddie Xavier, a gruff Teamster who drove a truck that delivered deli meat from New York and also worked as a checker on the

docks in Fox Point. Xavier grew up on the waterfront, in a crowded tenement with a large extended Portuguese family that had come to Rhode Island around the turn of the century from the Azores, an island chain off
the coast of Africa. One grandfather had cleaned trolleys; the other had
worked for the city of Providence, until he fell off a dump truck, landed on
his head, and went blind.

Xavier, who boxed at the Fox Point Boys Club, was well known around
the neighborhood for getting his people jobs with the city. Portuguese men
would show up at the Public Works garage, say that Eddie had sent them,
and be put to work on a garbage truck. Xavier used to complain to Larry
McGarry at Public Works that the Irish had a formula for handing out jobs:
the Irish in City Hall, the Italians on the highway, and the Portuguese picking up garbage.

When Cianci took office, Xavier became one of his most strident critics.
Xavier hated Cianci. Had Joe Doorley won, Xavier would have had tremendous pull. "I would've got everyone in Fox Point a job," he said wistfully.

Xavier led council inquiries into Cianci's firing of Lloyd Griffin and,
after Chief Ricci killed himself, into the selection of police recruits.

He shunned Cianci's entreaties. Once, at a reunion of the Fox Point
Boys Club at the Alpine Country Club, the mayor arrived and stood outside,
waiting for Xavier, who had also just arrived.

"You ain't walking in with me," said Xavier.

"Why not?" asked Cianci.

"Because I don't want these fucking people to think I'm with you."

Another time, during a heated budget debate, Cianci sent Xavier a note
on the council floor that said, "If you vote for the tax increase, I'll get your
girlfriend a job." Xavier crumpled the note and threw it on the floor, only to
have one of his enemies pick it up and give it to a reporter for *The Providence
Journal,* who wrote about it on the front page. The story, Xavier said rue-
fully, years later, "didn't help me with my wife. She still brings it up today."
(Xavier said the "girlfriend" was "just someone who hung around—she
liked politicians, and she could get free drinks.")

For sheer entertainment, there was no better show in town than City
Council meetings. One *Providence Journal* story took a blasé approach to a
typical night of bickering and infighting: "The city council got right down
to brass knuckles as it began its regular session last night." At that meeting
Xavier shouted down a pro-Cianci councilman during a parliamentary debate, yelling, "We don't need F. Lee Bailey to interpret our rules." And
Councilman Merola from Federal Hill, who had yet to be convicted of in-

surance fraud, demanded that the chief of police in Warwick publicly apologize for saying that the recent murder of a South Providence book-maker may have had Federal Hill connections. All his life, Merola complained, "I have always heard that killers come from Federal Hill. That is not a true fact." Merola's remarks were endorsed by another councilman, who said that he considered the murdered man a close personal friend, and criticized the newspaper for reporting that he had been a bookie.

In the spring of 1978, while the council dragged its feet on removing Haxton and Merola because of their criminal convictions, it also refused to endorse an ordinance to prohibit discrimination in employment and hous-ing against minorities, women, the elderly, and the handicapped, because the measure also included homosexuals. At a stormy public hearing, the council allowed opponents of the ordinance to speak at length until past 10 P.M., then limited supporters to three minutes each. The opponents in-cluded a Bible-thumping minister who equated homosexuals with murder-ers and a fireman who said that he wouldn't go into a burning building to save a homosexual.

It was no wonder that Cianci called the City Council "the Gong Show" and "one of the most incredible concentrations of stupidity in American politics."

In May, after Haxton and Merola were finally removed, and with Turchetta effectively gone because of his incarceration (though his wife still picked up his council paychecks), the council's anti-Cianci majority had shrunk from fifteen to twelve, with eleven Cianci supporters.

Cianci, conferring with Tony Bucci and Ronnie Glantz, began plotting to take the council.

On Sunday, July 9, the story about the Marquette rape accusation fi-nally broke. New Times, with a national circulation of 350,000, announced that it was publishing the story on the cover of its upcoming July 24 issue.

Cianci had known that the story was in the works, and he had dis-patched Herb DeSimone and Ron Glantz to New York in an effort to stop it. New Times's editor, Jon Larsen, was accustomed to taking on powerful leaders and corporate giants, but he said that he had never seen anything quite like the extraordinary performance of DeSimone and Glantz. They accused the reporter, Craig Waters, of offering money to Cianci's alleged victim and of coercing information from sources. They made what he con-sidered lawyerly arguments about the authenticity of the police reports, and threatened to sue if the magazine published the story.

"They didn't address the truth of the matter, they just questioned the validity of the copies of the police reports and tried to blackmail us by accusing Craig of unethical behavior," recalled Larsen. "The irony is that we weren't planning to put it on the cover. But when we walked out of there, I had what [Bob] Woodward would call a 'holy shit' moment."

The Providence Sunday Journal led the paper with a recap of the story, covering the allegations that its own reporters had looked into in January and the *New Times* account of how the *Journal*'s reporter had erred and the newspaper had decided not to print the story. The *Journal* also ran Cianci's entire statement of denial on top of the front page.

"I have never in my life been arrested, charged, indicted or placed before any court anywhere in the world for the commission of any criminal act," declared Cianci.

The day before the *Journal* published the story, its reporters and editors were once again locked in a battle with the mayor's office to obtain Cianci's comment. The mayor railed at the newspaper's Yankee owners. At one point, Glantz recalled, he shouted into the phone at a *Journal* editor about how "you work for those people."

That Saturday, after a meeting in which the *Journal*'s publisher, top editors, and lawyers decided to go with the story, one editor, Joel Rawson, recalled the publisher, John Watkins, saying that it was a shame because Cianci was a talented young man and this would end his career.

On Sunday, the day the *Journal* story appeared, Cianci received a hero's welcome at a Republican-party clambake in Scituate. Accompanied by his wife and their four-year-old daughter, Cianci was all smiles as he strolled about the outdoor picnic area, working the crowd, shaking hands, and predicting victory in November. Cianci painted himself as the victim of the media and "a political ploy" by his opponents.

"The media will stop at nothing to make a profit," he told five hundred cheering supporters. "If they can do this to the mayor of Providence, they can do it to anybody."

Glantz said later that he believed that Cianci succeeded in dampening the potentially devastating consequences of the story by keeping it from being reported earlier in 1978. By threatening lawsuits, capitalizing on the *Journal*'s misstep, and characterizing the story as a political ploy (there was never any evidence his opponents were behind it), Cianci put the media and his political foes on the defensive. When the story finally came out, he was able to paint himself as the victim. He didn't have to answer detailed questions about the accusation or explain the circumstances surrounding its withdrawal or the three-thousand-dollar settlement. It did not become a major issue in the campaign. *The Echo*, a local newspaper catering to the Italian-American community, dismissed the allegation as "another ethnic slur."

Cianci subsequently filed a seventy-two-million-dollar libel suit against *New Times*. A federal judge in New York threw it out, ruling that the article was accurate and protected under the First Amendment. Furthermore, the judge said, Cianci had failed to demonstrate that *New Times* had been guilty of malice, a necessary element of libel against a public figure such as Cianci. Cianci appealed, complaining, "I have been denied my day in court." The Second Circuit Court of Appeals reinstated the suit and sent it back to the lower court for trial to resolve the factual disputes. The appellate court, while holding that Cianci still faced a "heavy burden" in proving libel, said that the *New Times* story did not include Cianci's explanation of the civil settlement and implied that the three-thousand-dollar payment was made prior to and was the primary reason for the decision not to prosecute. The appellate court said that the judge could still dismiss the case after further discovery, but that the lower court "was not justified in lowering the boom on Mayor Cianci when it did."

As the suit progressed through discovery, Cianci gave his account of that night with Bandlow in sealed depositions, some of which later became public. For the first time, he acknowledged that he had paid Bandlow three thousand dollars, that he had introduced himself to her as she walked on the sidewalk near Marquette, that he later drove her to his house and spent the evening with her, and that there had been a gun in the house. But he adamantly denied raping her. Cianci also said that he had taken a lie-detector test, but said in a deposition that he could not remember whether he was advised of the results. After taking the test, he testified, he recalled that the person who administered it said that "I had nothing to be concerned about. I did just fine." Cianci refused to answer questions concerning his efforts in the winter of 1977–78 to stop *The Providence Journal* and *New Times* from publishing the story.

Early in 1981, the owners of the now-defunct *New Times* settled the lawsuit for eighty-five hundred dollars and a letter of apology. The magazine's publisher, George A. Hirsch, recalled the settlement as "minimal" and the letter of apology as "soft." *New Times*, which had always had trouble attracting advertisers because its muckraking alienated corporate advertisers, had folded early in 1979, for reasons unrelated to the Cianci story, and its lawyers wanted to get rid of the lawsuit to avoid the expense of a trial, said Hirsch. The money from the settlement went to Cianci's New York lawyers, who later sought another two hundred and twelve thousand dollars in unpaid legal bills from him. (Cianci called this a "misunderstanding" that was subsequently resolved.) The letter of apology went up on the wall in the mayor's office.

In the summer of 1978, when the *New Times* story was published, it was the talk of the town in Providence, drawing reporters from outside, including *The New York Times*. After overheated speculation, Rhode Island's largest magazine distributor decided not to carry the telltale issue of *New Times*, for fear of a lawsuit. "Don't forget," the distributor explained to *New Times*'s publisher, "he's still the mayor of this town."

That left it to Skip Chernov, the broken-down rock promoter, to bring the magazine to Providence. In the four years since Cianci's election as the anticorruption candidate, the fortunes of the man who had helped Cianci expose corruption at the Civic Center had declined as precipitously as Cianci's had improved.

Chernov had been blacklisted as a concert promoter and suffered a heart attack, divorce, and bankruptcy. He had started an ill-fated minor-league basketball team, the Providence Shooting Stars, which he lost one night when he got drunk in a bar and signed it away. His drinking and drug use had landed him in the hospital. After he got out, in spring 1978, Chernov launched a quixotic campaign for mayor, challenging Cianci in the Republican primary. He sold his beloved '50 Hudson Hornet and other personal belongings and raised four thousand dollars, which he spent on modest advertising and buying people drinks in bars. One of the candidate's first acts was to be arrested outside City Hall for handing out leaflets critical of Ronnie Glantz.

Chernov blamed Cianci for the loss of his last business, a popular Mexican restaurant near Brown University named Tortilla Flats. After Cianci took office, Chernov said that the mayor blocked his permit to expand the restaurant, which he needed to stay in business. Glantz confirmed this, years later. Chernov recalled storming down to City Hall and confronting Cianci, who icily told him that it would be better if he left town. The *New Times*'s George Hirsch, who heard from newsdealers that Cianci was pressuring them not to carry the issue, hired a pilot in Connecticut to fly the magazines in. The pilot was a no-nonsense air force veteran who had flown combat missions, Hirsch recalled. When apprised of the tense situation in

Rhode Island, he told Hirsch, "Don't worry. Those magazines will get in there."

THE PROVIDENCE CITY COUNCIL met in an ornate, wood-paneled room on the third floor of City Hall that was part theater and part courtroom.

The council chambers had wooden benches, like a courtroom, and a wooden railing with a swinging gate that divided the participants from the spectators. In front of the rail, twenty-six antique wooden desks were arranged in two rows, in a semicircle facing the president's desk, which was on a raised podium, like the judge's seat. Upstairs was a theaterlike balcony with additional seating for crowded meetings. The wood paneling ran halfway up the walls to the ceiling. The remainder of the walls had once been adorned with elaborately painted designs, like movie palaces of old, but were now covered with ugly asbestos tiles.

On Wednesday night, July 12, three days after the *New Times* story broke, council members filtered in as they always did. In the weeks since Haxton's and Merola's ouster, Eddie Xavier and Vinny Cirelli would walk upstairs and peek out from the balcony to make sure they had enough guys. If they did, the two men might not go in, and go out for a beer instead.

On this night, however, they just went in. The mayor, who seldom attended council meetings, sat downstairs in his second-floor office with Ron Glantz, listening through a stereo speaker that picked up what was being said from a microphone in the chamber.

As the roll was called, Glantz and Cianci realized that the Democrats didn't have their usual majority. Haxton's and Merola's vacancies had yet to be filled. Turchetta was in prison. And three other anti-Cianci Democrats were in the hospital, one with a back injury suffered on the golf course.

They did a quick head count and realized what the Democrats upstairs hadn't yet. There were eleven pro-Cianci councilmen and only nine opponents. As Larry McGarry used to say, "When you got the votes, you got the votes."

Glantz sent a low-level aide upstairs with a stack of ordinances, representing some thirty appointments to various city posts and boards that the council had been sitting on. If these appointments were approved, Cianci would instantly gain control of several powerful instruments of government—from the Board of Licenses, which regulated bars and restaurants, to the Board of Contract and Supply, which approved major city purchases, to the Board of Park Commissioners, which had denied Cianci credit for improvements to the city's parks and zoo.

The meeting was already under way when Xavier and Cirelli realized their mistake. The Democrats tried to adjourn. But Cianci's forces, drilled by Glantz, were ready. Armed with the city charter and *Robert's Rules of Order*, they pressed forward with Cianci's nominations. Stunned and in disarray, the anti-Cianci Democrats bolted for the exits, hoping to deny the mayor a quorum. There were shouts of "Get off the floor!" and "Get behind the rail!" When one councilman lingered on the threshold, another councilman shoved him out into the hallway before he could be counted.

A crowd of 150 people quickly caught on to the coup d'état in the making and started whooping and hollering, adding to the chaos. The city clerk picked up her note-taking equipment and walked out, too, reasoning that there couldn't be a roll-call vote for her to record without a quorum.

The anti-Cianci Democrats fled down the street to a popular downtown watering hole, Murphy's, which was known in Providence as a Jewish deli with an Irish name run by a Greek. But they had miscalculated, and Glantz knew it. He maintained that a quorum existed when the meeting began, and remained in effect because nobody ever officially challenged it.

As the rump Cianci council—eight Democrats, two Republicans, and one Independent—started approving each of the mayor's thirty appointees by individual roll-call votes, the Democrats who had adjourned to Murphy's learned what was happening and rushed back to City Hall. One of them, John Garan, who was running for mayor, repeatedly whipped up the jeering, frenzied crowd by accusing Cianci of trying to illegally railroad his appointments through.

Cianci sat downstairs in his office with Glantz and a handful of advisers, like a spider at the center of his web. He gloated and laughed hysterically as messengers brought him news of his unfolding coup.

"Watch," he joked, "one of them is going to pick up the phone and get Turchetta to vote from fucking prison."

Meanwhile, frantic phone calls were being made from the mayor's office, telling his new appointees to hurry down to City Hall. Cianci wanted to swear them in as quickly as possible.

A list of the new appointees telegraphed the new world order at City Hall.

Cianci had won over two black councilmen, who normally voted against him, by appointing eight minorities. (Cianci was no Abraham Lincoln, said one of the two councilmen, who explained that he backed Cianci "to ensure that our people got in.") Cianci had secured other Democratic votes by giving Tony Bucci the appointments that he wanted; they included Bucci's uncle Carmine to the Parks Commission and his Fourth Ward crony Slim DiBello to the Board of Licenses. And Cianci had punished Larry McGarry by knocking McGarry's ally Snack McManus off the tax board. Altogether, Cianci picked off five chairmen and changed the face of fifteen boards and commissions that night. The coup quickly became known as the Wednesday Night Massacre.

"Some call it a massacre," said Cianci. "Some call it a coup. I just prefer to call it a victory for the people."

The Wednesday Night Massacre awakened memories of the Bloodless Revolution of 1935, a legendary turning point in Rhode Island politics, when the state's urban Democrats used shrewd parliamentary tactics to seize power at the State House.

Until 1935, the old Yankee Republicans had ruled through a malapportioned state Senate that gave small communities like West Greenwich, with 485 people, the same representation as Providence, with 275,000. Consequently, the rural communities dominated the Senate. And thanks to a law engineered by Republican leader Charles "Boss" Brayton back in 1901, which weakened the power of the governor, all state patronage was controlled by the Senate, which even had the power to appoint department heads in the City of Providence. The Democrats, fueled by the tide of immigrants and fired by the Great Depression and Franklin Roosevelt's New Deal, were agitating for reform. But the Republicans were ruthless. A few years earlier, a Republican operative had broken up a Democratic filibuster by throwing a stink bomb into the Senate chamber.

It appeared that the Republicans, with a 22–20 Senate majority, would continue to reign when the General Assembly convened on a chilly New Year's Day in 1935. But a group of mostly Irish-American Democratic leaders from the cities had met with the Democratic governor, Theodore Francis Green, and hatched a plan.

When the Senate met, the presiding officer, Democratic lieutenant governor Robert Quinn, refused to swear in two Republicans from rural towns where the election results had been contested. With the Senate thus deadlocked, 20–20, Quinn swiftly appointed a recount committee. Governor Green, assisted by two dozen burly state troopers, ordered the state vault opened, had the ballots recounted, and determined that the Democratic candidates had won both seats. They were immediately sworn in, giving the Democrats a majority in both houses. That night Governor Green pushed through a sweeping reorganization of state government, replaced the entire Supreme Court, and wrested control of the State House from the rural Republicans once and for all.

Rhode Island's Bloodless Revolution sent reverberations across the country. *The New York Times* applauded it. But the conservative *Chicago Daily Tribune* condemned it as unconstitutional; its editor, Colonel Robert McCormick, ordered one star cut out of the American flag.

Cianci's Wednesday Night Massacre inspired similar mixed reaction, on a local scale. The mayor's supporters called it a dazzling coup, a shrewd maneuver worthy of Rhode Island's old-fashioned political bosses. The furious Democrats called it a "shoddy trick," and challenged Cianci in court. Glantz, who defended the mayor in court, brought in two expert witnesses from the American Institute of Parliamentarians, in Des Moines, Iowa, to debate the finer points of *Robert's Rules of Order*. Then, to put *Robert's Rules* in the context of the Providence City Council, Glantz said that Eddie Xavier was so dumb that he "thinks a caucus is what's left when you shoot a moose."

While the judge weighed his decision, he ordered the fifteen city boards and commissions affected not to transact any official business. That threw City Hall, already reeling from yet another budget crisis, with its cash shortages and threats of layoffs, into further turmoil. Glantz warned that deposed members who attempted to reclaim their positions would be forcibly removed from meetings, if necessary.

Two days after the massacre, Skip Chernov appeared before the Board of Licenses to confirm that he did not need a peddler's license to sell his fourteen hundred copies of *New Times* magazine, which were at that moment en route to Rhode Island. Chernov was greeted by two dueling Boards of Licenses, attempting to conduct separate meetings at the same table and trying to outshout each other under the watchful eyes of television cameras and police officers posted there in case things got out of hand. Unable to get a clear answer, Chernov went ahead without a license. Two of his vendors hawked the magazine, with Cianci's smiling face on the cover, on the sidewalks beneath the mayor's office, without incident.

Meanwhile, Providence was running out of money. The council needed to meet again, to pass a budget. But the Democrats were fearful of another Cianci ambush. Then, reversing course, they met and tried to undo Cianci's appointments, creating even more confusion for the courts to unravel.

With all the uproar, council meetings had taken on the aura of the Christians against the lions. Hundreds of spectators crowded the hot, smoky chamber to boo and shout and rain catcalls onto the floor, regardless of who was speaking or which side they were on. City workers serenaded the council with a thunderous chorus of "M-I-C-K-E-Y M-O-U-S-E." The police sent a paddy wagon to City Hall to arrest one spectator who had climbed over the wooden rail, jabbering incoherently; he later told the police that he didn't know it was a crime to disrupt a City Council meeting.

Before the meeting, Glantz had predicted that ailing Silver Lake councilman Louis Stravato, who had missed the Wednesday Night Massacre because of a slipped disc, would be there.

Stravato, who had spent the last seventeen days in the hospital, did not disappoint. Signing himself out of the hospital, against his doctor's advice, he was pushed into the council chambers in a wheelchair, his arms shaking and his brow sweating, then helped onto a walker, and, finally, into his council seat. "I'm here at my own risk," he announced. "I feel that the meeting on the twelfth was illegal."

Spectators winced each time Stravato rose to speak. Although his voice was strong, his hands trembled and he had to be supported by a nurse so that he wouldn't collapse. He vented much of his anger at Tony Bucci, who, he said, had asked him, in Bucci's downtown law office two weeks before the massacre, to back Cianci. Bucci had since denied that, prompting the councilman to invoke a point of personal privilege to respond.

"Mr. Bucci, you are the liar, and I challenge you anywhere, anytime," said Stravato, his voice rising.

With that, Stravato slumped down and was taken back to the hospital, where he spent another few weeks recuperating.

The day after the meeting, a superior-court judge ruled in favor of Cianci and said that the appointments were legal. The judge also criticized the Democrats who walked out of the meeting for trying to "thwart the proper conduct of business." But two weeks later the Rhode Island Supreme Court reversed that decision and ruled the Wednesday Night Massacre illegal.

Francis Darigan, Cianci's leading Democratic challenger for mayor, said that Cianci "took his best shot and lost. It was almost like he was in a crap game and he tried to roll a seven while everybody else was looking the other way."

The mayor vowed to fight all the way to the United States Supreme Court, if necessary. His supporters sued in federal court, accusing the council of crossing "the fine line between democracy and anarchy." Meanwhile, the *Journal* reported that Slim DiBello and another Cianci appointee had collected city paychecks while their appointments were in limbo.

THE FUROR OVER the Wednesday Night Massacre had barely died down when the mayor's 1978 reelection campaign heated up. In September Cianci cruised to victory in the Republican primary over Skip Chernov, who mustered only seventy-three votes. The mayor would face a more formidable challenger in November in Democratic city chairman Frank Darigan, who won his primary convincingly over Larry McGarry and Federal Hill lawyer Frank Caprio. Determined not to repeat the mistakes of 1974, the defeated Democrats vowed to unite behind Darigan. "I'll make a flat prediction," McGarry said of Cianci. "This guy is going to get bombed." (This truly was Mr. Democrat's last hurrah; he receded from city politics and was appointed by Governor Garrahy to the state racing commission, where he could follow his other love, the ponies.)

Throughout the campaign the polls showed Cianci and Darigan neck and neck, with a large percentage of voters undecided. Even the bookies were offering even money—not an auspicious sign for an incumbent mayor. Councilman Vinny Cirelli, one of Cianci's leading foes, was even more confident—when mayoral aide Joe Vileno stopped by the Old Timer's Tap for a drink, Cirelli offered to put up five hundred dollars, at three-to-one odds against Cianci.

Darigan hammered away at Cianci for raising taxes every year, for running budget deficits, for mishandling the blizzard, and for handing out city contracts to cronies like Norm Roussel, his political advertising man. Addressing a large Democratic gathering at the 1025 Club, Darigan shouted, "I'm going to eat this guy up like he's never been eaten before." As fourteen hundred party faithful dug into their macaroni and chicken, the Rhode Island secretary of state predicted that Cianci was "going out on his backside" and that nothing less than the "survival of the Democratic party in the city of Providence" was at stake. The state treasurer dismissed Cianci as a *spacone*, which Silver Lake power broker Vincent Igliozzi, Darigan's campaign manager, defined as "a flashy, boastful big shot."

Cianci fired back that Providence was moving in the right direction under his leadership. He pointed to new construction projects around the city and the revitalization of Federal Hill and other neighborhoods and blamed the intransigence of the City Council for the city's fiscal problems. The month before the election, Cianci attended the reopening of the restored Ocean State Performing Arts Center, a once-opulent downtown movie palace that he had rescued from demolition. The mayor beamed as Ethel Merman belted out "There's No Business Like Show Business."

Privately, Cianci was worried. It had been a tumultuous year, beginning with Robert Ricci's suicide and continuing through the blizzard and the *New Times* story and the Wednesday Night Massacre. Although Darigan didn't make an issue of the Marquette matter, it hovered in the background, an unknown variable. Vandals scrawled "Vote Rapist" on the mayor's campaign signs. Officials at Brown were angry when the Providence police questioned employees at the university's Women's Center about one such incident.

But Cianci was not without advantages. His charisma shone through the city's political turmoil. Voters liked him. Greeted by thunderous applause when he entered the 1025 Club during a banquet for the Federal Hill Little League, the mayor sat at the head table with deposed Federal Hill councilman Anthony Merola, who was pursuing his comeback after his conviction for insurance fraud. Shaking hands with supporters, Cianci noted: "I have been doing this ever since we were elected. Darigan is trying to do in six weeks what I have been doing for four years."

Cianci adviser Patrick Conley, a historian and Irish Democrat who had defected to Cianci after a spat with Governor Garrahy, viewed Darigan as too reserved for the more image-conscious politics of the seventies. Handsome, decent, and moral, Darigan would have been a picture-perfect candidate in the fifties, before television transformed American politics. Pitted against the glib Cianci, however, Darigan was too stiff, said Conley—"an eight-by-ten glossy."

Darigan had other problems. Despite the public show of togetherness, he knew that the Democratic party was not truly united. Cianci had made a strong push for Italian Democratic voters, doling out patronage and steering millions of federal dollars into the voter-rich neighborhoods that formed what he called the Fertile Crescent—an arc stretching across the northern part of the city from Silver Lake to Federal Hill to the North End to Mount Pleasant and Smith Hill. He also courted the public-employee unions and pulled off a historic feat by winning both the labor endorsement and the endorsement of *The Providence Journal.* The newspaper noted his shortcomings as an administrator but praised the mayor for "seizing opportunities where others saw only despair."

Tony Bucci, the Fourth Ward's Democratic boss, was strong with Cianci. Although Darigan was the Democratic nominee, he couldn't even get Democratic leaders in T.B.'s ward to pose for pictures with him. One Sunday morning shortly before the election, Darigan recalled, he was driving through the deserted streets of the Fourth Ward, past Cianci's campaign headquarters on Branch Avenue, when he saw Bucci and another Cianci lieutenant, Councilman Charles Mansolillo, emerging with stacks of red-and-white bumper stickers. The stickers said: GET THE GARLIC OUT OF CITY HALL. VOTE DARIGAN MAYOR.

Similar signs had sprouted on Federal Hill shortly before the 1974 election—signs that Cianci's then campaign manager, Mickey Farina, would years later attribute to the Cianci campaign. A few days before the 1978 election, the bumper stickers that Darigan had seen appeared throughout the North End and elsewhere. Some were plastered on Cianci campaign posters; others were distributed at Mount Pleasant High School.

Incredibly, when the *Journal* wrote about the mysterious bumper stickers and Darigan denied responsibility, he failed to disclose what he had seen. Later, he would acknowledge that that was a mistake. But he had chosen to campaign on the issues and thought that the voters would see through the ploy. Instead, he said, the stickers helped inflame the passions of Italian-American voters, playing into their historical mistreatment at the hands of the Irish bosses.

Three days before the election, Cianci publicly welcomed another old ally back into the fold—mail-ballot king Lloyd Griffin, whose magic had been instrumental in Cianci's narrow 1974 victory. Fired two years earlier as building inspector, the opportunistic Griffin, now a South Providence city councilman, said that he was supporting Cianci because he viewed the mayor as more vulnerable, and thus more willing to compromise than the Democrats. Griffin also felt that Cianci was more supportive of hiring minority police officers—ironically one of the factors in the mayor's police-hiring dispute with the late Chief Ricci. And Griffin was angered by a flyer circulating in black neighborhoods that attributed his firing to his being black. It wasn't racism, said Griffin—just politics.

Conley nicknamed him "Satchel" after seeing the lanky, six-foot-three-inch Griffin, who resembled the great Negro League pitcher Satchel Paige, stride into the mayor's office with a carpetbag and dump hundreds of mail ballots on Cianci's desk. Griffin, said Conley, loved it.

Cianci was still nervous going into election day. One campaign operative remembers staying up all night guarding the mayor's campaign headquarters in the Fifth Ward so nobody would cut the phone lines—something that had happened earlier in the campaign. "If you don't have your phones on election day," the aide said, "you're dead." As a preemptive measure, he asked the state Board of Elections—located, fittingly, across Branch Avenue from Providence's North Burial Grounds—to impound the voting machines after the polls closed.

Late that afternoon Darigan was standing vigil outside the John F. Kennedy School in the Fifth Ward, at the state's largest Democratic polling place, when the mayor's limousine pulled up and Cianci bounded out. The two men shook hands coldly. The mayor stayed for less than an hour. As he left, Darigan observed confidently: "There's the look of a worried man. We chased the mayor out of here." Darigan was counting on wards like the Fifth, Joe Doorley's old stronghold. He hoped that his criticisms of Cianci's soaring taxes would resonate with the solid middle-class voters of Mount Pleasant and Elmhurst, around Providence College.

That night, after the polls closed at 9 P.M., Cianci's campaign supporters gathered nervously in the ballroom at the Holiday Inn and waited for the returns. There were anxious whispers about the Marquette rape allegations, and all of the other negatives that had besieged the mayor in 1978. Cianci remained incommunicado. Roussel paced about the ballroom, smoking and chewing gum at the same time. He tried to remain upbeat, but when a reporter apprised him that the bookies had the mayor at even money, Roussel's smile vanished. "They're crazy!"

Darigan's forces weren't overly confident either. The night before the election, Joe Vileno had stopped by the Old Timer's Tap and tried to take Vinny Cirelli up on his earlier five-hundred-dollar bet against Cianci. But Cirelli refused. And Darigan, during his rounds on election day, had stopped at one polling place in the Fifth Ward to find the chief of police, Angelo Ricci (no relation to Robert Ricci), standing outside, leading the charge for Cianci.

Sure enough, shortly after 10 P.M., the first returns came in, and they were from the Fifth Ward. Cianci won one of the most populous Democratic wards in Rhode Island by about a hundred votes. At the Holiday Inn Angelo Ricci started hugging people and the celebration began. Cianci rolled to a stunning victory. He captured 56 percent of the vote, taking nine of the city's thirteen wards. He had outspent Darigan seven to one, including $107,000 to $7,000 on political advertising in the final month.

"We fought a machine four years ago and we barely won!" shouted an exultant Cianci. "Four years later we fought the machine and we pounded them."

Amidst the drinking and dancing and celebrating, one weary but relieved man leaned against a wall and sighed. "My Gawd," he said. "Now I can go to Vegas in peace."

Cianci's foes on the City Council awoke the morning after to the grim reality.

"The voters made Little Caesar a little bigger, that's what they did," grumbled Eddie Xavier. "I tell you, there will be a lot of heads rolling."

Vinny Cirelli, whose Sixth Ward had joined the surge to Cianci, retreated to his Old Timer's Tap on Mount Pleasant Avenue to grumble with his allies and drown his sorrows.

Cirelli and some of the other Democrats commiserated with Governor Garrahy. Cianci controls all the patronage, they complained. We need jobs. We don't know what to do. Garrahy responded, "Politics is the art of compromise."

A few days after the election Cirelli saw an unlikely sight: Buddy Cianci barreling through the door of the Old Timer's Tap. The mayor, stunned and elated by the size of his victory, was going through the wards of Providence, thanking people and trying to expand his base.

"Vinny, I need you," said Cianci. "Will you be with me? I'm Italian, you're Italian. Maybe we should join ranks and put the city where it belongs."

Cirelli decided that it was time to "bend." He even held a fund-raiser for Cianci. The mayor clambered up a stepladder onto the bar and said, "I never in my lifetime thought I'd be standing here, in Vinny Cirelli's bar, the Old Timer's Tap."

But there he stood, towering above his city, the undisputed prince of Providence.

CHAPTER FIVE

The Education of Ronnie Glantz

In the spring of 1979 there was a sense within Rhode Island's political world that Buddy Cianci was going places.

With his decisive reelection, he was positioned for a move up to the big leagues. The governor's seat seemed within his grasp in 1980. But the little mayor had even bigger ideas. He wanted to be vice president of the United States.

Late in March Cianci flew to Southern California for what he said was a vacation. But he was secretly there to audition for a spot on the 1980 Republican national ticket. He visited his old political benefactor, former president Ford, in Palm Springs, and also met with Ronald Reagan, one of the GOP contenders for president.

Cianci sold himself as someone who could win votes in traditionally Democratic areas—the urban, ethnic strongholds of the Northeast. Back in 1976 he had made no secret of his belief that Ford should have chosen as a running mate an urban Italian-American—he pointed to ex–Massachusetts governor John Volpe or Massachusetts congressman Silvio Conte—rather than Bob Dole. While the vice-presidential pipe dream never panned out, it spoke to Cianci's desire to move in high-powered circles. He might have been the mayor of Providence, but he was also someone who, when in Palm Springs, could drop in on Frank Sinatra.

No matter where Cianci went, though, Providence never seemed far behind. In Sinatra's Palm Springs home, Cianci noticed a picture of Raymond L. S. Patriarca, the New England mob boss. When Sinatra's bartender heard that Cianci was from Providence, he asked, "How's Raymond?"

Back in Providence, the grind of being mayor could be draining, despite Cianci's tremendous vigor. Shortly after his California trip Cianci was back at City Hall, welcoming a new card-and-gift shop downtown, announcing improvements to the dog pound, leading an antilitter campaign—the mundane tasks of being a mayor that seemed far removed from being a statesman.

"Governors aren't like this," he complained to aide Joe Vileno one day. "They can keep people at arm's length. Here the people lean over your desk and you can smell their armpits."

But in Providence Buddy was the man. When Sinatra wanted help getting a friend's child into Brown University, the Chairman of the Board turned to Cianci, not Patriarca. As Cianci told the story, according to former aide Paul Campbell, Sinatra called him one night, between sets of a concert, and asked the mayor to intercede at Brown. Cianci pulled some strings, and Sinatra's friend's kid became an Ivy Leaguer.

In the spring of 1979, when former San Francisco mayor Joseph Alioto came to the Verrazzano Day banquet, honoring Cianci as its man of the year, he paid homage to the prince of Providence. Cianci drove Alioto around Providence and, when he showed him the Fourth Ward, joked, "If Machiavelli were alive today, he would be a politician in the Fourth Ward."

Quipped Alioto: "Since they elected a [Republican] mayor, I'm sure that Machiavelli is alive and living in City Hall."

If Machiavelli had been around, he might have reminded Cianci of his dictum "The first impression that one gets of a ruler and of his brains is from seeing the men he has about him." Cianci, in his quest for power and a springboard to Washington, had surrounded himself with a motley crew—thugs and mob associates and political wheeler-dealers with their own scams and agendas.

He had married himelf to Tony Bucci, the Fourth Ward kingmaker who favored expensive silk shirts and used his political connections to build a lucrative downtown law practice. And Cianci relied on a cast of characters with names like Buckles and Blackjack to bring in the votes and sell campaign fund-raising tickets and help him control the patronage-rich Public Works Department, Larry McGarry's old power base.

When they weren't doing the mayor's bidding, they were extorting snowplow contractors and shaking down garbage-truck dealers and stealing asphalt and perfecting the art of the no-show job, a proud Providence tradition. They were looting city equipment, right down to the manhole covers, which were sold for scrap metal. They were trading contracts for cash, rigging bids, consorting with mobsters.

Ronald Glantz, Cianci's top aide, said that Cianci also tolerated corruption for another reason—because the mayor was the biggest crook of them all. Glantz said that he was an eyewitness to the corruption at City Hall—that he was Buddy's bagman.

LATE AT NIGHT the mayor's limousine would glide up to Ron Glantz's house on Overhill Road, on the East Side of Providence.

Glantz would be in bed when the phone rang, at 2 or 3 A.M. It was the mayor, saying that he was outside. Glantz would throw on a pair of jeans and a shirt, go downstairs, and slide into the backseat with Cianci. If the weather was warm, the mayor would tell his police driver to take a walk. In winter, Cianci would raise the glass divider so that he and Glantz could speak privately.

While the city slept, the mayor's mind was restlessly turning. He and Glantz would talk politics and strategy, trade gossip, laugh or bitch about who was screwing who at City Hall, plot and scheme. They would discuss bids and contracts and the thousand details involved in running a city.

Cianci leaned heavily on Glantz for information and advice, and to execute his orders. In the Mayor's War Room, as his office was known, Glantz was Cianci's top general. He was the city solicitor and the mayor's de facto chief of staff. He was Cianci's troubleshooter, handling crises with the city budget, going to Milwaukee to deal with the story of the Marquette rape accusation, and helping to orchestrate the Wednesday Night Massacre.

His detractors referred to him as "Mayor Glantz." One councilman called Glantz "the finest example of what a mayor or governor could want in terms of loyalty, ability, and political savvy—which is not to say that he's a fine human being."

Around City Hall, everyone called him Ronnie. He was a large, round-shouldered man with a quick wit and an easy smile, the political equivalent of a vaudeville act. His second cousin was Milton Berle. Glantz enjoyed power, was seduced by money and the good life, but also appreciated the humor in public service.

Once, when he was prosecuting Providence police cases as an assistant city solicitor under Joe Doorley, Glantz asked a witness to a South Providence grocery store shooting where the victim had been shot.

"In the chickens," the witness said.

Glantz, not sure he had heard right, asked again.

"In the chickens," the man repeated.

"Where's that?" asked the perplexed Glantz.

"Between the frozen food and the bread."

Glantz grew up in a Jewish neighborhood in South Providence. His father, who divorced his mother when Ronnie was twelve, managed a toy discounter and, Glantz remembered, "had the facility to make and lose money several times." The son became a lawyer, partly because he was idealistic and partly because his roommate at Boston University applied first. Glantz found that he liked constitutional law and the chance to help the underdog.

It was that spirit that inspired him to work in Joe Doorley's upstart campaign against the Democratic machine in 1964. Glantz's father also supported Doorley, even bringing in his cousin Milton Berle for a fundraiser. When Doorley won, he gave Ronnie a job as the fifth assistant city solicitor. Glantz was a bit player in the Doorley administration. Sometimes he'd drive the mayor to work or help out with the inventory at Doorley's Plantations Room at the Biltmore. Former Doorley officials remembered Glantz as a likeable guy who didn't always follow through and never told you anything you didn't want to hear.

The job permitted Glantz to witness firsthand the upheaval of the 1960s. He volunteered twelve hours a week as a legal adviser in South Providence, listening to residents' complaints about rats and sewage in their basement and trying to direct them to the appropriate city agency. He saw his old neighborhood, around Prairie Avenue, transformed into a war zone as protestors clashed with cops throwing tear-gas bombs.

Glantz also witnessed the city's mob culture up close. As a city lawyer assigned to police cases, he went to Pannone's Market in Silver Lake the day that bookies Rudy Marfeo and Anthony Melei were gunned down in 1968. He had never seen a dead body before, and he remembered picking his way around the bullet-riddled corpses in a state of shock. He also recalled the brouhaha that followed when Marfeo's family accused the cops of stealing Rudy's roll of money, which had vanished. Not long after that, he said, one of the officers bought a house in Narragansett.

Tony Bucci had been a partner in the law firm where Glantz had worked before going to City Hall, and the two remained friendly. When Bucci and Larry McGarry defected from Doorley in 1974, Glantz followed. He became the public face of Democrats for Cianci and a secret messenger between the McGarry faction and Buddy Cianci.

After Cianci won, he hired Glantz as a special adviser for legal affairs and stuck him in a small cubby in a back room of the mayor's executive offices. Then people started coming in, asking Glantz questions about this and that, how to get things done. Cianci reminded Glantz of Robert Redford in the movie *The Candidate*, who wins the election only to ask, "What do we do now?" Within a few months Glantz moved to the front office, to the large chamber just outside Cianci's door. Anyone going in to see the mayor had to pass by Glantz's desk. A new organizational chart showed most lines of authority flowing to Cianci through Glantz.

Glantz and Cianci would laugh and argue like a couple of frat brothers; an observer recalled one day seeing them fighting good-naturedly over a winning lottery ticket. When Cianci lost his temper, Glantz acted as a buffer between the mayor and his staff. He would defuse the tension by dancing around the office twirling an umbrella, in a pantomime of Gene Kelly in *Singin' in the Rain*, or pushing one of the secretaries down the hallway in her swivel chair. Once, Glantz came out of the mayor's office after an argument with Cianci, walked into a closet, shut the door, and let out a mock scream, then came out grinning.

Glantz had to laugh at the uproar that followed Cianci's decision in 1979 to cancel a concert at the Civic Center by the Who shortly after a stampede at a concert by the British rock group in Cincinnati killed eleven people. Cianci reveled in the national publicity he received, and Glantz led the cheers—"The mayor was on during San Francisco drive time," he exulted after one West Coast radio interview. When fans of the Who urged the mayor to reconsider, pointing out that the group's next concert in Buffalo had been fatality free, Cianci responded: "They perform in Cincinnati with eleven deaths and Buffalo with no deaths. That means when they perform, their average is 5.5 deaths." (Cianci eventually relented in the face of strong criticism, including rock fans chanting "Ayatollah Cianci" outside City Hall, but it was too late—the Who had decided they didn't want to play Providence.)

"Anybody that takes this business seriously, you're crazy," said Glantz, in a 1978 *Providence Journal* profile. "Politics is a hobby. The plotting and planning is fun. But the minute it becomes a profession, you have prostituted it."

Cianci began to rely more heavily on Glantz after his first year or so in office, when the mayor had a falling-out with his closest confidant, Mickey Farina.

Farina, the former Cranston real estate salesman, had been with Cianci from the beginning. He had managed his 1974 campaign and continued, after Cianci took office, to serve as his top political adviser. Cianci rewarded Farina by making him the director of Public Property, an influential department that handled city real estate and oversaw new construction and repairs to city buildings.

Elected as the anticorruption candidate, Cianci vowed to reform government. He opened previously secret board meetings, such as the Board of Contract and Supply, to the press and the public.

But that wasn't all that was wide open at City Hall.

One flight up from the mayor's office, on the third floor, Farina would throw parties that were well attended by city contractors. One contractor, Tommy Ricci, said that it was like a Dean Martin roast, with booze, broads, and merrymaking. Guys would sit around and talk about various scams— padding contracts, billing for phantom work. Eager to soak it all up, Farina picked the contractors' brains, recalled Ricci. "He wanted to learn quickly."

Eager to land city work, Ricci did his best to ingratiate himself with the director of Public Property. He said that he put a second floor on Farina's house in Cranston and did other work for him.

Cianci would stop by Farina's parties in Public Property and be envious, according to both Ricci and Glantz. He fumed that the cases of liquor weren't being sent to his office, and that Farina seemed to be building his own private fiefdom. Cianci wasn't stupid; he knew about Farina's dinners at the Old Canteen with city contractors, noticed the photographs on his walls of Farina with different people.

"Oh, you're doing pretty good," Cianci would mutter, drumming his pen furiously, according to Glantz.

Publicly, Cianci continued to emphasize running a clean government.

In the fall of 1975, during his first year as mayor, Cianci was in his office with Glantz, Farina, and an old friend, Anthony DiBiasio, a freelance contributor to *The Providence Journal*. DiBiasio was following Cianci around for a Sunday-magazine story about the mayor's style. According to DiBiasio's subsequent account, the mayor received a phone call from someone seeking his assistance. As Cianci greeted the unidentified caller, he scribbled the man's name on a piece of paper and held it up for Farina and Glantz to see.

"Watch it—that guy's a rat!" Farina exclaimed in a hoarse whisper.

Cianci listened for a while, then said, "Okay, let me tell you, I can't play it that way—you want it, you got to go to the boards like everyone else. I mean we just can't—"

The conversation continued until Cianci finally cut the caller off, saying, "Look, that's the way it's gotta be; give it a try that way, through channels, and see what you come up with. I'll help if I can, but it's got to go straight."

Hanging up, Cianci swiveled in his chair. "F'chrissakes, these guys are something else . . . all the time telling me how much they've done for me, and—"

"And it's usually the ones who didn't help when we needed it," interjected Farina.

"Regardless," continued Cianci. "I know you gotta treat people right, but I'm not going to screw up in this job over a guy like that."

"And you can't trust him, anyway," added Farina.

Cianci stood up and paced around his office. "What the hell, I—me and my mother—provided the bulk of the campaign money. Sure, others helped, but all I ever see and hear are these other names showing up for contracts and fees and everything, like they own me or the city."

He sat heavily back in his chair. "I want it up front, you hear?" Cianci continued, pointing at Farina and Glantz. "I'm not going to blow all this work for petty baloney like that. No way!"

Behind the scenes, Cianci's relationship with Farina was fraying. One day Glantz witnessed a blowup between the two men in the mayor's office. They started screaming and swearing at each other, then asked Glantz to leave. By early 1976 the break was public, though the reason remained a closely guarded secret. Cianci tried to fire Farina but couldn't, because he lacked the votes on the City Council.

Instead, Cianci tried to reassign Farina's purchasing power to a deputy who demonstrated his loyalty to the mayor by selling ten thousand dollars' worth of Cianci fund-raising tickets in the spring of 1977, many to city vendors. Shortly after the move, Farina struck back. He leaked a story to the *Journal*'s City Hall reporter, Doane Hulick, detailing how the deputy had often split up purchases from a chemical company with ties to Cianci—a tactic that circumvented the competitive-bidding requirement for purchases of $1,500 or more. For instance, when the Custom Chemical Corporation sold the city five fifty-five-gallon drums of antifreeze for $2,062, the purchase was split into two orders, each below the $1,500 bid threshold. Hulick found that Custom Chemical, one of whose partners was married to Cianci's cousin, and whose owners contributed generously to Citizens for Cianci, had seen its city business triple to $262,000 in the mayor's first two-plus years.

Glantz considered the split between Cianci and Farina a falling-out of thieves—Farina had gotten too greedy. Farina put the blame on Cianci and said that the two men began drifting apart after Farina urged the mayor to challenge John Chafee for the U.S. Senate in 1976, a suggestion Cianci rejected; Farina was no saint, but he had wanted to escape to Washington before the sewer of corruption in Providence sucked them in and made it harder to leave. In one instance, Farina allegedly learned from a City Hall janitor that Glantz had slipped into the Public Property office one weekend and steamed open envelopes containing sealed bids for a large garbage contract, in order to rig the bid for a company paying kickbacks.

Glantz said that Cianci feared Farina and what he knew. And Farina knew how to push Cianci's buttons. He told Glantz to tell "that fathead" that if Cianci did succeed in firing him, Farina would make a speech on the courthouse steps. Cianci ordered Glantz to have no further dealings with Farina.

Sitting in his limousine late at night, outside Glantz's house, Cianci would fret about Farina. "Is he going to the grand jury?" asked Cianci. "Do you think he's gonna do it?"

AFTER HIS REELECTION in 1978, Cianci finally mustered the council votes to oust Mickey Farina. The man who had been instrumental in Buddy's rise left City Hall quietly. There were no speeches, on the courthouse steps or elsewhere.

But the air of looseness remained as city business flowed to the mayor's cronies. Cianci's mentor, former attorney general Herbert DeSimone, received city legal work. His advertising guru, Normand Roussel, was hired to do promotional films, paid for with federal HUD funds. His Republican city chairman, Joseph DiSanto, received no-bid contracts for his family company, Henry Oil. (In 1979 another Cianci aide, Joseph Vileno, accused DiSanto of threatening to have him fired if he didn't steer emergency heating work to Henry Oil.)

The mayor's campaign contributors shared in the largesse, reaping lucrative city contracts for trash hauling, sewage-plant repairs, snow-plowing, street paving, street sweeping, school repairs, construction projects, school-bus contracts, city leases.

They would all gather regularly in the mayor's office for meetings of his campaign fund-raising committee. It was a large group, forty to fifty strong. All the department directors would attend, as well as contractors and subcontractors who worked for the city. Cianci would sit at his desk while his supporters reported their progress. The room was heavy with large stomachs and gold jewelry. The mayor's mother, Esther, sat at a card table, tracking ticket sales and collecting the money. Cash—legal then— was preferred.

If someone didn't sell enough tickets, Cianci would pressure them to sell more. Everyone was expected to contribute; the mayor was quick to remind people where their loyalty should lie, saying things like "Do you like your paycheck?" An internal Citizens for Cianci memo laid out a fund-raising strategy that included a birthday party for the mayor, "to allow people to pay homage."

Therese S. Kelly, who headed the mayor's Office of Community Development, said that Cianci once ordered her to fire an aide who had refused to buy a hundred-dollar fund-raising ticket. She bought a ticket for him instead. "It didn't surprise me at all," she later said, "because that was the way the mayor operated."

As a Republican in a Democratic city, Cianci always felt insecure about his position, and consequently he spent heavily on his campaigns. He saturated television and radio with ads and hired the best pollsters and consultants, top national GOP operatives like Fred Steeper, Gerald Ford's pollster, and Lynn Mueller.

Former aides said that Cianci also spent campaign funds on personal expenses, even the family butcher's bill. Rhode Island's campaign-finance laws were looser then; in nonelection years candidates did not have to report how they spent their money. The mayor's executive secretary, Margaret McClacken, his mother's good friend, paid the bills. His mother, a shrewd, tough businesswoman, controlled the campaign accounts.

At his desk next to the mayor's office, Ronnie Glantz later described sitting at the confluence of two rivers of cash—the city funds that flowed out to city contractors and the money that came flowing back to Cianci, like the tide pushing up Narragansett Bay. According to Glantz, a lot of money found its way to a safe in Cianci's mother's house. One day in 1979, he said, Cianci heard that someone might try to rob his mother's house, because there was $500,000 cash in the safe. Glantz said that the mayor called a friendly police officer and asked him to guard the house.

As Cianci's right-hand man, Glantz helped rig bids and fix contracts so that the mayor's men would receive the business. Glantz said that the mayor directed him to tailor the bid specifications for the city school-bus contract to fit one bidder, United Truck and Bus. The owner, Robert Doorley, was Joe Doorley's cousin, but he had no problem doing business with Cianci. According to Glantz, Cianci boasted that he had received a twenty-five-thousand-dollar payoff from Doorley.

Bruce Melucci, a former Cianci aide who was unaware of any behind-the-scenes machinations on the school-bus contract, remembered Doorley as a big campaign contributor who attended the mayor's ticket-committee meetings. Melucci also remembered Doorley's saying, "I'm the only bidder. How can I lose?" In Melucci's view, Cianci's "incessant demand for money" created an atmosphere ripe for abuse. "Everybody was trying to outdo each other, to look the best in the boss's eyes," Melucci said.

Other big contractors would pass by Glantz's desk to see the mayor. Glantz became friendly with Danny and Jack Capuano, brothers who ran a trash-hauling company; engineering executive Gene Castellucci, whose firm redesigned the city sewage plant; and contractor Tony Rosciti, who drove a Mercedes convertible.

Glantz would go to lunch up on the Hill with Castellucci, Rosciti, and Norm Roussel. He had drinks with the Capuanos at the Marriott and attended their Super Bowl party at a restaurant in Cranston. Glantz said that the contractors assumed that he knew everything that was going on and spoke freely of making payoffs to the mayor.

Glantz also heard it from the other end; Joe DiSanto would complain that Buddy got all the money and he got nothing.

Cianci, in his late-night discourses in the back of his limousine, or in his office, would tell Glantz that the Capuanos had kicked back hundreds of thousands of dollars for various trash-hauling and sludge-removal contracts. The mayor also confided to Glantz that he got $100,000 from Tony Rosciti for a big street-sweeping contract. Glantz said that Cianci told him about the kickbacks partly because he needed Glantz, as his city solicitor, to help dot the i's and cross the t's to make the contracts look legitimate. Often Cianci would tell Glantz that he wanted him to sign something first, adding, "I'm not signing anything until your name is on it." The mayor, ever the prosecutor, was paranoid about being discovered, said Glantz. Had he covered his tracks well enough? Would the *Journal* find out?

But Glantz believed that arrogance also drove Cianci to confide in him—he enjoyed proving that he could outfox anyone and showing off how well he could work the levers of power. Cianci equated money with power, said Glantz, so he needed to brag about his financial conquests.

When Farina faded from the picture, Glantz and Joe DiSanto became the mayor's confidants. Glantz said that they would discuss ways of writing the bid specifications so that the desired contractor would win, or splitting up a big job into smaller, no-bid jobs that fell under the fifteen-hundred-dollar threshold for competitive bids.

Another favorite trick was the "emergency contract." If a water main burst, or a school roof sprang a leak, city officials would exaggerate the severity of the problem and declare a fake emergency. Then a contractor could be picked without going through competitive bidding, and bill as much as he wanted. Glantz recalled Cianci, DiSanto, and Rosciti, on the sidewalk outside Glantz's stepfather's funeral, discussing one fake emergency, involving a downtown aqueduct.

As the dirty deals multiplied, Glantz found himself drawn further into the mayor's inner circle.

One day, said Glantz, he and Cianci were visiting DiSanto, who was hospitalized with back trouble, when another big booster, Jaguar dealer Jake Kaplan, came by the hospital room and handed the mayor a thousand dollars in cash. Glantz didn't know what the money was for—it could have been a legitimate campaign contribution or it could have been a bribe, he said. Kaplan, a flamboyant former car racer who drove a Rolls-Royce, leased property to the city.

Another time, Glantz said, Cianci called him into his office and instructed him to drive to the Marriott Hotel and pick up a package from James Forte, a partner in a construction company that repaired city sidewalks. As Glantz described it, it was late on a weekday afternoon. He drove the short distance from City Hall to the Marriott, which was behind the State House, and waited in a quiet corner of the large parking lot. Forte pulled his car in. Glantz got out and walked over to Forte's car. Without getting out, Forte wordlessly handed over a package wrapped in tinfoil, then drove away. Glantz brought the package to City Hall, where Cianci and DiSanto were waiting, and handed it to Cianci, who opened it to reveal stacks of hundred-dollar bills. The mayor counted ten thousand dollars and gave a thousand apiece to Glantz and DiSanto.

One of Cianci's former police drivers recalled walking into Glantz's office one day, while Glantz was next door in the mayor's office, and seeing his desk covered with stacks of money tied in rubber bands. Glantz's fur coat was draped over the chair. Since the mayor's office was right through the doorway, the driver found it hard to believe that the mayor wasn't aware of what was going on. Besides, the driver said, there were nights when he would drive Cianci around to various events—charity functions, political banquets, wakes—and the mayor would stand chatting with someone by the side of his limousine as he was leaving. Wordlessly, the person would casually drop a brick-shaped package wrapped in aluminum foil on the front seat. The brick would sit there as they made their rounds. "Guard that with your life," Cianci would say. At the end of the evening, the driver said, Cianci would gather it up with his papers and take it into his house.

Farina, no friend to Glantz, nevertheless felt that it was ridiculous to believe that Glantz could be doing this on his own; in his view, Cianci was corrupt, too, and paid close attention to the big-money city contracts and the actions of the influential Board of Contract and Supply. At some meetings, Glantz sat by the mayor's side.

As the money poured in, some stuck to Glantz's fingers. Given his position at the mayor's right hand, people were eager to be his friend. They would stop by, shake his hand, and palm him some cash. They would buy him dinner, send him flowers, drop off Christmas presents or a bottle of liquor. "We want you to have this," they would say.

He also became involved in his own scam, with Tony Bucci, to extort kickbacks for the purchase of city garbage trucks in the spring of 1979. The man paying the kickbacks was Joe Doorley's old pal North Providence car dealer Jimmy Notorantonio. But Jimmy Noto had bigger plans. In one of the wilder schemes of Cianci's first administration, Bucci was helping Notorantonio line up financing to build a sewage-sludge incinerator on the Providence waterfront—to turn trash into cash. Cianci was under pressure to address pollution problems at the aging Providence sewage plant. Greasy balls of sewage were washing up on the beaches down Narragansett Bay; sixty-five million gallons of raw sewage a day gushed into the bay. The federal Environmental Protection Agency was threatening massive fines. Meanwhile, the process of repairing the 1899 sewage plant was rife with corruption, from the kickbacks Glantz alleged had been paid for the contracts to no-show workers to the theft of equipment—everything from work gloves to sixty-pound cast-iron-and-steel valves. When Providence police investigating the thefts asked the plant's forty-two workers to take lie-detector tests, all forty-two refused, on the advice of counsel.

Jimmy Noto's scheme to help solve Cianci's sewage woes was elegant.

In a deal orchestrated by Glantz, the city would pay Notorantonio to take the sludge off its hands. Then Notorantonio, backed by a multimillion-dollar federal loan, would build an incinerator with state-of-the-art German technology and transform the sludge into flammable bricks that could be sold for fuel. His company was named Inge—for "I Never Get Enough." But the venture eventually collapsed in a tangle of lawsuits, fraud allegations, and criminal investigations. Someone even tried to blow up the unfinished incinerator, which never opened.

Meanwhile, Glantz moved on to other deals. He pursued outside business interests on the side, such as a partnership seeking to build a federally funded public-housing project. He began to feel invincible, like a fighter pilot who can't be shot down. But flying wasn't always fun.

In the fall of 1979, Glantz, DiSanto, and Cianci went in together on the purchase of a helicopter. The mayor was gearing up to run for governor, and he needed it to get around the state more quickly. But the partners also viewed it as a business proposition, figuring to make money by leasing it to the campaign and taking a tax write-off for depreciation.

Glantz and DiSanto were in the helicopter one day when it tried to take off in muggy air and nearly struck some utility wires. Another time, the chopper was lifting off from the Port of Providence, bearing Cianci to Woonsocket, in northern Rhode Island, when it struck a wire. The pilot brought the wobbling copter down in one of Jake Kaplan's car lots. Cianci started to get out when snarling guard dogs came rushing at him; he slammed the door and radioed the police for help.

WINDS OF CHANGE were blowing across Rhode Island. In the spring of 1980 the rotors of Buddy Cianci's helicopter stirred the air from Westerly to Woonsocket.

He was the can-do mayor of the comeback city, the energetic urban philosopher who could cut through red tape and bring home the bacon—fifty million dollars in downtown investment since taking office in 1975, supported by another ten million in city and federal funds.

He announced his candidacy with the slogan "What a governor he'll make." From his perch in the sky, Cianci could see the State House and, beyond the horizon, the United States Senate.

Although Providence still had a long way to go, Cianci was a genius at seeing the possibilities of arcane concepts like historic preservation and "intermodal transportation centers" (a fancy way of describing a downtown bus interchange). By personally pushing a handful of high-profile projects—the reopening of the Biltmore, the construction of a new banking office tower, the rejuvenation of Federal Hill—Cianci created a sense of excitement and progress that masked Providence's underlying corruption and fiscal chaos. In the process, he captured headlines and won votes. Cianci spoke of the "texture" of neighborhoods and of the importance of managing a city "like a violinist tuning a Stradivarius." He made people feel good about themselves, and for that they could overlook his flaws—if they could even see them in the all-encompassing whirlwind that was Buddy.

The mayor realized that Providence's stagnation had been a blessing in one sense—sparing its rich stock of historic buildings from the wrecking ball of urban renewal. In May he dazzled a national forum on historic preservation at the National Gallery in Washington with a witty presentation. The forum's participants, who included the vice president's wife, Joan Mondale, awoke from a slumberous series of speeches to take notice of the fast-talking, wisecracking mayor from Providence.

"Cities are great," proclaimed Cianci, "because they make love to people."

The crowd oohed and aahed as he showed them before-and-after slides of the rococo Ocean State Theater, which he had helped save from demolition.

"It kind of reminds you of being in Austria just before the war," narrated Cianci.

Another slide showed Cianci and his family walking down a Providence street. "That's a political picture," he quipped. "We'll keep that up for a while."

Kenneth Orenstein, Cianci's downtown development and preservation coordinator, recalled prepping the mayor to testify before Congress regarding tax credits for historic preservation. Cianci was a quick study who could take a few key words—noun, verb, adjective—and speak for fifteen minutes as if he owned the subject. After Cianci's congressional testimony, a staffer from the House Ways and Means Committee told Orenstein, "I've seen governors, senators, representatives—I've seen them all—but none better than your mayor."

Back home, advisers to the likeable two-term governor, J. Joseph Garrahy, scrutinized their private polls and cringed. Garrahy, the affable former beer salesman, product of the Irish Democratic machine in Providence and plaid-shirted hero of the Blizzard of '78, was surprisingly vulnerable. His focus groups found the dynamic Cianci scoring well as a leader compared with the more laid-back Garrahy, despite questions about Cianci's personal character and the integrity of his administration. In June 1980 Cianci's polls put him within three points of Garrahy, who six months earlier had led the mayor by eighteen points.

The helicopter became the indefatigable Cianci's trademark. He criss-crossed the state from dawn to well past dusk, barreling into banquet halls and senior-citizens luncheons, pumping hands at factory gates, gathering steam as the day unwound. "There's no schedule that can make me tired," he declared.

Cianci characterized his campaign with a joke about a chicken and a pig who decide to cook breakfast for their farmer. The chicken suggests bacon and eggs. The pig replies: "For you, that's a sacrifice. For me, it's a total commitment."

Despite the porcine imagery, Cianci was looking svelte. His Republican handlers had sought to "Yankee him up" for the campaign, one adviser recalled. He shed fifty pounds and traded his polyester suits and wide ties for blazers and khakis. His popularity surged when the mayor was barred from the historic Fourth of July parade in Bristol, Rhode Island.

The Bristol parade, dating back to 1785, was the oldest Fourth of July parade in the nation, a red, white, and blue pageant of Americana that drew several hundred thousand revelers to the picturesque old seaport on Narragansett Bay. Not wanting to be overrun by politicians, the parade's guardians had a policy of allowing only elected federal, state, and Bristol officials to march. Nevertheless, Cianci had marched every year since becoming mayor, tagging along with the Rhode Island Matadors, a Providence drum-and-bugle corps.

After the 1979 parade the organizers had written Cianci a letter "censuring" him for his participation. Now, in the weeks leading up to the 1980 parade, he was forbidden to march. As governor, Joe Garrahy could march—but not his challenger. Banned in Bristol, Cianci fired back with his own declaration of independence, vowing to show up anyway.

"I thought we're celebrating independence from tyranny," he said.

Five days before the parade, the Bristol Town Council voted unanimously to uphold the ban on Buddy. The police chief announced that two officers would be stationed at the parade's starting point to bar uninvited guests and arrest anyone who caused a disturbance.

"Let them arrest me," he said. "I am going to march to celebrate the joy of being an American."

Back in Providence, several of the mayor's men were also celebrating their constitutional rights—most notably the right to be presumed innocent and the right against self-incrimination.

In May seven men were indicted in a scam involving no-show jobs at the Department of Public Works. Several, including John D. Melvin, the city highway superintendent, had ties to mobsters. Melvin was on the job despite his arrest the previous year on unrelated charges of using a stolen credit card and kidnapping and beating a suspected mob informant with a wooden ax handle. One of the accused no-shows had testified as an alibi witness the previous year at the trial of mobsters Gerald and Harold Tillinghast for the execution of George Basmajian.

Anthony "Blackjack" DelSanto, an assistant highway superintendent and Cianci lieutenant, accused the Democratic attorney general of trying to smear the mayor. DelSanto's grand-jury appearance had turned sour when the prosecutor started grilling him about alleged mob control of various Providence nightclubs. At that point he refused to answer any more questions.

"They are trying to frame people," complained DelSanto. "I hang with a lot of 'wiseguys.' I grew up with them [on Federal Hill]. What they do on the side is their own business. . . . I don't know anything about organized crime. I work for a living." And in case anyone wondered, DelSanto added, the nickname "Blackjack" had been in his family for three generations.

Cianci had also testified to the grand jury, to explain a meeting that he had called with his department heads the previous fall to discuss the investigation. The mayor had gotten angry when he learned that the state police were conducting surveillance of alleged no-show employees on Federal Hill without telling him. Some of the workers had spotted the cops taking their pictures, and alerted Cianci. The mayor called Colonel Walter Stone, the legendary superintendent of the state police, to complain. Afterward, Cianci was bitter toward the state police. One day, while he was running for governor, Cianci was riding a horse in another parade when the animal defecated on the street. The mayor looked at a state trooper standing nearby and said, "Tell Stone that when I'm governor, he'll be cleaning this up."

The day before the Bristol parade in 1980 there was more bad news, this time in Cianci's police department. A lieutenant and a sergeant who headed the bad-check squad were indicted for recruiting mobster Dante Sciarra to intimidate a witness who had implicated the sergeant in a thirty-thousand-dollar bad-check scheme. Both police officers were active political supporters of the mayor. The sergeant, Robert C. Martini, sometimes spent his entire shift peddling hundred-dollar Cianci fund-raising tickets to businessmen on his beat rather than investigating bad-check complaints, according to his partner.

Former major John J. Leyden, who led the investigation, said that Cianci's police chief, Angelo Ricci, tried to squelch the case because Martini was a big fund-raiser for Cianci. When Leyden decided to wire up the informant so that he could tape Sciarra threatening him, the major deliberately didn't tell Ricci, because the chief was also part of the investigation, he said.

The Fourth of July dawned hot and hazy. Late in the morning the mayor's helicopter descended out of a sweltering sky on the town of Bristol.

"If they want to make an arrest, they'll have to prove that they're right," he had said a few days before. "If they're going to stop me, they will have to suffer the consequences personally."

The parade committee had voiced similar resolve. "Cianci comes down here looking like some rhinestone cowboy, but I'm not afraid of him," grumbled one committee member.

But when the mayor's helicopter touched down at Bristol High School, he was met only by Miss Rhode Island and her entourage, who climbed a hill to greet him. Town officials had backed down in the face of overwhelming public sentiment for Cianci. As the mayor rounded the corner onto red, white, and blue–striped Hope Street, near the parade's start, the crowd roared its approval.

"Hey, Buddy, you made it!"

"Congratulations, Governor!"

Sweating in the ninety-degree heat in his blue blazer and white pants, Cianci beamed as well-wishers mobbed him, offering hugs, kisses, handshakes, and cold drinks. Two women held up a banner that said BABES FOR BUDDY. A friend jokingly tried to slip a pair of plastic handcuffs on him. The crush of people forced Cianci to repeatedly fall behind the Matadors' color guard.

The mayor received by far the biggest cheers—bigger than the response for Governor Garrahy or Senators Chafee and Pell or Rhode Island's two congressmen. A record three hundred thousand spectators had turned out, twice what had been forecast, many eager to see what would happen to Buddy.

A few weeks after stealing the show in Bristol, Cianci spoke at the Republican National Convention in Detroit, where he blasted Jimmy Carter— "a president who promised plums four years ago and delivered us peanuts instead"—and praised Ronald Reagan. In the greenroom before going out, Cianci rubbed elbows with Billy Graham and Marie Osmond, and rehearsed in front of Wayne Newton. Cianci told Newton that if he lost the governor's race, maybe he could join the entertainer's Las Vegas act. Newton responded by predicting a Cianci victory.

Back home, while Cianci campaigned for governor, Ronnie Glantz was the de facto mayor. During a strategy session early in the year, the subject of the city's troubled finances had come up. Cianci couldn't afford a budget crisis this year, when he was running for governor. Glantz reassured Cianci that he could keep a lid on things. But he couldn't.

A summer of scandal, with the police and Public Works indictments, was followed by a fall of fiscal failings. In September officials conceded that the city was running a projected deficit of twelve million dollars. In October Cianci said he might have to lay off several hundred city workers. In protest, garbagemen staged a work slowdown. Trash piled up around the city. One East Sider complained, "If he wants to run the state, God help us."

Compounding his problems was the boorish nature lurking behind Cianci's charismatic exterior. That summer he publicly bullied the chairman of a citizens' review board looking into how he had spent millions of dollars in federal community-development funds. Afterward the chairman accused Cianci of practicing "gangster politics."

Cianci could be even worse in private, as officials at Brown University learned in the spring of 1980, when the mayor's nephew was denied admission.

Two of Cianci's nephews had applied to Brown. One was accepted, the other rejected. Before the letters went out, Brown admissions director James H. Rogers called the mayor, a courtesy he normally extended to prominent people. Cianci was furious. He screamed about the injustice of the decision, given everything that he had done for Brown, and shouted, "Don't you know who I am?" Rogers tried to speak, but Cianci kept cutting him off. Finally, the admissions director lost his temper and shouted into the phone, "Shut up, you jerk!"

There was a sudden silence. Then, calmly, Cianci said, "It's not nice to call the mayor a jerk," and hung up.

Not long afterward, Brown's athletic director, John Parry, learned that the city had delayed what should have been routine zoning variances for the university's new athletic complex, the Olney-Margolies Center. Shortly thereafter, said Parry, he encountered Cianci at the St. Joseph's Day parade and asked the mayor about the holdup. Cianci, according to Parry, replied that Brown's zoning application would sit for as long as his nephew's rejected application did.

Parry reported the threat to Howard Swearer, then Brown's president. Swearer talked to Cianci and told him that it didn't make sense for the mayor to act this way, especially since he was running for governor. The mayor relented. Brown got its variances, without admitting Cianci's nephew. (In later years, however, when Cianci told the story he implied that the nephew did get in.)

By early October the race for governor was essentially over. Three weeks before the election, polls showed Garrahy with more than 70 percent of the vote. Publicly, Cianci clung defiantly to hope and maintained his frenetic campaigning, but the helicopter had lost its lift. Earlier that year Jimmy Breslin, speaking at Roger Williams College in Bristol, had watched Cianci's aerial entrance in disbelief.

"What the fuck is that?" he asked his companion, Rhode Island writer Bill Reynolds.

"The mayor's helicopter," answered Reynolds.

Breslin shook his head. "If that was New York," he said, "we'd shoot the fucking thing down."

In the waning days, Cianci's campaign for governor went from bad to worse. Two weeks before the election the mayor issued layoff notices to nearly three hundred city workers. City Hall offices went dark as several hundred more workers walked out in protest. Glantz fumed when two Public Works engineers who had gotten pink slips refused to man the hurricane barrier during a storm that had sent floodwaters rising.

Shortly after that storm subsided, Glantz acknowledged to a *Providence Journal* reporter, four days before the election, that city taxpayers could face a midyear tax increase to plug the deficit. Then he headed to Yonkers, New York, to interview for the vacant city manager's job.

Cianci angrily denied Glantz's prediction, but the damage had been done. Close in the polls after his triumphant Fourth of July march, Cianci was swamped by Garrahy on election day. He lost every city and town in Rhode Island, and every ward in Providence. In fact, he carried just one polling place in Providence—St. Bart's Hall, in his native Silver Lake.

He greeted his tearful supporters in the seventeenth-floor Biltmore ballroom with humor and grace, invoking Abraham Lincoln and John F. Kennedy on the pain of defeat. He wanted to "show the people of the State of Rhode Island that I know how to lose, too." Then he smiled and said, "I really appreciate the overwhelming mandate from people all over the State of Rhode Island to continue my work in the City of Providence."

He had two years left in his term as mayor, but Cianci's loss was so lopsided, and Providence's financial problems so severe, that it seemed his days in City Hall were numbered, too.

Ronnie Glantz realized that it was time for him to leave. He was tired of the manic pace. And the feds were starting to circle City Hall. Subpoenas were flying around the building. Glantz recalled Cianci's calling in employees after their grand-jury testimony to debrief them, his pen tapping nervously on his desk.

Glantz was convinced that it was just a matter of time before someone got indicted. There was, he said, "an atmosphere of absolute looseness." One day, after he had stopped by Joe DiSanto's house to say that he'd had enough, the doorbell rang. It was a federal prosecutor and four FBI agents, stopping by to "chat."

Cianci also contemplated leaving. He angled for an ambassadorship from the newly elected president, Ronald Reagan, preferably to Italy. But his star had diminished. He was never seriously considered. With no Washington appointment forthcoming, Cianci put a halt to the speculation.

"My challenge is right here," he said. "I don't know what my political future will be, but I'm going to be here for a while."

Privately, Cianci was devastated by his first electoral defeat. It was a resounding personal rejection of a man who lived for public affirmation. In the days that followed, an aide recalled, Cianci sat morosely in his office, drinking vodka.

"Those sons of bitches," he said.

THE YEAR AFTER his ill-fated run for governor, Buddy Cianci returned to a city in disarray.

Providence was on the verge of bankruptcy. A committee of bankers and businessmen took control of the city's finances. Angry taxpayers demanded the mayor's resignation after he imposed a midyear tax hike. (Glantz's prediction had proven accurate.) Protected by a half-dozen policemen, Cianci marched through an angry mob at City Hall to beseech the City Council to approve his tax increase so that Providence wouldn't go the way of Cleveland, a bankrupt city whose polluted river had burst into flames.

The accompanying budget cuts and layoffs pushed the city's biggest labor union into open revolt. Much of the turmoil centered around the Department of Public Works, the department responsible for paving the roads, plowing the streets, fixing the sidewalks, collecting the trash, and maintaining the sewers, and the traditional dumping ground for political hacks and wiseguys.

Following his reelection in 1978, Cianci had put Democratic chairman Tony Bucci's brother-in-law, Clement Cesaro, in charge of Public Works. One of Cesaro's first actions had been to sign off on a deal orchestrated by Bucci to buy garbage trucks for the city from a North Providence car dealer—a deal that involved seventy-seven thousand dollars in kickbacks to Bucci and Glantz.

But by the middle of 1979, the Bucci-Cianci alliance had ended. Cesaro said later that the falling-out occurred because Cianci had broken a promise to Bucci to become a Democrat after the 1978 election. Others said that the split was inevitable, given the sizeable egos of the two men and Bucci's heavy-handed nature. Bucci, known as "Mr. Asphalt" after he took a case involving import restrictions on liquid asphalt all the way to the U.S. Supreme Court, had once threatened to put an opponent's political career "in a pine box." On nights the City Council met, Bucci would leave the light on in his downtown law office, which was visible from City Hall, to signal members how they should vote.

Stuck with Cesaro at Public Works, Cianci turned to two of his deputies, Edward "Buckles" Melise and Anthony "Blackjack" DelSanto. Their names would become catchphrases for the massive municipal corruption probes to follow, embodying the sense of lawlessness that overtook Buddy Cianci's City Hall in the early 1980s.

Buckles and Blackjack came from Federal Hill, where they served on the Thirteenth Ward Democratic Committee, which had endorsed Cianci. Cianci made them his men at Public Works. He put Buckles in charge of vermin control. Blackjack controlled the highways.

Bucci explained their rise this way: "Good waiters get good tips."

Buckles, who drove a pink Cadillac and had a weakness for crap games, was the more politically active of the two—and ultimately the one whom the authorities would zero in on. Cianci would refer to Buckles as a "dese, dem, and dose guy." As the city's chief rat exterminator, he was so enthusiastic that he bought rat poison in record quantities—twice as much as the City of Cleveland, which was four times as big. His program wound up feeding the rats instead of killing them. Bristling at criticism that he was incompetent, Buckles said that he had studied up on the subject—he had even gone to the library and "breezed" through a book about it.

Buckles and Blackjack would saunter into the mayor's office on city business in their jeans and leather jackets. DelSanto, a big man who enjoyed clowning around, would joke with the mayor's secretaries. "Is the mayor bothering you? Should I break his legs?" Cianci laughed along. The mayor who had met the queen of England and impishly given her a china plate depicting the Revolutionary War–era sloop *Providence,* which had fought the British, could also mix it up with Buckles and Blackjack.

According to Buckles's friend Tommy Ricci, the contractor who had grown up across the street from him on Gessler Street in Federal Hill, Buckles was one of Buddy's bagmen. Cianci's former police driver, who had recalled seeing money on Glantz's desk and Cianci's receipt of foil-wrapped packages on their evening rounds, also remembered sitting in the mayor's outer office on different occasions and seeing Buckles go into the mayor's office with a bag and leave emptyhanded.

But Buckles had a weakness for crap games and couldn't always be counted on to come back with the money. Ricci recalled accompanying Buckles on a gambling junket to Atlantic City, where many of the casino regulars knew him. The allure of the dice led to Ricci's taking over Buckles's collection duties for about a year in the late seventies. Every week, Ricci recalled, someone at City Hall would leave a shoebox with a list of names and Ricci would make his rounds. He'd throw a gym bag in the trunk of his Lincoln and then pop the trunk and let the contractor make his own deposit. He brought the bag back to City Hall in the early evening, after most workers had departed, and threw it on a table in a room where Cianci and a handful of aides were waiting.

Ricci described a system that was loose and disorganized. Sometimes, he said, he would palm the mayor a couple thousand dollars; on other occasions, he would give it to someone else. There were periodic shakeups, if someone was suspected of skimming, and as Cianci sought to insulate himself.

Ricci was an unshaven street philosopher, a hulking, scary-looking man with dirt under his fingernails and a line of tattoos marching up his muscular left forearm—a can, an eye, a screw, the letter *U*, and a question mark. "All I did was give kickbacks," he said. "Is that a crime or what?"

His father was a contractor, and when Ricci was seventeen he struck out on his own. While Joe Doorley was mayor, Ricci started getting small jobs with the city, such as fixing school roofs. He learned the nuances of City Hall—how to bid on a job and how to split a bigger job into two smaller jobs so that it wouldn't have to go out to bid. He learned that you could charge more when it was an "emergency contract." He set up a myriad of companies, including the Busy Bee Construction Company, to conceal how much city work he was actually getting.

Ricci also learned the value of politics. He bought sound equipment and put it on a used car for campaigns. The city work poured in. When Cianci challenged Doorley in 1974, Ricci publicly supported Doorley but privately hedged his bets, steering relatives, money, and cars with sound equipment to the Cianci campaign. When Cianci won, Ricci jumped on the bandwagon. He and his friend Caesar Brown, an electrician and chairman of the Seventh Ward Republican Committee in Silver Lake, threw fund-raising parties for Cianci.

As Ricci's influence grew, he received more and more city work. But after some negative publicity about a roof job at a school, he said, he had to slip Cianci twenty-five hundred dollars in cash, plus a box of expensive Cuban cigars, or "heaters," to get back on the list. Ricci said that he also did free work on Cianci's house before receptions for dignitaries—once for presidential candidate John Connally, another time for Henry Kissinger. Ricci said that he made his money back on one of the mayor's house jobs by padding a city contract to redo the Gessler Street swimming pool, in his and Buckles's old neighborhood. (Farina also was aware of Ricci's and Buckles's roles as bagmen, Buckles's gambling problem, and Ricci's gift to the mayor of a box of "Cuban heaters," as well as his padding on the Gessler Street pool job to cover work at Cianci's house.)

In 1977, Tommy Ricci got to meet Gerald Ford when the former president came to Providence for a Cianci fund-raiser. The evening represented a clash of the two cultures that made up Buddy's world. After a private City Hall reception for such dignitaries as John Chafee, John Pastore, Larry McGarry, the bishop of Providence, and prominent businessmen, Ford went to the Marriott, where Secret Service agents watched nervously as he shook hands with the likes of Ricci, city workers, and ward heelers.

After greeting Ford, Ricci and his pals left the ballroom and headed for the bar off the lobby of the Marriott. A woman joined them. A guy she had been with, who was drunk, got mad and took a swing at her. Then he charged Ricci's friends. In the melee that followed, the man staggered to his feet, a gun in one hand and a police radio in the other to call for help; he was an off-duty Providence cop. Someone punched him and he collapsed. Suddenly, the Marriott bar was filled with Providence police and Secret Service agents brandishing weapons.

Later, after being hauled down to the police station for questioning and then released, Ricci and his pals laughed. "Where else can you get arrested," he asked, "while visiting the president of the United States?"

Ricci was always on the lookout for new opportunities. In the years following the Blizzard of '78, he went to Buckles, who was in charge of snowplowing at Public Works, and got put on the list of "stand-by crews"—plowers who would be called in, and paid, when there was the threat of a storm. Ricci's annual Christmas parties became larger and livelier. He moved them from his garage on Hartford Avenue to nice restaurants. He hired bands and a magician. One year, as the magician performed, one of Ricci's friends shouted, "Can you turn snow into money? Tommy can!" Later it began to snow. The party-goers rushed out to get their plows.

In 1980, after Buckles stood by the mayor in his battle with Tony Bucci and Clem Cesaro, he was promoted to highway superintendent, the number-two job at Public Works. Another trusted Cianci ally, Joseph DiSanto, took over at Public Works after Cianci finally succeeded in forcing out Cesaro.

As the supervisor of 180 city workers and the overseer of snowplowing and street-paving contracts, Buckles was in a position to sell a lot of Cianci fund-raiser tickets. He was a regular at the mayor's cocktail parties and meetings of the tickets committee, his pink Caddy parked illegally outside City Hall.

One of Buckles's employees had also made rats his sworn enemy—as part of his Mafia induction ceremony. Blackjack's brother, William "Blackjack" DelSanto, also known as "Billy Black" to distinguish himself from his brother, was a *capo regime* in the Patriarca crime family. He was also a city "sidewalk inspector," a job that left him plenty of time to hang out with other wiseguys on the sidewalk in front of Tony's Colonial Market on Federal Hill. Early in 1979, the Rhode Island State Police tailed Billy Black and Raymond "Junior" Patriarca to the Boston headquarters of underboss

Gennaro "Jerry" Angiulo. He had also been present for a mob induction ceremony in Boston a few years earlier, when Angiulo had asked the inductee, "If your brother became a rat, would you kill him?"

What exactly Billy Black did as a sidewalk inspector, Buckles couldn't say, but he defended him as a good worker.

Buckles and Billy Black were also friendly with another notorious wiseguy, Bobo Marrapese, whom Buddy Cianci had once prosecuted for conspiracy to steal a camper, in the infamous Case of the Italian Wedding Soup. Bobo had come far in the decade since Cianci had sent him to prison. He ran a sizeable gambling and loan-sharking operation, and his rap sheet included arrests for threatening to kill someone, assault, possession of stolen goods, breaking and entering, larceny, and possession of a machine gun. He ran the Acorn Social Club, around the corner from Tony's Colonial Market. Through Buckles, Bobo also received city snowplowing work and had other deals cooking at Public Works.

In the summer of 1981, with his political fortunes sagging, Cianci counted heavily on allies like Buckles when he was confronted with a messy garbage strike. Although nobody realized it at first, the Great Garbage Strike would have an impact on the mayor's uncertain political fortunes.

UNDER COVER OF darkness on a warm summer night, a band of men slipped, commando-style, into the Public Works garages near the Providence waterfront and spirited away a dozen city garbage trucks.

They drove the trucks across town to an empty used-car lot, where a small army was gathering. About a dozen other trucks were already parked in the back of the fenced lot, hidden behind a blue school bus.

Inside the former showroom, about fifty-five men shuffled about nervously. A few minutes after 1 A.M., Buddy Cianci arrived. The mayor hurried inside. Someone closed the blinds. From the outside, the building appeared deserted in the half-light of a waning moon.

Cianci wore a short-sleeved blue shirt and no tie.

"We mean business and we're not going to let anyone stop you from doing your job," he barked. "You will be protected physically. We're not going to stand for any abuse. One hundred policemen will be here shortly. They will be carrying shotguns and they will be riding shotgun."

A few men laughed. There was a smattering of applause.

As if on cue, police cruisers suddenly filled the lot. Cianci urged the men outside, where they saw a squadron of Providence police officers forming in military ranks. Each officer carried a shotgun and wore a bandoleer of spare ammunition across his chest.

Cianci and city supervisors, one man wearing National Guard fatigues, exhorted the men to mount their garbage trucks. The sound and smell of diesel engines filled the night. Each truck carried a Teamsters driver, two garbage pickers, and a shotgun-toting policeman.

A supervisor shouted the command "Go, go, go," and the first truck lurched from the parking lot. The others followed.

And so it went, as Buddy Cianci deployed his troops through the sleeping streets of Providence to collect the garbage. A spring of labor discontent had boiled over into a bitter summer strike and reduced Providence to this—cops riding shotgun on garbage trucks.

When the garbagemen walked off the job, leaving uncollected trash to bake in ninety-five-degree heat, Cianci took a bold stand. He fired the workers and hired a private company to collect the trash, which he said would save the city money. Facing down the union's leader, Cianci declared: "This is Waterloo. Either for him or for me, but it's Waterloo. Hopefully, for him."

To guard against union violence and catch the protestors off guard, he staged his daring midnight ride of the garbage trucks, using Jake Kaplan's car lot. As the trucks rumbled through the city that night collecting the trash, Cianci rode around in a car getting updates from the front.

"We caught them with their pants down," gloated one Public Works supervisor.

Tommy Ricci, one of the commandos who had sneaked into the Public Works garage and taken the garbage trucks, was part of a crew that rode around the city that night watching for ambushes and communicating with radios. There had been reports that the union might use tractor-trailer trucks to block key intersections and ram the garbage trucks, but the threat never materialized. On Branch Avenue, a union man rammed his green pickup truck into a garbage truck. Ricci and his men pushed the pickup out of the way and called in a rescue for the injured man.

In the days that followed, strikers outside City Hall showered Cianci with curses and cries of "Maggot" as police bodyguards escorted him through a gauntlet outside his private entrance. The mayor, who had been sworn in for his second term protected by a bulletproof shield and rooftop snipers because of death threats, had round-the-clock police guards at his house.

The garbage strike was a drama that played out on multiple levels. On the surface, it was a classic standoff between the mayor and the powerful

Laborers' Union over the financial survival of Providence and its public employees. Behind the scenes, it was a tale rife with politics and corruption.

Privately, Cianci's advisers fiercely debated how strongly the mayor should oppose the union, according to former aide Bruce Melucci. Some warned against it, pointing out that the mayor had no strong grassroots Republican organization in Providence and therefore relied heavily on public employees. He shouldn't antagonize his power base, they argued. But others saw an opportunity for Cianci to win back taxpayers by taking a strong stand against the union and showing financial responsibility. He needed a bold gesture to revive his political career.

As the strike wore on, and the mayor's private polling showed him scoring points with the voters, Cianci was in no hurry to settle. Relaxing in his air-conditioned office one afternoon, nursing a Scotch, he said, "I have nowhere to go this summer." Another day, he took a leisurely horseback ride through Roger Williams Park.

Cianci's inner circle also profited from the strike.

His big boosters, the Capuanos, received the multimillion-dollar contract to take over garbage collection—a deal that Ronnie Glantz said was greased with a two-hundred-thousand-dollar kickback to Cianci.

With a private company picking up the trash, the city had no use for twenty-eight garbage trucks. Two years earlier, the city had bought new garbage trucks in a deal that involved kickbacks to Ronnie Glantz and Tony Bucci. So it was only fitting that the disposal of city trucks would also involve bribes. This time Jake Kaplan stepped in and brokered a deal to sell the trucks to Ralph's Truck World in New Hampshire—a deal that a federal indictment would later charge involved a fifteen-thousand-dollar kickback. Buckles Melise would later testify that during the strike, the buyer gave the fifteen thousand to Kaplan, who passed on ten thousand in cash to Buckles. According to Buckles, he brought the ten thousand to Joe DiSanto, who gave him half.

After sixteen days, the great garbage strike ended in victory for Cianci. Although the union won some concessions, the city's garbage collection remained with the Capuanos—at a substantial savings to the taxpayers, the mayor proclaimed.

"It's a crossroads for this city," the mayor declared. "All that mob can do what they want, but now they know one thing: they don't run this city, and they never will."

Cianci's popularity soared. The shotgun-toting cops had captured the public's imagination. The people didn't know that the shotguns were never loaded. It had all been a show, recalled one aide.

Several months later, Cianci was invited to speak to a conservative antilabor group in London about how he had broken the garbage strike.

"He talked about how he had sent Buckles down to the line to beat the shit out of guys," said Malcolm Farmer III, then a Republican councilman from the East Side. "He said how Buckles sledgehammered one guy and stuck his thumb in another guy's eye."

As Cianci told the story, upon his return to Providence, he roared with laughter. Using Buckles, he joked, was "great public policy."

EARLY IN 1982, Cianci gathered his closest advisers for a daylong strategy session about his political future.

One of his aides, Bruce Melucci, had written a long memo arguing that Cianci would have to abandon the Republican party to be reelected in November. Cianci was no longer strong enough to capture 50 percent of the vote in a one-on-one contest against a Democrat, Melucci concluded—the best he could hope for was 42 percent. Cianci also faced a strong challenge in the Republican party from East Side patrician Frederick Lippitt.

But there were drawbacks to leaving the Republican party. Cianci had nurtured strong Washington ties with the GOP, and still harbored national aspirations. And Cianci relished traveling in Republican circles. Henry Kissinger had been to his home. The previous year, Cianci had been seated next to Henry Cabot Lodge, the former U.S. senator who had been dislodged by John F. Kennedy, at a Massachusetts GOP luncheon in Boston. The blue-blooded Cabots and Lodges had dominated the state for generations; the Cabots spoke only to the Lodges, an old saying went, and the Lodges spoke only to God.

Cianci and Lodge were eating chowder when Lodge reached the bottom of the bowl, then picked it up and slurped the remaining broth.

"You do that just like an Italian," said Cianci.

"I am," replied Lodge.

Later, a perplexed Cianci asked Melucci what Lodge had meant by that. Melucci explained that Lodge was descended from an Italian navigator named Cabato, who had sailed from England with early Massachusetts Bay colonists.

Cianci didn't want to leave the Republican party. He believed that there was a place for both the Ciancis and the Lodges. So in the spring of 1982, he tried to keep Lippitt from entering the mayor's race. Privately, Cianci threatened to seek revenge by running as an Independent and savaging the GOP's entire statewide ticket. The party's elder statesman, Senator John Chafee, sent word back that if Cianci did that, his chances of obtaining a federal job if he lost would be zero.

Lippitt persisted in running. Cianci had good ideas, Lippitt said, but he was more interested in using the mayor's office as a stepping-stone than in the administrative details of running a city.

The numbers in a Republican primary were stacked against Cianci. There were only seventeen hundred registered Republican voters in Providence (compared with twenty-four thousand Democrats), and many of them were East Siders who had broken with the mayor. So Cianci tried to change the numbers. He and his lieutenants pressured city workers to sign forms disaffiliating themselves from the Democratic party so they could vote in the Republican primary.

Several workers called *The Providence Journal* to complain; some said that their jobs had been threatened if they didn't sign. Joseph DiSanto, who was heavily involved in the effort, denied any pressure; in fact, he said, many Democratic employees hadn't realized they could vote Republican and had been "happy to get the advice."

Still, convincing lifelong Democrats to vote Republican was slow going. When even Buckles Melise refused to sign, Melucci reported back to Cianci that the effort was hopeless.

In June Cianci made the break, announcing that he would run as an Independent. He said that he still regarded himself as a Republican but that he wanted to avoid a divisive primary against Lippitt. Democrat Frank Darigan, making his third run for mayor, was so frustrated by the maneuver that he went to Lippitt and tried to talk him out of running. "Fred, you're killing me," Darigan recalled telling Lippitt. "If you want to make changes, you're handing him the city by running. I can't beat him in a three-way race. You're handing the city back to this guy." But Lippitt, convinced he could win, stayed in the race.

That summer, the mayor launched the city's most ambitious public-works program in years, a $2.9 million blitz to repave streets and repair sidewalks. By election day, as Cianci campaigned with the slogan "Providence, you're looking good," the city had repaved one thousand streets and repaired two thousand sidewalks. The work was concentrated in neighborhoods that Cianci considered politically crucial—Mount Pleasant, Federal Hill, the North End, and the East Side. To pay for the crash program, Cianci "borrowed" federal funds that had been set aside for downtown and urban renewal, and for fixing substandard housing. When his political opponents accused Cianci of buying votes, his aides said with a straight face that there was nothing political about the program—the city was merely addressing a backlog of complaints about damaged sidewalks dating back to 1964.

"I won't say it's never been done. I did read *Boss*," quipped one Cianci official, referring to Mike Royko's book about Chicago mayor Richard Daley. "But you couldn't buy my vote by paving my sidewalk, even if I had one."

The program also offered Cianci's people new opportunities for graft.

Authorities would later investigate several hundred thousand dollars in overcharges by contractor Santi Campanella. A big Cianci booster, Campanella owned a yacht in Florida that the mayor would stay on. Years earlier, he had been partners with Raymond Patriarca and Frank Sinatra in the Berkshire Downs racetrack.

Meanwhile, Buckles Melise steered seven thousand tons of city asphalt, worth $150,000, to Bobo Marrapese's paving company, where it was used for private driveways, including that of a Mafia porn king. Buckles would send an emissary to Coventry Sand and Gravel. The man would flash his belt buckle, the signal that Buckles had sent him, then cart off a truckload of asphalt that would be billed to the city. Later, Buckles would meet Bobo at the Acorn Social Club to close the deal and receive his commission. This was the same bar where Bobo had killed mobster Dickie Callei in 1975, shooting him five times in the back, then stabbing the corpse for good measure.

One night in August 1982, at the height of the asphalt scheme and Cianci's reelection campaign, Bobo was drag-racing another mobster down Westminster Street when a Volkswagen cut him off. In the altercation that followed, the offending VW driver, a twenty-year-old man, was beaten to death with a baseball bat. (Charged with the murder a year later, Bobo initially agreed to plead guilty, then changed his mind, went to trial, and was acquitted.)

Buckles defended his city dealings with Bobo, explaining that his friendship with "the Marrapese family" dated back to their childhood on Federal Hill. "Mr. Marrapese always did his work and he did a good job," said Buckles. "What bothers me in the story, reading it, is using the word *organized crime.* I don't ever see anybody belonging to organized crime that worked for the City of Providence."

Other stories circulated within law enforcement about sidewalk scams. The state police looked into one involving Billy Black DelSanto, the Patriarca capo, in which city sidewalk inspectors went around Providence with sledgehammers, smashing sidewalks to create more work for private contractors.

Three days before the election, a *Providence Journal* editorial railed against Cianci's blatant attempt to hoodwink the voters.

Cianci also worked hard to hold on to the East Side. Having lost the WASP vote, he went after the area's large Jewish vote. Bruce Melucci, who had become Cianci's campaign manager on the strength of his early 1982 strategy memo, remembered the mayor's calling him in the middle of the night and asking how many Jewish voters there were in Providence. The mayor campaigned at synagogues and Jewish events, winning over voters, said Melucci, with his "brains and chutzpah."

One Saturday night Melucci was at home reading, enjoying a rare night off from the campaign, when his phone rang.

"Melucci," said the mayor, "do you want to go to the Philharmonic?"

"I didn't know you liked classical music," said Melucci.

"I don't."

"Then why are you going?" asked Melucci.

"I wanna be seen by the Jews," Cianci replied.

So off they went to the Philharmonic. During the concert, Melucci had to keep nudging Cianci, who was nodding off. Then, at intermission, Cianci sprang to life and worked the crowd in the lobby. Afterward, the mayor took the head of the United Jewish Appeal and his wife in his limousine to Leo's, a bar frequented by artists and journalists, where they stayed into the wee hours, drinking, eating burgers, and swapping stories.

The mayor also showed his resilience by winning labor's endorsement, one year after the bitter garbage strike. Since then, he had signed new labor contracts providing millions of dollars in raises to municipal workers, teachers, firefighters, and police.

The accommodation with the unions was not surprising. Despite his public posturing, Cianci privately acknowledged the power of the unions, particularly Laborers' boss Arthur E. Coia, a rough-hewn leader from the North End. Coia ran a mobbed-up union and answered personally to his friend Raymond Patriarca. Glantz recalled being in the mayor's office when Coia convinced Cianci to raise the city's contribution to the union's legal-defense fund, something that Cianci had criticized his predecessor, Joe Doorley, for doing. Glantz also said that Coia offered Cianci a job with the union after he left the mayor's office, just as the Laborers had hired Doorley after Cianci beat him.

Nothing moved in the union without Coia's okay. One source recalled being at Cianci's house one night at about 2 A.M. when the mayor was drinking with Coia and another union official. An early-winter snowstorm had struck Providence, and Cianci wanted the sanding trucks sent out. But Coia was refusing to allow the drivers to go until a contract matter was settled. At one point, Coia shouted at Cianci, "Listen to me, you cocksucker, I'll blow up your house." Cianci turned to his police bodyguard, who had just walked in with drinks for them, and replied, "You said that in front of a cop. He could arrest you." Coia looked at the officer and shot back, "He's my cousin. He's not going to arrest me." Before the night was out, the matter was resolved and the sanders went out.

Going into election day in 1982, Cianci trailed narrowly in the polls, but the race was too close to call. When the polls closed on election night, the mayor was convinced that he had lost. As upbeat as he was publicly, Cianci could be equally pessimistic in private. An aide, Paul Campbell, recalled being alone with him in the mayor's office that night. Cianci sat grimly at his desk, fidgeting with his pen, lamenting his defeat.

Later, Cianci was quiet as he watched the first returns come in. Two of the three Providence television stations predicted a Darigan victory. Then the mayor, who was politically astute counting votes, picked up on some of the numbers trickling in and realized he had a shot.

He carried the East Side, winding up with more Jewish votes, proportionally, than Italian votes. By the end of the night, Cianci led Darigan by 798 votes. Lippitt, who had faded down the stretch, was a distant third.

When Cianci realized that the race would come down to the nearly six thousand outstanding mail ballots, he was elated—because he had in his corner the maestro of mail ballots, Lloyd "Satchel" Griffin. His scheme to collect mail ballots by promising senior citizens a free bus trip to Atlantic City in 1974 had helped lift Cianci to victory over Joe Doorley. In 1978, he had delivered again.

At the start of the 1982 race, Griffin had professed neutrality. But then, eleven days before the election, state police troopers armed with shotguns raided Griffin's campaign headquarters in search of stolen mail ballots. They arrested and strip-searched a female Griffin volunteer. Two Darigan volunteers had complained that the woman had snatched two mail ballots from them in South Providence and threatened to have their windshields smashed if they persisted in trying to collect mail ballots on Lloyd Griffin's turf.

Three days later an angry Griffin declared his support of Cianci. "They've given me a little push," he declared.

Griffin brought in more than eight hundred mail ballots, assuring Cianci of victory. In the final tally, Cianci beat Darigan by 1,074 votes. Melucci's memo had proved prophetic—Cianci won with 42 percent of the vote.

It was a stunning political comeback. Triumphant at his inaugural address on January 3, 1983, Cianci proclaimed, "Like the characters in Homer's *Odyssey*, my supporters and I have engaged in an eight-year journey beset by challenges and tribulations."

"Buddy Cianci," observed a political foe, "is at his best when he is in trouble and at his worst when he is at the top."

As he began his third term, Buddy was back on top.

CHAPTER SIX

Nightmare on Power Street

*6*0 *Minutes* was just coming on in Raymond DeLeo's house in Bristol when he received a strange phone call from Buddy Cianci.

DeLeo, a wealthy contractor, had known Cianci for years, through Republican politics. But he didn't consider him a close friend. So he was perplexed when Cianci asked him to come to his house in Providence that Sunday night in March 1983. There was something odd about Cianci's voice. DeLeo asked what was going on.

"You've been fucking around with my wife," said Cianci.

In Providence, the mayor sat brooding by the fireplace in his rented carriage house on the corner of Power and Benefit Streets. His marriage had essentially been over for the last year or so, a casualty of too many late nights on the political circuit and his own infidelities. He and Sheila had recently gone to court to make it official.

Following his reelection in 1982, Cianci had moved into the rambling brick house at 33 Power Street, diagonally across from the imposing John Brown mansion. The carriage house had been built as a horse stable in 1902 by Providence utility baron Marsden Perry, known as "the man who owned Rhode Island."

The neighborhood fit Cianci's mood that night. H. P. Lovecraft, like Cianci a nocturnal creature, had spent most of his life wandering the ancient streets of College Hill, drawing inspiration for such tales of the macabre as *The Case of Charles Dexter Ward* and *The Shunned House*. Years earlier, a mournful Edgar Allan Poe had become smitten with a Benefit Street poetess, Sarah Helen Whitman, when he spied her picking roses in the moonlight. He courted her at the Providence Athenaeum, where he penned his famous poem "To Helen," but she later broke off their engagement because of his excessive drinking.

It was about 8:30 P.M. Deleo didn't realize that a modern Providence gothic tale was about to unfold as he pulled his Oldsmobile into the curving brick drive.

When DeLeo first heard Cianci's accusation on the phone, he thought that maybe the mayor was kidding. He agreed to come to Providence that night after Cianci told him that a mutual friend, former attorney general Herbert DeSimone, would also be there.

DeLeo walked up to the massive wooden front door and rang the bell. A uniformed Providence patrolman, James K. Hassett, answered. DeLeo stepped inside, into a spacious living room with a vaulted ceiling and tall, cathedral-like windows. The room had once served as a basketball court for the Fox Point Boys Club.

Cianci was on the phone, yelling at Sheila, who was in Florida. When he saw DeLeo, he shouted at the cop, "Frisk him!"

Hassett, who was Cianci's driver, turned DeLeo around, pushed him up against the door, spread-eagled with his palms against the wood, and patted him down. DeLeo had the impression that Hassett was checking to see if he was wearing a body wire.

"What the hell is this?" shouted a stunned DeLeo. "I thought I was coming to a meeting. Let me out of here."

Then, not saying a word, Hassett grabbed DeLeo's arm and directed him to a chair near the fireplace. Joseph DiSanto, a Cianci confidant and the director of Public Works, was sitting around the fireplace with William McGair, a former probate judge and Cianci's divorce lawyer. There were some drinks on the coffee table.

Cianci, who had been bellowing into the telephone, hung up and came into the room in shirtsleeves. He stood next to DeLeo's chair.

"You've been screwing around with my wife," he said. Then he slapped DeLeo in the head.

"Go ahead, strike me back," said Cianci. "You strike me back, you're gonna get a bullet in your head."

Out of the corner of his eye, DeLeo noticed Officer Hassett, who had positioned himself on the other side of his chair, move his hand to the holster on his hip.

Cianci kept smacking DeLeo about the head and daring him to hit back. He said that the men in the room would all swear that DeLeo had thrown the first punch. Like a Greek chorus, the men all agreed. DeLeo looked at Cianci in disbelief.

"I saw a crazed man," he later recalled. "I saw a lunatic."

■

RAYMOND DELEO WAS a self-made man.

A lifelong resident of Bristol, he lived with his wife on High Street, in an impressive house overlooking Narragansett Bay and decorated with Persian rugs and antique furniture.

DeLeo's parents had died young, leaving his older sister to raise him. In 1954 Hurricane Carol roared up the bay and devastated the historic seaport. The construction business that DeLeo had started on a shoestring received a lift from the rebuilding effort. As his business prospered, DeLeo also found time for politics. In the 1960s he was a leader of Nelson Rockefeller's presidential campaign organization in New England. He also headed the Bristol Republican Town Committee and met statewide politicians, including Herbert DeSimone.

DeSimone introduced DeLeo to his young protégé, Buddy Cianci. Every Fourth of July DeLeo threw a big party at his house, which was on the route of the famous Bristol parade. Cianci and other Republicans and friends would attend.

Before Cianci became mayor, DeLeo had consulted with him about representing him in a possible libel suit against the *Bristol Phoenix*. The newspaper had run an editorial cartoon depicting DeLeo sitting on the stone wall outside his house, pulling puppet strings with local GOP candidates attached like marionettes. DeLeo was angry because the cartoon resembled the cover drawing from Mario Puzo's novel about the Mafia *The Godfather*. But he never sued.

After Cianci became mayor, he discovered that DeLeo owned a motel in Hollywood Beach, Florida. He started calling DeLeo, asking if his family could go down and spend the week at the Mariner for free. DeLeo obliged.

The visits became regular. Sometimes Cianci would send his wife and daughter, Nicole, down alone. On other occasions, he would accompany them but stay on a friend's boat in nearby Fort Lauderdale. By the late 1970s, Sheila Cianci was going to Florida more often, and staying longer. DeLeo's sister, who ran the motel, began to resent her demands and the Ciancis' freeloading.

It was apparent that the Ciancis' marriage was in trouble. Sheila would complain to DeLeo that the mayor treated her badly and carried on with other women. According to DeLeo's later grand-jury testimony, Sheila told him "how she was abused by him to the point of attempting to strangle her, at one point." Years later DeLeo said that Cianci had come home drunk one night and threatened to throw his wife over the second-floor stair railing. She talked about getting a divorce but said that she was afraid of Buddy. She said that he had threatened her if she ever tried to take their daughter away.

Around the mayor's office it was no secret that Cianci's marriage was on the rocks. When Sheila was having a dinner or a birthday party for their daughter, she would call the mayor's office and beg the secretaries to make sure that Cianci came home on time. But he seldom did. His police drivers would come by the house on Blackstone Boulevard in the morning and listen as he and Sheila argued openly, yelling and cursing.

As things grew worse, Cianci stayed away more. He spent his nights going from one event to another, then out for a drink, then, after the bars closed, to a late-night coffee shop. One aide said that he hated going into Cianci's house, because of the tension and icy silences between the mayor and his wife.

"I was wrong in this marriage in many ways, many, many ways," he would later acknowledge to a grand jury, "and I've put my personal, political career, in many ways, apart from my family."

Asked in the grand jury if he had been involved with other women, he replied, "I'm not going to lie to you. Of course I was." Cianci also accused his wife of being unfaithful with several men, according to DeLeo.

Cianci always had a girlfriend, according to one of his former police drivers, who remembered dropping him off at the Marriott on various occasions or around the corner from the apartment of one particular woman who lived off Hope Street. An hour or two later, Cianci would call the driver to pick him up. Late one night during Cianci's first term, Ronnie Glantz said that he was in the car when the mayor had his police driver drop him at a woman's apartment on Benefit Street. The mayor went inside. Glantz said that he and the driver were sitting in the car nearby when they saw Doane Hulick, a reporter who covered City Hall for the *Journal*, go into the same building. Hulick, it turned out, also lived there; he had just missed bumping into the mayor. The former driver said that Cianci kept an unmarked city car with untraceable police plates in his garage for when he wanted to slip away on his own.

When Cianci finally did come home, Sheila told DeLeo, she would go through his pockets after he fell asleep and find room keys from different Providence hotels. She also reported finding packets of cash, and took some because Cianci was tight with his money.

A man who worked on Cianci's 1980 campaign for governor remembered going into the mayor's office one day and noticing a woman's foot under Cianci's desk. That night, when the man saw Cianci at Alarie's, he asked him about his visitor. The mayor laughed and replied, "I call those 'job applicants.' "

Finally, Sheila Cianci had had enough. She told Buddy that she wanted a divorce. The mayor convinced her to wait until after the 1982 election. In return, he agreed to pay her five hundred thousand dollars in their divorce settlement. About a year before the 1982 election, Sheila and Buddy signed a separation agreement. It called for Sheila to make a certain number of public appearances a month with Buddy. And the agreement stated that they would live separate and apart and date other people, as if they were not married.

Early in 1983, after Cianci was sworn in for a third term, Sheila and Buddy Cianci formally filed for divorce. On Tuesday, March 15, the Ciancis received a preliminary divorce decree. That Friday night, at a political fundraiser, according to DeLeo, Cianci picked up on some gossip between Joe DiSanto's wife and another woman that Sheila, who had been going to Ray DeLeo's motel in Florida, was having an affair with him.

Cianci was furious. His pride was wounded. He stewed over the five-hundred-thousand-dollar settlement. Over the weekend, he plotted his next move. On Sunday night he summoned DeLeo to Power Street.

AFTER HIS ROUGH greeting of DeLeo, Cianci got straight down to business.

He repeated his accusation that DeLeo had been fooling around with Sheila. He had Joe DiSanto relate what DiSanto's wife had heard at the mayor's fund-raiser Friday night.

Then Cianci turned to Bill McGair, his divorce lawyer, whom everyone called "Judge McGair" because of his former seat on the probate court. Cianci announced that the judge had some papers for DeLeo to sign—a confession that he had been sleeping with Sheila and an agreement that DeLeo would pay Cianci five hundred thousand dollars.

If DeLeo didn't sign, Cianci warned, "You're not gonna leave here tonight and you're gonna end up with a bullet in your head."

DeLeo, who was married, told Cianci that he had nothing to confess to, that he hadn't had an affair with Sheila.

Cianci repeated his threat, punctuating his words with slaps and punches. He spoke quickly, words tumbling over one another. He vowed to ruin DeLeo's business. He said that DeLeo would be found dead in the river. Cianci said that he had 255 policemen behind him and that the streets of Providence would not be safe for DeLeo. Cianci told DeLeo that he would always be looking over his shoulder and that he'd be picked up for some unsolved crime.

The mayor's eyes were bloodshot. Mucus ran from his left nostril, but Cianci was oblivious. DeLeo would later tell the state police, "I don't know whether he was just on some drug or something."

For the next two hours, Cianci stalked around his living room, verbally abusing and threatening DeLeo. He would be talking one moment, then lunge at DeLeo and strike him with his fist, or yank his hair, or kick him.

The police officer and the other men in the room said nothing. Based on their silence and Cianci's earlier threats, DeLeo dared not fight back or attempt to leave. He would later describe the feeling as if he were the mayor's prisoner.

Cianci's rage mounted. He threw liquor on DeLeo. He spit on him. He took his lit cigarette and tried to snuff it out in DeLeo's left eye. DeLeo flinched, and the glowing embers singed the corner of his eye. Ashes flaked into his eye, irritating it.

Cianci grabbed a fireplace log and raised it over DeLeo's head like a club. Joe DiSanto rushed over, and helped DeLeo fend off the blow.

As the night wore on, McGair recalled, Cianci spent more time going into the kitchen. McGair called Herbert DeSimone and urged him to come over. McGair hoped that DeSimone's "commanding presence could end the thing."

Six hundred miles away, in Florida, Sheila had also been frantically trying to reach DeSimone. She had been on the phone with Cianci when DeLeo arrived at Power Street. She had heard the doorbell ring, heard Cianci say, "Here he is now, Sheila," then heard the mayor shout at Patrolman Hassett to let DeLeo in and put him up against the wall and pat him down for a tape recorder or a gun. She had also heard DeLeo exclaim, "What is going on here?" followed by her ex-husband vowing, "Now I am going to beat the shit out of him, Sheila, I am going to kill this motherfucker." Terrified, Sheila had tried unsuccessfully to reach Vinny Vespia, then had called DeSimone and left an urgent message asking him to call her when he returned from the football game in Boston.

DeSimone arrived at about ten-thirty. Taking in the scene before him, from Cianci's crazed look to DeLeo's beat-up condition, he asked in a stunned voice, "What's happening here?"

Cianci, in an emotional voice, told DeSimone the DeLeo had been having an affair with Sheila. They walked toward DeLeo, as if to strike him again. But the taller and heavier DeSimone, who had been a star football lineman at Brown University in the 1950s, wrapped Cianci in a bear hug and led him into the kitchen. DiSanto motioned for DeLeo to leave quickly. But DeLeo didn't dare, because the policeman was standing between him and the door.

From time to time, Cianci would return to the living room and attack DeLeo. One time he picked up a heavy glass ashtray and flung it at DeLeo, who reached out and caught it.

Later, when Cianci was back in the kitchen, a woman knocked on the door to complain that DeLeo's car was blocking her driveway. The policeman took DeLeo's keys and went outside to move it. Cianci, hearing the noise, rushed out of the kitchen, bellowing, "You're not letting him get away, are you?"

When Officer Hassett came back inside, Cianci grabbed DeLeo's car keys.

About forty-five minutes after DeSimone arrived, at about eleven-fifteen, Hassett brought DeLeo into the kitchen, where Cianci sat at a table flanked by DeSimone and McGair. The mayor ordered him to stand at attention, his back to the range, then reviewed his demands.

DeLeo was to get Cianci a certified check for five hundred thousand dollars by Friday, or he'd be dead—"D-E-D," Cianci spelled it. "Make sure you understand that, DeLeo."

"Yes, I understand," DeLeo answered.

Cianci insisted that DeLeo repeat it. DeLeo was feeling dizzy and said that he couldn't but that he understood.

DeSimone, in his later grand-jury testimony, recalled Cianci's threatening to ruin DeLeo's business and screaming and crying and acting irrationally. But he said he was sure he didn't hear the mayor tell DeLeo that he would be "dead" if he didn't come up with the five hundred thousand.

McGair recalled Cianci's saying "D-E-D," but felt it was a reference to DeLeo's standing in the community, not to the "mortality aspect."

"C'mon, Buddy," DeSimone implored. "Let him go, let him go. Let's go and have some coffee. You need some coffee."

With that, Cianci finally allowed DeLeo to leave Power Street. It had been three hours since an unsuspecting DeLeo had walked through the mayor's door. Joe DiSanto suggested that he drive DeLeo home, since his clothes reeked of the alcohol that the mayor had thrown on him.

Back home in Bristol, DeLeo drove the short distance from his house to his office to collect his thoughts and clean himself up. It was past 2 A.M., and he was sitting at his desk, when the phone rang. It was Cianci. He sounded light-headed, almost giddy.

"Do you understand what happened, DeLeo? You know what I want? Get the five hundred thousand, or you're gonna be dead."

DeLeo hung up.

Back on Power Street, the mayor was in rough shape as the night wore on and he grasped the potential consequences of what he had done. He called his chief of police, Anthony Mancuso, who dispatched Lieutenant Richard Tamburini to Power Street to "keep the peace," fearing that Cianci might go after DeLeo again. It was nearly midnight when Tamburini arrived to find McGair and Lloyd Griffin, the flamboyant South Side councilman and one of the mayor's political supporters. McGair, who had taken Cianci out for coffee, left shortly thereafter. Tamburini and Griffin spent the night in the living room, dozing in armchairs and chatting. Periodically, a distraught and agitated Cianci would come downstairs in his robe, without his toupee, to get a drink or use the phone.

During that long night, Cianci called DeLeo's son and nephew demanding an affidavit attesting to Sheila's alleged infidelity. He called Sheila back and said that all of her friends were telling him everything and that DeLeo had broken down and cried and admitted everything. Cianci told her that DeLeo would pay for their divorce—that he would come up with five hundred thousand dollars by the end of the week or he would be dead: "D-E-D." Cianci also called Vespia, who had been his best man, and told him what had happened. Vespia, who in the Ciancis' divorce case had testified to their irreconcilable differences, was incredulous, especially when Cianci said that he had used a policeman to bring DeLeo into the house. "You're in big trouble," warned Vespia.

In Cianci's living room—the scene of the crime—Tamburini and Griffin agreed.

"The mayor's in a tight spot," said Griffin. "But he's gotten out of other tight spots before."

Early the next morning, a few aides arrived and urged him to pull himself together. Cianci, who had spent a sleepless night, was scheduled to make a television appearance at 9 A.M. At 8:45, he bounded down the stairs looking fresh and crisp in a suit and tie, clapping his hands, ready to go. Griffin looked at him approvingly and said, "Showtime!"

TWO DAYS LATER, on Tuesday morning, Lenore Siegel Steinberg was at home in West Palm Beach, Florida, packing for a trip to Providence later that day, when her phone rang. It was Buddy Cianci.

Steinberg, a former Barrrington socialite, was a friend of Sheila Cianci's. A former Broadway soprano, she had given up the stage to marry a wealthy Central Falls lace manufacturer. They had lived in an elegant house on fashionable Rumstick Road in Barrington, where she cut a flamboyant figure in her floor-length furs, large hats, and long gowns, always beige or white. She dismissed the other women in upscale Barrington as "Stepford wives," devoid of imagination and into tennis and sailing. Then her husband died in 1978, and she married a millionaire philanthropist and moved to West Palm Beach.

Steinberg listened as the mayor politely told her that Sheila and Ray DeLeo had been carrying on an affair for four years. Steinberg was surprised. She told Cianci that she didn't know anything about it.

"You're going to deny it?" snapped Cianci.

"Buddy, I don't know what you're talking about," she said.

"Well, you know, I'm in the midst of a divorce and giving my wife a lot of money, but after hearing this, I'll get him," said Cianci, before hanging up.

That evening Steinberg arrived in Providence. When she walked into the lobby of the Biltmore Hotel, Cianci was waiting for her with a uniformed Providence police officer wearing high black boots.

"I came to welcome you," Cianci told her.

Steinberg protested that she had to check in. Cianci shouted over her shoulder to the man behind the reception desk, "Check Mrs. Steinberg in."

The night was cold and the lobby empty, save for the policeman. Afraid to be alone with the mayor, Steinberg did not take her luggage to her room. Instead, she let him steer her up to L'Apogee, the Biltmore's elegant rooftop restaurant, which offered panoramic views of Providence.

Steinberg, who was famished, ordered dinner. The policeman stood nearby, until Cianci dismissed him. As Steinberg started to eat, she said, Cianci started raving like "a madman." He threatened to take her to court and send her to jail if she lied about Sheila and Ray DeLeo.

Cianci proceeded to tell her about what he had done to DeLeo at his house two nights earlier. He embellished the story, saying that he had had DeLeo tied to a chair and then beaten him "to a pulp." He boasted that he had put a loaded gun to DeLeo's head and threatened to pull the trigger. "I almost killed him, but it was worth it knowing that he had had an affair with my wife," Cianci told her.

Steinberg had lost her appetite. Cianci seemed to take a sadistic glee in describing the beating. He looked as pale as a ghost, the worst she'd ever seen him.

"Buddy, you're kidding me."

"I never kid," he replied. He told her that he would do terrible things to her, too, if she didn't "come up with the truth." He brought up the fact that Steinberg's previous husband had committed suicide at their house in Barrington. He said that he would start an investigation to prove that she and her husband had had a "love pact," that they had both agreed to shoot themselves, but she had backed out and killed him instead. Cianci also vowed to tell her current husband and wreck her marriage.

"I'm going to get back at you," said Cianci, "because you have a very big ego and you think you're very special and now that you have a fabulous husband, you're even worse."

It was past eleven when a horrified Steinberg finally got away from the mayor. In her room at the Biltmore, in Buddy Cianci's Providence, she was terrified and felt that she needed police protection. She called Vincent Vespia, the South Kingstown police chief and former state police detective who had been Cianci's best man. Vespia offered to have a police officer take her to the airport when she was finished with her business in Providence in a few days.

In the meantime, Steinberg was afraid to let the waiter in for room service. She was scared to take a taxi.

"I felt that Buddy would tow me away somewheres and beat me up or kill me," she said later.

AT FEW DAYS after Cianci assaulted him, DeLeo, experiencing headaches, went to a neurosurgeon. He was treated for injuries to his head and face, including burn marks around the left eye from Cianci's cigarette.

But DeLeo, a deeply private man, did not want to discuss his night on Power Street. In April a Providence television reporter came by his office and told him that the story was all over town. DeLeo said he didn't know what the reporter was talking about.

Worried, he went to an old Republican acquaintance, Lincoln C. Almond, the U.S. attorney for Rhode Island. At the time, Almond's office was investigating corruption in the Cianci administration. At a meeting in Almond's office one weekend, DeLeo described what had happened and expressed his fear that Cianci might try to set him up. Almond urged DeLeo to relax and to call him if he needed to talk again.

DeLeo went home, unaware that he had just set the wheels of justice in motion. Almond went to Colonel Walter Stone, superintendent of the Rhode Island State Police. Shortly after that, on April 18, 1983, two state police detectives appeared at DeLeo's office in Bristol and told him they were taking him to headquarters in Scituate to make a statement. DeLeo didn't want to go, but he agreed to after the police told him that he could go "the easy way or the hard way."

In Scituate DeLeo called his lawyer, who advised him to tell the truth. Over the next several hours, he reluctantly told his story. State prosecutors planned to put the case before a grand jury.

Meanwhile, Cianci had also swung into action. He dispatched one of his most trusted aides, Vito Russo, and a political ally, city councilman Lloyd Griffin, to visit DeLeo at his office. Their mission was to find out whether DeLeo had gone to the police, and what he intended to do.

When DeLeo described the incident, Russo was aghast. Russo had a doctorate in educational psychology and had known Sheila Cianci for years, since she had worked as a secretary at Marathon House, a substance-abuse treatment center that Russo had helped found.

According to DeLeo, Russo and Griffin told him that Cianci was threatening to make up a story that DeLeo had offered the mayor a bribe to help him collect money the city owed him for construction work years earlier. During the conversation, Russo referred to Cianci as a "sociopath." A few days before the assault, Russo said, Cianci had been elated about his divorce, proclaiming that he was a free man.

DeLeo told Russo and Griffin about his encounter with the state police. Griffin asked why he talked to them instead of demanding his lawyer.

It wasn't clear to DeLeo why Cianci had sent Griffin. The South Providence power broker had recently been tried, in a highly publicized case, for shooting a seventeen-year-old boy in the leg. Cianci had testified as a character witness for Griffin, who was acquitted.

The pressure on DeLeo intensified. On April 25, the night before he was scheduled to testify to the grand jury, lawyers for Cianci and DeLeo met at the attorney general's office with the AG, Dennis Roberts II, and other prosecutors and state police detectives assigned to the case. The lawyers brought along a "civil settlement" that had been brokered by Thomas Paolino, the retired supreme court justice who had also helped arrange the Ciancis' divorce. In it, DeLeo agreed not to press criminal charges and Cianci agreed not to sue DeLeo for alienation of affection. Without a sworn complaint from DeLeo, the lawyers argued that the criminal case should be dropped.

But the prosecutors didn't take the document seriously. No one, not even Buddy Cianci, had the right to negotiate a private settlement to a criminal matter. The attorney general made it clear that the case would go forward.

That same night, the story became public. Channel 12 reported that the grand jury was investigating an assault allegation against Cianci. DeLeo was not yet identified.

The next day DeLeo appeared before the grand jury and took the Fifth. Prosecutors immediately went upstairs to the presiding justice of the superior court for an order immunizing DeLeo.

DeLeo's lawyer, Irving Brodsky, fought the order. Brodsky, a former prosecutor, was close to Cianci; the two had worked together years earlier in the famous murder trial of Raymond Patriarca, the case involving the lying priest. Now, representing DeLeo, Brodsky took the immunity order upstairs to the Rhode Island Supreme Court.

A supreme court justice ruled in favor of the state. DeLeo was compelled to testify. The next day he told the grand jury about his nightmare on Power Street.

The other men who had been at Power Street that night—Joe DiSanto, Judge McGair, Herbert DeSimone—were paraded before the grand jury. "He was acting as Buddy Cianci, who was broken-hearted," testified McGair. Lloyd Griffin told grand jurors that Cianci was "like so many people—you don't realize what you've lost until you lose it."

Early in May, two state police detectives walked into the mayor's office to serve him with a grand-jury subpoena. Cianci saw them outside and thought they had come to arrest him. At first, he wouldn't let them in. He paced back and forth and spoke frantically into the telephone.

On May 5, in the Licht Judicial Complex, where he had launched his public career as a prosecutor, Cianci took his place before the grand jury.

He gave an extraordinary performance. Cianci began by reading a lengthy statement in which he described the pain of his divorce and his anger upon learning that his efforts to save his marriage had been sabotaged by the betrayal of Ray DeLeo, whom he'd thought of as a brother—a man who "shared in my most secret ambitions and dreams."

He said that he had learned of the affair on the day before the assault, when DeLeo's niece, whom Cianci had worked with in the attorney general's office, called looking for Sheila. The next day, Sunday, they had lunch. As a result of what he learned from her, Cianci said that he went through his wife's things at their old house—Sheila was in Florida—and found pictures showing DeLeo and Sheila at Disney World, and also in California.

The mayor described how he had found tape recordings, which Sheila had made on the advice of a psychic, that Buddy claimed captured the sounds of her having sex with DeLeo.

"This hearing is a secret one—and but for that secrecy, I would not be telling you all this, because I could never expose my wife and especially my daughter to the horror of what I heard on that tape," Cianci said. And he proceeded to play the tape for the grand jury.

DeLeo said later that Cianci performed "a tap-dance" before the grand jury, that he "lied through his teeth." DeLeo said that he and Cianci were never that close and that Cianci didn't find the alleged sex tapes until after he assaulted DeLeo—when he started scrambling for proof to justify his actions. Judge McGair, who was there, said that Cianci never mentioned the tapes on the night of the assault. Cianci's divorce lawyer said that he had been summoned to Power Street that evening by a phone call from Cianci, who felt betrayed and asked McGair, "How much did this thing [the divorce] cost me?" (McGair didn't have any formal papers for DeLeo to sign that night, he said—just notes that he'd scribbled on the back of an envelope.)

DeLeo maintained that the tapes Cianci found were of the psychic talking to Sheila and Sheila making unflattering comments about Cianci, not of people having sex. Notes that Sheila kept at the time indicate that on Wednesday, March 23—three days after the assault—she received a call from Judge Paolino, who said that he had gone by the house on Blackstone Boulevard with Cianci (Buddy and Sheila had both moved out so that the house could be sold). Cianci had seen the maid taking a basket out of the house, had looked inside, and had found the psychic tapes and some money-market statements from a broker; he was, according to Paolino, "like a madman." Sheila's notes also indicate that one of Cianci's cousins

had called her the day after the assault and warned Sheila to get everything out of the house before he found the tapes, because the cousin was
on a lot of them. After Cianci found the tapes, the same cousin reported to
Sheila that "Buddy is playing the tapes for everyone in the family and they
are all crying."

DeLeo said that he grew closer to Sheila after the assault, as they faced
Cianci's attempts to discredit them, and she told him more stories about
how Cianci had mistreated her during their marriage. But he said that they
were never lovers.

Others disagree. Some of the police investigators thought that the two
had had an affair. Vin Vespia, whose wife was close to Sheila, also believed
so, but told Sheila that it wasn't his place to judge her. But the prosecution
never considered the question relevant; Cianci and his wife had signed a
separation agreement nearly a year before the assault, stating that they
would live separate and apart, as if they weren't married.

Early on, the prosecutors and the state police made a decision to stick
to the facts of what happened on Power Street that night. They told one
another that this was going to be either a criminal prosecution or a soap
opera.

ON MAY 24, 1983, a Rhode Island grand jury indicted Mayor Vincent A.
Cianci, Jr., on charges of conspiracy, kidnapping, assault, assault with a
deadly weapon, and attempted extortion. His police bodyguard, James Hassett, was also indicted, for kidnapping and conspiracy to kidnap.

Later that afternoon Cianci faced the television cameras as they prepared to go live on the six o'clock news.

"I've had better Tuesdays," he muttered as he watched the technicians
set up their camera equipment. He got a laugh from some people standing
nearby. Noting the reaction, he repeated the line once the cameras started
rolling.

The case had become a full-blown media circus—Cianci's natural element. The mayor, who had kept a low profile during the grand-jury investigation, came out joking.

"I feel like I've been on *Dynasty, Dallas,* and *Falcon Crest* for the last
two months," he said. "I have had calls from NBC, ABC, and I expect one
from CBS about starring in a new television series. It will be called *Providence.*"

When middleweight boxing champ Marvin Hagler knocked out his opponent in the fourth round at the Civic Center, Cianci cracked, "There have been longer fights at my house."

Cianci refused to discuss the not-so-amusing details of what had actually happened on Power Street that night. It was "a personal domestic matter." Cianci was the cuckolded husband, betrayed by a close friend, reacting in a moment of understandable rage. Anyone else in his shoes would have done the same thing—or worse.

"I am a human being," he said. "I sweat. I feel. I cry. I laugh. I get angry. I am still going to run my city. They're not going to get me on a domestic matter involving a guy, my wife, and my daughter."

The media played into the mayor's strategy. Stories focused on his resilience and his roller-coaster career. Would Buddy survive this latest setback? Tune in tomorrow.

The national media came marching through Providence. One day, over lunch with political aide Bruce Melucci at the Biltmore's Falstaff Room, Cianci pulled a *Time* magazine out of his pocket. He flipped it open to a picture of him and Kevin White, the mayor of Boston, who was embroiled in his own corruption scandal. "I'll show you how to get excellent publicity," he joked.

"Too bad you didn't kill the guy," retorted Melucci. "You'd be in *Newsweek*, too."

The mayor shrugged and ordered another martini.

Behind the scenes, Cianci kept the pressure on his accusers. He hired Vincent O'Connell, a retired Providence police officer, to conduct surveillance on Sheila and DeLeo, and even on the state police and the prosecutors. Cianci wanted to know whom they were talking to.

During the grand-jury investigation prosecutor Susan McGuirl had noticed a mysterious dark sedan following her. It became so obvious that, when she went to lunch, she would make eye contact with the beefy driver, point to her watch, and hold up two fingers to indicate when she'd be back.

The day after Cianci's indictment, some prosecutors had their cars booted by the Providence police.

At times, it was like "Spy vs. Spy." One day O'Connell went by Sheila's house, only to run into the state police. Sometimes the state police and Cianci's private investigators would shadow each other.

Unlike Cianci, Ray DeLeo was uncomfortable in the public eye. He received hate mail and anonymous threatening phone calls. Someone left a dead fish in a paper bag on his doorstep. Cianci leaked a story to the press about Sheila's sex tapes, which he played for reporters in an off-the-record session. Another story detailed a trip that DeLeo and Sheila had supposedly taken to San Francisco.

Vinny O'Connell had unearthed that one, creating more turmoil in the process. The sheriff's office in Carmel, California, thinking that O'Connell was working as a Providence police detective on a case important to the mayor, had initially agreed to help him check the hotel where DeLeo and Sheila had supposedly stayed. But then the sheriff read about Cianci's case in a California newspaper and discovered that the mayor was actually the defendant. Furious, he alerted the Rhode Island State Police, who accused O'Connell of misrepresenting himself as a police officer.

It was a crazy time. The press camped outside DeLeo's office. The state police had a cruiser watching his house. And Cianci's private eyes, it seemed, followed him everywhere.

O'Connell recalled tailing Sheila and DeLeo to a restaurant in Massachusetts one night, but they spotted him and slipped out the back door.

One Sunday in the autumn of 1983 DeLeo was taking his nephew's wife to a New England Patriots game when he noticed a man sitting in a car outside his house, his face hidden by a newspaper. Driving away, DeLeo saw the parked car start to follow him. DeLeo gave the man the slip by pulling into a parking lot he was developing, and wound up following his follower. The detective finally managed to switch positions, and took photos of DeLeo and his companion. Later, Cianci showed the pictures to Sheila to taunt her, but Sheila recognized her as DeLeo's nephew's wife.

Behind his upbeat public persona, the mayor was frantic. He called and wrote Sheila constantly, alternately threatening to ruin her and DeLeo and pleading for another chance. He said that DeLeo would never leave his wife for Sheila, that he was too old for her, that he was headed to prison for some shady business dealings. No one, Cianci told Sheila, could love her as he could.

A former secretary, Sheila kept shorthand notes of some of Cianci's rambling conversations and tape-recorded others, later giving typewritten summaries to DeLeo as the case unfolded. "I know what is most important in life and it ain't being mayor, governor, or anything," Cianci said on the night of March 30. "It is to enjoy my wife and daughter." One day, urging Sheila to think about it, he offered to resign as mayor. "I will announce that I will never run again." A skeptical Sheila answered, "Then do it."

About a month after the assault, Buddy and Sheila met for lunch at

Camille's, on Federal Hill. The meeting quickly turned ugly. Sheila bolted from the restaurant, drove to their old house on Blackstone Boulevard, and locked herself in. According to a state police detective's grand-jury testimony, "the Mayor followed with his police entourage and started banging on the doors and ringing the doorbell and Mrs. Cianci became frightened to a point where both the state police were called and the Providence police."

Sheila was emotionally exhausted. On Christmas Day, she went to Power Street to pick up their daughter and had another tense encounter. Seated across from her in his den, Cianci rambled for a few hours about DeLeo and the case. At one point, she said, he pulled a money clip out of his left pocket, fanned out about thirty-seven hundred dollars, and asked if that was enough for her to deliver his message to DeLeo.

That night, Sheila said, Cianci called her and reiterated the threat that Lloyd Griffin and Vito Russo had previously warned DeLeo about—that the mayor would accuse DeLeo of paying bribes involving city construction projects. According to her notes, Sheila taped the call and later played it for Griffin and Russo. Griffin told Sheila not to worry about Cianci's threats to set up DeLeo because, in his view, "Buddy will probably plead."

The question of whether or not to go to trial weighed heavily on the mayor that winter. He sat up late in the house on Power Street, worrying. He vacillated between going to trial and cutting a deal. He didn't want to lose his office, but he feared going to jail.

Often Cianci called O'Connell in the middle of the night to vent. O'Connell, lying in bed with the receiver to his ear, would drowse off, only to awaken and hear the mayor, still talking.

BY EARLY 1984, as Cianci's case moved toward trial, there were more problems at City Hall.

State and federal investigations into corruption in the city's troubled Department of Public Works had picked up. Public Works employees and a private paving contractor were indicted. Others were called to testify before the grand jury. Edward "Buckles" Melise, Cianci's highway superintendent, took the Fifth.

One of the focal points was the mayor's controversial $1.2 million sidewalk- and street-repair blitz, which had boosted his reelection campaign in 1982. Investigators focused on several hundred thousand dollars' worth of overcharges by Campanella Construction, a big political supporter of the mayor's.

When Cianci vacationed in Florida, he often stayed in Fort Lauderdale on Santi Campanella's yacht. In fact, Cianci had gone there four days after his indictment to get away, making him a footnote in a grisly Florida murder.

The same day, May 28, 1983, Campanella's thirty-eight-year-old son, Santi Campanella, Jr., had vacated the yacht to make room for Cianci, who was scheduled to arrive later in the evening. That night, the younger Campanella was robbed and murdered in the parking lot of a Fort Lauderdale shopping mall by two male prostitutes, who stuffed his body into the trunk of his rented car, drove to Tennessee, and dumped the corpse down a well.

The mayor's name surfaced as the police tried to reconstruct the younger Campanella's final hours, though Cianci had never seen him during his stay.

Meanwhile, the mayor's ouster of a longtime political enemy, parks superintendent James Diamond, touched off a public furor. Diamond was a maverick who had won accolades for restoring the Victorian grandeur of Roger Williams Park and rebuilding the decrepit zoo. But he had long angered the mayor for refusing to bow to his political demands, such as selling fund-raising tickets, hiring political hacks, and putting Cianci's name on signs in city parks. Diamond's removal sparked a petition drive to recall Cianci from office. Diamond, accusing the mayor of running an administration that was "incompetent, immoral, and corrupt," helped lead the drive.

On March 1, 1984, recall advocates filed petitions at City Hall containing 19,760 signatures. But the mayor had more immediate concerns. Four days later he was scheduled to go on trial for the DeLeo assault.

In the courtroom the mayor wouldn't be able to spin things so easily. The prosecution planned to introduce Cianci's separation agreement to undermine his cuckolded-husband defense.

The mayor sought to introduce the Sheila sex tapes, as well as a Michigan State University voice expert to identify the participants. The state planned to counter by delving into the mayor's affairs.

Prosecutors were also prepared to resurrect an unsavory allegation from Cianci's past. In February, two state police detectives flew to Wisconsin to interview Ruth Bandlow, the woman who had accused Cianci of raping her at gunpoint in 1966. She agreed to fly to Rhode Island to testify as a character witness against Cianci.

Meanwhile, Cianci's lawyers were pressing for the charges against him to be thrown out, for lack of willing witnesses. Ray DeLeo wasn't eager to testify, they argued; he had signed an agreement not to sue Cianci and had only appeared before the grand jury after prosecutors immunized him against his will.

Meanwhile, another key witness, Lenore Steinberg, was getting cold feet. The previous spring, the West Palm Beach socialite had eagerly described to the grand jury how Cianci had attempted to extort a statement from her regarding DeLeo's alleged affair with Sheila. Now she said that she had not "appreciated the significance" of her testimony when she appeared before the grand jury. She did not wish to testify at Cianci's trial. The whole experience had been unpleasant for her and her family. She was terrified to return to Rhode Island, and her millionaire husband wasn't thrilled with the publicity detailing her previous husband's suicide—precisely what Cianci had threatened to stir up if she crossed him.

Concerned that Steinberg might skip the country, prosecutors had her subpoenaed as she returned home from her country club in West Palm Beach one afternoon. She was furious, shouting at her doorman and the Palm Beach investigator who served her.

On Wednesday, February 22, five days before Cianci's trial was scheduled to begin, Steinberg produced medical affidavits claiming that a digestive disorder had flared up from the stress of the case, and that she was unable to travel. A Palm Beach County judge was not convinced. He ordered her to Rhode Island to testify.

Meanwhile, Cianci had dispatched to Palm Beach one of his own lawyers, Frank Caprio, a onetime political adversary from Federal Hill. Caprio met Steinberg at the Breakers Hotel. She gave him a sworn statement saying that Cianci had never threatened her.

On the weekend before the trial was set to open, Cianci flew to London with Normand Roussel, his longtime political adman. As they made the rounds in London—dinner at the Marble Arch, a comedy club, a men's club where they sat smoking cigars—the topic was the same. Should he plead guilty?

There was a deal on the table: Cianci could plead no contest to the two assault charges, and the attorney general would drop the four remaining charges and recommend no jail time. Cianci wondered what the rest of his life would be like. Would it be the end of his once brilliant political career?

When he returned to Providence on Monday, Cianci was ready to plead. He even signed a form detailing a no-contest plea on the assault charges. But when he walked into court on Tuesday, he couldn't bring himself to do it. Smirking at the prosecutor, Susan McGuirl, Cianci stunned even his own lawyer by saying that he wanted to go to trial.

Vinny O'Connell, Cianci's private investigator, was urging him to fight. With the reluctance of key witnesses like Steinberg, he saw most of the charges melting away. Cianci was popular. And when the jurors heard about DeLeo's alleged affair with Sheila, O'Connell told him, they would decide in their hearts that Cianci had been justifiably provoked.

Patrick Conley, Cianci's aide, also encouraged Cianci to go to trial. He argued that the prosecution would never convince twelve jurors in Providence to convict him. The mayor's indictment had already wrecked Conley's "magnificent scheme" to catapult Cianci into the U.S. Senate—and get Conley back in the good graces of the Democrats from whom he had been estranged since going to work for the mayor. The year before, Conley had conceived a plan in which Cianci would support Democrat Joseph Walsh, the mayor of Warwick, in his 1984 campaign for governor. Then Cianci would become a Democrat and run for the Senate—against his nemesis, John Chafee—with the backing of Governor Walsh and Democratic House Speaker Matthew Smith, an old-style political boss from South Providence. Smith, who in the early eighties had blocked Cianci's efforts to pass legislation giving the city more fiscal flexibility, would benefit by then being able to handpick Cianci's successor as mayor. Conley said that he, Cianci, Walsh, and Smith met quietly a couple of times, once at Capriccio, another time at the Brown Faculty Club. Cianci was enthusiastic. Walsh confirmed that there were discussions. But then Cianci was indicted, and the magnificent scheme fell apart.

With an eye on his political fortunes, Cianci walked out of court that Tuesday ready to go to trial. He turned to O'Connell and said, "Let's go for it!" By Thursday, however, with the trial set to begin on Monday, Cianci was wavering again. The plea negotiations resumed.

On Friday the state police served Frank Caprio with a subpoena as he ate lunch at the Aurora Club, a private old-boys club of Providence pols and power brokers. On Monday morning prosecutors planned to question Caprio about his encounter with Steinberg at the Breakers.

The plea talks continued through the weekend. Cianci offered to plead guilty to the misdemeanor assault charge. The attorney general insisted that he plead to a felony count as well, and now he was no longer willing to promise that he wouldn't recommend jail time.

The mayor, notoriously indecisive, vacillated. His ally Lloyd Griffin, the councilman who had gone to trial the previous spring for shooting a teenager, warned him that the judge had a reputation for being strict—that he would probably send the mayor to prison for several years if he went to trial and was convicted.

The attorney general gave Cianci until 10 A.M. Monday to decide.

At the appointed hour, on March 5, 1984, Cianci walked into the Providence County Courthouse, which he had once patrolled as an ambitious young prosecutor, and pleaded guilty to assault and assault with a dangerous weapon.

The plea stunned the packed courtroom. Many of the spectators, including some of the mayor's closest advisers, had not known what he was going to do. Norm Roussel accompanied him to court believing that the mayor would go to trial. Afterward, Cianci said that he had acted for the sake of his ten-year-old daughter.

The judge, John Bourcier, read the first charge, the felony count accusing Cianci of attacking Raymond DeLeo with a lighted cigarette, an ashtray, and a fireplace log. The judge asked if it was true.

"Yes, it is, Your Honor," Cianci replied in a low voice.

BUDDY CIANCI LEFT City Hall in a trail of tears, a posse of lawmen nipping at his heels.

On Monday, April 23, 1984, the mayor received a five-year suspended prison sentence. Two nights later, now a convicted felon, Cianci followed the dictates of the new city charter he had helped push through and resigned before the City Council could push him out of his trophy-laden corner suite.

The framed photographs of Cianci with Gerald Ford, Nelson Rockefeller, Henry Kissinger, and Elizabeth Taylor were packed away in boxes. The desk and the black leather chair with the mayor's seal were carted off by Vito's Express. His office took on the atmosphere of a political wake.

"Ronald Reagan tells a story," he reminisced to reporters, "after he completed two successful terms as governor of California . . . of walking outside, getting into the backseat of his car, and there was no one to drive him.

"I don't know what my plans are. I don't know if I can practice law. I don't have an office. I don't even own a car. So if anybody sees me hitchhiking, I wish you would do me the courtesy and pick me up."

Outside City Hall, Rhode Island state troopers and Providence police officers stood guard to prevent the removal of records vital to law enforcement's autopsy of the Cianci years.

Two weeks earlier, the Providence chief of police, Anthony J. Mancuso, had held an extraordinary meeting in his office with the United States attorney for Rhode Island, top Rhode Island prosecutors, and leaders of the City Council. The topic was corruption. The mayor had not been invited.

Council members came away shocked. Mancuso displayed two lists— one of Public Works employees with criminal records, another of Public Works employees with ties to organized crime. They talked about corruption in other departments; about no-show jobs and bid rigging; about payoffs for jobs, promotions, and contracts. The feds needed to look no further than their own basement; one suspect no-bid contract involved a broken water main that flooded the cellar of the federal building downtown. Some of the very contractors under investigation had the streets around the offices of the U.S. attorney's and the FBI dug up for a year; like the lawmen, the contractors kept digging and digging and digging.

"The obvious feeling was that the pyramid ended at the top," recalled former councilman Nicholas Easton, a participant. "The ultimate objective was to bring down Buddy Cianci."

Despite the spreading stain, Cianci was determined to exit more gracefully than his staunch ally at Public Works, Buckles Melise, had. The week before Cianci left, Buckles unceremoniously wriggled out a window on the first floor of City Hall and fled from state troopers who had come to arrest him for extorting kickbacks from snowplowers. (Later he turned himself in.)

In one final flourish before bidding adieu, Cianci appointed his private investigator in the DeLeo case, Vinny O'Connell, as a Providence police major. Chief Mancuso refused to accept the appointment. He blasted Cianci for trying to plant O'Connell in the department to spy on the unfolding corruption probes. Cianci's public-safety director fired Mancuso. The chief refused to vacate his office. Finally, in the face of Cianci's impending departure, the public-safety director resigned. Mancuso stayed.

On April 25, 1984, five days before his forty-third birthday, as twilight fell over Providence, Vincent A. Cianci, Jr., stepped out of his office and strode to the second-floor landing on the grand staircase of City Hall. Several hundred supporters leaned against the lime-green walls and the marble pillars and hung over the balustrades above, cheering and weeping. The scene was carried live on all three Providence television stations.

Cianci's last official act was to order the massive, churchlike front doors of City Hall thrown open, so that he could leave the same way he had come in a decade earlier.

"There is no question everyone makes mistakes in their lives," he told them. "But one I never made is loving the City of Providence too much."

Later that night, Lloyd Griffin rallied the troops at a packed meeting in Cianci's downtown campaign headquarters. Guards were posted at the door to bar journalists, but a young Associated Press reporter slipped in, unnoticed. Griffin exhorted the people to show Cianci that they would support him if he tried to come back in the special election for mayor a few months from now. Buckles Melise wandered through the crowd.

"We all got a piece of the action while Buddy Cianci was mayor," shouted Griffin. "Some of us ate real big."

CHAPTER SEVEN

He Never Stopped Caring

It wasn't until a few days after his resignation, when he was sitting at home, that Buddy Cianci was hit by the enormity of his loss.

For the first time in nearly a decade, he couldn't pick up the phone and order something done. There was no limousine or police driver outside. The ex-mayor of Providence sat alone with his thoughts, in the house where he had assaulted Raymond DeLeo, powerless on Power Street.

He immediately began plotting his return.

Seven days after he resigned, Cianci received a tumultuous welcome on Federal Hill when he served as grand marshal of the St. Joseph's procession. He had hinted in advance that the crowd's reception would help him decide whether to run in the special election for mayor that summer, and he wasn't disappointed. The crowd surged forward when Cianci stepped out of his car. So many women rushed up to kiss him that he had to wipe the lipstick from his cheek. Many of the spectators moved with Cianci as the procession made its way down Atwells Avenue. An airplane flew over the Church of the Holy Ghost trailing a banner that read PROVIDENCE NEEDS CIANCI FOR PROGRESS.

The man who had been sworn in as acting mayor, City Council president Joseph R. Paolino, marched further back and passed in near silence.

Despite Cianci's rousing reception, the Italian-American newspaper *The Echo,* long a staunch supporter, urged him not to run if he truly loved Providence. Citing his assault conviction and "the unanswered question of corruption," *The Echo* said that Cianci risked becoming an embarrassment to his heritage. But Cianci forged ahead and declared that he would run again. Although the city charter had required him to resign following his conviction, he said that it didn't disqualify him from running again. He argued that he wasn't technically a convicted felon, because he hadn't been sent to prison.

Incredibly, Cianci invoked his eleven-year-old daughter, Nicole—the daughter he had neglected during his long hours as mayor—as his reason for running. Cianci said that he had met with Nicole and that she had urged him to run "because if you don't run for mayor, people would think you are a quitter and Ciancis aren't quitters."

But the Rhode Island Supreme Court didn't see it that way. In a 3–2 ruling, the court knocked Cianci off the ballot. The majority reasoned that it would be ludicrous to allow Cianci to fill out the term he had just been forced to surrender. The court was silent on the question of whether he could run in a future election.

Paul Campbell, a Cianci aide, says that they had campaign bumper stickers printed and the comeback campaign ready to roll. After the supreme court's ruling, Campbell recalls going to Cianci's house to discuss an appeal to the U.S. Supreme Court and an attempt to "reach out" to one of the justices in Washington. But Cianci ultimately decided not to appeal; it would have been expensive, and he faced long odds.

Ironically, the mayor had been done in by Providence's new home-rule charter, which he had pushed for to strengthen the powers of the mayor following his frequent battles with the Democratic City Council. A provision of the charter stated that felons could not serve as mayor. The chairman of the charter commission, Dr. Melvyn M. Gelch, had challenged Cianci's eligibility. A few days after the supreme court's ruling, a vitriolic Cianci called in to a radio talk show on WHJJ, on which Gelch, a neurosurgeon at Rhode Island Hospital, was the guest.

"Don't you own some land around Rhode Island Hospital?" asked Cianci.

"I do," replied Gelch.

"Yeah, and you're giving it to Rhode Island Hospital and taking a big tax deduction."

"No, I'm taking no tax deduction."

"You'd better not, Doctor, because we know about it."

"Buddy, the IRS knows about you, too. That two hundred thousand dollars a year."

"That was spent, Doctor, legitimately on campaign expenses—"

"Buddy, remember Al Capone went to jail for income-tax evasion, not for the other things."

"Doctor, you know something? You just can't stop being ethnic, can you? That's the problem with you."

"Now, Buddy, that's ridiculous. That's another wild attack."

"You know, you mention Al Capone, you mention me. I happen to be of Italian-American background and proud of it . . ."

Meanwhile, political life moved on without Buddy Cianci. Joseph Paolino, the twenty-nine-year-old son of a downtown real estate mogul, was elected mayor in the special election. Cianci faded from the spotlight. He dabbled in real estate, and he read a lot—he favored biographies of great men. He talked of writing his own book and about a variety of business ventures, including launching a regional airline. A few years after his departure, Cianci's name turned up on a list published by the state treasurer of forty-eight hundred people with unclaimed bank accounts. "When you're out of public office," he joked wryly, "they forget you in a hurry."

Later Cianci would liken the experience to "going through withdrawal." Friends would encounter him sitting forlornly in a bar or a restaurant, alone. "When you're in, you're in," he said heavily. "And when you're out, you're out." Rhode Island state police detectives doing drug surveillance began noticing Cianci driving his Mercedes late at night in Central Falls, a small, impoverished city near Providence that was gaining a reputation as the nation's cocaine capital. The one-square-mile city was home to a large number of immigrants from the Medellín section of Colombia, as well as several major drug dealers who were distributing cocaine throughout New England and as far as Montreal and Chicago.

Detective James C. Lynch, Jr., said that he saw Cianci perhaps half a dozen times as he was doing surveillance, and that other detectives also saw him. They thought it was unusual to see the ex-mayor cruising around Central Falls late at night, though they never saw him with any drug dealers or with drugs.

During the same period, in September 1986, the state police raided the home of a Warwick drug dealer, seizing more than one pound of cocaine, two ounces of marijuana, and eight thousand dollars in cash. Three detectives involved in the raid—Lynch, Captain James P. Mullen, and Sergeant Brian Andrews—said that a Mercedes in the garage belonged to Cianci. The dealer also did some work out of his house as an auto mechanic. The police tried to get the dealer to cooperate and tell them about his supplier and other customers, but he refused and later pleaded guilty. Cianci was never questioned.

Cianci's time in exile was a time for counting his losses, but also for healing old wounds.

Bruce Melucci, his former political adviser who had left on bitter terms, started seeing Cianci in Leo's. The two men reestablished a cordial relationship. Melucci, who had been struck by Cianci's loneliness even when he was mayor, thought that he seemed lost without the office that had come to define his life.

Skip Chernov, the fallen rock-and-roll promoter, had a drink with Cianci one night in the former Alarie's, now another bar. They discussed opening a jazz club together. The conversation turned to the old days, when Chernov had worn a wire into the Civic Center and Cianci had indicted Harold Copeland and then run as the anticorruption candidate. Chernov was bitter toward Cianci for having later turned on him, by blocking his efforts to expand Tortilla Flats, which had forced him out of business. Now, according to Chernov, Cianci said that he had done it because of Chernov's reputation as a rat—"You weren't a team player," Cianci told him.

Norm Roussel, his erstwhile adman, would eat lunch with Cianci on Fridays, at the Barnsider. Cianci would sit in the corner, depressed. Roussel would kid him that if he didn't cheer up, he wasn't going to buy him lunch. Cianci talked about how miserable he was, how he had let his career slip through his fingers. Roussel encouraged him to run for mayor again, but Cianci said no. Too little time had passed.

One day Cianci had martinis at the Left Bank restaurant with Bill Warner, the architect who had developed the original plans to relocate the downtown rivers and strip away the concrete that had smothered them. From their table the two men could track the progress of the ambitious project, which had begun during Cianci's first watch.

Warner had come up with the idea as an offshoot of the Capital Center Project, a city, state, and federal redevelopment effort to relocate the downtown railroad tracks and open up some thirty-five acres of prime land for development. Cianci, recognizing the potential and eager to tap into the federal funds that would pay for the bulk of the project, had eagerly signed on to the project. But within a few years he was gone.

As Cianci sat with Warner in the Left Bank, sipping his martini, the irony of his squandered opportunity could not have been lost on him. Minutes before Warner had come to the mayor's office to outline the river project, in 1983, Cianci had received the phone call notifying him of his indictment for the assault of Raymond DeLeo.

Although Cianci probably didn't realize it, his identity had been incorporated into a character that appeared on *Saturday Night Live* in the mid- to late 1980s—the Pathological Liar. Played by comedian Jon Lovitz, the spector, was charged with obtaining money under false pretenses. But the charges were later dropped, for lack of a speedy trial, and a judge ordered Blackjack reinstated at Public Works, with back pay.

The week before Cianci resigned, Edward "Buckles" Melise, Cianci's highway superintendent and campaign fund-raiser, was charged with extorting snowplow contractors, then indicted twice more after Cianci left, for stealing city asphalt and for approving paychecks for no-show workers. Following one indictment, Buckles led state police on a hundred-mile-an-hour car chase up Interstate 95 in his pink Cadillac before finally surrendering on Federal Hill. He pleaded guilty and went to prison.

Ron Glantz recalled having witnessed Cianci and Joe DiSanto argue about Buckles over lunch one day at the Old Canteen. Buckles was in prison, and his wife needed money. Glantz says that DiSanto brought up the fact that Cianci had promised to take care of him, by giving him five thousand dollars, and that they should pay him. But Cianci, according to Glantz, said, "Fuck him." DiSanto was upset, says Glantz, but Cianci didn't want to discuss it. Buckles subsequently testified against DiSanto and Jake Kaplan about the alleged fifteen-thousand-dollar kickback in the 1981 sale of the Providence garbage trucks. But they were acquitted.

The feds put a lot of pressure on DiSanto, Cianci's confidant and former Public Works director. In addition to the garbage-truck case, DiSanto also was indicted, with Richard Carroll, former chairman of the Water Supply Board, for extorting twenty-one thousand dollars from a plumbing-and-heating contractor. DiSanto beat that case, too. He was convicted by a jury, but the judge later threw out his conviction. DiSanto went to trial again, and this time was acquitted. (Carroll, his codefendant, was convicted and sent to prison.) In the midst of fighting the criminal charges, DiSanto was hauled into divorce court by his ex-wife, in a dispute over their property settlement. She accused him of bringing home a briefcase full of cash from a Cianci fund-raiser, and of storing cash in coffee cans in the basement of his house. DiSanto angrily denied the charges. Lincoln Almond, the U.S. attorney in Rhode Island, believed that DiSanto would have cooperated against Cianci had he been convicted. DiSanto was later convicted of state charges that he approved bogus overtime in Public Works. But by then the statute of limitations had expired on other possible crimes that Almond was looking at.

Cianci "kept close tabs on people," said Almond. In the fall of 1985, just before DiSanto went on trial the first time for the plumbing extortion, DiSanto and Cianci showed up at the U.S. attorney's office with a bizarre

Pathological Liar wore three-piece polyester suits and wide ties and bullied people to get what he wanted as he spun an increasingly improbable series of lies, punctuated with the exclamation "Yeah, that's the ticket!"

Cianci thought about leaving Providence. Then two things came to his rescue—a radio station and a woman.

About a year after Cianci's resignation, Ron St. Pierre, the program director at WHJJ, was leafing through a trade publication when he saw that the ex-mayor of Cleveland, Dennis Kucinich, had a successful Cleveland radio talk show. Chatting with his bosses, St. Pierre noted that Kucinich was popular, and he wasn't nearly as funny or as personable as Buddy Cianci. "Hey, Buddy's not doing anything right now," said St. Pierre. "Why don't we give him a call?"

On March 11, 1985, after a one-year hiatus, the Buddy Cianci Show moved from City Hall to the airwaves. The ex-mayor became the host of an afternoon drive-time talk-show on WHJJ. This was during the infancy of the modern era of talk radio, when Larry King and Dr. Ruth Westheimer were two of the big national names and a Denver talk-show host, Alan Berg, was gunned down by a crazed caller. In Rhode Island, WHJJ was the only station with an all-talk format and was looking to invigorate its lineup. (The station's midday host said that his best show ever had been a discussion about which way people put up their toilet paper.) In a state where politics is sport and everybody knows everybody else, Cianci was an instant hit.

One of Cianci's regular callers was "Ray from Lincoln"—left unspoken was his true identity, New England Mafia boss Raymond "Junior" Patriarca. Not that Ray ever called to chat about the good old days, like when he and Cianci had crossed paths in Maryland in pursuit of the priest who had been the elder Patriarca's alibi. Ray was like any other caller, offering his opinion on the issue of the day, from politics to taxes.

Smart, funny, and opinionated, Cianci became the bad boy of local radio, tossing out one-liners and skewering his political guests as he simultaneously settled old scores and boosted WHJJ's ratings. Unlike many hosts, Cianci screened his own calls and was quick to cut off those who disagreed with him. "Wait a minute," he interrupted one caller who challenged him. "I'll decide what's important on my show because I've got the microphone."

The smoke-filled, glass-walled radio booth became Cianci's Elba. Behind the microphone, he could pretend that he was back in the political arena—only this time with a seven-second delay button to silence his opponents. Some politicians, like Joe Paolino, whom Cianci liked to attack, refused to come on. Others ventured onto Cianci's show at their own risk, as young Patrick Kennedy learned in 1988 when he ran for state representative in Mount Pleasant. Kennedy, the son of Massachusetts senator Edward Kennedy, was an easy target for Cianci. Back in 1976 Ted Kennedy had blocked Senate confirmation of Cianci's mentor, Herbert DeSimone, to a federal judgeship. When Patrick Kennedy announced his candidacy, Cianci went after the Kennedys on his show. What had Patrick's father known about Chappaquiddick? How had a young woman drowned in the car accident while Ted swam away? What about Ted's alleged affairs with women? Why did he drink so much?

When Patrick Kennedy, a timid Providence College student, came on the show, Cianci ripped into him as a carpetbagger who didn't know his district. Before long, Cianci had Kennedy stumbling over street names in Mount Pleasant. Calls flooded in, asking the befuddled Kennedy if he knew where Jasmine Street was, or if he knew the Mahoney family. The show was a disaster. But Kennedy, backed by his family name and money, and a dose of sympathy from Cianci's attacks, went on to victory, the start of a successful political career that would carry him to Congress.

Cianci was making good money in radio, with little effort. Minutes before he was due on the air, he would call his frantic producer from his blue Mercedes convertible and cheerily report that it was "a top-down day." Then he'd roll into the station's parking lot in East Providence, carrying a newspaper or a magazine, and jump right into the show.

Cianci also found some personal stability in his life when he met Wendy Materna, a tall, pretty blonde. Despite her last name, Materna was descended from an old-line WASP family. A Daughter of the American Revolution, she traced her ancestry back to one of Rhode Island's first settlers, Colonel Benjamin Church, a famous Indian fighter who kept a diary chronicling the bloody King Philip's War in 1675–76, when the colonists wrested control of New England from its native inhabitants.

Born in Providence, Materna had moved around the country as a girl because her father was a navy pilot. Although she lived in Chicago, Providence remained her touchstone, the place she would return for holidays and to visit her grandparents, who lived on the East Side and had been big Cianci supporters. On Pearl Harbor Day in 1984, toward the end of Cianci's first year in exile, Materna met him in Capriccio during a visit to

Providence. The following year she moved to Rhode Island to take care of her elderly grandmother, who had had a stroke. She and Buddy began dating in the fall of 1985.

Materna, who had just turned thirty, found the older Cianci, who was forty-four, fascinating. He was funny and bright, kind and charming. Away from politics, he was calmer. Their relationship worked because she knew him as just Buddy, not the mayor. She was from Providence, but she wasn't a Providence girl. She was smart, savvy, and socially graceful. They enjoyed a nice life together. Cianci, who was doing well financially between his radio gig and his real estate ventures, bought a fifty-one-foot yacht, which he named the *Nicola*, after his daughter. In nice weather he and Materna spent weekends together on the boat, in Newport. They bought two cocker spaniels, Tucker and Belle. On Sunday nights Wendy cooked dinner for Buddy at his house.

When the mayor's job opened up again in 1986, Cianci vacillated. On the morning of the filing deadline, WHJJ bought a newspaper ad that said: "Run the show or run for office? Buddy's decision today." Forty minutes before the deadline, Cianci signed his declaration papers at the Café at Brooks, then decided not to file. He announced on the air that he would not run—for personal reasons, he emphasized, not because he was running away from a fight.

Materna knew that running again was always in the back of his mind. Cianci had vowed never to set foot in City Hall unless it was as mayor. But she also knew that it was a question of timing—not just politically, but personally. He had to, in her words, "rebuild to a good place from a bad place."

WHILE BUDDY CIANCI tried to move on, state and federal investigators were moving in on City Hall.

Investigators found a cornucopia of corruption and eventually indicted thirty people, many of them connected to the Department of Public Works. Twenty-two were convicted, and sixteen went to jail. Many of those convicted were low-level players, who had been involved in no-show jobs, bogus construction repairs, rigged snowplowing contracts, and stolen asphalt. Police divers even searched the Providence River for manhole covers that authorities suspected had been stolen for sale as scrap metal, then dumped when the police started closing in.

William "Blackjack" DelSanto, the Patriarca capo and city sidewalk in-

Pathological Liar wore three-piece polyester suits and wide ties and bullied people to get what he wanted as he spun an increasingly improbable series of lies, punctuated with the exclamation "Yeah, that's the ticket!"

Cianci thought about leaving Providence. Then two things came to his rescue—a radio station and a woman.

About a year after Cianci's resignation, Ron St. Pierre, the program director at WHJJ, was leafing through a trade publication when he saw that the ex-mayor of Cleveland, Dennis Kucinich, had a successful Cleveland radio talk show. Chatting with his bosses, St. Pierre noted that Kucinich was popular, and he wasn't nearly as funny or as personable as Buddy Cianci. "Hey, Buddy's not doing anything right now," said St. Pierre. "Why don't we give him a call?"

On March 11, 1985, after a one-year hiatus, the Buddy Cianci Show moved from City Hall to the airwaves. The ex-mayor became the host of an afternoon drive-time talk-show on WHJJ. This was during the infancy of the modern era of talk radio, when Larry King and Dr. Ruth Westheimer were two of the big national names and a Denver talk-show host, Alan Berg, was gunned down by a crazed caller. In Rhode Island, WHJJ was the only station with an all-talk format and was looking to invigorate its lineup. (The station's midday host said that his best show ever had been a discussion about which way people put up their toilet paper.) In a state where politics is sport and everybody knows everybody else, Cianci was an instant hit.

One of Cianci's regular callers was "Ray from Lincoln"—left unspoken was his true identity, New England Mafia boss Raymond "Junior" Patriarca. Not that Ray ever called to chat about the good old days, like when he and Cianci had crossed paths in Maryland in pursuit of the priest who had been the elder Patriarca's alibi. Ray was like any other caller, offering his opinion on the issue of the day, from politics to taxes.

Smart, funny, and opinionated, Cianci became the bad boy of local radio, tossing out one-liners and skewering his political guests as he simultaneously settled old scores and boosted WHJJ's ratings. Unlike many hosts, Cianci screened his own calls and was quick to cut off those who disagreed with him. "Wait a minute," he interrupted one caller who challenged him. "I'll decide what's important on my show because I've got the microphone."

The smoke-filled, glass-walled radio booth became Cianci's Elba. Behind the microphone, he could pretend that he was back in the political arena—only this time with a seven-second delay button to silence his opponents. Some politicians, like Joe Paolino, whom Cianci liked to attack, refused to come on. Others ventured onto Cianci's show at their own risk, as young Patrick Kennedy learned in 1988 when he ran for state representative in Mount Pleasant. Kennedy, the son of Massachusetts senator Edward Kennedy, was an easy target for Cianci. Back in 1976 Ted Kennedy had blocked Senate confirmation of Cianci's mentor, Herbert DeSimone, to a federal judgeship. When Patrick Kennedy announced his candidacy, Cianci went after the Kennedys on his show. What had Patrick's father known about Chappaquiddick? How had a young woman drowned in the car accident while Ted swam away? What about Ted's alleged affairs with women? Why did he drink so much?

When Patrick Kennedy, a timid Providence College student, came on the show, Cianci ripped into him as a carpetbagger who didn't know his district. Before long, Cianci had Kennedy stumbling over street names in Mount Pleasant. Calls flooded in, asking the befuddled Kennedy if he knew where Jasmine Street was, or if he knew the Mahoney family. The show was a disaster. But Kennedy, backed by his family name and money, and a dose of sympathy from Cianci's attacks, went on to victory, the start of a successful political career that would carry him to Congress.

Cianci was making good money in radio, with little effort. Minutes before he was due on the air, he would call his frantic producer from his blue Mercedes convertible and cheerily report that it was "a top-down day." Then he'd roll into the station's parking lot in East Providence, carrying a newspaper or a magazine, and jump right into the show.

Cianci also found some personal stability in his life when he met Wendy Materna, a tall, pretty blonde. Despite her last name, Materna was descended from an old-line WASP family. A Daughter of the American Revolution, she traced her ancestry back to one of Rhode Island's first settlers, Colonel Benjamin Church, a famous Indian fighter who kept a diary chronicling the bloody King Philip's War in 1675–76, when the colonists wrested control of New England from its native inhabitants.

Born in Providence, Materna had moved around the country as a girl because her father was a navy pilot. Although she lived in Chicago, Providence remained her touchstone, the place she would return for holidays and to visit her grandparents, who lived on the East Side and had been big Cianci supporters. On Pearl Harbor Day in 1984, toward the end of Cianci's first year in exile, Materna met him in Capriccio during a visit to

Providence. The following year she moved to Rhode Island to take care of her elderly grandmother, who had had a stroke. She and Buddy began dating in the fall of 1985.

Materna, who had just turned thirty, found the older Cianci, who was forty-four, fascinating. He was funny and bright, kind and charming. Away from politics, he was calmer. Their relationship worked because she knew him as just Buddy, not the mayor. She was from Providence, but she wasn't a Providence girl. She was smart, savvy, and socially graceful. They enjoyed a nice life together. Cianci, who was doing well financially between his radio gig and his real estate ventures, bought a fifty-one-foot yacht, which he named the *Nicola*, after his daughter. In nice weather he and Materna spent weekends together on the boat, in Newport. They bought two cocker spaniels, Tucker and Belle. On Sunday nights Wendy cooked dinner for Buddy at his house.

When the mayor's job opened up again in 1986, Cianci vacillated. On the morning of the filing deadline, WHJJ bought a newspaper ad that said: "Run the show or run for office? Buddy's decision today." Forty minutes before the deadline, Cianci signed his declaration papers at the Café at Brooks, then decided not to file. He announced on the air that he would not run—for personal reasons, he emphasized, not because he was running away from a fight.

Materna knew that running again was always in the back of his mind. Cianci had vowed never to set foot in City Hall unless it was as mayor. But she also knew that it was a question of timing—not just politically, but personally. He had to, in her words, "rebuild to a good place from a bad place."

WHILE BUDDY CIANCI tried to move on, state and federal investigators were moving in on City Hall.

Investigators found a cornucopia of corruption and eventually indicted thirty people, many of them connected to the Department of Public Works. Twenty-two were convicted, and sixteen went to jail. Many of those convicted were low-level players, who had been involved in no-show jobs, bogus construction repairs, rigged snowplowing contracts, and stolen asphalt. Police divers even searched the Providence River for manhole covers that authorities suspected had been stolen for sale as scrap metal, then dumped when the police started closing in.

William "Blackjack" DelSanto, the Patriarca capo and city sidewalk inspector, was charged with obtaining money under false pretenses. But the charges were later dropped, for lack of a speedy trial, and a judge ordered Blackjack reinstated at Public Works, with back pay.

The week before Cianci resigned, Edward "Buckles" Melise, Cianci's highway superintendent and campaign fund-raiser, was charged with extorting snowplow contractors, then indicted twice more after Cianci left, for stealing city asphalt and for approving paychecks for no-show workers. Following one indictment, Buckles led state police on a hundred-mile-an-hour car chase up Interstate 95 in his pink Cadillac before finally surrendering on Federal Hill. He pleaded guilty and went to prison.

Ron Glantz recalled having witnessed Cianci and Joe DiSanto argue about Buckles over lunch one day at the Old Canteen. Buckles was in prison, and his wife needed money. Glantz says that DiSanto brought up the fact that Cianci had promised to take care of him, by giving him five thousand dollars, and that they should pay him. But Cianci, according to Glantz, said, "Fuck him." DiSanto was upset, says Glantz, but Cianci didn't want to discuss it. Buckles subsequently testified against DiSanto and Jake Kaplan about the alleged fifteen-thousand-dollar kickback in the 1981 sale of the Providence garbage trucks. But they were acquitted.

The feds put a lot of pressure on DiSanto, Cianci's confidant and former Public Works director. In addition to the garbage-truck case, DiSanto also was indicted, with Richard Carroll, former chairman of the Water Supply Board, for extorting twenty-one thousand dollars from a plumbing-and-heating contractor. DiSanto beat that case, too. He was convicted by a jury, but the judge later threw out his conviction. DiSanto went to trial again, and this time was acquitted. (Carroll, his codefendant, was convicted and sent to prison.) In the midst of fighting the criminal charges, DiSanto was hauled into divorce court by his ex-wife, in a dispute over their property settlement. She accused him of bringing home a briefcase full of cash from a Cianci fund-raiser, and of storing cash in coffee cans in the basement of his house. DiSanto angrily denied the charges. Lincoln Almond, the U.S. attorney in Rhode Island, believed that DiSanto would have cooperated against Cianci had he been convicted. DiSanto was later convicted of state charges that he approved bogus overtime in Public Works. But by then the statute of limitations had expired on other possible crimes that Almond was looking at.

Cianci "kept close tabs on people," said Almond. In the fall of 1985, just before DiSanto went on trial the first time for the plumbing extortion, DiSanto and Cianci showed up at the U.S. attorney's office with a bizarre tale that illustrated the Byzantine nature of Rhode Island politics. DiSanto described a chance encounter that he had had the previous winter in Florida with a Rhode Island prosecutor, Henry Gemma, Jr. The respected chief of the attorney general's Criminal Division, Gemma had worked with Cianci when he was a prosecutor and had felt uncomfortable when he was assigned to the prosecution team in the DeLeo case. DiSanto and Gemma had a mutual friend, William Riccitelli, who was DiSanto's civil lawyer. Through Riccitelli, they bumped into each other one night in DiSanto's condominium in West Palm Beach. Then the story turned weird. DiSanto claimed that Riccitelli took him into another room and said that he could get the state charges against him dropped for a forty-thousand-dollar pay-off to the attorney general, Dennis Roberts II. DiSanto refused. Gemma and Roberts called the accusation ludicrous. Gemma speculated that DiSanto had made up the story to try to have the charges against him dismissed.

Contractor Tommy Ricci, the owner of the Busy Bee Construction Company, was also in the crosshairs of state and federal grand juries—for snowplowing contracts, for school-repair work, and for stealing city equipment. According to an informant, one dump truck went into the Public Works garage with the CITY OF PROVIDENCE seal on the door and came out with another seal that said BUSY BEE.

Dogged by investigators who seized his equipment, subpoenaed his records, summoned him repeatedly to the grand jury, and even snooped through his trash, Ricci refused to cooperate. Years later he self-published a book about his experiences, *In-Justice*, with a dagger dripping blood on the cover and a wintry picture of City Hall on the back with the caption "A decade of corruption emanates from within these once hallowed halls." Today Ricci freely admits that his city work skyrocketed as he contributed to Cianci.

Ricci said that he went to the grand jury twenty-seven times. The feds "wanted me to roll on Buddy." Once, a prosecutor put his arm around Ricci and said, "We're going to make you sing." Ricci, who had always been a ball buster, went into the courtroom and started singing "Fly Me to the Moon." After his grand-jury appearances, Ricci said he would stop by Cianci's house on Power Street to tell him what had happened. The feds offered him money and the return of his equipment to testify against Cianci, Ricci said, but he refused. He didn't want to be labeled a rat. Cianci cursed the prosecutors and urged Ricci to confront them. "Confront them yourself," Ricci replied.

Ricci was never convicted of any corruption charges. But he did plead guilty to income-tax evasion and did four months in federal prison. He said that he pleaded on the advice of his lawyer, who said that the feds were going to keep gunning for him, so he might as well get it over with. He said that he kept his mouth shut about Cianci.

Meanwhile, Ronnie Glantz had his own decisions to make.

In 1985, Glantz and Tony Bucci were indicted for extorting seventy-seven thousand dollars in kickbacks from businessman James Notorantonio for the 1979 purchase of garbage trucks. They refused overtures to cooperate. Glantz said that he talked it over with his wife but couldn't bring himself to be a rat. He and Bucci were tried and convicted in 1986. One month later Glantz was indicted again, for obstruction of justice and perjury. This crime concerned his lying to a grand jury to cover up his participation in a fraudulent land deal involving a proposed hazardous-waste recycling plant. Glantz went to trial again and was convicted in December 1986. The government's star witness was Glantz's partner in the recycling plant and another former Cianci confidant—Mickey Farina. Farina, who had pleaded guilty to making false statements, testified under a grant of immunity. He said that he turned on Glantz because his old friend had misrepresented him in his divorce back in 1978, by failing to file the divorce decree—which later complicated his second marriage. Glantz countered that he gave the decree to Farina, who didn't file it because he was trying to conceal his assets from an investigation.

Either way, Glantz was screwed. Early in 1987 he was sentenced to eleven years in federal prison; the soonest he would be eligible for parole was in four years. That spring, at the age of forty-nine, Ronnie Glantz, the onetime jokester of City Hall, reported to Allenwood Federal Prison Camp in Pennsylvania, leaving his wife and four children and East Side home for a bunk bed in a dormitory room with nineteen other convicts. Allenwood was no country club. Glantz was thrust into a militarylike regimen—breakfast at six, report to his prison job by eight, mandatory head counts at 4 P.M. and 7 P.M., standing at attention beside his bed; lights out at nine. He was locked up with New York mobsters and inner-city drug dealers. He learned to avoid the TV room, where fights often broke out, and to be wary in the telephone line, where an inmate coming off a bad call home—his wife was leaving him, his kids hated him—might erupt and take a swing at the nearest inmate. He witnessed the ganglike rivalries between the black inmates from Washington and those from Philadelphia and New York. One summer day Glantz was assigned to a work crew picking dandelions on the prison grounds. Some of the other inmates took some yeast from the kitchen and put it in a plastic garbage bag filled with dandelions and let it ferment in the sun to make dandelion wine. It was a far cry from the vintage wines that Glantz had enjoyed on Federal Hill during his years as the second-most powerful man in City Hall.

His first summer in prison, Glantz wrote to the Rhode Island State Police, offering information regarding the hazardous-waste plant that he had been a partner in. The state police sent two investigators to visit Glantz in Allenwood. He talked generally about the plant and also about the corruption at City Hall. He said that Buddy Cianci, Joe DiSanto, and Mickey Farina had solicited and received bribes from a number of contractors. He said that he had been present for their conversations and, in some cases, the actual payoffs. In exchange for immunity, he offered to provide details of bribes and bid rigging.

Captain Michael J. Urso, Jr., then detective commander of the state police, met with Glantz and came away feeling that his story carried "the ring of truth." Colonel Steven M. Pare, then a young detective and today the head of the state police, said that he found Glantz's accounts of City Hall corruption convincing, including his description of the various bribery schemes involving contractors, his role as the bagman, and his accounts of cash payoffs being turned over to the mayor.

Glantz received immunity and continued to talk to the authorities. That fall, U.S. attorney Lincoln Almond said publicly that Cianci's indictment was imminent, hoping to convince other witnesses to come forward. But it never happened. Although prosecutors didn't doubt that Glantz had been involved in corruption with Cianci, they were concerned about his credibility, given his perjury conviction. They also had trouble finding other witnesses to corroborate his story. The five-year statute of limitations was also a problem—the clock had run out on many of the alleged crimes that Glantz had described.

Publicly, Cianci seemed unperturbed by the ongoing scrutiny. "Frankly, the whole thing is getting a little boring," he said.

In February 1989 Almond announced the end of the Providence probe. He called the seven-year investigation a success, "despite the fact that some will go unpunished."

"It can be disappointing," said Almond, "but it happens quite often."

■

WHILE RONNIE GLANTZ sat in prison, Buddy Cianci became a high flier in the world of real estate and contemplated his future in politics. It was the late 1980s, a boom time, and there was money to be made if you had the right connections and a willingness to take risks.

Cianci speculated in South Providence land, bought and sold a downtown office building for a million-dollar profit in just eight months, and opened two restaurants. One, Flyer's, was near the airport in Warwick; the other, Trapper John's, near Rhode Island Hospital, had a *M*A*S*H* theme. Another deal, netting Cianci and his partners an $850,000 profit, was sketched out on a napkin over drinks in a bar. Flush from his success, Cianci bought his rented carriage house on Power Street for $625,000, outbidding the president of Fleet National Bank, Terrence Murray, and borrowed $200,000 to purchase his yacht, the *Nicola*.

Two of Cianci's former aides, Patrick Conley and Paul Campbell, brought him into the South Providence real estate ventures. Conley, the founder of the business, had attracted controversy when Cianci was mayor, for allegations that he received inside information from the mayor's office about property that the city was going to offer at tax sale. Neighborhood activists criticized their dealings for contributing to neighborhood blight. One tenement house that Cianci and his partners purchased was cited for several housing-code violations.

Conley said that he and Cianci formed a partnership with another man, a real estate broker, who picked up run-down property at tax sales. They named it Solid Investment; *Solid* stood for "Scavengers of Land in Decline." According to Conley, Cianci used his connections to obtain a two-hundred-thousand-dollar line of credit from First Bank & Trust, which had received city deposits when Cianci was mayor.

Cianci's foray into real estate also received a boost from two crooked businessmen, Joseph Mollicone, Jr., and Joseph Cerilli, high rollers who defined the greedy eighties in Rhode Island. Mollicone, the driving force behind the deal, was the son of a Federal Hill banker, "Puppy Dog" Mollicone, who had been Raymond Patriarca's personal banker.

In the early 1980s, when Cianci was mayor, Mollicone and Cerilli refurbished the historic Old Providence Journal Building. Cianci, who encouraged the project as part of his blueprint for downtown renewal, steered the city solicitor's and building inspector's offices into the building as paying tenants. Around the same time, Mollicone purchased Cianci's house on Blackstone Boulevard, during the mayor's divorce, for $345,000— a price that critics called high.

Mollicone and Cerilli would later allege that they paid off Cianci for his assistance. Mollicone said that they gave him seventy thousand dollars. Cerilli said that they gave him cash, after he left office, and booked it as "legal fees."

After Cianci left office, Mollicone helped him launch his real estate career by selling him two condominiums in a medical office building. Cianci had to put down only $1,000, borrowing the remaining $155,000 from Mollicone's bank. Later, in a standard transaction to delay capital-gains taxes, Cianci swapped the two condos to Mollicone for a restaurant near the airport, and became a restaurateur.

In the late 1980s Cianci's fortunes turned. After earning $780,000 in 1987 and $212,000 in 1988, he lost money over the next two years, as the real estate market declined and the restaurant business slumped. His house and his other properties were heavily mortgaged.

Meanwhile, the mayor's job was opening up. Joseph Paolino announced his candidacy for governor in 1990. In April Conley, who was also a prominent Rhode Island historian and a former Providence College professor, formed a nonprofit group called the City Symposium, to discuss economic and political issues facing Providence. But the group's real purpose was to convince Cianci, who was on the fence, to run for mayor. Besides Conley, the group consisted of old allies like Norm Roussel, Paul Campbell, and Frank Corrente, an accountant who had been city controller at the end of Buddy I, and Thomas Rossi, a state representative from the politically important Fourth Ward, Tony Bucci's old territory. Rossi was the only elected official to publicly support Cianci.

The City Symposium raised fifteen thousand dollars to conduct a poll of how voters would view a Cianci candidacy. Conley said that the poll found a die-hard core of 23 percent of the voters willing to support Cianci "even if he raped a girl in Kennedy Plaza or robbed a bank at gunpoint." The poll also showed other voters willing to consider Cianci, which gave him hope that they could pick up another 13 to 14 percent and win a three-way race. Cianci's consultants drew up a twenty-page strategy paper stressing the "second chance" theme. They assumed that 58 percent of the city's voters would never vote for Cianci, but that didn't matter. They were banking on a three-way race and needed just 34 percent of the vote.

But first they needed a candidate. In strategy sessions at the "Crime Castle," as some of his followers dubbed his house on Power Street, Cianci was hesitant. He knew that he would be a long shot, and worried about raising money, especially with his personal financial troubles. He confided to Wendy Materna that he wasn't sure he wanted to return to the craziness of politics. It had also been a turbulent year personally. His mother had died of throat cancer in 1989, on Mother's Day. And his sixteen-year-old daughter, Nicole, struggling with emotional problems stemming from her parents' divorce and her attempts to win her father's approval, had moved in with him.

But Materna knew Cianci too well. Although he seemed generally happy, there was an undercurrent to their conversations. For four years, she had listened to him begin his sentences, "When I was mayor . . ." Although she loved their life together, she gave him the final push.

A few weeks before the June filing deadline, Materna slipped into City Hall, incognito, to pick up blank nomination papers. She had just come off a boat from Prudence Island in Narragansett Bay, where her family had a summer home. She walked into the Board of Canvassers office, flecks of seaweed in her hair and salt spray on her face, and asked for papers for mayor. The workers looked curiously at the leggy blonde in shorts and baseball cap.

As the filing deadline approached, the public speculation about Buddy's plans intensified. Even President Bush, during a White House luncheon with reporters from around the country, asked *Providence Journal* political columnist M. Charles Bakst about Cianci. "Talk about a guy who liked to mix it up," Bush said.

On June 27, the filing deadline, Patrick Conley went to Cianci's house in the morning and found him lounging in bed. Conley had written an announcement speech. Cianci asked him to read it. Conley stood at the foot of Cianci's bed and delivered the speech in his deep, theatrical voice. Then he tossed it on the bed and left, saying: "Jeez, Buddy, you can win. Between now and the end of the day, grow some testicles."

Later, after lunch, Materna went to Power Street and found Cianci still in bed, and uncertain. "Let's go," she told him. He got up and got dressed. His driver took them to WHJJ for his show, which began at 3 P.M.

When the show started, a caller urged Cianci to run. Then another. And another. He got caught up in it. During a break, he turned to his driver and said, "Go to City Hall." The driver left with his nomination papers. Seventeen minutes before the 4 P.M. deadline, Cianci announced on the air that he was running for mayor. His live broadcast mysteriously popped up on every police radio in Providence, interrupting normal transmissions as police brass scrambled to figure out what was happening. One minute later,

Cianci's driver walked into City Hall and filed the papers in the Board of Canvassers office on the first floor.

Upstairs, in his second-floor office, Mayor Paolino leapt up when he heard the news. Paolino, expected to win the state Democratic-party endorsement for governor that night, headed for the door. "That does it," he declared to some aides. "Somebody's got to stop him. I'm going downstairs and file to run against him." But Paolino's aides urged him not to act so hastily, delaying him long enough so that he missed the deadline. (Cianci's advisers had concluded that he couldn't beat Paolino.)

About twenty minutes later, Cianci and Materna took a preliminary victory lap through City Hall, trailed by television cameras. He was cheered by city workers who rushed out of their offices and hung over the stairwell railings. Some cried.

Cianci's comeback bid made national headlines—and, local critics said, further embarrassed a city with a legacy of chicanery. (A few years earlier, the city had adopted the tourism slogan "Providence harbors the best," which some people said made the city sound like a haven for fugitives.) *The Wall Street Journal*, in a front-page story headlined AMAZING COMEBACK: BUDDY CIANCI IS TOAST OF PROVIDENCE, said that a Cianci comeback "would be the envy of Richard Nixon."

The campaign was vintage Cianci, part tent revival and part political mugging. His two hapless opponents, Fred Lippitt and Andrew Annaldo, never saw what hit them.

Over and over, a humble and self-deprecating Cianci sought voters' forgiveness. "Yes, I have sinned," he said. "But let he who is without sin cast the first stone. That's what the Bible says." Cianci preached that he was no Mother Teresa—but that he had "never stopped caring about Providence." When a *New York Times* reporter pressed him about past corruption, Cianci told him to go to the Rhode Island Historical Society. That was "ancient history."

But the past kept cropping up. Reporters asked Cianci about the corruption on his first watch and his assault of DeLeo. On a televised newsmakers program, the first question dealt with Cianci's alleged cocaine use—a rumor that had been strong at the time of his assault on DeLeo but that had never surfaced so publicly. During a televised debate, the *Journal*'s Charlie Bakst held up a Cianci campaign brochure promising to reduce crime and asked whether the voters could trust a criminal to accomplish that. Cianci remained calm in front of the camera and stayed on message—that he had paid a very public price for his mistake, and that he wanted to talk about the future.

Running as an Independent, Cianci was matched against the Democrat Annaldo, a young city councilman from the Fourth Ward, and the venerable Lippitt, the seventy-three-year-old East Side patrician he had beaten in a three-way race in 1982.

Neither man was very articulate, and the nimble Cianci made them appear even more wooden. Standing between his two bickering opponents in one debate, Cianci listened as they accused each other of dipping into special pension deals at taxpayer expense, then unleashed the campaign's most memorable line: "I'm getting caught in the crossfire here between the Little Dipper and the Big Dipper." In another debate, at Brown University, Cianci skewered Annaldo's plan to force tax-exempt colleges and other institutions to pay more money to the city for police and fire protection. Taxing religious institutions, Cianci quipped, had been settled "when the people came in with high hats and turkeys."

Moments before one televised debate, as the candidates were standing in the television studio, sources said that Cianci leaned over and made a derogatory remark about the unmarried Lippitt's reputed homosexuality, rattling him. Prior to another debate, during an angry verbal exchange in the parking lot with the bachelor Annaldo, Cianci ripped into Andy "and his boyfriends."

Behind the scenes, the campaign was marked by skulduggery and financial perils.

One night, Lippitt said years later, he was leaving a fund-raiser at the Roger Williams Park Casino when some volunteers in another car noticed that he was being followed. They tailed that car and traced the license plate to an off-duty Providence policeman who was working for Cianci. Later that night they followed the car back to Cianci's house. (After the election, Lippitt said that Frank Corrente admitted that they had had him followed, to see whom he met with.)

In the campaign's final weeks, covert smear campaigns emerged against two of the candidates—Lippitt and Annaldo. One weekend, flyers calling Lippitt's Yankee ancestors "slave traders" mysteriously appeared in black neighborhoods in South Providence. Another day, someone delivered tape recordings to *The Providence Journal* of intercepted car-phone conversations between Annaldo and a Democratic fund-raiser, spiced with salty language but otherwise not incriminating. All three candidates denied any responsibility.

Heading down the stretch, Cianci was running out of funds. Between campaign stops he was on his car phone, trying to borrow money. On October 19 Conley, Roussel, and another supporter cosigned a hundred-thousand-dollar note to get him across the finish line.

Operating out of a cavernous abandoned supermarket on Branch Avenue, the Cianci campaign made up with manpower what it lacked in money. His New York political consultants were amazed at how quickly Cianci could turn out dozens of volunteers if he needed phone calls made or envelopes stuffed.

One volunteer was Steven Antonson, a twenty-seven-year-old electrician from Elmhurst. Antonson had grown up in a Doorley family, down the street from Joe Doorley's father. His parents had hated Buddy Cianci. But Steven, who had developed an interest in politics through his grandfather, the head of maintenance at the State House, admired Cianci as a brilliant politician. After Cianci declared his candidacy in 1990, Antonson went to an organizational meeting at his campaign headquarters, in an abandoned hardware store on Branch Avenue. Cianci gave a rousing speech, and Antonson was dazzled. This was the man to learn from—the man to teach him how to be a politician.

Antonson signed on as an advance man and quickly became indoctrinated in the wily ways of Buddy. One of his first tasks was to get Cianci into the St. Bartholomew's Feast parade in Silver Lake that summer. But even though Cianci had grown up in Silver Lake, the priest refused to invite him. Cianci would ruin the parade, he said. Antonson didn't know what the priest meant—until Cianci showed up anyway. The parade began uneventfully, with Cianci marching and waving. Then, suddenly, Cianci stopped marching and stood in the middle of the street, shaking hands. The front section of the parade kept going. But the entire parade behind him came to a halt. Cianci waited patiently, until seventy-five yards had opened up between him and the front of the parade, then resumed marching. At the end of the parade, Cianci turned to his advance man and said, "Antonson, did you see what I did?" Antonson was puzzled, so Cianci explained. "Everyone saw me. The only view they had was of me coming up the street." Antonson, realizing that he was right, laughed.

Antonson was awed by Cianci's ability to soak up information, to remember names and faces and dates, and to count votes with mathematical precision. When Antonson mentioned that he had graduated from Mount Pleasant High School in 1980, Cianci remembered that the school's basketball team had won the championship that year, and he named the principal. One day, campaigning at a supermarket, Antonson was handing out silver Cianci key chains when Cianci grabbed him and pulled him over in front of the dairy case. As the two men stood side by side, staring up at the milk cartons, Cianci said: "Antonson, what's wrong with you? Those key chains cost 75.9 cents apiece. You're giving them to people who don't vote."

As the campaign gathered momentum, Antonson found himself spending more time with Cianci. One of his jobs was to get the candidate out of bed in the morning. One Sunday, when Antonson made his wake-up call, Cianci asked if he'd gotten the newspaper. Antonson went outside, got the paper off his stoop, and came back to the phone. "Are there any articles about me?" Cianci asked. Antonson sat in his bed next to his wife, who was half asleep, and paged through the paper until he found an article about Cianci. "Read it to me," Cianci commanded. By now, Antonson's wife, Lori, was fuming. She sat up in bed and made such a commotion that Antonson had to hang up. "If he can't read his own paper," she snapped, "then he shouldn't be mayor."

Antonson got to know Cianci's insecurities and eccentricities, including his need to be loved. Elated after a successful visit to an electrical-workers banquet, Cianci wouldn't leave, even after the hall emptied out. "They loved me," he told Antonson. "Didn't they love me?"

He also never seemed to carry any money; Pat Conley joked that Cianci was like crime: "He never pays." One hot day, in a church basement on Smith Street, Cianci asked Antonson if he wanted a drink. Antonson said he'd like a Coke, then waited expectantly. "What's wrong?" asked Cianci. "The bar's over there." Another time Cianci had Antonson on his boat, anchored at Shooter's, on India Point, and offered him a drink. Antonson said he'd have a Coke. Cianci asked insistently if he wanted something stronger, but Antonson kept declining. Finally, Cianci said: "You're lucky you didn't ask for a drink. If you had, I would've told you to leave. When you drink, you say stuff you shouldn't say. Drinking makes you stupid." Cianci, who often drank vodka during the campaign, also advised, "If you're gonna drink, drink vodka. They can't smell it."

Cianci had one last lesson for Antonson: "The only thing I ask of you is that you're loyal. I've gotta be able to trust you. Otherwise, I don't need you around me."

Cianci's entire campaign in 1990 targeted the "leaners." During a brainstorming session, Cianci suggested inviting all of Providence's unde-cided voters to his house for a cookout. His consultants vetoed the idea, not wanting to alienate his core supporters. Outspent on television adver-tising, Cianci countered with a cheaper, yet sophisticated, direct-mail cam-paign that focused on undecided voters, by issue and by neighborhood.

Meanwhile, Tom Rossi, Cianci's campaign manager, identified thousands of voters likely to vote against Cianci, and sent postcards to their addresses. Several thousand came back as undeliverable. Two weeks before the elec-tion, Rossi went to the Board of Canvassers and challenged the eligibility of thirty-five hundred voters. The board disqualified about seven hundred likely anti-Cianci voters. Cianci went on to win the election by 317 votes—a victory that would not be cemented until five days before Christmas, when the Rhode Island Supreme Court this time ruled in his favor on the question of whether a convicted felon could hold office.

On election night, with the outcome still in doubt, Cianci turned to Wendy Materna and said, "I want no tears." But it had never entered her mind that he might lose. Later that night, when the returns were more en-couraging, a joyous Cianci got down on one knee in his yard and asked Ma-terna to marry him. She would laugh later at the memory. It was his first serious marriage proposal but not the last. As Buddy Cianci prepared to be-come mayor again, their relationship had entered a new phase.

CHAPTER EIGHT

Zorba the Mayor

Buddy II, as the second reign of Vincent A. Cianci, Jr., was known, began under two circus tents outside his carriage house on Power Street.

At one minute past midnight on January 7, 1991, Cianci was sworn in as mayor in front of more than five hundred friends and well-wishers. Wendy Materna and his daughter, Nicole, stood by his side. Cianci felt as if he had gone to sleep for six years and just woken up, as if his time in exile had been nothing more than a bad dream.

He regained office lacking a mandate, and knowing that he would have to consolidate his power. He humbly pledged to be "a different kind of mayor," to recruit the best people for his administration this time, and to foster "unity and togetherness." One Saturday night in early January he was at City Hall, cleaning his office with a small group of aides. He called them together and said: "I've been through hard times, so I know what it's like. If you have a problem, I want you to come to me."

He hired Joseph Almagno, the respected former Providence school superintendent who had supported Annaldo in the election, as his chief of staff. Some of Almagno's closest friends advised him not to take the job. They warned him that Cianci was using him to gain legitimacy. But Almagno wanted to believe that Cianci had changed; he wanted him to succeed, for the sake of Providence. Publicly, Almagno praised Cianci's "superior intellectual ability" and his vision for the city. "I am thoroughly convinced that he will put people in critical positions that will reflect a government of integrity. He has no other way to go." Privately, Almagno told Cianci that he would resign if he saw any sign of impropriety.

"Joe Almagno is a classy guy," said one city official. "He won't stand for any shenanigans. If he goes, and it's not health or something, then you got to start asking questions."

Joining Almagno in the mayor's new inner circle were Frank Corrente, the campaign deputy treasurer, who became director of administration, and Tom Rossi, the campaign manager, who was named policy coordinator.

Corrente and Rossi were more hard-core political operators than Almagno. Before jumping on Cianci's winning bandwagon, both men had been political outcasts—Corrente from Paolino's City Hall, Rossi from the North End political machine. After Cianci's victory, Corrente and Rossi stood together at a fund-raiser at the Metacomet Country Club and laughed as they watched all of the political players who had been against them come streaming in the door. Cianci was the only show in town now, they gloated, and everyone had to "buy a ticket to the dance," as Rossi put it.

Publicly magnanimous in victory, Cianci showed a nastier side in private. One night at a function at the Biltmore he approached ex-councilman Malcolm Farmer III, a former ally who had supported Lippitt in the recent campaign. According to Farmer, Cianci warned, "You'd better not have a drink and back out of your driveway."

After Cianci took office, he summoned all of the department directors, holdovers from the previous administration, to the aldermens' chambers at City Hall. There was a chill in the air as he marched in, like a general reviewing his troops.

"I just want you to know that I'm the fucking mayor," he said. "I'm going to be examining every fucking résumé and looking at all you fucking people."

Their survival depended on their loyalty to him, Cianci said. He was putting everyone on notice; he called it "putting the monkey" on their back. After an unannounced visit to the Public Works garages to dress down the man in charge of snowplowing, the mayor told a reporter, "He knows that I know that he knows that I know."

Despite his bluster, Cianci didn't simply bully people. He co-opted his enemies. He hired Nick Easton, his former council critic and potential rival who had sought the Democratic nomination for mayor in 1990, as the city's deputy building inspector. He put Fred Lippitt on a budget task force. He kept the head of the city's Democratic party on the city payroll and hired the chairman of the city's Republican party. Neither party would endorse a candidate for mayor in 1994.

Cianci had a saying: "Marry your enemies and fuck your friends."

His first day back, he was in a playful mood. He made impromptu visits to the tax assessor's office and the dog pound and toured City Hall, where he took note of the many Paolino pictures still hanging in offices. Then, relaxing in his old, familiar corner office, he kidded with Tom Rossi, who had just returned from a meeting with the state's mayors to discuss fiscal problems.

"Lots of tales of woe, Tommy?" asked Cianci.

"Woe? We had to stop a lot of them from jumping out the windows," replied Rossi.

The mayor fielded dozens of phone calls. His secretary said that a man had called to complain that he was being hassled by his ex-wife and wanted the mayor's help.

"I guess I know what he's talking about," said Cianci. "Call him back."

Cianci's cocker spaniel, Tucker, darted into the room, followed by Wendy Materna.

"Hey, Tucker," he called, his eyes shining. The dog raced up to Cianci, then ran into a back office, then ran into the mayor's private bathroom.

"Go get George," said Cianci, throwing a plastic squeeze-toy replica of George Bush in a Santa Claus suit. "He loves that."

After the corruption that had disgraced his first reign, Cianci vowed to be more hands-on. He showed up for one meeting of the Board of Contract and Supply, in the City Council chambers, and grilled employees for three hours about city purchases, right down to a basketball backboard at Central High School.

"A fifty-nine-hundred-dollar change order from an engineering company raises my eyebrows," Cianci lectured one official. "And you see that reporter over there? Well, he is gonna write all kinds of stories about us if we can't answer questions later on about why we approved these things."

"Where is someone from the Parks Department?" he demanded. Looking around the room as he smoked a cigarette, Cianci spotted a man sitting in the back, wearing a trench coat. He worked for the Parks Department. "Who are you? Come up here. Why don't you take your coat off. You might get a cold and then you'd have to go on worker's comp. Can you tell me what this trash-hauling contract is about? Who is this SDS Disposal?"

The man didn't know.

"Well, what is this charge of fifty dollars a pull? What's a pull, anyway? I want to know what a pull is."

In his first months back, Cianci was confronted with familiar challenges. Providence was in the doldrums, with downtown buildings boarded up and nighttime streets lifeless. The critically acclaimed Trinity Repertory Theater was on the verge of bankruptcy. The Civic Center was in decline. Despite Cianci's efforts during his first administration to reclaim pockets of downtown, such as the Biltmore Hotel and the Providence Performing Arts Center, the 1980s economic boom had passed by the city's aging core. Jobs and people had continued to flee.

Cianci's hopes of paying for new programs were hamstrung by a growing budget deficit and a recession compounded by a statewide banking crisis. The same week that he took office, the governor closed forty-five privately insured banks and credit unions, touching off the worst banking disaster in Rhode Island since the Great Depression.

The system's private insurer had failed after one banker, Cianci's former business associate Joseph Mollicone, absconded with thirteen million dollars shortly after election day in 1990, prompting a run on the banks. He was last seen at Boston's Logan Airport, but some speculated that he had been murdered by mobsters who had banked with him.

Against that backdrop, Cianci went about trying to restore his city. To be successful, he said, a mayor had to address four things: housing, jobs, crime, and schools. Those four things—"and maybe a little excitement now and then."

The first four things proved rather intractable, given the city's high poverty rate and the lack of money, though Cianci did boast of bringing the crime rate down. But the mayor was never at a loss for creating excitement.

As part of his inaugural festivities, he brought in actor Hal Linden to headline a Broadway revue at the Providence Performing Arts Center, as a band outside played the theme from *The Godfather*. Over lunch at Toscano's with a *Los Angeles Times* reporter, Cianci downed a vodka trimmed with six tiny cocktail onions and spoke of Providence as "simpatico, a responsibility, your mistress, your wife, whatever you want to call it. . . . This is like a second coming." As for the challenges ahead, he said, "I have the testicular fortitude to do what has to be done."

In his first year he plugged the budget deficit by pushing a tax increase through a reluctant City Council. He proposed an ambitious hundred-million-dollar "Providence Plan," to replace old housing and spruce up the city over the next several years—where the money would come from was less clear. He rescued Trinity Rep with a two-hundred-thousand-dollar city loan.

Cianci also preached the need to redistribute the wealth of the suburbs to Providence, the heart of the city-state, which added so much to the vitality of Rhode Island.

"Elephants cost a lot to feed these days," he told a Chamber of Commerce breakfast. "Even the birds don't sing for nothing. They want to charge you a fee."

Looking around the room, filled with suburban business types, Cianci continued: "Now, I like the people who live in Barrington and East Greenwich. But think about it. They come into Providence in the morning to drop off their children at Moses Brown or the Wheeler School—great taxpayers for the city. Then they go to the Providence Public Library to drop off a book that's overdue. Then they say, 'Let's go see Grandma at the hospital.' Then maybe they go to the zoo to see the penguins. And then end up saying, 'Why don't we go catch something at Trinity tonight?' But you know who pays for all those services? The taxpayer in Providence, the elderly lady sweeping in front of her house, because the city can't afford to provide the street sweepers anymore."

Privately, the mayor could be more caustic, fueled by his resentment and envy of the old Yankee elite. During a meeting in his office with Rhode Island Hospital executives, who wanted to start a South Providence job-training program, he harangued them for not living in Providence.

Another time, seeking corporate assistance for the city, the mayor attended a breakfast meeting at the Turks Head Club, a preserve of Providence's old-line business establishment. The president of Narragansett Electric was there. So were the head of the gas company, the publisher of *The Providence Journal,* bankers, lawyers, and corporate executives.

As Cianci later told the story, disparagingly: "These guys get up early. They were eating eggs. I had tomato juice and coffee." At one point, he turned to Alan Hassenfeld, chief executive of the Hasbro toy company, which his father had started, and lectured him: "Let's get one thing straight. You make fucking toys. I run a city. I have a police department, a fire department. You make fucking toys. And the only reason you do that is because your father left you the company, because you're a member of the Lucky Sperm Club."

Given Cianci's legacy of corruption, suburban lawmakers were reluctant to throw money into the urban sinkhole. But the mayor found a sympathetic ear in the new Democratic governor, Bruce Sundlun.

The son of a tough, self-made Jewish lawyer from the East Side, Sundlun was a wealthy executive who had run a Providence television station and developed an interest in political office later in life. He had served on the business task force that rescued Cianci's city from the brink of bankruptcy in the early 1980s, and later sold his carriage house on Power Street to Cianci. He had spent millions of dollars on three campaigns for governor, finally winning in 1990.

Arrogant and imperious, Sundlun was in his sixties and on his third wife but still had an eye for younger blondes. While he was governor, an illegitimate college-aged daughter popped up threatening a paternity suit, and state environmental officials investigated him for shooting raccoons at his Newport estate.

Cianci and Sundlun struck up a jocular friendship. The mayor teased the governor about his wooden style. Sundlun, who wanted to be one of the political guys, kidded Cianci about his toupees. Sundlun rode to Providence's rescue with a bundle of state aid—with less accountability for how it was spent than some leaders would have liked.

The irony was that Sundlun, as a businessman in the early eighties, had served on the Providence Review Commission, which had been created to rescue the city from bankruptcy and Cianci's fiscal mismanagement. The city's finances had been in such a shambles, Sundlun recalled, that there were "hundreds, thousands" of uncashed checks stuffed in desk drawers throughout City Hall. But as governor in the nineties, Sundlun believed that the state's fortunes were inextricably linked to the city's, and he considered Cianci the only one with the political skills to hold the city together.

Sundlun's favorite story about Cianci's showmanship involved the time that the mayor was "discovered" by a Hollywood producer. It happened in the early eighties, when Sundlun, then chairman of Outlet Communications, brought executives from Columbia Pictures to the mayor's office when they were in Providence on business. For about an hour, Cianci regaled the executives with political yarns and one-liners. Afterward, Ray Stark, producer of the movie *Funny Girl,* pulled Sundlun aside and asked, "Is this guy for real?" Then he asked how much Cianci made. Sundlun told him. Stark replied: "You tell that guy that I'll pay him two hundred fifty thousand dollars, give him a three-year contract, and run him in a sitcom. We'll call it *The Mayor.*" Stark insisted that he was serious, that Cianci had real talent. But though Cianci was flattered and would tell the story for years, he wasn't ready to give up the political stage.

The mayor was a master at grabbing what he liked to call "other people's money." And he could be a showoff about it. Sitting in his office with union leaders, he hatched a scheme on the spot to get state funds for a project. According to Rick Brooks, president of Rhode Island's United Nurses & Allied Professionals union, Cianci turned to the union men and said:

"Watch this. I'm going to call the governor, convince him to come up with the money, and make him think it's his idea."

Brooks watched as Cianci got Sundlun on the phone and schmoozed him. "Hi, Bruce . . . great things in the works . . . great opportunity for the governor to show his support of the unions." All the while, Cianci was winking and waggling his eyebrows at the union men—showing them that the governor was going for it.

Walking into Cianci's office, said Brooks, could be like stepping into a Fellini film.

When a Westin Hotel was being built in Providence in the early 1990s, Brooks's union set up a meeting with a hotel executive from Florida to discuss jobs for low-income residents. As they waited in the mayor's anteroom, the straitlaced exec found himself being entertained with card tricks by Walter Miller, a disheveled, gap-toothed denizen of downtown who had become Cianci's unofficial mascot. Walter, who was also a racetrack tout, loved Buddy. He hung around in the outer office, prompting one secretary to light a candle to cover his body odor, and carried a battered boom box plastered with Cianci bumper stickers. He liked to make up songs about Buddy, which he sang in a fast, scratchy voice. Once, when Umberto Crenca, the artistic director of AS220, a nonprofit arts center and café downtown, came to see Cianci about renegotiating a city loan, the mayor told him, "I'm going to have you negotiate with Walter." He put them in a room off the mayor's office, where Miller proceeded to scribble numbers and gibberish on a piece of paper as Crenca made his pitch. Finally, Cianci, who had been agreeable to the deal all along, came in and asked, "Okay, Walter, what did you decide?" Miller said that Crenca seemed like a nice guy and gave him the thumbs-up.

When Cianci finally arrived for the Westin meeting, he made a fuss over the exec, then called out to Walter: "Make the noise. Make the noise." Walter made a gurgling, clicking sound deep in his throat.

The meeting moved into the mayor's office, where Cianci launched into a monologue spiced with jokes and lewd remarks. He was simultaneously charming and subtly menacing. "I met your CEO a few weeks ago," he began. "Nice guy. Smooth as a minister's dick."

Eventually, Cianci got to the point. The Westin was a public hotel, and the mayor expected the company to work with the unions and hire Providence residents. "I still control the liquor licenses in this city, and I've never yet seen a hotel that's been able to make money selling iced tea," he said.

Cianci ended by arranging a police escort to the airport, so the man wouldn't miss his plane. The mayor sent the dumbstruck executive off with a coffee-table picture book of Providence, which he autographed "To my friend Harry."

Other establishments that served the mayor did not always fare so well.

One of the mayor's favorite haunts was Amsterdam's Rotisserie and Bar, a trendy yuppie spot on South Main Street. The mayor's limo would glide up to the curb, where a line of customers waited on the sidewalk, and sweep past with his entourage as the wait staff hurried to clear a prime table.

Cianci ordered a steak, read the newspaper, held court. He drank B&B on the rocks, from a snifter. Often he would leave without paying the tab, said the owner, Peter Dupre, who wrote it off as "the cost of doing business."

Toward the end of his first year back in office, on December 16, 1991, Cianci tried to breeze in as usual, this time with Wendy Materna and another couple. There was music that night, and the place was crowded. Although Cianci had come for dinner, the bouncer, who was new, refused to let him in without paying the two-dollar cover charge. Cianci argued in vain, telling the bouncer, "I'm the mayor of Providence, here." Then he walked away. A short time later, the city fire marshal pulled up in a big red van, accompanied by a fire truck, its lights flashing. Amsterdam's was closed down for overcrowding. Two days later, its temporary entertainment license was suspended.

On the advice of a patron who worked for the city, Dupre went to City Hall to make peace with the mayor. He had made an appointment for the morning but was kept waiting most of the day. Finally, late in the afternoon, Dupre was shown into Cianci's office. As Dupre later described it, their fifteen-minute meeting was not pleasant.

Cianci asked Dupre if he was aware that Amsterdam's had exceeded the legal occupancy limit. Dupre tried to explain that the bouncer had a clicker to count the people coming in and out. Cianci didn't want to hear it. Then the mayor changed tack.

"I have it on good authority that you're selling drugs in that place," Dupre recalled Cianci's telling him.

Horrified, Dupre protested that it wasn't true.

"Well, if I say you're selling drugs, you're selling drugs," Cianci insisted.

The mayor chastised Dupre for his bouncer's disrespectful behavior and threatened to run the restaurateur out of town on the next bus. Dupre tried to be humble and low-key, but every time he tried to explain, Cianci cut him off. "You don't want to get into a pissing match with me," said Cianci, "because you're a cup of water, and I'm Niagara Falls."

Eventually, Amsterdam's was allowed to reopen. The restaurant was fined $250 for overcrowding. And Dupre, on the advice of his City Hall patron, donated $250 to Cianci's campaign. Until he closed Amsterdam's and went back to New York a few years later—largely because of Cianci, he said—Dupre lived with the lingering fear that he might be set up with drugs someday.

Although Dupre and his partners kept their mouths shut, word spread quickly through Providence's restaurant community. Other club owners approached him sympathetically and said, "You think you're the only one?"

JOSH FENTON KNEW that he had arrived as a member of the loyal opposition to Buddy Cianci when he started seeing the unmarked police cars outside his house.

Elected to the City Council in 1990, at the age of twenty-seven, Fenton was bright and brash and full of questions. Why, for instance, did city employees who worked outdoors receive a paid day off when the temperature hit ninety degrees? Why were elected officials allowed to collect pensions from the municipal labor union whose contracts they ratified? Why were more than 90 percent of the city's firefighters going out on costly disability pensions? And why was the mayor, with his million-dollar staff and personal expense account and four police drivers and city limousine, always trying to raise taxes instead of cutting costs?

As the only Independent on the otherwise all-Democratic City Council, Fenton was the de facto minority leader. As a minority of one, he sometimes questioned the council's actions as well; for instance, holding its annual Christmas party at Andino's, a Federal Hill restaurant owned by a convicted mob killer. (The killer's picture appeared in an old state police organizational chart of the Providence Mafia that Fenton had found one day, jammed in the back of a file cabinet in his office at the state Department of Environmental Management.)

If Fenton seemed politically savvy beyond his years, perhaps it was because he had worked in Washington as an aide to two U.S. senators,

Maine's George Mitchell and Rhode Island's John Chafee. After a difficult childhood in Providence's Mount Hope neighborhood, a pocket of lower-income families and blacks amidst the wealth of the East Side, Fenton won a scholarship to Suffield Academy, a Connecticut prep school. In 1990, newly married, he ran for council in his old neighborhood, part of the Third Ward, and beat the Democratic incumbent by sixteen votes.

The council was an elected position; Fenton's full-time job was as a state environmental lobbyist. He was also working on a master's degree in environmental studies at Brown University; for his thesis he was analyzing the quality of life and health risks in Providence's twenty-five neighborhoods.

On the City Council in the early 1990s, Fenton emerged as Cianci's leading critic. He questioned government waste, generous spending on the mayor's cronies, and Cianci's giveaways to the politically powerful unions. He called the mayor "a spending maniac," more interested in his self-aggrandizement than in cutting the city's runaway labor costs. As a result, Fenton argued, Providence was "wallpapered with FOR SALE signs" as the middle class fled to the suburbs, further eroding the city's tax base, its neighborhoods, and its schools.

Cianci tried to dismiss him as "a youthful and ambitious politician." But Fenton remained an effective critic. In 1991 he helped lead a council revolt against Cianci's efforts to raise taxes. But the mayor, who had been outmaneuvering the council when Fenton was in grammar school, persuaded four members to change their votes at the last minute, and prevailed.

In Fenton's view, he was a mystery to Cianci. What did he want? Following his dictum to "marry your enemies," the mayor offered Fenton a city job, running the Parks Department. He declined.

Late one night in the spring of 1991 Fenton and his wife were walking down Thayer Street, near Brown, when they saw Cianci sitting alone in Andrea's. He motioned them in. This was shortly after Desert Storm. Cianci told them how he had recently met with Kuwait's consulate general about establishing some sort of relationship between Kuwait and Providence. He asked Fenton if he would like to go to Kuwait, to represent the city; of course, everything would be paid for.

Fenton never did get to Kuwait. He remained in Providence, pushing the mayor. In the summer of 1992, Fenton was increasingly frustrated by Cianci's failure to tackle the city's fiscal problems. One night he was on the telephone with Rita Williams, the councilwoman from the neighboring Second Ward, discussing the latest budget impasse.

"Why don't we just freeze taxes?" said Williams.

"I'll second that," said Fenton.

Out of that grew the Zero Eight—eight of the council's fifteen members rebelling against Cianci. The next day, a Wednesday, Fenton typed a letter calling for a special council meeting, with a cover letter pledging to vote for a tax freeze. He asked everyone to sign it, so it would be harder to back out.

The meeting was set for that Friday, July 24, at 5:30 P.M. Cianci requested a special council meeting of his own the same day at five—in the mayor's chambers.

Fenton and several other council members skipped the meeting with the mayor, fearing that it would violate the state's open-meetings law. A previous meeting with the mayor and council members had turned ugly. In that session, Cianci had bluntly told one councilwoman that she owed him her vote because he had given her boyfriend a city job. He called another councilwoman a hypocrite because she and her husband collectively had three government Blue Cross plans. Then he stalked over to his bar, poured himself a double Scotch, and asked a council staff member, "How do you work with these people?"

Still, several council members did show up that Friday in the mayor's office, including Rita Williams and other members of the Zero Eight.

Cianci, flanked by his top aides—Almagno, Corrente, and Rossi—was seated at his desk when the meeting began, but he quickly began pacing around the room. He demanded to know what they proposed to cut from the budget if they refused to pass his tax increase. Someone suggested closing unnecessary fire stations; one of Fenton's most persistent criticisms was that the Fire Department was overstaffed.

The mayor turned to Williams and threw rapid-fire questions at her, like a prosecutor. "Which stations do you want me to cut? Tell me which ones, which ones do you want to cut? . . . You sit in that [mayor's] chair and tell me what to do."

Williams offered to close a station in her ward. "Fine," said Cianci. "Send a letter to your area and see if it gets support."

Williams also suggested reducing Fire Department overtime. Cianci countered that he could cut the Downtown Providence Improvement Association, which her husband ran. Offended, Williams stood up to leave.

"Walk out and abdicate your responsibility," snarled Cianci.

She came back.

The meeting wore on, as surly union members gathered one floor up in the council chambers and railed against the Zero Eight.

When the meeting with Cianci finally broke up, after two and a half hours, several of the council members appeared dazed. The mayor's "brain-washing exercise," as one called it, had been hard to resist. Even Williams, who had suggested the freeze, was weakening.

Walking into the council chambers, Williams, Fenton, and the rest of the Zero Eight were confronted by five hundred screaming, cursing union members. Fenton looked around at the line of uniformed police officers that held back the crowd and wondered how quickly the unionized police would come to his defense if something happened. Before the meeting, some firefighters had burned Fenton in effigy.

Then the chant began: "Councilwoman Williams, why don't you lay off your husband?"

Fenton cajoled Williams to stick to her commitment and not hang the rest of them out to dry. He promised to go door-to-door with her in her ward and support her. Fenton, who had been in the U.S. Senate with Chafee in 1986 during the historic tax-reform debate, said that this was as dramatic as anything he'd witnessed.

Not wanting to waste any time, the council voted. Fenton wasn't sure which way Williams would go. When her turn came, she voted against Cianci. The Zero Eight had held. Fenton knew that the balance of power had shifted when Local 1033's business agent, who had always ignored him, suggested that they have lunch.

"The city just changed directions," Fenton declared, exultant.

Downstairs, listening on the speaker in his office, Cianci was furious. As Fenton later put it: "The king wasn't the king for a while. It stung."

Fenton had emerged as a potential rival to Cianci in 1994. On Friday nights his former boss and Cianci's old nemesis, John Chafee, would call him at home to offer encouragement. In 1993, with Fenton considering a run for mayor, Senator Chafee cosponsored a political fund-raiser for him along with another political heavyweight and onetime Cianci rival, former governor Joe Garrahy.

Fenton began to notice cars outside his house on the East Side, off-duty cops or firefighters behind the wheel. Some were the men he had criticized for obtaining fraudulent disability pensions. Often, he said, he was watched by Providence patrolman Rodney Patterson, who had been assigned by Cianci to an elite anticorruption unit when the mayor returned to office.

(Patterson and two other members of the five-officer unit had criminal records.) Meanwhile, Fenton said, a union official who served on the board of the United Way, where his wife worked, tried to have her fired.

For the most part, it was merely a nuisance. The one time Fenton feared for his life was when an ex-cop whose disability pension he had questioned left a message on his answering machine, threatening to kill him. Fenton told some state police detectives he knew. After they had a chat with the ex-cop, he left Fenton alone.

After several months, Fenton got tired of being followed all the time. He complained to Frank Corrente and threatened to hold a press conference and show pictures that he had taken of the cars. Corrente denied that they were responsible but promised to look into it. Afterward, said Fenton, the harassment stopped.

Following the Zero Eight vote, Cianci, as promised, eliminated the Downtown Providence Improvement Association, run by Rita Williams's husband. Lyman Williams was demoted to a Public Works maintenance job. The following year, after he underwent double-bypass heart surgery, the city fought his efforts to collect worker's compensation.

Two policemen in Cianci's anticorruption unit, Rodney Patterson and Nic Ricamo, started following Lyman Williams. According to Williams, on Yom Kippur they followed him to his synagogue in Barrington and later videotaped him as he relaxed on his boat in a nearby marina. Cianci publicly charged that the tapes showed Williams working on his boat, proving that he had filed a fraudulent worker's-comp claim. But the city never produced the tapes to back up the mayor's claim. Instead, after the case dragged on for two years, the case was settled in Williams's favor.

The mayor did make one last overture, the Williamses said. After Lyman Williams recovered from his surgery, Cianci offered him his job back—on the condition that the Second Ward Democratic Committee, which Lyman Williams chaired, back Cianci in 1994. "No one works for me who doesn't support me," said Cianci.

Lyman Williams refused and took early retirement instead.

Meanwhile, as a result of Cianci's failure to address the city's longer-term financial problems, he failed to win a tax increase in 1992, which further depleted the city of needed revenue. In the opinion of the council's auditor, Stephen Woerner, that set the city on a downward spiral. To compensate, the mayor embarked on a series of questionable moves that would jeopardize the city's long-term financial health for years to come—most notably, drastically reducing the city's annual contributions to the pension system. By decade's end, the system would be underfunded by several hundred million dollars. As a result, the Providence Renaissance that began to emerge in the mid-1990s was built on quicksand.

Meanwhile, Cianci was preoccupied with being Providence's head cheerleader. To inject more life into the city center, he flew to Anchorage, Alaska, in 1992 to woo the 1996 National Figure Skating Championships. Three weeks later, Cianci landed the Bruins, a minor-league hockey team from Maine, for Providence and helped the team sell three thousand season tickets before its first game that fall. "Anything we can do to put a little life and money into the downtown area has to be considered a plus," he said.

The Providence Bruins were a hit. During their first winter, in 1992–93, they played before ten thousand fans a night at the Civic Center. Cianci was a regular, if habitually late, fan. As the hockey players chased the puck around the ice, the mayor would make a grand entrance to his seats at center ice, carrying a bottle of champagne and squiring Wendy Materna.

Trailing behind was the mayor's court jester, Walter Miller, who carried a plastic totem pole. During lulls in the action, Walter would riffle a worn deck of cards and entertain the mayor with card tricks. "What number do ya like, Mayor, what number do ya like?" prattled Walter.

But not even Cianci's showmanship, or Walter's sleight of hand, could make the mayor's financial problems disappear. Buddy, like his city, was nearly broke.

IN 1992, AS the tax debate with the City Council raged, Cianci was fighting another battle; this one, which played out behind the scenes, was to avoid personal bankruptcy. Creditors were banging on his door, threatening to foreclose on his house, seeking to attach his salary.

The real estate empire he had built while in exile had collapsed as a result of the recession and the state banking crisis. His two restaurants had gone out of business, leaving a trail of debts. His million-dollar house on Power Street was heavily mortgaged. He owed about $700,000 on the failed restaurant near the airport. He had a $140,000 note on his yacht. A personal financial statement prepared during the summer of 1992, while he was battling the Zero Eight, revealed a negative net worth of $1.4 million.

Declaring bankruptcy might have made sense financially, but it would have been devastating politically, especially for a mayor trying to shake a reputation for fiscal recklessness. Instead, Cianci relied on a web of aides, city employees, lawyers who represented the city, and businessmen. Wendy Materna also helped, cosigning on the $140,000 loan with him; this gave her an interest in his yacht, which already carried $189,000 in debt. He also borrowed heavily from Wendy Materna.

In December 1992 Cianci sold a piece of his house, which had been divided into condominium units, to Michael Kent, who operated several bars in Providence, for $200,000, averting foreclosure. The mayor said that he paid rent to Kent, which in effect made Kent the mayor's landlord. The arrangement raised questions among Providence police officers and other club operators, who felt that the city wasn't aggressive dealing with rowdyism and underage drinking at Kent's bars.

The mayor also used city lawyers to help negotiate with his creditors, and he borrowed money from city employees, most notably Frank Corrente and another aide, Artin H. Coloian.

Through the 1990s Corrente and Coloian lent the mayor $150,000 between them, according to federal court proceedings. Corrente and Coloian also worked quietly to help dig Cianci out of debt—holding meetings, dealing with various parties, and trying to regulate the mayor's spending.

For all his maneuvering, the financial fate of Buddy Cianci ultimately came down to whether the Hooters girls would save him. Early in 1993, Hooters, the national restaurant chain known for its busty waitresses, was considering leasing Cianci's defunct airport restaurant. The mayor had already staved off foreclosure by going to Hartford, Connecticut, and convincing the president of Northeast Savings Bank, which held a $700,000 note on the property, to reduce his debt to about $400,000. Coloian then lined up a local financier, Gregory Demetrekas, to lend Cianci the money to repay the bank. Now the mayor, who also owed more than $70,000 in back taxes, needed a paying tenant so that he could make his loan payments to Demetrekas. Enter Hooters, which had been called America's first "breastaurant." The deal almost fell through when Hooters executives rejected the location, feeling that it wouldn't attract enough traffic. Cianci's representatives convinced the franchisees to appeal to Hooters headquarters in Atlanta. The businessmen flew to Atlanta on April 1 and won the approval of the company's chairman just hours before his son was killed in a plane crash along with NASCAR racing champion Alan Kulwicki. Had the meeting been any later, the deal might never have been approved. Instead, the mayor had wriggled out of another financial jam.

Meanwhile, old Cianci allies like Pat Conley and adman Norm Roussel felt the sting from their financial ties to the mayor. Conley wound up declaring bankruptcy and losing property in South Providence that he and his wife had put up as collateral for some of his business ventures with Cianci, whom he subsequently sued. One day when Conley was in court, he said, he bumped into Roussel, who had been sued by a bank and ordered to repay $124,000 on the campaign loan he had cosigned for the mayor during his 1990 comeback. Roussel subsequently closed his advertising firm, which Cianci had used in each of his mayoral campaigns, and declared bankruptcy. He soon found a job at City Hall as Cianci's $50,000-a-year communications coordinator. Cianci said that the job had nothing to do with the loan, and that he had repaid it himself.

"Buddy is like crime," a bitter Conley said. "He never pays."

Wendy Materna could attest to that. She said she grew accustomed to walking into restaurants with the mayor and never having anyone present him with a bill. Even Materna's longtime family dentist, a political junkie, didn't send her a bill for nine years, to ingratiate himself with Cianci, she said.

Adding to Cianci's financial turmoil, the state receiver for Joe Mollicone's failed bank sued Cianci, seeking repayment of $150,000 in unpaid loans. Cianci fretted about the publicity, given Mollicone's notoriety as a $13 million embezzler, and said that he barely knew him.

Then, in the spring of 1992, Mollicone resurfaced, turning himself in to the authorities; he had been hiding in Salt Lake City for the past eighteen months. At a neighborhood groundbreaking in Mount Hope, Cianci made a crack to Josh Fenton about an ethics complaint that had been filed against the councilman; Fenton shot back that he heard things weren't going well with Mollicone in the grand jury. Cianci, he said, turned white and walked away quickly, then came back and apologized.

His critics wondered how he managed to support his extravagant lifestyle, the house, the boat, and his other debts on his annual mayor's salary of $114,000. It didn't add up. Josh Fenton gathered public records about the mayor's finances—his mortgages, his yacht registration, his campaign-finance reports, and his state ethics commission filings—and went to Lincoln Almond, who was still the U.S. attorney for Rhode Island. "How do these two things jibe?" asked Fenton. Almond was sympathetic; he said that he'd been investigating Cianci for years.

Cianci lived "on the brink," said Roussel, "because he enjoys the finer things in life." He didn't let his debts diminish his quality of life. The mayor used public funds to eat in fancy restaurants and spent campaign funds on meals, trips, hair grooming, Christmas gifts for family members, even birthday parties for his young grandchildren, featuring Danoe the Clown and Barney the Dinosaur.

City vendors were also happy to help; the pony-ride concessionaire at Roger Williams Park gave Cianci a deal on pony rides for his granddaughter's seventh birthday. Later, Coloian would note that the children at the birthday parties were future voters. Cianci justified the expenditures, saying, "Everything in my life is political."

According to one party to the discussions, Corrente, who doubled as Cianci's campaign treasurer, asked about the tax implications of the mayor's taking an interest-free loan from the campaign. A tax adviser warned that the IRS would regard it as income if he didn't make regular payments on the loan and pay interest.

The blurry line between the mayor's private and political finances caught the eye of the IRS, which audited both. No public action ever resulted; privately, Cianci boasted that he came through the audit clean. When a city auditor questioned Cianci's public spending on restaurants, Corrente brushed him off; when the auditor persisted, his job was eliminated.

Even the Mayor's Own Marinara Sauce, sold to benefit the mayor's nonprofit scholarship fund for needy college-bound Providence youths, straddled Cianci's personal and political finances. In 1995, he started a private company, Capital Innovations, to market his marinara sauce and other products. Since the company's books are private, it is impossible to determine how much money went to the mayor for expenses before proceeds from the sale of the sauce went to the scholarship fund. Capital Innovations sold sauce to the Friends of Cianci campaign organization, which used the sauce at fund-raising events and also for handing out to dignitaries. The mayor also used Capital Innovations to pay some of his daughter's personal expenses; after she got into an auto accident, the Providence police said that her car insurance had been paid by Capital Innovations. And the company was paid "finder's fees" by Incanto Soprano, a Providence company run by two old Cianci friends that produced olive oil from a vineyard in the Puglia region of southern Italy. Cianci said that the fees were for his help in brokering the sale of olive oil to a food wholesaler in Maryland. A few years later, Incanto Soprano—Italian for "enchantment of the highest order"—began producing the Mayor's Own Extra Virgin Olive Oil to benefit his scholarship fund. When the mayor held a press conference to unveil the olive oil, Incanto Soprano was delinquent on a

$50,000 economic-development loan from the city. The city held off on foreclosure after the company said that it had a $75,000 order in the works, for 1,876 cases of the Mayor's Own Extra Virgin Olive Oil, which was bound for Providence on a freighter from Naples.

Corrente was quickly establishing himself as the mayor's go-to guy at City Hall. A native of the North End, where his father had worked in a macaroni factory, Corrente controlled jobs, contracts, union negotiations, and the mayor's campaign fund. Hired by Joe Doorley in the sixties, Corrente rose to the position of city controller under Cianci and was a loyal political fund-raiser; he also grew familiar with the grand jury, answering a number of document subpoenas during the myriad corruption probes that marked Buddy I. He had an old-school political mentality, bred in the North End and the Fifth Ward—you helped your friends. The lines defining ethical conduct were blurry. When Corrente's wife, Thelma, a Providence school nurse, received a promotion and became the School Department's health services administrator, a school board member said that she was pressured by Frank, which he denied.

Corrente negotiated city labor contracts with the Laborers' Union, whose national general president, Arthur A. Coia, was an old family friend. Corrente's son, a lawyer, was married to Coia's daughter and worked at Coia's law firm, which did union legal work. "It's better to negotiate with a friend than with an adversary," said Corrente. When the Laborers' legal-defense fund, which the city funded, bought a Providence office building from a partnership that included Corrente and Coia for $2.3 million, Corrente denied any conflict. He had been unaware of the details of the transaction, or even the identity of the buyer, he said. The sale occurred in the fall of 1994; the following month, the U.S. Justice Department notified Coia that it was planning a government takeover of the 770,000-member union because it was controlled by the Mafia. (Coia, a big supporter and labor confidant of President Clinton who was an overnight guest in the Lincoln Bedroom, subsequently convinced the Justice Department to allow him to supervise his own cleanup despite the fact that federal prosecutors had identified him as a mob puppet.)

While Cianci was out cutting ribbons and holding press conferences, Corrente saw that things ran smoothly and protected the mayor from embarrassment. As Corrente explained his job to another aide, "All you have to do, boss, is make sure the king's ass is firmly in the chair."

An accountant by trade, Corrente was a gangster at heart. People referred to him as the mayor's "strong arm." He favored hallway meetings, paranoid that his office was bugged, and spoke in a high-pitched, staccato voice, frequently mangling his sentences, to Cianci's amusement. Subpoenaed to appear before a grand jury investigating a city employee, he said nonchalantly, "I don't care if I have to go to jail—as long as it says on my gravestone, 'He was a stand-up guy.' " Still, he was well liked by many people, including Cianci's opponents, because he was a man of his word who got things done.

Corrente, who had made money from real estate investments, said that he didn't need the paycheck at City Hall; he could always retire and play golf. But he liked the power and the action. A wiry man in his sixties, with a silvery toupee, the married Corrente chased younger women. He had long-running affairs with at least two City Hall employees. He heaped gifts upon them. Both women received raises and promotions that set their coworkers grumbling. City employees would corner Cianci at events and complain that they wanted a raise like Frank's girlfriend had gotten.

It made for a long-running soap opera at City Hall, as the rival mistresses confronted each other, or Corrente's wife stormed into the building to confront her cheating husband and the other women. One time Corrente took one of his girlfriends to Cape Cod, where she left her tennis bracelet in their hotel room. The hotel called Corrente's wife to report that they had found her bracelet, which sent her charging down to City Hall to yell at Frank.

Artin Coloian, the other aide who had helped bail Cianci out of his financial mess, also had a reputation as a ladies' man. After one affair went bad, the spurned woman threw a drink in his face at City Hall. Unlike Corrente, however, Coloian was young and single, favoring designer suits and fine cigars. Once, when he was working as a junior aide to Senator John Chafee, Coloian bought a Ford Taurus, drove up to Cambridge, Massachusetts, to the Harvard University bookstore, and purchased a Harvard sticker for the window. Josh Fenton, who also worked for Chafee, recalled Coloian's telling him that he hoped the sticker would impress chicks.

Coloian had grown up poor, a member of Providence's sizeable Armenian community. In his teens he hustled odd jobs and painted houses, saved his money, and started buying and selling cars and real estate. His love of politics brought him under the wing of successful businessmen who helped him along. His involvement in the city's Republican party led him to a job in Senator Chafee's Providence office and, later, to City Hall.

Coloian, who was in his late twenties, became a favorite of Cianci, who had addressed his graduating class at Mount Pleasant High School in 1982. Unlike the mayor's more senior aides, he often accompanied Cianci on his late-night rambles through Providence's bar scene. He handled a variety of chores for his boss, including arranging private fund-raising parties. Wendy Materna recalled Coloian as someone who "made himself useful . . . Artie would say, 'Boss, I'll handle that.' Once, when I got a traffic ticket, Buddy said, 'Artie will handle that for you.' "

Corrente and Coloian also had various moonlighting enterprises.

Corrente still did some accounting for old clients, including a tow-truck operator who got onto the lucrative police tow list. He also owned real estate, including property that he leased to a city agency and a used-car lot that he rented to some former Public Works employees with mob ties who had been convicted of corruption stemming from Buddy I.

Coloian, who had recently become a lawyer, did some immigration law on the side. He continued to dabble in real estate, including apartments that he offered for rent to city employees. And he bought some billboards, which councilman Josh Fenton had previously sought to tax to raise city revenues.

Corrente and Coloian didn't like or trust each other. Though on the surface they treated each other politely, behind each other's back they played sneaky games, trying to curry favor with the mayor. Corrente once told someone that he did certain things for the mayor, and Coloian did the things that Corrente wouldn't do.

Both men undercut Joe Almagno, the gentlemanly chief of staff who had been recruited to lend integrity to the Cianci administration. Corrente would argue with Almagno about patronage and promotions. Coloian would bring up decisions that he knew Almagno had already made in front of the mayor, who would get angry that he hadn't been consulted. Although Almagno continued to sit next to the mayor at directors' meetings, Cianci started skipping over him and going right to Corrente.

In the summer of 1993 Almagno resigned. As part of the ensuing staff shake-up, Corrente emerged as the clear number-two man at City Hall. Coloian was promoted to executive assistant; his salary jumped from forty-four thousand to sixty thousand dollars.

Publicly, Almagno said all the right things about pursuing other options and departing on good terms. Privately, he told someone close to him, "I'm getting out before this all blows up."

■

FIRE IS A SYMBOL of life and rebirth, death and destruction. It illuminates and it burns. In the mid-1990s, fire became the defining element of Buddy Cianci and his reborn Renaissance City.

On soft summer nights, the fragrant smell of wood smoke curled around the city's historic architecture. Down the center of the Providence River a line of ethereal fires bloomed in iron braziers on pillars. Music, from opera to New Age, crackled through the air along with the sparks lifting toward heaven. Venetian gondolas plied the waters.

This was WaterFire, a soaring, meditative experience that attracted international attention and drew thousands to the waterfront. The creation of local artist and sculptor Barnaby Evans, WaterFire was hailed by publications ranging from *Granta* to a Brazilian magazine as one of the must-see events in the United States.

A Berkeley, California, native who went to Brown, Evans was intrigued by the duality of water and fire, their lifegiving aspects and their mutually destructive qualities—water extinguishes fire, fire evaporates water. He thought of ways to fuse the two into something that would attract people downtown at night, to enjoy the newly opened Waterplace Park. He hated how the city emptied after dark, leaving behind "a scary, desolate feeling." Evans wanted to fill the darkness with hope. Then he had it: beacon fires reflected in the waters, summoning people back to Providence.

WaterFire debuted on New Year's Eve in 1994, as part of Providence's First Night celebration. It was such a hit that Evans, with Cianci's enthusiastic backing, brought it back for good in the summer of 1996.

Cianci could often be found where the crowds were thickest, holding court at an outdoor table at Cafe Nuovo, a chic restaurant in the new brick-and-glass office tower rising from a triangle of land where the ancient Moshassuck and Woonasquatucket Rivers flowed into the Providence River on its journey to Narragansett Bay and the sea.

WaterFire showcased the New Providence, a trendy city to live in and visit with its vibrant arts scene, world-class restaurants, and Old World flavor. Providence became the paradigm for the New American city, defined by culture rather than manufacturing. The comeback city and the comeback mayor were profiled in national publications. Cianci spoke at urban-planning seminars from Wilmington, Delaware, to San Diego. He attributed Providence's turnaround to cheerleading and the city's strong-mayor form of government, which enabled him to cut through red tape and exert real leadership.

"You have to get people to join in the mission," he said. "You have to get them to drink the Kool-Aid."

Cianci became the messianic mayor, an urban Moses who had moved rivers.

The story of Providence's turnaround is actually more complicated. It offers a case study in urban planning and how a city can reinvent itself by focusing on its heritage—in Providence's case, as a historic seafaring power.

When architect Bill Warner first suggested the daring plan to move the rivers, in 1983, skeptics dismissed it as the "Moses plan." But through a fortuitous series of breaks and a heroic partnership of architects, engineers, government bureaucrats, business leaders, and elected city, state, and federal officials, the Moses plan came to pass. Cianci had endorsed the idea in its early stages, before leaving office in 1984. For too long the city had turned its back on its greatest natural resource, its waterfront, which had grown seedy, weedy, and filthy.

The Moses plan flowed from another ambitious idea that had been kicking around since the early 1900s—to move the railroad tracks that bisected Providence. For nearly a hundred years, the tracks, elevated on an earthen embankment known as the Chinese Wall, had cut off downtown from the State House, half a mile away. The land in between had become an unsightly jungle of freight yards and parking lots.

In colonial times, this wasteland had been the Great Salt Cove that Roger Williams saw when he paddled up the Providence River. He founded his colony near its shore. Over time, as seafaring gave way to manufacturing, the cove was filled in around the edges for wharves and factories. In the latter part of the nineteenth century the cove was taken over and eventually filled in completely by the rapacious railroads. Older, affluent East Siders, who remembered the elliptical Cove Basin with its elegant promenades and waterfront festivals, had fought the railroads. Mayor Thomas Doyle, who objected to the Chinese Wall, called the cove "holy water." The city's superintendent of health said that a large body of tidewater was healthy because it helped circulate fresh air through an increasingly foul factory city; filling in the cove, he warned, would literally make Providence sick. But the cove, neglected by the railroads, had grown rank with industrial waste and sewage. The railroad interests controlled the City Council, which voted to turn over the cove lands. The last of the cove was filled in 1892.

Within a few decades, various lone visionaries began proposing different ideas to move the railroad tracks and rejuvenate the old cove lands. One utopian plan called for bringing back the cove and building a new City Hall on a manmade island in the center, reached by meandering footpaths. During the Great Depression, a local radio broadcast noted that the city's founders had passed up an opportunity to lay out Providence like Venice, with water highways "where long, swan-like gondolas might have glided." But the broadcast praised industry, concluding, "If our forefathers did not conceive the creation of a little Venice, they did make a little Rome out of a marsh, a lagoon and seven surrounding hills."

Around 1910, a Canadian railroad executive, Charles Melville Hays, envisioned Providence as the eastern terminus of a new transcontinental rail system that would challenge the monopoly of Wall Street tycoon J. Pierpoint Morgan. Providence's leaders, eager to compete with Boston, feted Hays with sumptuous dinners at the University Club and lined up two million dollars in public financing for the project, which would have created a new rail line and a new port. But then Hays took a business trip to London. When it was time to return home, he refused to sail on a ship owned by a Morgan syndicate. Instead, in April 1912, Hays booked passage on the maiden voyage of the *Titanic.* The Providence plan went down with him.

After World War II, rail-relocation plans were revived in earnest, but a lack of financing delayed their implementation. When Joseph Doorley, Jr., became mayor in 1965, he opposed the move, arguing that the money would be better spent on rebuilding the neighborhoods. When Buddy Cianci ran against Doorley in 1974, he trumpeted a plan by a Rhode Island School of Design professor to move the railroad tracks and uncover the river. But once again there was no money.

The breakthrough finally came in 1978. The Federal Railroad Administration had begun a five-year, $1.5 billion upgrade of rail service from Boston to Washington. Ron Marsella, executive director of the Providence Foundation, a nonprofit Chamber of Commerce affiliate, wondered if the federal government would pay to move the tracks in Providence instead of simply rebuilding them. His idea quickly caught on with U.S. senator Claiborne Pell, a railroad buff. Pell called the governor, Joe Garrahy, who was also enthusiastic. Bruce Sundlun, the president of the Providence Foundation, took the idea to Cianci, whose response was, "Hey, if the federal government's going to pay for it, let's do it." With the key local leaders on board, Pell lobbied in Washington and won approval.

Cianci and Garrahy also lobbied Washington, as they prepared to run against each other for governor in 1980. Their political rivalry created the comical scene of their aides flying home together from meetings in Washington, then rushing to City Hall and the State House to see whose boss could get out the first press release.

Leaders realized that they needed a vehicle to shepherd the project, one that would be free of politics so that it could take a longer view. For all of Cianci's enthusiasm, one former aide said, he was skeptical at first because of the long time frame. "In this business, two years is long-term," Cianci said.

In 1980 the quasi-public Capital Center Commission was created, its members appointed by the governor, the mayor, and the Providence Foundation. "The project had to survive the politicians of the time," Cianci recalled in the 1990s. "Little did I know that I'd still be here."

The city committed $4.6 million to the project; the federal government paid 70 percent of the overall $100 million price tag. Cianci presided over the groundbreaking on February 16, 1983—one month before he assaulted Raymond DeLeo.

That same month, the Providence Foundation's new executive director, Kenneth Orenstein, panicked when he reviewed the plans and saw that Capital Center engineers had proposed paving over the entire Providence River to create a new road. The idea was not new. In 1946, a city planner had suggested putting a highway over the river so that "the foul open sewer, which runs through the heart of the city, will finally be subjugated."

Much of the Providence River had already been "subjugated." The Crawford Street Bridge, which spanned a 1,147-foot stretch of the river behind the post office, was listed in the *Guinness Book of World Records* as the world's widest bridge. Behind it was Suicide Circle, a congested rotary at the base of College Hill where cars jockeyed around the tall stone pillar of the World War I memorial.

Orenstein called Warner, who was studying potential waterfront uses for the Providence Foundation. "Look," he said, "you've got to come up with something. They're going to pave the river."

Warner, who had moved out of Providence after realizing that spring had come and gone without his noticing, sat by the woodstove on his eighty-acre farm in southern Rhode Island one rainy Sunday afternoon. In a few hours he sketched out a plan to uncover the river and replace the wide bridge with a series of smaller, graceful bridges. Later, refining the plan, Warner moved the river out from underneath the post office, placed the confluence of the three rivers one hundred yards to the east, eliminated Suicide Circle, and removed the Crawford Street Bridge. It looked good on paper.

In the ensuing months, Orenstein and Warner peddled the plan to all of the key players. Some were resistant. One city planner threatened to walk out of a meeting if Orenstein didn't put the plan back in his briefcase. This is when someone derisively dubbed it the Moses plan.

Cianci grasped the potential, even if the plan didn't come at the best time for him personally. In the spring of 1983, minutes before he was scheduled to meet with Orenstein and state officials to hear the plan, Cianci received word that he was going to be indicted for assaulting DeLeo. The mayor went ahead with the meeting but seemed clearly agitated. Although the planners had seen him lose his temper before, Cianci seemed angrier than usual. Unaware of the impending DeLeo indictment, Orenstein listened as the mayor shouted that the state had been keeping him out of the loop on the river plan.

Finally Cianci calmed down and embraced the idea. That fall, he and Governor Garrahy announced a feasibility study of the river plan. Recognizing its revolutionary nature, the National Endowment for the Arts also provided a grant.

The rest of the Moses plan was history—but not Buddy Cianci's history. Their paths diverged as the mayor went into exile, then, like the rechanneled rivers, flowed together again in the early 1990s. By then, the project, which cost forty million dollars, most of it paid for by the federal government, was nearly complete. As the crowning touch, designers created WaterPlace Park, a one-acre pond where the old Cove Basin had been. The pond, a bulge in the Woonasquatucket River, was graced by a concrete amphitheater and encircled by promenades that continued along the newly exposed rivers.

In the summer of 1994, WaterPlace Park was dedicated with the release of one hundred white doves. While most of the politicians and dignitaries arrived by land, Cianci came by sea. He and Wendy Materna motored up the Providence River from India Point in the *Nicola*'s inflatable dinghy and circled the pond to the cheers of construction workers.

Materna smiled with a practiced ease as the cameras clicked. For the past four years, she had been the unofficial first lady of Providence, a lithe, graceful presence by the mayor's side. She had danced with him at the policemen's ball and subbed for him when he was late for speaking engagements. She had smashed a bottle of champagne to christen a new fireboat. She had suggested that he bottle his own marinara sauce and sell it for charity, like Paul Newman, and even gave him her recipe to use.

Cianci's first few years back in office had been good ones, bathed in the glow of redemption. On summer weekends, he and Materna would hole up on his boat, in Newport or Block Island. He would arrive at the dock in Newport at 10:30 on Friday night and Materna would have everything prepared: music, candlelight, chilled cocktails. Late at night, the mayor would pace the docks and walk their cocker spaniels, Tucker and Belle, unwinding and enjoying the solitude. Sunday evenings, after the tourists had departed, were the best, as he savored the peace and the sunset over Narragansett Bay. But as Cianci's term wore on, there were more and more weekends that he would head back to Providence early to attend one event or another.

Materna had also put up with Cianci's late nights and his childish temper, his drinking and his infidelities. She had caught him cheating on her many times, she said, and also suffered his verbal abuse and inconsiderate behavior. She remembered screaming at him in his house on Power Street one night at 4 A.M., so angry that she started throwing things. She had also worked to build a relationship with Cianci's teenage daughter, Nicole, but it wasn't always easy.

Some of the mayor's aides likened Materna to Henry Higgins, trying to teach Cianci's Eliza Doolittle the social graces and smooth over the rough edges. One friend of Cianci's said that she gave him structure. Materna joked that wasn't in the back room with the "old boys." She was "Wendy the WASP, the blond doll he'd pull off the shelf to give him legitimacy." He called her Gwendolyn.

She had seen how insecure Cianci could be behind the public bravado, and the conflicted nature of his heritage—the rich boy in Silver Lake, the Italian kid at Moses Brown. One time they went into the Squantum Club, a private old-boys club in East Providence, where the father of one of Cianci's Moses Brown chums, another Italian-American, hugged Cianci and said, "Who'd have thunk it—a little guinea boy like you growing up to be mayor."

Mortified, Materna looked at Cianci. After the man walked away, Cianci said to her, "You don't get it, do you?" The man had meant it as a compliment.

Buddy's election night proposal had become a running joke. He had proposed "many times" since then and even given her a few rings, she said, but he never followed through. He would tell Wendy not to worry, but she wanted more in her life. She was thirty-eight—Buddy was fifty-three—and she wanted to get married and have a family. Wendy's voyage up the Providence River with Buddy that summer day in 1994 was in many ways reflective of their nine years together—buoyant and exciting, with tricky currents beneath. Although she loved him, she also felt that there was "too much water under the bridge—so much heartache."

The previous winter, she had gone to Florida to stay with her mother and thaw out after coming down with pneumonia. Cianci had promised to come down and meet her, but he never did. In January she met a man named Christian Johannsen at a valet-parking stand outside a restaurant where she had gone to eat with her parents. He gave her his business card. In Providence, Materna said, she never looked at another man; out in nightclubs like Sh-Booms, she and her girlfriends would joke about how one of "Buddy's baby-sitters" always seemed to be around.

Materna called Johannsen, who worked in Miami as an investment banker, and they went out. "It was the first time that somebody had taken me to dinner in nine years," she said. Before things could go any further, she received a frantic call from Cianci. A Providence patrolman, Steven Shaw, had been shot and killed apprehending a robbery suspect, and he wanted her to return for the funeral. "Please come back," she recalled Cianci's telling her. "I need you." Still nursing her pneumonia, Materna flew back to Rhode Island in early February and marched in the funeral procession behind the casket with Cianci and Governor Sundlun. It was a gray day, wet and snowy.

Later that month, they had what she called their "first big serious talk" about their relationship. Once again, he said that he would marry her. In March Materna went back to Florida for six weeks and kindled a romance with Johannsen. Cianci, she said, apparently became suspicious and found out—how, she didn't know, because she didn't tell him.

In the coming months, Materna shuttled between Florida and Rhode Island, Christian and Buddy, never staying in one place too long. Cianci began pushing her to get married, only now she had another suitor. She felt conflicted between her need to move on and the strong pull of her relationship with Buddy—and with Providence. Growing up as a navy brat, she had always felt Providence was her home base, her touchstone. She had good friends and "a great little life" there. And Cianci, for all the pain of their relationship, had transformed her into a much more confident person—"He gave me the world." She had become a polished public speaker and a doer, serving on a multitude of charitable boards and learning how to get things accomplished. She had gotten involved with the Providence Preservation Society, the Providence Performing Arts Center, the library, the schools, the dog pound. The political whirl with Cianci was "exciting, thrilling, exhausting." It was, she said, "like being the bride at every party, every night." But there was also the heartache, and the realization that Buddy was never going to change and make her a true bride.

"There's nobody better for you than me," he'd tell her. But she was hesitant. She envisioned herself staying with him, sitting at home alone on Power Street and growing old while he was out at political events or with other women. Cianci signed them up for couples therapy, and they started going to see a man in Cranston; the mayor's police chauffeur would drive them, discreetly parking the limousine in a garage near the office. To Materna, the sessions were comical. The therapist parroted Cianci so much that they should have been sitting on the couch together, she joked; it was as if the mayor had told him what to say. The therapist would compare Johannsen to a doctor who had come on the scene to highlight the problems in her relationship with Cianci. But you don't marry the doctor, the therapist said—you use him to fix the relationship, and then you send the doctor away. Within the mayor's office, one aide said, there was talk that Cianci had "gotten to" the therapist.

One night, over dinner at the Old Canteen, Wendy asked, "Why do you act the way you do?" She couldn't understand how he could have such a big heart, be so kind and wonderful and loving, and yet behave so horribly. Then it hit her. "What happened with your father?" she asked. Cianci burst into tears. He didn't go into detail about his father, or talk about the things that Wendy had heard on other occasions about Dr. Cianci's girlfriends, or how he could be aloof and demanding. Instead, Buddy spoke tearfully about the last time he had seen his father alive, when Buddy boarded the train in Providence to join the army in 1967. His father had died a short time later, on the Fourth of July. The Fourth had always been an awkward day for Wendy when she was with Buddy, because it was her favorite holiday.

It was an election year, and Materna came back from Florida for a fund-raiser in May and again for the mayor's official announcement in June. Then, as the summer wore on, she said, "I sat up there [in Providence] and went crazy." Cianci's proposal became a public issue; she told the *Journal* that she was thinking about it. "It literally became a show," she recalled. "We'd go to a fund-raiser, and it would be like George Burns and Gracie Allen. Buddy would say, 'She wants me to marry her.' I'd laugh."

Behind the scenes, Cianci was turning up the pressure. He started calling Materna's mother in Chicago and charming her, talking for hours. Materna, who had struggled in the past to get Cianci to spend any time with her parents when they were in town, was annoyed. "He's really fabulous, Wendy," her mother would say. An exasperated Materna replied, "He's been making me cry for nine years, and you call him fabulous?"

Cianci was "very, very angry" with her, Materna recalled. One day her Florida boyfriend, Johannsen, chased away a private detective who showed up snooping at his office in Miami. In a conversation with Materna, she said, Cianci took credit for sending the detective, and also relayed information from credit reports that he had somehow obtained on Johannsen. Cianci even described how her new beau walked and how he dressed. Materna suspected that the phone at her apartment in Providence was tapped, because Cianci would repeat back to her verbatim conversations that she had had with Johannsen, who would be asking when she was coming back to Florida. The mayor also threatened to plant drugs on her boyfriend and tip off the police, though she considered that an idle threat—she had heard Cianci say the same thing many times before about political rivals or anyone else who angered him.

Art Coloian began talking to her, telling her that she had "better behave." One day, she said, he took her to lunch and told her to "keep my head on straight." Materna laughed. A Providence police officer said he received a phone message from Coloian one day, asking him to go to Florida on a matter involving Materna. But the police officer, who had just worked an overnight shift, said that he ducked the call.

In the summer of 1994, during the month following her dinghy ride with Cianci to dedicate WaterPlace Park, Materna vacillated between her two suitors. She was, she recalled, "all over the place emotionally." She wasn't happy in Rhode Island. She wasn't happy in Florida. She didn't want to leave Providence, but she didn't feel that she could stay with Cianci, even though she loved him. Finally, she and Johannsen agreed to get married in Barbados on Saturday, September 10.

As the wedding approached, Materna's emotional turmoil grew. Just before Labor Day weekend, miserable in Florida, she put her marriage plans on hold and called Cianci and said that she wanted to come home. Cianci arranged a flight. When she stepped off the plane in Rhode Island, Cianci was standing on the gangway of the airport with their two dogs,

Tucker and Belle. But rather than being touched by the scene, she grew angry when she saw that the dogs had bows on their heads—something she had always hated, one more sign of how little attention Cianci paid her. She pulled the bows off the dogs' heads and told Cianci that she wanted him to take her home. Surprised, Cianci said, "I thought you came home to get married." She said no, that she wanted to be left alone to think. After he dropped her at her apartment, she retreated to her cousin's house on Prudence Island for the weekend, where she realized that she had made a mistake. She called Johannsen and they agreed to go forward with the wedding.

That Tuesday, Materna went to Power Street to break the news to Cianci. He was devastated, she said. Late in the afternoon, they took a walk along the waterfront at India Point. Cianci sobbed, she said, as they grieved over the end of their relationship. A few days later, she flew back to Florida. Before Materna left for Barbados on Friday, Cianci sent a courier to hand-deliver a letter, asking her not to go through with it. But it was too late.

Cianci was wild with grief. Devastated, he poured his heart out to close friends, including his longtime secretary, Carol Agugiaro, who was surprised to see such a vulnerable side to the hard-charging mayor. Bruce Sundlun said that it was "the only time I've ever seen him knocked off his feet." According to Sundlun, Cianci said that it was "the worst blow and the worst mistake he had ever made."

Even after she married, Materna said, Cianci continued to call, asking, "When are you coming back?" In what she described as one of the low points of their relationship, Cianci sent Tucker and Belle to live at the Providence dog pound for ten months, at the instigation of an old girlfriend whom Cianci had left for Materna years before and who had moved back in and wanted no reminders of Wendy. When Materna found out, she was furious. Around the same time, Cianci received an insurance settlement for some damage to his boat; because Materna had lent him money on the boat to help him out of his early-nineties financial troubles, she had to sign off on the check. She agreed to do so, she said, in return for Cianci's releasing the dogs to her custody. She hired a lawyer and wound up spending five thousand dollars to get Tucker and Belle out of the Providence pound and bring them to live with her at her new home in Key Biscayne.

The day that Wendy walked down the aisle in Barbados, Buddy campaigned for reelection at the Providence Waterfront Festival, where he kissed a pig named Petunia.

Petunia was at a booth to raise money for charity; people could pay a dollar for a ballot and vote for the politician they wanted to see kiss the swine. Cianci won in a landslide. Puckering up for the cameras, he joked, "I've kissed a lotta pigs in my life."

Cianci had an easy race that year. His would-be challenger, councilman Josh Fenton, had decided to retire from politics; his wife was pregnant, and he wanted a normal family life. Still, the mayor campaigned on, trailed by a PBS camera crew filming a segment on him for a documentary on American politics, *Vote for Me*.

"I'm running for my fifth term," Cianci told his PBS interviewer. "That's a long time. You've really and truly gotta want it and love it. You've gotta be dedicated to it. And you've gotta like to do what I'm about to do in that crowd right now."

Later, after he'd kissed the pig, Cianci was back in his limo, riding to another campaign stop. "All fame and power, I guess, is fleeting," he said. "It goes and it comes. . . . I've been in and out, back in again, and I can tell you—when you're out, you're out."

At another stop, a woman asked innocently, "How's Wendy?"

"She's, uh, getting married today, in Barbados or someplace," he replied.

Embarrassed, the woman said, "I didn't know that."

"Yeah, she met a guy—good luck to 'em."

Later, at another stop, a man dressed like Uncle Sam asked about Wendy. Cianci said she was getting married, then told Uncle Sam, "Yeah, bad move—for me. . . . It isn't a very good day for me, you know."

Back in his limousine, Cianci looked sad. "Kinda lonely today, just alone, place to place, from one advance man to the next one. But if you don't like it, you shouldn't be in it. My whole life has been the city, so it's tough for me to say that I don't want to do things in it."

The limousine drove past the State House, where a bride and groom stood outside, posing for wedding pictures. "Oh, look at this, a bride," he said softly. "Stop, we'll go say hello to the bride. Isn't that nice."

Chuckling, Cianci got out.

"That's the prettiest sight I've seen," he called out. "I only see demonstrations here, you know, and riots and things."

Cianci shook the groom's hand and pecked the bride on the cheek. He stood with the newlyweds for a picture, his smile frozen in place.

VINCENT ALBERT CIANCI, JR.
454 Laurel Hill Avenue, Cranston, R .I.

Form I: Baseball, Football, *Moses Brown News*.
Form II: Baseball, Football, Glee Club, Chess Club.
Form III: Baseball, Football, Wrestling, Snack Bar Committee.
Form IV: Baseball, Letter in Football, Wrestling, Glee Club, Snack Bar Committee, *Quaker*.
Form V: Letter in Football, Letter in Wrestling, Letter in Baseball, Glee Club, *Quaker*.

"The grey mare is the better horse."

Everyone on the campus has noticed the "Buddha." A day student for seven years, Buddy threw away the carefree life and became a boarder in his senior year. Football and wrestling are his bread and butter, and nobody will ever forget his beautifully executed pass interception against St. George's. Buddy is a plugger in everything he does and spends many a night burning the midnight oil. Of course on open weekends "Buddha" seeks relaxation as most hard-working individuals do. Bud has been able to do what no other Moses Brown man has ever done — pin Jerry Zeoli, and in thirty seconds flat. Last winter he learned a lesson in the business world. His Laurel Avenue Tavern was closed down after one gala weekend. While he did not give his all for dear old Moses Brown, he gave more than most — his two front teeth.

"Everyone on the campus has noticed the 'Buddha.'"
Moses Brown yearbook, 1958

WRESTLING

Row 1: R. B. Chaser, J. D. Richardson, H. S. Thornley, F. T. Rooks, II, Captain; V. A. Cianci, Jr., J. R. Nixon, D. P. Lind, Jr.   Row 2: D. R. Hazen, W. D. Nixen, W. N. Mattiek, V. Johnson, Coach; J. C. Towle, Manager; A. F. Vincent, S. S. Harding. Not in picture: A. C. Ray.

It was on the wrestling mat that Cianci (front row, third from right) learned some of the moves that would serve him well in politics.
Moses Brown yearbook

The ivy-covered halls of Moses Brown were a world away from Italian Silver Lake for Cianci (third row from front, fourth from left), who strove to fit in with the WASP sons of privilege.   Moses Brown yearbook

Before Providence was Buddy's town, it belonged to New England mob boss Raymond L. S. Patriarca, whose control of cops, judges, and politicians earned him a reputation as the unofficial mayor of Providence.

William L. Rooney, *The Providence Journal*

Bookmaker Rudolph Marfeo's 1968 murder in Pannone's Market, near where Cianci grew up, was the culmination of a bloody mob war that would draw the future mayor into the prosecution of Patriarca.

Providence Police Department Photo

Mayor Joseph Doorley, who once stood on the ramparts of Lyndon Johnson's Great Society, saw his fortunes decline along with his city's, culminating in a 1974 mutiny in the ranks of the mighty Democratic machine. *The Providence Journal*

Cianci anounced his candidacy for mayor in the spring of 1974. He ran as the anticorruption candidate. "The Providence River is like the Democratic machine that has been running this city—namely, it stinks," he said. *The Providence Journal*

Cianci poses with his wife, Sheila, and daughter Nicole at home in January 1975, shortly before being sworn in as Providence's first Italian-American mayor. *The Providence Journal*

Mr. Democrat, Larry McGarry (in wheelchair), visits Cianci in the mayor's office
on inauguration day 1975.

Thomas D. Stevens, *The Providence Journal*

Cianci became the ringmaster of the circus
at City Hall and an ally of President Ford.
Some said that Cianci had the potential
to become the first Italian-American in
the Oval Office.   Circus: *The Providence Journal*;
Cianci and Ford: Associated Press

The mayor, seeking to revitalize the dormant downtown,
invited the press along for
a 1977 police raid of an
adult bookstore.

Michael Kelly, *The Providence Journal*

Cianci and John Chafee, seen here in 1980 when
Cianci ran for governor, dueled behind the
scenes in 1976 for a coveted U.S. Senate seat.

William K. Daby, *The Providence Journal*

The mayor leads the Brown
University band on a 1976
downtown trolley tour as
they play tunes by the
Providence-born showman
George M. Cohan.

William L. Rooney, *The Providence Journal*

"Let them arrest me," Cianci declared when the Bristol town fathers attempted to ban him from the Fourth of July parade. "I am going to march to celebrate the joy of being an American."

Andy Dickerman,
The Providence Journal

Ronald Glantz was the mayor's Mr. Fix-It—and, Glantz later said, his accomplice in bribery. Glantz went to prison for his own scam involving kickbacks for the purchase of garbage trucks.

Richard Benjamin, *The Providence Journal*

Cianci makes Frank Sinatra, whose father was a firefighter, an honorary fire chief in 1979. The wiseguys turned out when Sinatra, who was friendly with Raymond Patriarca, performed in Providence. After Sinatra's death in 1998, the flag over City Hall flew at half-mast.

The Providence Journal

A relentless campaigner, Cianci crisscrossed Rhode Island when he ran for governor in 1980. "I would attend the opening of an envelope," he said.

Andy Dickerman, *The Providence Journal*

Seeking to break a nasty 1981 strike, the mayor deployed armed police officers to ride shotgun during the midnight ride of the garbage trucks.

John L. Hanlon, *The Providence Journal*

Buckles Melise (below, right), shown during the 1981 sanitation strike, was mobster Bobo Marrapese's man at Public Works and also a loyal Cianci fund-raiser. The mayor joked that it was "great public policy" when Buckles sledgehammered a striking garbage worker.

Peter Morgan, *The Providence Journal*

Bristol contractor Raymond DeLeo (right) described the night that the mayor assaulted him for an alleged affair with Cianci's wife: "I saw a crazed man. I saw a lunatic."

Thomas D. Stevens,
The Providence Journal

The mayor, standing next to state prosecutor Susan McGuirl, receives a five-year suspended prison sentence after pleading no contest to felony assault of DeLeo. The plea forced him to resign and was widely viewed as the end of his political career.

William L. Rooney, *The Providence Journal*

One week after resigning as mayor in 1984, Cianci serves as grand marshal at the St. Joseph's Day parade on Federal Hill and receives a hero's welcome.

The Providence Journal

Cianci and girlfriend Wendy
Materna outside his Power
Street house in 1990, celebrating a political comeback
that *The Wall Street Journal*
said "would be the envy of
Richard Nixon."

Bob Thayer, *The Providence Journal*

WaterFire, the creation of
artist Barnaby Evans, won
international acclaim and
became a signature event of
Buddy Cianci's trend-setting
Renaissance.

Sandor Bodo, *The Providence Journal*

WaterPlace Park, dedicated in 1994 on the site of the Great Salt Cove of colonial times, helped make Providence a national model for urban renewal. *Money* and other magazines called it one of America's most livable cities.
The Providence Journal

Cianci, flanked by longtime ad man Norm Roussel, gets a hug from Wendy Materna after announcing for reelection in 1994. Materna faced her own decision—about whether to marry the mayor and stay in Providence.

Bob Thayer, *The Providence Journal*

The mayor kisses a pig named Petunia, a moment captured in the acclaimed PBS documentary on American politics *Vote for Me*. The documentary crowned Cianci "the King of Retail."

Bob Thayer, *The Providence Journal*

Cianci flew to Palm Beach, Florida, in 1997 in an effort to convince New England Patriots owner Robert Kraft to move his NFL franchise to Providence.   Glenn Osmundson, *The Providence Journal*

Actor Anthony Quinn, who moved to Rhode Island in 1995, came to regard the effervescent Cianci as a son. "I don't know of any artist or man in the world who has the dreams for a place that Buddy has for Providence," Quinn said.   William K. Daby, *The Providence Journal*

The mayor stands outside his carriage house on Power Street, dubbed by associates the "Crime Castle." In 1999, the FBI appeared at his doorstep.

Bob Thayer,
The Providence Journal

Frank Corrente, Cianci's top aide and campaign treasurer, helped rescue the mayor from bankruptcy. Corrente craved power and younger women at City Hall.   Mary Murphy, *The Providence Journal*

Edward Voccola (right), with Plunder Dome codefendant Richard Autiello, was accused of paying bribes to lease his auto-body shop, which was near a strip club, to the city as a registration center for schoolchildren. A witness against him in an insurance-fraud case was sent black roses and an animal tongue.   Mary Murphy, *The Providence Journal*

Businessman Antonio Freitas
spent a year undercover for the
FBI, armed with hidden
cameras and microphones
as he penetrated a web of
City Hall corruption.
Mary Murphy, *The Providence Journal*

Cianci's appointees to lead the city
tax board, Joseph Pannone (above)
and David Ead (right), found
themselves sharing a jail cell the day
Operation Plunder Dome became
public. The pair would become key
figures in the case against the mayor.
The Providence Journal

On the opening day of his epic racketeering trial, Cianci and his lawyer Richard Egbert choose to walk from the Biltmore (right) to the federal courthouse on the opposite end of Kennedy Plaza. City Hall is behind the mayor.

Kathy Borchers, *The Providence Journal*

Under indictment for racketeering, Cianci visited Ground Zero in New York two weeks after the September 11 terrorist attacks, along with his city photographer and videographer.

Peter Goldberg

The government's team
in Operation Plunder
Dome. FBI agent Dennis
Aiken is flanked by
prosecutors Terrence
Donnelly (left) and
Richard Rose (right).

Kathy Borchers,
The Providence Journal

The defense team has lunch in
the mayor's anteroom during
the trial. At the end of the second
week of jury deliberations,
Egbert offers encouragement.

Peter Goldberg

The nation's longest-serving active mayor ponders his fate after his conviction prompts him not to seek a seventh term. "I was convicted," he said, "of being the mayor." Peter Goldberg

In December 2002, Cianci checked out of the Biltmore and reported to federal prison in Fort Dix, New Jersey—which he called "a very, very inexpensive spa."

Gretchen Ertl, *The Providence Journal*

WENDY WAS GONE, but Buddy still had Providence.

He was reelected easily in 1994, and his love affair with his city flourished. As the Renaissance took shape, his approval rating soared past 80 percent.

There was a new convention center and new hotels. The upscale Providence Place Mall opened, a handsome brick structure that stretched from downtown to the State House. Fleet Bank financed an outdoor public ice-skating rink outside City Hall; the mayor, not wanting to embarrass himself at the dedication ceremonies, hired a personal skating instructor.

"We have moved more than railroad tracks and rivers," he proclaimed. "We have moved the hearts and souls of an entire city."

The old downtown core remained a problem, though there were signs of life. He declared downtown an arts-and-entertainment district, modeled after a program in Dublin, Ireland, and pushed for tax credits for artists and developers to rehab old buildings into lofts. He wanted to bring residents back downtown. But financing remained difficult, and progress slow. For all the attention focused on Cianci's program of tax breaks for artists, only a handful actually moved downtown to take advantage. More artists were moving into cheaper old mill space in neighboring Pawtucket. When the mayor boasted that Providence had more artists per capita than any city in America, he was counting the art students at the Rhode Island School of Design, according to Patricia McLaughlin, his downtown economic czar. Still, as the river-relocation project had shown, change sometimes came slowly. Nobody could fault Cianci for his grand ideas.

Zorba the Greek was impressed by the mayor's vision.

In 1995, actor Anthony Quinn moved to Rhode Island and settled on a waterfront estate in Bristol to paint and sculpt. Quinn had met Cianci in 1986, while performing *Zorba the Greek* in Providence. Cianci had shown him around the drab city, which singer Bette Midler once called "the pits," and enthusiastically pointed out how they were going to move these rivers and restore those historic buildings.

Quinn thought that Cianci was nuts, but he listened with good humor. He had been a mayor, at least in the movies, and he knew that it was a tough role. In *The Secret of Santa Vittoria* Quinn had played an amiable drunk who unexpectedly becomes mayor of his Italian wine-making village during World War II and must contend with Nazis intent on looting the village's vintage wines.

When Quinn moved to Rhode Island, he renewed his acquaintance with Cianci. The two grew as close as father and son, Zorba the Elder and Zorba the Younger, dining and drinking and laughing late into the night up on Federal Hill.

"I don't know of any artist or man in the world who has the dreams for a place that Buddy has for Providence," said Quinn. "He made all his dreams come true. He's a miracle man."

In the 1970s, Cianci said, mayors were social workers; in the 1990s they were entrepreneurs. A Wellesley College urban-studies professor, Wilbur C. Rich, concluded that mayors in postindustrial cities had to be salesmen who could create excitement to promote their city as a good place to live, work, and play.

"Buddy Cianci has mastered the technique of creating the show particularly well," Rich wrote in a book on mayoral leadership in middle-sized American cities. "To say he is the life of the party in Providence is an understatement. . . . Cianci has come close to melding his personality with the so-called New Providence." As a result, the public was willing to put up with Cianci's "idiosyncrasies and self-serving behavior. He is the merchant of the New Providence. Shameless boosterism is now the norm in Providence."

Cianci could be over the top, telling *The New York Times* that Providence was "the Florence of America," or returning from a mayors' conference in San Francisco and ordering his economic-development director, John Palmieri, to get cracking on a Chinatown for Providence. Undeterred by Providence's negligible Chinese population, Cianci shouted, "I want pagodas!"

But the mayor's enthusiasm was infectious. Providence became trendy. Publications as diverse as *Money* magazine and *Swing*, a magazine for the twenty-something set, rated Providence as one of the best cities in America in which to live. *Utne Reader* ranked Providence as one of the country's ten most enlightened cities. *Esquire* and the *Journal of Food & Wine* raved about Providence's restaurants, many of which had been nurtured by an aggressive city loan program. *Food & Wine* rated the city's restaurants ahead of Boston's.

As the longest-serving active mayor in the country of a city with more than one hundred thousand people, Cianci presented himself as a statesman. "You know, Winston Churchill once said that a politician gives people what they want and a statesman gives them what they need," Cianci told *The New York Times* in 1997. "This is the only time in my career I'll be able to make them converge."

Cianci became something of a national cult figure as the roguish savior of Providence. A frequent guest on the ribald *Imus in the Morning* radio program, he went toe-to-toe with the acerbic Don Imus, who was not known for suffering fools gladly.

Imus teased Cianci about wearing an ankle bracelet and finding thumbs in the mayor's marinara sauce. Cianci pledged to rename Clown Alley, the street beside the Civic Center where the circus unloaded, Imus Way—for a price. Cianci would have his public-relations people work for days writing material before an Imus appearance, but he was also quick at ad-libbing.

"Did you set someone on fire?" asked Imus, who liked bringing up Cianci's assault conviction.

"I set people on fire every night," shot back Cianci.

Afterward, puffing so hard on a Barclay cigarette that he left teeth marks on the filter, a charged-up Cianci crowed about the line all day. "You just have to stay with him," he boasted to a friend. "He's not hard to out-flank."

Cianci pitched Providence on Broadway and in Hollywood, on the *Today* show and *The Tonight Show with Jay Leno*. His face beamed out from the display window of Cartier on Fifth Avenue in Manhattan, on a jar of the Mayor's Own Marinara Sauce wreathed in gems. When First Lady Hillary Rodham Clinton came to Providence in 1997, Cianci presented her with a jar of his sauce and told her to give the White House chef a night off and open it for her and the president. He prepared an authentic Italian meal in the kitchen of his house on Power Street for the PBS cooking show *Ciao Italia*. The creator of the Fox television cartoon *The Family Guy*—a graduate of the Rhode Island School of Design—featured a Buddy Cianci Junior High School on the show.

He lobbied for an expansion of the Providence Performing Arts Center, to accommodate big Broadway shows, and helped convince the producer of *The Phantom of the Opera* to commit to bringing the show to Providence, to help the theater pay for the renovation.

To Lynn Singleton, PPAC's executive director, the mayor's star power was a valuable commodity. When the Broadway producer of *Saturday Night Fever* was in town for a theater workshop, he told Singleton that he'd been reading about the mayor, and that he seemed like "a hot shit." Singleton picked up the phone and arranged an immediate meeting with Cianci, who schmoozed him over drinks in the mayor's office. A few years later, when *Saturday Night Fever* went on tour, Providence was one of the first cities booked.

Cianci was an intuitive performer, someone who "could hit the mark," said Singleton. Like all great productions, the Providence Renaissance was a collaboration—but Cianci was the star.

At his 1995 inaugural ball at PPAC, Cianci sang his old radio theme song, "Rhode Island Is Famous for You," with Robert Goulet. A few years later, when Goulet was performing in *Camelot* at PPAC, Singleton found the actor and his wife waiting expectantly for the mayor at the cast party after the show.

Frantically, Singleton raced downstairs and called the Providence police station and asked them to track down the mayor. It was past 10 P.M. A tired Cianci called back from his limousine a few minutes later, on his way home after attending several events. He grumbled at Singleton's request. But five minutes later the reenergized mayor breezed into the theater and charmed the Goulets. When Singleton last saw them, Cianci was herding the couple into his limousine for a midnight tour of the zoo.

Every Christmas season, Singleton took Cianci to New York to see a show and attend an annual party of theater managers. One year, hoping to snare *The Lion King* for a trial production before it went on tour, Singleton arranged dinner with Cianci and the head of Touring Disney, Tony McLean, at Le Cirque.

Singleton wanted the city to offer Disney a hundred thousand dollars toward expenses to get *The Lion King*, arguing that it would pay off economically over the course of a two-month run. Cianci was skeptical. "Why would I want to give Disney a hundred thousand dollars?" he asked.

They went to dinner, Singleton anticipating a disaster. Over drinks, Cianci asked McLean where Disney was going to mount *The Lion King*. McLean said Denver. Cianci, his municipal pride wounded, paused in midmartini.

"Denver!" he exploded. "Why would you want to go to Denver? There's nothing there but cows and mountains. I'll give you two hundred fifty thousand to open the show in Providence."

McLean, flabbergasted, said that he would have to check with his bosses. The dinner proceeded, and Cianci poured on the charm. The owner of Le Cirque, who had received an award from Cianci in Providence honoring the contributions of Italian-Americans to the culinary arts, sent free desserts to their table.

The Lion King stayed in Denver, where it had already been committed, but Cianci had made his point. He wanted Providence to play in the big leagues.

When there was talk of Robert Redford's Sundance Cinemas building an arts movie house in downtown Providence, Cianci flew to Utah and spent the night at Redford's ranch. The two of them even went horseback riding—Buddy Cassidy and the Sundance Kid. That project, too, never panned out, due to a lack of financing.

The mayor's love of the spotlight was evident one night in Lupo's Heartbreak Hotel, a rock club, when Little Richard was performing. Cianci had a bad cold and sat slumped at his table, his forehead nearly touching the tabletop. Then, down onstage, Little Richard said that he wanted to thank his good friend Buddy Cianci for the warm welcome, and the mayor's head shot up as if he'd been injected with adrenaline. He bounded down onto the stage and wound up dancing and singing with Little Richard on top of his piano.

One night in April 1996, Cianci showed up for a Bob Dylan concert at the Strand, a downtown nightclub. Toward the end of the show, the mayor sent word backstage that he wanted to meet Dylan, only to hear back from the tour manager that the only people the enigmatic rock star had agreed to meet in recent years were the prime minister of Israel and President Clinton. Cianci, who had been drinking, marched backstage with his entourage, his toupee slipping down his forehead, to confront the tour manager, who demanded to know who the hell he thought he was coming back there.

"I'll tell you who I am," Cianci said matter-of-factly, sticking out his hand. "I'm the mayor of this town. I'm the guy who can make sure that the police don't search those two tour buses out there for the next couple of hours."

"No problem, Mr. Mayor," replied the manager, who dutifully introduced Cianci to Bob Dylan when he came offstage.

But not every star was taken with the mayor. One night, while Carol Channing was performing at PPAC, Cianci and his entourage showed up. They were hanging around backstage when the actress's stage manager, according to his later account, asked Cianci to put out his cigarette, because Channing was sensitive to smoke.

A nasty encounter ensued, in which the stage manager accused Cianci of calling him "a fucking faggot." The story hit the newspaper a few days later, and Cianci denied it. Channing refused to accept a key to the city.

According to a city worker who moonlighted as a security guard at the Biltmore Hotel, he was on duty one night that week when he saw a city policeman loyal to Cianci going through the stage manager's room. The cop told the security guard that he was trying to dig up dirt in case the man caused any more trouble. Then the cop asked the guard to call the police and report an attemped break-in of the man's room, so that the police would have an excuse to question the stage manager and obtain personal information about him.

Cianci's charisma and vision could be offset by his ego and temper. The mayor could be, in the words of a former secretary who nevertheless admired him, a *cafone*, an Italian expression for an ill-mannered pig who takes what he wants.

One night, in the Capital Grille, a drunken Cianci gave a Nazi salute to a dictatorial State House politician, the House majority leader, and shouted, "Heil Hitler!" The restaurant was crowded with politicians and businessmen. Furious, the majority leader held up the city's legislation for weeks.

Another time, the mayor confronted a state senator from Providence in the restaurant Mediterraneo, upset with her for something, and reminded her that he had several hundred police officers working for him.

Cianci could also be nasty to the people who had helped him look good. One night, at a party at WaterFire creator Barnaby Evans's home, the mayor stood in the back, interrupting the other speakers and speaking coarsely. He leaned over a railing and shook it and said that he'd better send the building inspector down. Later, when Evans tried to present him with a WaterFire poster, Cianci snapped that he already had several.

Cianci had a love-hate relationship with Arnold "Buff" Chace, Jr., the downtown developer who was trying to rehab historic buildings into loft space.

Chace was not your typical developer. He was the wealthy scion of an old Yankee textile manufacturing family—one of the few families not to move their mills south during the early 1900s to capitalize on cheaper labor costs. (His great-great-grandmother Elizabeth Buffum Chace had been a famous nineteenth-century abolitionist and women's suffragist.) Chace could remember, as a boy, his father's lobbying the Eisenhower administration for protectionist rules to guard against the incoming flood of cheap Asian textiles. Later, as his father's efforts failed, his father would bring home bolts of corduroy and beautiful fabric as the family's New England mills shut down.

Still, the family was by no means destitute. In the 1960s they sold their company, Berkshire Hathaway, to financier Warren Buffett. Buff Chace dabbled in filmmaking and later became interested in Buddhism. He became a developer after agreeing to manage some family land on Cape Cod, and with the help of renowned Miami architect Andres Duany developed an award-winning shopping center, Mashpee Commons.

In 1991, the year Buddy Cianci returned to office, Chace read in the newspaper that a block of old buildings behind City Hall was going to be auctioned. He drove downtown with his twins, who were eight or nine, and looked around. His daughter Sarah said, "Why don't you do this, Dad?" That, he said later with a laugh, was "the kiss of death."

Chace brought Duany to Providence in late 1991 for a *charette*, a brainstorming session that ignited the movement to transform downtown into an arts district. Duany marveled at the historic architecture and recommended creating artists' lofts to bring people back downtown. Cianci, who endorsed the *charette*, called it "urban group therapy."

Chace, out of a sense of noblesse oblige rather than a desire for a quick profit, spent the 1990s trudging forward against tremendous odds. It was nearly impossible to find financing to restore the old buildings and create affordable loft space. It was tough to create the necessary critical mass to make downtown a residential draw. And despite Cianci's vision and his ballyhooed arts district, the mayor didn't always make it easy.

Chace urged Cianci to take a bold step by condemning the first floors of some of the buildings, to pave the way for stores and specialty shops that would make renovating the upper floors financially feasible, and to provide the amenities that people upstairs would want. A dialogue began, he said, "but then we started to see all the old political relationships" with the big downtown landowners, who had sat on their property for years. Nothing happened.

One of the problems that Chace saw was that there was no thoughtful approach to restoring downtown. It was a helter-skelter process that depended on the mood of the mayor, who could be capricious. It didn't help that Chace was a member of Cianci's hated Lucky Sperm Club, a term that he would throw out while berating Chace. Cianci would grow impatient with Chace, saying that he was unrealistic. In one meeting, the mayor lost his temper and scattered the blueprints that Chace had brought.

One day, Chace asked the city's economic-development director, John Palmieri, why the mayor was holding up approval of tax credits critical to a restoration project.

"Well, Buff, the mayor is trying to decide whether to fuck you or not," said Palmieri. When Chace asked him why, Palmieri replied, "Just think of fifteenth-century Padua."

Palmieri and Chace would often commiserate about the mayor. The long-suffering Palmieri had seen the mayor's brilliance and also borne the brunt of his anger. The mayor was a taskmaster, a perfectionist; he didn't want to hear about obstacles, but bulldozed ahead, making things happen for Providence through sheer force of will.

Cianci would torture Palmieri and others at his regular directors' meetings, which became dreaded events. Once, angry with his Public Works director, Cianci whipped open the newspaper classified section and started reading jobs that began with *P*—pastry maker, plumber. . . . Then he said, "I don't see any jobs in here for Public Works director." Another time, Cianci flew into a rage and yelled about how he'd tried to be nice to them, but that hadn't worked. Then, quoting Machiavelli, he said, "It's better to be feared than loved."

The directors, twenty or thirty people, sat in rows of chairs lined up in front of the mayor's desk. They would stand when Cianci addressed them, like schoolchildren being quizzed by the teacher. If the mayor was in a good mood, his directors would laugh quickly at his jokes, hoping to keep him happy. If a particular director became a pariah, there was an instinctive tendency among the others to disassociate themselves from that person, like the weakest animal in the herd. Palmieri learned to "take the hit," to weigh the abuse against the overall enjoyment of his job, which paid well, and the need to provide for his family.

Palmieri had also enjoyed good times with the mayor, like the trip to Manhattan to meet with Calvin Klein executives considering a distribution center in Providence. Cianci, who had his police driver and limousine, received a New York City police escort through midtown Manhattan, making Palmieri feel like some Third World head of state visiting the United Nations.

That night the Calvin Klein people arranged for the mayor and his party to dine at Rao's, a trendy Italian restaurant in Harlem that drew celebrities and required reservations months in advance. Later, Cianci spoke disparagingly of the place, grousing that he could get better food cheaper at the Rosario Club in Silver Lake, from Italian-speaking women with kerchiefs on their heads. That night, he got into an argument with the owner, who also had his own pasta sauce. The mayor scoffed when the owner boasted that his sauce had been ranked by *Consumer Reports*. "*Consumer Reports?*" said Cianci. "Who reads *Consumer Reports* for pasta sauce?"

The Calvin Klein warehouse never came to Providence. Palmieri knew that you couldn't win them all, but he had also seen the mayor scare away business with his overeagerness and need for headlines. In one instance, Palmieri said, the mayor prematurely announced that a New Bedford, Massachusetts, manufacturer of leather handbags for Coach was coming to Providence. The company, which had pursued low-key talks because of labor issues, didn't come.

One of the biggest disasters where Cianci jumped the gun involved Pfizer, the pharmaceutical giant. In 1998 Governor Lincoln Almond and state economic officials had been talking for months with Pfizer about opening a plant at Fields Point. Pfizer, not wanting to alarm out-of-state workers who might be affected until the deal was finalized, had insisted on absolute secrecy. Finally, the talks reached the point where Almond, reluctantly, had to tell Cianci. The next thing they knew, Cianci was trumpeting the Pfizer deal on the front page of *The Providence Journal.* That day, company officials privately told the governor that they were pulling out.

If Bruce Sundlun had been an ally to Cianci, his successor, Linc Almond, was an enemy. Republican allies in the 1970s, Cianci and Almond had broken up in the 1980s, when Almond, as U.S. attorney, investigated City Hall corruption. Cianci ordered workers at the Civic Center not to allow the governor's limousine to park inside when Almond attended events there. One night, the governor's state police driver threatened to arrest a Civic Center employee over the matter. Another night, Cianci arrived to find Almond's limo parked inside, and boxed him in with his own limo. Then the mayor berated an arena official: "Do you know that I can fire you, or are you just stupid? How many times do I have to tell you—the governor doesn't park here. It's my building."

In 1997 Cianci and Almond clashed over a highly publicized effort to lure the New England Patriots football team to Providence. The talks became a media frenzy, intensified by the fact that they occurred during the Patriots' run to the Super Bowl in New Orleans. Robert Kraft, the Patriots owner, was playing wannabe hosts Providence and Hartford off against Boston, hoping to win generous taxpayer subsidies. Almond, who was unwilling to give the team the millions that Kraft was seeking, watched in annoyance as the Patriots tried an end run with Cianci. The mayor, who boasted of his finesse in prying loose "other people's money," lacked the authority to commit the necessary state financing. But he created plenty of havoc. He even followed the Krafts to New Orleans, with former governor Phil Noel, a lawyer involved in downtown development. Later, Cianci told Palmieri about his wild time in the Big Easy, including a description of the voluptuous madam who ran a nightclub that he had visited. The state ultimately rejected a deal with the Patriots. The Krafts committed to Hartford instead. Cianci, speaking from Florence, Italy, where he was arranging for Providence to borrow Renaissance paintings from the Uffizi Gallery, reacted with a line that put a new twist on the Broadway musical *Damn Yankees*, in which Lola, once the "ugliest woman in Providence, Rhode Island," sells her soul to the Devil to become beautiful. Cracked Cianci, "You can marry an ugly woman for enough money, I guess." (Or not. The Krafts would later leave Hartford at the altar for a new stadium next to their old one in Foxboro, Massachusetts.)

Other corporate executives shied away from Providence, either because of Buddy's histrionics or because they were wary of corruption.

Terry Murray, the chairman of Fleet National Bank, considered it unfortunate that a leader of Cianci's intellect would exploit rather than seek to reform a political culture defined by "getting your brother-in-law a job"—preferably a no-show job. Addressing the annual Chamber of Commerce dinner in 1996, Murray said that Rhode Island, despite its recent strides, still lagged behind other parts of the country because of its bloated and inefficient government. He singled out the excessive amount of money spent on disability pensions for police officers and firefighters, but the message was obscured by the messenger—a wealthy corporate executive. "Terry Murray says 'You're paying your firefighters too much,' " Cianci later scoffed. "Well, okay, Terry, but you're not the one to be telling them that, making fourteen million."

But if Murray's speech bombed, the problems lingered. From his perch high atop the old Superman Building—when he wasn't in Boston, where Fleet was moving its corporate headquarters—Murray shook his head as Cianci patched together his budgets with gimmicks while failing to address the underlying rot in City Hall. "When Buddy goes," Murray predicted in a private conversation one day, "it will be like taking the canvas off a lobster boil. There's a lot of steam built up, and the smells are enormous."

Cianci was a fabulous promoter who had served Providence well in some respects, Murray believed. But beneath the façade was a bullying quality that held back the Good Buddy. Cianci embodied the story *The Picture of Dorian Gray*, about a man who continues to look young and fit as his portrait decays and grows ugly: at City Hall, the mayor's handlers unveiled a portrait of a young, svelte Cianci. "It's like somewhere he sold his soul and made a pact with the devil to be mayor for the rest of his life," said Murray. "Buddy has more retainers than Rudy Giuliani. But after a while, the whole routine with the limousine gets old. What excites him when he gets up in the morning?" One day, Murray was standing in line at a wake when the mayor cut in line to join him and proceeded to describe, in graphic sexual detail, how he was exhausted because he'd just spent the past forty-eight hours "shacked up" at the Congress Inn, a motel off Interstate 95 in rural West Greenwich.

Michael Rich, a political-science professor at Brown University, received a firsthand lesson in how Cianci operated when the mayor drafted him to run the Providence Plan, a public-private consortium to help revitalize the city. Rich found the mayor eloquent in painting a vision of what cities should be, but heavy-handed in implementing his ideas. He functioned like an old-fashioned machine boss, bullying executives and trying to control everything.

One morning Rich and a Fleet Bank executive organized a breakfast meeting at the Turks Head Club of about fifteen top business leaders. Rich gave his spiel about the importance of getting the business community involved, but the response was lukewarm. "A dozen or more people at major institutions told me that they were very supportive of our goals, but that as long as Buddy Cianci was the mayor, they wouldn't give a nickel," said Rich. "It was a question of trust, and of whether the money would go to support a 'special friend' or company on his political donor list."

At one of Cianci's infamous directors' meetings, Rich was a few minutes into a presentation on strategic planning when Frank Corrente cut him off, saying, "Okay, Professor, I'm sure we could talk about this all day, but we've got more important things." Then the discussion shifted to jobs in the Fire Department.

Rich remembered Cianci ending a directors' meeting by asking for a rundown of "who's been good to us, who can we help, and who's been bad, who can we stick it to." For instance, if someone the mayor had a problem with had applied for a zoning variance or a building permit, he might say, "There's no way this is going through," or "Find a way to slap a code violation on them."

Rich, who had more autonomy, resisted efforts at political meddling. Someone from the mayor's office would point out that Rich hadn't hung the mayor's picture on the wall in his office; he stuck it in a file cabinet. Corrente would grumble at Rich's refusal to hire unqualified people, saying that he had "all these people" he needed to help out. Art Coloian asked him to use a particular printer for his next newsletter who had been "good to the mayor." Rich refused.

One day Rich made a comment, possibly to a Brown student writing a term paper, that the only way for the Providence Plan to succeed would be with a new mayor. The remark got back to Cianci, who had Rich pulled out of a meeting and brought to the mayor's office. For the next two and a half hours, Rich said, Cianci screamed at him, got in his face, swearing, and jabbed his finger at him. The mayor shouted that he wasn't going to let some "chicken-shit professor" run him down. Rich replied that he wasn't being disloyal—"I'm just not into this old-style form of governing." That further enraged Cianci. Rich sat there as the mayor ranted, the fireplace-log episode with Raymond DeLeo going through his mind.

Rich finally resigned and left Providence to become a professor at Emory University in Atlanta. Looking back, he said, "As far as Providence has come, imagine where it could be if you had a mayor who was a real partner-maker. You'd be blowing other cities off the map."

IN 1998 BUDDY CIANCI ran unopposed for mayor and was reelected to a record sixth term. He started the race with just one opponent, a downtown businessman named Pat Cortellessa, who claimed that he had been shaken down by Frank Corrente. Cortellessa was just a minor irritant, but the mayor didn't need to hear his accusations of corruption in the Renaissance City.

One summer day Art Coloian rounded up some of the mayor's aides at City Hall and took them to the mayor's campaign headquarters. They spent the day, on city time, checking the names and addresses of people who had signed Cortellessa's nomination papers. Buddy's blitzkrieg resulted in the Board of Canvassers invalidating several signatures. Cortellessa was knocked off the ballot.

The mayor had more important concerns. He was going Hollywood.

The motion-picture industry, which had had a strong presence in Providence during the silent-film era in the 1920s, was rediscovering the city. From Michael Corrente's *Federal Hill* to the Farrelly brothers' *There's Something About Mary* to Steven Spielberg's historic slave drama, *Amistad,* the city became a Hollywood set.

Personally, Cianci disliked *Federal Hill,* for its portrayal of mobsters. But when the film won international awards, he publicly embraced Corrente, who, it turned out, was a distant cousin of Frank Corrente's, from suburban Coventry. When Michael Corrente chose to film *American Buffalo,* starring Dustin Hoffman, in Pawtucket instead of Providence, Cianci was upset. In 1995 he launched the Providence Film Commission. Two years later, Cianci began sponsoring an annual "Rhode Island Night" at the Century Plaza Hotel in Los Angeles, during a major film-industry convention. The event featured homegrown Rhode Island stars like actor James Woods, from Warwick, and homegrown foods: clam cakes, Del's frozen lemonade, coffee milk, and, of course, the mayor's marinara sauce.

"Providence has been making locations for years," said Cianci, who sold himself as the mayor of a film-friendly community. He would personally cut through red tape and do what it took to accommodate moviemakers. For the movie *Dumb & Dumber,* filmmaker Peter Farrelly said that Cianci offered to shut down Interstate 95 so that Farrelly and his brother could film the opening scene of Jim Carrey and Jeff Daniels driving out of Providence—an offer the Farrellys declined for the potential traffic tie-ups it would create. (The fact that some of the Teamsters on local film crews had Mafia ties only added to the allure of Providence as a place where life imitated art.)

The mayor loved the spotlight. When *Meet Joe Black,* starring Brad Pitt and Anthony Hopkins, was being filmed at the waterfront Aldrich mansion in Warwick, members of the film crew had to wave Cianci's yacht away after he cruised into camera range.

The crowning moment came when NBC chose Providence as the location for a prime-time television series, *Providence,* a feel-good drama about a Beverly Hills plastic surgeon who returns to her roots on the East Side. The producer said that he picked Providence because he liked the name, as in "divine Providence." The show, with its loving shots of WaterPlace Park and the city's historic architecture bathed in golden light, became a ratings success and a tourism bonanza. Cianci even wangled a cameo, playing himself. He judged a cooking contest featuring his ubiquitous marinara sauce. At national mayors' conferences, Cianci joked, the mayor of Baltimore would lament that his city got stuck with the TV series *Homicide.*

In the spring of 1997, *Homicide* star Melissa Leo came to Providence to film a low-budget thriller that had been pulled together with the assistance of the mayor's film commission. She played a Medicaid-fraud investigator who uncovers a serial killer who is a government official. The film crew used the mayor's office as the serial killer's office, bringing in a tank of piranha. There was also a boat chase scene down the Providence River. To keep the water levels up for filming, Cianci ordered the Fox Point Hurricane

Barrier closed, to keep in the tide. That caused a crisis at the adjacent power plant, which relied on the outflowing water to power its turbines. During filming one afternoon, frantic Narragansett Electric officials called the city to report that the turbines were overheating and would seize up if the hurricane barrier wasn't reopened. The filming was completed, the barrier opened, and the crisis averted.

The following year, in the spring of 1997, Cianci attended the movie's premiere at the Showcase Cinemas in Warwick. Several hundred men and women in tuxedos and evening gowns mingled in the theater and drank a champagne toast. Cianci said that he was "honored, after all I've been through, that you chose my offices to film a movie called *Code of Ethics.*"

Within a year, another film crew would set up shop in the basement of an industrial building in the city's faded West Broadway neighborhood. But there would be no announcement or press release. The mayor didn't even know.

Operation Plunder Dome had come to the Renaissance City for an extended run.

CHAPTER NINE

Mr. Freon

Buddy Cianci was walking out of the Capital Grille in late 1995 when he bumped into a ghost from his past.

"How ya doin', Mayor?" asked a man with a drawl like molasses.

Dennis Aiken, the FBI agent from Mississippi, was back.

For once the mayor was speechless. He turned pale under his pancake makeup. Aiken, smiling, noticed that Cianci was carrying a paper bag. He wondered, half jokingly, what was inside.

Cianci nodded curtly and hurried out of the restaurant. The redneck FBI agent definitely did not fit into the mayor's blueprint for the Providence Renaissance.

Cianci would have been even less pleased to see Aiken had he followed the FBI agent's career.

After leaving Providence in 1981, Aiken had risen through the ranks to become the FBI's foremost authority on public corruption. The head of the Bureau's Public Corruption Unit in Washington, he had helped design undercover operations that nailed California legislators, Florida mobsters, Mississippi county supervisors, and Washington, D.C., police officers. In the California case, agents posing as corrupt lobbyists had bribed state legislators in Sacramento to pass a meaningless bill. Then, to prevent the embarrassment of having the governor sign the bill into law, Aiken had instructed the agents to go back to the legislators and say that they'd changed their mind. The lawmakers dutifully took another sixty thousand to kill the bill.

"Greed," Aiken would say, "overcomes common sense every time."

Aiken had learned from the FBI agent who worked on Abscam, the famous sting of congressmen in the late 1970s, that undercover investigations were the way to go. The success rate was 95 percent, compared to just

5 percent for cases of "historic corruption," where investigators try to un-ravel shadowy transactions that have already occurred, usually one-on-one, with untraceable cash.

Aiken had been back in Providence for about a year when he ran into Cianci. He could still remember his wife's dropping him off for work that first day. Standing in front of City Hall, briefcase in hand like the other busi-nessmen hurrying past him, Aiken felt like he'd never left.

His wife, Cheryl, thought that he'd hate it. Aiken had had a big job and a bright future in Washington. He worked just a few blocks from the White House and met regularly with the FBI director. He had been involved in some of the Bureau's most sensitive cases, from the ethics probe of Ronald Reagan's attorney general, Edwin Meese, to the investigation of dirty tricks in the 1992 presidential campaign of Ross Perot. Now he was back on the streets of Providence, as a field agent.

But that's what Aiken wanted. He was a tenacious investigator who hated desk work. When the Bureau offered an initiative to put several hun-dred senior agents back in the field, allowing them to keep their manage-ment pay, Aiken eagerly accepted.

He asked to be sent to Rhode Island, his wife's home state. He was forty-two years old, with two young children, and he'd moved eight times in his career. It was time to put down some roots.

Aiken knew that he would never be lacking for work, given Rhode Is-land's incestuous politics and its notorious history of insider deals. Rhode Island was "Louisiana North." He asked his supervisor not to assign him any cases; he would find his own.

The FBI office in Providence, which employs about twenty agents, had moved since Aiken's last tour. Now it was on the ninth floor of an office building diagonally across the street from City Hall—a move that had not gone unnoticed in the mayor's office, where one aide joked that the FBI had relocated to better keep an eye on Cianci.

Cianci's paranoia was understandable, given the numerous investiga-tions that had targeted him through the years.

In the early 1990s, during an argument with an aide, the mayor had snapped, "You wouldn't do very well in front of the grand jury."

In the mid-1990s, in an FBI investigation dubbed Operation Crocodile Smile, undercover agents attended the mayor's political fund-raisers, pos-ing as businessmen with flashy clothes and cars and girlfriends.

As part of that probe, in 1995, an agent calling himself Marco ap-proached Cianci in Capriccio, an upscale Italian bar and restaurant, one of the mayor's regular haunts. Wearing a wire, Marco tried to ingratiate himself with Cianci. Marco discussed his interest in landing a contract to do construction work at Providence schools. Cianci didn't bite. He told Marco to talk to the appropriate city officials. And if any city official tried to shake him down, Cianci said forcefully, the mayor would personally "cut his cock off." Later, the mayor laughingly introduced Marco to the Rhode Island Republican party chairman as an undercover FBI agent.

To Cianci, everything was personal. The feds were out to get him. They were jealous of his success, eager to bring him down. It was a vendetta, rooted in his Italian heritage and his split with the WASPs who controlled the Republican party in Rhode Island.

Cianci made no secret of his hatred for Governor Lincoln C. Almond, who had investigated him as U.S. attorney in the 1980s. Privately, the mayor also blamed the state GOP's elder statesman, U.S. senator John Chafee, who, in 1976, had taken the Senate seat that Cianci had coveted.

Aiken didn't see the world through the lens of the mayor's old grudges and paranoia. He viewed things as more black and white. Corruption was a line in the sand that you just didn't cross. Otherwise, honest citizens couldn't be assured of fair treatment, no matter how popular their leaders. Digging beneath the glitzy surface of the Providence Renaissance was in some ways reminiscent of turning a shovel in the rich black soil of his native Mississippi, where a good-ole-boy network of white southerners had ruled.

Aiken was born in 1952 in Clarksdale, in the Mississippi Delta, about seventy-five miles south of Memphis. The railroad tracks ran through the center of town, dividing the ruling whites from the disenfranchised blacks. His father, a farm-equipment salesman who worked with blacks, would sneak across the railroad tracks at night to visit black friends. Instilled with his parents' sense of fairness, young Dennis found it hard to understand when the town fathers filled in the public swimming pool with dirt rather than accept blacks, or built private schools the year after federal marshals integrated the public schools. Aiken played trumpet in an all-white rock band, the Avengers, covering Motown songs.

At the height of racial tensions, the teenage Aiken was sitting in his Southern Baptist church one Sunday. A rumor was going around that blacks were going to integrate the church. There were fears of violence. Then the door swung open and in walked Hal Fabriz, a six-foot-nine FBI agent stationed in Clarksdale, and a parishioner.

"There'll be no trouble today," said Aiken's mother. "The FBI is here." That was when Aiken decided to become an FBI agent.

He graduated from the University of Mississippi with an accounting degree, then, too young to become an agent, joined the FBI as a clerk in Washington in 1974. He was twenty-one.

His first case was Watergate.

Aiken's role was strictly clerical—compiling a database of witness interviews—but his enthusiasm was evident when he called his mother to break the news that he was helping to investigate the president of the United States, Richard M. Nixon. His mother paused for a long moment, then cautioned her son, "Y'all be careful up there."

When he turned twenty-three, Aiken took the agent's exam and was assigned to Houston, where he worked on the FBI's bank-robbery and fugitive squad. He also bagged his first corrupt public official, Houston's assistant police chief, for soliciting a twenty-five-thousand-dollar bribe to fix a case. Aiken went into prison to tape an informant discussing the payoff, then arrested the assistant chief after he had taken the bribe, in uniform.

After three years in Houston, when he came up for a transfer, Aiken heard a rumor that he was going to be sent to New York and begged his supervisor to send him somewhere else. That's how he wound up in Rhode Island the first time.

At first Rhode Island was culture shock, in everything from the weather to the accents. It was hard for Aiken, with his distinctive southern accent, to blend in, making "pretext calls," where an agent anonymously calls someone's office to verify employment or some other piece of background information. But Aiken had a folksy way about him that disarmed reluctant witnesses, combined with a direct, persistent manner that convinced people he wasn't going to go away until he got the truth or read them their rights.

After reading that the speaker of the Rhode Island House was redecorating his State House office, Aiken struck up a rapport with the furniture salesman and convinced him to testify about how he had bribed the speaker. One morning Aiken appeared at the speaker's home with a search warrant, went upstairs to his bedroom, and cut a swatch of carpet from under the bed matching the carpet in his State House office.

The speaker was indicted, but the case, tried twice in Boston because of heavy publicity, ended in two hung juries. When Aiken returned to Rhode Island in 1994, he and his wife bought a house in the suburb of Cumberland. The former speaker, long out of politics, lived nearby. Aiken's father-in-law, a retired court administrator, had sworn Buddy Cianci into the bar in 1967.

Back in Rhode Island, Aiken wanted to believe that Cianci had redeemed himself, that the Providence Renaissance was real. But the more he poked around, the more he heard the same things he'd heard in the early 1980s—that City Hall was for sale.

If Cianci painted the Renaissance as a triumphant effort to raise Providence's self-esteem, Aiken viewed the underlying corruption as sapping the city's moral strength.

One of the first things that Aiken did after he came back to Providence was review the intelligence on the mayor to see if there were any viable cases to pursue.

One day he stopped by a local television station, WJAR–Channel 10, to pick up a tape of Cianci speaking on a Sunday-morning newsmakers show. Jim Taricani, a veteran investigative reporter who had known Aiken in the early 1980s, was surprised to see him again.

"Still chasing Buddy?" he asked.

"I never give up," replied Aiken.

But all the suspicions and leads in the world wouldn't get Aiken inside City Hall. He needed a guide.

EDDIE VOCCOLA WAS the merry prankster of Providence auto-body shop owners.

In a seedy business rife with tales of stolen cars and insurance scams, Voccola had a certain panache. Once, an insurance appraiser climbed up onto Voccola's roof to inspect a claim of storm damage but couldn't find any. Voccola asked him to look again. The appraiser said that he still couldn't see anything. Voccola took down the ladder, marooning the man on the roof, and told him to look harder.

Other insurance adjusters swapped stories of being locked in one of the maze of rooms above Voccola's Federal Auto Body, or being stuffed in the trunk of a car. In 1971 Voccola and his brother, John, a former Cranston city councilman and mayoral candidate, accosted a Connecticut insurance investigator who stopped by the garage to verify a lost wage statement. As John choked the man with his own necktie, Eddie forced him up against the wall with a chair and started punching him.

"Let's boff him!" yelled Eddie.

"I'm going to put you in a pine box!" screamed John.

The investigator staggered from the garage, Eddie shouting after him: "This is Rhode Island—I'll blow up your car and kill you."

Voccola's methods may not have been taught at the Harvard Business School, but no one could argue with his success. When Dennis Aiken returned to Providence in 1994, he couldn't help noticing the niche that Voccola had carved for himself in Buddy Cianci's Renaissance.

Five months after Cianci returned to office, he had signed a $750,000 lease for the School Department to rent Voccola's garage as a registration center for Providence schoolchildren. The lease was renewed in 1994, despite complaints about the unsatisfactory conditions and high rent. Parents and children were forced to stand in line in stifling auto bays that had once borne witness to various crimes, in a dilapidated neighborhood down the street from a strip club. The floors were concrete. The bathrooms were hard to reach. There weren't enough seats.

When Julia Steiny, a maverick School Board member and East Side playwright, fought the lease, hoping to steer more dollars to impoverished educational programs, she was warned by a school official not to buck City Hall. After the lease was renewed, Cianci dumped her from the School Board. Steiny equated the experience to "walking into a scene from *The Godfather,* and you didn't have any guns."

Around the same time, the Providence Recreation Department leased a cinder-block building that Voccola owned next to his body shop as a recreation center for senior citizens. By the spring of 1995, Voccola had the schoolkids signing up for classes in one garage and the old folks doing arts and crafts around the corner.

Then, in April, Voccola was indicted for insurance fraud. Federal postal inspectors, spying from a nearby rooftop, had watched as Voccola's men towed cars from his garage to another building down the street, then smashed them up. Voccola was charged with using five "hit cars" to accumulate $128,000 worth of bogus accident claims. Voccola was also charged with trying to persuade a witness to lie to the grand jury.

Even as Voccola was negotiating another real estate deal with the city, a federal prosecutor pointed out at his bail hearing that a government witness had received an animal tongue in the mail, been sent roses spray-painted black, and received the telephone numbers of local funeral homes on her pager.

Voccola pleaded guilty and was sent to prison for thirty-three months. On his way to prison, he received another taxpayer-financed lease—eight thousand dollars a month to rent space to store janitorial supplies for Providence schools. The feds wound up garnishing his city rent check to help cover his half million dollars in fines from the criminal conviction.

In all, Voccola took the taxpayers of Providence for a $2.2 million ride in the 1990s. The bulk of the money came from a School Department that couldn't afford to properly educate its largely poor, non-English-speaking students. While Cianci spoke boldly of improving the schools and bringing middle-class families back to Providence, the reality was underpaid teachers, overcrowded classrooms, crumbling school buildings, a shortage of textbooks, and underfunded arts and music programs.

Meanwhile, Cianci distanced himself from the growing public controversy over the city's dealings with Voccola. When reporters sought explanations, the mayor's minions played stupid.

Dennis Aiken smelled a bribe. Then he found Roger Cavaca.

Cavaca, Voccola's longtime office manager and partner in crime, had been convicted with Voccola in the insurance-fraud case, and sentenced to eighteen months in prison. But instead of reporting to prison at Fort Dix, New Jersey, in January 1996, as ordered, Cavaca fled.

For the next year, Cavaca moved around the country, supported in part, the authorities said later, by about four hundred dollars a week from Voccola's daughter. The feds, who monitored Voccola's prison telephone conversations with his daughter, believed that Voccola had seen Cavaca weakening and urged him to run before he started talking to the feds.

But then, for some reason, the money stopped. Cavaca, tired of being a fugitive, started negotiating through his son in Rhode Island to surrender. In return, he offered a laundry list of crimes that he could shed light on—from scams involving vinyl siding and food stamps to public corruption involving Voccola and City Hall.

Prosecutors said that there would be no deal unless Cavaca turned himself in. But then the U.S. marshals caught up with him in North Carolina, in 1997. He was arrested and brought back to Rhode Island. That summer, Dennis Aiken drove to the federal detention center in Central Falls to debrief Cavaca.

Sitting in a private visitors' room, Aiken came face-to-face with a flat, expressionless man in his fifties who had the faded pallor of concrete. For twenty-four years, Cavaca had blended into Eddie Voccola's world, had seen every confidence trick with those vacant eyes. Now, facing an additional five years in prison, he told Aiken about the Providence school-registration center.

In the winter of 1991, before the lease was signed, Cavaca said that Voccola had instructed him to measure the garage for the School Department. Voccola explained that he needed the building's dimensions so that when the city advertised for public bids, the specifications could be drawn to fit the garage.

Voccola told Cavaca that he had arranged the deal with Frank Corrente at the Blue Grotto, on Federal Hill. Voccola confided that he was paying bribes to Corrente, Cianci's "errand boy."

Cavaca also told Aiken about an incident in 1992, when Voccola had sent him to the bank to cash a seventy-five-hundred-dollar check, saying that Corrente was coming by the garage to "pick up an envelope." Cavaca brought the cash back to Voccola and watched him put it in an envelope and write "Frank C." on it, then put it in the office safe. A day or two later, Cavacca said, he buzzed Corrente into the garage, then watched him and Voccola go into Voccola's office. Later, after Corrente had left, Cavaca said, he had to get something out of the safe and noticed that the envelope was gone.

Aiken knew that Cavaca was a veteran con man with incentive to lie to reduce his prison time. So the agent tested him repeatedly, trying to catch him in a lie. But he said that he never did. The clincher came when Aiken subpoenaed Voccola's bank records and found a check for seventy-five hundred dollars in 1992.

The check was a significant breakthrough. Not long after Aiken discovered it, a grand jury was convened to investigate Voccola, Corrente, and the lease.

ONE OF THE lessons that Dennis Aiken tried to teach younger agents was the importance of "shaking the bushes." You never knew what might fall out.

Early in 1998 the investigation of the Voccola lease was grinding along. City officials weren't eager to talk. Aiken knew that he needed more than Cavaca to get to Cianci or Corrente, and Voccola was unlikely to flip.

So he kept shaking the bushes—and Tony Freitas fell out.

Antonio R. Freitas ran a million-dollar company, JKL Engineering, that installed heating and air-conditioning systems, but he fancied himself "a little bit of a renegade." As a young man starting out in business, he had received a visit from two Providence building inspectors who began reciting a litany of costly improvements that his building needed to conform to code. One inspector advised that Freitas could either do the repairs or make the problem go away for "two hundred bananas."

Freitas, a naïve kid of twenty-two, looked perplexed. "Why would you want two hundred bananas?" he asked.

"Kid, look at me," the inspector said, rubbing his fingers together. "I mean two hundred *bananas*."

When Freitas finally caught on, he was furious. He had grown up in the Azores, where corrupt government bureaucrats under the Portuguese dictator Antonio Salazar always had their hands out for a *grata*. When an immigration official had tried shaking him down for his visa to the United States, the thirteen-year-old Freitas flashed him some money, then shoved it back in his pocket when the official handed over the visa first. Now, concealing his anger, Freitas told the Providence building inspectors to come back in a week. They returned, smiling. Freitas led them into the back of his shop, where his coworkers had just uncrated some air conditioners, and called out: "Hey, are those two boxes ready yet? Let's put them in." The smiles vanished from the inspectors' faces. Freitas grabbed a two-by-four and chased them out of the building, screaming, "I'll throw you in the Providence River!"

Freitas's office was just down the street from Eddie Voccola's garage. Cavaca had seen Freitas at Voccola's garage, talking to Joseph Pannone, the chairman of the Providence Board of Tax Assessment Review. Cavaca said that Voccola had bribed Pannone to lower his taxes, and thought that Freitas may have, too.

Aiken wanted to size up Freitas, and see how he'd react to the accusation. The FBI agent was also aware, through reading the newspaper, that Freitas was angry with the School Department. The grand-jury investigation of Voccola had become public, increasing pressure on the city to find a new home for the school-registration center. Freitas had put in a low bid to move it to a building that he owned, but he had been rejected. The registration center remained, at least temporarily, in Voccola's garage.

The paperwork for Freitas's spurned school bid was strewn on the floor of his office when Aiken stopped by. It was January 27, 1998, the day before Freitas's forty-ninth birthday. For an hour Aiken listened to Freitas rant about the lease in his heavy Portuguese accent. Then Aiken asked Freitas if he had ever bribed Joe Pannone for help with his taxes. Freitas was appalled. He said that he had met Pannone at Voccola's garage a few years earlier, when he had stopped by to check on repairs to one of his trucks. Freitas had mentioned a mix-up on his taxes, and Pannone had offered to help straighten things out. After the problem was resolved, Pannone had even stopped by Freitas's office and mentioned that he was about to take his annual winter trip to Florida. But Freitas failed to pick up on the hint that he should throw Pannone some spending money for his assistance.

Freitas told Aiken that he would take a lie-detector test. Aiken countered that Freitas could invite Pannone over and ask him directly if Freitas had ever given him a bribe. The FBI agent could secretly tape the conversation. If Freitas had bribed Pannone, Aiken reasoned, he wouldn't want to do that.

But Freitas didn't flinch. "I have a better idea. Why don't I wear a wire? Then I can help you clean up this city."

Now Aiken was convinced of Freitas's honesty—but worried about his sanity. What person in his right mind would agree to wear a wire in Providence?

Aiken knew from experience that not everyone is capable of working undercover. It takes brains and guts. He also needed to know that he could control Freitas—that he wouldn't do something crazy to jeopardize the operation or their safety.

In the coming weeks, as Aiken felt out Freitas, he liked what he saw. He seemed smart enough and gutsy enough to pull it off. Freitas was also an honest businessman, not someone cooperating to avoid prosecution, so he would be more credible. When Aiken said that the FBI would be willing to pay Freitas for the time that his undercover work would take away from his business, Freitas said no. He didn't want any money; he just wanted to clean the "cockroaches" out of City Hall. Aiken liked that Freitas was established in the community. He would be less likely to arouse suspicion than an outsider like Marco. Their biggest challenge would be passing Freitas off as a corrupt businessman, after he had been so publicly critical of City Hall. Aiken reasoned that Freitas would be the man who had seen the light, who was willing to pay bribes and needed a teacher. He already had an entrée to City Hall—Joe Pannone, the tax official he had met at Voccola's garage. The FBI would install hidden cameras in Freitas's office and wire him up for visits to City Hall with the latest in miniaturized gadgetry and record his lessons in corruption.

To shield Freitas's identity in internal FBI paperwork, Aiken had to assign him a code name. He chose the name of a chemical coolant found in the air conditioners that Freitas installed; Freitas became Mr. Freon.

Aiken also needed a name for the investigation. FBI undercover operations are named the way hurricanes are. Aiken was brainstorming at his kitchen table one day when his teenage daughter, Karlene, mentioned the black dome atop City Hall, fringed with green copper. Aiken thought about what went on beneath the dome. He named the investigation Operation Plunder Dome.

AT THE AGE of seventy-five, Joseph Pannone had not lost his taste for money or the things that it could buy in Providence—a seat on the city tax board, the fried calamari at Andino's on Federal Hill, blow jobs from a young hooker.

Tony Freitas and the FBI could not have found a more willing teacher.

"Understand, there's nothing for nothing," Pannone told Freitas. "There's no free lunches. It's money that counts, Tony."

People too curious about his business had *picca naso*—nose trouble. A deputy assessor who helped him fix people's taxes "bends, know what I mean? I just show some green and she's all right."

Discussing the secretary for a lawyer he did corrupt deals with, Pannone said: "Ah, he's been banging her for years. . . . I wouldn't even screw that broad. . . . She's got to be at least forty."

Freitas called him Uncle Joe. The stooped Pannone, with his white hair and thick glasses, reminded him of "the guy who did the movie *Oh, God!* . . . [George] Burns."

"Hey, I'm learning with Uncle Joe," Freitas said.

"Money talks, bullshit walks," Pannone answered.

"Hey, I like those pants you have on, Uncle Joe," Freitas said one day.

"You want to buy them?"

The married Pannone was a man on the make. He received twenty-five-dollar blow jobs from a young, blond exotic dancer at the Satin Doll, who serviced him in an office above an auto showroom whose owner Pannone had assisted in lowering his taxes. Pannone also had an older girlfriend who worked at the city water-supply board.

Pannone's relationship with Freitas began in April 1998, after Freitas left a message for him at the tax assessor's office at City Hall.

Freitas had filed an application with the Board of Tax Assessment Review to lower his taxes on some boarded-up buildings he had purchased. He was legitimately entitled to the reductions, since he had fixed up the property. But Aiken wanted him to approach Pannone through the back door, to see what would happen.

One day, Pannone showed up, unannounced, at JKL Engineering. The visit surprised Freitas and Aiken. The FBI wasn't ready to start recording their conversations. After Pannone left, Freitas called Aiken in a panic. Pannone had talked about how the mayor was taking money, how Corrente was the mayor's bagman, how Voccola had paid bribes—everything that Aiken wanted to hear. But it sounded too good to be true.

"Tony, if it's not on tape, it didn't happen," said Aiken.

"I'll get him back here, and he'll say the same things," vowed Freitas.

Pannone came back, many times. He had served on the tax board since the early 1980s, when Cianci first appointed him, and had known Cianci when the mayor was a little boy, playing at Joe's sister's house after school with her son. Pannone was from the Italian working-class neighborhood of Eagle Park, where he had run a fish-and-chips restaurant for years and been active in ward politics. The weekly meetings at City Hall gave him something to do in retirement, and he also liked the free Blue Cross coverage.

Pannone was a *spaccone*, a wannabe. When he wasn't attending to tax-board business, he hustled Cianci campaign tickets and his own deals. He was a harmless-looking old Italian man, serving in relative obscurity on a little-noticed board, one of the mayor's foot soldiers. He hung around City Hall, wandering in and out of various offices, and was a frequent visitor to Frank Corrente's. He called himself an "in-between man" who facilitated deals and took his own cut, much as Corrente acted, on a higher level, as the mayor's in-between man.

"Buddy doesn't take nothing," Pannone explained one day. The money, he said, went through Corrente.

Lubricated by cash from Freitas, Pannone was eager to show him the ropes and pass on lessons that he claimed to have learned from Cianci.

"Know what the mayor told me one time? There was a café on Cranston Street that wanted to give me two thousand dollars to stay open until two o'clock [in the morning]. I said, 'Buddy, I can get you two thousand.' " The mayor advised him to be careful, Pannone confided. "He said to me, 'Joe, I want to tell you something. You know we're friends a hundred years. Never talk on the telephone—' "

"He should know," Freitas interjected. "He was a prosecutor."

"He said, 'Never talk on the phone, never get a check, but get cash when you're one-on-one.' I said, 'Well, okay, Mayor.' He said, 'I just want to clue you in.' "

Pannone may have seemed like a doddering old fool, puffing himself up behind the mayor's back to grab some cash. But he had been around City Hall a long time. Behind his bluster, much of what Pannone said rang true to Aiken, particularly his comments about the voracious Cianci campaign fund-raising machine and its influence over city jobs, promotions, contracts, and favors.

"Boy, I'm telling you," Freitas said one day. "It's like a movie."

"Yeah, I'll tell ya, Providence," said Pannone. "I'm gonna tell ya this has been going on since day one. But it was small." In the old days, if you wanted a job with the city, Pannone said, you gave your first week's pay to your councilman and said, "Thank you for the job." But now "there's no control no more. Now see my job? My job I got? I give [Cianci] a thousand dollars every year. . . . And then the tickets I sell, that makes him happy."

Some of the money came in by check and went into the campaign. The rest, in cash (which was illegal under Rhode Island election law), "goes south," said Pannone.

"Yeah, cash, good," Pannone said as Freitas counted out $250 for two tickets to a Cianci fund-raiser.

Ironically, that same day, the mayor announced the apprehension of two small-time bank robbers who had been hitting Providence banks. "They didn't even take what you can make at a decent fund-raiser," joked Cianci.

Pannone said of Cianci: "He's into the green. He's got that boat. He's got to fix his hair. . . . I'd like to have the money that he gets that is not registered. You know what I mean? Just handed to him."

Pannone and Freitas would meet in an office in the basement of JKL Engineering, which the FBI equipped with hidden cameras and microphones. On one of his first visits, Pannone sat down on a wire coat hanger and leaped up, shouting: "Jeez. That thing went right up my ass." He moved to a second chair in front of Freitas's desk, where the camera angle turned out to be so good that Freitas left the hanger where it was for months, so that Pannone would always take the other seat.

Aiken monitored their conversations from a utility closet down the hall, where he had a television monitor and wore headphones. One day, early in the investigation, he was sitting in the closet, listening to Pannone and Freitas, when two meter readers showed up from Narragansett Electric.

The FBI agent couldn't see them coming. Freitas jumped up and announced their presence, stalling them for a few minutes, giving Aiken time to think. Aiken realized that if the women screamed and gave him away, the operation could be blown; he might even have to arrest Pannone on the spot, well before they managed to penetrate City Hall.

The two Narragansett Electric women proceeded down the hallway and opened the door to find Aiken sitting there, headphones in place, index finger to his lips. He flashed his badge and asked them to remain quiet, as Freitas hustled Pannone out of his office. Then Aiken told the meter readers that Freitas was helping him catch a dangerous drug dealer; his life would be in danger if they told anyone. They left, shaken but promising not to breathe a word.

Freitas continued to meet with Pannone through the spring, summer, and fall of 1998. Pannone, secure in Freitas's basement, spilled the secrets of City Hall.

He described how he had saved a convicted felon and mob associate, Paulie Calenda, sixteen thousand dollars a year in taxes, by lowering the assessments on three buildings he owned—one of which had burned in an arson fire. Coincidentally, Calenda received the tax break just before going to federal prison for possession of an Uzi submachine gun. Pannone explained that the Calenda tax deal had gone through a lawyer who represented taxpayers before the board, John Scungio—a guy "so fucking cheap, it ain't even funny."

Pannone also discussed his reliance on the deputy assessor, Rosemary Glancy—"the fat girl"—to do the numbers on illicit tax breaks. In return, he'd throw her fifty or a hundred bucks, and take her to lunch at Andino's on Federal Hill.

"Have you seen her? Rosemary? She's like this, you know," said Pannone, spreading his arms wide. "Three hundred pounds. Well, somebody says that fucking Joe, he's getting hard up. But, heh, she's my right arm."

Over lunch at Andino's one day—Pannone favored the "fried calamaris"—he described how he and Glancy had commiserated over the School Department's decision to reject Freitas's bid for a lease. "I said, 'That's a joke, Rosemary.' She said, 'Everything in Providence is a joke.' 'If you don't pay, forget it. And that's not right.' And Rosemary goes, 'You're right, Joe, but what are you gonna do? What are you gonna do?' "

Pannone told Freitas that he had lost out on the lease because he didn't pay. Voccola, he said, "used to give them money every fucking week." Pannone volunteered that Voccola had also taken care of him, for lowering his property taxes. He boasted how he had outfoxed Dennis Aiken when the FBI agent questioned him about Cavaca's allegations that he took kickbacks.

On October 2, 1998, as Freitas counted out twenty-four hundred dollars in bribes, Pannone said that Aiken would never pin the Voccola bribes on him, just as he'd never know about the money from Freitas—"unless you got spies here," he added, laughing.

Another time, Pannone walked in and joked about whether Freitas had a hidden camera in his office. Freitas pointed at the concealed camera and said that it was right there.

Pannone's willingness to reveal secrets became a running joke between Aiken and Freitas. One day Pannone not only described a half-million-dollar tax break that involved a bribe directly to Cianci—he obligingly spelled the taxpayer's name.

From his perch in the utility closet, Aiken would call Freitas on his cell phone and tell him what to ask Pannone. One day, Aiken challenged Freitas to find out where Pannone hid his money. Within minutes Pannone revealed that he kept it in the drawer of the nightstand beside his bed—under a picture of a saint. "My wife doesn't even know that," said Pannone, laughing. "I just told you a secret, Goddammit."

Aside from providing the FBI with a road map to Providence corruption, Pannone also hooked Freitas up with Frank Corrente, the number-two man at City Hall.

Pannone told Corrente that Freitas was willing to kick back at least twenty-five thousand dollars a year for a school lease. To get Corrente's attention, Freitas put cash in an envelope—three hundred one time, eight hundred another—and gave it to Pannone to deliver to Corrente.

"See, I'm taking myself out of the picture," said Pannone. "I want you to be tight with Frank. . . . I want that name Tony Frazier [sic] to sink in his head."

Freitas began meeting directly with Corrente in his office at City Hall. Pannone warned Freitas to be careful discussing money—Corrente was still spooked by the Voccola investigation, and wary of FBI bugs. "He didn't know if you gotta pig on you," said Pannone, using slang for a hidden wire. Corrente was so paranoid about someone eavesdropping that he would say no to a bribe even as he took it. He inhabited a culture, explained Pannone, where "no, no, no means yes, yes, yes."

Corrente's paranoia was evident the first time Freitas visited him. He started touching Freitas on the chest, as if checking for wires. Freitas took Corrente's hand and moved it down to his crotch. He was sending Corrente a message, he explained later: "If you don't trust me, touch me there." Corrente snatched his hand away and said, "Are you crazy?"

But Corrente didn't count on Freitas carrying a briefcase with a hidden camera inside.

On December 3, 1998, the camera captured Corrente taking a thousand-dollar payoff from Freitas, in return for his help securing a School Department lease. A month later, on January 3, 1999, Freitas dropped another envelope containing a thousand dollars on Corrente's desk.

"What the fuck are you doing?" asked Corrente, sounding exasperated. "It's not necessary. Do you hear me?"

"Frank, I appreciate," said Freitas, in his broken English.

The telephone interrupted Corrente's protests. Corrente waved his hand, as if in disgust, and answered the call. While Corrente was on the phone, Freitas picked up the envelope and counted the money, fanning the hundred-dollar bills for the camera, then put it back on the desk.

Corrente, still talking on the phone, picked up the envelope and slid it quickly into his desk drawer. When he hung up, he called an official at the School Department and directed him not to give Freitas any trouble on the lease.

"See, I'm smart," Corrente boasted to Freitas afterward. "I know how to talk. I said, 'Do you got any objections?' He says, 'No.' I said, 'Well, I think it's a good idea.' "

"Uncle Frank," said Freitas.

"See, I don't say do it," Corrente explained. "I just have to say it's a good idea. . . . They absolutely know what the fuck I mean."

BY EARLY 1999, the stress of working undercover was taking its toll on Tony Freitas. It had been a year since Dennis Aiken had come to visit, a year of juggling the demands of his business with hours spent cultivating the mayor's men. He and his wife, Nancy, who had assumed a larger role in helping to run JKL Engineering, were edgy from the strain. Freitas would feel so drained that he had to lie down during the day to rest.

He worried about being discovered. One day, while he was in his office with Aiken, Freitas's secretary paged him with a call from a Mr. Freon. He was startled to hear his FBI code name, but it was a coincidence—the caller was an out-of-town salesman with an air-conditioning-equipment supplier.

Freitas also worried that he might walk into a setup. Dennis Aiken was always down the hall when Freitas met with city officials at JKL Engineering, but meetings away from the office were nerve-wracking. Whenever Freitas finished, he would call Aiken on his cell phone and give him the signal that he was all right—"Hallelujah." One day Aiken worried when Freitas failed to report in for a long time after attending a Cianci fund-raiser at the Biltmore Hotel.

The scariest moments were when Freitas met with David Ead, vice chairman of the Providence Board of Tax Assessment Review.

Ead was an ex-Providence cop, an intimidating grizzly bear of a man, weighing more than 350 pounds. He was also vice chairman of the Providence Democratic Committee, an organization that had been co-opted by Cianci. Ead ran a vending-machine business and traded on his political connections to place hundreds of juice, soda, and snack machines in Providence schools and police headquarters, recreation centers, city and state office buildings—even the federal courthouse downtown.

Cianci had appointed Ead to the tax board in 1994. Ead—his name rhymed with *greed*—helped Pannone shake down taxpayers who came before the board.

As Freitas burrowed deeper into the corrupt recesses of City Hall, he told Pannone that he needed a way to come up with more cash for all the bribes he was paying. Pannone introduced him to Ead, whose Doris Vending was swimming in cash. The trunk of Ead's Cadillac sagged from the weight of bags of coins that flowed from his machines like the jackpot at Foxwoods Casino, a favored haunt.

Ead outlined a money-laundering scheme. Freitas would pretend to buy soda machines for JKL Engineering. Ead would supply him with phony invoices. Freitas would write a check to Doris Vending. Ead would cash the check and give money back to Freitas—minus a 10 percent "handling" fee.

Unlike the loose-lipped, cartoonish Pannone, Ead was guarded and menacing. He occasionally lumbered around with a gun tucked in his waistband, and told Freitas that he had a cousin who was a well-known mob associate, Joe Badway, who had been Raymond Patriarca's driver. (This being Providence, Badway ran a notorious auto-body shop near Eddie Voccola's. Badway had also been one of Patriarca's supporters who had raced Buddy Cianci to Maryland years earlier, when the young prosecutor had outsmarted the lying priest in the mob boss's murder trial.)

Freitas found it unnerving to visit Doris Vending, a ramshackle, barn-like building on Manton Avenue, in the North End. The only way in was through a thick steel door, bearing a sign warning that trespassers would be shot. There were bars on the windows. Ead called it his fortress.

"See these walls? They're all one foot thick," he boasted one January day, sitting inside his dark, cavelike office, crowded with boxes of candy and trinkets and hung with pictures of famous Rhode Island politicians, from John Chafee to Buddy Cianci. "This is better than a bank down here. In fact, if you go downstairs, I got vaults that banks have."

Once, Ead became suspicious about the way Freitas had positioned his briefcase, on the couch beside Ead's desk. He stared at the briefcase. Freitas thought that Ead had spotted the tiny camera hidden in the handle. Freitas grabbed the briefcase and opened it, then pulled out some paperwork he wanted to show Ead regarding the soda machines he was pretending to buy. Ead relaxed.

Ead warned Freitas not to trust people like Joe Pannone, who talked too much, or Frank Corrente, who had drawn heat from the feds on the Voccola lease. If Freitas had a payoff to make, he should call Corrente and tell him to stop by to pick up the "pizza" and "soda." Deal on our own turf, Ead advised; as an ex-cop, he knew what the feds were capable of.

"Nothing says they can't go down to City Hall with a key, open the door, go up to Frank's office and put a bug in and he'll never know what's happening," said Ead. "You could never get into this building. When I go home at night, my head is rested. You can't even break into it. So, but you can get into City Hall with a key. Everybody has a key."

A few days later, David Ead unwittingly became Dennis Aiken's key to the mayor's office. Back at Doris Vending, Freitas told Ead of his interest in purchasing two vacant lots from the city, under a program that Cianci had created to combat urban blight.

"I'll go to the mayor for you," said Ead. He told Freitas to close the office door, then hashed out a proposal to bring to Cianci—one that called for the city to sell Freitas the lots for a thousand dollars apiece, and for Freitas to give Ead a ten-thousand-dollar payoff to bring to "the man downtown."

"I do business direct," Ead later boasted. "Eliminate all the middlemen . . . even eliminate Frank."

Ead said that he was acting "strictly as a delivery boy"—his play was to ingratiate himself with Cianci, so he could land a part-time city job and qualify for a pension and free Blue Cross. The mayor was open to deals, explained Ead, because he had "a business mentality." Only recently, Ead said, he had pulled off a great deal involving a half-million-dollar tax break on some abandoned property.

The deal sounded familiar. The previous fall, Freitas had attended a Cianci fund-raiser at the Biltmore with Ead and Pannone. The mayor had stopped by their table to say hello, and mentioned to Ead, "I took care of that for you." Later Pannone confided to Freitas that the matter involved a big tax break that had required the mayor's approval. Ead had "taken care of" Cianci, said Pannone.

Ead met with Cianci to discuss Freitas's interest in purchasing the lots. He showed the mayor photos documenting the nice job that Freitas had done improving the West Broadway neighborhood. In February Ead reported back to Freitas that Cianci was willing to do the deal for a ten-thousand-dollar payoff.

Aiken zeroed in on the anticipated payoff. He sent agents to follow Ead to City Hall when he met with Cianci. But the agents couldn't monitor what went on inside the mayor's office.

It was time to get the key.

Fortuitously for the FBI, Freitas had done air-conditioning work in City Hall, and he had the blueprints to the building. One day Freitas and an undercover FBI agent, disguised as a JKL Engineering workman and carrying a toolbox, went into City Hall in work clothes, to work on the ventilation system.

Freitas told the city's property director that he needed to get into the attic. A custodian handed him the keys to City Hall, on a large metal ring with tags marking which doors they opened. One key opened a door in the dusty archives, on the fifth floor, that led into the attic. Freitas unlocked the door. He and the agent climbed into the upper reaches of City Hall, underneath the Plunder Dome, a vast, musty space honeycombed with air ducts and smelling of a bygone era. There, out of sight, they made a wax impression of the key to the mayor's office.

Aiken had gathered enough evidence to obtain a warrant to bug Cianci's inner sanctum. The plan was to send a team of workmen into City Hall during the day and have them hide in the attic until nightfall. Then, under cover of darkness, the team would slip into the mayor's office and plant hidden microphones and cameras. If all went according to plan, Aiken hoped to capture Cianci on camera when Ead delivered the ten thousand dollars.

But before the FBI could move in, the deal fell apart. One of the lots was inadvertently sold to someone else. Then, on March 9, Ead received an anonymous call from a woman who warned him to watch out for Tony Freitas, because he was working for the FBI.

Ead checked his caller ID and traced the call to a pay phone in East Providence. Ead thought he recognized the woman as one of Pannone's girlfriends, who lived in East Providence. Ead was angry with Pannone for double-crossing him, by not sharing the bribes from Freitas, and had cut him out of the loop. Maybe this was Pannone's way of getting even.

Still, the call spooked Ead. Four days later, he showed up at Freitas's office and said that he was going to return twelve hundred dollars that Freitas had given him for voting to lower his taxes. He tried to explain that he didn't have a broker's license, so he couldn't receive cash legally. Ead also said: "There's no big guy involved here. I was just testing you. . . . There's no ten grand to give nobody." At the end of the meeting, Ead asked Freitas to walk him to his car. In the parking lot, unaware that Freitas was wearing a body wire, Ead described the woman's call accusing Freitas of being with the FBI. Freitas laughed it off, joking that he was really working for the CIA. But later, as he and Aiken discussed the conversation, they knew that Mr. Freon's work was finished.

At dawn on April 28, 1999, fifty FBI agents from Providence and Boston assembled in offices in downtown Providence, within sight of City Hall. They were armed with warrants to search several city offices for records, as well as Pannone's home and Ead's office. The agents awaited Dennis Aiken's orders.

The next move would be up to David Ead.

CHAPTER TEN

Toads in the Basement

David Ead's eyes narrowed as he steered his battered brown Cadillac through the early-morning traffic on Manton Avenue and spotted the strange white car parked in front of Doris Vending.

Two men in suits sat waiting in the front seat. It was seven o'clock, the hour that Ead usually arrived to open up his vending-machine business.

Since the early 1970s, Ead had operated Doris Vending at the busy intersection of Manton and Chalkstone Avenues. The building, surrounded by a chain-link fence and padlocked gates, blended into the neighborhood of sagging triple-deckers and used-car lots. Faded campaign signs from last November's election still hung on the fence.

Ead noticed that the white car had no front license plate. He turned his Cadillac around to circle the block and approach the car from behind. The white car followed. Ead drove slowly around the block and parked. The white car parked. It had a Massachusetts plate. The two suits got out and walked over to Ead's car.

One of the men smiled and said in a southern drawl, "What are you doing, trying to escape?"

Dennis Aiken and the other FBI agent slid into the backseat of Ead's Cadillac. Aiken said that they knew about his corrupt dealings with Joe Pannone and Tony Freitas.

Ead denied it. Aiken showed him a photograph of Ead meeting with Freitas inside Doris Vending.

"How'd you get that picture?" asked Ead. "My office is like a bank."

Aiken laughed.

Ead and the two agents went inside Doris Vending, through a dim storage room stuffed with old gumball and toy machines. In Ead's office, decorated with autographed pictures of politicians, a photo of Ead with his

Providence Police Academy Class of '63, and pinups of Marilyn Monroe, Aiken laid it out.

The FBI had Ead on tape, discussing bribes and taking payoffs from Tony Freitas. They knew all about the money laundering and the phantom soda machines. And they knew about the ten thousand dollars that Ead had promised to deliver to Cianci for the vacant lots. Aiken told Ead that he wanted him to wear a wire and bring the ten thousand to "the man downtown." Aiken had the money in his briefcase.

"I can't do that," Ead protested. "I can probably do that to Frank Corrente or Art Coloian, but not the mayor."

Aiken handcuffed him and told him that if he didn't cooperate, he would face prison and financial ruin. He could be charged with money laundering and lose his business. Ead asked them to take the cuffs off so they could talk. A gambler most of his life, Ead was stalling for time, trying to figure his next play. But this wasn't Willie Marfeo's crap game on Federal Hill or the blackjack table at Foxwoods Casino. Ead was confused. He thought Aiken was bluffing.

By now, Ead's wife of thirty-four years, Doris, for whom the business was named, had arrived for work, too. In her youth, Doris had reminded Ead of Marilyn Monroe. Now she was ready to take a heart attack, as they say in Rhode Island. Another relative of Ead's came in and started trying to reach his lawyer.

Ead and Aiken went back and forth, with Ead saying that he couldn't do it and Aiken telling him that he was in serious trouble if he didn't try.

Meanwhile, the agents who had massed in the FBI's downtown offices waited for instructions. Aiken knew that he couldn't keep fifty agents a secret in Providence for long. After half an hour, it was apparent to Aiken that Ead had slipped into denial. He wasn't willing to cooperate. The handcuffs went back on.

Aiken signaled the other agents to move in on City Hall. He also flashed word to agents following Joseph Pannone, who had just dropped his wife off for work at a jewelry shop in Olneyville. Agents in three unmarked cars surrounded the seventy-six-year-old Pannone's car as he drove down River Avenue. They handcuffed him and took him to his house, where they searched his bedroom and seized about sixteen hundred dollars in cash—including five hundred that Pannone had raised selling tickets to Cianci's birthday fund-raiser party scheduled for the next evening at the Biltmore.

Then Aiken headed to Power Street, for his unannounced appointment with the mayor. It was about nine o'clock on a lovely spring morning, the kind of day that brings joggers out along Benefit Street. Here Cianci's Renaissance was in full flower. The National Historic Preservation Trust had booked its 2001 national convention in Providence. Big celebrations were already being planned for September, when Cianci would become the longest-serving mayor in the city's history. He was at the peak of his popularity, fueling speculation that he might run for governor or U.S. senator.

Aiken's shadow fell across the mayor's doorstep. He parked in Cianci's impressive brick drive and rang the doorbell. Aiken knew it was early for the mayor—that Cianci wouldn't normally appear at City Hall for at least another few hours. But Aiken wanted to be sure to catch him.

Their brief encounter was reminiscent of the times, years ago, that the young mayor and the young agent had met in the corridors of City Hall, when Cianci would ask why he was there and Aiken would answer that he was trying to root out corruption.

Cianci had no witty rejoinders this time. Aiken informed him that he was conducting an investigation and asked the mayor if he would like to answer a few questions. They looked at each other, the irresistible force and the immovable object. Cianci looked at Aiken's tape recorder and said that he wasn't talking into that thing. Then he bid Aiken farewell.

Continuing his rounds, Aiken drove down the hill to City Hall to supervise the FBI's search for tax records. Now that Plunder Dome was out in the open, the mayor's men were going to have to choose sides.

LATER THAT MORNING the chairman and vice chairman of the Providence Board of Tax Assessment Review found themselves holding an impromptu meeting—in a holding cell in the basement of the Providence Post Office on Kennedy Plaza.

Joe Pannone and David Ead were neighborhood guys, rooted in the gritty world of Providence ward politics. Jail was a new experience. Two young Hispanic men, arrested on drug charges, shared the roomy cell. One sat on a toilet, behind a partition.

Ead looked sullen and didn't say much. Pannone chattered nervously.

"They got me, they got me," said Pannone, looking dazed and disoriented.

Ead told Pannone how Aiken had asked him to bring ten thousand dollars to the mayor. "I told him to screw," said Ead.

"I'm glad you told him that," answered Pannone. "The mayor's a good guy. He doesn't deserve that."

Meanwhile, Cianci remained bunkered on Power Street, talking on the telephone to his lawyers and aides, tracking the day's mad developments. FBI agents were seizing records from the tax assessor, the tax collector, the building inspector, the Planning Department, the School Department. City officials huddled in small knots in the corridors, as agents turned away confused citizens trying to pay their taxes. A few blocks away, at the city Planning Department, the director turned up his collar and donned sunglasses, to hide from the TV cameras, he joked. Another city worker, leaving a downtown café, deadpanned that he was going back to work to burn some records.

As the day wore on, there was still no sign of Cianci at City Hall. Finally, near the top of the six o'clock news, the mayor materialized for a news conference in his office and attempted to calm the hysteria.

"We're on a roll in this city," he said. "We are experiencing a renaissance." Then he made a Monica Lewinsky joke: "You're not going to find any stains on this jacket."

Cianci had never been close friends with Ead and Pannone, but now he also sought to distance himself from them politically. Yes, he had appointed them to the tax board, and yes, "the buck stops here." But Cianci had had little or nothing to do with the tax board, he said; he certainly never told Pannone or Ead what to do. Pannone was "an old gentleman I haven't seen in years." Ead was "a political animal," a Democratic City Committee official whom the mayor had appointed in the interest of maintaining political harmony.

Although the rough-edged Pannone and Ead were out of Cianci's league, the mayor relied on people like them for power. They were loyalists in Buddy's Brigade, the ones who helped with the campaigns and lent financial support, part of the army of city workers, appointees, vendors, neighborhood folks, and supplicants who made Cianci a political untouchable. He commanded their loyalty with patronage and small favors, the mother's milk of politics.

The son of a tailor, Pannone had spent his whole life in Eagle Park, a working-class Italian neighborhood near Providence College. He was the proprietor of the Dairy Del and later ran Carrie's, a popular fish-and-chips restaurant, named for his wife. He had always been involved in politics in the Fourteenth Ward, part of the fractious North End. Cianci had courted Pannone's support in the 1970s, when the mayor was battling the remnants of the Democratic machine. Pannone had known Cianci since the mayor's childhood, when little Buddy played with Joe's nephew at Joe's sister Millie's house, a few blocks from the Ciancis'. Years later, Pannone recalled, the mayor would joke, "I gotta reappoint Joe because his sister used to make me spaghetti."

Pannone remembered the first time Cianci ran for mayor, against Joe Doorley in 1974. A friend who worked for the city asked Pannone to put up a big Doorley sign outside Carrie's. Pannone was reluctant, because he knew Cianci, but the friend pleaded with him, saying that he could lose his job. After Cianci beat Doorley and took office, Pannone said, a black limousine pulled into the parking lot of Carrie's one day. "I say to myself, 'Oh, geez, here we go.' Buddy gets out and says, 'Joe, what happened?' I said, 'Buddy, I voted for you, but I owed a guy a favor.' Buddy says, 'Tell me who made him put the sign up and I'll fire him.' I said, 'Nah, that's not my style.' "

In the early 1980s Pannone sold Carrie's and retired. Cianci appointed him to the tax board. Pannone enjoyed the job; it gave him somewhere to go on Mondays and made him feel important. In later years, he got himself a police-style badge, identifying him as the chairman of the tax board. He liked riding around Providence, checking on property, schmoozing with people, wheeling and dealing. One of his haunts was Eddie Voccola's garage, where he occasionally picked up envelopes of cash, for helping lower Voccola's property taxes.

Pannone also kept busy with other part-time jobs, which occasionally landed him in trouble. He lost a state patronage job as a urine inspector at Lincoln Greyhound Park because he rarely showed up. Another job, as a bus driver, also landed him in trouble when he drove the jurors during the 1983 gangland murder trial of mobster Louis "Baby Shacks" Manocchio.

Manocchio, who had been on the lam for more than a decade, traveling in Europe and occasionally disguising himself by wearing women's clothes, was being tried for accessory to murder in the 1968 shotgun slayings of bookies Rudy Marfeo and Anthony Melei at Pannone's Market. That was the famous murder case in which Buddy Cianci, as a young prosecutor, had crossed paths with New England mob boss Raymond L. S. Patriarca. Joe Pannone was not related to the proprietors of Pannone's Market, but one of the jurors claimed that he had told them he was related to one of the victims, Melei. Manocchio, who was convicted, moved for a new trial, in part because of Pannone's allegedly prejudicial remarks. Pannone, testifying in court, denied telling the jurors anything; Manocchio lost his bid for a new trial.

On April 28, 1999, Pannone was back in court, this time as a defendant. That afternoon, marshals finally released him and Ead from their basement holding cell and led them into a federal courtroom in handcuffs for their arraignment.

The judge explained to Pannone the terms of his fifty-thousand-dollar bail—that he would forfeit the money if he violated his bail conditions. Pannone, playing the tough guy, interrupted the judge, joking that if he met his bail conditions, "you'll give me fifty thousand."

Outside the courthouse, Pannone tried to hold his blue jacket in front of his face to block the news photographers—but he held it at the wrong angle. Pannone, fiercely proud and old-school, was embarrassed by his arrest and all the publicity. It brought shame on his family—his wife and their two grown children, who lived in a two-family house next door to his neatly tended white ranch house.

After he was indicted with Ead and Rosemary Glancy, the deputy tax assessor, on charges of fixing people's taxes, Pannone refused to cut a deal with the feds. He vowed to "take the heat" for his confederates. He wouldn't be a rat. Then his lawyer started showing him the Freitas videotapes and explained the facts of life: at the age of seventy-six, Pannone was looking at a likely death sentence in federal prison. He also saw that his confederates were on tape, and reasoned that he couldn't protect them.

Around Thanksgiving he had a chat with his family. John Scungio, the lawyer who had paid off Pannone in one crooked tax deal, had recently agreed to cooperate—the first Plunder Dome defendant to plead guilty. Pannone's family urged him to come forward. The Sunday after Thanksgiving, David Ead stopped by Pannone's house, trying to keep him in the fold. Ead showed him a police report in which the owner of a Providence nightclub had accused Tony Freitas of threatening him with a gun. The FBI's star witness wasn't so clean after all, Ead argued. He told Pannone not to worry—the feds were going to have to drop the charges.

But it was too late. Pannone asked Ead to go away. He had decided to plead guilty.

DAVID EAD KNEW what it was like to be on the right side of the law.

In the 1960s, before he started his vending business and got involved in City Hall politics and crimes, Ead had been a Providence patrolman, and a good one. He had a fistful of commendations to prove it: for apprehending a ring of burglars, arresting a suspect for assault with a dangerous weapon, rescuing an elderly woman from a burning building, and catching a car thief before the owner even knew his car had been stolen.

His looks alone could strike fear into a suspect. He was six foot one and 225 pounds, a boxer in the police academy who was not afraid to mix it up. On patrol in Federal Hill one day, Ead decided to settle an old score with a bookie who had whacked him across the face with a pool cue when he was a boy. Ead slammed the man against a brick wall a few times, then dragged him down to police headquarters and flushed his head in the toilet. "What goes around comes around, you boob," he said.

Ead was a throwback to the Providence of gangsters and hustlers and bare-knuckles politicians. He grew up on Federal Hill, the son of an Italian mother and a Palestinian father who had emigrated from the West Bank and ran a small market on the Hill. As a boy, Ead looked out his bedroom window one night and saw two gunmen fleeing through the alley after a mob hit; one ditched his weapon in a trash can. Ead kept his mouth shut. As a teenager in the 1950s, Ead sold the *Providence Evening Bulletin* for a nickel in the bars along Atwells Avenue and downtown—Doorley's Pub, the hoodlum joints, the raucous sailor bars. Providence was a brawling, wide-open town. Ead met the great Rocky Marciano in Manny Almeida's Tap, and got the champ's autograph. He saw the actor Gregory Peck step out of a big Lincoln for a screening of his new movie, *Moby Dick*, at the Majestic Theater. He lost his virginity in a bar one New Year's Eve, when a barmaid pulled him into the back room.

As a young police officer, Ead was assigned to a new tactical squad whose job was to patrol Providence's high-crime areas in unmarked cars, gathering intelligence on burglars, thieves, and assorted thugs. On the side, he put coin-operated gumball machines in variety stores and gas stations. With an elderly mother and a young family to support, Ead left the force after four years to pursue the vending business full-time.

He thrived in the cutthroat competition, building Doris Vending up to six hundred soda, juice, and snack machines in Rhode Island, Massachusetts, and Connecticut. He was a sharp businessman, sometimes accused of chiseling his customers out of their commissions—including the Association for the Blind, which was supposed to share in the profits from his machines in state government offices. In 1994, when a state banking crisis put his business in jeopardy, the city bailed him out with a seventy-five-thousand-dollar low-interest loan.

"The money is the god," he told Tony Freitas.

He liked to play the part of a high roller. After leaving the force, he would go around to Willie Marfeo's crap game. Later, he became a big blackjack player at the Foxwoods Casino. Ead had friends on both sides of the law. When Frank Sinatra performed at the Providence Civic Center in the 1970s, a wiseguy pal got Ead's mother a front-row seat. At a later Sinatra concert, Ead's friend the Providence police chief let him in the back door of the Civic Center, as Buddy Cianci was presenting the Chairman of the Board with an honorary Providence fire chief's helmet. When the Chairman of the Board died in 1998, shortly after Freitas began working undercover for the FBI, Ead mourned along with most of Providence, the city where Sinatra, a friend to Raymond Patriarca, had once said: "I always like being in Providence. I have a lot of friends here." Cianci ordered the flag above City Hall flown at half-mast. "He may be gone," said the mayor, "but I don't think he'll ever really leave."

Ead was also a political operator, which is how he met Cianci.

In the early 1980s, when Cianci was warring with city Democratic boss Tony Bucci, Ead, the party vice chairman, was one of the Democrats who fought Bucci, whom he called "a shakedown artist." At one raucous City Committee meeting, Ead threatened to punch out Bucci's brother-in-law, who kept shoving him. Ead recalled Cianci's courting his support, showing up at a party Ead threw at the Shriners hall in Cranston, and presenting Ead's seventy-five-year-old mother with a key to the city.

In 1990, when Cianci launched his political comeback, Ead said that he received a desperate phone call from an aide reporting that the campaign was "getting light—light of funds." Ead and his cousin drove in his Cadillac Brougham to the Civic Center and met Cianci, who slid into the backseat and accepted five hundred dollars in cash from Ead. Later in the campaign, Ead said he also donated at least twelve hundred dollars' worth of soda and refreshments to Cianci's campaign headquarters.

After Cianci won, Ead began attending the mayor's fund-raisers and selling campaign tickets. He also started lobbying Cianci to put him on the city payroll, so he could qualify for a pension and Blue Cross insurance. The mayor did appoint him to the tax board in 1993, which gave him free Blue Cross, but it was a nonpaying job. Ead kept angling for something better but saw the plums going to other people.

Ead complained to his new friend tax assessor Tom Rossi that Frank Corrente didn't seem to like him. Rossi said that Ead needed to contribute more—and that Corrente and Cianci preferred cash. Following Rossi's advice, Ead said that he put five hundred dollars cash in an envelope and gave it to Corrente. Shortly thereafter, Ead was watching the Columbus Day parade on Federal Hill when Cianci, marching down Atwells Avenue, veered over and thanked him.

Ead began searching for other ways to ingratiate himself with the mayor. During a visit to the dentist, another opportunity presented itself. The dental hygienist was married to a young man, Christopher Ise, whose aunt used to live next door to Ead. The wife said that Ise had graduated from college with a degree in urban planning and historic preservation but that he was having trouble finding a job in his field. He was working at a Borders bookstore in Cranston.

Ead offered to help and eventually, according to his story, met with the mayor and reported that Ise would be willing to make a five-thousand-dollar "contribution" to Cianci's campaign. (The legal annual limit was one thousand dollars.) Ead brought Ise around to Cianci's office for an interview, warning him not to say anything in front of the mayor about the money. During the interview, Cianci called a city planning official and told him to hire Ise immediately.

A month or so later, after Ise had started work, Ead called him up and said it was time to fork over the five thousand.

Ise, an artsy-looking young man with a shaved head and black, horn-rimmed glasses, debated what to do. Although he had grown up in Providence, he had purposely not looked for work there, searching instead in cities like Boston and New York. Now Ise was being asked to kick back for a job in the city he had hoped to escape. It didn't seem right, Ise reflected, but he needed the job. And it beat working at Borders. Ise's friends told him not to worry; that's how things worked in Providence.

Ise rounded up the money, borrowing some from his sister. He told her that it was for a career-development program. He gave the five thousand to Ead; after that, he didn't want to know what happened to it. Ise didn't know whether the money went to Cianci or whether Ead kept it and Cianci had hired him as a political favor to Ead.

Ead would later give the following account of what he did with the money: After Ise gave him the five thousand dollars, Ead called Cianci to report that the "situation" with Mr. Ise was "all set." Cianci told him to come down. Ead walked into the mayor's office feeling uneasy. He pointed to his pocket, where the money was hidden, and told Cianci, "I got it over here." The mayor told him not to be nervous, and sent him to give it to Art Coloian.

Ead had known Coloian for years. A friend of Ead's daughter, Coloian had started coming around Doris Vending, and the two had become friendly. Ead had a picture of himself with Coloian on his office wall and a copy of Coloian's acceptance letter to law school.

Ead said that he took the money to Coloian, who put it in his drawer; before leaving he asked Coloian to make sure that the kid didn't get laid off. Ead fretted about the city's screwing Ise because, he said, two of Ise's relatives were old-time bookmakers on Federal Hill.

The following year, in 1998, Ead worked another crooked deal in which he described going directly to the mayor. This was the alleged ten-thousand-dollar payoff that had cropped up on the Freitas tapes—the one in which the city had resolved a delinquent five-hundred-thousand-dollar tax debt on the estate of the late buckle manufacturer Fernando Ronci.

The lawyer for the Ronci estate was Angelo "Jerry" Mosca, Jr., a long-time State House insider and lobbyist. Ead knew Mosca, who had represented Doris Vending in a dispute with the state over unpaid sales taxes.

Ead went to Cianci and helped arrange a settlement that was actually reasonable. In return for a hundred-thousand-dollar payment from the Ronci estate, the city would waive the remaining four hundred thousand in back taxes, which had accumulated over the past three decades because of a mistaken assessment. According to Ead, he also told the mayor that his approval would be appreciated—to the tune of a ten-thousand-dollar "campaign contribution." Those were "nice words," Ead later explained. "You can't expect to walk into the mayor's office, with the American flag on one side and the Rhode Island flag on the other, and say, 'Here's the bribe.' "

After the settlement had been arranged, Ead said, he received a phone call from Frank Corrente, who said the mayor had told him that Ead had something to deliver. Ead reported that it would be coming soon. "Well, you know the mayor," Ead recalled Corrente saying. "He's on my back. Do your best."

In a scene reminiscent of Tony Freitas's dealings with Corrente, Ead described taking the ten thousand in cash from Mosca to Corrente, who opened a big envelope and put his hands to his lips to be quiet. As Ead dropped the money in the envelope, he said he joked that they should have also taken twenty-five thousand for the mayor from the hundred-thousand-dollar settlement.

Not long after that, Ead and Cianci were at a fund-raiser for the mayor at Blake's Tavern, hosted by Rosemary Glancy on behalf of her brother, who was seeking a police promotion. On his way out, according to Ead, Cianci shook his hand and said, "I heard what you told Frank," and laughed.

Ead wasn't laughing in the summer of 1999.

Following his arrest, he had made yet another effort to land a City Hall job—this time for his wife. Ead was willing to keep his mouth shut and take the hit, but he wanted to make sure that his wife was provided for if he went to prison. Ead sent someone to see Coloian. But Coloian rejected his request; he didn't even want to hear Ead's name.

That summer, Ead would meet with his lawyer, James E. O'Neil, to watch the Freitas tapes. O'Neil, a former federal prosecutor and Rhode Island attorney general who had investigated corruption in Cianci's first administration, saw it as his job to "educate" Ead about the evidence and the conspiracy law under which he'd been indicted.

Ead, embarrassed by his newfound notoriety, tried to lie low. He kept going to the 8:30 Sunday mass at St. Augustine's in Mount Pleasant, but he stopped taking communion. One day as he was leaving church, he saw Frank Corrente "walk in like Moses," going to communion, shaking hands with judges and politicians, telling them that he'd be all right. Ead hung near the back of the church. Did he go to confession? "Nah, the priest is a friend of the mayor's."

Ead, still in denial, tried to divine his future by going to psychics.

He consulted first with an Italian woman named Maryann, a retired state worker whom his wife had seen do readings at a park in Providence. Embarrassed that people might think he was crazy, he talked to her on the telephone. Afterward, he'd send her twenty bucks for a half-hour reading. The psychic gave Ead her read on Plunder Dome.

"Jim O'Neil's a good man, but he can only take you so far down the road," Ead recalled Maryann telling him. "You're going to have to cooperate." She did not see Ead going to prison and predicted a bumpy ride for Cianci: "It looks like he's going, then it looks like he's not, then it looks like he is."

Not satisfied, Ead sought a second opinion.

He went to a young, dark-haired Iranian woman who worked out of her house in a working-class Italian neighborhood in Cranston. The woman looked at the furrows on Ead's massive brow, studied his hands, then rolled her eyes back in her head until her pupils disappeared and only the whites showed. In Ead's vernacular, she advised: "You're in big trouble.

Your name will be shit for a long time. I don't see jail for you, but I see some hectic times."

Ead didn't go back to the Iranian woman. He was too freaked out by the eyeball thing. Plus, she charged thirty bucks.

Ultimately, it was Jerry Mosca who would determine Ead's fortunes.

Mosca was an old-timer at the Rhode Island State House, a former legislative counsel who had boasted to Ead about how the bribery game was played. As a lobbyist for the insurance industry, Mosca said, he had paid off various legislative leaders. He described how he would have a relative in New York cash checks, or cash checks himself in small amounts from different bank accounts, to come up with the money for bribes. After handling the Ronci estate, Mosca had paid Ead and Pannone another bribe to lower the property taxes on his Chalkstone Avenue law office.

Not long after his arrest, Ead was driving down the Pleasant Valley Parkway when he passed Mosca's stately brick home. His Cadillac with the special license plate LEG COUNSEL EMERITUS 1 was parked in the driveway. Mosca, a stooped man with thick glasses and receding white hair, was outside, watering his lawn. Ead pulled over to talk.

"Remember, there's only ten tickets you bought," said Ead. He was referring to their cover story, worked out in a previous meeting, that the ten thousand dollars Mosca had given Ead was for ten thousand-dollar Cianci fund-raising tickets.

Mosca told Ead that he had lied to the FBI and the grand jury about the bribe. Ead said that he was glad. Mosca hugged Ead and promised to take their secret "to the grave."

In early December, a day or so after Joe Pannone pleaded guilty, a trembling Mosca showed up at Ead's house. They got into Mosca's car and went for a ride. Mosca said that he hated Pannone's guts for ratting on them. Ead reassured Mosca that they would be okay, as long as they stuck to their story that the ten thousand had been for campaign tickets. Mosca became so nervous that he stopped the car. Ead told him to start driving again; he didn't want them to be seen together.

Not long after that, Dennis Aiken flew to Mosca's winter home in Florida to personally deliver a message: "We gotcha." Mosca could either cooperate or become the next one indicted.

Back in Providence a short time later, Aiken saw Ead eating lunch with his lawyer, Jim O'Neil, in the atrium of the Fleet Center downtown. He nudged Ead playfully and said, "David, I got your boy, Mosca." Ead didn't say anything, but the color had gone out of his face.

On January 19, 2000, Mosca pleaded guilty to extortion charges and agreed to cooperate.

On Valentine's Day, shortly before his trial was scheduled to begin, David Ead pleaded guilty to charges that he had arranged bribes with Buddy Cianci. The mayor's identity was cloaked in prosecutor-speak—"E1," for Executive 1—or described in Ead's words as "the man downtown."

But there was no doubt in Providence who that meant.

THE WEEK AFTER Operation Plunder Dome became public, Cianci went on the Imus show and scoffed at "Wonder Dome."

An Imus sidekick teased that if the mayor couldn't get a cameo on the TV show *Providence*, perhaps he could make *America's Most Wanted*. Imus pointed out that the show was broadcasting that morning from Scranton, Pennsylvania—where the mayor "never put a cigarette out on somebody's forehead."

"You know, Imus, it's nice to be with you, because you should entitle your show *Mad About Everything*," quipped Cianci. The mayor recapped the investigation, which he said was focused on some low-level city officials accused of lowering people's tax bills. Cianci pointed out that he wasn't involved.

"You're awfully quick to defend yourself," needled Imus. "Nobody made any accusations."

"No, no one made any accusations," replied Cianci. "But I know you, Imus, because the first damn thing you'll do is, you'll be blaming me for bombing a school bus in Kosovo in about a minute."

Imus asked Cianci if he'd still be there the next time the radio show broadcast from Providence.

"Unless I get appointed to run against you in the morning, you know, with another radio show or something," said Cianci. The mayor noted that this was his tenth appearance on *Imus*. "I should get a pension for this."

That night Cianci was inducted into the Rhode Island Heritage Hall of Fame. It was a vintage Rhode Island moment. One of the other inductees, posthumously, was the former mayor of Pawtucket Thomas P. McCoy, who had been one of Rhode Island's most notorious political bosses in the 1920s and 1930s. The president of the Hall of Fame was Manuel Gorriaran, Jr., the first husband of Cianci's ex-wife, Sheila. Cianci was introduced by his former aide Patrick Conley, who praised him as the greatest mayor in Providence history. Conley ignored Plunder Dome, calling Cianci's induction "your ultimate vindication." Conley didn't say that he had helped orchestrate Cianci's selection, in return for a promise from the mayor to appoint him to the Providence Heritage Harbor Commission, which was planning a waterfront museum, and to consider helping Conley's troubled stepson, who had a drug problem, get back on the Providence police force. (The mayor followed through on the first promise but not the second.)

"It's a very big night for me, because I've had a checkered career, and I've been up, down, and all around," said Cianci.

The Plunder Dome investigation complicated Cianci's future plans. The mayor had always thrived on challenges, and his easy reelection in 1998 had felt anticlimactic. Privately, he had begun to struggle with the idea of a life after City Hall. The long nights and endless weekends packed with public appearances were gruelling, despite his remarkable energy and stamina. Behind the public bravado was a gnawing loneliness, a void that Cianci sought to fill with his job and with late nights of carousing and a string of girlfriends. Aides joked about his whirlwind affairs; he once flew to a Caribbean island with one woman, then left her and met another woman on another island. In Providence, there were occasions when one woman would be leaving his house or boat as another one was arriving.

"There's gotta be a life out there," he would later reflect. "And the life can't be every day being consumed by this office, which I love very much."

As much as Cianci loved being mayor—was addicted to the power and the pomp and the celebrity, the ability to make things happen, the turnaround in Providence's fortunes—he was pushing sixty, and had been doing this for most of his adult life. He was the longest-serving active mayor in the country among cities with populations of 100,000 or more. And in September, on his 6,584th day in office, Cianci became Providence's longest-serving mayor ever. The milestone made Cianci more aware of his place in history—and of his mortality.

Cianci liked to compare himself to the previous record holder, nineteenth-century mayor Thomas A. Doyle. A self-styled maverick Republican, Doyle had taken office near the end of the Civil War, thanks to a split in the Democratic party. He had lived on Benefit Street, a block from Cianci's house, and was known as a charismatic, energetic mayor who feuded with the City Council. Doyle was voted out of office in 1869 after being criticized for, among other things, extravagance with city funds—

only to make a triumphant comeback a year later. He oversaw the construction of City Hall, the development of Roger Williams Park, the formation of a professional police department, and the creation of a state-of-the-art sewage system. During Doyle's eighteen-year tenure, Providence doubled in wealth and population. Doyle died in office, after suffering a cerebral hemorrhage while horseback riding.

On September 23, 1999, as Cianci hosted a dinner for visiting Italian artists and artisans from Florence, aides with laptop computers tuned in to the official NASA clock to mark the exact time that Doyle had expired, at 9:26 P.M., on his 6,584th day in office. When the moment came, the guests raised their glasses of Italian sparkling wine in a toast to the new reigning longest-serving mayor, Buddy Cianci.

In the early 1990s Cianci had told a city councilwoman that he wanted to be "mayor for life." Now, as the decade drew to a close, he wasn't so sure. He contemplated life as an elder statesman, writing his memoirs, traveling, lecturing—maybe another radio talk show. He formed a non-profit organization, the Vincent A. Cianci Jr. Library & Archive, to raise money for an urban-research center and think tank. The idea was to merge his marinara-sauce scholarship fund with the research-center fund, providing a pool of money to support his various endeavors—and his own continuing reign as Providence's Buddy emeritus.

But could Buddy walk away? And would Plunder Dome allow him to leave on his terms?

Cianci's emotions welled up one August day as he spoke to his long-time secretary, Carol Agugiaro, who was retiring. Agugiaro had been with him from the beginning, first in the attorney general's office, when he was a prosecutor, and then through the roller-coaster rides of Buddies I and II.

A trim, pleasant woman, Agugiaro could still remember Cianci's first inauguration day, in 1975, when his eyes shone with the excitement of a child on Christmas morning. There was a sense of family then. Cianci was kind and funny. He would talk to anyone, from corporate executives to Jimmy the Balloon Man, a retarded denizen of downtown who would wander in for a cup of coffee. Agugiaro had witnessed the growing tension in the office, the nonstop power struggles and political battles, the mayor's rages, his disintegrating family life. She had fielded the phone calls from Sheila, begging her to make sure Buddy came home for Nicole's birthday party. She had seen it all come apart, with the mayor's felony conviction, and then watched him put it all back together, with his amazing comeback.

Sitting outside the mayor's door in the nineties, Agugiaro had seen Cianci's visions materialize in the Providence Renaissance, and his dark excesses consume him. She had handled his travel arrangements and taken the angry phone calls, like the time the phone in his hotel room in Miami didn't work, and he called on his cell phone, screaming at her to call the front desk to fix it. She had seen the girlfriends come and go, and had listened to him pour his heart out after Wendy Materna left him. She had seen the emptiness underlying the larger-than-life public persona, the man who, if he was sitting in his office at night, before going out, needed someone else to be there.

Agugiaro had also seen the corruption investigators come and go. In the 1980s, a state police detective asked her if she'd ever seen anyone carrying a bag or satchel into the mayor's office. "You mean with money sticking out?" she asked derisively.

She had been one of the first people the FBI visited in the days after the raid on City Hall, in the spring of 1999. Two agents had walked into the mayor's office one morning and flipped their badges, just like in the movies. They knew where she sat and how to pronounce her name. They all went into Ronnie Glantz's old office, next to the mayor's. As staffers walked by the open door and gawked, the agents quizzed Agugiaro about people's comings and goings, and the mayor's contacts with David Ead and Joe Pannone. Someone called Cianci at home to alert him.

That summer, Agugiaro put in her notice that she was retiring. She had worked in City Hall for twenty-four years and was burned out. It was time to enjoy her family and grandchildren. On her last day, August 6, she and Cianci spoke in the mayor's anteroom.

"I can't believe you're leaving," he said.

Cianci gave her some advice about stocks and investments, then grew somber.

"You're doing the right thing," he told her. "I'm so tired of this. I'm tired of having to go to the opening of an envelope. I'm getting run-down. I'm sick of kissing little old ladies who spit all over you."

Cianci envied Agugiaro for having a family to go home to. "What do I have?" he said. "Nothing."

But Cianci also found it hard to let go of the office. If he left, he told Agugiaro, he would miss his city cell phone, the limousine, the police protection.

Cianci hugged Agugiaro good-bye and walked back into his office.

■

CIANCI HAD OTHER things on his mind in the summer of 1999. The Plunder Dome grand jury had widened its investigation to examine the mayor's membership in the University Club, a private East Side preserve of Providence's movers and shakers.

Perched near the foot of College Hill, overlooking the historic First Baptist Church, the University Club was steeped in tradition. Founded in 1899 for "literary, scientific, artistic and social purposes," its first directors included the governor of Rhode Island, the president of Brown University, and the Episcopal bishop of Rhode Island. Dignitaries from Walter Camp, father of American college football, to Bill Clinton had visited the handsome brick mansion on Benefit Street, which stood on the site of an old burial ground reputed to be haunted by ghosts.

Cianci had applied for a University Club membership in the 1970s, after he became mayor. His sponsors included John Chafee and two members of the Rhode Island Supreme Court. But the club buried his application. The snub was more political than ethnic—one of the leading anti-Cianci members was Edmund Mauro, a successful Italian-American businessman who had been a big Joe Doorley supporter. Still, the rejection stung. He recruited politically influential friends, such as Herbert DeSimone, the former Rhode Island attorney general, and business leader Bruce Sundlun, a future Rhode Island governor, to lobby on his behalf, to no avail.

Living just a few blocks away, Cianci was reminded of his rejection whenever he drove by and saw the white flag with the club's crest fluttering in the breeze. An aide recalls driving by with him during the 1990 campaign, and Cianci muttering: "Those fucking guys. I'm gonna show them. I'll be the mayor again, and they're going to have to answer to me."

After Cianci regained office, the president of the Greater Providence Chamber of Commerce, James Hagan, made discreet inquiries on Cianci's behalf. But by now, attitudes toward Cianci had hardened in the wake of his corrupt first administration. A few years later, word got back to Cianci that the club had hired comedian Charlie Hall and members of his Ocean State Follies troupe to perform at its Christmas party. One actor, a Cianci look-alike, had come in pretending to be the mayor and brought the official greetings of the city, drawing a huge laugh. Cianci's rejection was common knowledge among club members.

Then, in the summer of 1998, the club embarked on a million-dollar renovation of its nearly two-hundred-year-old home. The job required permits from the City of Providence. One day near the end of July, Cianci was going through his mail when he glanced at the agenda for the city's Building Board of Review. The University Club was on the docket, seeking routine construction variances.

A vengeful mayor exploded. He called the city's building inspector and two members of the building board and told them that he wanted the variances rejected. When the board met on July 30, he dispatched a trusted aide, deputy city solicitor Patricia McLaughlin, to the meeting. Although the club's architects had been meeting for months with the building inspector and believed everything was on track, a handful of key variances were rejected when the board met.

Afterward, board member Steven Antonson and building inspector Ramzi Loqa went into Loqa's office and called Cianci to report the rejection. Antonson told Cianci that the rejection was going to cost the club $250,000. "Well, that is because of fucking Mauro," retorted Cianci.

Cianci wasn't finished with the University Club. When the club appealed the city's decision to the state building board, the mayor called Loqa from his boat on Block Island and ordered Loqa not to miss the meeting. He promised him a 10 percent raise if he succeeded in blocking the club. "Make sure you go," barked Cianci. "No excuses. No vacation, no sick leave. You have to go."

The club won at the state level. Cianci vowed to appeal all the way to the Rhode Island Supreme Court. That would keep the club shuttered for months and jeopardize a bank loan that club officials had taken out to pay for the renovations.

The club's leaders tried to make peace. On August 18, 1998, two club officers came to Cianci's office. One leader, Alan Gelfuso, stuck a Cianci campaign bumper sticker on the back of his suit, hoping to lighten the mood. The other, club president Jerry Sansiveri, had a letter of apology for the club's past treatment of the mayor—including the 1996 Christmas skit, which Sansiveri blamed on "the guest comedian."

Rather than appeasing Cianci, the letter set him off. He raged and cursed. He vowed to have the police ticket cars outside the club "all night and all day." He demanded that Eddie Mauro, who had blackballed him in the seventies, be thrown out. He also threatened to yank the club's liquor license and turn it into a "BYOB club"—bring your own bottle. When he wanted to speak to the city's liquor-board chairman, who was legally blind, Cianci shouted, "Get the blind man on the phone." As he screamed at the club leaders, Frank Corrente stood behind the mayor's right shoulder, motioning wildly for them to leave.

Cianci pointed out that the letter they had brought was the first official communication he had received in more than two decades concerning his rejection. "How long does Emily Post say it should take to answer a letter?" he asked. "Two, three weeks?"

Gelfuso said that things had changed and that the mayor should consider becoming a member. Cianci swore that he wanted no part of the club. Then he uttered what could pass as a proverb for Providence: "Be careful how you act. The toe you stepped on yesterday may be connected to the ass you have to kiss today."

Shortly thereafter, the mayor obtained a University Club membership directory. After a meeting in his office to discuss Providence tourism, Cianci went through the book with Jim Hagan from the Chamber of Commerce. It was like taking a trip through your high school yearbook, Hagan later recalled, as Cianci offered running commentary: "This guy's nice. . . . This guy's a jerk. . . . This guy's a moron."

Early in September, the University Club's Board of Governors voted to offer Cianci an honorary lifetime membership—only the second such membership the club had ever extended. (The first had gone to a Catholic cleric.) Some members objected, feeling that it was a shakedown. But Gelfuso argued that they had better make peace with the mayor if they hoped to reopen. Those opposed skipped the meeting, since a unanimous vote was required.

On September 11, 1998, Sansiveri returned to the mayor's office and presented him with a letter informing him of his membership. As an honorary member, he would not have to pay any dues or membership fees, though he would be responsible for meals. The mayor seemed pleased and asked if the membership was for him personally or for the office of mayor. It was for him personally, as long as he lived. Six days later, the city dropped its fight against the University Club. McLaughlin told Loqa that the battle was over—the club had given Cianci a membership. The club reopened that fall.

Ironically, one of the contractors on the University Club renovations that summer was Tony Freitas, who did the ventilation system. When the job was delayed, the general contractor alluded to some problems with

City Hall. That fall, in a taped conversation in Freitas's office, Rosemary Glancy confided that Cianci had also ordered a city appraiser to give the University Club a hard look. "The mayor's on their ass," said Glancy. "He must have got a bad dinner over there." Dennis Aiken had also heard about the mayor's membership from another source. The following spring, when Plunder Dome became public, the FBI seized records from the building inspector and began questioning people.

One of the first people questioned was Ramzi Loqa, the building inspector from Baghdad. Raised in the repressive society of Iraq, Loqa had come to the United States in the early 1970s to study engineering and later went to work for the city. A timid man with a bad hairpiece, he had grown accustomed to Cianci's belittling and abusive behavior. Fearing the mayor more than the FBI, he denied that Cianci had pressured him. Later, Loqa said, he filled Cianci in on how he had held back, and the mayor sounded pleased. But then Aiken came back to Loqa and called him a liar. After talking it over with his wife and his lawyer, Loqa agreed to cooperate.

Steve Antonson was also feeling the pressure from both sides.

Shortly after the FBI raid on City Hall, Antonson was sitting at home watching the television news when he saw Cianci interviewed about the University Club. The mayor denied having spoken to anyone on the building board about the club's variances prior to the vote. Antonson leaped up and said, "Oh, shit." An expressive man, he began talking aloud to himself. "I know he talked to me. What the hell is he lying for?"

Antonson had come a long way since joining the mayor's 1990 comeback campaign, hoping to learn about politics. After the election, he recalled, Cianci had seemed stunned when Antonson turned down a City Hall job. "What's wrong with you?" Cianci demanded. "Why the fuck did you get involved with me?"

"All I wanted to do is learn about politics," he replied.

"You mean to tell me you don't want anything?"

Antonson explained that he made more money as an electrician. Cianci seemed offended. After he regained City Hall, Cianci helped Antonson's wife get a job as a police dispatcher—one that she was quick to point out she was qualified for. When the mayor saw Antonson, he'd say: "You're gonna work for me, Antonson. I'm gonna get you." Early in 1992, Antonson received a call from the business agent for the electricians union, which assigned work, and was told that he was being moved to the Providence Civic Center as the chief electrician, on the mayor's demand. Antonson protested that he didn't want to go, but his union bosses told him he had to; they didn't want to anger Cianci. Shortly after he started, Antonson saw Cianci there. "See, Antonson," the mayor said, "I told you you'd work for me. This is my building, you know."

Antonson renewed the relationship that had developed during the '90 campaign. Cianci would show up for Civic Center events and sit on a couch outside the operations office, in the concrete tunnel beneath the stands, bantering with Antonson and the other workers. When the National Figure Skating Championships came to town, along with the ABC Sports television cameras, Cianci asked Antonson, "Whaddya think about a TV at my seat? So if the camera hits me, I can watch myself." Antonson installed the television, then watched as the mayor wreaked havoc. Spectators complained that the TV was too loud. Figure-skating officials complained about the mayor's late, attention-getting arrivals, which distracted the skaters.

One night, Cianci asked Antonson if he would like to become his personal electrician. The previous one, Caesar Brown, had died. "Do you want to fill his shoes?" asked Cianci. "They're big shoes to fill." Antonson began doing odd jobs, sometimes at odd hours, at the mayor's house and on the mayor's boat, always for free. There were funny, aggravating times. Antonson went over to the house on Christmas Eve to fix the lights on Cianci's Christmas tree. He endured the middle-of-the-night phone calls from the lonely, obsessive man who would call repeatedly, saying, "Antonson, now, you know, my lights are not on. When are you going to fix them?" Often, the air-conditioning ducts on Cianci's boat would become clogged with seawater. One Sunday morning, Antonson received a panicky call from Cianci on his boat, anchored in Jamestown. "There's smoke!" wailed Cianci. "I can't see." Antonson told him to put out the fire and promised to come down after church. Cianci asked how long that would take.

"Obviously, you haven't been in a while," replied Antonson.

"Don't fuck with me, Antonson. Never mind church."

Antonson skipped church and hurried to Jamestown to rewire the boat's electrical system. When the problem was fixed, Cianci beamed. "That's my electrician!" The mayor was always after him to go for a cruise, but Antonson, who was easily seasick and thought the boat was "a piece of shit," put him off. Cianci usually kept the boat anchored at a marina in Warren; sometimes he would have his city limousine brought down, so that he could decide whether to return to Providence by land or by sea.

Cianci also appointed Antonson to replace the late Caesar Brown on the Providence Building Board of Review. The mayor told him that it was a very important board, dealing with safety issues. And, "you're gonna get paid for doing nothing." Plus, free Blue Cross. "You have to pay attention," Cianci told him. Antonson agreed, on one condition. If it was a safety issue, he didn't want to get any phone calls from someone looking for a favor. He told the mayor: "I'm an honest guy. I'll serve as long as I can do the honest thing." Cianci agreed.

The mayor had kept his word until the summer of 1998, when he called about the University Club. Antonson didn't understand why Cianci was so worked up, but he called repeatedly. "Remember, I appoint people to this board. You get Blue Cross. You get a check. You always said safety was important. Well, this is it." Still, Antonson never thought that what he was doing was illegal; he didn't believe that the mayor would put him in that position.

The following spring, after watching Cianci lie on television, Antonson saw him at a Providence Bruins hockey game. The mayor was standing behind the glass near one of the goals, where he liked to harass an American Hockey League goal judge who had once been his police driver. Without turning around, Cianci rocked back on his heels and said, "If the FBI asks you anything about the University Club, we never talked. Do you understand, Antonson? Loyalty."

Not long after that, Dennis Aiken called. "You're not a target, you're a witness," he said. Two days later, after two sleepless nights, Antonson put on a tie and walked into the FBI offices, passing through a door with a combination lock and a metal detector in a small reception room with photographs of America's Ten Most Wanted criminals. Aiken showed him into a room with another agent, and began questioning him about the University Club. After ten minutes of evasive answers, Aiken blew up.

"Listen, kid," he shouted. "Did you know obstruction of justice is five years? Do you want to go to jail for that piece-of-shit mayor? You're a liar. Don't ever cheat on your wife, because you can't lie."

Aiken turned to the other agent and asked, "Can he lie?" The agent replied, "He sucks as a liar." Aiken said that they could tear up their notes and start over, or Antonson could keep playing games and take his chances. "My advice, if you don't want to go to jail, is to start over. You've got a family. What's wrong with you?"

Antonson relented and told them everything he knew about the University Club. As the agents explained extortion, Antonson realized that this could be the end of Buddy Cianci. Aiken said that they would need him to testify. Antonson felt relieved to get the truth out, but also scared about how the mayor and his cronies would react. He was even more petrified a month or so later, in August 1999, when Aiken brought him to testify before the grand jury in the federal courthouse opposite City Hall. Grasping him firmly by the arm, Aiken pulled Antonson into a waiting room holding about a dozen City Hall officials, who had been subpoenaed to produce records. Then Aiken pulled him out of the room and put him in another room, by himself.

"Do you know why I did that?" asked Aiken. "So all those people will see you. It will get back to him. It'll kill him. All those little people are going to run back like little servants. So I know he'll call you."

Antonson didn't share Aiken's enthusiasm. "Oh my God," he thought. "I'm a dead man."

Sure enough, when he got home, there were messages from the mayor's office. Antonson called Aiken, who came down to his house with a tape recorder. "Listen, we gotta record this," the agent said. "Do you want your life back? We gotta get him on tape."

Aiken told Antonson to tell Cianci that he had not yet testified; there had been a screwup and the feds wanted him to come back tomorrow. Standing by his kitchen sink in his house in suburban East Greenwich, Antonson dialed the mayor's private line. Cianci quickly came on the line and began coaching Antonson on how to testify.

"Nobody ever talked to you about not giving them anything," said Cianci. "That's what I'm gonna tell them when I talk to them. . . . I never fucking talked to you once."

Cianci reassured him that Ramzi Loqa had already talked to the FBI twice, and denied everything. When Antonson hesitated, Cianci said, "What, are you losing your balls now? . . . Don't let those guys intimidate you. Don't be a volunteer for the U.S. government."

"No, I'm not," replied Antonson.

"Who the fuck do they think they are?" growled Cianci.

As they spoke, Antonson realized that Cianci was intimidating him—and that he always had. Antonson sensed the disappointment in the mayor's voice, and felt as though he had failed him. He listened as Cianci criticized the feds. "They operate with great deceit—and great trickery."

Cianci told Antonson that he would take a lie-detector test. "By the way," said Cianci in parting, "don't volunteer anything."

When Antonson hung up, his face was flushed; he felt drained and exhilarated. "My God," said Aiken. "Does he do this to you all the time? He really intimidates you."

The next day Antonson called back. Once again, the conversation was recorded. This time an agitated Antonson told Cianci that the FBI had shown him some of the Freitas tapes. The mayor responded, "I'm not on any tapes."

"Mayor, I'm not gonna lie for you," said Antonson. "I can't."

"I didn't ask you to lie for me," replied Cianci.

"I can't. I mean, the shit they have is unreal."

"Steven, Steven, I never asked you to lie for me," said Cianci.

"You know, I'm an honest person . . . and it's fucking me up . . . destroying my family. . . . I feel fucked."

Cianci acknowledged that he had called him prior to the building-board meeting—but only to ask if the University Club was on the agenda, not to tell him how to vote. The conversation deteriorated quickly. Antonson was shouting and on the verge of tears. "You used my honesty!" he said.

Cianci, the canny ex-prosecutor, seemed to realize what was happening. "Did I ever ask you to change your vote on anything?" he asked.

"On what, Mayor?"

"On the University Club?"

"No, no, that night you called, you asked me to deny every goddamned fucking item," replied Antonson.

"Oh, Steven, come on."

"No, I can't lie, Mayor."

"Well, well, then don't lie."

Near the end of their conversation, Antonson was nearly sobbing.

"I got involved in frickin' politics for the honesty of it," he said.

"I totally agree," said Cianci, reassuringly.

When he hung up this time, Antonson felt like he'd hurt Cianci. The mayor couldn't stand people not liking him, and Antonson had rejected him.

Aiken smiled and said, "Steven, you got your life back. You really told the bastard off."

A FEW WEEKS after his conversations with Antonson, Cianci got into a tussle with *The Sopranos*.

In anticipation of its season premiere, the producers of the hit HBO series were planning promotional events in twenty-three cities, including Providence. In September an HBO official contacted the mayor's office, asking to purchase several cases of the Mayor's Own Marinara Sauce. Cianci fired back a sharp letter refusing to have anything to do with *The Sopranos*. Although he had never seen the show, which depicted the life of a dysfunctional New Jersey Mafia family, the mayor bristled at what he considered its negative stereotyping of Italian-Americans.

One of the show's writers and producers, Robin Green, was from Providence. In college she had double-dated with Junior Patriarca. The show's creator, David Chase, also had a Providence connection: his grandmother Theresa Melfi had emigrated from Italy and lived in Providence before moving to New Jersey.

An HBO executive wrote to Cianci to point out that many prominent Italian-American politicans supported *The Sopranos*, including Alfonse D'Amato, Mario Cuomo, and Rudolph Giuliani. Cianci retorted that D'Amato and Cuomo had been voted out of office, and asserted that Giuliani, who had campaigned with Cianci on Federal Hill in 1998, did not endorse the show. *The Sopranos* event in Providence was canceled.

"For us to celebrate that in this city, after we've done all this work to rid ourselves of this image, doesn't do us any public good," said Cianci.

Besides, who needed *The Sopranos* when you had the real thing? In March 2000, federal prosecutors began playing tapes in the first Plunder Dome trial.

The trial offered the first public glimpses of the explosive Freitas tapes, including Joe Pannone's comments that Cianci used Corrente as his bagman and how the mayor had schooled him in the art of bribery: "Never talk on the phone, never get a check, but get cash when you're one-on-one." The case involved charges that Pannone, David Ead, and Rosemary Glancy had conspired to lower Freitas's property taxes for bribes. But Pannone and Ead had pleaded guilty, leaving Glancy to stand trial alone.

Glancy was not your typical corrupt public official, but she was a typical city worker. A heavyset woman with grayish hair that she usually wore swept back in a ponytail, she had worked at City Hall for twenty-six of her forty-seven years. She lived with her sister, who also worked for the city, in the house where they had grown up, in Mount Pleasant, a neighborhood of tidy middle-class homes inhabited by Irish and Italians. Two of her brothers were Providence police officers; another brother was a dispatcher for the Rhode Island State Police.

Glancy spent a lot of her free time in Muldowney's Pub, where she tended bar, cheered on her beloved Boston Red Sox, and brought home-cooked meals on Christmas and Thanksgiving for patrons who had nowhere else to go. Located downtown on Empire Street, Muldowney's was not like the yuppie fern bars or artsy cafés that had popped up as part of the Providence Renaissance. It was an old shot-and-beer joint that offered karaoke on Monday nights and that had, over the years, catered to the down-and-out. The bar stool beside the lottery machine belonged to a man from Mississippi named Paul, an itinerant carpenter who had gone blind in Providence in the early 1970s and just stayed. Marylana, a homeless woman who wore flowery hats, sipped vodka, and dragged on Marlboros, kept a live snake in her bosom and took afternoon naps in one of the booths. When she was found strangled and stabbed to death in Burnside Park one night, in front of the federal courthouse, her friends at Muldowney's passed the hat and paid for a proper Christian burial, with a funeral mass at the Cathedral of Saints Peter and Paul.

This was Rosemary Glancy's world. In 1993, she had been featured as one of *The Providence Journal*'s Christmastime "Good Folk," for her charitable work with the homeless and people afflicted with spina bifida. After her indictment, her friends rallied to her support, throwing a time that drew more than two hundred people and raised more than five thousand dollars. A homeless man pressed one hundred dollars in crinkled bills into her hand, and when she resisted, said: "Rosemary, when I was hungry, you always made sure I ate. At Christmas, when I was lost, you found me. You treated me like I was someone. Now it's my time to help you."

Glancy was also part of the "go along to get along" culture that had pervaded City Hall for decades. You followed orders, didn't ask questions, looked the other way, and contributed to the mayor. As a lowly clerk in the 1970s, Glancy could remember being up for a five-dollar-a-week raise. Before she got it, she had to go into Cianci's office and raise her right hand, in a perversion of the pledge of allegiance, and swear her loyalty to the mayor. In the 1990s, as the deputy assessor, she organized fund-raisers for Cianci, geared toward winning her brother John a promotion in the police department, where advancement was widely seen as being tied to political contributions.

Pannone enlisted Glancy in his corrupt tax-fixing schemes. She was the one who knew how to make the numbers work. She wasn't taking the kind of money that Pannone and Ead were, but she wasn't stupid. Pannone had called her "the fat girl," the one who "bends" if he showed her "a little green." He'd throw her fifty bucks here, a hundred there, and take her out to lunch; Andino's, on Federal Hill, was a favorite spot.

Her lawyer, Kevin Bristow, an earnest ex-prosecutor, tried to paint Glancy's conduct as more reflective of the political culture of City Hall than blatant corruption. Unlike Pannone and Ead, Glancy had not been caught on tape taking money. It was primarily the word of Pannone, a proven liar and cheat, that he had shared the bribe money with her. But unlike Pannone and Ead, Glancy couldn't cut a deal with the feds because she had nothing to give up—she was, Bristow argued, "the smallest fish in the pond." That was underscored when Bristow tried to call Pannone and Ead to testify at Glancy's trial. Bristow wanted to attack their credibility and raise doubts that they had, in fact, passed bribe money along to Glancy. But although their plea agreements required them to testify for the government, it did not require them to testify for a defendant. Ead and Pannone both took the Fifth.

One moment on tape helped do Glancy in. In October 1998, when Freitas was working undercover, paying bribes to Pannone, Dennis Aiken decided to put her to the test. He had Freitas ask her to stop by his office to explain the tax savings he had achieved after paying twenty-four thousand dollars in bribes to Pannone. How much Glancy knew—or chose not to know—became evident as she and Pannone met with Freitas at JKL Engineering. When Freitas thanked them for their help on his taxes, Pannone replied, "And it ain't stopped yet." Glancy looked at Pannone, held up her hand, and said, *"Stai zitto"*—Italian for "shut up."

"I'm Irish," she added, with a husky laugh. Then she repeated, *"Stai zitto."*

Nor did it help her when Glancy peered around at Freitas's finished basement and advised him to lie about it to the city's revaluation inspectors.

"Is that honest services being performed in the basement of JKL?" asked prosecutor Richard W. Rose, in his closing argument. "She conducted a dishonest-services seminar, soup to nuts, A to Z: How to Cheat Providence Taxpayers."

Noting the nature of the conspiracy law, which requires only that someone participate in a corrupt scheme, Rose thundered that it didn't matter whether Glancy "sold the city out for cash, out of misguided loyalty or for lunch."

Glancy never took the stand in her own defense. She had taken to drinking heavily since her indictment, and as she sat at the defense table, her whole body shook visibly, from nerves. During a recess one day, an elderly woman walked up to her on a downtown street, called her a criminal, and spat in her face. Glancy was "at the end of the line," Bristow later said. She was physically incapable of testifying for hours.

The trial lasted eight days, drawing national attention and an overflow crowd to the tiny courtroom. On March 16, 2000, the jury began deliberating. The next day was St. Patrick's Day, an auspicious day for Glancy, who normally spent the holiday serving up green beer at Muldowney's. Waiting outside the courtroom, she joked nervously that she would dance a jig on the steps of City Hall if she were acquitted. But a few hours later, the jury returned with guilty verdicts on all seven counts of extortion, conspiracy, and mail fraud. A devastated Glancy was sentenced to thirty-three months in federal prison.

She didn't last a month.

Shortly after reporting to prison in Danbury, Connecticut, Glancy hurt her leg while working at her prison job—sweeping up goose droppings left by the hundreds of geese that would fly into the prison exercise yard every morning to eat the grass. Glancy's lower leg began to swell. Within weeks she was flown to a prison hospital in Carswell, Texas—the nation's only federal prison hospital for female inmates. But that facility couldn't treat her, and Glancy wound up in a community hospital in Fort Worth, handcuffed to the rail of her hospital bed. Her years in City Hall had taught her that it would do no good to complain to the prison guards; "Bubba doesn't explain," she said.

Glancy was diagnosed with terminal liver and kidney failure. The doctors gave her just weeks to live. Over the next twelve days, with Bristow, her lawyer, working around the clock, and backing from federal prosecutors and Rhode Island's congressional delegation, Glancy won what may have been the speediest "compassionate release" in the history of the federal Bureau of Prisons.

In October 2000 Rosemary Glancy returned home to Providence to die.

She was checked in to a private room in Rhode Island Hospital under an assumed name, Maria Rodriguez. One afternoon she chatted amiably as she lay in her bed. An intravenous line carrying blood was hooked up to her arm. Her eyes flitted from the row of flower arrangements on the windowsill to the television show *Law & Order*, where two prosecutors talked about squeezing a woman to force her to cooperate.

Glancy talked about her years as a city assessor, slogging through run-down houses and murky cellars, some of them flooded. She voiced regret for her trip into Tony Freitas's basement. And she described the poisonous atmosphere in City Hall, where, for years, asbestos had crawled out of the pipes. She was bitter toward Cianci and the other big shots at City Hall, whom she held responsible for the corrupt system that she had gotten caught up in. "The greedy got richer and the poor people got screwed," she said.

Glancy lingered for another few months, prompting complaints from local radio talk-show callers that she had duped the system. A woman with an oxygen tank had been spotted dining at Mediterraneo; suspicious callers mistakenly thought it was Glancy.

Rosemary Glancy died of liver failure on January 12, 2001. She was forty-eight.

Hundreds of people attended her funeral at the Church of the Assumption of the Blessed Virgin Mary, a once-Irish parish now dominated by Latinos in the city's downtrodden West End. The mourners came from all walks of life—cops, judges, the poor. Father Daniel Trainor, widely known for his work among the city's poor, criticized the "ambitious prosecutors" who had targeted Glancy. She was "a good person" who had been afraid to speak up, a woman who became ensnared in Providence's "petty politics."

Cianci, in Washington on business, said that he otherwise would have attended Glancy's funeral. He said that her life shouldn't have been judged by the fact that she had "once or twice" gotten caught up in "some bad things." He seemed uncomfortable when asked to comment on the fact that some people blamed him for Glancy's tragic end.

"Well, I can't help the fact that she died," he said. "I don't think I caused that. I think the buck stops at my desk, but I wasn't involved in any wrongdoing. . . . There's no reason to indict me."

TWO DAYS AFTER Rosemary Glancy was laid to rest, Joe Pannone sat mournfully in the visitors' room at the federal prison in Fort Devens, Massachusetts. The prison stood on a former military base—where Buddy Cianci had commanded the stockade as a young army officer—in a forlorn, wooded patch of north-central Massachusetts. On this raw afternoon, the prison was shrouded in fog.

It wasn't supposed to have ended this way for Uncle Joe.

After he decided to cooperate, he started losing his friends. And after his taped statements about Cianci were played at Glancy's trial, the mayor dismissed him and David Ead as "*Goodfellas* wannabes."

Now here he was, in prison, hanging around with the real goodfellas. He shuffled into the visitors' room, a stooped, white-haired man with Coke-bottle glasses, George Burns in a green prison jumpsuit. Across the room, another elderly, bespectacled inmate waved to the ex-chairman of the Providence tax board.

"That's Jerry Angiulo," said Pannone, referring to the former Boston Mafia boss. "He has a lot of power in here. He calls guards 'fags' and 'fairies' and gets away with it. If I said that, they'd put me in the hole."

Pannone had met Angiulo through another mobster imprisoned there, Anthony "the Saint" St. Laurent, a major Rhode Island bookmaker and loan shark. The Saint had tried to avoid prison by citing a chronic bowel condition that required up to forty enemas a day, which invited a new nickname—"Public Enema Number One."

When the Saint heard what Pannone was in for, he was impressed.

"Hey, you made a lot of money, huh?" asked the Saint.

"I wish I did," replied Pannone.

In the pill line one day, the Saint introduced Pannone to Angiulo as "Mr. Plunder Dome." Angiulo's eyes lit up.

"Are you the mayor of Providence?" he asked.

Pannone was seventy-eight years old and doing five years in prison—a possible life sentence at his age. Prosecutors had revoked his deal after a series of disastrous meetings in which he fumbled and contradicted himself, complained of headaches and stress, and lamented that his friends considered him a rat. During one session, Pannone told the FBI agents what was all too apparent—that he was a lousy "testifier." Ultimately, the feds didn't need Joe Pannone—he had said it all on tape. So following emergency triple-bypass heart surgery—covered by his city Blue Cross—Pannone was packed off to prison. He felt that the judge had made an example of him.

"When the judge looked at me, I thought he was looking at the mayor," said Pannone.

Now he was spending his golden years in a Darwinian world of murderers, drug dealers, and rapists, where inmates fought over what television show to watch and guards periodically tapped on the bars with rubber mallets to check for tampering. On foggy days like this, the inmates were not allowed outside. That was fine with Pannone, who couldn't stand looking at the fences.

"They're making a hardened criminal out of me," he said, laughing nervously. "I could be a boss in here if I wanted to. I'm already half a boss. I control these guys—a bag of rice, a bag of candy, a can of soda. They respect me."

The feds were never going to nail Buddy, Pannone predicted, because "Buddy's very smart. They're not going to get him, and I'll tell you why. They got me and the others on tape. They don't have tapes on the mayor."

EARLY IN 2001, the man who had launched Operation Plunder Dome, Tony Freitas, started following developments in the case from a state prison cell.

The man who had set out to bring down the mayor had been defeated by his own volatile nature, exacerbated by the stress of his year undercover. His third wife, Nancy, had filed for divorce in November 1999, seven months after the City Hall investigation became public. They continued to work together at JKL Engineering, but the situation was tense. Nancy Freitas said that the strain of her husband's role in Operation Plunder Dome had helped destroy their ten-year marriage.

In December the FBI started an inquiry into possible witness intimidation of Freitas by the Providence Police Department, in its handling of two complaints against him. In one complaint, Freitas had lost his temper in the city building inspector's office after believing that he was being hassled over a building permit. In the other, the owner of a nightclub near JKL Engineering accused Freitas of threatening him with a gun during an argument over a boundary dispute. Later the club owner, a Cianci supporter, admitted that he never saw a gun. But Cianci, who had watched a videotape of the incident from the club's security camera, implied otherwise. The mayor gloated that Freitas "got himself on tape . . . doing bad things."

A few months later, during jury selection in the trial of Rosemary Glancy, Freitas was arrested for punching his wife in the face during an argument in the office. As he was booked at police headquarters, some cops fed up with City Hall corruption and meddling in police promotions shook his hand and embraced him. Freitas was fingerprinted and locked up, then handcuffed to a suspected murderer and driven to court by Patrolman Bruce Glancy, the brother of Rosemary, whom Freitas was about to testify against.

"I need this like I need a hole in the head," lamented Freitas.

Freitas, who had been feted as a civic hero and lectured at the FBI Academy in Quantico, Virginia, found his two previous marriages, which had also ended amid allegations of abuse, held up to public scrutiny. The head of the Rhode Island chapter of Common Cause, which had honored Freitas for his corruption-fighting efforts, said that his arrest showed that everyone is flawed. The award, explained a saddened H. Philip West, "doesn't say that someone is a saint, only that they've made an extraordinary contribution to public life."

Freitas was arrested again in April 2000, for violating a no-contact order with his wife, and again in May, after she accused him of grabbing her and kissing her in the office. That arrest followed a call from the FBI's Dennis Aiken to the Providence police, notifying them that Freitas had threatened to kill his wife, her friend, and himself. Freitas went to Butler Hospital to seek counseling. A psychological evaluation found him to be highly intelligent, "with a high energy level and a high level of emotional expressiveness," a man under a great deal of stress from his role in Operation Plunder Dome and his divorce.

Nancy Freitas was troubled that her husband's enemies were "focusing on Tony and his temper, and not the criminals" at City Hall. She spoke of the risks that her husband had taken, and how she had lived through the unnerving experience with him. But she had given him plenty of chances, and "he just can't seem to get a handle on his behavior . . . the stress was too much for him and he just went over the edge."

Freitas pleaded no contest to domestic assault and served ten days in prison and sixty days in home confinement. In December he was arrested again, this time charged with assaulting his girlfriend—a black belt in karate who, he claimed, had actually assaulted him because he wanted to break up. The arrest violated Freitas's probation. On February 1, 2001, he began serving a four-month prison term.

As Freitas sat in his prison cell, his paranoia grew. He saw conspiracies everywhere. He felt that he'd been set up. The attorney general, he believed, was too cozy politically with Cianci. The judge was a personal friend of the mayor's. To Freitas, it showed that "the cockroaches" were out to get him. He read a book about the early European explorers in the New World, and the corruption of the merchants who enriched themselves at the expense of the people. When they were caught, he noted with satisfaction, they were hanged. Corruption in Rhode Island "has taken a big hit" as a result of Operation Plunder Dome, he said. "This is a lesson for future politicians."

Then, contemplating his circumstances, he added: "Never for a million years did I think I would be doing time in jail. I always looked at myself as the good guy."

BY EARLY 2001, Buddy Cianci was hearing footsteps.

Six people had been convicted of corruption charges involving tax scams. A federal judge, in sentencing Pannone and Glancy in the summer of 2000, had lashed out at the mayor for presiding over the most corrupt administration in Rhode Island's long and checkered history. Corruption, declared Judge Ronald R. Lagueux, "comes from the top." City Hall was a place where "nothing gets done unless money changes hands."

Cianci criticized the judge's remarks as unfounded and prejudicial. Privately, he grumbled that Lagueux was a former aide to John Chafee, out to settle an old score. The mayor enlisted Harvard lawyer Alan Dershowitz, who had clashed with Lagueux while representing Claus von Bulow, to attack the judge. And he pointed gleefully to the past arrest of Lagueux's son, a Rhode Island state police detective, for stealing three submachine guns. (A grand jury later chose not to indict him.)

Meanwhile, Cianci worried about Frank Corrente, who had retired abruptly in the summer of 1999, a few months after the FBI raid on City Hall. On the morning of the raid, two FBI agents had walked into Corrente's office and shown him a photograph taken from the Freitas videotape, of him taking a bribe. Corrente had excused himself quickly and left City Hall, telling a reporter in the hallway that he was going to play golf. On June 29, 2000, Corrente was indicted with Pannone for taking bribes from Freitas. Cianci, the picture of confidence five days later as he rode a white police horse in the Bristol Fourth of July parade, wondered privately what Corrente would do. One night Cianci had dinner in Massachusetts to discuss strategy with his lawyer, Richard Egbert; his chief of staff, Art Coloian; and Coloian's lawyer. The feeling was that Corrente would flip, because he couldn't stand to go to prison at his age. The mayor and the others discussed ways to discredit Corrente by bringing up some of his shady dealings.

Ironically, the feds had a contrary view. They thought it unlikely that

Corrente would cut a deal. He was too old-school. Although family members urged him to cooperate, and one of his lawyers talked to prosecutors about a deal involving no jail time, Corrente refused to deal. He hired a new lawyer, C. Leonard O'Brien, a former Vietnam War–era protester who didn't believe in cutting deals with prosecutors.

O'Brien's mistrust of the government increased early in 2001, when a local television reporter, Channel 10's Jim Taricani, aired portions of a secret FBI videotape showing Corrente taking a thousand-dollar bribe from Tony Freitas in his City Hall office. O'Brien believed that the feds may have leaked the tape to put more pressure on Corrente. The U.S. attorney's office responded that the tapes were in the possession of defense lawyers and Plunder Dome defendants, any of whom might have leaked it, perhaps to discredit the government. The chief judge of the federal district court in Rhode Island, Ernest C. Torres, later appointed a special prosecutor to pursue the leak. Meanwhile, O'Brien hired his own private detective to investigate.

Cianci kept in touch with Corrente, who in his retirement still liked to stop by City Hall to see people and check on his girlfriends. The objective, according to another top Cianci aide, was to "keep Frank close."

The feds were also putting pressure on Coloian. Coloian recalled walking down the street near City Hall during the spring of 2000 to meet some friends for dinner at Capriccio. Richard Rose, the lead Plunder Dome prosecutor, pulled up in his car and rolled down the window.

"How come you're not taking the limo?" Rose asked.

"Why don't you give me a ride?" replied Coloian.

"I'll give you a ride," said Rose.

Coloian climbed in and they bantered on the short ride to the restaurant, studiously avoiding the biggest subject between them—Operation Plunder Dome. As Coloian got out of the car, he quipped, "I'd invite you in for a drink, but that probably wouldn't be a good idea under the circumstances."

Meanwhile, Cianci pushed ahead with the Renaissance. In his annual State of the City address to the City Council in March, the mayor sketched out his vision for the future, including his ambitious "New Cities" plan. The program included plans to transform the industrial South Providence waterfront into a mecca for cruise ships, condos, shops, and restaurants and cover Interstate 95 downtown to create forty new acres of land for development. Critics said that Cianci should finish fixing the old city before embarking on new ones, that his New Cities was nothing more than fanciful artist's renderings—more sizzle than substance.

After the speech the mayor's chief of policy, William Collins, stood in the hallway outside the council chambers. A former *Providence Journal* reporter, Collins had covered downtown development in the 1970s and written a story in 1980 about the mayor's "War Room" and abuse of power. A few years later Collins, who had a degree in urban planning, went to work for Cianci, and he returned to City Hall with him in 1991. A wonkish, bespectacled man, Collins spoke of a calmer, more mature Cianci, a mayor with extraordinary vision and the ability to wield power effectively to push Providence forward.

In drafting the State of the City speech, Collins and Cianci had held long, reflective discussions about the future. They talked about capitalizing on Providence's proximity to Boston, and its cheaper cost of living and quality of life, to attract new businesses. They spoke of the city's central location, between medical-research centers Boston and New Haven, home to Yale University, as an incentive to create a biotechnology-research park affiliated with Brown University's medical school and the city's hospitals. Providence was a traditionally working-class city struggling to remake itself as a magnet for higher-paying jobs and college graduates. The Renaissance was a fragile work in progress; it required "constant replenishment," said Collins. "Otherwise, the lights will go out."

"We've got to keep hitting home runs," said Collins. "The mayor is the best person to do that. I don't know if I could tell the feds doing Plunder Dome this, but he's too important to the future of Providence. He's an enormously valuable asset."

The mayor that Collins knew, beckoning from the spires of his New Cities, would never involve himself with the likes of David Ead or Joseph Pannone. They were, said Collins, "toads in the basement."

CHAPTER ELEVEN

Buddy's Inferno

Davio's, the bar in the Biltmore Hotel, drew an eclectic nighttime crowd—tourists, conventioneers, gays, traveling salesmen, and Brown University professors.

In the spring of 2001 Buddy Cianci could be found many a night drinking alone there. A few years before, when the playwright Arthur Miller was in town to receive an award, Cianci had read the scene from *Death of a Salesman* where Willy Loman describes meeting the mayor of Providence in the lobby of his hotel. Now Cianci seemed to be playing the role of the salesman, reminiscing about the days he "knocked 'em cold in Providence," as another cigarette burned down and he waited for the curtain to fall.

The previous fall, Cianci had sold his beloved carriage house on Power Street and moved into the Presidential Suite at the Biltmore. If the mayor's life had become a lounge act, then Davio's was, he joked, his living room. The cynics said that Cianci was liquidating his assets before the feds swooped in. The mayor insisted that he had simply grown tired of rattling around in a big, empty house, all alone. Besides, he quipped, living at the Biltmore meant never having to buy another roll of toilet paper.

One of the people who got to know Buddy after dark was Laurel Casey, a cabaret singer who performed Friday nights at Davio's. A tall, angular woman in her late forties, Casey usually wore a slinky black evening dress and matching gloves. Casey did her irreverent best to re-create the avant-garde café society of 1920s Berlin. She was just as likely to flash her breasts, dance on the bar, or insult her patrons—anything to shake them out of their middle-class sensibilities. She patterned her act on the cabaret performers of Weimar Germany, who had skewered the Nazis on their rise to power. One of Casey's favorite targets was the WASP elite, and Cianci loved it.

Casey viewed the mayor as a kindred spirit. Like her, he was a show-man, always onstage, uncomfortable when the spotlight was turned off. "When we're alone, it's like we disappear, because no one's watching," she explained. Behind Cianci's sad basset-hound eyes, Casey saw a vulnerable boy who wanted to be loved, who needed to feel important.

She had moved to Providence in 2000 from Newport because Cianci supported artists, understood them because he was one. But that didn't stop Casey from satirizing the Providence Renaissance as skin-deep, or telling her audience that she lived between a Vietnamese restaurant and a crack house on the South Side. The mayor would shout back, "One step at a time, Laurel."

Late one night Cianci came in with some friends and Casey started lampooning them as a bunch of no-neck thugs. The mayor egged her on, urging her to "do that thing that got you fired" from a previous gig, meaning flashing her breasts. Laughing, Cianci guaranteed her that his companions would all throw twenty-dollar bills if she did. Instead, Casey mooned them; the mayor seemed shocked, taken aback. But that's what true cabaret was about, she believed—a slap in the face of convention.

On other nights, Casey would coax Cianci to join her. Reluctantly, en-couraged by the applause of the audience—some tourists from Omaha, perhaps, or men in town for a turf-management convention—the mayor would get up and tell a few jokes or sing a song, like an old vaudevillian. On those nights, it seemed, Cianci managed to forget the growing shadow of Plunder Dome. It was as if he'd been transported back to his childhood, when he sang and tap-danced in Celia Moreau's Kiddie Revue.

One night Cianci and Casey performed a duet of one of the mayor's fa-vorite songs, "It Had to Be You." Cianci also liked "Mountain Greenery," "The Man That Got Away," and "Big Spender," with its opening line, "The minute you walked in the joint." These were songs that spoke to the Provi-dence of his youth and his imagination—a brassy, romantic world of film-noir light and shadows. There was a poetry to his sitting in the Biltmore, a former Jazz Age hotel where a teenage Raymond Patriarca had been a bell-boy and where Cianci had announced his first candidacy for mayor, back in 1974.

When Casey complained about her stagnating singing career and mused about moving to Los Angeles, the mayor encouraged her to stay.

"Being a cult figure in Providence, Rhode Island, is no small thing, Laurel."

Less than a hundred yards away from the Biltmore, on the eighth floor of the Fleet office tower facing Kennedy Plaza, the lights burned after hours in the offices of the United States attorney, Margaret E. Curran. For months a team of federal prosecutors under Curran—her top deputy, Craig Moore; Richard Rose, the lead Plunder Dome prosecutor; and Terrence Donnelly, another prosecutor who had joined the case—had been writing and rewriting the draft of a racketeering indictment against the mayor.

For the past two years, since the conclusion of Tony Freitas's undercover work, a federal grand jury had sifted through hundreds of boxes of evidence and heard from more than 150 witnesses. Dennis Aiken likened the investigation to turning over rocks and seeing what would crawl out. The grand jury had issued nearly three hundred subpoenas and scrutinized virtually every corner of city government—from the mayor's office to the police department and the School Department to obscure city boards and agencies to the city's loan program for some of the Renaissance's glitzy restaurants. The acclaimed Trinity Repertory Company had even received a subpoena for records, as investigators explored whether city tow-truck operators had laundered payoffs through donations to the theater that Cianci had done so much to support. But it had been slow going in a city where the culture of corruption was deeply ingrained. Curran joked that there were only two degrees of separation in Providence; as a result, she said, "Nobody gave information above a whisper."

The Freitas tapes had changed the equation, but the tapes alone didn't give them the mayor. Early on, when Pannone started describing City Hall payoffs, Moore had warned people in the office that he didn't want to hear the "R word." They were still a long way from building a racketeering case against Cianci; he wasn't on the tapes. The feds viewed the mayor as a smart, experienced criminal who had insulated himself so well that nobody could point to any specific crime that he had committed. His subordinates could carry out his wishes with just a wink and a nod, even as Cianci personally spurned advances by people he didn't trust, like the undercover FBI agent Marco in 1995.

But the more Pannone told Freitas about how the money went through Corrente to Cianci, the more convinced the feds became that they had the makings of a racketeering case. By early 2001 the investigators believed that they had uncovered a pattern of corruption that the RICO statute was designed to address, with Cianci as the Mafia-like boss. But a seasoned prosecutor knew that there were two universes: what may have actually happened, and what could be proven in court.

Putting an indictment together was laborious. The prosecutors had to make hard choices about what to put in and what to leave out. There were heated discussions over evidence and witnesses, over who might be willing to cooperate and who wouldn't. The draft indictment also went to the Justice Department in Washington, which must approve all RICO cases. Early in 2001 Moore, Rose, and Donnelly closeted themselves in a conference room for a week and went through the lengthy indictment, line by line. It was reminiscent of an old law-school exercise of drafting an "elements sheet," with the elements of each crime written across the top of the page and the evidence filled in underneath.

They emerged with a lengthy document that accused Cianci of being the Tony Soprano of City Hall—of running a criminal enterprise out of the mayor's office that, during the 1990s, had extorted more than two million dollars in kickbacks for jobs, contracts, and favors. The draft indictment accused Cianci of conspiring with Frank Corrente to extort $1.2 million from Edward Voccola for the School Department registration center, and another $250,000 in campaign contributions from tow-truck operators to maintain their lucrative place on the police department tow list. The mayor was also accused of conspiring to take three bribes arranged by David Ead—$10,000 for the vacant lots that Freitas had wanted to purchase from the city; $10,000 from the estate of Fernando Ronci to resolve a half-million-dollar tax debt; and $5,000 from a city job-seeker, Christopher Ise. Last, the indictment accused the mayor of extorting an honorary lifetime membership from the University Club, and of witness tampering for urging Steven Antonson to lie to investigators about how the mayor had ordered the club's building variances blocked.

The indictment also charged Corrente, Voccola, Pannone, and Richard Autiello, the leader of the tow-truck operators, with being participants in Cianci's criminal enterprise. Corrente and Pannone were accused of taking payoffs from Freitas. Voccola was accused of bribery and money laundering. Autiello, Corrente's good friend and a leading Cianci supporter who had the contract to service city police cars, was charged with taking $5,000 to help a woman's son get onto the Providence police force, despite a criminal record. The mayor's chief of staff, Art Coloian, was charged with serving as bagman for the Ise bribe, but not with racketeering, which required at least two underlying criminal charges.

In March, not long after Cianci gave his State of the City address, federal prosecutors invited him to address another forum—the Plunder Dome grand jury. They warned he didn't have much time; indictments were coming soon. Cianci was tempted, confident that he could explain away the feds' suspicions and outsmart his pursuers. But his lawyer would never allow it. Cianci turned down the invitation.

The federal cloud overshadowed a Cianci fund-raiser at the Biltmore that month, which was sparsely attended compared with previous bashes. Some of the people who came admitted quietly that they were there to hedge their bets. "Say he doesn't go down," explained Providence police sergeant Bob Bennett, the head of internal affairs, as he munched on hors d'oeuvres. "I'd like to think that he'd remember the people who were here tonight."

Sharky Almagno, the former Silver Lake councilman who had been with Cianci from the beginning and was the city's inspector of weights and measures, said that he'd be "stunned—stunned" if the mayor were convicted of anything. "An indictment doesn't mean anything. I've got that kind of faith in the man." He dismissed the videotape of Corrente taking money from Freitas. "Talk about entrapment."

Lawyer Walter Stone, a cochair of the fund-raiser, gave a speech in which he said that he supported Cianci because he had a 60 percent approval rating, because nobody was running against him, and because the corruption probe had been going on for two and a half years with no resolution in sight. "I find it most offensive," said Stone. "Either indict his ass, try him and convict him, or leave him alone." The crowd cheered.

On Monday, April 2, the grand jury assembled in the John O. Pastore Building, across Kennedy Plaza from City Hall. Channel 12's Jack White, a veteran newspaper and television reporter, had been staking out the courthouse since Friday, told by his sources that the mayor's indictment was imminent. On Monday morning White arrived with a large satellite truck and another satellite truck from his sister station in Boston. As the day wore on, all Cianci had to do was glance out his office window to see the growing media contingent. The chief judge for the federal district of Rhode Island, Ernest C. Torres, also noticed the photographers outside and fretted that there had been a leak in the grand jury. Torres, who ran a tight courthouse, groused that he seemed to be the last person in Providence to know of the coming indictment.

Later that day the grand jury voted to indict Cianci and his alleged co-conspirators. The indictment remained sealed, to give the FBI time to arrest Voccola, who was considered a flight risk because of his extensive criminal record.

Bustling about the courthouse, Richard Rose smiled enigmatically at the reporters who had gathered in the clerk's office. He deflected their questions with quips and an enthusiastic scouting report on Duke University's basketball team, which was playing for the national championship that night. An avid basketball fan and former player in his youth (when he was twelve years old he once hit a lucky hook shot over Providence College All-American Marvin Barnes while fooling around in Alumni Hall), Rose regarded the federal courthouse as his home court. "I got game," he liked to say, the brash talk of the streets of South Providence, where he had grown up poor, black, and fatherless.

Rose, only the second black federal prosecutor in Rhode Island history, had journeyed far for his court date with Cianci. The last time he had sought an encounter with the mayor was back in the spring of 1975, Cianci's first year in office. Rose was a sixteen-year-old sophomore at Central High School, a truant who spent a lot of time hanging around downtown, then a wasteland dominated by X-rated movie theaters. When the Paris Cinema, where Rose liked to watch kung-fu movies and blaxploitation flicks like *Superfly*, also switched to X-rated films, Rose complained to any public official who would listen. He and a classmate collected more than fifteen hundred signatures on a petition. When Rose saw that the mayor was appearing on a television broadcast from Burnside Park, outside the federal courthouse, he went downtown and tried to speak to Cianci but was turned away. "The mayor is trying to get people into the city," Rose told a reporter. "These movies aren't helping."

That same spring Rose's social-studies teacher lectured him about the fact that he was the smartest kid in class but never came to school. Rose had already spent five years in a Catholic orphanage in rural Smithfield; his mother, who collected welfare and worked odd jobs while struggling to raise five children alone, put him in the orphanage when he was eleven because she couldn't control him and wanted to keep him away from the drugs and street crime decimating South Providence. Now, back in the city, Rose was adrift again. His teacher pressed him: What was he going to do with his life? Rose said that he wanted to be a lawyer. The teacher told him to go down to the courthouse and write a report about what he saw. Rose went to the Providence County Courthouse on Benefit Street and walked into a courtroom where the lawyers were picking a jury in Rhode Island's first death-penalty case in more than a century, since an Irish immigrant had been hanged for the 1843 murder of a textile baron that he probably didn't commit.

The judge was curious about the skinny black kid and let Rose sit with the press through the trial. The defendant, a state-prison escapee, had shot a Bristol fish peddler outside a Providence housing project. Rose was riveted by the spectacle of the trial, the theatrics of the lawyers—"the whole Perry Mason thing." He thought to himself, "I can definitely do that."

The following year, after his seventeenth birthday, Rose passed the high school equivalency exam, dropped out of Central, and joined the marines. The discipline was jarring—life as a private, he said, was "one of the worst existences in the world"—but it helped turn his life around. He spent five years in the marines, then graduated from the Community College of Rhode Island, Rhode Island College, and Northeastern University Law School in Boston. He joined one of Boston's hottest law firms, Mintz, Levin, Cohn, Ferris, Glovsky and Popeo, telling a partner in his job interview, "Mintz, Levin is like me—we're both young and cocky." As the firm's only Rhode Island lawyer, Rose wound up working directly with the firm's chairman, R. Robert Popeo, a former federal prosecutor and nationally known criminal-defense lawyer. First the City of Pawtucket hired Popeo to conduct a forensic audit following a federal corruption probe that sent the mayor, Brian Sarault, to prison for shaking down contractors. Later Rose joined the defense team in one of the biggest corruption cases in Rhode Island history, against former governor Edward D. DiPrete.

DiPrete, who had been governor in the mid- to late 1980s, and his son, Dennis, faced state charges in the mid-1990s that they had run the Rhode Island State House as a racketeering enterprise. The ex-governor was accused of extorting contractors, including a ten-thousand-dollar payoff that he inadvertently threw away at a fast-food restaurant after eating a roast-beef sandwich; when he discovered his mistake, the governor drove back to the restaurant and retrieved the cash from the trash can in the parking lot. Popeo represented Dennis DiPrete, while another top-rated Boston defense lawyer, Richard Egbert—Cianci's future lawyer—represented the former governor. Popeo taught Rose to be prepared, to know his case inside out. Walking into the state police financial-crimes unit and surveying the hundreds of boxes of evidence, Popeo told Rose: "Our defense is in there somewhere. I just don't know where right now." Rose spent about a year plowing through those boxes. His efforts helped lay the groundwork for Popeo and Egbert to show that state prosecutors had concealed critical evidence favorable to the DiPretes, then attempted to cover it up. The former governor eventually pleaded guilty to eighteen felony corruption charges, but because of the prosecutorial bungling, he landed a good deal, doing only a year in prison. By then Rose, who was pushing forty and eager for trial experience, had moved on to the U.S. attorney's office in Providence.

A deeply religious man, Rose worshiped at the Mount Hope Community Baptist Church and approached his job with a missionarylike zeal that bordered on arrogance. He alienated defense lawyers in a major drug-trafficking case by telling them, "You're in my house now." Later he and one of the lawyers nearly came to blows. During Rosemary Glancy's trial, her defense lawyer, Kevin Bristow, told the jurors that he wasn't going to "bounce around" like Rose. Spinning and hopping around the courtroom, modulating his voice from a roar to a whisper, pointing an accusing finger in the trembling Glancy's face, Rose spoke passionately in his closing argument about the toll of corruption on honest government and equal opportunity. Afterward, he teased Bristow, "You didn't like my Chuck Berry?"

Smart and flamboyant, favoring bow ties that complemented his scholarly round wire glasses, Rose had a flair for zeroing in on the pertinent fact or incriminating detail that would stick in a juror's mind. In one case he seized on the fact that the defendant had hidden drugs in a child's room, in a box of Grizzly Graham cookies.

As Providence's first black assistant U.S. attorney in three decades, Rose was always conscious of his position and his race. Whenever he walked into a courtroom, he felt as though he were the one being judged. He urged other minorities in law enforcement to serve as role models and spoke to inner-city youths about overcoming obstacles. Rose exhorted a banquet of minority police officers: "Know your history. Take responsibility for your role in history."

Rose discovered the racial divide when he was in the third grade, in the 1960s, being bused from South Providence to the Italian North End; one day angry whites rocked his school bus and shouted, "Nigger, go home!" As a prosecutor, he decorated his office with an autographed picture of Muhammad Ali, the front page of a nineteenth-century abolitionist newspaper, and a yellowed legal document settling a lawsuit with the payment of a male slave.

Sometimes he wondered if he was doing the right thing, prosecuting black criminals from his old neighborhood for a government that imprisoned a disproportionate number of minorities. One of his first cases involved a seventy-three-year-old crack dealer who had peddled drugs from a tenement next door to where Rose once lived. After the man was convicted and sentenced to fifteen years in prison—more than a suburban white drug dealer might have gotten—an anguished Rose drove by his old neighborhood. He saw two little girls his daughter's age, sitting on the front porch of the crack dealer's tenement, and knew that he had made the right choice.

When Dennis Aiken needed a prosecutor to work with in Operation Plunder Dome, early in Tony Freitas's undercover work, he had been happy when the U.S. attorney's office suggested Rose. Aiken thought that Rose was gutsy, unafraid of a tough case. When Aiken first pitched Plunder Dome, Rose had some concerns. Taking on Buddy Cianci in Providence wouldn't be easy. There would be a lot of noise, tremendous pressure. When it was over, Aiken told Rose, "Somebody's gonna leave town." But as Rose watched the tapes of Freitas and Pannone, he saw the potential. This was the kind of case he lived for. "Let's go," he told Aiken. "Let's play."

As Rose helped shepherd the undercover phase of the investigation, he would run into Cianci around town, at various events or nightspots. A few days before Operation Plunder Dome had become public, in 1998, the mayor had seen Rose at a banquet of the minority police officers' association at the Biltmore. Cianci, who knew that Rose shared his taste for fine cigars, had made a big show of presenting Rose with an Ovo, a Dominican cigar. Rose, knowing that the FBI was about to execute search warrants at City Hall, turned the cigar over to Aiken and filed an internal report documenting his contact with the target of an investigation.

Now, three years after he had begun building the case against the mayor, just before court closed for the day on April 2, 2001, Rose's work was finally unveiled—a ninety-seven-count indictment of Cianci and his alleged confederates. The indictment reduced the mayor's well-worn nickname to a moblike alias: "Vincent A. Cianci Jr., a/k/a 'Buddy.' "

As word of the mayor's indictment flashed across Providence and beyond, a private lawyer who was Rose's best friend, Casby Harrison, was leaving work when a man approached him outside his office in South Providence. The man identified himself as a private detective, working for Frank Corrente. He was investigating the leak to Channel 10 of the video of Corrente taking money.

The detective asked Harrison if Rose had ever shown him any of the secret Plunder Dome videotapes. Harrison had seen a tape the previous spring—the same one that had been leaked to Channel 10. He and his wife had stopped by Rose's house after dinner one night and found him at work, reviewing a Plunder Dome tape. Rose had invited Harrison to watch, curious as to his reaction. But the tape was under a court-ordered seal. This being Providence, where a secret is something you tell one person at a time, word had gotten back to the defense camp. Harrison, stunned by the detective's questions, refused to say anything. Instead, he went home and warned Rose.

A chagrined Rose knew that he would have to confess his transgression to his superiors, and to the judge and the defense. He could face court sanctions for his lapse in judgment. In the biggest case of his career, Rose had given Cianci an opening to counterattack. The indictment was only a few hours old, and already the pressure on the prosecutor had been ratcheted up. When Rose told Rhode Island attorney general Sheldon Whitehouse, the former U.S. attorney who had hired him, Whitehouse said, "You have given the world's biggest ball buster a giant nutcracker."

BUDDY CIANCI WAS also feeling the pressure. The mayor was agitated as he sat in his private conference room, with its mahogany bar and richly varnished wainscoting. Outside, reporters and television cameras waited in his office. It was Monday night. A few hours earlier, after his indictment had become public, the mayor's aides had received 911 pages to rush back to City Hall. Now, in the remobilized Cianci War Room, the mayor chain-smoked as he went over his statement with his lawyer, Richard Egbert, and his longtime confidant Charles Mansolillo.

Finally, it was showtime. The mayor strode into his office and stood behind the lectern on his desk, under the white glare of the television lights.

"I've had better Mondays," he said, an echo of his line, following his indictment nearly two decades earlier for the assault of Raymond DeLeo, that he'd had better Tuesdays. The mayor waved the ninety-seven-page indictment defiantly and thundered, "Ninety-seven times zero is zero." The government's case was "based on self-serving statements by criminals seeking to save their own skins." Cianci vowed that the indictment would not deter him from doing his job, including a date at the White House on Thursday with President Bush for a summit of American mayors on "the New American City."

The room was packed with reporters and with Cianci supporters, who lent it the air of a church revival. Robert Farrow, an African-American

Methodist bishop who called himself the mayor's spiritual adviser, stood behind him, chanting, "Amen."

"I said before there are no stains on this jacket, and there are still no stains on this jacket," he said. "I'm going to fight this as far as I can. I'm going to go all the way to the Supreme Court, to The Hague, wherever they want to go."

Richard Egbert, Cianci's lawyer, stepped to the mayor's podium and declared of the indictment: "This is the government's best shot. They won't get to control the way the case is tried."

A television reporter asked Egbert if he would seek a change of venue to another city because of the intense negative publicity. It was one of the rare moments that the taciturn Egbert smiled. "Who would want to leave this wonderful city?" said Egbert. "Who better to judge the mayor than a jury of his peers?"

Afterward, away from the cameras in the privacy of his conference room, Cianci slumped in his chair, lit the first of three Merits in ten minutes, and inhaled deeply. His voice dropped to a hush and his eyes reddened as he described a phone call from his daughter, Nicole, who cried when she heard about the indictment.

"Yeah, it hurts," Cianci told Karen Lee Ziner, a *Providence Journal* reporter. "The first day is the toughest. Then it gets better."

Thirty minutes later Cianci headed up to the tony Oyster Bar, one of his regular haunts on Federal Hill, packed tonight with his people. The owner, Frank DiBiase, was a good friend, his restaurant the beneficiary of a start-up loan from the city.

This was where the mayor would fight the government's racketeering case—not just in the courtroom, but here, amid the friends of Cianci and the fat of the Providence Renaissance. Here, in the long, narrow Oyster Bar with its stamped tin ceilings and linen tablecloths, live lobster tank and waiters hurrying past with trays of stuffed oysters swimming in butter and bread crumbs. Holding a cigarette in one hand and a snifter of brandy— "cough medicine"—in the other, Cianci drew strength from the steady stream of supporters who shook his hand and kissed his cheeks.

The day after his indictment, Cianci received an e-mail from Laurel Casey, who wrote: "You're the hero of the community. I'm plugging for you." She and her friend Deborah Zaki, the wife of a wealthy East Side doctor, went to a print shop and ordered several hundred FREE BUDDY bumper stickers. But the next day Zaki's husband was found murdered, shot to death in his bedroom. Debbie Zaki, who had cited spousal abuse in an earlier but never-finalized divorce proceeding, quickly emerged as a leading suspect. The state police questioned Casey, who had been her yoga instructor. Mrs. Zaki was never charged, and the murder remained unsolved. She and Casey were so distressed that they never picked up the FREE BUDDY bumper stickers. Casey did hang a LEAVE BUDDY ALONE sign in the window of her apartment; shortly after that she was evicted by her landlord, an Old World Italian man who thought that she was a prostitute because of the slinky evening gowns she wore for her cabaret shows. She found a new place and continued to worry about Buddy. "If he leaves, I leave," she vowed. "I can't imagine the city without him."

For Cianci, especially in times of adversity, the show must go on. The next day, he flew to Washington for the annual gathering of the U.S. Conference of Mayors, where he was to moderate a seminar entitled "The American City: Competitive Assets and Investment Opportunities."

Trailed by a flock of Providence reporters and camera crews, Cianci was the center of attention. His fellow mayors gave him a warm and sympathetic welcome.

"People get indicted in this business," shrugged Oakland mayor Jerry Brown. "Buddy's a good guy."

Discussing Cianci with a colleague, Akron mayor Donald Plusquellic said, "You know, the worst scumbag drug dealer in Akron that's been busted and convicted twenty-seven times is still entitled to the presumption of innocence the twenty-eighth time he's arrested."

When Cianci saw the mayor of Reno, Jeff Griffin, he joked, "Hey, they still got those prostitution houses out there?"

"Six blocks from the state capital," replied Griffin.

Later, Griffin said: "I heard they [the FBI] were sneaking around there in City Hall. . . . You do this job and you're going to get people mad at you—sometimes the feds."

Meanwhile, at the White House, Bush officials were deflecting questions about whether Cianci was still welcome to join the other mayors with the president in the Rose Garden. When Bush's chief of staff, Andrew Card, heard of the indictment, he declared brightly, "Buddy!"

"His career has been a roller coaster at other times, and I guess this is one of those roller-coaster moments," said Card, who had known Cianci since Card's days as a Massachusetts state legislator in the 1970s.

Cianci insisted that he would go to the White House to meet Bush, just as he'd met Bill Clinton and Bush's father and Ronald Reagan and Jimmy Carter and Gerald Ford.

But other mayors pulled him aside privately and said, "Hey, don't embarrass the president." Finally, Cianci got the message. He skipped the White House reception and left Washington early on Thursday, explaining that he had to get home early for his arraignment the next day.

The following morning the mayor waded through one of the biggest forests of cameras and microphones outside a Providence courthouse since Newport socialite Claus von Bulow's 1985 murder trial.

A television reporter promptly handed Cianci a setup line. "Are you concerned about the media circus?" he asked.

"What, are you calling yourself a clown?" the mayor deadpanned.

Cianci pleaded not guilty and was released on a fifty-thousand-dollar unsecured bond. The judge gave the mayor the standard instructions to refrain from excessive use of alcohol and the use of illegal drugs. Then Cianci reported to the U.S. marshal's office, where he was fingerprinted and forced to remove his toupee for a mug shot.

The Monday after his indictment Cianci launched his counterattack. That day Rose sent Judge Lagueux and the defense lawyers a letter acknowledging his mistake with the videotape. Rose said that he had also shown the tape to his sister, to elicit her reaction, but that he had not given any of the tapes to anyone, including Channel 10.

That night, Cianci and Art Coloian called reporters at home to tip them off to the news, even providing Rose's home address and phone number and urging them to hurry over because "the TV trucks are rolling." It was a time-honored tactic that the mayor employed in his dealings with the media; through the years, many a reporter had received a late-night phone call from Cianci, who would bark the reporter's last name in a gravelly voice, then announce, "This is your mayor." Often he would have a tip regarding one of his enemies, prefaced by "You didn't get this from me . . ."

The story about Rose and the tape was all over that night's eleven o'clock news and on the front page of the next morning's *Providence Journal*. Rose's lapse in judgment didn't rise to the level of misconduct that would jeopardize the government's case, but it did give Cianci an opening to turn the tables on his accusers.

On Tuesday morning the mayor went on the Don Imus show and ripped into the prosecution. "When I was a prosecutor, I never showed tapes that were sealed and sacrosanct," Cianci told Imus. "It's outrageous. It's cuckoo."

Imus agreed. The mayor milked it. "I guess Blockbuster's was closed that night," he quipped. "He had a little party at his house. I wonder if he sold popcorn."

Since his indictment, Cianci pointed out, Rose had been caught showing secret tapes, the judge had recused himself (after having called Cianci corrupt), and the government's star witness, Tony Freitas, was in jail.

"Absolutely, not guilty," Cianci pleaded before Imus and a national radio audience. "It's like Mario Puzo wrote that indictment. Awful . . . these people come off as holier than thou and they are the leaders of the free world, and, by the way, when you go against the United States of America, the federal government, they bring out the FBI, the IRS, the Coast Guard, the National Guard, the Navy SEALs. And there you are, alone, fighting this stuff."

The mayor also went after Dennis Aiken, the lead FBI agent. In the affidavit supporting his search warrant, Aiken had acknowledged having been censured in 1982 as part of an internal FBI investigation for lying about signing an internal document on behalf of another employee. Aiken later called it a mistake that was "stupid" and "embarrassing" but noted that he was promoted the following week. On *Imus*, Cianci inflated the matter, saying that Aiken had signed an affidavit admitting that he had obtained money under false pretenses, adding, "This is what you're fighting here."

Aiken, who was driving to work, heard Cianci on the radio and was furious. Walking past City Hall to his office a short time later, Aiken saw Cianci's staff administrator, Christopher Nocera, and told him to deliver a message to "your piece-of-shit mayor"—to stop lying about him on the radio, or else Aiken might sue.

Richard Egbert wrote to the U.S. attorney to condemn Aiken's behavior, and released copies of the letter to the press. Cianci took the opportunity to further embellish his accusations against Aiken, telling a *Providence Journal* reporter that the FBI agent had signed an affidavit saying that he lied—"whether it was about money, women, I don't know. . . . We go from tapes that are being released, private showings, sneak previews, now we go to witnesses being intimidated on the streets," fumed Cianci. "Don't forget, this man was armed."

Was the mayor suggesting that Aiken had brandished his weapon?

"I didn't say that," shouted Cianci. "He was armed! . . . He's an armed agent of the federal government. And it had nothing to do with the case. It had to do with him personally."

Of course, with Cianci, everything was personal. But his actions also served to spin the potential jury pool, deflect attention from the racketeering charges, and put the focus on the government's tactics. Shortly after the case became public, the mayor had publicly criticized Aiken, then sent word to the FBI agent, through an intermediary, that he was sorry and shouldn't have done it, according to Aiken. The agent tried to ignore Cianci. He viewed it as part of the mayor's strategy to discredit him and the FBI and discourage potential witnesses from cooperating. But when he heard Cianci on *Imus,* he and his family were upset. Cianci, Aiken reflected later, "likes to play head games, and I wouldn't play his head games. I bit once, and I shouldn't have."

ON SEPTEMBER 11, 2001, Buddy Cianci was at home, talking by phone on a local radio talk show, when the second hijacked airliner crashed into the World Trade Center. Like millions of Americans, he flipped on his television to watch the unfolding horror of the terrorist attacks on New York and Washington.

The next day, in the confusing aftermath, the world spotlight shone briefly on Providence, where authorities searched an Amtrak train suspected of carrying terrorists.

Earlier, police had surrounded the Westin Copley Hotel in Boston, where a band of terrorists were believed to be holed up. In the confusing reports that followed, four suspects were reported to have boarded an Amtrak train bound for Washington.

Television cameras captured the drama live as the train was stopped and surrounded in Providence. Police cars and undercover cars swerved down Gaspee Street, blocking off the train station just beneath the glittering white marble dome of the State House. Shoppers carrying Nordstrom's bags from the nearby Providence Place Mall gawked as more than fifty police officers swarmed into the station, some with bomb-sniffing dogs straining at their leashes.

At one point there was an unconfirmed report that one of the terrorists had slipped away from the train and was on the loose in Providence.

Into this pandemonium streaked the mayor's black limousine, cutting through the blockade and screeching to a halt in front. Cianci stepped out and marched into the train station to take charge. A while later a squadron of police marched out with a terrified, bearded Sikh wearing a green turban. He was arrested for possession of a ceremonial dagger. They escorted him through an angry mob of cursing, spitting people. Meanwhile, Cianci went before the cameras and briefed the nation on the situation.

In the weeks that followed, Cianci embraced the war on terrorism to the exclusion of all else—especially nagging questions about Operation Plunder Dome. Appearing on the Sunday-morning *Truman Taylor Show*, Cianci was eager to talk about terrorism prevention. But when the questioning turned to Plunder Dome, the mayor showed a side that he rarely revealed in public. Sidestepping Taylor's questions, Cianci pulled out some American flag pins and handed one to Taylor.

"See, I can't believe that a popular man like you is here with a national crisis, and you don't have a flag you're wearing," he said.

Taylor, a courtly, white-haired veteran broadcaster, gently persisted, and the mayor turned churlish.

"You don't even wear a flag," snapped Cianci. "I came here to assure people that we have task forces and everything else and you use it as a ploy to get me on to ask about Plunder Dome so your ratings go up and you get more for this show. . . . We have more people for brunch in my apartment than are watching." Growing redder and redder, Cianci sneered: "Put the pin on, will you? Show you're an American, at least."

When Taylor asked Cianci if he intended to fight in court rather than resign and strike a plea bargain, the mayor's eyebrows flared. "That's what America is about, isn't it? That's what our liberties are about, our freedoms are about, presumption of innocence, those things that terrorists want to take away from us."

By the end of the show, Cianci was out of control. "You think President Bush is going to sit back and not fight terrorists?" he asked. "You know something, they'll never come here because they like you. You're a terrorist."

Two weeks after September 11, the mayor decided that it was time to go to Ground Zero.

One morning, the mayor's limousine roared out of Providence, leading a convoy of six police cruisers with flashing lights and a truck bearing medical supplies and equipment for the rescue workers in New York. The procession made its way down Interstate 95. By the time they reached Connecticut, the policemen were talking back and forth on their radios about how embarrassing it was to have their lights flashing.

During a rest stop in Darien, where the mayor cheerfully bought everyone coffee, the officers discovered that the truck had a flat tire. They stalled fixing it so that the mayor would go on without them.

In the Bronx Cianci's motorcade, sans truck, started blowing through red lights, lights and sirens going, and roared into Manhattan. The Providence officers were mortified. The New York drivers were not pleased. When Cianci got stuck in traffic around Thirty-fourth Street, lights still flashing, angry New Yorkers started yelling and cursing.

"What the fuck are you doing?" shouted a motorist.

"We're here to help you people," an aide to the Providence police commissioner replied.

"Fuck you!" someone yelled back.

"The mayor of Providence is here," he tried to explain.

"Who the fuck cares?"

The mayor had asked a Providence officer with a friend in the New York Police Department to get them into Ground Zero, which was tightly guarded. The New York cop came through.

Passing through a checkpoint, Cianci made his way down West Street, through a shattered world of glass and steel, powdered in soot and ash that covered his shiny black shoes. The mayor pointed out the twisted metal beams and blown-out windows.

They turned a corner and beheld what had been the World Trade Center. The small party from Providence was awestruck.

Then the mayor's photographer took out his camera. The videographer, who normally filmed Providence traffic court for a cult show on cable access, *Caught in Providence*, hefted his camera. Cianci whipped off his white hard hat and began striking heroic poses among the ruins.

Later he pulled out his cell phone and made some calls. Cianci had been trying all day to line up a meeting with the mayor of New York, but Rudy Giuliani, not surprisingly, was too busy.

Then the mayor walked over to Amanda Milkovits, *The Providence Journal*'s police reporter, who was overcome by the scene. Cianci put his arm around her in a comforting way. "Whaddya think of our first date?" he said. "Not too romantic, huh?"

Before they left, Cianci had his photographer take his picture with Milkovits, and later sent it to her, just as he had had his picture taken thousands of times in thousands of settings with thousands of people over the years.

■

BACK AT CITY Hall, it was business as usual.

As Cianci prepared for his trial, he continued to preside over the Renaissance and project an image of a strong, confident leader moving Providence forward. He compared his racketeering indictment to the inevitable turbulence one experiences on a long-distance flight; just as the plane finally lands, he predicted, he and the city would ultimately reach their destination, unscathed.

The citizens of Providence showed little outrage. There was no public call for his resignation, just a tolerant and cynical, wait-and-see attitude from people who had seen it all before. Sure, Cianci was probably guilty, they said, but look at all the wonderful things he had done for the city. "This is Rhode Island, where every politician is a candidate for 'Movie of the Week,' " one woman told *The Boston Globe*. "The mayor's got pluck, and not only that, he's got wits. He's an excellent person, and he's done well for the city. Corruption? Corruption is everywhere." A waiter at a downtown restaurant said that the public sentiment was to leave Buddy alone. "Providence wouldn't be where it is today without the mayor's charisma," he said. "If there was a Providence coin, Buddy Cianci's face would be on it."

Cianci's approval rating actually went up after his indictment, from 60 to 64 percent, making him the most popular politician in Rhode Island. At the same time, 80 percent of those surveyed by a Brown University pollster felt that corruption in Providence was a problem, and half considered Cianci dishonest. The results showed that "honesty isn't a job requirement for a Rhode Island politician," according to an Associated Press story that ran in *The Washington Post*. Matt Lauer, a former Providence television newsman who had covered Cianci in the early 1980s, framed the paradox when he asked the mayor, in an interview for the *Today* show, if it was possible that he could love Providence and steal from it.

A delegation of government officials from Africa seemed bemused by Cianci's roguish image when they visited Providence in the summer of 2001. The leaders, from Nigeria, Cameroon, and other nations, were on a tour, sponsored by the U.S. State Department, to study government corruption. Rhode Island had been chosen for its historic reputation and also because of Operation Plunder Dome. The Africans met with Dennis Aiken, who talked about the FBI's investigative techniques. They were fascinated by Cianci; some wanted to meet him. But there was no time. The next day the delegates left Providence for the next stop on their U.S. corruption tour: Louisiana.

In Providence the big question, besides whether Buddy would survive, was whether the Renaissance could survive without him. The jury was divided. Some viewed the Renaissance as fragile, something that Cianci had willed into existence with his dynamic salesmanship, a work in progress that would wither away without him. Business leaders said that a critical mass had been reached, and that Providence's comeback could continue without Cianci—though his value in attracting development and generating excitement should not be discounted. But critics viewed the Renaissance as a façade concealing the rot of corruption that held the city back from true greatness. Lincoln Chafee, the former mayor of Warwick, who had succeeded his late father as U.S. senator, said that corporate executives had told him they avoided Providence because of Cianci and the stigma of corruption. Business leaders who backed Cianci or failed to speak out were cowardly enablers.

As the holidays approached, Cianci preferred to cultivate his Father Christmas image—until the Boston Pops tried to play Scrooge. For years, the mayor had taken center stage at the Pops' annual Christmas concert at the Providence Civic Center. In 2001, in need of perhaps more holiday cheer as his trial approached, he became infuriated when he learned that Civic Center officials were planning to cancel the Pops that year. Because so many free tickets were given out—to people in the community, and also to political cronies of all affiliations—the concert had become a perennial money loser. Cianci ordered that the show must go on—until he discovered that the Pops planned to replace him in his annual reading of " 'Twas the Night Before Christmas" with a professional actor. Cianci pointed out that *he* was a professional actor, with a Screen Actors Guild card from his guest stint on the TV show *Providence.* The Pops tried to appease Cianci by offering to let him be the guest conductor, but he ordered the show canceled. Finally, after aides told him how embarrassing a cancellation would be if the real story got out, he backed down. The Pops performed, with the mayor as their guest conductor.

On a rainy January morning in 2002, a few months before Cianci's trial was set to begin, Buff Chace sat in his downtown office and reflected on the Buddy Question. Chace, the Yankee patrician who had struggled for the past decade to rehab historic downtown buildings, was frustrated by what he called "the unfinished Renaissance."

"I don't think we'll be successful about developing ourselves until there's a process," he said. "Buddy is a throwback from the modern way. I briefly considered running for mayor a few years ago, out of frustration.

And I thought that the approach would have been not to criticize Buddy, but to praise him for what he has done and to say that now it is time for a new set of skills." Ironically, when Cianci had auctioned off his job for a day at a recent Trinity Repertory fund-raiser, Chace had made the winning bid, six thousand dollars. "You can be mayor for a day," Cianci had said. "You can take a ride in the helicopter. You can even go to the police and tell the colonel, 'You're not doing a good job.' " Chace's cousin piped up that the mayor also controlled the tax assessor's office. If he were mayor, Chace said, he would have created a clear process for developers to follow, replacing the byzantine path that shifted according to the whims of the mayor. Chace, who had sought unsuccessfully to create collaboration among rival downtown landowners and political factions, believed that cooperation was counter to Cianci's modus operandi. "My theory is that he's always created power by keeping people apart, so that everyone has to go to him. He's furious if you try to develop a relationship with the City Council."

On the wall behind Chace hung a huge, color-coded map of Providence, divided into wards bearing the names of each council member, like individual fiefdoms. Chace said that things had gotten worse since the mayor's indictment. Behind his public bravado, Cianci was distracted and unfocused. Projects had stalled. Part of the problem was the economic recession, particularly in the wake of the September 11 terrorist attacks. But there was also a sense of paralysis because of the uncertainty over Cianci's future. Relations were said to be strained between the mayor and his top downtown-development aide, Patricia McLaughlin, who was a witness against him on the University Club extortion charges.

Cianci, seeking to burnish his image as his trial approached, was even more prone to creating policy by press conference; Chace laughed as he recalled a recent news conference in which a hotel developer said that he hoped to break ground within three years. "Buddy's head jerked around," said Chace; the mayor interrupted to say that he expected the project to start sooner. Chace, a gentle, soft-spoken man in his early fifties with a full, brown beard, sighed and said, "Buddy has launched a huge PR campaign over the next ninety days to make us think that we can't live without him."

Chace, an investor in the Biltmore Hotel, where Cianci lived, was joined by the hotel's principal owner, John Cullen, who had just gotten off the red-eye from San Diego. Cullen ran a large pension-fund group, Greenfield Partners, which invested in hotels and real estate across America and also helped manage the pension funds of General Electric and Honeywell.

His mother managed the Biltmore and, he joked, sometimes swiped the mayor's newspapers from outside his Presidential Suite.

"Buddy has done a great job generating interest, and he is as pro-development as any urban mayor I've ever met," said Cullen. "Problem is, the city needs him to be like the old Buddy, to pick one project and bring it to conclusion." When the Providence River was moved, or the Convention Center was built, it was because of a remarkable alignment of forces. But with Cianci's future unclear, and an election year coming, and the resulting realignment of political forces, Cullen feared stagnation and a loss of momentum. He acknowledged that the city's corrupt image was also a deterrent to business investment, although he considered that reputation overblown and credited Cianci with making Providence "a major-league city." Still, Cullen, who had spent sixty-one million dollars on hotels around the country in the past nine months, was reluctant to invest in Providence, because of the tortuous political climate. "Buff finds the hardest buildings to do," said Cullen. "He's a bored, rich guy who does it out of a sense of noblesse oblige. I've taken his money and invested it in Sun Valley and San Diego. It's hard to allocate more capital for Providence until there's more cooperation." Cullen said that most investors would laugh off Chace's projects. "Single-digit returns, with heavy politics, wouldn't make it onto my desk, let alone off of it."

As maddening as the business climate could be, Cullen, who spent more than two hundred days a year on the road, also loved Providence. He enjoyed its small scale, its fine restaurants, its sense of history, and its rebellious spirit. Sometimes he took day trips from his home in Annapolis, Maryland, catching a 6 A.M. flight from Baltimore, spending the day, having a great meal in a great restaurant, and returning home by 10 P.M. "Some of the things I like least about Providence I also enjoy the most. It's one of the most sophisticated small towns in America. It has all the best urban experiences of New York, Chicago, or Boston, the dining and culture, without the negatives: congestion, urban anger, crime. You rarely find a city with such natural barriers, confining it so that all the economic variables can ricochet to create a great urban center. It's confined by the highways, by Brown and College Hill, the rivers and the bay. . . . You have a city with all these different people . . . all forced to live with one another. I think that's fun. The success and the problem of Providence is that it's contained naturally. It's the biggest small town I know. Unlike many other places, politics is one of the city's great industries. If they could find a way to turn it into money . . ." His voice trailed off as he laughed in agreement with the suggestion that some had.

"From the end of the mill era until 1975, Providence lost its way," said Cullen. "Then it decided to return to its roots as an incubator, and to that spirit of defiance, of going against the grain. They moved a *river*. It's incredible how they mustered the force, the capital to defy the conventional wisdom. That's a strength. However, if misdirected, it can be incredibly bad."

People in Providence loved Cianci because Cianci was a reflection of Providence, in all its glory and contradictions. "A mayor reflects every part of his community, which is why Daley could never be mayor of New York, and Giuliani could never be mayor of Boston," said Cullen. "Providence made Buddy. And Providence will go to the finish line with him, kicking and screaming and loving every minute."

In the weeks leading up to the trial, Cianci increased his already frenetic pace. He raced around Providence attending news conferences, banquets, groundbreakings, art openings, weddings, wakes. If a garage door opened in Silver Lake, one city councilman joked, the mayor was there to take credit. After the power went out at Rhode Island Hospital, the mayor came striding down the darkened corridors, patients cheering his name. When the workers at the Biltmore threatened to strike, he mediated a settlement, averting cancellation of a wedding reception and winning an invitation from the grateful bride. Posing for a photograph with former state transportation directors, he cracked, "Which one of you guys did I grab the most money from?" Then he helped them blow out the candles on a cake marking the agency's one hundredth birthday and quipped, "I wish your pensions all get bigger." At a groundbreaking for a new Brooks drugstore in the North End, Cianci declined to climb into the bulldozer; he told a funny story about how something had gone wrong when he took the controls of a bulldozer at the groundbreaking for the new police station. The next thing he knew, a building being torn down had burst into flames. Wherever Cianci went, people shook his hand, patted his back, said they were praying for him, honked their horns, shouted "Bud-dee!"

In late February Cianci stood on the courthouse steps after a pretrial hearing and cut off reporters' questions, announcing that he had to go to the Purim parade, a Jewish festival on the East Side. He turned to *Journal* columnist Charlie Bakst, who is Jewish, and said: "Why don't you follow me? Come on, Bakst, it's your kind of day." The veteran political columnist had followed Cianci's career from way back, and been one of his most persistent critics. "Buddy Cianci is bright, energetic and funny," Bakst wrote after Cianci announced his 1990 comeback. "So why is the prospect of his return as mayor—even his running for mayor—so troubling? Perhaps it is because elections should be appeals to the conscience and ideals of the community, to the best within us, not to the dark side of society that makes celebrities of criminals and embraces as heroes those who abuse the public's trust."

Though Cianci would privately, and sometimes publicly, curse Bakst—using him as a foil in his populist-tinged attacks on *The Providence Journal*—he also believed in the dictum that you kept your friends close and your enemies closer. The irascible mayor and the curmudgeonly columnist were like an old married couple, often kibbitzing at various events. Every Rosh Hashanah, Bakst gave the mayor a challah, which he looked forward to receiving. Cianci told Bakst that he wanted to find someone willing to open a kosher restaurant in Providence.

Bakst was sitting in the *Journal*'s newsroom, after the court hearing, when his phone rang. It was Cianci, offering him a ride to the Purim festivities. The mayor's police-chauffeured limousine already was outside the *Journal* building on Fountain Street, which Cianci had often threatened to rename Cianci Way. Bakst got in. Joining the mayor in the backseat, Bakst was surprised to see him studying briefing papers on Purim. The holiday celebrates the Old Testament story of how the Jewish queen of Persia, Esther, saved the Jews from being massacred by the evil prime minister, Haman, who was hanged instead. Cianci and Bakst discussed the finer points of Purim; for instance, the three-cornered pastries, *hamantaschen*, which represented Haman's three-cornered hat. Bakst asked Cianci what he knew about Purim. "I know that every year I go," the mayor replied. "I know that you remind me of Haman." As Cianci rustled his briefing papers, Bakst said, "You don't have to tell them the story. They'll know the story." "Yeah," replied Cianci, "but they have to know I know it!"

The parade had already stepped off when the mayor's limousine arrived at the Jewish Community Center, across from Brown Stadium. Cianci bounded out of the car and joined in the merry scene—clowns, noisemakers, klezmer music, people dancing in the street, someone in a duck suit, another person in a rabbit costume, a group of young boys in yarmulkes. The mayor shook hands with a rabbi outside the Providence Hebrew Day School. People smiled and posed for pictures with Cianci, hugging and kissing him. An old man taking pictures rushed up to greet him; Cianci had appointed his son "Mayor of Taft Avenue" many years ago. "You're still that!" Cianci declared, beaming. "No one can ever take that away from you!"

After the parade Cianci addressed the crowd. He spoke eloquently about how the Jewish people, through the years, had shown "tremendous bravery, determination, and strength in the face, by the way, of great adversity." In farewell, he shouted, "Shalom." To loud cheers, the mayor climbed back into his limousine, Bakst in tow. As they returned downtown, the mayor elated from the warm reception, Bakst steered the conversation back to Plunder Dome. He asked if Cianci felt ashamed for being in court that morning. The mood was shattered. "Charlie, happy Purim," the mayor said abruptly, ending the conversation.

As his trial approached, Cianci was waging two campaigns—one aimed at the jury pool, another for his reelection in November. He spoke confidently of being acquitted, then going on to win a record seventh term. After that, he would leave City Hall on his own terms, to travel, write his memoirs, host a radio talk show, and oversee the Vincent A. Cianci Jr. Library & Archives. Even with the baggage of a criminal trial in an election year, Cianci would be hard to beat in November. A host of civic leaders and would-be mayoral candidates who felt privately that it was time for a change dared not say so publicly, fearing retribution. Instead, they waited to see what would happen. Many doubted that the prosecution could convince a jury in Providence to convict the irrepressible Cianci.

Only one man dared enter the ring against Cianci. In February David Cicilline, a wealthy criminal-defense lawyer and liberal state representative from the East Side who drove a Rolls-Royce, announced his candidacy for mayor. Promising "no more business as usual," Cicilline pledged not to accept campaign contributions from city workers and to address the ills behind the Renaissance—corruption, unsafe neighborhoods, poor schools. Cicilline was an intriguing candidate. A short, cherubic man in his early forties, he had many of the demographic bases of the old and new Providences covered—he was half Jewish, half Italian, conversant in Spanish, openly gay, and the son of a prominent mob lawyer, Jack Cicilline, who had been Mayor Joe Doorley's chief policy adviser in the 1960s. As a college student at Brown University, the younger Cicilline had cofounded the College Democrats with two classmates—John F. Kennedy, Jr., and William Mondale, son of the former vice president. Cicilline also was friendly with

Plunder Dome prosecutor Richard Rose; the two men cotaught a class, "Advanced Criminal Procedure," at Roger Williams University Law School.

Cicilline vowed to run a grassroots campaign and not to be intimidated by Cianci. With Cicilline expected to make a strong showing on the East Side and Cianci likely to do well in the Italian wards, both men saw that the campaign could hinge on the growing Hispanic vote. Cicilline spent a lot of time walking the city's Hispanic neighborhoods and put his campaign headquarters in South Providence. Cianci, using the power of his office, appointed Hispanics to city posts, including a liaison to the Latino community, and steered city funds to Hispanic community groups. Cianci, who had learned since his narrow upset of Joe Doorley never to take an election for granted, was clearly bothered by Cicilline's criticisms. A few weeks before his trial began, Cianci and Cicilline met at a ribbon cutting for new, lead-free housing in a blighted South Providence neighborhood. Cianci threw his arm playfully around Cicilline's shoulders and told his photographer to take their picture. A few days later, sitting in his office, Cianci pulled out the photo of himself and Cicilline and showed it to a reporter. "That was a good event," he said, an edge to his voice. "Cicilline says I'm not doing enough in the neighborhoods."

Privately, Cianci predicted that Cicilline wouldn't even win the gay vote. Gays didn't respect him, Cianci contended, because he had been slow to come out. Actually, Cicilline was well regarded in the gay community, which took pride in having an openly gay candidate for mayor; if he won, Providence would surpass Tempe, Arizona, as the largest city in the United States with a gay mayor. But Cianci had also done a lot to support the gay community. Since the mid-1990s, he had employed a gay liaison, supported health insurance for city workers with same-sex partners, and been visible in Providence's vibrant gay community—marching in the Pride Parade, flying the pink flag atop City Hall, and showing up at other events. The mayor, who had been accused of making homophobic remarks about past opponents and even Carol Channing's stage manager, also recognized the value of gays to the city's Renaissance image as a trendy arts community. And the sizeable gay community, estimated at 10 percent of the electorate, voted. *Girlfriends* magazine rated Providence as a gay-friendly city. A few weeks before his trial, Cianci appeared on *The O'Reilly Factor,* a national conservative talk show on Fox Television, and defended his decision to order reluctant firefighters to send a truck to the Pride Parade; some firefighters had balked, fearing that people would think that they were gay, and had hired the ACLU to sue the city. Afterward Cianci received hate mail for his defense of gays—"from a ring of trailer parks around the country," he joked.

Beyond his political motivation for embracing the gay community, Cianci also seemed to enjoy the support that he found there, especially as the shadow of Operation Plunder Dome grew. A few weeks after his indictment, on the night of his sixtieth birthday, Cianci stopped by a gay nightclub, Pulse, near Rhode Island Hospital. It was late, and nearly naked men danced around poles. Patrons stuffed dollar bills in their waistbands. Lady Chablis, the female impersonator from Savannah, Georgia, who was made famous by the best-selling book *Midnight in the Garden of Good and Evil*, was the featured performer. The mayor, who arrived alone except for one of his advance men, invited Rudy Cheeks, a columnist from the alternative weekly *Providence Phoenix*, and his wife, Susan, to join him at his table up front. Cheeks, who had known the mayor for years, thought that he seemed more subdued than usual. He sat there, smoking and drinking, trading quips with Lady Chablis, and basking in the adulation of patrons who shook his hand and offered their unqualified support.

Cianci, Cicilline later joked, "spent more time in gay bars than me."

Another night shortly after his indictment, after the Gay Ball at the Biltmore, the party spilled over into the mayor's Presidential Suite. Twice after midnight Cianci summoned an aide to bring cases of champagne for him and his guests, including a group of transvestites in dresses. That summer the mayor showed up at a gay nightclub downtown owned by his City Hall gay liaison, for the Ocean State Leather contest.

The emcee, *Village Voice* sex columnist Tristan Taormino, was impressed by the solidarity of Rhode Island's community. "How many leatherpeople can there be in the smallest state in the country?" she later wrote. "The answer is *plenty*, and what they lack in numbers, they more than make up for in passion."

Shortly after the leather sashes were draped on the winners, Cianci showed up to make a speech. The mayor was surrounded by whip-toting dominatrixes and a sea of leather jockstraps, chaps, and bizarre props (a Dunkin' Donuts box, a *Star Wars* light saber). When he finished speaking, Cianci giddily asked one of the drag queens to do a special number for him, and she obliged.

Rudy Giuliani would never show up at such an event in a million years, let alone be as gracious as Mayor Cianci, marveled Taormino. "Racketeering, schmacketeering, his recent indictment has yet to overshadow his gay-positive attitude," she wrote. "The mayor used the word 'transgendered' so many times that I wanted to marry him."

In the weeks leading up to his trial, in the spring of 2002, Cianci was invited to a drag queen's dream—Liza Minnelli's star-studded wedding in New York. Cianci had met Minnelli's fiancé through Anthony Quinn.

As the mayor emerged from the Waldorf, amid the throng of celebrities, he suddenly heard people chanting, "Bud-dee, Bud-dee!" Cianci looked over to see a group of drag queens from the weekly Sunday brunch at Intermezzo in Providence. They had driven down to New York to stand outside the Waldorf for a glimpse of Liza.

Despite the frenetic pace, there was also a pathetic, almost tragic quality to Cianci's rambles. He was like Frank Sinatra in his later years, still capable of brilliance but unable to hit the high notes consistently. There were also signs that the mayor was using cocaine, according to a former aide who spent a lot of time with him during that period.

A few days after Cianci's indictment, the aide said, he was in the Presidential Suite at the Biltmore, packing the mayor's cologne and other toiletries for his trip to the U.S. mayors' conference in Washington, when he noticed a white plastic bag containing three narrow clear-plastic bags with white powder. The bag was at the bottom of the mayor's black carry-on travel bag. The aide, who said that he was familiar with cocaine from college, said that he tasted the powder, and it was cocaine.

The aide said that he held up one of the plastic bags to show another Cianci aide and asked, "Hey, what's this?" The other aide smiled and replied, "Oh, that's the mayor's special foot powder." (The second aide confirmed the incident, but said that he didn't know what was actually in the bag, and that he had never seen Cianci use cocaine.)

The first aide recalled other occasions when he would brush white powder off the lapels of the mayor's suit as he stepped out of the Presidential Suite. A month or so after Cianci's indictment, the aide said, he was at the Black Heritage Ball at the Westin Hotel. Upstairs, near the piano bar, the mayor went into a small men's room that was empty and ordered the aide to guard the door. When the aide stood outside, Cianci told him to stand inside the door. The aide complied. As he stood there, he said, Cianci went into the stall and the aide listened to him snorting. The mayor was quick and nobody tried to come in, the aide said.

Other former aides said that they had never seen Cianci use drugs.

They dismissed the rumors as false, emanating from the mayor's energetic lifestyle and late nights on the town.

At times Cianci's drinking become more evident.

Cianci had always been a heavy drinker, but for the most part he wasn't sloppy. He had an amazing tolerance for alcohol. During morning press conferences he would have brandy in his coffee, at lunchtime a few glasses of wine. He often sipped what appeared to be ice water from a clear glass with his name inscribed in gold letters; it was actually chilled vodka or tequila. When he showed up at the Civic Center, an official was ready with his "apple juice"—a glass of Jack Daniel's.

As his trial loomed, Cianci could often be found sitting morosely at the bar in Davio's or Mediterraneo. Laurel Casey saw him a few times in Davio's in January 2002, and he was drinking quite a bit of bourbon. He was sullen and insular, not gregarious. When she asked him about the trial, he was stoic, saying, "I'll be fine."

A few weeks before his trial, the mayor's timing was off when he ventured into an Aretha Franklin concert at the Providence Performing Arts Center.

Cianci had attended quite a few events that night, from a banquet in West Warwick to something in nearby Seekonk, Massachusetts. At each stop, according to an advance person who accompanied him, the mayor had at least two Scotches. By the time he reached PPAC, the aide estimated, it was up to at least eight to ten. At the theater, as Cianci waited in the wings to give Franklin a key to the city, he had another.

Franklin was wrapping up "Freeway of Love," toward the end of her set, when Cianci stumbled onstage. "Aretha," he called out. "I'm the mayor of Providence, and even I couldn't get a ticket."

Franklin seemed taken aback. She stopped singing and leaned against the piano, her other hand on her hip. There was an awkward, frozen silence in the crowd as the mayor presented her with the key to the city and a jar of his marinara sauce. Then Cianci told the renowned Queen of Soul that it was great to have "the Soul of Queen" in Providence for such a terrific concert.

Afterward, Cianci asked an aide how he had done. The aide didn't want to tell him the truth, so he fudged. But the mayor knew.

"Well, she was an uptight bitch," he snapped. "Her show's over. She's seen better days."

CHAPTER TWELVE

Pomp and Circumstantial Evidence

One week before his sixty-first birthday, on April 23, 2002, the reputed godfather of Providence City Hall awoke in the Presidential Suite at the Biltmore. Judgment day had arrived for Buddy Cianci.

The trappings of one of the mayor's Renaissance pageants were already evident outside his fifteenth-floor windows, from the photographers staking out their positions in front of the gray courthouse to the crowd of spectators lining up for a seat in the courtroom for the opening arguments to the buses emblazoned with ads from a local television station that screamed, OPERATION PLUNDER DOME: CIANCI ON TRIAL.

On the mayor's bathroom counter, on Styrofoam heads, were the hairpieces that he rotated, depending on the occasion. On this morning, Cianci selected a silvery gray toupee that he had begun wearing in recent months, one that gave him a more distinguished, statesmanlike bearing. There was a backup toupee with longer hair, for when his remaining real hair grew out on the sides and in the back; an older, darker toupee; and a swirly, salt-and-pepper one, which he wore to blizzards, fires, and crime scenes, known as "the tousled piece." The mayor's hair began life halfway around the globe, on the heads of peasant women in China, where corrupt public officials were executed by hanging. The women wrapped their hair in turbans, to protect it from the oxidizing effect of air and sunshine, then sold it to companies that stripped out the color and recolored it. Low-paid wig makers then wove the strands by hand, mixing in synthetic fibers for white hair, to create luxuriously thatched hairpieces that sold for a few thousand dollars. Cianci sent his toupees by limousine to Squire's Hair Salon, near Brown University, where the stylists referred to them as BIB—"Buddy in a box." If Cianci were convicted and sent to prison, he would be stripped of his toupees. Although Cianci's rugs were famous in Rhode Island—"hair helper," he called them—in prison they would be considered a disguise.

After the toupee, which was applied with double-sided adhesive tape, came a layer of bronze makeup, to darken Cianci's ghostly complexion for the television cameras. Downstairs, in a mobile radio studio in a converted camper parked near the courthouse, WHJJ talk-show host John DePetro previewed the trial for Don Imus. DePetro referred to the case as "Operation Thugs and Bad Rugs." With his makeup-induced tan, Cianci "looks like he should be playing mixed doubles in Boca," DePetro quipped. Outside the courthouse, the mayor's court jester, Walter Miller, performed card tricks in a red, white, and blue stovepipe hat that glittered with sequins. "Pannone's a phony, he's throwing the baloney," chanted Miller, riffling his cards. "Four of hearts, Buddy's innocent." He turned over a four of clubs. "Well, it's a four."

Toupee in place and makeup applied, resplendent in a charcoal suit with a gold city seal and a tiny American flag pinned to the lapel, Cianci made his way downstairs to his limousine for the ride around Kennedy Plaza. It was with a sense of disbelief that he climbed the steps of the federal courthouse, nodding and waving to cheering spectators, to go on trial for racketeering. The RICO law had been designed to go after Mafia bosses, who ordered beatings and murders; to accuse the mayor of running a racketeering enterprise out of City Hall, he said, was "nuts." A few weeks earlier, sitting in the privacy of his office (a gag order prevented him from discussing the charges publicly before and during the trial), Cianci had dissected the government's case. "I've read through the discovery," he said, "and they don't have one person giving me any money. Now, they have someone saying he gave Coloian money, or Corrente money, to give to me—not that I believe it—but there's no way they gave any money to me. That's bullshit." The alleged extortion of $250,000 in campaign contributions from tow-truck operators? "I don't even know those guys. They're big, burly guys who go into the worst neighborhoods, risk a bullet for a tow. They're going to be intimidated by me?" Edward Voccola's suspicious School Department lease? "I sign hundreds of leases. The only time I get involved is if somebody has a question. I found in our files a report that Judge Brodsky did, recommending we sign that lease. He's a respected judge, a former prosecutor." Thirty years earlier Cianci had helped Irving Brodsky prosecute Raymond Patriarca; after becoming mayor, Cianci had named Brodsky city solicitor and later appointed him a housing-court judge. (Brodsky had died in 2000.) With his impending trial, Cianci's life had come full circle. The onetime mob prosecutor was being prosecuted under a law inspired by gangsters like Patriarca.

The mayor warmed to his defense. "Let's talk about the University Club," he said. "If you took the facts, took my name out of it and made it Mayor X, and presented it as an essay on the bar exam, what would you do? You'd indict the club leaders for attempted bribery. If I'm a prick, if I'm the ogre they think I am, do you think it would have taken me twenty-five years to fuck them?" The city had opposed the club for safety reasons. "When I'm eighty-five and sitting in Scalabrini Green [nursing home], I don't want two guys walking up to me and handing me a subpoena because there was a fire and three people died."

The phone rang before Cianci could address the witness-tampering charge involving Steve Antonson or the RICO charges themselves, which accused the mayor of using underlings to commit crimes on his behalf. That was the most worrisome aspect of the case for the mayor—the Antonson tapes and the overarching nature of RICO. He worried that the tapes could make jurors more inclined to believe the other charges. His lawyers had asked the judge for a separate trial on the University Club counts, arguing that they didn't fit the pattern of the other alleged bribes and could prejudice the jury. But the judge disagreed. So now Cianci's strategy was to downplay the University Club affair. His lawyer Richard Egbert characterized it as "two kids fighting in the sandbox." In Providence a jury might find it a stretch to criminalize the mayor's legendary vindictiveness. Cianci liked to tell a joke in which he was sitting in prison with a group of inmates, swapping stories about what they were in for. One prisoner robbed a bank. Another killed someone. A third embezzled a million dollars. And the mayor? "I'm in because I got into the University Club." But the Antonson tapes, on which a surly Cianci tells a witness to lie to the FBI, might not be so amusing to a jury being asked to decide whether the mayor was a criminal mastermind.

Inside the courthouse, in the small, brightly lit courtroom of chief U.S. district judge Ernest C. Torres, the lawyers were gathering. An upright oar painted silver, beside the Rhode Island flag with the motto "Hope," signaled that it was also an admiralty court. In the mid-1990s some independent filmmakers had cast the mayor to play the judge in a courtroom drama based on the bloody Prohibition shooting of rumrunners by the Coast Guard in Narragansett Bay. But the financing fell through.

Richard Rose marched in carrying a thick black binder labeled "Battle Plan." The pressure on the prosecutor had increased since his faux pas in showing friends the Plunder Dome videotape. The previous summer, a judge had fined him five hundred dollars and suspended him from the case for thirty days.

In the months that followed, Rose had braced himself for the possibility of being fired or having the case taken away from him. His superiors in Providence were supportive, but he worried about what someone in the Justice Department in Washington might do, given the magnitude of the case. The previous fall, Rose had attended the annual banquet of the NAACP in Providence at the Marriott. Cianci was one of the speakers. At one point during his speech, the mayor looked pointedly across the large room at Rose's table and said, "And I guarantee you one thing—I'll be back next year!"

It wasn't until the last few months before the trial that Rose felt confident that the case would remain his. As he entered the courtroom, a few of the defense lawyers grumbled in the hallway about a recent message Rose had put on his answering machine at work, saying that he was off "doing the Lord's work." Rose said later that he had meant the message to be tongue in cheek, but the pretrial tension was evident.

Rose knew that he had a lot to prove—not just the charges against Cianci and his codefendants, Frank Corrente, Edward Voccola, and Richard Autiello, but also about his own abilities. He had never lost a trial to a lead defendant as a prosecutor, but the stakes had never been so high. If he failed, he worried that some people would say that he hadn't been up to it—that he was there because he was black. He could quote the lyrics to rapper Eminem's song "Lose Yourself," about a man who has one shot at glory:

> Would you capture it . . . or just let it slip?
> His palms are sweaty, knees weak, arms are heavy
> There's vomit on his sweater already, Mom's spaghetti.

Rose didn't want spaghetti sauce on his shirt. But he also looked forward to the battle. There weren't many jobs that carried the adrenaline rush of athletics; a trial was Rose's opportunity "to put it all on the line."

In the hallway outside the courtroom, Richard Egbert hitched up his pants like a gunfighter. A short, fifty-five-year-old man with a bristly mustache and round wire-rimmed glasses, Egbert, one of the top criminal-defense lawyers in the Northeast, was "the guy you don't want to see represent the guy you arrested," said the retired detective commander of the Rhode Island State Police Brian Andrews. A manic worker, Egbert would awake at four o'clock in the morning and read documents, then walk around the city at dawn, along the restored waterfront and among the glittering skyscrapers of the Renaissance City.

Providence was not like Egbert's home base of Boston. It was smaller, more intimate. For all the years that Egbert had been coming down to Rhode Island, he still found it strange to see his face staring out from a newspaper box, or have passersby stop him on the street and urge him to keep up the good fight. He had defended prominent Rhode Island mobsters and politicians, including the former governor Edward DiPrete; the mayor of North Providence, who was acquitted of taking bribes from developers; and the chief justice of the state supreme court, who was impeached for consorting with mobsters.

Egbert also was no stranger to federal corruption probes of Buddy Cianci's City Hall; in the 1980s he had represented two of Cianci's former top aides, Ronald Glantz and Joseph DiSanto. In fact, with Glantz listed as a potential government witness in the Plunder Dome trial, to testify to past corruption, the government had tried unsuccessfully to have Egbert disqualified as Cianci's lawyer. (The judge ruled that Glantz's testimony would be inadmissible unless Cianci took the stand in his defense and denied ever having taken any bribes, a decision that had not yet been made. If Glantz did testify, Egbert would have to step aside and permit another defense lawyer to cross-examine him.)

The son of a Jewish garment worker and a housewife who traced their roots to Nazi-occupied Austria, Egbert grew up around Boston and came of age during the turbulent sixties. As a student at the University of Massachusetts he had seen his best friend's head split open by a policeman's baton during an antiwar protest, a searing memory that served to remind him of his adversary in the courtroom—"a government out of control." A plaque hanging in Egbert's office, from a client acquitted in a bank-fraud case, said, ACT LIKE A SICILIAN AND THINK LIKE A JEW. Egbert saw himself as a check against the power of prosecutors and the police. When a mob client discovered a bugging device in his car, Egbert sent photocopies to state and federal law enforcement agencies until the FBI sheepishly claimed it. One of his favorite movies was *My Cousin Vinny.*

In the courtroom Egbert was a tenacious cross-examiner, someone who would methodically exhume every skeleton from a government witness's closet and then reassemble it, piece by piece, in front of the jury. His withering interrogation of mob informant Billy Ferle, in a 1988 trial in Providence, had helped mobster Bobo Marrapese—whom Cianci had once prosecuted—win acquittal for the baseball-bat murder of a motorist after a traffic altercation. Ferle, Bobo's alleged accomplice, kept saying that "Bobo made me do it." Egbert pounded away at Ferle as if he were the speed bag that the lawyer pummeled at home. He demanded to know whether Ferle would also attribute the sun's coming up in the morning to Bobo. A defeated Ferle agreed. When Egbert sat down, he knew he had nailed it. He turned to Bobo, who said, "I'm so happy I could burn a church." The case had been memorable for another reason; during the trial Egbert had met his third and current wife, Patty, a dentist, at a local restaurant. When she came to court to watch, she noticed Bobo's "satanic eyebrows" as he looked her over and told Egbert to make sure his client didn't look at the jurors.

One of the biggest trials in Providence history took place in a Beaux Arts granite courthouse that stood where Abraham Lincoln once spoke. The one-hundred-year-old building, richly appointed in marble, mahogany, and oak, had recently been restored to its original grandeur by a contractor who had gotten immunity for admitting to bribes to the former governor Edward DiPrete for earlier government work. Until recently the soda machines at federal court had been supplied by David Ead's vending company.

Every seat in the courtroom was taken as the lawyers in *United States* v. *Cianci* prepared to deliver their opening arguments. Down the hall, more people sat in the "remote room," where a large, flat-screen television had been erected in an unused courtroom to handle the overflow. Televised proceedings were rare in federal court, which still banned cameras; another notable case where a video feed had been used because of strong public interest was the trial of Oklahoma City bomber Timothy McVeigh.

Mary Tassone, a sixty-six-year-old retired artificial-fruit maker and veteran court watcher, wore Spectator Badge Number One. She had been attending trials for years and was on a first-name basis with the courthouse personnel and most of the lawyers. "It's better than sitting home and watching soap operas, right?" she said. Tassone would have liked to have been on Cianci's jury, or any jury, but she was too well known around the courthouse. The previous month she had gotten excited when she was summoned for jury duty in state court. "They asked me what I do. I said, 'I go to court.' So they threw me off. They told me my name could come up again in three years. I said, 'I'll be dead in three years.' " Tassone, who had no rooting interest in Cianci's trial, handicapped the case: "The only thing they've got him on is the University Club, isn't it? They don't have him on tape. They don't have him on video." But she was making no predictions. "Never underestimate a jury," she said sagely, "or what they might do."

It had taken three days to pick a jury of eight men and four women. Only one juror lived in Providence, and she was a Texan who had attended Brown University. The process revealed the interwoven nature of Providence. One prospective juror, John F. Smollins, had run for mayor as an Independent in 1974, when Cianci beat Joe Doorley, challenging the candidates to a one-mile footrace to City Hall. (Nobody showed up.) He went to the same church as Frank Corrente. He had once had his car repaired by Richard Autiello. He knew Edward Voccola. He was excused. Another juror, a retired naval-police officer in Newport, said that Cianci had attended his twenty-fifth wedding anniversary celebration at the Jamestown Country Club in 1975—but the juror couldn't remember why Cianci came, who invited him, or whether they had even spoken. "I was half in the bag," he explained. He made the cut.

The trial was expected to last two months or more, and Cianci worried about the negative publicity that it would generate for Providence. He was determined to maintain a vigorous public schedule, to show that he was still in control. During the lunch recess on the first day of jury selection, Cianci hurried over to an Urban League of Rhode Island luncheon, where he was applauded for saying, "Even the United States of America couldn't keep me away!" That night he attended a book sale at a branch of the Providence Public Library, where he purchased a book on Harry Truman, one of his favorite politicians, and *The Law of Mass Communications: Freedom and Control of the Broadcast Media.* The next morning, on his way to court, Cianci stopped off at the Fleet Skating Center to celebrate Bike to Work Day, clambering on an oversized tricycle for a quick photo op.

Beyond establishing Cianci's guilt or innocence, the trial would also be a referendum on the Providence Renaissance. To Richard Rose, the Renaissance was a façade; to Richard Egbert, it was Exhibit A in the mayor's defense. Those themes became apparent in their opening arguments.

This was a case, said Rose, about a mayor who ran a criminal enterprise out of City Hall. He pointed at Cianci—"the head of the criminal enterprise"—and Corrente, sitting to the mayor's left—"the bagman."

"Cianci's criminal enterprise collected illegal contributions and cash in exchange for hundreds of thousands of dollars in tax breaks, jobs, leases, and city contracts," said Rose, speaking in a measured yet forceful voice. "Indeed, when defendant Cianci wanted a private club membership and the club said no, he used his criminal enterprise to take one."

Egbert, when his turn came, tore into the government's case as a house of cards, constructed by witnesses who were "liars, cheats, and thieves."

"These are people who have been committing crimes since the day they could breathe," thundered Egbert in his raspy, booming voice. "They would con anyone. They would lie to their friends, their family. They would lie to the government and they are people who will lie to you."

Egbert might have considered calling the author Tom Wolfe as a character witness. Speaking on the eve of the trial at a Brown University conference on "The City: No Limits," Wolfe praised the Providence Renaissance as an example of how cities can be reborn through the arts as opposed to factory jobs. In the new "psychology economy," said Wolfe, "money is exchanged for an experience, not a product. You bring home nothing— except an experience, a gratification." Cities are "the stage for ambition. Nobody in the country has ever understood this better than Mayor Cianci of Providence."

Meanwhile, light-years from leafy College Hill, in the gritty streets of Manton near Ead's vending office, the brief for the prosecution was filed by Keven McKenna, a political gadfly and former municipal judge, as he declared his candidacy for mayor. Standing in a parking lot near St. Teresa of Avila Church, McKenna contrasted Cianci's illusory Renaissance with the downtrodden neighborhoods. "Real City is not the city of Nobel Prize winners teaching at tax-exempted universities. Real City is a city of the high school dropouts living in three-deckers. Real City is not the soothing glow of WaterFire. It is the slinking shadows of rats running around the neighborhood garbage piles under a disappearing moon."

Indeed, the proliferation of rats was a growing concern in the neighborhoods. One frustrated letter writer complained that City Hall was not doing enough to address the problem, and that the rats would soon outnumber the humans in Providence. (Where was Buckles Melise and his truckload of rat poison when you needed him?) That spring Cianci sent city residents a newsletter calling rats "Providence's Public Enemy Number 1." Rats, the mayor wrote, "carry innumerable diseases and expose us to unspeakable filth. They contribute nothing of value to society. Rats feed on garbage and if you provide access, they will surely take advantage of it."

And the vermin problem was about to get worse. The government's first witness was a 365-pound rat named David Ead.

LATE ON TUESDAY afternoon, after the opening arguments, Ead lumbered to the stand. The decision to call him as the leadoff witness came as a surprise, given his liabilities and the other evidence. But it also made sense. The public had focused on the Freitas tapes as the heart of the government's case. But they weren't—Cianci wasn't on them. Eight of the twelve counts against him related to the three bribes that Ead said he had arranged with the mayor—the five thousand dollars for Christopher Ise's job, the ten thousand for the Ronci tax settlement, and the proposed ten thousand for the Freitas vacant lots.

Over the next three days Cianci sat grimly as Ead described his efforts to ingratiate himself with the mayor. He described how the relationship progressed from politics to payoffs, from free soda for Cianci's campaign headquarters to an illicit campaign contribution in the backseat of Ead's Cadillac, an acknowledgment of a payoff at the Columbus Day parade on Federal Hill, Ead's desire for a city pension and free Blue Cross, a box of fine cigars for the mayor at Christmas, a shared laugh over a payoff, and discussions of extortion and bribery. The jurors also got their first glimpse of the Freitas tapes. Rose played a tape in which Ead boasted: "Anytime I have to do business, I go direct to the mayor . . . he and I have been buddies for twenty-five years."

Ead also described walking into the mayor's office and voicing frustration over the resistance of city tax officials to the Ronci tax settlement. "Vincenzo, you've got all stupid people working at City Hall," he recalled telling Cianci.

During a recess, Egbert mocked Ead's testimony. "Vincenzo," he said, laughing. "I like that."

Before the trial, Egbert had been laying his trap for the mayor's accuser.

Digging into Ead's background, Egbert found that Ead liked to gamble at the Foxwoods Casino, in southeastern Connecticut. Since the casino, the world's largest, was run by the Mashantucket Pequots, a sovereign nation, it wasn't easy to subpoena patrons' gambling records. The casino treated them as confidential, like bank records. But Egbert wanted to pursue a defense that Ead had gambled away the bribe money he claimed had gone to the mayor.

The year before, Cianci had hired an advance aide who had been a hotel supervisor at Foxwoods. The week before jury selection, Cianci and Egbert summoned the aide and asked him how gambling records were kept. Then they asked him to use his connections and see what he could find out.

The aide drove down to Foxwoods late one night and logged on to a friend's computer after 11 P.M., when he would be less likely to be detected. Since a printout would be traced to his friend, the aide copied down Ead's gambling information longhand on a yellow legal pad. That first night, he reviewed thirty days. The next day, Cianci sent him back to get more. The aide wound up at Foxwoods four nights in a row and eventually copied down a more extensive gambling history on Ead. That weekend, staying with a friend in Connecticut, the aide was getting ten or more calls a day from Cianci, who would ask, "Whaddya got?"

Early Monday morning the aide returned to Providence, made copies of his notes, and rushed them up to Egbert's room at the Biltmore. That week, aided by knowing exactly what to ask for, Egbert subpoenaed Ead's gambling records.

The following Thursday, after Rose finished questioning Ead, Egbert strode to the lawyer's podium.

"Good afternoon, Mr. Ead," said Egbert.

After a few preliminaries, Egbert got down to business. He asked Ead about his 450 visits to the Foxwoods and Mohegan Sun casinos in the past year and a half.

"I can't believe it's that many times," replied Ead.

"How many times? Have a guess—a hundred?"

Egbert reached for a thick computer printout and plopped it down on the podium with a loud thunk. For the first time in days, Cianci broke into a broad smile. Egbert asked some more questions, then threw another number at Ead.

"Would you be surprised to learn that you gambled eight hundred seventy thousand dollars in the past three years?"

"I have no idea where you get those figures," replied Ead.

Egbert ticked off the dates that Ead had spent at Foxwoods in December 1999, when his bail restrictions supposedly limited his travel: December 2, 3, 4, 5, 6, 7, 8, 9, 11, 12, 13, 14, 16, 17, 19, 20, 22, 25, 26, 27, 28, 29, and 30. "That's indicative of someone with a gambling problem, isn't it?"

Ead disagreed.

During the afternoon recess Rose was visibly distressed. He complained to the judge that he hadn't been provided with the Foxwoods documents. Egbert pointed out that this was cross-examination; under the rules of evidence, the defense didn't have to share its information with the prosecution until it began presenting its case. Egbert smirked as Rose complained, to no avail.

Rose had expected Egbert to beat up Ead, but the extent of Ead's gambling came as a surprise. The prosecution team realized that this was a potentially devastating blow, one that they would have to respond to somehow. Without access to the Foxwoods information, they wondered what Egbert actually had. During the recess, the prosecutors huddled with Dennis Aiken, who was following the trial from a seat at the prosecution table. An FBI agent started making phone calls, reaching out to retired law enforcement agents who worked in security at Foxwoods.

Meanwhile, in the hallway, an upbeat Cianci autographed spectators' courtroom badges and winked at reporters. "You ain't seen nothing yet," he said.

For the next day and a half, Egbert hammered away at Ead as a money-grubber who had lied about the mayor to avoid prison and save his vending business. He mocked Ead's account of having given Cianci five hundred dollars in cash in the back of an automobile during the mayor's 1990 campaign.

"That's a lot of money," said Ead.

"To you?" asked Egbert.

"To him," replied Ead.

"That's about five minutes at the blackjack table for you," Egbert shot back.

Later Egbert walked over behind Cianci and put his hands on the mayor's shoulders.

"If the mayor was corrupt enough to take five thousand from a young man when he and his wife are hardly supporting themselves, if the mayor takes ten thousand to assist [the tax break], if the mayor takes ten thousand to assist [the real estate deal], then why didn't you just buy a job instead of running around? Why didn't you just say, 'Buddy, give me a stinking job for ten grand?' "

"I wouldn't talk to him that way."

" '*Vincenzo*,' " said Egbert, " 'give me a stinking job for ten grand!' "

"That's not my way," said Ead.

"You didn't do it because you knew the mayor would have thrown you out of his office," Egbert shouted.

"No, that's not right."

The inarticulate Ead had trouble keeping up with Egbert, who mocked his expressions. When Ead referred to a political maneuver against a rival tax-board member as a "pork chop," Egbert hit him with a flurry of questions ending with the quip, "You gave her a reverse pork chop."

Judge Torres, who also had trouble keeping a straight face, had to remind spectators at one point to stifle their laughter. "This is not a sporting event," he said.

But Cianci was jubilant. Egbert, he crowed, had ripped through Ead "like a chainsaw."

Near the end of his second and last day on the stand with Egbert, Ead fought back in his clumsy way. Ead described a Christmastime meeting he had in the mayor's office to discuss finding Christopher Ise a job. Ead said that he brought Cianci a box of cigars. As they spoke, an elderly Italian gentleman walked into Cianci's office and cried, "Thank you very much, Vincenzo!"

The man, said Ead, dropped to his knees and kissed the mayor's hand. Ead looked at Cianci and said, "I haven't seen that in a long time."

Egbert zeroed in. "When was the last time you saw that?"

"The *Godfather* movie," deadpanned Ead.

The courtroom erupted in laughter.

AFTER THE OPENING fireworks surrounding David Ead, the trial settled into a plodding rhythm interspersed with moments of high drama and low comedy. Hoping to repair some of the damage that Egbert had done to Ead, Rose called two witnesses who corroborated parts of Ead's story.

Christopher Ise, the city planner, described how Ead had used his influence with Cianci to get him hired, including bringing him to the mayor's office for a job interview. During the interview, Cianci telephoned the city's deputy planning director, Thomas Deller, and ordered him to create a position for Ise. Ead told Ise not to mention the five thousand in front of Cianci. When the interview concluded, Ise testified, he went outside while Ead stayed behind to speak privately with Cianci. Deller followed Ise to the stand and corroborated his story about being ordered by Cianci to hire him. Deller also backed up a key part of Ead's story about the vacant lots that Tony Freitas had wanted to buy from the city. When the deal hit a snag, Cianci called Deller and told him not to give Ead a hard time. Subsequently, after one of the two lots Freitas wanted was mistakenly sold to someone else, Deller heard Cianci say to Ead, "Tell Tony I owe him one."

During his cross-examinations of Ise and Deller, Egbert established that neither had any firsthand knowledge that Cianci's motives were corrupt. Ise said that he didn't know what Ead did with the five thousand. Deller wasn't privy to any discussions between Cianci and Ead regarding a payoff for the vacant lots. Egbert tried to show that Cianci helped Ead because he was vice chairman of the city Democratic party, and because both propositions made sense—Ise was qualified, and Freitas was going to restore two blighted lots.

Next, Rose turned to the University Club. Patricia McLaughlin, Ramzi Loqa, and other city officials described how angry Cianci had been, and how he had ordered them to keep the club from reopening. Loqa also testified that he had initially lied to the FBI about the mayor's involvement because he was afraid of Cianci. Alan Gelfuso, the club's vice president, testified about the club's attempts to pacify Cianci, culminating in its decision to offer him a lifetime honorary membership.

Egbert, trying to show that the matter was all about payback, not extortion, brought out Cianci's memorable line to the club's leaders: "Be careful how you act. The toe you stepped on yesterday may be connected to the ass you have to kiss today." Before the trial was over, one Providence entrepreneur would be selling T-shirts imprinted with that slogan. Later, during jury deliberations, Cianci stood outside the courthouse, smoking a cigarette and chuckling at the memory of his one-liner. "I remember saying that. It was a pretty good line. Of course, it may not be so good for me now."

In Providence there was a thin line between crime and comedy. One of the details about the University Club saga that emerged from the testimony was Cianci's anger at having been the butt of jokes at the club's Christmas party. In a letter of apology, the club's leaders blamed the "guest comedian." The comedian, Charlie Hall, was in the courtroom, covering the trial as the sketch artist for local television stations. As Hall sketched Patricia McLaughlin, he listened to her testify how Cianci had telephoned the comedian, in front of the club's leaders, to ask about the Christmas skit. This was during Bill Clinton's impeachment crisis; Hall would later remember that the mayor began the conversation with a few Monica Lewinsky jokes. Hall told Cianci that he had told some jokes about the mayor's not being a member—material, Cianci pointed out with prosecutorial zeal, that could only have come from someone at the club.

Hall had been questioned briefly by the FBI's Dennis Aiken, but he hadn't made the witness list. During breaks in the testimony, Cianci and Hall would kibbitz in the hallway. The mayor and the comedian had a history; they even shared an uncle. Back in the seventies, when Hall was eighteen, he had worked for the mayor's office, directing a summer camp for senior citizens. Hall, who favored floral Hawaiian shirts in court, had been doing Cianci impressions since his student days at the Rhode Island School of Design. He had also played goalie on the RISD hockey team, nicknamed the Nads (so that students could cheer "Go, Nads!"), a zany bunch that later made Cianci their honorary coach. Hall had a standard repertoire of Buddy jokes—the toupee, the sauce, the thugs. Cianci would smile publicly, then approach Hall privately and grouse, "Why the fuck are you busting my balls?" How could Hall not? Through the years, the mayor's antics had provided inspiration for Hall's Ocean State Follies, a comedy cabaret that spoofed Rhode Island's accent, its eccentricities, and its political chicanery.

"We're incestuous," quipped Hall. "And I mean that in the nicest possible way. The state is just one big, smoky back room."

Even in Hall's world of comedy, one hand washed the other. His work as a courtroom sketch artist provided him with plenty of fresh material for his Follies. In his spare time he worked on a musical, called *Buddy*, and drew cartoons about the trial. Cianci got a kick out of showing reporters one of Hall's cartoons, in which two skeptical, cigar-smoking plutocrats ask Jesus Christ why he thinks he deserves to be a member of the University Club.

One day Cianci walked over to Hall during a recess and said playfully, "You make me look fat." Hall knew all about critics; his most terrifying moment as a sketch artist had come during the murder trial of mobster Harold Tillinghast. The artist didn't dare make Tillinghast look fat. "You know what happens when an artist gets a mobster mad at him?" said Hall. "He wakes up the next morning with a drawing of a horse's head in his bed."

The Providence Journal ran a short item in its trial notebook about Hall's days working for Cianci. With all the testimony from city officials, cops, and tow-truck operators about having to make campaign contributions, Hall remembered when he had worked for the city in the seventies, and how his weekly paycheck of $150 had come with $5 Cianci fund-raiser tickets attached. Hall had been upset; "It seemed like a quid pro quo." But when he complained, his boss told him that that was how the game was played in Providence.

The morning that the newspaper item ran, Egbert confronted Hall outside the courtroom and threatened to slap him with a witness subpoena if there were any more negative stories—which would have barred the artist from covering the trial. Hall was stunned. He stood there, waiting for the punch line. But Egbert wasn't laughing.

IN PROVIDENCE, EVERYTHING had a price—especially doing the right thing.

That's how Steve Antonson felt as he walked into the courtroom late in the second week of the trial. A stocky, rawboned man with a craggy face, he avoided the mayor's piercing stare as he took the witness stand.

Once an untouchable because he was the mayor's boy, Antonson had become a pariah once his cooperation became known. His coworkers at the Civic Center called him a rat. His schedule started getting changed around. He watched Cianci on the television news, saying that he barely knew Steve Antonson. When Cianci attended a concert one night, his police driver told Antonson to stay away from the mayor, as another aide and the chief of police, Barney Prignano, glared.

Things weren't much better at home. His wife, who never liked Cianci's late-night phone calls, was furious with Antonson for having gotten himself mixed up with the mayor. She told Aiken that if anything happened to her husband, either a heart attack from the stress or some physical harm from one of Cianci's cronies, she would kill him, and the mayor. Antonson's mother, who also worried for her son's safety, started telling people that he was her nephew. His father, a temporary city electrical inspector, was passed over for permanent openings. And his thirteen-year-old, Stevie, took it hard. One day, his teacher came into the classroom wearing a Cianci mask and, looking at the boy, asked if anyone recognized the face. Stevie, who had been a water boy for the Providence Bruins and ridden in the victory parade with the mayor after the team won the 1999 American Hockey League championship, even started getting the cold shoulder from Civic Center employees. Eventually, the boy quit. One day during Cianci's trial, Antonson was driving with his son, who grew quiet and then said that he needed to ask him something about Plunder Dome.

"Did you take any money?" he asked. Antonson said no. "Did you do anything illegal?" Antonson said he hadn't. "Then I don't care what they write about you," the boy answered, "as long as you're my father."

Antonson's ordeal had worsened after Cianci's indictment. A few weeks later, a woman who worked at a Civic Center refreshment stand accused him of sexual harassment. Antonson, an affectionate person, said that it was an innocent hug, something that he had done before. People who knew him found the accusation to be out of character and the timing suspicious. Antonson was fired. The Civic Center's acting executive director, Lawrence Lepore, was a former Providence cop under investigation by the state police for stealing gold from a pawnshop raid. Ironically, when Lepore was subsequently indicted, during Cianci's trial, he was allowed to remain on the job. He presided over meetings in a conference room decorated with a picture of Harold C. Copeland, the Civic Center's first director, whom Cianci had gotten indicted for soliciting a bribe from Skip Chernov, back in the days when the mayor was the anticorruption candidate. (The portrait came down after Chernov complained.)

Antonson was dying for a cigarette as he testified. He was bolstered by his bond with Dennis Aiken. Before the trial, he had given the FBI agent a bronze pin with the mayor's seal, which Cianci had given Antonson. "When you clean out the government," he told Aiken, "you can give me this pin back."

But Steve Antonson's long-awaited opportunity to tell his story turned into a disaster. Things started fine, with Richard Rose asking him to relate what had happened with the University Club. Then Rose played the tapes of Antonson's phone conversations with Cianci. In the courtroom, people listened intently. Antonson looked at the mayor, who was watching the script of their conversations as it scrolled across his video monitor. Afterward, several of the jurors stared, expressionless, at the mayor. As Antonson left the courtroom for the afternoon recess, Cianci stood and gazed at him, tapping his fingers on the back of his chair.

Antonson started to walk out the exit for a cigarette, then halted when he smelled Cianci's cologne. A court sheriff let him go out the other door. Antonson stood smoking on the courthouse steps, outside the entrance, while Cianci stood about ten yards away, smoking outside the exit. Then the mayor threw down his cigarette and headed back into the courthouse, past Antonson.

"Steven, are you okay?" he asked.

"Yeah, I'm all right."

Back inside, Richard Egbert went after Antonson. He asked about the sexual-harassment complaint that had gotten him fired.

"It's more like a sexual-assault claim, isn't it?" asked Egbert—"that you grabbed a woman's crotch, put your tongue in her ear" and jumped over a desk, "rubbed your body against her," and pinned her against a wall?

Antonson told Egbert that the allegations were false. Egbert asked Antonson if he thought his firing could be related to his cooperation with the FBI. "I'm not really sure," replied Antonson. "It could."

Then, in a confusing series of questions worthy of the Abbott and Costello routine "Who's on First?" Egbert asked Antonson about his statements, on the tapes, where he had agreed with Cianci that he told the truth about the University Club. Although Antonson had been playing along at the time, he got all twisted around by Egbert's questions, and agreed that the mayor had told the truth.

It was late afternoon when Egbert finished. Court broke for the day. Upstairs, in an office used by the prosecution, Rose seemed upset with Antonson's performance. He and Aiken argued about whether to put Antonson back on the stand the next morning, to clear up the confusion in his testimony, as Judge Torres had suggested. Rose snapped for someone to get Antonson out of there. Aiken told Antonson to come back tomorrow.

The next morning, Antonson was waiting in the hallway to retake the stand when Aiken suddenly burst out of the courtroom and said: "It's over. You can go home." Antonson went home frustrated. After a year of keeping everything he'd been through bottled up inside, he didn't understand why he hadn't been allowed to tell his story. He called Aiken and complained that they had made him look like an idiot. Aiken was apologetic; he said that Rose had fucked up, and caught hell for it.

But Antonson also understood. The night before he testified, he had met with Rose in the U.S. attorney's office. Rose had said how tired he was. Antonson knew exactly how he felt.

THE SAME DAY that the Antonson tapes were played in court, prosecutors revealed the existence of another explosive tape—one in which Frank Corrente allegedly discussed corruption at City Hall with another former top Cianci aide, Thomas Rossi.

Working with the FBI, Rossi had agreed to wear a wire in the summer of 1999. A few days after Corrente retired in the face of Operation Plunder Dome, prosecutors said that he "reached out" to Rossi to find out what he knew about the investigation. It was surprising that the normally suspicious Corrente would have wanted to talk to Rossi, who was perceived in the mayor's office as a loose cannon and a disgruntled former aide, someone who had lost out to Corrente in their early 1990s power struggle. But Corrente was angry and discouraged, having just given up a position of power that he craved. He also may have been bitter toward Cianci, feeling that he'd been pushed out of City Hall because of the growing scandal.

Corrente and Rossi met on July 7, 1999, at a Dunkin' Donuts near Corrente's house in Cranston. It was a fitting spot for the rendezvous. It seemed as if there was a Dunkin' Donuts on every corner in the state, reinforcing Rhode Island's position as one of the most obese states in the nation. In the months following his indictment, Cianci had negotiated a million-dollar marketing deal renaming the financially troubled Providence Civic Center the Dunkin' Donuts Center; at a ceremony featuring a dancing donut, the mayor had raised the donut chain's ubiquitous orange and fuchsia colors above the building where his cronies were in the process of harassing Steve Antonson.

The Dunkin' Donuts tape quickly became a cause célèbre in Cianci's trial. That Thursday morning, before the jury came in and testimony resumed, the lawyers debated whether the jury should hear any of the one-hour tape, which the government had edited down to thirty minutes. Prosecutor Terrence Donnelly argued that the tape was important evidence in showing that Cianci and Corrente ran a criminal enterprise at City Hall. On the tape Corrente said that he and Coloian had loaned Cianci $150,000, and the money—at least Corrente's share—had never been repaid. The financial relationship could help prosecutors show the mayor's need for money, as well as help explain Corrente's role as the mayor's bagman. Corrente also talked on the tape about how he and Cianci used campaign funds, about the School Department lease with Edward Voccola, and about his control over the Providence Police Department. For example, Corrente said that he could use police officers to check motorists' license plates, and that he had quashed a police investigation into whether the mayor's chief of staff, Art Coloian, had assaulted his girlfriend.

The defense lawyers vociferously fought introduction of the tape. Voccola's lawyer, William Murphy, said that Rossi had been playing "Mickey the Dunce," trying to get Corrente to say something incriminating. Egbert called it "triple quadruple hearsay"—locker-room talk that even included a discussion of the mayor's sex life. Corrente's lawyer, Len O'Brien, complained that the tape was filled with "salacious gossip." So naturally the public and the press were eager to hear it. But Judge Torres reserved judgment, postponing Rossi's appearance on the stand.

Beyond the Dunkin' Donuts tape, Rossi's anticipated testimony promised to connect Cianci and Corrente to the shakedown of tow-truck operators and bribes from Eddie Voccola. In the early 1990s, shortly after Cianci regained office, Rossi described attending a meeting in which Corrente told a leader of the towing association that members would have to increase their contributions to five thousand dollars a year to remain on the police list. Rossi also said that he had been privy to a meeting between Corrente and Voccola in 1991, and Voccola had agreed to pay "cash kickbacks" to Cianci, through Corrente, if the School Department rented his garage. Later, after the lease was signed, Rossi said that he saw Voccola outside Corrente's office at City Hall one day with a brown Stop & Shop bag; Voccola said that he had a bag of "scarole" and that he had to see Frank. Privately, Rossi was telling people that Corrente and Cianci had had an arrangement: Cianci would work off his personal debts to Corrente by allowing him to pocket some of the bribe money.

While prosecutors believed the essence of what Rossi was telling them, he had problems. Rossi had a reputation for craving attention and for exaggerating. With memories of David Ead perhaps fresh in their minds, the prosecutors didn't want to risk having Rossi's revelations overshadowed by a withering Egbert cross-examination. Cianci's defense team was calling people all over town, trying to dig up dirt on Rossi. Egbert sarcastically referred to him as "Rossi to the rescue," noting how he so conveniently popped up throughout the case. In addition to the towers and the Voccola lease, Rossi also claimed to have dealt with one of the leaders of the University Club when they were having problems with Cianci—something that the club official had denied on the stand.

And yet some of what Rossi said had been corroborated by others. For example, Joseph Pannone had told the FBI of having seen Voccola at City Hall, paying his "juice" for the school lease. And tow-truck operator Kenneth Rocha testified that Rossi was present when Corrente demanded that the towers increase their contributions to Cianci.

Over the next three weeks, as the trial plodded on, Rossi hovered in the background. Judge Torres pondered the matter carefully, asking all of the lawyers to submit written briefs. Three weeks after the prosecution had sought to introduce the Rossi tape, Torres ruled that he would allow portions of it to be played, specifically Corrente's comments about Cianci's personal finances and the mayor's use of campaign funds. But first the government would have to lay a sufficient foundation, by showing that Corrente had made the statements as a coconspirator in furtherance of the conspiracy. Otherwise, the statements would be inadmissible hearsay. As the trial moved on, the prosecutors had to decide: How badly did they want the Rossi tape? And how much was it going to cost? Ultimately, they decided the price was too high. Rossi was never called.

Rossi's disappearance underscored the challenge facing the prosecution or how thin the government's case was, depending on your point of view. Legal analysts said that the case had been "overcharged" with the hope of pressuring Corrente to turn on the mayor. But it hadn't happened. As witness after witness testified to various sordid dealings, from illegal campaign contributions to payoffs for city jobs to the questionable circumstances surrounding Voccola's school lease, Egbert kept pointing to the lack of evidence against Cianci. There was testimony that Corrente had shaken down the towers and arranged bribes with Voccola—but not with Cianci himself. He either was not involved or had insulated himself so well that no witness could testify to the mayor's knowledge, at least in those two instances. Prosecutors did point to one piece of circumstantial evidence regarding the towers—a memo from Cianci's campaign bookkeeper indicating that the mayor paid close attention to the money coming in. To bypass the legal campaign limit of one thousand dollars a year, towers testified that they made contributions in the names of others, including young children, which was illegal in Rhode Island. When two towers inadvertently gave too much in their own names and the campaign had to return thirty-four hundred dollars, Cianci's campaign bookkeeper sought Corrente's help in rounding up replacement checks. "I know that the mayor does not want to part with that without money being replaced," she wrote. The prosecution argued that Corrente acted on the mayor's behalf, since the towers' contributions flowed to Friends of Cianci for the mayor's benefit.

Likewise, in the case of Voccola's school lease, tracing a path to the mayor proved difficult. City officials testified that Corrente had ordered them to steer the lease to Voccola, even having them rewrite the bid specifications and arranging for Voccola to receive his monthly rent checks in advance—a courtesy previously extended only to the Catholic Church. And Roger Cavaca, Voccola's longtime employee, testified that Voccola had told him about paying bribes to Corrente. Cavaca also described the time he cashed the $7,500 check for Voccola and watched him put the money in an envelope marked "Frank C." shortly before Corrente stopped by the garage to see Voccola. That was the check that had helped Dennis Aiken launch the Plunder Dome investigation. But Judge Torres would not allow Cavaca to say in front of the jury that Voccola had described Corrente as "Cianci's errand boy." Without additional evidence tying Cianci into the lease conspiracy, Torres ruled that Cavaca's statement was hearsay.

Still, as the Voccola lease was dissected, an unflattering portrait of the culture at City Hall emerged. Mark Dunham, the School Department's finance director, said that he initially lied to the FBI about Corrente's involvement because he feared for his job; when Dunham tried to get the city out of the Voccola lease when it came up for renewal, Corrente called him and screamed, "Are you fucking nuts?" Alan Sepe, the acting property director, said that he, too, had lied to investigators about Corrente's role because "I wanted to be a stand-up person—I didn't want to be a rat."

Eddie Voccola, who often sat slumbering during the trial, lived in a world divided between rats and stand-up guys. He had a disdain for the media, which had latched onto the squat, no-necked Voccola as the quintessential Rhode Island thug. In the privacy of the room reserved for defendants during court breaks, he would complain about the press but also talk about which female reporters he'd like to fuck. Voccola was a funny man, regaling his codefendants with stories, like the one about the time he had stranded the insurance adjuster on the roof. And he was more cultured than one might think. He had traveled widely in Europe and would engage Cianci in discourses about the prosecution's Machiavellian tactics and ancient Roman history. During a break in Roger Cavaca's testimony, Voccola complained about what a smooth talker his former employee was. Asked to describe the safe where Voccola allegedly stored bribe money, Cavaca had deadpanned, "It's a large metal object with a lock on it." Said Voccola: "The fuckin' guy talks better than Cicero." Chimed in Cianci, "And Ovid, too."

One morning, while the lawyers were preparing for court in the defendants' conference room, Voccola and Cianci got into a heated debate about who made the best marinara sauce. The two went back and forth. Voccola told Cianci he needed to put meat in his sauce. Cianci emphasized the importance of the carrots, to counteract the acidity of the tomatoes. Voccola said that it wasn't real red gravy if it had carrots. By the end, the lawyers were shaking their heads and smiling, and even Cianci was laughing hysterically. But one day Voccola encountered some digestive distress that wasn't so funny. Shortly after court convened one afternoon, his lawyer asked the judge for an emergency recess. As Voccola waddled out of the courtroom toward the bathroom, Egbert chanted, "Go, Eddie, go!" When Voccola returned, Egbert teased, "Well, Eddie, at least no one can say you're full of crap now."

The day after Cavaca's testimony, Don Imus parachuted into Providence, bringing more comic relief. Broadcasting his show on Friday morning live from the top-floor ballroom of the Biltmore—Cianci's living room—Imus cracked: "Obviously, he's guilty. The question is, can they prove it?" More than eight hundred people crowded into the ballroom, beneath the golden ceiling, to watch Imus and his sidekicks skewer the city's rich history of mobsters and corrupt politicians. Imus lamented that he had to leave after the show for a wedding in Connecticut; otherwise he'd "hang out and launder some money." Outside, a man hawked FREE BUDDY T-shirts that had been made in Raymond Patriarca's former Federal Hill headquarters, now a tattoo parlor. When Cianci made his entrance at eight-thirty he was greeted by enthusiastic applause. Some people rose to their feet. The audience, some of whom had been waiting in line since 5 A.M., included the Chamber of Commerce president, who had testified for the government about the University Club, and a retired state police detective who had investigated Cianci's assault of Raymond DeLeo.

Cianci told Imus that the trial had not interfered with his duties as mayor. Imus cut in to ask if those duties included opening the mail—"just an envelope joke," he added, when the mayor appeared baffled. "See that? I'm innocent," replied Cianci. The mayor launched into a lengthy monologue about Providence—the Renaissance, the rivers, the restaurants—until Imus interrupted, "Are you on amphetamines?"

When Cianci professed his innocence, Imus grinned and shot back, "You can say you're not guilty, but they can still have something on you." Imus told Cianci that he hoped he "got off." The mayor corrected him— "found not guilty."

THE MONDAY AFTER Imus came to town, Buddy Cianci's former chief of police sauntered into the courthouse to testify under a grant of immunity.

Urbano Prignano, Jr., had served five tempestuous years as chief, years marked by scandals involving missing evidence, including gold and cocaine; loose control of automobiles seized from drug dealers; political favoritism in promotions; and paranoia and low morale. To his critics, Prignano presided over a corrupt department where justice was for sale, where the mayor's friends were protected and his enemies spied on. Several of Cianci's City Council foes through the years had stories about being followed by the police. The day before Operation Plunder Dome became public, the police union had voted no confidence in Prignano following the discovery of a hidden surveillance camera at a police substation, apparently planted to catch whoever was posting unflattering messages about the chief on the bulletin board. Prignano had resigned under fire in 2001, as the widening federal probe explored payoffs for police promotions and case fixing.

Politics in the police department had been a reality since the early Cianci years, when the mayor had had City Council president Robert Haxton arrested and chief Robert Ricci committed suicide amidst allegations that Cianci had pressured him to hire unqualified recruits. The Plunder Dome investigation had turned up more recent allegations. Rosemary Glancy had been busy raising money for the mayor to help her brother's chances at being promoted. David Ead told investigators that he went to Art Coloian, who threw a big fund-raiser for Cianci attended by cops, on behalf of a friend willing to donate five thousand for a promotion to major. Coloian, he said, told him that he had to be kidding, that a major's job cost twenty thousand.

During the trial, Major Dennis Simoneau, who had been passed over for advancement, testified that he started contributing to Cianci, at Prignano's urging, and was subsequently promoted after donating about three thousand over the next few years. (On cross-examination, Egbert raised another reason for the delay of Simoneau's promotion—his involvement in a drunken episode at the police union hall in 1978, when disgruntled officers had fired their service revolvers at a picture of Cianci on the wall.) Prignano said that the politics predated Cianci, accusing the Irish cops who controlled things under Joe Doorley of each memorizing sections of the promotional exams and passing them on to their friends.

A stumpy man who looked like Fred Flintstone and answered to the nickname Barney, Prignano had been a streetwise cop who specialized in wiretaps. In the late seventies, he had served as Cianci's bodyguard. A Silver Lake native, the future chief had played Babe Ruth ball with Joseph Mollicone, the future embezzler, and had once been treated by Cianci's father after being hit in the head by a baseball bat while playing catcher. Many were surprised when Cianci chose him to be chief; he had skipped the ranks of lieutenant and captain. Prignano, who had an explosive temper, blew up at a reporter who wrote about his meteoric rise, thinking that the reporter meant mediocre. Because Prignano was so unpolished, an arrogant young lieutenant with his own ambitions of being chief, John Ryan, was promoted to captain and served as the department's public mouthpiece.

When *The Providence Journal* wrote stories questioning Prignano's friendship with a convicted felon and bail bondsman, Wayne David Collins, Jr., who had been involved in the armed robbery of a Cranston fur salon, Prignano pointed angrily to the wall, where Cianci's picture hung, and shouted: "I work for him—and he's a convicted felon. So if you wanna bang me, bang me for that." Collins had the run of the chief's office, to the point where he once sat in the chief's chair when Prignano wasn't there, feet up on the desk, as he dished dirt to a reporter about the alleged mob ties of one of Cianci's political enemies.

Prignano was being called to testify about charges that Corrente and Autiello had extorted a five-thousand-dollar bribe from the mother of a police recruit who had had several run-ins with the law, but was still admitted to the Police Academy, only to withdraw due to injury. The recruit was subsequently denied entrance to the next academy class, after other senior officers learned about his troubled past. Autiello lobbied Prignano to reinstate him. So did Ryan, who ran the academy and had his own allegedly corrupt relationship with Autiello. (Autiello, who had a multimillion-dollar contract to repair city police vehicles that Ryan administered, bought Ryan a car and gave it to him at a discount, according to court records.) Prignano, who was offended by the recruit's arrest for impersonating a police officer, refused to reinstate him. Still, Autiello told the angry mother to forget about getting her money back.

But where had the five thousand gone? The mother, Mary Maggiacomo, testified that she had given the money, in hundred-dollar bills, to Autiello, after Autiello told her that she couldn't expect to get her son onto the Providence police force without contributing to Cianci. Another police officer testified that Prignano had gone to a meeting with Corrente at City Hall to discuss police recruits. Now Richard Rose was calling Prignano to close the loop. In his opening argument Rose said that Prignano and Corrente had argued over Maggiacomo's hiring. According to a law enforcement source, Prignano had told the FBI that Corrente asked him about re-instating Maggiacomo, and the chief had said he couldn't.

But the combustible Prignano refused to stick to the story. Perhaps he didn't want to betray Corrente, who had been instrumental in making him chief. Or perhaps it was simply because he didn't like Richard Rose, who he felt didn't treat him with the proper respect. With Barney, you never knew. In any event, a few days before his testimony, he strolled into the court-house, loudly proclaiming, "I'm a hostile witness." He was there to be im-munized, compelling his testimony. And he was in a combative mood. He went after *Providence Journal* investigative reporter Bill Malinowski, who had written several exposés about police corruption, saying, "You don't write the truth about me because my name ends in a vowel." Malinowski pointed out that his own name ended in a vowel. Prignano said it didn't, so Malinowski spelled it out for him. "Well, it's the wrong vowel," snapped Prignano.

A few nights earlier, during a meeting with Rose and Aiken in the U.S. attorney's office, Prignano had gotten upset over some of the questions that the prosecutor planned to ask. Prignano threatened to take the Fifth. Rose said that he might have to get into Prignano's recent, messy divorce. (Prignano's wife had discovered his affair with a woman who worked at the city dog pound—a woman who had ended up with an automobile that the police had impounded from a drug dealer.) Prignano accused Rose of ruining his personal life. "Why don't you just pull down my pants and give it to me up the ass?" Prignano recalled shouting. The session ended after Prignano threatened to ruin Rose's personal life by bringing up things from the prosecutor's past.

Outside on the courthouse steps Prignano chattered nervously about his upcoming testimony. He seemed upset that the feds wouldn't tell him what else they knew about the Maggiacomo bribe. As a cop, he said, he'd like to know. When he heard about the bribe, he said, he grabbed Ryan by the lapels, shook him, and screamed, "Did you take the fucking money?" Ryan, who had signed his own proffer with the feds, earning him the nick-name Captain Canary, denied it. Prignano said that the feds were out to crucify him because he wouldn't tell them what they wanted to hear. He insisted that Corrente had never talked to him about Maggiacomo. If he had, Prignano said, he would've told Corrente: "Look, Frank, I don't need this kid. I've already got enough fucking assholes working for me."

Prignano's testimony was widely anticipated. People stopped by the courthouse and asked the clerk when Barney would be going on. When Prignano finally took the stand that Monday morning, he seemed more nervous than defiant. From the moment Rose began questioning Prignano, their mutual contempt was evident. Prignano said that Autiello had lobbied him about Maggiacomo, but Corrente hadn't. Rose hammered away at the mayor's strong political influence over the police department, and the need to contribute to Cianci's campaign to get ahead, as illustrated by the eight thousand dollars that Prignano had donated in the nineties. Prignano described the meeting in the mayor's office when Cianci decided to make him chief, and how the mayor had first played a little joke by telling him that someone else was getting the job. Prignano conceded that Cianci called the shots on high-level promotions, but insisted, to Rose's incredulity, that he, too, had input.

"You promoted him?" Rose asked about one major.

"I think so," answered Prignano.

"You made that decision?" insisted Rose.

"I didn't say that. I said I promoted him. Promoting is when you stand in front of the guy and pin on the badge."

In the spectator benches Lou Pulner, a lawyer doing television analysis of the trial, leaned over to Prignano's lawyer and whispered, "Did your client have a lobotomy?"

When Prignano stepped down at the lunch recess, Aiken approached him and said something about sticking to his story. After lunch, when Prignano retook the stand, Rose elicited testimony that the chief had given some officers advance copies of their promotional exams. One was Sergeant Tonya King, a black officer whom Rose had praised six years earlier as a pioneer. Noting that there had never been a minority female sergeant in Providence, Rose had said in a speech to the Rhode Island Minority Police Association, attended by Prignano: "We have not given up hope. If the results of the latest sergeant's exam hold true, we won't have to wait much longer."

The reasons for Prignano's actions were never fully explored, nor were they linked to anyone at City Hall. Ryan, who had his own credibility problems, was never called to testify. But the damage—to Prignano's reputation and his tarnished department—was done.

"I'm not proud of that," he told Rose softly. "It's one of my dark days in the police department in my thirty-four years."

Prignano's testimony brought more heat than light to the proceedings. But as he stepped down, some jurors shook their heads. They wondered why Cianci had ever made him chief.

AS THE TRIAL moved toward its climax—the playing of the Freitas tapes—the tensions between the prosecution and the defense grew. On several occasions, defense lawyers complained about Rose's facial gestures and his tendency to make gurgling noises during cross-examinations. Judge Torres admonished Rose for his behavior. "Some of your facial expressions need to be restrained," he warned.

The normally even-tempered Torres was growing impatient with the frequent bickering. One day he angrily warned that another outburst would bring consequences. He was regarded as a conservative, fair, and even-handed judge, determined to move the trial along and maintain a strict decorum. "If you watched the O. J. Simpson trial," Torres said at the trial's outset, "I can assure you that this will not be anything like that." But the judge also had an impish sense of humor. One day, during a sidebar with the lawyers, out of earshot of the jury and courtroom spectators, Egbert accidentally stepped on Donnelly's toes. Rose glared. Torres asked what was wrong, and Egbert told him. "Be careful," the judge warned, "because the toe you step on today could be connected to the ass you have to kiss tomorrow." Egbert smiled and replied, "Not on your life!"

With the government nearing the end of its case and preparing to call Tony Freitas, the judge faced a pivotal decision: whether to admit the Freitas-Pannone tapes. Uncle Joe, with his explosive statements about Cianci's involvement in bribery, was an unwelcome presence in the courtroom for the mayor. The defense lawyers fought hard to keep him out, arguing that Pannone's statements were hearsay, and prejudicial. But as a coconspirator, Pannone's statements could be used against his alleged confederates—provided that the prosecution had introduced independent evidence of a racketeering enterprise.

While the judge weighed his decision, prosecutors called another witness, a surprise they hoped to use to rehabilitate David Ead—the director of table games at the Foxwoods Casino. Backed by a stack of computer printouts, Richard Tesler rebutted Egbert's assertion that Ead had gambled $897,000 in the past three years. In fact, Tesler testified, Ead had actually won $155,000 during the past decade. The revelation stunned the courtroom; there was an audible gasp from one spectator. Foxwoods rated Ead as a steady gambler but not a high roller. He was a pretty good blackjack player who won more than he lost. Tesler explained that the $897,000 was a misleading figure, a cumulative number of bets as opposed to actual wins or losses. Egbert, during his cross-examination, tried to suggest that Ead had manipulated his gambling chips, to launder bribe money, but Tesler rejected the possibility. The prosecution team felt that they had scored with Tesler's testimony, though that remained to be seen. Tesler also testified that Ead had visited the casino more than a thousand times in the past decade.

The next day Joseph Pannone, now seventy-nine, shuffled into court to be sentenced. A codefendant in the racketeering case, he had pleaded guilty before the trial. He looked frail in his blue prison work shirt and had trouble hearing. Given Pannone's age and poor health, Torres gave him a concurrent term, meaning that he would serve no additional prison time beyond his original five-year sentence and be eligible for release in two more years. As federal marshals led him from the courtroom to drive him back to prison, the people in the courtroom wondered: Was this the end of Uncle Joe? Would Torres allow the Pannone tapes to be played? And if he did, would Pannone testify for the defense?

In preparation for that possibility, Cianci and Egbert had been cultivating an unlikely source—radio talk-show host John DePetro, who had spent the last two years portraying the mayor as the Tony Soprano of City Hall and who, in covering the investigation, had befriended Joe Pannone. To his critics, DePetro was a typical talk-show wiseass and a shameless self-promoter. He called himself the Independent Man, after the statue atop the Rhode Island State House that symbolized the state's maverick spirit, and referred to his wife as the Independent Wife and his children as the Independent Children. A native Rhode Islander, DePetro had been making good money in radio sales in Manhattan, working for WABC. But he yearned for his own talk show and in 1999 returned home to take over the midday slot on WHJJ, Cianci's old station. DePetro latched onto Plunder Dome as the case was heating up. His show could be heard blaring from portable radios in offices throughout City Hall.

DePetro's constant Buddy bashing irritated Cianci. DePetro would repeat rumors about the investigation and, early on, posted updates on his website predicting the mayor's imminent indictment. He asked listeners to e-mail their favorite Buddy stories; one claimed to have been in Cianci's house in the early eighties and seen Hitler's *Mein Kampf* on the mayor's bookshelf. One night Cianci confronted DePetro in a bar and, according to DePetro, grabbed him hard by the arm. Another time, DePetro and Art Coloian, the mayor's chief of staff, had a Friday night dust-up in the men's room at Raphael's, an upscale downtown restaurant.

As Operation Plunder Dome had unfolded, DePetro had gotten to know several of the key players, including Tony Freitas, David Ead, Steve Antonson, Eddie Voccola, and, most notably, Joe Pannone. One day shortly after Pannone's indictment, when he was ducking other reporters, DePetro went over to his house and they had a long conversation. Pannone and his family took a liking to DePetro.

During Rosemary Glancy's trial, DePetro ran a contest and took the winner to lunch at the infamous Andino's, where Glancy and Pannone had discussed City Hall corruption over the fried calamari. After lunch De-Petro brought the contestant to court, where she got to meet Pannone, who was there taking the Fifth. One day DePetro was over at Pannone's house when the bumbling tax official tried to put a tape in his VCR of a Frank Sinatra concert—and unwittingly inserted one of the FBI's under-cover tapes of him and Freitas. After Pannone was sent away, DePetro vis-ited him in prison. About four months before Cianci's trial, the special counsel appointed by Judge Torres to investigate how the Plunder Dome tape was leaked to Channel 10 subpoenaed DePetro. WHJJ's lawyer fought the subpoena, invoking DePetro's journalistic privilege, but he was ulti-mately compelled to testify in a deposition, where he said he didn't know how the television station obtained the tape. "John DePetro is a journalist," scoffed Richard Egbert, "like My Cousin Vinny is a lawyer."

But now Egbert needed DePetro. On the morning of opening argu-ments, DePetro was sitting in WHJJ's Winnebago in downtown Provi-dence, where he would be broadcasting during the trial, when a constable walked in. DePetro had just been on *Imus in the Morning*, previewing the trial and joking about Operation Thugs and Bad Rugs. "Great show," the constable said, and handed DePetro a subpoena to testify as a witness for Buddy Cianci.

As a potential witness, DePetro was barred from the courtroom. That came as a blow to someone who had lived professionally for this moment, who said that he prayed that Cianci would take the stand. When Judge Tor-res announced the DePetro ban later that morning, Cianci cast a satisfied look toward the press gallery. During the lunch break between opening ar-guments, Torres heard an appeal in his chambers from WHJJ's lawyer, protesting the ban on First Amendment grounds. The judge seemed sympathetic, but Egbert insisted that DePetro had information that could be helpful to Cianci. DePetro remained locked out of the trial as Egbert put off his lawyer's efforts to work something out.

DePetro wondered why Cianci wanted him to testify, and whether the mayor was yanking his chain. In fact, Egbert was genuinely interested in calling DePetro—but he and Cianci also enjoyed yanking his chain. Egbert had received portions of DePetro's deposition from the special counsel investigating the leaked Plunder Dome video, and believed DePetro could contradict some of the things that Pannone had said to Freitas. Egbert kept trying to meet with DePetro, to ask him about his conversations with Pannone, but DePetro refused. After about a week, Egbert finally agreed to let DePetro back in the courtroom, on a limited basis. But the threat of being barred again hung over the talk-show host, to Cianci's amusement. "Hey, Semi-Independent Man," the mayor would hail him in the corridor. Cianci started calling him "Semi" for short. Periodically Cianci or Egbert would pull DePetro aside and insist they were sincere about calling him. Egbert promised to let him back in the courtroom if DePetro agreed to talk to him. Later in the trial, when the debate over the Rossi-Corrente tape surfaced, Egbert stormed into DePetro's radio trailer. The lawyer was upset about how DePetro had egged on a caller speculating about the reference to the mayor's sex life. Egbert said that he ought to punch DePetro in the nose. Then he told him to cut out that "bisexual bullshit."

The day after Memorial Day, as the trial moved into its sixth week, Torres finally ruled on the Pannone-Freitas tapes. He said that the government had presented evidence linking Cianci and Corrente to a racketeering conspiracy; therefore, the Pannone tapes could be played.

THE JUDGE'S RULING came after Tony Freitas had already been on the stand for two days, testifying to his meetings with Corrente as prosecutors played those tapes.

It had been ironic to hear Rose urge Freitas, when he first took the stand, to speak directly into the microphone. After weeks of often tedious testimony the jurors appeared eager to see the tapes, and curious about Freitas. After one tape was played, a juror interrupted to ask that the monitor in front of Freitas be lowered so that he could see his face. Outside the courthouse, spectators waited in line for a courtroom seat and cheered

Freitas, who smiled and waved. One day, though, Freitas left the court-house to find a parking ticket on his Jeep Cherokee; none of the other cars around him had tickets.

The Corrente tapes captured the chaos in the office of the mayor's number-two man. The phone rang constantly. Amidst running the city and scheming with Freitas, Corrente was preoccupied with a new house he was building in Cranston, car repairs, cooking pasta and beans, and fending off an unwanted caller. "Did you tell that guy I'm not coming in today?" he barked at his secretary. "Then why did he call again?" One day the power went out in his office. Another day he railed against "the fucking Jews."

Turning to the Pannone tapes, the prosecution hoped to weave to-gether the various strands of the racketeering enterprise that Cianci had allegedly presided over. The jurors listened as Pannone's raspy voice guided them: "There are no free lunches. It's the money that counts, Tony." "God bless the mayor. You can't point the finger at him and say he did it. Frank's in the middle." Or the advice he recalled receiving from Cianci: "Never talk on the phone, never get a check, but get cash when you're one-on-one."

Pannone might have just been some old blowhard, puffing himself up behind the mayor's back, but he was right about how things worked at City Hall. He had delivered on his promise to set Freitas up with Corrente, and accurately predicted that Corrente, paranoid of bugs, would talk like he didn't want the money even as he took it from Freitas. (" 'No, no, no' means 'yes, yes, yes.' ") It was telling that Corrente would take money from Freitas, whom he hardly knew, when he had just been investigated for tak-ing bribes from Eddie Voccola. Was that the act of someone who had never palmed an envelope? And Pannone was right about the Cianci campaign's taking of illegal cash. When Freitas gave Corrente a cash contribution, it never showed up in the mayor's campaign reports. The money, Pannone said, "goes south." (The government also introduced evidence of cash col-lected at a fund-raiser that Rosemary Glancy had cosponsored.)

The jury had been watching tapes and listening to Freitas weave his tale of sleaze at City Hall for four days when Egbert rose to question the government's star witness. Freitas would be harder to attack than David Ead because everything he had done was on tape. But Egbert wasn't going after Freitas—he was going after the absent Pannone. Cianci's lawyer knew that he wasn't going to have the opportunity to question Pannone directly. Uncle Joe was through talking; his lawyer had informed Egbert that Pan-

none would take the Fifth. If Egbert was going to attack Pannone's asser-
tions that Cianci ran a criminal enterprise, he was going to have to do it
through Freitas, by contrasting the statesmanlike mayor with his buffoon-
ish tax-board chairman.

In a masterful performance, seemingly ad-libbed but meticulously
planned, Egbert attempted to deconstruct Joseph Pannone. Distilling several hundred hours of tape, Egbert spent part of one day and most of the
next painting him as a boastful liar who had exaggerated his ties to Cianci
and other powerful politicians. Reading from transcripts of tapes that the
government had not played, Egbert highlighted particularly absurd moments. He had the judge and jury laughing as he recounted Pannone's description of visiting a woman whose brother had died in the house. "So I
closed his eyes, right? I said, 'See Joan, your brother's dead. Why don't you
give him to my friend at Pontarelli's [funeral home].' " The sister, looking
for her brother's will, went to a cedar chest where, according to Pannone,
"he had four hundred thousand dollars in that fucking chest." Then Egbert, trying to show how easily confused Pannone was, pointed to another
conversation in which he said, "The mayor had a cedar chest full of fucking money."

Egbert zeroed in on Pannone's allegation that a former Rhode Island
governor, Philip Noel, had used his influence with Cianci to secure a substantial tax break for an upscale East Side retirement home. The FBI had, in
fact, investigated the matter, but nobody had been charged. Pannone also
said that Cianci and Noel "go out screwing together." Later, Egbert would
call Noel to the stand to deny it, in effect putting an ex-governor's word up
against the conniving Pannone's. Egbert questioned Pannone's claim that
he had clout with judges and with an influential North End state senator,
Dominick Ruggerio. (Egbert failed to mention the incident that had made
Ruggerio part of Rhode Island political folklore—shoplifting condoms from
a CVS drugstore by stuffing them in his sock, which earned him the nickname "Rubbers.")

Egbert also delved into the curious case of a coin-laundry owner
named John J. Izzo, a family friend of Pannone's who liked prostitutes. In
June 1998 Izzo was arrested for soliciting an undercover policewoman.
Izzo, who was married, had been arrested once before for solicitation. He
turned to Pannone, who later told Freitas that he had passed along a bribe
to Corrente to fix the case. Izzo pleaded no contest and his case was filed for
a year, which meant it would be erased from his record if he stayed out of

trouble. It was not an unusual disposition, prompting Egbert to question the alleged fix.

The prosecution countered that what had actually happened was murkier, demonstrating that in spite of his braggadocio, Pannone wasn't as clueless as Egbert would have the jury believe. Izzo had given a thousand dollars in cash to Pannone, who had taken Izzo to Corrente's office and then gone in alone while Izzo waited outside. Fatefully, Freitas had also come to see Corrente that day and found himself in the reception area with Pannone and Izzo. His hidden recorder captured Corrente's coming out and chastising Izzo and Pannone for not going to court with a lawyer whom Corrente had arranged to represent Izzo at a hearing that day. Corrente told them that the lawyer had just gone over to court with Art Coloian. Later, with Freitas still there, Coloian came in and said that the case had been postponed and that Corrente would call and find out the new date. Izzo went to court the following month and pleaded no contest. Egbert would later call the judge and the undercover policewoman to testify that nobody approached them to fix the case. Corrente's role in the case, and the fate of Izzo's thousand bucks, remained a mystery.

On Monday morning, June 3, six weeks after the trial began, Freitas stepped down from the witness stand. Shortly after that, the government rested. The defendants moved immediately for judgments of acquittal, arguing that the government hadn't proven its racketeering case. Although such motions are routine, Torres questioned the prosecution closely on whether the evidence spelled RICO.

A prosecution brief presented the government's view of City Hall: "Cianci was the head of a criminal business, in effect, the CEO. Corrente was his vice-president, responsible for overseeing daily operations. The other defendants were responsible for various aspects of that business. Pannone was responsible for taxes, along with David Ead. Autiello was responsible for the towers. Those defendants also handled 'walk-in customers'—like Ise and Maggiacomo. And Voccola was responsible for ensuring a steady flow of cash, obtaining city funds on a corrupt lease, laundering those funds into cash, and making sure the cash made its way back to the CEO—through the vice president." In court, Terrence Donnelly summed it up: "If a leader sets up a scheme and then has other people carry it out, he's on the hook, whether it's John Gotti or Vincent Cianci."

But where, the defense lawyers asked, was the proof that Cianci had organized any scheme? There was no evidence linking the mayor to the

Voccola lease or the alleged extortion of tow-truck operators. There was no proof that Cianci, Corrente, Autiello, and Voccola had an agreement to run a criminal enterprise—no tapes or testimony of meetings or conversations. There was, at best, the three bribes alleged by David Ead—"sporadic unconnected episodes"—and the University Club charges, which also didn't fit into any pattern of criminal activity. As for Pannone's statements, the defense urged the judge to look at the corruption that Pannone knew about firsthand, most of it involving the tax board. The government was trying to inflate "a cesspool of corruption" into a "Great Swamp."

The defense was fighting an uphill battle. Cianci and his codefendants were attacking the very essence of RICO, which reversed the legal notion that someone cannot be convicted for a crime he didn't commit by being held responsible for the crimes of his coconspirators. Enacted by Congress in 1970 to combat organized crime, at a time when Cianci was a mob prosecutor, the Racketeer Influenced and Corrupt Organizations Act was considered the atomic bomb in a prosecutor's arsenal. RICO grew out of the Kefauver hearings into the Mafia in the fifties and the McClellan hearings in the sixties, in which Joseph Valachi exposed the inner workings of the mob and identified Raymond Patriarca as one of the nation's top bosses. The hearings had revealed the mob's infiltration of legitimate businesses and how Mafia bosses had made themselves virtually untouchable by insulating themselves from the crimes committed by their underlings. A new approach was needed, one that targeted the entire organization.

RICO was drafted by G. Robert Blakey, a former mob prosecutor for U.S. attorney general Robert Kennedy and later special counsel to McClellan's U.S. Senate Judiciary Subcommittee on Criminal Laws and Procedures. As a prosecutor, Blakey had read the FBI reports on the illegal bugging of Patriarca's Federal Hill office. But while RICO was designed to nail mobsters like Patriarca, McClellan directed Blakey to draft it more broadly. Hearings had also shown that the Mafia could not survive without corrupting public officials. The law targeted "any person" who engaged in racketeering activity, not, Blakey later joked, "any person whose name ends in a vowel." Still, many believed that the acronym RICO was inspired by Edward G. Robinson's gangster Caesar Enrico Bandello, in the movie *Little Caesar*, who said as he lay dying, "Mother of Mercy, is this the end of Rico?" Blakey, a gangster-movie buff, pointed to a less remembered character from the film, Big Boy, the shadowy upper-world figure behind the rackets who is not brought to justice. The RICO statute, wrote Blakey, "was designed to change the ending of the movie. Racketeers—like Rico—should not be shot by the police. They are entitled to due process. Big Boys—racketeers as much as their underworld counterparts—should not be above the law."

Cianci and his defenders sought to portray the government's use of RICO against a mayor as an abuse of power. RICO was a "runaway train," they complained. Egbert criticized it as the "kitchen-sink" approach—"just throw all kinds of disparate, unconnected allegations against the wall and see what sticks." But while RICO had faced a number of court challenges over the years, the U.S. Supreme Court had affirmed its application beyond organized crime. Prosecutors had successfully used RICO against street gangs, neo-Nazis, corporate executives, Wall Street inside traders, and corrupt politicians who employed a moblike hierarchy. The Justice Department brought more RICO cases against corrupt public officials than it did against mobsters; public-corruption cases were the largest single category of RICO cases. Said Blakey, "We learned by studying organized crime, but RICO transcended that to attack corrupt systems, including political ones. Mayors, governors, police chiefs, senators, congressmen—all have been convicted where the political entity is the enterprise." Former Boston Mafia underboss Gennaro Angiulo offered his own sobering analysis of the RICO law that would eventually land him in prison with Joseph Pannone. In a conversation bugged by the FBI, Angiulo complained, "Under RICO, no matter who . . . we are, if we're together, they'll get every . . . one of us."

Blakey, now a law professor at Notre Dame, said that he had received a call after Cianci's indictment from someone in the mayor's defense camp, asking if he saw any grounds for challenging how the indictment had been drawn. He said that he couldn't find any. Blakey, whose knowledge of Rhode Island dated back to Raymond Patriarca's heyday, had also represented an out-of-state contractor drawn into a federal corruption probe in neighboring Johnston in the mid-nineties. The case, laced as it was with the state's incestuous politics, reinforced Blakey's belief that "Rhode Island is more corrupt than Vietnam."

The day after the arguments over judgments of acquittal, Judge Torres refused to dismiss the racketeering charges against Buddy Cianci, Frank Corrente, and Richard Autiello. But he threw out the charges against Edward Voccola, ruling that while there was evidence that he had paid bribes and laundered money, the government had not proven that Voccola was part of a racketeering enterprise. If anything, Torres said, Voccola was at cross-purposes, since he was the one allegedly paying the bribes. (Because of the statute of limitations, the feds had been unable to charge Voccola separately with paying bribes or with money laundering.)

After hugging Cianci and his other codefendants in the defendants' room, Voccola walked out of the courthouse a free man. "We're going to miss you," Cianci said to Voccola's lawyer. Voccola celebrated by making up a story for the *Journal*'s Tracy Breton about a fictitious victory party at his house for ninety people, featuring lobster and roast beef. (Later, when friends complained that they hadn't been invited, Voccola had a real party.)

Torres also threw out some of the lesser charges against the mayor. He dismissed charges accusing him of direct involvement in the extortion of the tow-truck operators but said that the mayor could still be held accountable, under RICO, of approving the shakedown. (By the time the case reached the jury, the judge would also throw out the RICO charge against Cianci regarding the Voccola lease.) Torres also tossed the witness-tampering charges regarding Steven Antonson because of Richard Rose's failure to clarify Antonson's confusing testimony during Egbert's cross-examination.

Trial analyst Daniel I. Small, a former federal prosecutor in Boston who had defended former Louisiana governor Edwin Edwards on corruption charges, called the judge's ruling an embarrassment for the government and an important victory for the defense. "But you can win battles and still lose the war," he said.

It didn't take the defense long to present its case—a handful of minor witnesses. A hearing expert testified about Frank Corrente's impaired hearing, part of a defense argument that he hadn't grasped everything that Freitas had said in his heavy Portuguese accent. Reporters covering the trial joked that it was the "hear no evil" defense.

The judge shot down Egbert's attempt to play the 1995 FBI tape in which Cianci told "Marco," the undercover agent posing as a businessman trying to do business with the city, that he would castrate anyone who tried to shake him down. Before he ruled, Torres warned Egbert that playing the tape—and introducing evidence that the mayor was above bribes—would open the door for the government to introduce evidence of corruption in Cianci's first administration.

The prosecution had a list of familiar faces from Buddy's past all teed up, from Ronnie Glantz to Ruth Bandlow, the woman who had accused him of raping her at gunpoint when he was a law student at Marquette. Egbert asked the judge if that door would also be opened if the mayor took the stand. That depends, Torres replied, on what Cianci would testify to.

Up until the trial's last few weeks, Cianci held out the possibility of taking the stand. He felt that he could explain things away and show the jury how far removed he had been from the Joe Pannones and the David Eads. The risk, said one adviser, was that Cianci might not shut up, and say something damaging. But because he was so quick and intelligent and confident that he could pull it off, the prosecutors thought that there was a chance.

Richard Rose prepped for a possible cross-examination. If Cianci testified, he would have to be perfect. The prosecutors thought that Cianci would have trouble reconciling certain things. For instance, the mayor claimed to be unaware of the small details of what went on at City Hall— and yet he followed things so closely that he spotted the University Club on the agenda of the obscure Building Board of Review and involved himself in the hiring of a low-level city worker, Christopher Ise, and in the sale of two city-owned vacant lots to Tony Freitas.

Ultimately, the mayor chose not to testify. Aside from the risks, another factor was a belief that he was ahead—that Egbert had sown reasonable doubt in the minds of the jurors with his attacks on the credibility of Ead and Pannone.

Instead, the defense rested with another face from the mayor's past— Eddie Xavier, the old political warhorse and former councilman from Fox Point. In the early days, Xavier had been one of Cianci's sworn enemies. He had been one of the Democratic leaders in 1978, during the famous Wednesday Night Massacre, when Ronnie Glantz called him so dumb that he probably thought a caucus was a dead moose.

Like many old adversaries, Xavier had made his peace with Cianci. He ran the city's Office of Emergency Management.

In the middle of the afternoon, Xavier trudged into the courthouse in work clothes, his plaid shirt partially soaked from a sudden rainstorm that had swept Kennedy Plaza. After taking the stand, he pointed out that he had taken half a vacation day to appear on Cianci's behalf.

His testimony was brief. As a member of the Friends of Cianci campaign committee, Xavier said that he had never seen Pannone at meetings to distribute fund-raising tickets.

After a few minutes, Xavier stepped down from the stand, and Torres joked, "Enjoy the rest of your vacation."

■

RENAISSANCE CITY—OR a City for Sale?

In their closing arguments, Richard Rose and Richard Egbert painted contrasting views of Buddy Cianci and Providence.

"The evidence shows that the price of admission was often five thousand dollars," said Rose. "Want a job? Five thousand. Want to be on the tow list? Five thousand. Want to grease the chairman of the tax board? Five thousand. It was a city for sale, where anything could be had for a price."

(Rose need not have looked any further than the packed spectator benches for proof—a former state legislator and his girlfriend had paid two people waiting in line five hundred dollars for their courtroom seats.)

Richard Egbert took a more reflective tone, telling the jury about a stroll that he had taken around downtown Providence that dawn, as he contemplated his closing. "I walked around, looking at some of the things—the Westin Hotel, the Providence Place Mall, the Convention Center, the rivers moved. . . . I realized that this, in fact, is a Renaissance City." The mayor, said Egbert, "was the leader, the backbone, the visionary."

Rose reminded the jurors that people like David Ead and Joseph Pannone were Cianci's men. "It's not like a coach who gets a team and inherits the players," he said. "He picked 'em and he reappointed 'em. Why? Because they were stand-up guys." And if David Ead was making it up about meeting with Cianci on bribes, Rose asked, then why didn't he just keep it simple and say he'd delivered the money directly to the mayor, instead of to Corrente and Coloian?

Egbert asked the jurors to imagine a trial in simpler times, in a colonial village where everyone knew everyone else. "So when Joe Pannone walked into the courtroom in that village in 1650, . . . people could say, 'Oh, there goes Joe Pannone the Liar, who would sell you the Brooklyn Bridge.' And when David Ead walked in, they could say, 'There goes David Ead. He's the one who lives around the corner and stole from this store and that store and didn't pay his taxes and gambled at Foxwoods night and day and was there on Christmas.' "

That same day, a new Brown University poll found that over half the voters in Rhode Island thought Cianci was guilty, but 67 percent felt he showed strong leadership. The pollster, political scientist Darrell West, attributed the dichotomy to "the Houdini quality of Buddy Cianci. People see him as someone who is able to escape from impossible situations."

Across the river behind the courthouse, three RISD sculpture students raised a fourteen-foot-high inflatable Buddy constructed from thirty yards of silicone-coated nylon and inflated with a leaf blower. Cianci was popular among RISD students; every year at graduation he would waive the penalties on overdue parking tickets for those who had paid the original fines. "I could do more, but this year I can't," he had quipped the previous year, alluding to his indictment. The balloon Buddy, the product of a final class project to create a public monument or memorial, looked out across Providence, a sash across his chest proclaiming, "Serving the city since 1974."

Would the jury burst the mayor's balloon, or set him free? The jurors had gotten the case after three hours of mind-numbing instructions from the judge on the intricacies of racketeering and conspiracy and "extortion under color of official right."

"You just earned credit for a year in law school," Cianci quipped to reporters in the hallway. On a more somber note, he grumbled: "If you gave the jurors an exam right now, they'd probably score about thirty. And these people have my life in their hands."

The week ended with no verdict. The jury had been out for three days. That Saturday night the mayor served as grand marshal for the Rhode Island Festival of Pride parade, celebrating the gay community.

As darkness fell over the city, a few thousand people lined Francis Street, which ran from the foot of the State House along the length of Providence Place Mall. The pulsing music and flashing lights of the floats gave the street the feel of a carnival midway. "Enjoy the great city of Providence! Enjoy this great city of diversity!" shouted Cianci. "Let's get on with the parade!"

The mayor climbed onto the back of a Saab convertible with a busty blond drag queen, BB Hayes, who was actually a hairdresser from North Providence. The procession moved slowly through a tunnel of noise, as the mayor, electrified, reached out to shake outthrust hands. The parade made its way downtown, past the Biltmore and through darkened streets with pockets of activity outside gay bars. On Weybosset Street the crowd thickened again, as several hundred raucous people waited outside the flashing marquee of the Providence Performing Arts Center. The car moved past a building where three nearly naked men in towels danced on the fire escape.

Cianci got out at the theater, shaking hands. One man said, "I'm lighting a candle for you." Humble and grateful, the mayor worked his way through the adoring crowd and went inside Intermezzo, a stylish bistro. He sat at the corner of the bar, nursing a Courvoisier and B&B and smoking a cigarette.

An inveterate gossip and raconteur, Cianci held court for more than an hour, reminiscing about past political battles and his current predicament. He talked about how he had finally been able to get some sleep last night, then woke up that morning and was channel surfing when he came across the movie *Moonstruck* and got lost in it for a while, laughing and forgetting. "I love that movie, with the wolf and the moon. It's so Italian."

"Heyyy, El-le-gance," Cianci called to a man who sang show tunes at Intermezzo on Wednesday nights.

Two drag queens came over to have their picture taken with the mayor, whose official photographer hovered nearby. "They're actually guys, you know," said Cianci, chuckling.

The mayor fretted about a *Journal* photographer who had taken his picture earlier, in the parade. "This is going to hurt me with the jurors—oh, he likes gays," he said.

Cianci held a bemused live-and-let-live attitude toward gays, he said. His open-door policy was a continuation of the tolerance that had marked Providence since its creation, by Roger Williams, as a haven for religious freedom that welcomed Quakers and Jews and other outcasts. The mayor admitted that he cultivated gays for political reasons, then shrugged and said, "Hey, I haven't lived my life on the straight and narrow, so who am I to question them?"

Judgment day was never far from Cianci's thoughts. He replayed scenes from the trial, laughing about Pannone's wacky comments and then saying plaintively, "They can't convict me on that!" There was a sense of disbelief that it had come to this, that such a motley cast of characters— Pannone, Ead, Freitas—had put the mighty mayor in such a jam.

If he was acquitted, Cianci said, he was going to take the half million dollars in his campaign fund and throw a series of parties throughout the city—for blacks, Hispanics, people in wheelchairs, the blind, the deaf. "People say it's a victory if I'm acquitted. It's not a victory. It's harassment. They've been after me for seven years. They spent twenty million dollars. Why? Because I wanted to be a U.S. senator."

The mayor's bitterness toward the WASPs surfaced. John Chafee was a big thief, grumbled Cianci. "I can tell you a deal where he took four hundred grand," he continued, holding up four fingers. "As a U.S. senator." He reflected on an early turning point in his life—the decision not to run against Chafee in 1976. "I thought I had more time," he said regretfully. "There's a lesson there. When opportunity comes, grab it!" He slammed his fist on the bar.

It was approaching midnight. Someone had invited Cianci to stop by Mirabar, a gay nightclub around the corner. The mayor, a reporter, and a woman filming a documentary about Cianci's life piled into his limousine for the short ride.

There was a line out the door to get in, but one of the mayor's advance men was already inside. Soon a side door opened and Cianci's party was ushered inside, into a small, dark room packed with humanity and throbbing with ear-splitting music. The darkness flashed with strobe lights, illuminating near-naked men dancing on a raised platform decorated with balloons. Cianci's uniformed police driver with the high leather boots stood against the back wall.

Someone put a white spotlight on Cianci, who wore an olive sport jacket and tan slacks and a tie, and introduced the mayor of Providence. There were screams of delight. Cianci stood modestly, his thumb hooked in his pocket, acknowledging the praise.

Later, sitting at a small table in the corner, the mayor laughed and shouted to be heard above the noise. "How many laws do you think are being broken in here tonight?" he said with a laugh. "I had lunch in the Old Canteen today. Little old Italian ladies. Can you imagine them in here?"

His photographer, who had walked over from Intermezzo, joked that this was life in the Renaissance City. "More like ancient Rome," quipped Cianci.

Later, as Cianci was leaving Mirabar, a young man from Connecticut, wearing a red T-shirt that said FRUITCAKE, shook the mayor's hand and said, "You're the best thing to happen to Providence in thirty years."

THE DELIBERATIONS DRAGGED on through the following week. Channel 12 started running a jury clock superimposed on the screen during newscasts. Potential candidates for mayor watched the clock and the calendar as the June 26 filing deadline approached. City Hall fell into an early summer state of suspended animation. The mayor holed up most of the time in his office, unable to venture more than ten minutes from the courthouse in case the jury came back.

Sitting at his desk a few minutes before noon one day, the mayor was on the speakerphone with his police chief, Richard Sullivan, talking about a fake pipe bomb at Hope High School. Sullivan was explaining that the janitor had found the bomb in a bathroom and, thinking it was real, brought it to the principal's office. Cianci rolled his eyes. He told Sullivan to have extra officers there that night for graduation, then hung up to watch the noon news, his eyes flitting back and forth between two televisions tuned to two different stations. The reporters at Hope High reported that the bomb was real. "Oh, Christ," said Cianci, "get me Sullivan on the phone again." When Sullivan was back on the phone, Cianci barked, "Didn't you tell the media it was a fake?" The chief said that they were doing that now. "Well, you missed the noon news."

A few minutes later, a delegation was shown into the mayor's office prior to a press conference touting the city's latest acquisition—a Russian nuclear submarine from the cold war, to be anchored at India Point as a tourist attraction. One of the visitors was the daughter-in-law of former Soviet leader Nikita Khrushchev, whose son taught at Brown. The sub was featured in an upcoming Hollywood movie, *K-19: The Widowmaker,* starring Harrison Ford. Hopefully, Cianci said, Ford would come to Providence for the movie's premiere in July. "You always need to have a submarine around," quipped Cianci. "You may need to get out of town in a hurry."

On some days, the mayor would come across Kennedy Plaza and hold court with the reporters awaiting the verdict. "Here we are," he said one day with a sigh, "waiting for a judge to tell us what extortion is."

Cianci sat on the granite steps. Inside, the jurors had asked the judge to clarify the definition of *extortion.* The warm sunshine angled across the front of the courthouse and beat down on the mayor. "I can take the heat," he said. "Inside and outside the courtroom."

He surveyed the skyline of his city, which he had known since he was a boy, coming downtown with his mother for singing lessons in Celia Moreau's studio behind City Hall. He pointed to the top of the Art Deco Fleet Tower, noting that it had been built during the Roaring Twenties with a rooftop docking station for dirigibles. He reminisced about distant political battles and bygone machine bosses. He talked about his time as a prosecutor, when his longest wait for a verdict had been two days, in the trial of armored-car robber John Gary Robichaud. He told stories of his army days, when he was commander of the military stockade at Fort Devens—"where Joe Pannone is now," he added, laughing harshly.

A Splash Duck Tours bus rolled past the courthouse. The driver was telling the passengers on his microphone that this was where the mayor of Providence was on trial, then spotted Cianci and exclaimed, "Hey, there he is now!" Cianci waved as the tourists snapped pictures.

As the vigil wore on, the media contingent had grown. The weedy vacant lot from which John DePetro continued to broadcast his radio show had become an RV city filled with television trucks from throughout New England.

Cianci took in the scene and muttered: "Look at them. Waiting for blood."

AS CHANNEL 12'S jury clock ticked, the jurors sat in the deliberation room, shielded behind a wooden door guarded by a federal marshal.

The morning that Cianci sat outside commenting on the media's bloodlust was the seventh day of deliberations. The jury had finally begun hashing out the blockbuster charges, counts 1 and 2: RICO conspiracy and RICO.

The eight women and four men on the jury had spent a week and a half getting to this point, arduously working their way through a ten-page verdict sheet that required them to answer eighty-three separate questions of guilt or innocence regarding Cianci, Corrente, and Autiello.

After nearly seven weeks of testimony from sixty-one witnesses and 721 exhibits, the case was in the hands of a cross section of Rhode Islanders. They were teachers and social workers, a cab driver, a store manager, a retired policeman, a laborer, a forklift operator, a physical therapist, and a worker at the Rhode Island Central Landfill. The lone Providence resident, a Brown graduate whose parents were lawyers in her native Houston, Texas, was elected forewoman.

It wasn't like in the movies, one jury later reflected. They worked hard, taking twenty-minute lunch breaks and carefully considering the law and the evidence. They read and reread the law, trying to understand the elements of conspiracy and extortion and the subtle distinctions between racketeering and racketeering conspiracy. They listened to a tape recording of Judge Torres's instructions over and over.

They began with the easiest charges, the ones in which Corrente was on tape, taking bribes. They were unmoved by Corrente's arguments of entrapment and poor hearing. "He seemed to hear when it was convenient," noted one juror. And he still took the money from Freitas. They also voted to convict Corrente and Autiello of bribery conspiracy for demanding campaign contributions from the tow-truck operators, based in part on Autiello's role in collecting the money and Corrente's knowledge as campaign chairman, as indicated in Cianci campaign records. But they were skeptical of the government's key witness, tower Kenneth Rocha, who had described a meeting in which Corrente had demanded the money, and acquitted Corrente and Autiello of extorting the towers. The jury also convicted Autiello of conspiring to extort five thousand dollars from the mother of the police recruit, though they acquitted him of taking the actual bribe, because of the mystery of what happened to the money. (One juror said that the jurors debated their own theories of who got the money, with some suspecting that it went to Captain Ryan.)

The jurors spent a lot of time fighting over the extortion and bribery counts involving Cianci and David Ead. Many generally believed Ead, but not beyond a reasonable doubt. He was too sleazy, and his gambling was troubling. One juror said that some felt a bit "conned" by Egbert after the Foxwoods official testified that Ead's gambling wasn't as bad as the defense had implied. But it was bad enough. When Egbert ticked off the number of days that Ead had been to Foxwoods, then asked if he thought he had a gambling problem, "Ead looked like he was trying to answer 'What's the distance between Neptune and Pluto?' " said the juror. "Maybe Ead was right. But a lot of us felt that the standard of proof fell just short. We were being asked to convict Buddy Cianci solely on the word of David Ead."

After a few days of heated debate, the jury voted to acquit Cianci of the eight counts regarding the Ead bribes.

The most contentious part of the deliberations concerned the University Club. The initial vote was 6–6. For nearly three days the jurors debated whether the mayor had extorted a membership. Voices were raised and tempers frayed. Some of the jurors, many of whom weren't the type to belong to the University Club, had trouble relating to its affluent members as victims. The debate came down to why the club had offered Cianci an honorary membership. If it was to make a friend, then a majority felt that it wasn't extortion. But if it was to get the club's variances approved to reopen, it was. They focused on the testimony of club leader Alan Gelfuso. It was here that their frustration with Richard Rose was most apparent, said two of the jurors. As they went over a transcript of Gelfuso's testimony, they wished that Rose had asked one more question and gotten the club's motives explicitly on the record. By the end of the third day, the vote had shifted to 9–3 to acquit. But the three remaining holdouts were adamant. Finally, exasperated, the jury set the University Club aside and moved on to the RICO counts.

By this point, the jurors felt as if they were the ones in prison. One day, after two of them got into a heated argument, one read his horoscope from a tabloid aloud to the others: "You will be explosive in your temper." The jurors burst into laughter, momentarily easing the tension. Although they generally kept the window blinds shut, one of the court sheriffs joked one day that they should open them and let the people outside see them duking it out.

There had been days, during the long and, at times, tedious testimony, that the jurors had longed to escape. They joked about hiding from the sheriff in the two bathrooms off the deliberation room, then opening the second-floor window to make him think that they had jumped. One day, during a recess, there was a commotion in the jury lounge when one of the jurors looked out the window and saw one of the towers, who had testified, in action. "Hey, Matarese is towing someone's car!" someone shouted. Everyone rushed to the window to see.

Since the jurors weren't supposed to discuss the testimony, they made small talk. Often they would discuss the combatants. They noticed when Voccola was asleep and when Corrente came to court one day with his lips swollen (an allergic reaction to medication). They liked Judge Torres, who they felt ran a strict but fair courtroom; once, when the bickering among the lawyers got out of hand, the judge threatened to send them all to the principal's office. They also studied the lawyers. They liked Egbert, his smooth, confident manner, and were at times annoyed by Rose's histrionics; whenever he got ticked off during a defense lawyer's questioning, noted one juror, Rose would sit at the prosecution table and pull on his socks. During breaks, the jurors would imitate Egbert hitching up his pants or Rose tugging at his socks. One day, after watching the two lawyers go at it, the jurors joked that if it came to fisticuffs, they'd bet on Rose, because he was heavier and had a longer reach. Then someone said, "What if [Bill] Murphy [Voccola's lawyer] jumps in?"

As they listened to the witnesses, the jurors also formed impressions of Cianci's City Hall—impressions that came into play as they considered the RICO counts. One was struck by the number of city employees with immunity. Some looked like they hadn't graduated from high school, said one juror. As they testified, noted another, "you could see the wheels turning, wondering, 'How can I answer this so that if Buddy isn't convicted, I won't lose my job?' "

Given the contentious discussions over some of the underlying charges, the jurors dreaded the time when they would have to resolve the RICO count. But it turned out to be simpler than they had expected. To be convicted of racketeering, a defendant had to be found guilty of at least two predicate acts. Since the jury had not found Cianci guilty of any specific crime, he was acquitted of count 2. But his two alleged confederates, Corrente and Autiello, were convicted.

That left Count 1: RICO conspiracy.

In his instructions, Judge Torres had explained that a defendant could be convicted of racketeering conspiracy if he was knowingly a part of the plan. He did not have to be found guilty of committing any of the actual crimes or even be aware of all of the details of the criminal enterprise. "Each member of the conspiracy may perform separate and distinct acts and at different times," said Torres. "Some may perform major roles; some minor roles."

The evidence of a conspiracy did not have to be direct. It could be shown through circumstantial evidence, which one juror would later observe isn't as sexy as on television, when there is always a smoking gun. After the tapes that they had seen during the trial, one juror wondered: "How come they can't wire Cianci's office? Why can't they wire the big man?"

As the jurors closed in on a verdict, they considered what the mayor had known. Although the evidence had not been sufficient, in their eyes, to link him beyond a reasonable doubt to Corrente or Ead or Pannone, the accumulation of their corrupt acts, and their association with the mayor, was damning. Even if the people beneath him were sleazy and had their own little scams, the jurors found it hard to believe that all of this could have gone on without Cianci's knowledge, or that he didn't benefit. It was so blatant, said one juror, and the mayor kept an eye on things, such as the building-board agenda from which he had learned of the University Club's application. As another juror put it during deliberations, "This guy knows how many rolls of toilet paper there are in City Hall."

Although they didn't believe everything that Joe Pannone had said on the tapes, two jurors said that they found him generally credible about how corruption worked at City Hall—and his words were backed up by Corrente's actions caught on tape. One juror also pointed to Freitas's testimony about attending a Cianci fund-raiser, where the mayor had mentioned to Ead that he had taken care of a particular matter. Other testimony indicated that Cianci had been referring to the Ronci estate-tax deal, and that he had been involved in that matter, as well as in the hiring of Christopher Ise.

Another decisive piece of evidence, according to the two jurors, sprang from a matter that they were still stuck on—the University Club. Although they could not agree on the extortion count regarding the club, the jury was troubled by the Steve Antonson tapes. It sounded to them as if Cianci had told Antonson to lie to investigators. Even though the judge had thrown out the witness-tampering charges against Cianci, because of Rose's failure to clarify Antonson's testimony, the jury was still free to consider the evidence for the remaining charges.

As they neared a verdict on Count 1, the jurors kept coming back to the Antonson tapes. Cianci, said one juror, "was very, very unbelievable."

SHORTLY BEFORE NOON on Monday, June 24, Judge Torres's clerk handed him a note. He was presiding over the start of the bribery trial of Art Coloian, accused of serving as the mayor's bagman for the Christopher Ise bribe. Richard Rose was questioning David Ead all over again. The judge broke early for lunch. Coloian left the defendant's table. At about twelve-thirty Cianci, Corrente, and Autiello replaced him. The mayor's hand shook as he poured himself a cup of water from the pitcher.

Four federal marshals posted themselves beside the defendants, and the jury was brought in. Mary Dole, the forewoman, handed the verdict sheet to the judge's clerk, who stepped to the lectern beneath Torres and announced the verdict.

"Count 1, racketeering conspiracy, as to Vincent A. Cianci Jr.—guilty."

As the clerk continued to read the roll, the mayor, his face ashen, methodically checked off each charge with his pen, never looking up. Corrente, seated to his left, exhaled and shook his head in disbelief.

Cianci's surprise grew as he marked off the string of "not guiltys" that followed his initial conviction.

The jurors, who had deadlocked on the University Club charges, were also in disbelief when Torres sent them back to resolve their differences. They walked back into the deliberation room and looked at one another as if to say, "Now what do we do?" For the next three hours they prodded the

three holdouts to show them the evidence that Cianci was guilty. They finally helped break the impasse by convincing the three tired jurors that a
vote to acquit was not a vote that Cianci was innocent—only that the government had failed to prove it beyond a reasonable doubt.

Meanwhile, court security shooed reporters and spectators out of the
courthouse. Cianci and his codefendants and their lawyers remained incommunicado inside. Outside, about two hundred people gathered in disbelief in Kennedy Plaza. Many had hurried from downtown office buildings to
witness a moment in Providence history. A businessman said that people
would remember this day in Providence the way people remembered where
they were on September 11, 2001, or the day that President Kennedy was
shot. A young legal intern said that she had expected the mayor to be found
not guilty. "I think everyone kind of knew he was doing things, but I think
that what he has done for the city overshadowed that he was a crook." But
Pat Cortellessa, the last man to attempt to run for mayor against Cianci, before he had been knocked off the ballot, said that he had a case of champagne on ice. "It's a victory party for the people of Providence who fought
corruption, kickbacks, and bribes," said Cortellessa, who had attended the
trial every day.

Two dozen uniformed police officers and plainclothes detectives lined
the street. Many asked reporters hopefully if this meant that the reign of
Buddy Cianci was over.

It was small comfort when the jury came back late in the afternoon
and acquitted Cianci of the remaining University Club charges. At about
4 P.M. court was adjourned. The loquacious Cianci seemed in a daze as he
walked past the reporters in the corridor. "How you doin'?" he murmured
as he walked past them.

The mayor walked, blinking, outside into the bright sunshine. He was
greeted by a polite smattering of applause from the crowd and a few lonely
cries of "Buddy!" Managing a small smile, Cianci waved and climbed into
his waiting Lincoln Town Car with a deflated Egbert. The car drove a few
feet, then stopped to pick up another lawyer, who would handle the
mayor's appeal, and roared off.

In the days and weeks ahead, as Cianci prepared to leave office and
steeled himself for prison, he would tick off all the charges he had been acquitted of and puzzle over the one that he hadn't.

"What was I convicted of?" he asked plaintively, to anyone who would
listen.

Then he answered his own question. "I was convicted of being the mayor."

The jurors, besieged by reporters, did not speak publicly about their deliberations. Later, when asked to respond to Cianci's lament about being found not guilty of twenty-nine out of thirty charges (it was actually eleven of twelve, with five having been thrown out by the judge), one juror said: "Well, he was darn lucky. He's like John Gotti. His suit's a little slick."

THERE WAS AN elegiac quality to Cianci's final days in office in the summer of 2002. In September he faced sentencing. Until then, at least, he was still the mayor.

On June 26, two days after his conviction, he faced a decision. It was the filing deadline for candidates for mayor. The notoriously indecisive Cianci wrestled with whether to announce for reelection, on the chance that the judge might throw out the jury's verdict. Others advised him not to antagonize Torres, who might interpret a decision to run as a sign of defiance that would weigh against him at sentencing. At six that morning, he contemplated running as a Democrat. But early that afternoon he announced that he would not run. A record nineteen candidates, many of whom had been waiting for his decision, rushed to file for mayor.

"I thought I could win," he said. "But by four o'clock today, I can't honestly say to the people that I can be their mayor for the next four years."

Journal columnist Charlie Bakst came into the mayor's office and congratulated Cianci on his decision. The two men chatted. Cianci was hoping to remain free during his appeal and talked about writing his memoirs.

"Nixon said the best writing is done in prison," interjected Bakst.

"Only you could say that, Charlie. Obviously you've never been there because we don't get great writing from you." Cianci roared with laughter, his aides and other reporters joining in.

Later that day, after a long, rambling press conference carried live by all three Providence television stations, the lame-duck mayor did what he had always done. He made the rounds. In the afternoon, he addressed the Classical High School graduation at the Veterans Memorial Auditorium. Waiting in the wings as the band played "Pomp and Circumstance," Cianci bounded onto the stage to raucous applause.

"This is a very big day for you and an equally big day for me," he said, as he awarded three graduates one-thousand-dollar scholarships from his marinara-sauce fund.

That night Cianci made a pilgrimage to the Rosario Club in Silver Lake, where his first campaign, against Joe Doorley, had ignited when he went there to address supporters of Franny Brown. The occasion was a meeting of the Democratic City Committee, which had gathered to endorse candidates. The assembled ward bosses, many of whom had formed the backbone of Cianci's political machine and who, no doubt, would have endorsed him again, gave him a warm welcome. When the mayor spoke, he was a study in humility.

"You're the ones who go out and get the votes," he said. "It's wonderful to go on television and give a great speech and talk about policy, but you're the ones in the trenches. There's a lot to be said about that. It's called democracy. . . . People from all walks of life, all races, all colors, all creeds coming together to express their interest in the governance of their city and their state. And it happens all across America. It happens in Iowa as you see the presidential caucuses, and it happens in Silver Lake."

In parting, Cianci pointed to the bar and noted the pictures on the wall—of Frank Sinatra and the Rat Pack, of himself. Then he gestured to a statue in an alcove, saying, "To guide you in your deliberations, you have the Virgin Mary over there." The mayor urged them to "stay all night. It took them nine days to talk about me. Don't rush to judgment."

On the Fourth of July he sought solace at the Bristol parade, where his 1980 campaign for governor had peaked, and where he had always basked in the adulation of the crowd. But despite another warm reception, he couldn't entirely escape the shadow of his conviction. The parade paused in front of Raymond DeLeo's house on High Street, where, as always, a large party was in progress. Several young men in the front yard began serenading him. To the tune of "For He's a Jolly Good Fellow," they sang, "For he's a RICO felon, for he's a RICO felon . . . which nobody can deny." Cianci was so uncomfortable that he directed an aide to tell the band to start playing, to drown them out.

At the end of July, on a sweltering afternoon, Cianci journeyed to the Second Ward, on the East Side, to dedicate Francis Brown Square. Brown had died, but his widow and children and other old political hands came out for what turned into a retrospective on Providence politics. Cianci reminisced about how Brown's primary challenge of Doorley had opened the door for his election, and lamented the fact that few people in Providence remembered the political kingmaker Larry McGarry, Mr. Democrat. Cianci recalled attending McGarry's wake in 1995 and asking his police driver if he had ever heard of McGarry. The driver responded, "Who's Larry

McGarry?" Cianci shook his head sadly. Later, as he was leaving, the *Journal*'s Charlie Bakst pointed out that Cianci had been the anticorruption candidate back then. "Still am," Cianci replied curtly.

On August 21 David Ead was sentenced to home confinement, fined ten thousand dollars, and ordered to pay sixty thousand in restitution to the City of Providence. The judge, Ronald Lagueux, surprised Ead by ordering him to stay away from Foxwoods or any other form of gambling for the duration of his sentence. "You've beaten the odds up till now, but you can't indefinitely," said Lagueux. Ead, who cried in relief at avoiding prison, soon began complaining about the hefty restitution. He said that it would take him longer to pay the money back if he couldn't win some at the blackjack table.

In passing sentence, Lagueux said that he believed Ead's testimony, and that it established that "there were, indeed, stains on the mayor's jacket." At the same time, Cianci stood in front of City Hall, unveiling a high-tech police crime-fighting vehicle equipped with a rooftop camera that he said could be "zoomed right into the mayor's office." He declined to discuss Lagueux's remarks.

The week before his sentencing, Cianci attended a farewell party with a few hundred old friends and former adversaries in the ballroom atop the Biltmore. He talked about how his entire career had been wrapped up in the old hotel, dating back to 1974 and his first announcement for mayor in the Garden Room downstairs.

"I started in the Garden Room, and I ended up in the ballroom," he said. "I like living in the Biltmore because I can look out at most of the city you've created." Cianci quoted from a *New Yorker* story published that week about his trial, which referred to Providence as "the most resuscitated city in America." He pointed to a recent *Town & Country* article recommending six cities to visit: Barcelona, Florence, Venice, Los Angeles, Paris—and Providence. "We're confident, moving in the right direction. We believe in ourselves. That's the best legacy that any mayor could expect."

After his speech, Cianci chatted about the *New Yorker* story and some unflattering references to Freitas. The mayor shook his head in disgust. "Freitas is a nut," he said. "Aiken got Freitas and worked through Rose because he wanted me so bad—because he couldn't get me the first time. After that I guess they taught a course at the FBI Academy: How Not to Run a Corruption Investigation. At least that's what I heard."

Sentencing day, September 5, 2002, dawned sunny and bright, another beautiful day in the Renaissance City. Before dawn Cianci and a few family members slipped into the mayor's office for a quiet farewell breakfast.

Later that morning, Cianci stood before Judge Torres and was sentenced to five years and four months in prison.

Judge Torres said that he was "struck by the parallels between the story of Dr. Jekyll and Mr. Hyde. There appear to be two very different Buddy Ciancis. The first Buddy Cianci is a skilled, charismatic political figure, one of the most talented Rhode Island has ever seen. . . . Then there's the Buddy Cianci who's been portrayed here. That's the Buddy Cianci who was mayor of an administration that was corrupt at all levels. That's the Buddy Cianci who committed an egregious breach of the public trust by . . . operating the city that Buddy Cianci was supposed to serve as a criminal enterprise to line his own pockets. My job is to sentence the second Buddy Cianci. Because the first Buddy Cianci wouldn't be here."

Cianci spoke briefly. He maintained his innocence, vowed to appeal, and thanked the judge for his fairness throughout the trial. "It's an unfortunate situation," he said. "I'm sorry, obviously, that it's come to this. . . . I have dedicated myself to the City of Providence in many ways. . . . I love the city.

"I never intended to do anything wrong."

As the noon hour passed and the sentence was imposed, the office of mayor officially passed from Cianci's hands for the second time. While he was still inside the courthouse, the black Lincoln Town Car with the number-one license plate drove away, leaving Cianci to get a ride back to the Biltmore in a friend's beat-up Nissan Maxima.

But Cianci did not go gently. The judge had one final surprise. He gave Cianci a ninety-day stay of execution, allowing him to ask the First Circuit Court of Appeals to permit him to remain free during his appeal. As Cianci left the courthouse, legal minds raced to digest the consequences of the stay of execution. The city charter called for Cianci to lose office upon sentencing. But if the judge had delayed execution of the sentence, did that mean Cianci was legally out of office? Asked on the courthouse steps if he was still the mayor, Cianci replied, "Yes, I'm still the mayor. . . . I guess they won't be able to have their meeting in ten minutes," meaning the swearing in of City Council president John Lombardi as the new mayor.

Over at City Hall, while Cianci headed back to the Biltmore, his city solicitor, Charles Mansolillo, raced through the corridors. Mansolillo was engaged in heated discussions with Lombardi and his advisers, and also talking to Cianci and his lawyers by phone. As the honor guard gathered outside the packed council chambers, there was a sense of a coup d'état in the air.

But shortly after 1 P.M., Cianci agreed that his time had passed. Across the street at the Biltmore, he adjourned to the bar at Davio's, where he nursed a drink, smoked a cigarette, and held court. He already had a gig lined up as a radio talk-show host until he had to report to prison in December—unless, God willing, the appellate court allowed him to remain free on appeal. Cianci looked up at the barroom television and watched his replacement being sworn in. "Look at him," said Cianci, chuckling. "He's sweating."

The following Tuesday, Citizen Cianci was having his hair done up at his East Side salon when filmmaker Michael Corrente, who knew the owner, called to chat. Corrente, who was planning to make a movie about Cianci's life, soon found himself on the phone with the ex-mayor.

"The judge cut me some slack," Cianci said.

"I heard," replied Corrente.

The mayor chuckled. "Dr. Jekyll and Mr. Hyde. Dr. Jekyll and Mr. Hyde. The cocksucker. He didn't give me two fuckin' paychecks, though."

The Last Hurrah

In the months following his sentencing and removal from office, Vincent A. Cianci, Jr., took comfort in the cocoon of Buddy World.

His lawyers appealed to the First Circuit Court of Appeals in Boston, asking that Cianci be allowed to remain free on appeal. He needed a decision before December 6, the deadline that Judge Torres had set for Cianci to report to prison.

Meanwhile, the federal Bureau of Prisons was preparing Cianci's bed. He was issued an inmate number, 05000-070 (the last three digits signifying Rhode Island), and put in a database of prisoners. His status was listed as "in transit." But everyone in Providence knew where Buddy was.

He remained in the Presidential Suite at the Biltmore, a visible presence in Providence. He traded his black city limousine and police driver for a red minivan and a retired policeman as his chauffeur. His archives— several hundred boxes of papers, trophies, and memorabilia—gathered dust on the upper floor of an old mill building on Branch Avenue, above a World Gym and an adult bookstore. He still ate and drank at Mediterraneo and haunted the bar in Davio's, at the Biltmore.

The week after his sentencing, Cianci started cohosting a morning talk show on local radio station WPRO. The move stirred the usual controversy about glorifying criminals but also boosted the station's ratings. Besides the money, Cianci appreciated the distraction from thinking about prison, and the opportunity to take shots at his enemies. A bonus was the time slot—it allowed him to go *mano a microphone* with his nemesis at WHJJ, John "the Independent Man" DePetro.

The once-mighty mayor found himself reduced to competing with a reviled talk-show host. On the airwaves he remained a polarizing force. His supporters lamented that Cianci had been wrongly convicted, and that the

Providence Renaissance would not survive without him. But a growing number of Providencians had grown tired of Cianci's act and felt that it was time for a new mayor to carry the city forward.

It galled Cianci to see government march on without him.

He spent a lot of time on the air sniping at his successor, John Lombardi. As the City Council president, Lombardi had questioned the mayor's bloated personal staff, which was bigger than the mayor of Boston's. Immediately after Lombardi was sworn in, he dispatched aides, accompanied by uniformed policemen, to fire Cianci aides whose positions had been cut from the budget.

During his first week in office Lombardi led a reporter into the mayor's office, which seemed larger without the large Oriental carpet and Cianci's trophies and celebrity photos. Mousetraps were scattered about the bare wooden floor, to cope with a rodent-infestation problem. Lombardi, a tall, dignified man who had grown up orphaned on Federal Hill, seemed gratified to be serving as mayor, an office he had considered running for but then decided against, on his wife's wishes. He talked about the temptation of power, how he had been in a restaurant having lunch and a man at another table had tried to pick up the check. Lombardi said that he practically had to fight the man before he got the message.

Lombardi had also watched in amusement as several Cianci loyalists now attempted to ingratiate themselves with him. One, Cianci's acting police chief, asked the new mayor if there was anything he could do. Lombardi suggested that the chief try to get to the bottom of reports that Cianci had used the police to follow his enemies on the council. The chief promised to look into it.

The new mayor lowered his voice, as if the office still belonged to Cianci, and confided that he thought the room might be bugged.

A few weeks later, Lombardi demoted the police chief and fired Cianci's public-safety director. The next morning Cianci had the fired official on his radio show.

Cianci was also hired to do election-night commentary on Channel 6, Providence's bottom-rated television station. The response was so negative that two other election-night commentators—a former lieutenant governor and a college professor—refused to show up, saying that a corrupt politician shouldn't be provided such a platform.

On September 10 David Cicilline decisively won a four-way Democratic primary. With no meaningful opposition in November, the victory assured the forty-one-year-old Cicilline, the gay, Jewish-Italian son of a mob lawyer, of becoming the next mayor of Providence. Cicilline represented a break with the past and signified a new era of diversity, political observers said.

His father, Jack Cicilline, who had been Joe Doorley's top policy aide back in the 1960s before becoming a mob lawyer, had remained in the background, not wanting to tarnish his son's image. But one old family friend of the father's who turned up at Cicilline's campaign headquarters election night was Buckles Melise, Cianci's former highway superintendent. Buckles, who had been arrested on a bad-check warrant the previous month, could still be found, most days, hanging out on Federal Hill.

Behind his upbeat public persona, Cianci was morose about the prospect of prison as the weeks slipped by with no word from the appeals court. The Bureau of Prisons assigned him to the Elkton prison in Lisbon, Ohio, a bleak spot in rural Appalachia, where locals hunted squirrels outside the fences. The prison was in the district of former congressman James A. Traficant, Jr., who was serving time in neighboring Pennsylvania following his corruption conviction—and campaigning for reelection.

One night, Cianci came into Murphy's Deli for a corned-beef sandwich and commiserated with Scott MacKay, a veteran *Providence Journal* political reporter, about his fate. "It's all drug dealers," he said of the Elkton prison population.

On a brighter note, he told MacKay that his radio show was doing well. "My ratings are up," he said.

But that was small consolation, he added, if he had to "go away."

Cianci wasn't his usual snappy self when he appeared on the Don Imus show. When Imus congratulated him on getting married, Cianci didn't catch on, saying that he wasn't getting married. "Oh, yes, you are," said Imus, a reference to his impending prison date.

Cianci also seemed puzzled when Imus asked, "Have you ever watched *Soul Train?*" Cianci said that he hadn't. "You will," Imus predicted.

Cianci told Imus how the jury had found him not guilty twenty-nine times. But this wasn't the First Circuit. Imus joked that the jury should have read the twenty-nine "not guiltys" first before socking him with the one "guilty." When Cianci sought to downplay the lone count he was convicted of, Imus pointed out that the feds had gotten Al Capone on his taxes.

"I'm not Al Capone," said Cianci plaintively.

Four days after a *Providence Journal* story detailing conditions at Elkton,

Cianci launched a campaign to be transferred to a prison closer to Rhode Island.

He invoked the need to be near his daughter, Nicole, who was in a drug-rehab center.

Born in 1974, the year her father first became mayor, Nicole Cianci had had a hard life. Trotted out for campaign commercials from the time she was a baby, she had struggled to win her father's attention as he pursued his political ambitions and ran the city. Alternatively spoiled and ignored by her father, Nicole later had to endure the very nasty and public breakup of her parents' marriage, compounded by news of Cianci's ugly assault of Raymond DeLeo.

In her teens, Nicole developed a drug problem, said Cianci's former girlfriend Wendy Materna. In her early twenties she became the unwed mother of two children. She depended on her father for financial support. She was listed as a director of a private company that Cianci formed to handle his marinara sauce; the company paid for her car insurance. Aides recalled the mayor's dismissive attitude toward Nicole when she came by City Hall. She often relied on Cianci's aides and police drivers. Aides said that they admired her efforts to be a good parent, but that it was hard. The drug problem persisted.

During the summer of her father's Plunder Dome trial, Nicole reported to the police that a boyfriend had beaten her up. She appeared in court for her father's sentencing, a girl of twenty-eight with straight blond hair and reddened eyes hidden behind sunglasses. A few days later, she was found wandering incoherently on Branch Avenue. She checked in to a residential drug-treatment center in rural Exeter, under an assumed name. Her mother, Sheila, took the grandchildren.

In November, seeking a new prison assignment, Buddy and Nicole Cianci wrote letters to Rhode Island congressmen Patrick Kennedy and James Langevin, asking them to intercede. "Being closer to Nicole and providing a solid base of family support is not only crucial to Nicole, but to me as well," wrote Cianci.

Cianci, who said that he had created a trust to provide for his daughter and grandchildren in the event of his death or imprisonment, acknowledged that his "preoccupation" with himself had harmed his daughter. But he said that Nicole had been there for him since his indictment in Operation Plunder Dome, and now he wanted to be there for her.

Nicole wrote that the prospect of her father going to prison was difficult, "because I love him unconditionally."

Arlene Violet, the former nun and attorney general who was friendly with Sheila and Nicole and knew the grandchildren, was incensed after the letters became public. As host of a popular afternoon talk show on WHJJ, she blasted Cianci on the air for ignoring Nicole and his grandchildren and now using them to help himself. She charged that Cianci, after his conviction, had sent an aide to his daughter's home to tell them to go on welfare. "Shame on you, Buddy Cianci!" she shouted.

A Cianci family tragedy quickly became a public spectacle. David Ead, who was on home confinement, phoned Violet's show to call Cianci "a scumbag."

The next morning Cianci went on his radio show and called Violet a liar. Cianci's accountant called in to say that Cianci paid Nicole's rent, car insurance, and medical insurance. Nicole's former landlord reported that Cianci had paid his daughter's rent and bought her a car. Callers even questioned whether Violet was a lesbian; Cianci's cohost, Steve Kass, snapped: "What the hell does she know about raising children? What would she know about tough love?"

DePetro joined the fray, asking listeners whether they believed Violet, his WHJJ colleague and a former attorney general, or Cianci, a convicted felon and "pathological liar." Tony Freitas weighed in, writing a letter to the Bureau of Prisons urging that Cianci's request be denied. He accused Cianci of using Nicole's "unfortunate situation for his own personal gain."

The next day Cianci met a *Journal* reporter at the bar at Davio's to deliver a handwritten letter from Nicole attacking Violet for her public remarks, and accusing her of "telling lies about my father."

The following week, after Congressmen Patrick Kennedy and James Langevin intervened with the Bureau of Prisons for Nicole's sake, Cianci was reassigned to the federal prison in Fort Dix, New Jersey.

During Thanksgiving week, Cianci had dinner with Wendy Materna, now Wendy Johannsen, who was in town with her family visiting relatives. After a period of homesickness for Providence, she had made a new life for herself in Florida. She and her husband had a son, Christian, who had his mother's thick blond hair and blue eyes. The bitterness of her breakup with Cianci had faded, and they remained friendly. (When Cianci called shortly after his indictment, Wendy's five-year-old had gotten on the phone and said, "Buddy, I thought you were in jail," prompting a chuckle from the mayor.)

"How tragic it is for this man who has so much talent to end up in prison," she reflected. "The years I spent with him were the highest of the highs and the lowest of the lows."

The day before Thanksgiving, Cianci was at the eye doctor's when he received a call from the lawyer handling his appeal, Terry MacFadyen. "I have some bad news," MacFadyen told him. "We lost the appeal."

The day after Thanksgiving, Cianci went on the radio for the last time and said good-bye.

"You'll always be our Buddy," sobbed Anne from North Providence. "Please don't give up."

Cianci tried to remain upbeat. He said that he'd be back in four or five years, maybe less if he won the appeal of his conviction. He said he might lose weight, learn Spanish, quit smoking, cut back on his drinking. "There's no alcohol there, there's no good wine," he said.

"Probably the wine list is fairly limited," said his sidekick, Steve Kass.

Said Cianci, "It's like going to a very, very inexpensive spa."

Only one of the callers who got through was glad that Cianci was going to prison. "You betrayed the public trust," he said. "You committed the worst crime any man could commit—an elected official who was corrupt."

But Kass cut the man off.

"If you're that vindictive or that mean-spirited, take it out on somebody else. . . . Go kick someone in a wheelchair."

THE DAY BEFORE he left for prison, Cianci sat in the Biltmore and did a live interview on NBC's *Today* show with Matt Lauer, who had covered Cianci as a young Providence television reporter in the early 1980s.

"I've had better Wednesdays, Thursdays, and Fridays," Cianci told Lauer. After his Plunder Dome indictment Cianci had said that he'd had better Mondays. After his indictment for assaulting Raymond DeLeo, he'd said that he'd had better Tuesdays. He was running out of days.

The next day, Thursday, December 5, as a snowstorm moved up the East Coast, Buddy Cianci checked out of Providence. Fat white flakes fell outside the Biltmore. Christmas carols filled the air. Skaters glided around the ice rink across the street. Cianci, his face puffier and older-looking, said how surreal the day seemed.

His longtime employee and errand boy, retired police officer Bob Lovell, drove him to New Jersey. As they headed south on Interstate 95, Cianci called a producer for *60 Minutes* to request a sneak preview of a segment about him scheduled to air that Sunday. But the producer told him it was against the show's policy.

Cianci had no need to worry. En route to prison, he still had the ability to spin *60 Minutes*. In a rosy profile that painted Cianci as the victim of overzealous prosecutors, Morley Safer allowed the ex-mayor to rewrite his ugly assault on DeLeo. The cigarette, said Cianci, "wasn't even lit. Just threw it at him. End of story."

By the time the profile ran on Sunday night, Cianci would be an inmate, in a harsh new world where the senior prisoners dictated what shows to watch in the television room. Another former Rhode Island public official who had done time at Fort Dix recalled watching inmates use a "lock in the sock"—a combination lock stuffed into a sock—to settle fights over the television. Cianci would be sleeping in a twenty-by-twenty-five-foot room with bunk beds housing a dozen or so other convicts. Many were drug dealers and illegal aliens, with a sprinkling of mobsters. Lights-out was at 11 P.M. Prisoners got up between 5 and 6 A.M.

"You're basically losing your life," said the former Rhode Island convict. "All the things that are part of who you are are gone. Buddy lived a twenty-four-hour day. He was everywhere. Now he's nowhere."

Cianci and Lovell spent the night in Trenton. The next morning, with eight inches of snow blanketing the sprawling prison and military-base complex in southern New Jersey, Lovell pulled up to a military checkpoint at the entrance to the base. The guards would not allow Cianci to take in the cigarettes and novel that he carried.

Lovell had been with Cianci since 1974, when they walked a police picket line together to protest "No Dough Joe" Doorley's refusal to buy new police uniforms. He had fought back tears outside the courtroom prior to Cianci's sentencing.

"Good-bye," said Cianci, hugging Lovell. "Thanks for all your help."

Buddy Cianci climbed into a white prison van with tinted windows. The van drove off across the flat, barren landscape, carrying away the prince of Providence.

Shortly before I began work on *The Prince of Providence*, I was sitting in Buddy Cianci's office, listening to the mayor talk about a Caribbean dictator.

"Take Trujillo," said Cianci gleefully. "Now he was a bastard."

Cianci, who had been indicted a few weeks earlier, was unwinding after a press conference with his friend Anthony Quinn to promote the Providence Latin American Film Festival. Rafael Trujillo, the notorious Dominican Republic dictator from 1930 to 1961, had come up because Quinn was supposed to play him in a movie being shot in Puerto Rico that summer. Cianci had dug up an old biography of Trujillo that he had read years ago, when he said he was considering President Reagan's offer to become the United States ambassador to the Dominican Republic.

"I flew down to look around," he recalled. "I went with Ellsworth Bunker, who wrote their constitution. He was the U.S. ambassador to Vietnam. Jeb Bush was in the delegation. We flew down on Air Force Two. You couldn't drink the water, but there was a big swimming pool at our hotel. Palm trees all around. People wore white suits. I had just lost the race for governor and I was gonna bail. I went to the palace and met the president. I also met the mayor of Santo Domingo. We went to his inauguration. I remember riding in the mayor's limousine and suddenly hundreds of people surround the car and start rocking it. I thought, 'Shit! It's a revolution!' The mayor says, 'No, they *like* you when they do that!' These crazy fucking people are trying to lift up the car and carry it, to show how much they love you."

Cianci laughed and took a quick drag on his cigarette. Then he returned to Trujillo.

"A Ph.D. student at Columbia University in New York was writing his thesis about the misfortunes of the dictatorship. He had published some pretty unflattering things about Trujillo. One day, Trujillo sent a plane to New York. Two guys went up to Columbia and hustled the student into a car, then drove him to La Guardia and put him on the plane. They had diplomatic immunity, so no one asked any questions. That night the guy was at Trujillo's compound. Trujillo comes in, wearing the boots, waving the swagger stick. They're out by a swimming pool, which is filled with piranha. Trujillo says, 'Tell me how shitty I am for my country. You say I'm a mean bastard? I'm going to show you how mean I am.' Then they throw him in the pool.

The water is thrashing with piranha and sharks, eating the shit out of the guy, right down to the bones. Dead.

"You know how they finally nailed Trujillo? The pilots gave him up. They got fired from their jobs, so they gave him up. That was the beginning of the end for Trujillo. When word got out, public opinion turned against him."

Cianci laughed, a throaty chuckle. "What a banana republic," he said, grinning. "We need more of that around here."

Those two stories—the adoring throng rocking his limousine, the despotic dictator punishing a critic—reflected the two sides of the mayor. Writing a book about Cianci gave me the opportunity to witness both sides firsthand.

As I went about my research into this complex character, he and I engaged in the traditional dance between journalist and politician. On some days, he would invite me in to share some of his stories—though always selectively, for this most public of figures managed to glide through his high-profile career without really addressing the most personal or controversial aspects of his life. On other occasions, he would shut me out and call me "the novelist" or a "mercenary." Journalists write books about politicians all the time, but Cianci tried to make it sound as if I was acting unethically in doing so. When he learned that I was writing this book, he called Howard Sutton, the publisher of *The Providence Journal,* and tried to have me ordered off the project. Later, Cianci complained to *The Boston Globe*'s Alex Beam that I was "stalking" him—showing up at his press conferences and other public events and trying to ask him questions about his personal life. When I mentioned that to Brown University political science professor Darrell West, the author of a biography of Rhode Island congressman Patrick Kennedy, Darrell told me that that's what all biographers must do.

Just before his trial, when he learned that the movie rights to the book had been optioned, Cianci confronted me after a press conference at Prospect Park, near the statue of Roger Williams with his hand outstretched over downtown. A television reporter asked him what he thought of the movie deal. The mayor, seeing me standing with the other reporters, pulled me into the picture, put his arm around me, and squeezed me hard on the back of the neck. Then, with the cameras rolling, the mayor proceeded, in classic Cianci fashion, to turn the tables by trying to interview me about how much money I was getting. We sparred playfully for a minute or two and then he dismissed me, saying, "Go play in the traffic now." The film clip later appeared in a *60 Minutes* profile of Cianci.

Then there was the Saturday night, in the midst of the jury's deliberations, that I decided to go watch the mayor serve as grand marshal in the Providence gay-pride parade. Cianci was seated in the back of a convertible with a drag queen when he saw me standing on the sidewalk. "Stanton, is that you?" he barked. "Get in!" I dutifully climbed into the front seat and rode through the rest of the parade with him, then joined him for drinks at a restaurant, followed by an impromptu trip to a gay nightclub with flashing strobe lights and half-naked men dancing on stage. He was, as I'd seen him on many other occasions, surprisingly relaxed given the enormous pressure he was under, a gifted raconteur with a remarkable capacity to compartmentalize.

The unqualified love that Cianci inspired in many people was evident that night in the steady stream of admirers, as was the underlying loneliness that so many of his former aides had described. As the evening wore on, he became boozy and sentimental. In the club, where the music was so loud that he had to put his mouth up to my ear and shout to be heard, Cianci told me: "You're a good shit. I'm sorry I've been such a prick, but I've been under a lot of pressure. I hope for the sake of your children that you make a million dollars on the book." Later, riding back to the Biltmore in his limousine, Cianci seemed tired as he dropped me off in front of Haven Brothers, the silver diner on wheels next to City Hall. The next day was Father's Day, and we wished one another a happy Father's Day. He told me to give him a call, and that he would talk to me.

But he never did formally cooperate with this book, which is not surprising. For years, Cianci had talked about writing his own book. He would needle me about how big an advance he thought I had gotten, and ask how much money I was going to give him.

"What do I get out of talking to you except agita?" he asked me one day in August 2002, about a month after his conviction, as he was preparing to leave office and be sentenced to prison.

It was a muggy afternoon. The mayor's office was unusually quiet. Cianci sat in his shirtsleeves in his air-conditioned office, which felt like a meat locker, signing papers and going through his mail. He picked up a letter from a literary agent and read it aloud, then dropped it on his desk and said, "I get these all the time."

The mayor launched into a lengthy discussion of the publishing industry— how there are fifty-six thousand titles published every year, and most sell fewer than five thousand copies, et cetera. Cianci told me that his story should command "a healthy six figures." When I said that I'd gotten nowhere near that, he looked at me incredulously and shouted, "How could you sell yourself so cheap?" I replied that I was approaching this project as a chance to expand myself as a journalist by writing about a subject that fascinated me; I wanted to be fairly compensated, but it wasn't all about the money. "Why not?" he said.

Outside, the wind was picking up and greenish-black clouds darkened the sky. Rain began to smack against the windows.

"The books that really sell today are the tell-all autobiographies," Cianci said. "I reread Lee Iacocca's book a few days ago. What makes that book is the personal stuff, Henry Ford calling him a Jew. You won't have my stories—the stories about

Frank Sinatra's visits to Providence, the time I helped him get someone into Brown. You need the behind-the-scenes stuff. I'll tell you what: we'll call Random House right now, get a new deal, write the book together, get a six-hundred-thousand-dollar advance. I guarantee you that by five P.M. they'll rip up your contract and we'll have a new one.

"My story is the story of a man who becomes mayor, has political battles. He beats up his wife's lover, has to leave office. He comes back, brings back the city. Then he runs into some other bullshit with the feds. He's kind of a rogue. Maybe he wins his appeal. . . ."

Thunder rumbled above City Hall and lightning flashed outside. Cianci, his voice a similar low rumble, continued, "It's like thunder and lightning. Your book will have the lightning, but it won't have the thun-derrrr."

But when you live as large a life as Buddy Cianci, your stories are everywhere—from the old political wards to the glitzy Providence Renaissance bistros, in the cracks and crevices of Providence itself. Everybody in Rhode Island, it seems, has a Buddy story. I was inundated. While some people were reluctant to talk, out of loyalty or for fear of incurring Cianci's wrath, many more were eager. Some spoke anonymously, because they still have to live in Rhode Island. They shared their stories, good and bad, fond and outrageous. I have tried to weave their stories into a tapestry of Providence and of a gifted and flawed man who embodied both the corruption and the rebirth of an American city. In the words of Willie Stark in *All the King's Men:* "Dirt makes grass grow; a diamond ain't a thing in the world but a piece of dirt that got awful hot. And God-a-Mighty picked up a handful of dirt and blew on it and made you and me and George Washington."

Love him or hate him—and with Buddy Cianci there is no middle ground—most would agree that Providence won't be the same without him. Even after he went away, many hungered for news of his life in prison. He worked in the prison kitchen, lost more than twenty pounds, and was still very bitter about his conviction. "I'm locked in the kitchen eight hours a day," he wrote Wendy Materna, noting that this was his 110th day behind bars. "Prison is no fun, but an eye opener," he wrote Mark Silberstein of the *East Side Monthly.* "There are some nice people here. And, then again, there are those who do not have too many branches on the family tree." The mayor remained hopeful for his appeal.

Meanwhile, the new mayor, David Cicilline, was confronted with a fifty-nine-million-dollar budget deficit that he attributed to the excesses of the Cianci years. Cicilline struggled to change a culture where "everything was a favor and a handshake." When former New York mayor Rudy Giuliani, whom Cianci had once feted on Federal Hill, visited Providence, he signed his new autobiography for Cicilline and said, "Good luck cleaning up your town."

Still, many in Providence said that they wouldn't bet against Cianci's winning his appeal and making yet another comeback. He has, after all, kept his Presidential Suite at the Biltmore. Shortly before he checked out, Cianci teased the reporters who had chronicled his exploits over the years and served as his foils. "You're gonna miss me," he said.

I hope that I have succeeded in capturing the thunder and the lightning that was Buddy—a dynamic spark both destructive and illuminating.

Buddy Cianci, though he never formally agreed to cooperate with this book, provided considerable information in numerous interviews and encounters during the nearly four years that Operation Plunder Dome played out. We spoke in his ornate office at City Hall, in his limousine riding around Providence, and at various events throughout the city: speeches, groundbreakings, dedications, fund-raisers, parties, parades, and press conferences. I had ample opportunity to observe the King of Retail up close and in his element—politicking, schmoozing, joking, raging, cajoling, bullying, reminiscing, and painting his vision of Providence.

Early in 2000, shortly before his indictment, Cianci discussed his early career, philosophy, and style during a two-hour lunch at Davio's. He also invited me to ride around with him one night, and to attend one of his directors' meetings at City Hall. I also spoke to him quite a bit during his trial: in the hallway outside the courtroom, on the courthouse steps during rambling discourses with reporters, and in his office as he awaited the jury's verdict.

I interviewed many people who worked for and supported the mayor, including Carol Agugiaro and her husband, Joe Agugiaro, Sharky Almagno, Paul Campbell, Artin H. Coloian, Patrick Conley, Raymond Dettore, Mickey Farina, Melissa Forrest, Rosemary Glancy, Ron Glantz, Charles Mansolillo, William McGair, Patricia McLaughlin, Bruce Melucci, John Palmieri, Urbano Prignano, Jr., Thomas Rossi, Normand Roussel, Carl Stenberg, and Joe Vileno, as well as others who wish to remain anonymous.

I also interviewed several past and present members of the Providence City Council who have been with Cianci or against him, or both, over the years. They include Luis Aponte, Vin Cirelli, Raymond Cola, Nick Easton, Joshua Fenton, Sanford Gorodetsky, John Lombardi, Robert Lynch, John Murphy, Rita Williams, Balbina Young, and Ed Xavier. I also talked to Steve Woerner, who worked as the council's auditor in the early 1990s, and James Lombardi, who succeeded him.

Wendy Materna, Vincent Vespia, Jr., Herbert DeSimone, and Bruce Sundlun provided me with insights into the personal Buddy, as did others who wish to remain anonymous.

Many journalists who have known Cianci through the years shared their insights, including past and present *Providence Journal* colleagues M. Charles Bakst,

Scott MacKay, Bob Kerr, Doane Hulick, Ken Mingis, and Karen Lee Ziner. Also, Jim Taricani of WJAR–Channel 10, Jack White of WPRI–Channel 12, Jim Hummel from WLNE–Channel 6, and Rudy Cheeks and Chip Young, a.k.a. Philippe & Jorge, columnists for the *Providence Phoenix.*

The archives of *The Providence Journal* and the defunct *Evening Bulletin* provided an exhaustive day-by-day account of Cianci's career and the various issues confronting Providence over the past four decades. I found several books helpful in understanding Cianci, urban politics, and Providence's history and comeback. *The Prince,* by Machiavelli, was a valuable primer, as was *The Portable Renaissance Reader,* edited by James Bruce Ross and Mary Martin McLaughlin. *Governing Middle-Sized American Cities,* edited by Wilbur Rich, devotes a chapter to Cianci and the Providence Renaissance. Two useful sources on the Providence Renaissance were *Interface: Providence,* a 1974 study of the center city conducted by Professor Gerald Howes and his team of design students at the Rhode Island School of Design, and a 2002 booklet compiled by architect William Warner, *An Abbreviated History of the Waterplace Park and River Relocation Projects.* Three valuable resources on local history were *Rhode Island: A History,* by William G. McLoughlin; *Rhode Island,* by George H. Kellner and J. Stanley Lemons; and the Rhode Island Century series, by Scott MacKay and Jody McPhillips, which ran in *The Providence Journal* throughout 1999. Also, *Downtown Providence,* an architectural inventory compiled by the Rhode Island Historical Preservation Commission, and *Downtown Providence in the Twentieth Century,* by Joe Fuoco and A. J. Lothrop.

As chief of *The Providence Journal's* investigative team, I covered Operation Plunder Dome from the day it became public, on April 28, 1999. Over the next three and a half years, as the case unfolded, I got to know the players. My investigative colleagues and I broke stories concerning the evidence against the mayor, the University Club affair, the city's tow-truck operators, Edward Voccola's dealings with the city, and the mayor's personal use of campaign funds, which led to a state grand-jury probe and a civil consent order in which the mayor agreed to repay $7,400 in improper campaign expenditures and his campaign organization paid a $22,000 civil fine.

Prologue: A Knock on the Door

I interviewed W. Dennis Aiken about his early experiences as an FBI agent in Rhode Island. Cianci and Bruce Sundlun told me the story of the mayor's having been offered a sitcom, in the early 1980s. A former aide told me about the mayor's "to-go cups." A source told me of Aiken's visit to Cianci's house on the morning of April 28, 1999, and three other sources confirmed it.

Chapter One: The Prosecutor, the Priest, and the Mob Boss

In an interview with me, Cianci mentioned his race to Maryland to uncover the truth about Father Moriarty. I filled in the details by interviewing Bobby Stevenson, the Providence police detective who accompanied him; former prosecutors Richard Israel and William Dimitri; former state police detective Vincent Vespia, Jr.; Monsignor William O'Donnell and Margaret McNeill at St. Ignatius in Oxon Hill, Maryland; and Allan Densford, the father of the girl who was baptized. (Stacy Lynn Densford grew up, married, and recently had her second daughter; she works as a hotel manager in Dallas, Texas. The Father Moriarty story has become part of Densford-family folklore.) Two key actors in the drama, Father Moriarty and prosecutor Irving Brodsky, are dead.

Brian Andrews, retired detective commander of the Rhode Island State Police, shared his insights and documents detailing Raymond Patriarca's criminal career and the influence of the Mafia in Rhode Island—including a transcript of Colonel Walter Stone's 1963 congressional testimony. I obtained a transcript of Patriarca's 1959 congressional testimony, in which he was questioned by Bobby Kennedy, from the John F. Kennedy Library in Boston. Lionel Benjamin, a retired state police major, told me about Frank Sinatra, Mia Farrow, and the tale of Damon Runyon's widow's diamond ring. Vinny Teresa, in *My Life in the Mafia,* described Patriarca's ties to Papa Doc Duvalier.

I also read old state police reports chronicling Patriarca's career back to his bootlegging days, and FBI reports summarizing conversations in Patriarca's vending office from the illegal bugging ordered by J. Edgar Hoover in the early 1960s, as part of Bobby Kennedy's war on organized crime. The mob boss's hatred of Kennedy is apparent. In one conversation, after President John F. Kennedy's assassination, Patriarca lamented that his brother Bobby hadn't also been "whacked."

I learned about the Mafia in general and the Marfeo-Patriarca wars in particular from retired state police detective Vincent Vespia, Jr.; retired state police major Lionel Benjamin; former Providence police officers Vincent O'Connell, Don Kennedy, and Howard Luther; former Rhode Island attorneys general Herbert DeSimone and Richard Israel; and two Federal Hill sources who wish to remain anonymous.

A number of people talked to me about Cianci's family and childhood, most notably his aunt Josephine Antocicco. His cousin Norma Lynch told me the story of Buddy's telling his second-grade class he wanted to be president. Cianci, in comments to me and to other reporters over the years, talked about growing up and going to Moses Brown. Other sources, including aides and friends, talked to me about things that he told them about his childhood. Old-timers in Silver Lake also told me about the family. Wendy Materna offered insights into Cianci's relationship with his father and his father's womanizing, as did other sources who requested anonymity. Michael Traficante and Pasquale and Millie DeSocio talked about Buddy's youth. Mary Ann Sorrentino remembered him as a childhood performer. His music teacher, Celia Moreau, who has since died, talked about Buddy's performances in stories published in the *Journal*. *The Italo-Americans of Rhode Island*, published in the 1930s, offered biographical sketches of Cianci family members.

I learned about Silver Lake from many of its natives: Sharky Almagno, John Cicilline, Ronald and Christopher Del Sesto, Stephen Fortunato, Orlando Giansanti, Jr., Vincent Igliozzi, Teresa Merolli, Ralph Pappitto, Urbano Prignano, Jr., Fred Santagata, and Mike Traficante. Charlie Pisaturo sent me local historical articles. I also read Father Stephen Almagno's book chronicling the history of St. Bartholomew's, *The Days of Our Lives*.

I interviewed several schoolmates and teachers of Cianci's at Moses Brown, most notably Robert Ellis Smith, Jerry Zeoli, King O'Dell, Steve Fortunato, Walter Nason, and Edmund Armstrong. Also, Barry Fain, Stephen Ham, George Kilborn, Frank Robinson, Doug Marquis, and Donald Shaghalian. I went through the yearbooks for the years he attended. Former Mount Pleasant wrestler John A. Volpe and his coach, Lou Marciano, talked about Cianci's wrestling career.

For Buddy's career as a prosecutor, I talked to Vin Vespia, Steve Fortunato, Herb DeSimone, Richard Israel, William Dimitri, and Slater Allen.

Chapter Two: The Anticorruption Candidate

I talked at length to Skip Chernov about his life and the Harold Copeland case before his death late in 2001, and read an unpublished manuscript that Chernov had written about his life. I also read stories published at the time in *The Providence Journal-Bulletin*, including two longer profiles, "Up from Rock 'n' Roll" by George Popkin in 1971 and "The Rise and Fall of a Boy Wonder," by Carol Stocker in 1976. I also talked to his former partner Bruce Goldstein; Morris Nathanson, who designed the Incredible Organ Pub; Chernov's former lawyers Milton Stanzler and Jim O'Neil; former Rhode Island attorney general Richard Israel; and former state police detective Vincent Vespia, Jr. I also read Chernov's and Goldstein's 1973 state police statements about Copeland, and the court file of a subsequent civil suit by Chernov against the Civic Center over lost concert business.

Chernov's account of being pressured to change his testimony by a member of the Civic Center Authority was corroborated by his lawyer, Jim O'Neil. When Chernov sued the Civic Center, O'Neil told me that he saw a memo, written by a lawyer for Chernov's business partner. The memo described the meeting, which Chernov had told me about, in which Lloyd Bliss, deputy chairman of the Civic Center Authority, told Chernov that he could resume promoting concerts if he changed his testimony about Copeland.

I found background information on Joe Doorley in the Doorley Archives at Providence College, including letters, speeches, biographical sketches, and materials about urban renewal in the 1960s. I also interviewed his top policy aide, John Cicilline, and political allies of Doorley and Larry McGarry, including Ray Devitt, John Murphy, and Ed Xavier, as well as Francis Darigan, who challenged Doorley in the 1974 primary. Dr. Paul O'Malley at Providence College, who worked in Darigan's campaign, provided background about the Democratic machine and the texture of life in postwar Providence, as did Nick Easton, who is doing a doctorate in political science on political machines, and Dr. Patrick T. Conley. *Journal* colleague Scott MacKay gave me a research paper written by Providence College graduate student Carl Antonucci about the Doorley-McGarry split and the 1974 campaign. I showed the paper to Cianci one day during the Plunder Dome trial, and he talked about the 1974 race.

Several sources talked about Doorley's drinking, including Farina, Glantz, Murphy, and Xavier. Murphy and Xavier, both of whom served on Doorley's campaign committee, told me that Doorley's campaign advisers talked to the mayor about controlling his drinking during the campaign. Xavier also described Doorley's drinking buddies joking about Cianci. Farina described the Old Canteen encounter between Cianci and Doorley, and Vin Vespia, who heard about it from Cianci, corroborated it.

I also talked to Vin Vespia, Mickey Farina, and two other sources who wish to remain anonymous about the relationship between Buddy Cianci and Sheila Bentley.

The intrigue of the Cianci campaign was described to me by Ron Glantz, Mickey Farina, and Sharky Almagno. There were also stories in the newspaper at the time about the formation of Friends of Cianci. Cianci and Farina told me about the fateful Rosario Club meeting on primary night. Farina and Glantz described the clandestine van rendezvous. Herb DeSimone and Jean Coughlin talked to me about the campaign in general. Two sources told me about Lloyd Griffin's Atlantic City ploy in securing absentee ballots, including a former Cianci aide who heard the story from Cianci. A source who was at the hotel on election night told me about Cianci's comment to his mother. Cianci told me about McGarry's being carried into his house to meet with him after the election; McGarry told the *Journal* at the time about the meeting.

Chapter Three: The Art of Politics

Cianci's workout with the city softball team was described in a *Providence Journal* story and photo-essay. For the inauguration, I drew on the *Journal*'s coverage and also looked at pictures in a file in the newspaper's library.

The Robert Haxton affair was chronicled in the *Journal,* including an in-depth story by Lorraine Hopkins that ran on November 14, 1976. I also interviewed Ron Glantz, Major John J. Leyden of the Providence police, and Francis Darigan.

For vignettes about the mayor's style, I interviewed several former aides and others. Joe Agugiaro described the mayor's trip to Nashville to lobby for the Fraternal Order of Police convention, including the al dente story, which was also referred to in a *Journal* story about Cianci. Joe Vileno was in the mayor's office when he slid out of his chair in reaction to the news that the Biltmore had closed. Vileno also told me about the mayor's pressuring the banks to cash senior citizens' Social Security checks. Another former aide, who wishes to remain anonymous, described the meeting with Antoinette Downing, which was also referred to in newspaper clippings. Cianci told me the story of the City Hall janitor stealing the aldermen's chairs that turned up in the antique store. Two sources told me the story of the mayor's losing his temper and throwing chairs in his outer office. Barney Prignano and Carol and Joseph Agugiaro described Cianci's interaction with his police drivers.

Nick Easton and Ken Orenstein described the problems with the mayor's Office of Community Development.

Cianci, Herb DeSimone, and federal appeals judge Bruce Selya, Chafee's 1976 campaign chairman, described Cianci's jockeying with Chafee for the U.S. Senate seat in 1976. Joe Vileno described the GOP function at the West Valley Inn in West Warwick, when Chafee upstaged Cianci. A source with ties to both Cianci and Chafee also talked to me about the behind-the-scenes drama.

Norm Roussel described accompanying Cianci to Kansas City to speak at the 1976 Republican National Convention.

For the account of Chief Ricci's suicide, I interviewed two of the police officials who found his body, John Leyden and Ted Collins, as well as Ron Glantz, who described the phone call from Cianci in which the mayor wondered whether Ricci had left a note. A Cianci aide who requested anonymity described being angry at the mayor following Ricci's death. I also read the extensive *Journal* coverage.

Chapter Four: Operation Snow Job

For the story of the Marquette rape accusation, I drew on federal court records that emerged during Cianci's libel suit against *New Times* magazine, including the July 24, 1978, *New Times* article by Craig Waters and interrogatories in which Cianci said that he paid his accuser three thousand dollars. (Cianci has said that the civil settlement had nothing to do with the district attorney's decision not to charge him criminally.) I also obtained police and prosecution records from 1966, including the alleged victim's handwritten statement, a Wisconsin State Crime Laboratory report, and a police summary stating that Cianci had failed a polygraph test three times and that his accuser passed the test. The police summary also quotes a crime-lab investigator calling it "one of the most clear-cut cases of rape he had ever processed," and the Milwaukee district attorney at the time, Hugh O'Connell, calling it one of the more "dastardly" crimes he had ever seen, but that "due to a lack of evidence prosecution was almost impossible."

In researching the events of 1978, I interviewed Ron Glantz and Herb DeSimone about their trip to Milwaukee; Milwaukee lawyer Alan Eisenberg, a law-school classmate of Cianci's; Chuck Hauser, then executive editor of *The Providence Journal;* Joel Rawson, another editor; and *Journal* reporters Doane Hulick and Bert Wade. I also talked to Paul Giacobbe, then a television reporter for WJAR–Channel 10, and obtained footage of a televised interview that he did in 1978 with Ruth Bandlow.

In researching the Blizzard of '78, I consulted *Journal* clips, including a special section that the newspaper later published, and a Channel 10 television documentary. I also interviewed Cianci and Glantz, who both blamed Governor Garrahy for the delays in plowing Providence, and a Cianci aide who was snowbound at City Hall.

Glantz told me about the falling-out between Cianci and McGarry, which was also evident in McGarry's public criticisms of Cianci in 1978.

The Wednesday Night Massacre was described to me by Glantz; another Cianci aide who requested anonymity; Ray Dettore, one of the Cianci appointees sworn in that night; and council members Ed Xavier, Joe Cirelli, and Charles Mansolillo. I also read *Journal* stories about the massacre and its aftermath. My description of the 1935 Bloodless Revolution is based on McLoughlin's *Rhode Island: A History,* and *Pride Without Prejudice: The Life of John O. Pastore,* by Ruth S. Morgenthau.

Cianci aide Joe Vileno told me about trying to make bets on the election with Vinny Cirelli at the Old Timer's Tap. Cirelli told me about making peace with Cianci after the 1978 election and described the fund-raiser where Cianci stood on the bar.

Chapter Five: The Education of Ronnie Glantz

I interviewed Ronnie Glantz extensively about his role in Cianci's first administration and the corruption that engulfed it. His allegations of payoffs to Cianci from specific contractors are also contained in a 1987 state police report that I obtained and in court papers filed by the government in Operation Plunder Dome, offering a preview of what Glantz would have testified to if he had been called. (Glantz could only have been called as a rebuttal witness by the government if Cianci had taken the stand and opened the door to evidence of earlier corruption.) James A. Forte, the contractor whom Glantz alleges gave him ten thousand dollars to deliver to Cianci, later pleaded guilty to paying fifteen thousand in bribes in 1990 to city officials in neighboring Pawtucket. The other contractors named in the state police report and in the court papers include Jack and Danny Capuano, Tony Rosciti, Gene Castellucci, and Robert Doorley. Those documents also name Joe DiSanto as a bribe recipient.

Several people described the close relationship between Cianci and Glantz, including Carol Agugiaro, who also told me how Glantz would clown around in the office. Jim Taricani told me about seeing Glantz and Cianci arguing in the mayor's office one day over a winning lottery ticket.

In a March 28, 1979, story, *The Providence Journal*'s Doane Hulick quoted political sources that Cianci was in California pitching himself as a possible vice-presidential nominee to Ronald Reagan and Gerald Ford; Cianci said the trip was nonpolitical. Two sources told me that Cianci was, in fact, interested in the vice presidency; one said that he came home "pissed off" that it hadn't worked out.

Wendy Materna, David Ead, and another source told me of hearing Cianci describe his visit to Frank Sinatra's house in Palm Springs, including the reference to Raymond Patriarca. Ead and the source recalled Cianci's saying in the early 1980s that Patriarca's picture was on the wall. Materna said she heard the story several times in later years, with the bartender asking about Patriarca but no reference to his picture on the wall. Paul Campbell told me the story of how Cianci helped Sinatra's friend's child who wanted to attend Brown University; another source confirmed it. Joe Vileno told me about Cianci's telling him that governors weren't like mayors, because they could keep people at arm's length. I've heard Cianci say similar things. Cianci's exchange with former San Francisco mayor Joseph Alioto was written about in *The Providence Journal* on May 21, 1979.

Glantz and contractor Thomas Ricci described Mickey Farina's City Hall parties with city contractors. The subsequent falling-out between Cianci and Farina—though not the reason why—was reported in *The Providence Journal*. I spoke to Glantz and Farina.

The *Journal* wrote stories about Cianci's fund-raising operation, including one on July 8, 1984, by Katherine Gregg and Ira Chinoy, that cited the internal strategy memo and quoted Therese Kelly about how employees were pressured to buy fund-raising tickets. Several Cianci aides told me the same thing, as did police major John J. Leyden, who says that the mayor pressured him. A former aide told me the story of Cianci asking aides if they liked their paycheck. Former Cianci aide Bruce Melucci described the ticket-committee meetings. Glantz, Melucci, and Carol Agugiaro told me that Buckles Melise was a regular and a strong ticket seller. A former aide told me that Cianci spent campaign funds to pay the butcher's bill.

Glantz told me about the time that Cianci asked a policeman to watch his mother's house because there was five hundred thousand dollars in cash in the safe; he also told the state police about that, according to a 1987 state police memo summarizing an interview in federal prison in Allenwood, Pennsylvania, with Glantz.

Tommy Ricci corroborates Glantz's description of how games were played with bid specifications, emergency contracts, and splitting bigger jobs into smaller ones to avoid competitive bidding. He also told me about meeting President Ford; the bar melee at the Marriott was confirmed by a retired police official.

Jimmy Notorantonio's trash-into-cash scheme is documented in court records and newspaper accounts. When Noto was sentenced to prison, he drove to Lewisburg, Pennsylvania, with his good friend Joe Doorley.

I interviewed two Cianci aides, Patrick T. Conley and Paul Campbell, regarding the 1980 governor's race. Cianci told me the story of his helicopter's emergency landing at the Port of Providence and the guard dogs. *Providence Journal* sports columnist Bill Reynolds was with Jimmy Breslin for the comments on Cianci's helicopter. Chafee's former chief of staff David Griswold and a former Cianci aide both told me of Cianci's interest in an ambassadorship from Ronald Reagan but said that the mayor was never seriously considered.

Retired major Lionel Benjamin of the Rhode Island State Police told me about Cianci's anger over not being clued in about the state police investigation of no-show city workers. Another law enforcement source told me about Cianci's crack that Colonel Walter Stone would have to clean up after his horse once Cianci became governor. Former major John Leyden of the Providence Police Department told me about the investigation of the bad-check cops loyal to Cianci and the interference he faced from the police chief.

Two former Brown University officials, admissions director James Rogers and athletic director John Parry, talked about Cianci's reaction after his nephew was rejected. Another source confirmed Cianci's anger. (The Brown president at the time, Howard Swearer, is dead.) Cianci's Moses Brown classmate Robert Ellis Smith said that Cianci later told him the story, leaving the impression that the rejected nephew got in.

Mac Farmer told me the story of Tony Bucci's leaving his office light on to signal the City Council.

Retired state police captain Brian Andrews told me about following Patriarca and Blackjack DelSanto to Boston. I also have testimony from Nino Cucinotta describing the Boston Mafia induction ceremony. Jim Diamond, who worked for Attorney General Richard Israel, said that another Israel supporter described to him his conversation with Cianci about why the mayor would tolerate an underworld figure on the city payroll.

Bruce Melucci, Cianci's 1982 campaign manager, told me about the campaign strategy; he also told me the story of Cianci and Henry Cabot Lodge. Melucci told me that the shotguns the police carried in the garbage strike were not loaded.

Arthur F. Coia's ties to Patriarca were documented years later in court records and union disciplinary proceedings.

Chapter Six: Nightmare on Power Street

My account of Buddy Cianci's assault of Raymond DeLeo, and the mayor's alleged attempt to pressure Lenore Steinberg, is drawn primarily from court records in the case—grand-jury testimony and state police statements. My *Providence Journal* colleague Tracy Breton, who covered the original case, conducted a lengthy interview with DeLeo for a 2002 newspaper story that we worked on together. I subsequently interviewed DeLeo. I also spoke to William McGair and Herbert DeSimone, who were there that night; Lieutenant Richard Tamburini; Vincent O'Connell, who worked for Cianci as a private detective on the case; and other sources connected to the case who wish to remain anonymous. Cianci's only comment to me about that night on Power Street, made shortly before he went to prison, was "Remember, I never actually hit him with that fireplace log." I also read notes that Sheila kept over a period of several months following the assault, thanks to a source.

DeLeo and former Cianci aides described the mayor's crumbling marriage, including his infidelities, which Cianci acknowledged in his grand-jury testimony.

Norm Roussel, in an interview with me, described his weekend in London with Cianci shortly before the mayor pleaded no contest.

The intensifying corruption investigations of City Hall were well documented in *The Providence Journal* and state and federal indictments. Nick Easton described the meeting of state and federal authorities in the police chief's office to discuss corruption.

Chapter Seven: He Never Stopped Caring

Cianci has described his time in exile in various interviews during his years out of office and after his comeback. His failed comeback in 1984 was well documented in the *Journal,* including his rousing reception at the St. Joseph's Day parade. Aide Paul Campbell also told me about the comeback effort. Patrick Conley, Norm Roussel, Bruce Melucci, and Skip Chernov told me about their encounters with Cianci in exile. Cianci talked about having martinis with Bill Warner. A well-placed source confirmed that Cianci was one of the inspirations for the Pathological Liar character on *Saturday Night Live.*

Ron St. Pierre, then with WHJJ radio, told me about Cianci's hiring as a talkshow host; he also confirmed that everyone knew that the caller "Ray from Lincoln" was mob boss Raymond "Junior" Patriarca. Cianci's on-air roasting of Patrick Kennedy is recounted in Darrell West's biography of Patrick Kennedy. I was able to observe Cianci and the smoke-filled radio booth firsthand; in the winter of 1987–88 I did a weekly sports-talk show on college basketball with hosts Dick & Dave, immediately following Cianci's show.

Wendy Materna told me about her background and her relationship with Cianci.

I relied on interviews, court files, and *Journal* stories in recapping the state and federal corruption investigations of City Hall. I talked to Ronald Glantz, Thomas Ricci, former U.S. attorney Lincoln Almond, former federal prosecutor and Rhode Island attorney general James E. O'Neil, retired state police major Michael Urso, and other former members of law enforcement who requested anonymity. I also obtained a July 21, 1987, state police memo from Urso to Colonel Walter Stone, summarizing his meeting with Glantz at the Allenwood Federal Prison Camp.

There is an inconsistency in the matter of whether Cianci paid Buckles Melise five thousand dollars to keep him from testifying. Federal prosecutors, in court papers filed in Operation Plunder Dome, said that Glantz would testify that Cianci paid Melise. Glantz told me that Cianci had promised to pay Melise but subsequently refused, triggering an argument with Joe DiSanto over lunch at the Old Canteen. DiSanto, who wanted Melise taken care of, according to Glantz, later went on trial and Melise testified against him. DiSanto would not talk to me.

The Henry Gemma matter was covered by *The Providence Journal* and also described by Arlene Violet in her book, *Convictions.*

Two of Cianci's real estate partners, Patrick Conley and Paul Campbell, told me about their business ventures in the late 1980s. I also read news stories in the early 1990s describing his business dealings and personal finances during that period. Joseph Cerilli's allegations of bribing Cianci are contained in Cerilli's state grand-jury testimony in another corruption case, involving former governor Edward D. DiPrete. Joseph Mollicone's bribery allegations were described in court papers filed by federal prosecutors in Operation Plunder Dome.

Conley, Campbell, Tom Rossi, Wendy Materna, and Steven Antonson talked to me about the 1990 comeback, as did other advisers who requested anonymity. I also interviewed Fred Lippitt and read the *Journal*'s coverage of the campaign and subsequent court challenge.

Chapter Eight: Zorba the Mayor

Carol Agugiaro described the weekend meeting in the mayor's office when Cianci regained office. Two sources told me of warning Joe Almagno not to work for Cianci, and of his later statement that he was getting out before "this all blows up." John Palmieri described the chilly directors' meeting. Several former aides described Cianci's saying, "Marry your enemies and fuck your friends." Cianci told me the story of the Turks Head Club meeting with corporate executives.

The Amsterdam's incident was described to me by Peter Dupre, two of his business associates, and two patrons who were there that night and saw Cianci argue with the doorman. Cianci's girlfriend Wendy Materna told me that she was there and that there was a disagreement over the cover charge, which she felt they shouldn't have had to pay since they were going in for dinner. She said that she was unaware of anything that happened afterward.

Regarding the early 1990s wars with the City Council, I interviewed Joshua Fenton, Rita and Lyman Williams, Steve Woerner, Tom Rossi, John Lombardi, and Balbina Young.

In researching the mayor's personal finances, I talked to several people involved in negotiating various financial deals and obtained letters, financial statements, and an IRS document requesting records for an audit. I also relied on real estate records and published accounts in *The Providence Journal* detailing the mayor's personal finances. I also obtained records, which I used in a 2000 newspaper story, detailing the mayor's use of campaign funds to pay for his grandchildren's birthday parties, as well as Christmas presents and Christmas dinners at his house.

Several former aides described the relationship between Cianci and Corrente; one, who requested anonymity, recalled Corrente's saying that their job was to "make sure the king's ass is firmly in the chair," a quote confirmed by another source, and also that Corrente wanted it written on his tombstone that he was a stand-up guy. Several aides confirmed Corrente's turbulent affairs with women at City Hall, and his rivalry with Artin Coloian.

The section on the Providence Renaissance is based on newspaper clippings, architect William Warner's booklet *An Abbreviated History of the Waterplace Park and River Relocation Projects*, and interviews with Cianci; Ken Orenstein, former director of the Providence Foundation; Lynn Singleton, executive director of the Providence Performing Arts Center; and several former mayoral aides, including Paul Campbell and Patricia McLaughlin. I also attended a twentieth-anniversary press conference about the project, in April 2002, at which Warner and other key players reminisced. *The Boston Globe*'s Dick Lehr shared his notes from a Buddy profile in which he described the mayor after his appearance on the Don Imus radio show.

Wendy Materna told me about her life with Buddy and their breakup. Carol Agugiaro, Bruce Sundlun, and former aides also described the relationship and the affect of the breakup on Cianci.

I interviewed Anthony Quinn before his death in 2002. A source told me about the police officer's searching the hotel room of Carol Channing's stage manager. The then Rhode Island Senate majority leader, Paul Kelly, described one of his senators telling him how Cianci told her at Mediterraneo that he had several hundred police officers who worked for him. Former *Journal* reporter C. J. Chivers, now with *The New York Times*, was at Barnaby Evans's home the night that Buddy behaved boorishly.

Buff Chace told me about his efforts to refurbish downtown buildings. John Palmieri and another source also described Cianci's clashes with Chace. Palmieri and Tom Rossi described the mayor's stormy directors' meetings. Palmieri and another aide told me about the Calvin Klein trip to New York; Cianci told me about the dinner at Rao's.

Former governor Lincoln Almond and officials in his administration described their clashes with Cianci over economic development, including the New England Patriots deal. Michael Rich, former head of the Providence Foundation, told me about the reluctance of the business community to deal with Cianci.

Former Cianci aide Melissa Forrest told me that Art Coloian pulled workers out of City Hall to orchestrate a drive to knock mayoral challenger Pat Cortellessa off the ballot in 1998.

A source who was there described the Bob Dylan concert at the Strand.

Cianci and Paul Campbell, who ran the mayor's film commission, talked about the mayor's efforts to woo Hollywood.

Chapter Nine: Mr. Freon

I interviewed FBI special agent W. Dennis Aiken and cooperating witness Antonio R. Freitas about the genesis of Operation Plunder Dome and Freitas's year undercover. I also relied on extensive court records in the case, including videotapes and transcripts of videotapes of Freitas's dealings with Joseph Pannone, David Ead, and Frank Corrente. Former federal prosecutor James E. O'Neil told me about working with Aiken on the Edward Manning case.

The material on Edward Voccola is based on court records and extensive interviews that I conducted for a two-part *Providence Journal* series that I coauthored with David Herzog, which was published on May 7 and 8, 2000.

Cianci talked to me about his dislike of Linc Almond and John Chafee, which he has made no secret of. A former aide told me of the mayor's comment "You wouldn't do very well in front of the grand jury." The undercover FBI agent "Marco" was disclosed in Cianci's trial by his defense lawyer, Richard Egbert, who argued that it showed that the mayor would not tolerate corruption.

Chapter Ten: Toads in the Basement

Dennis Aiken and David Ead described the scene at Doris Vending on the morning of April 28, 1999. Four sources told me of Aiken's encounter with Cianci at the mayor's house that same morning. Ead and his lawyer, James E. O'Neil, and Joseph Pannone described being in the holding cell that morning. I was at City Hall that day when the search warrants were being executed and in court that afternoon for Ead's and Pannone's arraignment. My *Journal* colleague Bill Malinowski and I visited Ead at Doris Vending shortly after his arrest, and also interviewed Pannone's daughter, Debbie Pannone.

In subsequent interviews, Ead and Pannone talked to me about their backgrounds; one interview was conducted with Pannone after he was sent to prison in Fort Devens, Massachusetts. I was present when Pannone exchanged waves in the prison visitors' room with Mafia underboss Jerry Angiulo. I also interviewed Ead's former police partner, retired Providence major Pasquale "Pat" Rocchio, and former major John J. Leyden about Ead's days as a police officer. Ead gave me copies of his police commendations.

Bill Malinowski and I also interviewed Christopher Ise for a *Journal* story on October 15, 2000, that detailed the three bribes that Ead told the feds he arranged with the mayor.

Cianci talked to me about his aspirations of opening a library and archive. Carol Agugiaro told me about her farewell conversation with Cianci when she retired.

The account of the University Club affair is based on court testimony, trial exhibits, the tape recordings of the mayor's two telephone conversations with Steven Antonson, and my own interviews for an extensive *Providence Journal* story that I wrote on July 18, 1999.

Cianci talked to me early in 2001 about his feud with the producers of *The Sopranos*.

I covered Rosemary Glancy's case, including her trial in 2001, and interviewed her many times, including in her hospital room, with my colleague Tracy Breton, just after her release from prison and a few months before her death.

Chapter Eleven: Buddy's Inferno

I interviewed Laurel Casey. She also gave me a copy of a video documentary about a year in her life that includes footage of Cianci—*Laurel Casey: The Hurting Truth*, by Xaque Gruber.

I was at City Hall the night of Cianci's indictment for his press conference. My *Journal* colleague Karen Lee Ziner was with the mayor afterward in his back office and later that night at the Oyster Bar. For an account of Cianci's trip to the U.S. mayors' conference in Washington, I relied on the reporting of the *Journal*'s Washington bureau chief, John Mulligan.

I was one of the reporters who received phone calls at home from the mayor's office the night that the story about Richard Rose showing the Plunder Dome videotape broke. I spoke to Cianci the next day, when he accused Dennis Aiken of getting out of line with Chris Nocera. I also wrote the earlier stories about the dispute between Cianci and Tony Freitas. The background on Richard Rose is based on interviews I did with Rose, friends, and lawyers, including former U.S. attorney Sheldon

Whitehouse and Clifford Montiero, president of the Providence chapter of the NAACP, as well as Rose's public comments, in speeches and in a March 24, 1998, Q&A with the *Journal*'s Karen A. Davis.

I interviewed Amanda Milkovits, *The Providence Journal*'s police reporter who accompanied Cianci to Ground Zero in New York, about the trip. I was at the Providence train station the day after September 11, when Cianci showed up for the arrest of the terrorist suspect. I obtained a tape of *The Truman Taylor Show*.

I covered Cianci at a variety of public events in the weeks and months leading up to his trial, and engaged in private conversations with him afterward. An aide described his late-night party at the Biltmore following the Gay Ball. I read Tristan Taormino's August 10, 2001, column in *The Village Voice* about Cianci's attendance at the Ocean State Leather Contest. I was in Cianci's office when he was going through his mail and found his invitation to Liza Minnelli's wedding; Lynn Singleton of the Providence Performing Arts Center told me about the Providence drag queens calling Buddy's name outside the Waldorf in New York.

Two sources at the Providence Civic Center told me about the Boston Pops.

Two aides who were there described the episode involving "the mayor's special foot powder." One of them also described the incident in the Westin men's room and brushing white powder off Cianci's lapel.

An aide described Cianci's drinking and comments on the night of the Aretha Franklin concert. Several concertgoers told me about witnessing the mayor's antics, including his reference to her as "the soul of queen."

Chapter Twelve: Pomp and Circumstantial Evidence

I covered the trial of Buddy Cianci for *The Providence Journal*. Much of this chapter is based on my observations inside and outside the courtroom. Background on Richard Egbert came from conversations that we had during the trial, from a *Providence Journal* profile that I did with three other reporters in 1998, and from profiles prior to the trial by Bill Malinowski in the *Journal* and Ian Donnis in the *Providence Phoenix*. I also interviewed defense lawyers C. Leonard O'Brien and Richard Bicki.

A source told me how Cianci dispatched an aide to the Foxwoods Casino to ferret out David Ead's gambling records.

I interviewed G. Robert Blakey about the RICO law and Cianci's case.

The account of Barney Prignano's clash with prosecutor Richard Rose is based on my interviews with Prignano and his lawyer, Stephen Famiglietti. Dennis Aiken and Steven Antonson talked to me after the trial about Antonson's decision to cooperate. I interviewed John DePetro and his lawyer, Joseph Cavanagh (who has also represented my newspaper), regarding the Plunder Dome subpoena.

I was with Cianci at the gay-pride parade on June 15, 2002, and later that night at Intermezzo and Mirabar.

I interviewed two of the jurors after the case about their deliberations.

I was in the courtroom when Cianci was sentenced, spoke to him on the courthouse steps about the confusion over whether he was still the mayor, and then hurried over to City Hall to observe the confusion and last-minute negotiations over the change in power.

Michael Corrente, who has optioned this book for a movie, told me about his phone conversation with Cianci after the mayor was sentenced, in which Cianci made the crack about Jekyll and Hyde and asked why didn't he get two paychecks.

Epilogue: The Last Hurrah

I interviewed John Lombardi in the mayor's office shortly after he replaced Cianci. Sources saw Buckles Melise at Cicilline's campaign headquarters on primary night.

Wendy Materna talked to me about Nicole Cianci, as did Carol Agugiaro and other former Cianci aides who requested anonymity. So did Arlene Violet, who is a friend of Cianci's ex-wife, Sheila Bentley. Cianci, in his letter seeking a new prison assignment, acknowledged his daughter's problems and his own failings as a father, which he said he was eager to make up for. Police reports document the alleged assault of Nicole by her boyfriend. Former *Journal* reporter Jonathan Rockoff and I discovered that a company created by Cianci to handle his marinara sauce had paid Nicole's car insurance after she was involved in an accident. We obtained police records documenting this and also interviewed the driver of the other car.

A former Rhode Island public official who had been incarcerated at Fort Dix talked to me about conditions there, and what Cianci could expect.

Bob Lovell told reporters about Cianci's journey to prison.

BIBLIOGRAPHY

Almagno, R. Stephen. *The Days of Our Lives: St. Bartholomew's Parish, Providence, Rhode Island, 1907–1969.* Providence: St. Bartholomew's Church, 1976.

Antonucci, Carl. "The Doorley-McGarry Split and Its Impact on the Providence Mayoral Election of November 1974." Providence College, Graduate Research Seminar, May 14, 1997.

Beck, Sam. *Manny Almeida's Ringside Lounge.* Providence: Gavea-Brown Publications, 1992.

Blakey, G. Robert, and Thomas A. Perry. "An Analysis of the Myths That Bolster Efforts to Rewrite RICO and the Various Proposals for Reform: 'Mother of God— Is This the End of RICO?' " *Vanderbilt Law Review* 43 (1990): 851.

Breslin, Jimmy. "Jerry the Booster." In *The World of Jimmy Breslin.* New York: Ballantine, 1969.

Campbell, Paul, and Patrick T. Conley. *Providence: A Pictorial History.* Virginia Beach, Va.: Donning, 1982.

Chapple, Bennett. *"What Cheer" in Rhode Island.* Providence: Chapple, 1911.

Conley, Patrick T. *The Irish in Rhode Island.* Providence: The Rhode Island Heritage Commission and the Rhode Island Publications Society, 1986.

Fuller, Frank E. *Shadows of the Elms: Reminiscences of Moses Brown School.* Providence: Moses Brown School, 1983.

Fuoco, Joe. *Federal Hill.* Dover, N.H.: Arcadia, 1996.

Fuoco, Joe, and A. J. Lothrop. *Downtown Providence in the Twentieth Century.* Charleston, S.C.: Arcadia, 1998.

———. *Knightsville and Silver Lake.* Dover, N.H.: Arcadia, 1998.

Hayman, Robert W. *Catholicism in Rhode Island and the Diocese of Providence.* Providence: Diocese of Providence, 1982.

Holli, Melvin G. *The American Mayor.* University Park: Pennsylvania State University Press, 1999.

Jacobs, Jane. *The Death and Life of Great American Cities.* New York: Random House, 1961.

Kellner, George H., and J. Stanley Lemons. *Rhode Island: The Independent State.* Woodland Hills, Calif.: Windsor Publications in cooperation with the Rhode Island Historical Society, 1982.

King, Moses. *King's Pocket-book of Providence.* Cambridge, Mass.: Tibbitts & Shaw, 1882.

Kirk, William. *A Modern City.* Chicago: University of Chicago Press, 1909.

Lehr, Dick, and Gerard O'Neill. *The Underboss: The Rise and Fall of a Mafia Family.* New York: St. Martin's, 1989.

Liebling, A. J. *Wayward Pressman.* Garden City, N.Y.: Doubleday, 1947.

Machiavelli, Niccolò. *The Prince and The Discourses.* New York: Modern Library, 1950.

MacKay, Scott, and Jody McPhillips. "The Rhode Island Century." *Providence Journal* newspaper series, 1999.

Maiocco, Carmen. *Downcity: Downtown Providence in the 1950s.* Carmen Maiocco, 1997.

Mangione, Jerre, and Ben Morreale. *La Storia: Five Centuries of the Italian American Experience.* New York: HarperCollins, 1992.

McLoughlin, William G. "Providence: The Confident Years, 1890–1920." *Rhode Island History,* May 1993.

———. *Rhode Island: A History.* New York: Norton, 1986.

Morgenthau, Ruth S. *Pride without Prejudice: The Life of John O. Pastore.* Providence: Rhode Island Historical Society, 1989.

Paxton, William. *Moses Brown School: A History of Its Third Half-Century.* Providence: Moses Brown School, 1974.

Pesaturo, Ubaldo. *The Italo-Americans in Rhode Island: Their Contributions and Achievements.* Providence: Ubaldo Pesaturo, 1936.

Providence Journal. Blizzard. Providence: Providence Journal Company, 1978.

Rhode Island School of Design. *Interface: Providence.* Providence: Rhode Island School of Design, 1974.

Ricci, Tommy. *In-Justice.* Johnston, R.I.: Seedling Publications, 1992.

Rich, Wilbur C. "Vincent Cianci and Boosterism in Providence, Rhode Island." In *Governing Middle-Sized Cities: Studies in Mayoral Leadership,* ed. James Bowers and Wilbur C. Rich. Boulder, Colo.: Lynne Rienner, 2000.

Ross, James Bruce, and Mary Martin McLaughlin, eds. *The Portable Renaissance Reader.* New York: Viking, 1953.

Santoro, Carmela. *The Italians in Rhode Island.* Providence: Rhode Island Heritage Society, 1990.

Simister, Florence Parker. *Streets of the City: An Anecdotal History of Providence.* Providence: Mowbray, 1969.

Smith, Judith. *Family Connections: A History of Italian and Jewish Immigrant Lives in Providence, Rhode Island, 1900–1940.* Albany: State University of New York Press, 1985.

Stillwell, Margaret Bingham. *The Pageant of Benefit Street Down Through the Years.* Providence: Akerman-Standard, 1945.

Teresa, Vincent. *My Life in the Mafia*. Garden City, N.Y.: Doubleday, 1973.

Violet, Arlene. *Convictions*. New York: Random House, 1988.

West, Darrell M. *Patrick Kennedy: The Rise to Power.* Upper Saddle River, N.J.: Prentice Hall, 2001.

Woodward, William McKenzie. *Downtown Providence.* Providence: Rhode Island Historical Preservation Commission, 1981.

ACKNOWLEDGMENTS

The story of Buddy Cianci could not have been told without the generous support of many people. Although the mayor was not enthused about this project, I am grateful for the time that he did spend with me in the year leading up to his trial and also during the nine days that the jury was deliberating his fate.

I was lucky to find a terrific agent in Andrew Blauner, who was always there with advice and encouragement, and a superb editor at Random House in Jonathan Karp, who pushed me in many ways to make this a better book. With Jon's support, I expanded my initial focus on Operation Plunder Dome and went back to Cianci's early years, which I believe made for a richer and more complex tale. I'd also like to thank Amelia Zalcman, Jonathan Jao, Barbara Bachman, and Steve Messina at Random House for their efforts.

I have been blessed with wonderful colleagues and editors in my eighteen years at *The Providence Journal,* a newspaper whose proud heritage includes such distinguished journalists as A. J. Liebling, Ben Bagdikian, and Jules Witcover. I would like to thank the *Journal*'s publisher, Howard Sutton, for standing up for me when Cianci tried to stop me from doing this book. I owe a special debt to Tracy Breton, a good friend and classy colleague on the investigative team who introduced me to Raymond DeLeo, Ronald Glantz, and others. I also couldn't have survived this without the friendship and counsel of another investigative colleague, Bill Malinowski, the best partner in crime a journalist could hope to have. I would also like to acknowledge the support over the years of a man I've kicked many a trash can with, the *Journal*'s executive editor, Joel Rawson. And if it weren't for Tom Heslin, the *Journal*'s metro managing editor, I might still be covering the Friars. Thanks, Tom, for your patience, wisdom, and insightful editing over the years, and for teaching me THWTB: "The hard way's the best." And thanks to my former I-team colleague David Herzog, whose journalism students at the University of Missouri probably won't believe his stories about Eddie Voccola. I'd also like to thank Mary Murphy for her friendship and her marvelous photography throughout Plunder Dome, and for my book-jacket photo. Thanks also to *Journal* photo editor Mike Delaney and Maureen Aldrich for their assistance in rounding up the photos for this book. Several other colleagues provided advice, shared information, and offered moral support: Linda Borg, Ged Carbone, Hilary Horton, Bob Kerr, Jennifer Levitz, Peter Lord, Kevin McNamara, Amanda Milkovits, G. Wayne Miller, Tom Mooney, Mark Patinkin, Bill Reynolds, and Karen Lee Ziner. And a special thanks to Scott MacKay, my former Rhode Island history classmate at URI, and M. Charles Bakst, both of whom read the manuscript and offered valuable feedback. I'm also grateful to former *Journal* editor Chuck Hauser and former colleagues Chris Chivers, Doane Hulick, Mark Johnson, and Jon Rockoff. Linda Henderson's library staff at the *Journal* also deserves thanks, particularly Jennifer Hazard and Christina Siwy.

Jack White of Channel 12 and Jim Taricani of Channel 10 were generous in sharing their knowledge of Providence, the Mafia, and Cianci's early years, and also in providing tapes of key events, for which I am grateful. I'd also like to thank the Ocean State Follies' Charlie Hall, the *Providence Phoenix*'s Rudy Cheeks, and WPRO's Ron St. Pierre for their Buddy stories. Thanks also to Dan Yorke of WPRO for his assistance and copies of broadcast tapes. And thanks to Cherry Arnold of Big Orange Films for her encouragement, and best wishes for success with her Cianci documentary. I'd also like to thank Dick Lehr and Brian Mooney of *The Boston Globe* for their help and encouragement, and Evan Osnos of the *Chicago Tribune*.

I interviewed dozens of people who have known or worked for Buddy Cianci through the years, but some stand out. I appreciate the generous time and insights of Carol and Joe Agugiaro, Sharky Almagno, Paul Campbell, Buff Chace, Raymond DeLeo, Nick Easton, Stephen Fortunato, Ron Glantz, Wendy Materna, Bruce Melucci, John Palmieri, Normand Roussel, and Vin Vespia. There are others who wished to remain anonymous—you know who you are. Thank you. I would also like to thank the members of Cianci's staff for their graciousness, particularly Beryl Kenyon, Linda Verhulst, and Pat Zompa. And thanks to Artin Coloian, who was helpful even though he was more intent on finding out what I knew than telling me everything he knew.

I'd like to thank Brian Andrews, retired detective commander of the Rhode Island State Police, for his help and for lunches at Mike's Kitchen, and Bobby Stevenson for sharing his memories of his trip to Maryland with

Cianci in pursuit of the lying priest. I'd also like to thank Mike Urso and Pete Benjamin, retired members of the Rhode Island State Police, and the current head of the state police, Colonel Steve Pare. Thanks also to East Providence police chief Gary Dias and Johnston police chief Richard Tamburini. I also appreciate the memories shared by retired Providence police officers Ted Collins, Jack Leyden, Howard Luther, and Vincent O'Connell. Jack Cicilline's memories of the Doorley administration, the mob, and growing up in Providence enriched this book tremendously. I also appreciate all those who helped me understand the immigrant culture and ethnic politics that shaped Providence in the early and middle twentieth century, including Patrick Conley, Francis Darigan, Christopher and Ronald Del Sesto, Orlando Giansanti Jr., Vincent Igliozzi, Teresa Merolli, Ralph Pappito, Fred Santagata, and Michael Traficante. I'd like to thank Robert Ellis Smith for his recollections of Cianci's years at Moses Brown, and the president of Moses Brown, Joanne Hoffman, and her gracious faculty and staff for their assistance. And thanks to Ken Orenstein and Cliff Wood for their perspectives on downtown redevelopment. Thanks also to Jim Barfoot and Paul Giaccobe.

I would like to thank several of the key figures in Operation Plunder Dome for their willingness to talk to me. Dennis Aiken shared his experiences investigating public corruption. Richard Rose talked about his life. Also, Steven Antonson, David Ead, Tony Freitas, and Joseph Pannone. Several of the lawyers were as helpful as they could be given the legal constraints of the case. I'd particularly like to thank Richard Bicki, Kevin Bristow, and Len O'Brien. And thanks to John DePetro of WHJJ radio and his lawyer, Joe Cavanagh.

Thanks to the talented Peter Goldberg for his wonderful Cianci photos. And thanks to the staffs of the William H. Hall Free Library in Cranston and the Providence Athenaeum for providing me sanctuary.

I'd also like to thank Michael Corrente for his enthusiasm and support.

I am indebted to three people who passed away during this project— Skip Chernov, Rosemary Glancy, and Victoria Lederberg.

Finally, I'm indebted to my sister, Ann, and brother-in-law, Kevin, for hanging in there through the tough times. This book is in memory of my parents, Mary and Earl, who taught me to seek the truth. It is dedicated to my wife, Susan, to whom I owe everything.

INDEX

MIKE STANTON heads the investigative reporting team at *The Providence Journal*, Rhode Island's leading newspaper. He has broken stories about mobsters, a crooked governor and a crooked Supreme Court judge, wayward cops and prosecutors, and sleazy bankers and developers. Stanton has also written for *The Washington Post*, the *Columbia Journalism Review*, and *The Boston Globe*. He shared the 1994 Pulitzer Prize for investigative reporting, exposing widespread corruption at the Rhode Island Supreme Court. In 1997, he received the Master Reporter Award, for career achievement, from the New England Society of Newspaper Editors. He has also won prizes from Investigative Reporters and Editors, the American Society of Newspaper Editors, and the Associated Press. He is a graduate of Syracuse University and Northwestern University's Medill School of Journalism. Stanton lives in Rhode Island with his wife, Susan Hodgin, and their two children.

ABOUT THE TYPE

This book was set in Photina, a typeface designed by
José Mendoza in 1971. It is a very elegant design with
high legibility, and its close character fit has made it a
popular choice for use in quality magazines and art
gallery publications.